Guidelines
for Office Microsoft® 2013

Nancy Muir | **Anita Verno**

WRITER, AUTHOR, INSTRUCTOR
SEATTLE, WASHINGTON

ASSOCIATE PROFESSOR
INFORMATION TECHNOLOGY
BERGEN COMMUNITY COLLEGE
PARAMUS, NEW JERSEY

PARADIGM
EDUCATION SOLUTIONS

St. Paul

Managing Editor	Christine Hurney
Director of Production	Timothy W. Larson
Senior Editor	Cheryl Drivdahl
Contributing Writers	Jan Marrelli, Rob Neilly, and Doug Burden
Production Editor	Sarah Kearin
Cover Designer	Valerie King
Text Designer	Leslie Anderson
Design and Production Specialists	Jack Ross and Valerie King
Copy Editor	Crystal Bullen, DPS Associates
Testers	Margaret Cooksey and Jeff Johnson
Indexer	Schroeder Indexing Services
VP & Director of Digital Projects	Chuck Bratton
Digital Projects Manager	Tom Modl

Acknowledgements: Charles Adams, II, Danville Community College, Danville, VA; **Carla Anderson**, National College, Lynchburg, VA; **Vicki Badgley**, South Arkansas Community College, El Dorado, AR; **Stephen J. Baltes**, Randolph Community College, Asheboro, NC; **Sara P. Beakley-Mercill**, Scottsdale Community College, Chandler, AZ; **Linda Bettinger**, Southeast Community College, Lincoln, NE; **Ann Blackman**, Parkland College, Champaign, IL; **Larry Bush**, University of Cincinnati, Clermont College, Amelia, OH; **Miles Cannon**, Lanier Technical College, Oakwood, GA; **Sue Canter**, Guilford Technical Community College, Jamestown, NC; **Carol Cornforth**, West Virginia Northern Community College, Wheeling, WV; **Tim Ellis**, Schoolcraft College, Liconia, MI; **Philip Feinberg**, Palomar Community College, San Marcos, CA; **Clara Groeper**, Illinois Central College, East Peoria, IL; **Dana King**, Heartland Community College, Normal, IL; **Irvin LaFleur**, Lanier Technical College, Cumming, GA; **Leslie Martin**, Gaston College, Dallas, NC; **Judy A. McLaney**, Lurleen B. Wallace Community College, Opp, AL; **Deborah Miller**, Augusta Technical College, Augusta, GA; **LeAnn Moreno**, Minnesota State College, Southeast, Red Wing, MN; **Patricia Partyka**, Schoolcraft College, Prudenville, MI; **Angela Payne**, Southwest Tennessee Community College, Memphis, TN; **Jocelyn S. Pinkard**, Arlington Career Institute, Grand Prairie, TX; **Donna Reffit**, Jefferson Community College, Shelbyville, KY; **Felicia Reynolds**, Broward Community College, Pembroke Pines, FL; **Libby Rogers**, New River Community and Technical College, Greenbrier Valley Campus, Lewisburg, WV; **William Roxbury**, National College, Stow, OH; Reuel Sample, National College, Knoxville, TN; **Karen Spray**, Northeast Community College, Norfolk, NE; **Wanda Stuparits**, Lanier Technical College, Cumming, GA; **Casey Thompson**, Wiregrass Georgia Technical College, Douglas, GA; **Brandon Walker**, Kanawha Valley Community and Technical College, South Charleston, WV; **Carolyn Walker**, Greenville Technical College, Greenville, SC; **Fathia Williams**, Fletcher Technical Community College, Houma, LA; **Regina Young**, Wiregrass Georgia Technical College, Valdosta, GA.

Photo Credits: See page 712.

Care has been taken to verify the accuracy of information presented in this book. However, the authors, editors, and publisher cannot accept responsibility for Web, e-mail, newsgroup, or chat room subject matter or content, or for consequences from application of the information in this book, and make no warranty, expressed or implied, with respect to its content.

Trademarks: Some of the product names and company names included in this book have been used for identification purposes only and may be trademarks or registered trade names of their respective manufacturers and sellers. For example, Access, Excel, Internet Explorer, Microsoft, Outlook, OneNote, PowerPoint, and Windows are trademarks or registered trademarks of Microsoft Corporation in the United States and/or other countries. The authors, editors, and publisher disclaim any affiliation, association, or connection with, or sponsorship or endorsement by, such owners.

We have made every effort to trace the ownership of all copyrighted material and to secure permission from copyright holders. In the event of any question arising as to the use of any material, we will be pleased to make the necessary corrections in future printings. Thanks are due to the aforementioned authors, publishers, and agents for permission to use the materials indicated.

ISBN 978-0-76385-255-9 (text)
ISBN 978-0-76385-258-0 (text & disc)
ISBN 978-0-76385-262-7 (eBook)

© 2014 by Paradigm Publishing, Inc.
875 Montreal Way
St. Paul, MN 55102
Email: educate@emcp.com
Website: www.paradigmcollege.com

Printed in the United States of America

22 21 20 19 18 17 16 15 14   5 6 7 8 9 10

CONTENTS

Preface

Learning how to use software should be a simple, straightforward, and intuitive experience—right? We think so too, and that's why we developed *Guidelines for Microsoft® Office*.

We listened to what students and instructors were saying about how they wanted to learn and teach the Office suite of applications. What we heard time and again was that people wanted an easy-to-understand book about Office basics that they could use without feeling overwhelmed.

The first edition of this book was the result. In this second edition, *Guidelines for Microsoft® Office 2013*, we apply those basics to the newest version of the Office suite. As in the first edition, you will find a step-by-step, visual approach that will help you quickly learn the key features of the Office applications, building knowledge in a logical and easy-to-follow way. For every skill, you will have the option of playing a Skills Video to see and hear the steps demonstrated on screen. Structured end-of-chapter and end-of-module activities and projects will help reinforce what you have learned and assess how well you can apply your new skills to realistic work and school situations. As you work through the skills, exercises, and projects in each chapter, you will gain confidence and proficiency.

Clear and Simple Learning

Guidelines 2013 offers a simple path to mastering the basics of Office 2013, Windows 8, and Internet Explorer 10. This path is designed with you in mind and created to support you in a number of ways. First, you prepare to succeed in the course by learning how to use Outlook to manage your schedules, SkyDrive to manage and share files, OneNote to take notes, and the Print Screen key, Snipping Tool, and Clipping Tool to take screen captures. Next, you learn essential computer hardware and software concepts, Windows and Internet basics, and important Office features that you will encounter frequently when working in the major Office applications.

In the Word, Excel, Access, and PowerPoint modules, you focus on completing tasks using the ribbon, which displays tools and commands organized into tabs and groups based on common tasks. In addition, you find out about keystroke combinations and shortcut menus that can be used as alternative ways to get things done. By the time you complete this book, you will be familiar with all the basic tools the ribbon offers and understand the advantages of several different shortcut methods.

In the introduction to each chapter, read the list of skills to preview what you will accomplish as you work through the chapter. Also read the list of files you will need from the Student Resources disc, and look at the image of the final document or file you will produce.

Each skill is presented in a two- or four-page layout with steps on the left page and screenshots on the right page. In the screenshots, callouts showing you where to click are numbered to match the steps. By reading the steps and studying the screenshots, you can easily complete every task covered in this book. When you have finished a skill, compare your file against the Completed Skill image showing you what the file should look like.

Interesting Step-by-Step Application

The modules of this book that address the main Office programs (Word, Excel, Access, and PowerPoint) follow an engaging scenario involving the business of running a chocolate museum. This scenario offers you the opportunity to complete tasks related to creating exhibits, managing fund-raising efforts, and maintaining a gift shop.

Each file you create in this scenario has a goal—to communicate, to educate, to manage, or to entertain. When you reach the end of each chapter, you will have created useful materials and learned Office features and skills along the way.

Student Resources Disc

The data files you will use to complete the skills in this book, Skills Videos illustrating the steps in the skills, and a glossary are all provided on the Student Resources disc that accompanies this textbook. See the "Guidelines for Getting Started" section on pages 2–3 of this book for information about using the disc and setting up your computer system. See Module 2, Project 1, pages 166–168 for guided instruction on copying the data file folders from the Student Resources disc to a storage medium (such as a USB flash drive, SkyDrive account, or computer hard disk).

SNAP Training and Assessment

SNAP is a Web-based program offering an interactive venue for learning Microsoft Office 2013, Windows 8, and Internet Explorer 10. SNAP course materials include the Skills Videos; skill exams and performance evaluations that you complete live in the Office applications; interactive versions of the multiple-choice Features Review assessments; a concept exam question bank; and new Grade It activities that allow you to complete selected end-of-chapter exercises live in the Office application. (*NOTE: Textbook features that are available in SNAP are indicated by a SNAP or SNAP Grade It logo in the margin.*) SNAP delivers these course materials in a learning management system that includes an online grade book and course planning tools. For more information and to access SNAP materials that you have purchased for this course, go to snap2013.emcp.com.

Additional Student Resources

Book-specific Website   Go to the Internet Resource Center at www.ParadigmCollege.net/Guidelines13 to find learning tools and reference materials that support this book. You can access the same data files that are on the Student Resources disc, along with study aids, web links, and tips for using computers effectively in academic and workplace settings.

Online eBook   You can travel light by accessing the entire contents of this book through the online eBook. The Guidelines 2013 eBook includes hyperlinks to the Skills Videos and dynamic navigation tools that allow you to bookmark, highlight, take notes, and jump to specific pages.

Additional Instructor Resources

Instructor's Guide and Disc   Instructor support for Guidelines 2013 includes the Instructor's Guide and Instructor Resources Disc package. This package contains course planning materials, such as syllabus suggestions and Lesson Plans with teaching hints; PowerPoint presentations with lecture notes; and assessment resources, including the ExamView® Assessment Suite with concepts exam question banks, an overview of available assessment venues, live model answers for chapter activities, live and PDF model answers for end-of-chapter exercises, and rubrics.

Internet Resource Center for Instructors   With the exception of the ExamView® materials (which are available on the Instructor Resources disc only), the contents of the Instructor's Guide and Instructor Resources Disc package are also available in the password-protected instructor area of the Internet Resource Center at www.ParadigmCollege.net/Guidelines13.

Blackboard Cartridge   This set of files allows instructors to create a personalized Blackboard website for their course and provides course content, tests, and the mechanisms for establishing e-discussions and online group conferences. Available content includes a syllabus, concept exam question banks, PowerPoint presentations, and supplementary course materials. Upon request, the files can be available within 24–48 hours. Hosting the site is the responsibility of the educational institution.

INTRODUCTION

Your Digital Toolkit

 Chapter 2, Skill 2, of Module 2 teaches you how to copy a module's folder of files from the Student Resources disc to your hard disk, flash drive, SkyDrive, or other storage medium. You will need one of those files for Chapter 2 of this module.

In this book, you learn to use several computer application programs (also called *apps*) that combine to make an application *suite*. This suite of programs is called Microsoft Office 2013. The programs you learn to use, also referred to as *software*, work with your operating system to enable you to perform various types of tasks. The programs in the suite include Word, a word processing program; Excel, a spreadsheet program; Access, a database program; OneNote, an electronic notebook program; Outlook, a personal information manager; and PowerPoint, a presentation program. You also learn the basic features of the Windows 8 operating system and the Web browsers Internet Explorer, Chrome, and Mozilla Firefox.

The Guidelines Book Package

Your book comes with a Student Resources disc that contains (1) files required for completing the activities and (2) Skills Videos that, step by step, demonstrate each skill in the book. You also need access to a computer that has an Internet connection and the Windows 8 operating system with Microsoft Office 2013 software installed. The data files, along with additional references and resources, are also available at the book's website at www.ParadigmCollege.net/Guidelines13.

Hardware and Software Requirements

Your book is designed for a computer running a standard installation of the Microsoft Office 365 Home Premium or Small Business and the Microsoft Windows 8 (Windows 8 Pro, Windows 8 Enterprise, Windows RT) operating system. To run this suite and operating system effectively, your computer should have the following capabilities:

- 1 gigahertz (GHz) processor or higher; 1 gigabyte (GB) RAM (32-bit) or 2 GB RAM (64-bit)
- CD/DVD drive, USB port and USB flash drive, SkyDrive account with a live Internet connection, or other removable storage medium
- 3 GB of available hard-disk space
- .NET version 3.5, 4.0, or 4.5
- DirectX10 graphics card

- Minimum 1024 x 576 monitor resolution (or 1366 x 768 to use the Windows 8 Snap feature)
- Computer mouse, multi-touch device, or other compatible pointing device

Start-Up and Shut-Down Procedures

You need to know how to turn the computer on and off and, depending on where you will store your course work, how to insert a CD or DVD and flash drive, and how to access SkyDrive.

- **To turn on the computer:** Press the power button ⏻ , which loads the Windows 8 operating system. You may need to log in using an assigned user name and password.
- **To insert a CD or DVD:** Press the Open button on the front panel of the CD or DVD drive and the tray opens. Place the disc in the tray with the disc label facing up. Press the Open button again to close the tray.
- **To insert a flash drive:** Insert your flash drive into a USB port. Note that there is only one way to insert the flash drive, so you may have to flip it over so that it fits. Do not force the flash drive into the port. If you need help ejecting the flash drive, check with your instructor.
- **To access SkyDrive:** Refer to Chapter 2—Using SkyDrive.
- **To turn off the computer:** When you are finished working with your computer, press Win + C, click Settings, click Power, and then click Shut Down.

CPU
monitor
printer
DVD drive
power button
mouse
keyboard
open button, DVD drive
laptop
storage media
USB port (front, back or side of computer)

Started

Using the Student Resources Disc

The Student Resources disc that comes with your book contains videos demonstrating the steps for each skill in the book. You can use the videos to preview the skills before you start working or to clarify how to perform the steps if you have difficulty completing a skill. To run the skills video, your computer needs to have a web browser and the Adobe Flash Player plugin installed. Flash Player is automatically installed with Windows 8 and is also available free of charge from Adobe online at get.adobe.com/flashplayer.

The Student Resources disc also contains files you need to complete the module or chapter skills, chapter assessments, and module assessments. Module 2, Chapter 2 teaches you how to download or copy each module's folder of files from the disc to your hard disk, flash drive, SkyDrive, or other storage medium. Note that you don't need any student data files for Module 1.

Starting an Office 2013 Application Program

The first module in your book uses the Outlook and OneNote programs. To start Outlook or another program in the Office suite, follow these steps:

1 Press Win + C to display the Charms bar.

2 Click the Search charm.

3 Type the name of the app in the search box.

4 Click *Apps* in the Search pane if it is not already selected.

5 Click the name of the app in the Apps results list.

Chapter 1

Managing Your Time with Microsoft Outlook 2013

Developing good organizational and time management skills can help you succeed in both school and your career. Personal information management software, such as Outlook, can simplify the organization of personal and business activities and help you stay on top of things. Outlook contains tools for organizing appointments, managing email, and keeping track of people.

One aspect of managing time involves keeping an organized schedule. Calendar is an Outlook scheduling tool that you can use to keep track of appointments, create reminders about events, and schedule meetings.

Knowing where to quickly find email addresses or phone numbers for personal and business contacts is also an essential organizational and time management skill. People is an Outlook tool for creating an electronic address book that stores contact information for the people you communicate with. Because People is linked to your Outlook email address book and the Outlook Social Connector, you can stay up-to-date on your social networks without leaving Outlook.

You may have noticed that a Calendar app and a People app are installed with Windows 8. These apps are also designed to help you manage your time. However the focus of this chapter is Outlook, which is part of the Microsoft Office 2013 suite.

Skills You Learn

1 Open Outlook and use Peeks
2 Display the Calendar
3 Schedule an appointment
4 Schedule a meeting
5 Add people
6 Search for people and appointments

Files You Need
For these skills, you do not need any student data files.

What You Create
In this chapter, you learn how to use Outlook to organize your personal, school, and career life. You schedule an appointment and a meeting in Outlook's digital Calendar. You then send an electronic invitation to others, inviting them to attend a scheduled meeting. You also add your personal and business contacts to Outlook's People list and you learn how to always have schedule and contact information at your fingertips.

Scheduled Appointment

Completed Skill 3

Scheduled Meeting

Completed Skill 4

People

Completed Skill 5

Introduction

Open Outlook and Use Peeks

 I_C1_S01

Outlook contains four main views—Mail, Calendar, People, and Tasks. When you start Outlook, Mail view displays by default. Use the Navigation bar in the bottom left of the screen to switch to Calendar view. You can also use a feature called Peeks to view your Calendar, People, or Tasks without having to switch views.

Steps

1-4 *Another Way*
You may have an Outlook 2013 tile on the Start screen. If you do, click this tile to start Outlook 2013.

▶**Tip** See page 3 for an illustration of Steps 1–4.

▶**Tip** To pin Outlook 2013 to your Start screen, right-click *Outlook 2013* in the Apps results list and then click *Pin to Start*.

▶**Tip** If you do not have an Outlook account, you will be prompted to set one up.

▶**Tip** When a peek is pinned within a view, it only displays in that view. For example, if you want to see the Calendar peek in both the Mail view and the People view, you will need to pin it in both views.

1 From the Start screen, press Win + C to display the Charms bar.

2 Click *Search* in the Charms bar.

3 Type Outlook in the search box.

4 Click *Outlook 2013* in the Apps results list.

5 Hover over the Calendar button in the Navigation bar to peek at the Calendar.

6 Move the mouse off the Calendar button to make the Calendar peek disappear.

7 Hover over the Calendar button again to reopen the Calendar peek.

8 Click the Dock the peek button to pin the Calendar peek to the right edge of the Outlook window.

9 Click the Remove the peek button to remove the Calendar peek.

Taking It Further

Customizing the Look of Your Navigation Bar By default, the Navigation bar displays buttons for four views: Mail, Calendar, People, and Tasks. The number of view buttons displayed and the order in which the buttons appear can be changed by clicking the ellipsis ••• on the Navigation bar and then clicking *Navigation Options*. To change how many buttons appear, change the maximum number of visible items. To change the order in which the buttons appear, click a button and then click the Move Up or Move Down button.

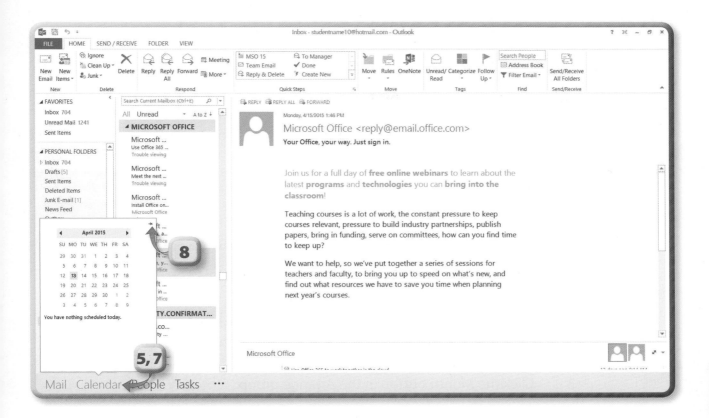

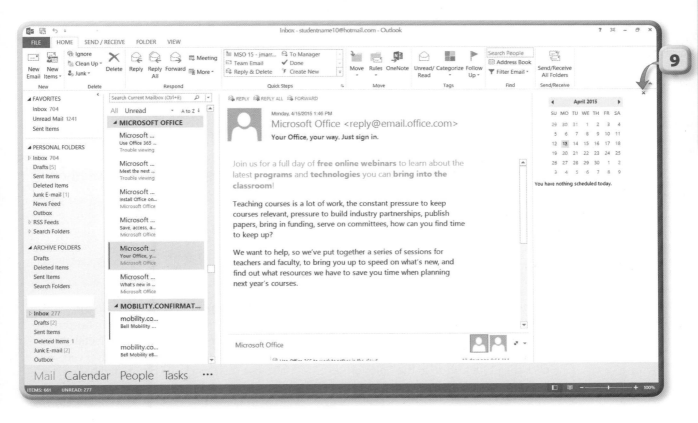

Introduction

Introduction

Video I_C1_S02

Display the Calendar

You can display your calendar in a daily, weekly, or monthly view. You can also navigate to different days using buttons on the HOME tab or using the Date Navigator. While you are viewing your calendar, you are also able to view your local weather forecast on the Weather bar.

Steps

1 Shortcut
Display Calendar
Ctrl + 2

▶**Tip** To move forward or backward a day in Day view, or to move to the next or previous month in Month view, you can use the Forward and Back navigation buttons.

▶**Tip** If you do not see the Date Navigator, click the Folder Pane Minimize/Maximize button.

▶**Tip** To add another city to the Weather bar, click the down arrow next to the city, click *Add Location,* type the name of the city, and then press Enter.

▶**Tip** Depending on the size of your monitor screen, you may need to minimize the Folder pane to see Tomorrow on the Weather bar.

1 With Outlook open, click the Calendar button on the Navigation bar to display Calendar view.

2 Click the Day button in the Arrange group on the HOME tab.

3 Click the Month button in the Arrange group.

4 Click the Next 7 Days button in the Go To group.

5 Click tomorrow's date in the Date Navigator at the top of the Folder pane.

6 Click the Today button in the Go To group to display your calendar for today.

7 Hover over Today on the Weather bar to display additional weather details.

8 Hover over Tomorrow on the Weather bar to display additional weather details.

Taking It Further

Customizing the Look of Your Calendar   The VIEW tab contains many options for customizing the look of your calendar. To change the background color, click the Color button in the Color group and then click a background color. You can change the time intervals shown in the Calendar by clicking the Time Scale button in the Arrangement group and selecting an interval from the drop-down list. You can also use the Time Scale button to change the time zone.

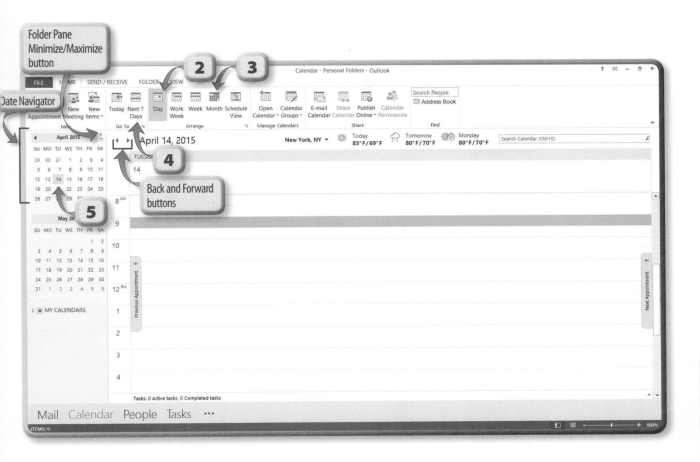

Folder Pane Minimize/Maximize button

Date Navigator

Back and Forward buttons

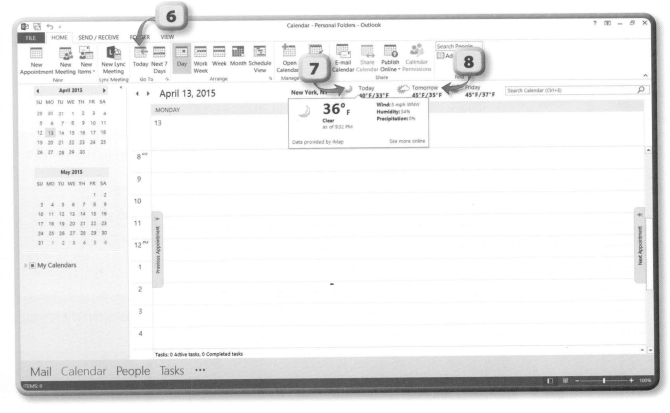

Introduction

Introduction

Video ▶ I_C1_S03

Schedule an Appointment

Your Outlook Calendar can help keep you organized when you use it to schedule appointments. An appointment is any activity that you schedule in your calendar with a starting time and an ending time. You can schedule homework assignments and exams as appointments. If you specify an appointment location, it is shown in parentheses next to the appointment information. You can also set an appointment reminder to help you remember the appointment. You can add appointments in any view.

Steps

1 With Outlook Calendar open, click the Today button in the Go To group on the HOME tab.

2 If Day view is not active, click the Day button in the Arrange group.

3 Shortcut
Create New Appointment
Ctrl + N

3 Click the New Appointment button in the New group.

4 Type Dentist Appointment in the *Subject* text box and then press the Tab key.

5 Type Main Office in the *Location* text box.

6 Click the *Start time* option box arrow and click *2:00 PM* in the drop-down list. (Scroll as needed to display *2:00 PM* in the list.)

▶ **Tip** Click the *All day event* check box if the activity lasts the entire day and does not have a start or end time, such as a vacation day.

7 Click the *End time* option box arrow and click *3:00 PM (1 hour)* in the drop-down list.

▶ **Tip** Choose another date for *End time* in order to schedule a multiple-day appointment, such as a vacation or conference.

8 Click the *Reminder* option box arrow in the Options group on the APPOINTMENT tab.

▶ **Tip** In the Options group, use the Recurrence button to enter an appointment that occurs on a regular basis, such as daily, weekly, monthly, or yearly.

9 Click *1 hour* in the drop-down list.

10 Click the Save & Close button in the Actions group on the APPOINTMENT tab.

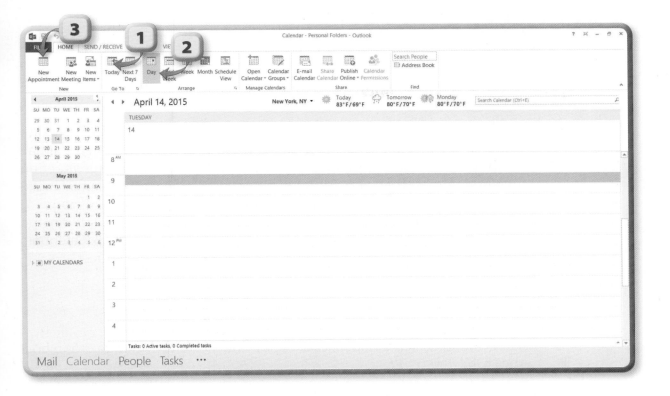

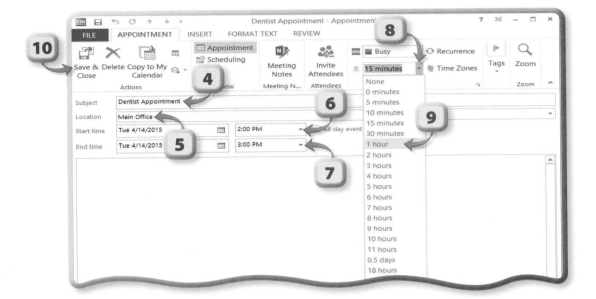

Taking It Further

Organizing Your Calendar To help organize your school schedule, you can create appointments for project due dates and homework assignments. You may want to add reminders to these appointments to help you get your work finished on time. You can also plan your course work by creating a multiple-day appointment with the subject *Chapter 1* to show which days you plan to work on this chapter.

Introduction

Introduction

Schedule a Meeting

Video   I_C1_S04

If you need to schedule a meeting, you can use Outlook Calendar to send out a meeting request. A meeting request is an appointment that is sent to other people and can include the meeting location and other important information about the meeting, such as its topic and goals. Sending a meeting request is one way you can integrate the Outlook Calendar and Email tools. Responses to your meeting requests appear in your email Inbox folder. Recipients can respond to a meeting request by adding the meeting to their Outlook Calendars or by declining the request.

Steps

1 With Outlook Calendar open, click the Day button in the Arrange group on the HOME tab.

2 Click the New Meeting button in the New group.

3 Type Project Meeting in the *Subject* text box and then press the Tab key.

4 Type Conference Room A in the *Location* text box.

5 Click the Calendar button in the *Start time* text box and then click the date that is one week from today in the drop-down list. The date displayed in the *End time* text box also changes.

6 Click the *Start time* option box arrow and then click *1:00 PM* in the drop-down list.

7 Click the *End time* option box arrow and then click *3:00 PM (2 hours)* in the drop-down list.

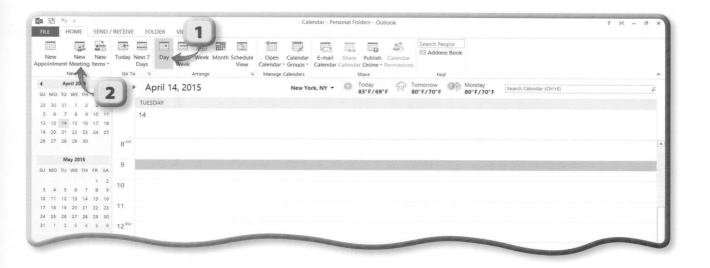

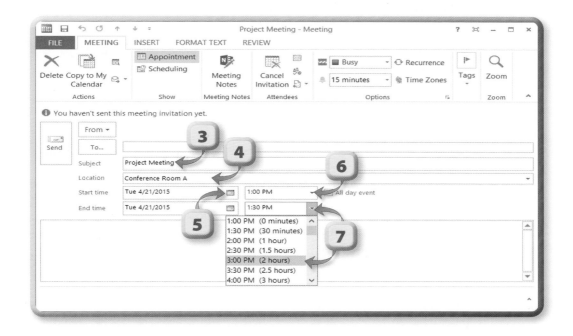

More

Introduction

▶Tip You can also click the To button to select email addresses from your Address Book.

▶Tip Separate email addresses with a comma (,) or semi-colon (;) if you are inviting more than one person to the meeting.

8   Type Please bring your research notes. in the body of the meeting request.

9   Exchange email addresses with a classmate and type the classmate's email address in the *To* text box. ***NOTE:*** *For steps 9–14, you must be using Outlook as your email client. These steps will work with either a desktop or web-based version of Outlook that has been configured for your personal use.*

10   Click the Send button.

11   Click the Mail button in the Navigation bar to check your email.

12   Double-click the new email you received from your classmate.

13   Click the Accept button arrow.

14   In the drop-down list, click *Send the Response Now* to respond to the meeting request.

Taking It Further

Configuring Outlook   Outlook needs to be set up or configured for a specific user. If you are using Outlook on a shared computer, you will need to log in to Outlook before you can use it. However, for security purposes most schools do not permit students to configure Outlook.

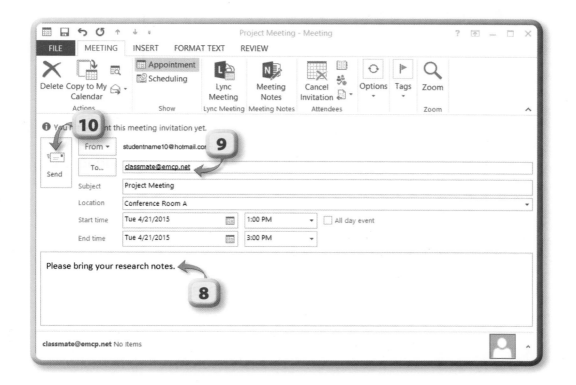

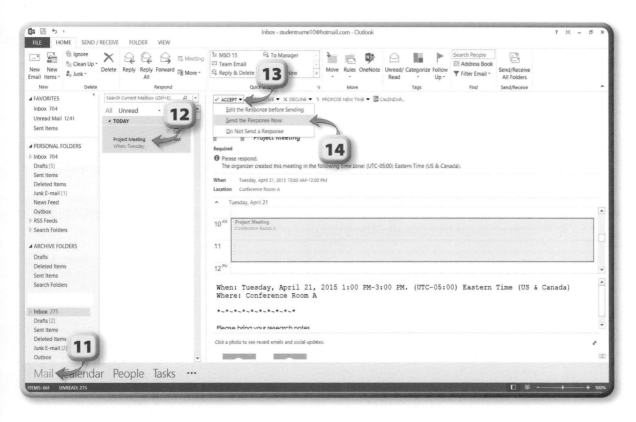

Introduction

Introduction

Skill 5

Add People

Video | I_C1_S05

People is an Outlook tool that you can use to organize and save information about the people and businesses that you communicate with. The information you enter about a person or business can include just the contact's name and email address, or it can include additional information, such as the contact's street address, cell phone number, picture, and birthday.

Steps

① Shortcut
Display People
Ctrl + 3

▶**Tip** The *File as* text box is completed automatically after you enter the full name. This entry is used to organize the People list in alphabetical order.

▶**Tip** The *Display as* text box is completed automatically after you enter the email address.

▶**Tip** When you receive an email message in Outlook, you can add the sender as a new contact by right-clicking the person's name at the top of the message and then clicking *Add to Outlook Contacts.*

1 With Outlook open, click the People button in the Navigation bar to display People view.

2 Click the New Contact button in the New group on the HOME tab.

3 Type Michaela Williams in the *Full Name* text box.

4 Type Align Computers in the *Company* text box.

5 Type m.williams@emcp.net in the *E-mail* text box.

6 Type (561) 555-2322 in the *Business* text box.

7 Click the Save & Close button in the Actions group on the CONTACT tab.

8 Click the Business Card button in the Current View group on the HOME tab to change to Business Card view.

Taking It Further

Adding a Picture You can add a picture of your contact to help you quickly connect a face to a name or a logo to a business contact. If both the sender and the recipient use Microsoft Outlook 2013, 2010, or 2007, the person's picture will appear in the email message header. To add a picture, click the image icon in the New Contact window, browse to locate the picture that you want to add, and then double-click the file name.

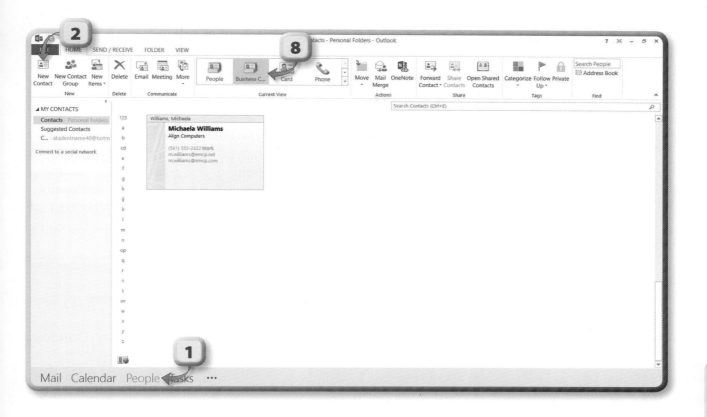

Introduction

Introduction

Skill 6

Video | _C1_S06

Search for People and Appointments

Being organized means having information at your fingertips and knowing how best to manage it. With Outlook, you can easily find people and appointments by using the *Search Contacts* and *Search* *Calendar* text boxes. You only need to type in the information you are looking for—and you can even search using partial information. For example, you can type part of a business name or phone number.

Steps

1 With Outlook open, click the Calendar button in the Navigation bar.

2 Click in the *Search Calendar* text box and type Dentist Appointment. Outlook displays the appointment you created in Skill 3.

3 Double-click the appointment.

4 Change the appointment start time to *2:30 PM*.

5 Change the appointment end time to *4:00 PM*.

6 Click the Save & Close button in the Actions group.

7 Click the People button in the Navigation bar.

8 Click in the *Search Contacts* text box and type (561. Outlook displays the Michaela Williams contact.

9 Click the Close Search button in the Close group on the SEARCH TOOLS SEARCH tab.

10 Click the Close button to close Outlook.

2 *Shortcut*

Open *Search Calendar* Text Box
Ctrl + E

▶**Tip** You can refine your search by using the buttons on the SEARCH TOOLS SEARCH tab.

8 *Shortcut*

Open *Search Contacts* Text Box
Ctrl + E

Taking It Further

Exploring the SEARCH TOOLS SEARCH Tab
When you click in the *Search Contacts* text box or *Search Calendar* text box, the SEARCH TOOLS SEARCH tab appears, enabling you to refine your search. Commands in the Scope group specify which Outlook folders are included in your search. Use commands in the Refine group to narrow your search. Commands in the Options group allow you to reuse previous searches, saving you the time and effort of retyping search criteria. For example, click the Recent Searches button and you will find the search you conducted in this skill in the drop-down list.

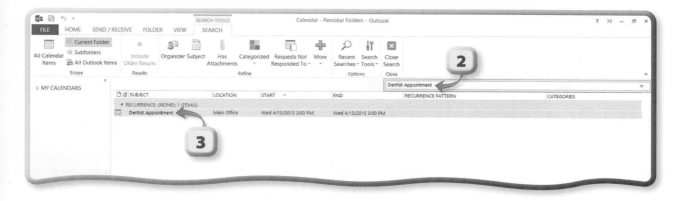

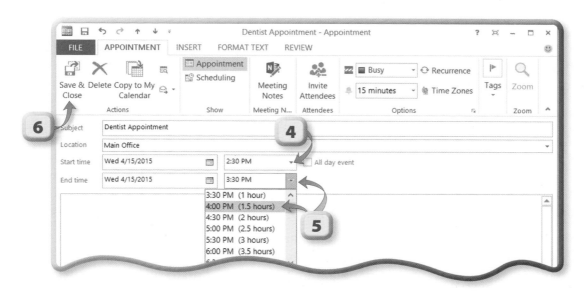

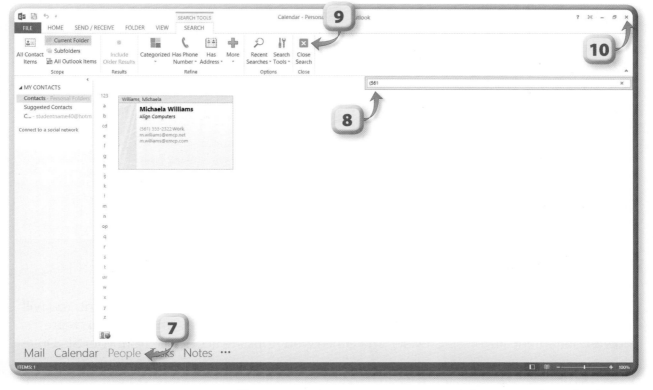

Chapter 2

Using SkyDrive

SkyDrive is a service offered by Microsoft that allows you to upload files to an online storage area. The online storage area is called a *cloud* or *cloud storage*. At the time of publication of this textbook, SkyDrive allows you to use up to 7 GB of storage for free. Additional storage space can be purchased.

When you install SkyDrive, a SkyDrive folder is automatically created on your computer. You can access this folder from the File Explorer just like you access all of your other files. You can also access your SkyDrive files from the website SkyDrive.live.com. The SkyDrive folder on your computer makes it easy to access files you have saved to the cloud from your computer, but the real advantage to using SkyDrive is being able to access your files from any computing device that has Internet access. For example, if you save a file to SkyDrive from your school or work computer, you can access that file from your home computer without having to email the file or use a flash drive or other portable storage device. For another example, you can store photos in your SkyDrive folder and then access them from your smartphone. Any file you put in your SkyDrive folder is automatically synced to all of your computing devices that have SkyDrive.

Files stored in your SkyDrive folder can also be shared with others. You can decide whether the people you are sharing with can just read a file or can also edit a file. Using SkyDrive is a great way to collaborate on a project or document without having to be in the same location or having to email files back and forth.

Skills You Learn

1   Create a SkyDrive account
2   Sign in to and out of SkyDrive
3   Manage files and folders on SkyDrive
4   Edit files using Office Web Apps
5   Create files using Office Web Apps
6   Share files on SkyDrive

Files You Need
For these skills, you need the following student data file.

M0-C2-S3-Vacation.docx

What You Create
In this chapter, you will create a SkyDrive account and then add a file to your account. You will also create and rename a folder and learn to use the Office Web Apps, which let you create and edit documents in a web browser. The Office Web Apps are accessible from your SkyDrive account.

SkyDrive Sign-in Page

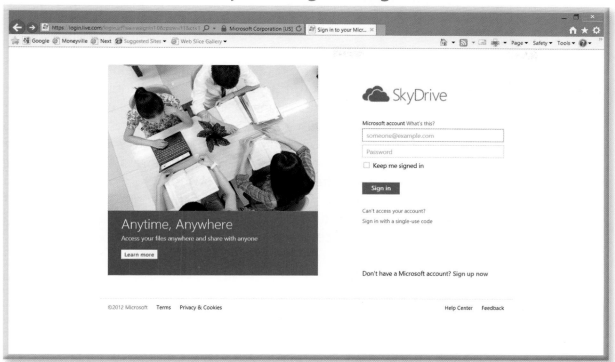

SkyDrive Cloud Storage Window

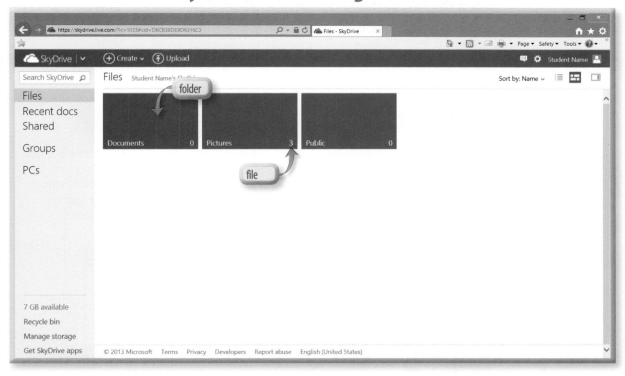

Introduction

Skill 1

Video I_C2_S01

Create a SkyDrive Account

Creating a SkyDrive account will allow you to store your files online in the cloud, making them easily accessible from any computing device. To create a SkyDrive account, you will need to go to the SkyDrive website and create a Microsoft account. A Microsoft account allows you to sign in to services such as SkyDrive and Hotmail. Your Microsoft account consists of a login, which is your email address, and a password you create. If you already have a Hotmail address, Xbox LIVE account, or Windows Phone, you can use the same login and password for SkyDrive.

Steps

1 Click the Desktop tile in the Start screen.

2 Click the Internet Explorer button, located on the Windows Taskbar, to start the Internet Explorer web browser.

3 Select the text in the Address bar, type skydrive.live.com, and then press Enter to display the home page for SkyDrive.

▶ **Tip** If you have a Microsoft account, skip to Skill 2.

4 Click the Sign up now link to display a Microsoft account form.

Taking It Further

Using SkyDrive's Auto Sync Feature
This chapter focuses on using SkyDrive's web interface so you can learn about its many features in a public lab. However, if you are working on your home computer, SkyDrive will sync with the File Explorer so that you will be able to access your SkyDrive account just like you access any folder on your computer. Note that the Auto Sync feature may be turned off on public computers to avoid unintentional sharing of files.

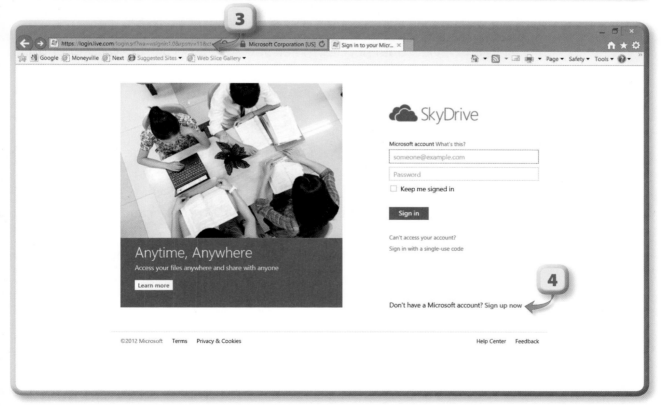

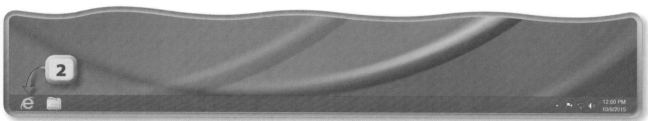

Introduction

5 In the *First Name* text box, type your first name and then press the Tab key.

6 In the *Last Name* text box, type your last name and then press the Tab key.

7 Click the *Birth date* option box arrows to select your birth date in the drop-down lists.

8 Click the *Gender* option box arrow and select *Male* or *Female*.

9 In the *Microsoft account name* text box, type your email address and then press the Tab key.

▶ **Tip** Create a password that is not easy for others to guess. Secure passwords contain at least eight characters, upper- and lowercase letters and a combination of numbers, letters, and special characters.

10 In the *Create a password* text box, type your password and then press the Tab key.

11 In the *Reenter password* text box, type your password again and then press the Tab key.

12 In the *Phone number* text box, type your phone number.

▶ **Tip** You may want to click to the clear the *Send me email with promotional offers from Microsoft* check box if you do not want to receive emails from Microsoft.

13 In the *ZIP code* text box, enter your zip code.

14 Click the <u>Microsoft services agreement</u> and the <u>privacy & cookies statement</u> links and review both policies. When you are ready, click the I accept button.

15 In the *Help us make sure you're not a robot* text box, type the displayed characters.

16 Click the I accept button to create your account. A message displays indicating that a verification email will be sent to you.

17 Open your email account and locate the SkyDrive verification email.

18 Click the link in the email to finish setting up your SkyDrive account.

Introduction

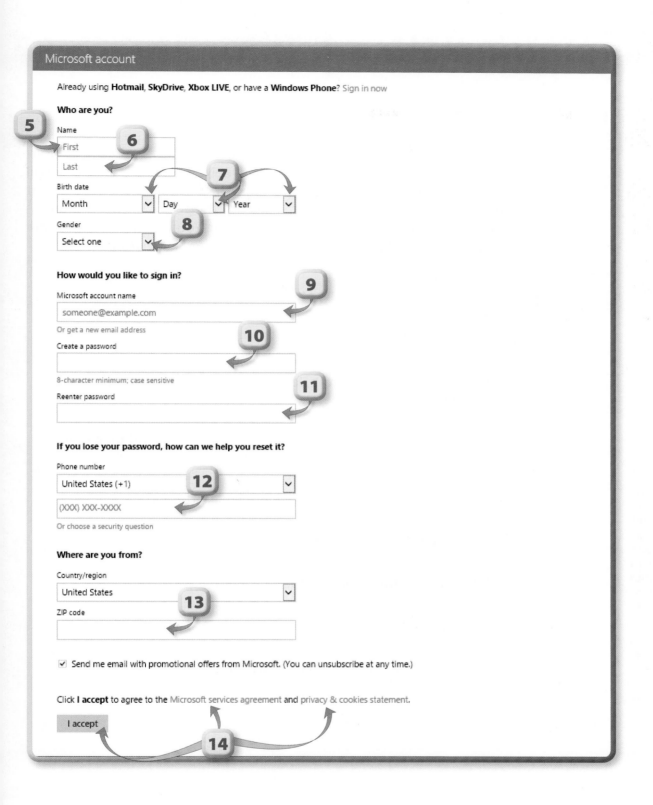

Introduction

Sign In to and Out of SkyDrive

 I_C2_S02

Now that you have created a SkyDrive account, you are able to store your files (such as documents, photos, and videos) in the cloud. You can sign in to the SkyDrive account you created in Skill 1 from the SkyDrive web page or from a Microsoft application, such as Word or OneNote. In this skill, you will sign in to your SkyDrive account using the web browser Internet Explorer. You will also learn to sign out of your SkyDrive account.

Steps

1 Click the Desktop tile in the Start screen.

2 Click the Internet Explorer button, located on the Windows Taskbar, to start the Internet Explorer web browser.

3 Select the text in the Address bar, type skydrive.live.com, and then press Enter to display the home page for SkyDrive.

4 In the *Microsoft account* text box, type your email address.

5 In the *Password* text box, type your password.

6 Click the Sign in button to display the SkyDrive window.

7 Click your account name.

8 Click the *Sign out* option to sign out of your SkyDrive account.

▶ **Tip** Click the *Keep me signed in* check box to save your Microsoft account and password on your computer. Note that you should enable this option only on a secure personal computer, never on a public or shared computer.

▶ **Tip** If the sign-in page is showing a Microsoft account that is not yours, highlight the text in the text box before entering your email address.

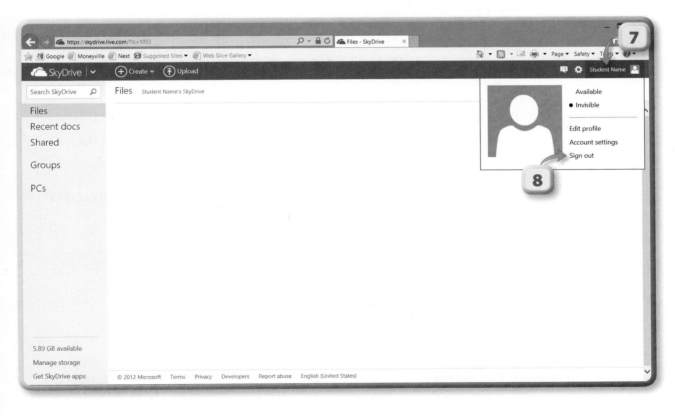

Introduction

Skill 3

Manage Files and Folders on SkyDrive

Video I_C2_S03

After you sign in to your SkyDrive account, you can upload files to your cloud storage area. Uploaded files can be viewed as tiles, similar to those on the Windows 8 Start screen, or they can be viewed in Details view. Details view displays information about the files, such as the date the file was created and the file size. It is a good idea to organize uploaded files into folders so that they are easy to find. An uploaded file can be moved to a folder by dragging the file to the folder. Folders and files should have meaningful names, and they can be renamed in SkyDrive. You can view the contents of files online or by downloading them to your computer.

Steps

▶ **Tip** Recall that the URL for the SkyDrive home page is *skydrive.live.com* (see Skill 2, Step 3).

1 Start Internet Explorer, go to the SkyDrive home page, and then sign in to SkyDrive.

2 Click the Upload button to display the Choose File to Upload dialog box.

3 Insert your Student Resources disc into your disc drive and navigate to the student data file named **M0-C2-S3-Vacation.docx** in the Module0-Introduction folder.

4 Click **M0-C2-S3-Vacation.docx** to select the file.

5 Click the Open button to upload the file.

▶ **Tip** To view additional details about a file or to add comments, click the Expand Pane button.

6 Click the Details button to display the contents of your SkyDrive account in a list with details such as the last date modified and the size.

7 Click the Tiles button to display a tile-based layout.

8 Click the Create button.

9 Click the *Folder* option.

Taking It Further

Sorting Files By default, SkyDrive folders are displayed in ascending alphabetical order, followed by any files not in folders, also in ascending alphabetical order. You can change how files are sorted by clicking the *Sort by* down-pointing arrow and selecting an option, such as *Date created* or *Size*. Select *Descending* to display the files in reverse order.

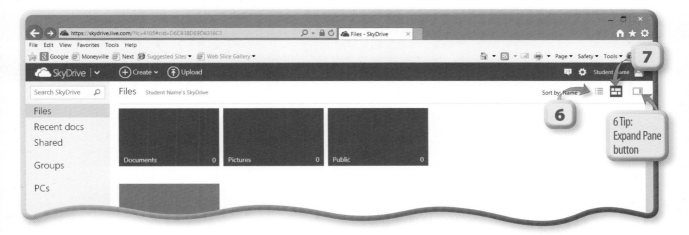

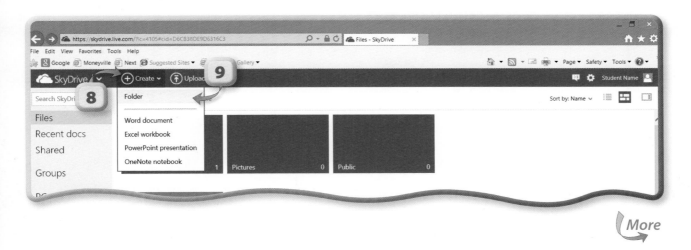

More

Introduction

Tip Folder names should be descriptive of the folder contents.

10 Type Destinations to replace the *New folder* placeholder text.

11 Drag the **M0-C2-S3-Vacation.docx** file to the Documents folder. The Documents folder now shows it contains one file.

12 Right-click the *Destinations* folder.

Tip To delete a file or folder, right-click it and then click *Delete*.

13 Click the *Rename* option.

14 Type Vacation and then press Enter to rename the folder.

15 Double-click the *Vacation* folder to open it.

16 Move your mouse over the M0-C2-S3-Vacation tile.

17 Click the check box in the top right corner of the M0-C2-S3-Vacation tile to select the file.

18 Click the Download button to download the file to your computer.

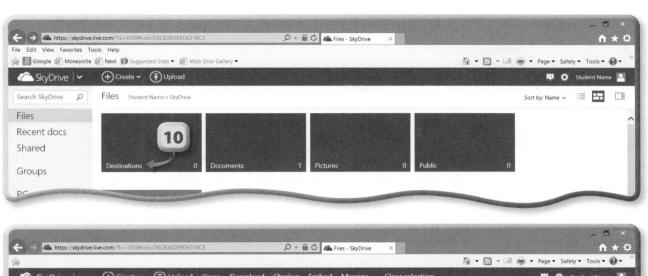

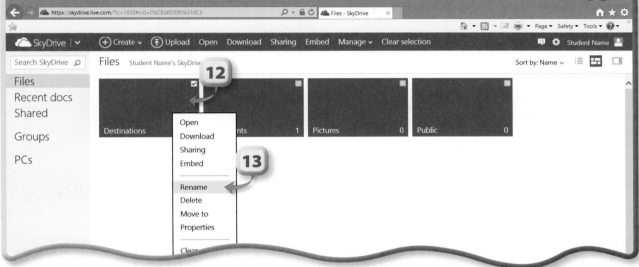

Introduction

Introduction

Skill 4

Edit Files Using Office Web Apps

 I_C2_S04

Office Web Apps are web-based versions of the Microsoft Office applications Word, Excel, PowerPoint, and OneNote. You can access these apps from your SkyDrive account. This allows you to create, open, edit, and save a file in one of the Office Web Apps, such as Word, without having to have the Office application installed on your computer. The Office Web Apps do not have all the features of the full Office applications, but you can do basic editing and formatting.

Steps

1 Sign in to your SkyDrive account if it is not already open.

2 Click the *Vacation* folder if it is not already open.

3 Click the check box in the top right corner of the Lastname-M0-C2-S3-Vacation tile to select the file.

4 Click the Open button arrow.

5 Click *Open in Word Web App* to view the file.

6 Click the EDIT DOCUMENT tab and then click the *Edit in Word Web App* option to display the document in the Microsoft Word Web App.

7 Double-click the word *Spring* to select it.

8 Type Summer and then press the spacebar to replace the selected text.

9 Click the Exit button in the document window to display the SkyDrive window.

3–5 *Another Way*
Click anywhere in the Lastname-M0-C2-S3-Vacation tile to open the file in the Microsoft Word Web App.

▶**Tip** The options available in the Open button drop-down menu will vary depending on the selected file. For example, if an Excel file was selected, the *Open in Excel Web App* option would be available.

▶**Tip** If you have Microsoft Office installed on your computer, you can use the *Open* option box arrow and choose to open a file using the Office Web App or the installed version of the software.

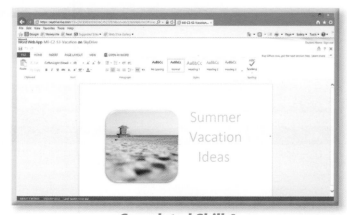

Completed Skill 4

Introduction

Skill 5

Create Files Using Office Web Apps

 Video I_C2_S05

In Skill 4, you edited an existing file using the Word Web App. You can also create files using the Office Web Apps. The Office Web Apps allow you to create a Word document, Excel workbook, PowerPoint presentation, or OneNote notebook from a web browser without having to have the Office applications installed on your computer. Once you have created a document, you can store the file on SkyDrive and then edit or share the file. When you create a file using the Office Web Apps, you have to name the file before you can work in it.

Steps

1   Sign in to your SkyDrive account if it is not already open.

2   Click the *Vacation* folder if it is not already open.

3   Click the Create button.

4   Click the *Word document* option.

5   Type Destinations in the *New Microsoft Word document* text box.

6   Click the Create button.

7   Type Vacation Destinations and then press the Enter key.

8   Click the Bullets button in the Paragraph group on the HOME tab.

9   Type San Diego and then press the Enter key.

▶**Tip** Before you save your document, you can click the Spelling button in the Spelling group to spell check your work.

10   Type Miami and then press the Enter key twice.

11   Click the Save button.

12   Click the Exit button in the document window to close the document and display the Destinations file in the SkyDrive window.

Completed Skill 5

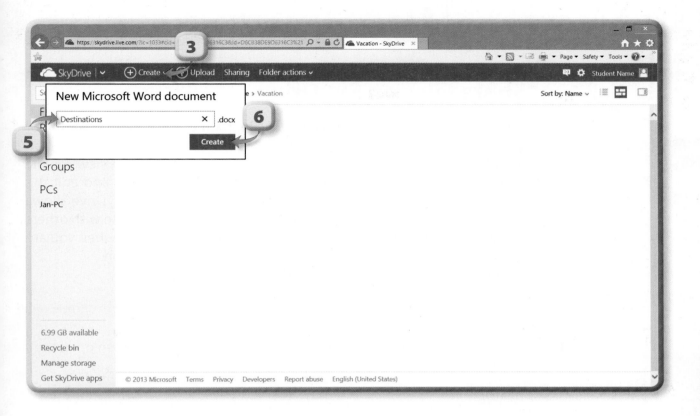

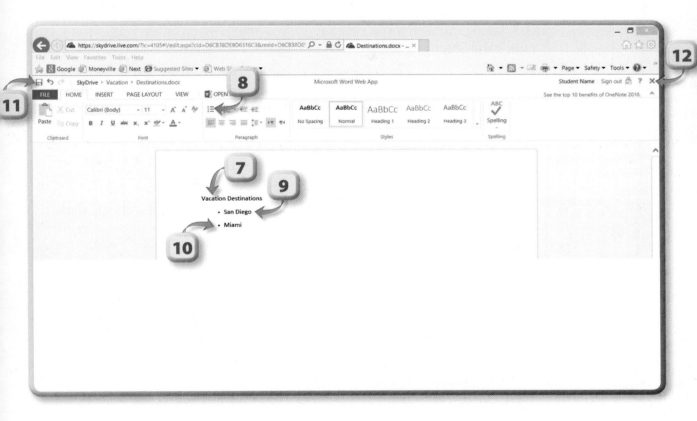

Introduction

Share Files on SkyDrive

Video | C2_S06

If your files are stored on SkyDrive, you can easily share files with your friends, classmates, and coworkers. If your files are large in size, as many photos and PowerPoint presentations are, you can send an email link to the SkyDrive location of the file. You can also post a link to the file on a social networking site, such as Facebook, LinkedIn, or Twitter. When you share a file, you can allow recipients to view the file or allow them to view and edit the file. Sharing files on SkyDrive allows you to easily collaborate with others on a single document when you are not in the same location.

Steps

1. Sign in to your SkyDrive account if it is not already open and then open the Vacation folder.

2. Click the check box in the top right corner of the Destinations tile to select the file.

3. Click the Sharing button.

4. Click the *Send email* option if it is not selected. Exchange email addresses with a classmate and type the classmate's email address in the *To* text box.

5. In the *Include a personal message (optional)* text box, type Please add to the destination list.

6. If necessary, click the *Recipients can edit* check box to insert a check mark.

7. Click the Share button to send the link.

8. Check your email account.

9. Double-click the new email you received from your classmate.

10. Click the Destinations.docx link to open the file in the Microsoft Word Web App.

11. Close the document. Sign out of SkyDrive and then close the browser window.

▶**Tip** To share the same link with more than one person, return to the SkyDrive main window, click *Groups* in the left pane, create a group, and then send the link to the group.

▶**Tip** Click *Post to* if you want to post the link on a social networking site instead of emailing the link.

▶**Tip** You may be asked to complete a security check before sharing the link.

▶**Tip** Click the EDIT DOCUMENT tab to edit the shared document.

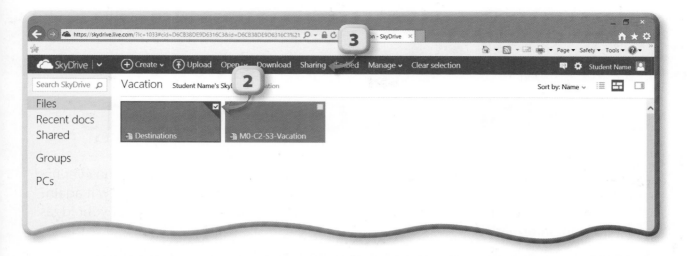

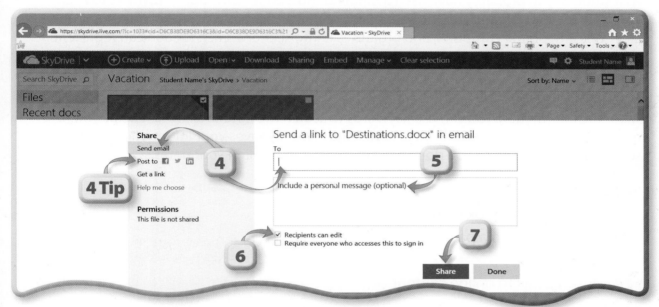

Chapter 3

Using Microsoft OneNote 2013

Do you ever take notes and then lose the piece of paper you wrote them on? Do you ever find a great website and then have to spend time searching for it when you want to view it again? One way to avoid these problems is to use OneNote as a digital notebook for all of your ideas and important information.

As a student, you probably have used a binder or notebook with subject dividers to keep your course notes organized. OneNote builds on the same idea, but stores your notebook electronically, on the computer, and organizes it into sections. Each section can represent a different subject and contain one or more pages.

OneNote has many advantages over a paper notebook. You are able to type information or copy from a website or other document. You are also able to easily delete, move, update, and share the information. You can use keywords to search the notebook, which helps you to quickly find what you need. Plus, OneNote automatically saves your information, including source web addresses, so you don't have to worry about losing your notes.

Skills You Learn

1   Create a notebook with sections
2   Add content to a page
3   Tag notes
4   Insert a link to online content

Files You Need

For these skills, you do not need any student data files.

What You Create

In this chapter, you create a digital notebook and organize the notebook into sections. You add and fill pages, flag important notes with tags, and include links to outside content. We suggest that once you know how to use OneNote, you make a section for each module in this textbook. As you work through the textbook, use the pages in each notebook section for your assignments and study notes.

Digital Notebook

Completed Skill 4

Introduction

Skill 1

Create a Notebook with Sections

Video I_C3_S01

In OneNote, you can create a digital notebook to collect all of your notes and information in one place. You can then search for information quickly and easily. Each new notebook you create consists of one section and one page. By default, the page contains a page header area. Below the page header area, OneNote lists the date and time that you created the page.

Steps

1 Another Way
You may have a OneNote 2013 tile on the Start screen. If you do, you can click this tile to start OneNote.

▶**Tip** You may be asked to sign in to your account when you open OneNote.

7–9 Another Way
To save your notebook on your computer, click *Computer*, click the Create in a different folder link, browse to the appropriate location, type the name of the notebook in the text box, and then click the Create button.

▶**Tip** Selecting SkyDrive as the storage location for your OneNote notebook will make the notebook available from all of your computing devices including your smartphone, tablet, and laptop.

1 From the Start screen, press Win + C to display the Charms bar.

2 Click the Search charm.

3 Type onenote in the search box.

4 Click *OneNote 2013* in the Apps results list.

5 Click the FILE tab.

6 Click the *New* option.

7 Click *Student Name's SkyDrive* to save your notebook on your SkyDrive. **NOTE:** *You will see your name instead of* Student Name.

8 Type Lastname Guidelines in the *Notebook Name* text box, but replace *Lastname* with your last name.

9 Click the Create Notebook button.

10 Click *Not now* in the displayed dialog box.

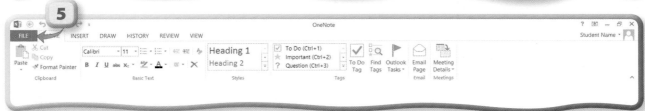

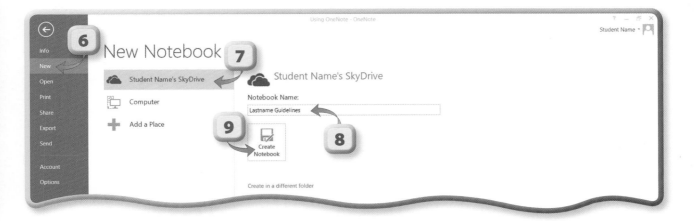

11 Right-click the New Section 1 tab and then click the *Rename* option.

12 Type Introduction Toolkit and press Enter. Use this OneNote section for your notes from the Introduction section of this textbook.

13 Point to the right of the Introduction Toolkit tab until you see the Create a New Section tab and then click the Create a New Section tab.

14 Type Module 1 Computing Essentials and then press Enter. Use this section for your notes from Module 1 of this textbook.

15 If you are not continuing on to the next skill, click the Close button.

Taking It Further

Sharing a Notebook   Sharing a notebook allows you to collaborate with others on projects without having to be in the same room or having to email files back and forth. When you select SkyDrive as the place to save your notebook, you will be prompted to invite others to share your notebook. You will need to type the email addresses of the people you are sharing with or select their names from your address book. You can also specify if they are able to edit the notebook or just view it. To share a notebook after you have created it, click the FILE tab, click the *Share* option, and then type the email address of the person you would like to share the notebook with in the *Invite People* text box.

Completed Skill 1

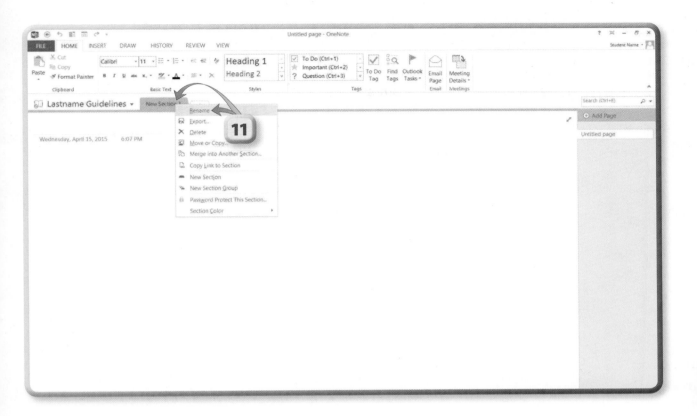

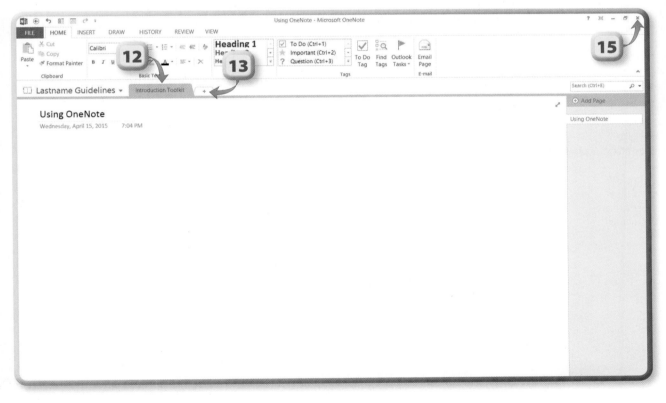

Introduction

Skill 2

Add Content to a Page

Video   I_C3_S02

You can add data anywhere on a notebook page. To create a note, click the spot on the page where you want the note to appear and then start typing. OneNote creates a box called a *note container* around each block of text that you type.

The content in a note container is not limited to text—you can also add pictures, tables, equations, files, screenshots, web links, audio, video, and original drawings. You can also move and size note containers.

Steps

1 With your Guidelines OneNote notebook open, click the Introduction Toolkit tab, if it is not already selected.

2 Type Using OneNote in the page header area to change the name of the page.

3 Click a blank area of the page below the current time and type Data can be added anywhere on a page.

4 Click a blank area of the page below and to the right of the note container you created in Step 3 and type The box around the text you type is called a note container.

5 If you are not continuing on to the next skill, click the Close button.

▶**Tip** The default colors of the tabs in OneNote may vary and may not match the colors shown on the opposite page.

▶**Tip** Each page header also appears on its corresponding page tab in the right pane. If you leave the page header blank, the text in the first line of your notes automatically becomes the page header.

▶**Tip** To organize your notes, you can move note containers. Hover your mouse pointer over the top bar until the mouse pointer turns into a four-headed arrow and then drag the container to move it to another location on the page.

Taking It Further

Creating and Naming New Pages
Typically, a section in a paper notebook consists of more than one page. To add a new page to the current section of your OneNote notebook, click the Add Page button at the top of the page tabs. You can navigate among pages by clicking a page tab in the right pane. When naming a page, keep in mind that page names should be meaningful and should reflect the page content. You can change the page name by typing text in the page header.

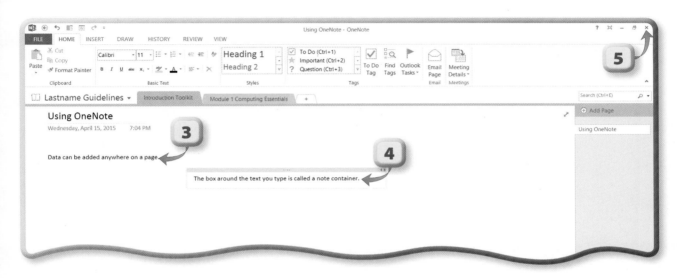

Completed Skill 2

Introduction

Introduction

> Skill 3

Tag Notes

 I_C3_S03

When you are taking a lot of notes, it is useful to be able to flag important notes so you can go back to them quickly. OneNote makes this easy by providing several predefined note tags, such as *Important* and

To Do. Use these predefined note tags to organize your notes. You can also create your own custom note tags and then create a summary of tagged items.

Steps

1 With your Guidelines OneNote notebook open, click the Introduction Toolkit tab, if it is not already selected.

2 Click the note container containing the text *Data can be added anywhere on a page*.

3 Click the HOME tab.

4 Click the More button in the Tags gallery in the Tags group.

5 Click the *Important* option.

▶**Tip** Click *Customize Tags* in the Tags gallery to create your own custom note tag.

6 Click the note container containing the text *The box around the text you type is called a note container*.

7 Click the More arrow in the Tags gallery.

▶**Tip** To remove a tag, select the note container and then click *Remove Tag* in the Tags gallery.

8 Click the *Definition* option.

9 Click the Find Tags button in the Tags group to display the Tags Summary task pane.

▶**Tip** The Tags Summary task pane shows all tagged items. Use the *Group tags by* and *Search* drop-down arrows to filter the tags. Use the Refresh Results button to update the Tags Summary after adding or removing tags.

10 Click the Close button in the Tags Summary task pane.

11 Click the Close button in the OneNote window if you are not continuing on to the next skill.

Completed Skill 3

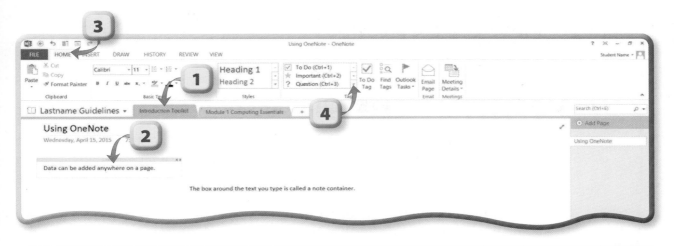

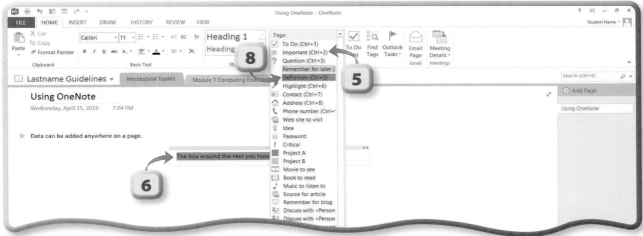

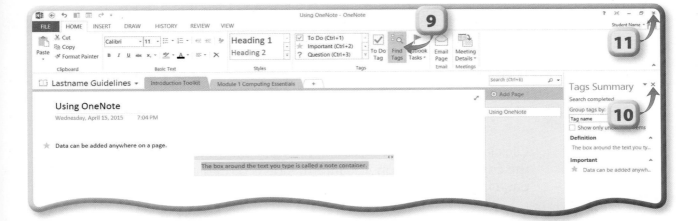

Taking It Further

Creating and Using a To-Do List   If you need to create a task or to-do list, use the *To Do* tag. This tag adds a check box to the left of the content in a note container. You can then create a To Do list on a separate page by clicking the Find Tags button, collapsing all tags shown except the *To Do* tags, and then clicking the Create Summary Page button at the bottom of the Tags Summary task pane. Once you create this list, you can use it to keep track of which tasks are completed and which remain. To indicate that you have done a task, click the check box next to the item to insert a check mark.

Introduction

Skill 4

Video I_C3_S04

Insert a Link to Online Content

When researching on the Web, you can copy useful information from a web page to a OneNote page. OneNote creates a note container for the pasted information. A great feature of OneNote is that, when you paste that information into the OneNote page, it automatically places the website's location (URL) in the note container. Having the URL with your research notes ensures that you know where the information came from and saves you time in documenting your research sources. Plus, you can easily go back to the website by clicking the link on the OneNote page.

Steps

1 With your Guidelines OneNote notebook open, click the Introduction Toolkit tab, if it is not already selected.

2 Click in a blank area of the page below the existing note containers and type www.emcp.net/OneNote.

3 Click the www.emcp.net/OneNote link to display the web page in your browser window.

4 On the displayed web page, triple-click the text below *OneNote Tip* to select it.

5 Press Ctrl + C to copy the selected information to your Clipboard.

6 Close the browser window.

7 Click in a blank area of the *Using OneNote* page and press Ctrl + V to paste the copied information. The information is pasted along with the URL of the page from which the information was copied.

8 Click the Close button to close OneNote.

▶ **Tip** Create a list of the websites in your notebook pages by tagging them *Web sites to visit*. Later, you can create a Tags Summary list of all such websites. If you add links, click the Refresh Results button to update the list.

Taking It Further

Using OneNote to Create a Research Paper   Start by creating note containers with your research notes. You can then move and tag note containers to organize your notes. Once your research is organized, click the FILE tab and then click the *Export* option to export your notes into a Word document. Alternatively, click the title bar of the note container, press Ctrl + C to copy the contents, and then switch to the Word document and press Ctrl + V to paste them.

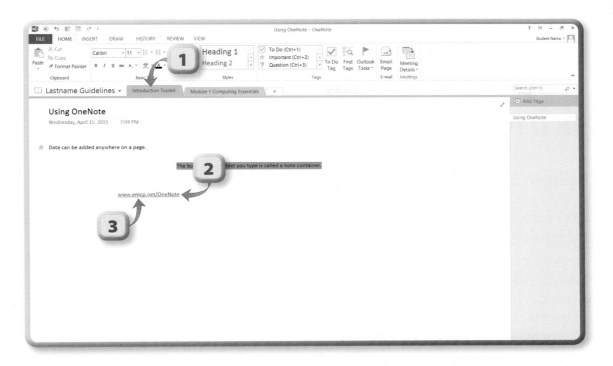

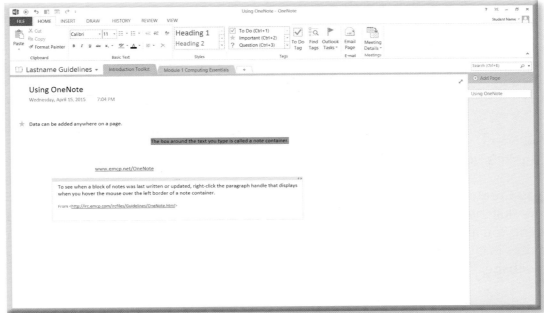

Completed Skill 4

Introduction

Chapter 4

Taking Screenshots

A screenshot captures a picture of your computer monitor screen. You can use screenshots to create a simple instruction manual by inserting the screenshots in a document and adding callouts or labels to point out specific items in the pictures. You can also attach a screenshot to an email message.

As you work through this textbook, if you have difficulty or encounter an error message, you can take a screenshot and send it to your instructor. After reviewing the screenshot, your instructor can help you to learn what went wrong or can explain how to fix the error. Your instructor may also want you to take a screenshot to confirm that you have completed some of the skills or assessments in this textbook.

You can take a screenshot of the entire desktop by using the Print Screen key. The Print Screen key copies the screenshot to the Clipboard. A temporary storage area, the Clipboard holds the screen image so that you can paste it into a file. For example, you could paste it into a WordPad document. You can also save a screenshot as a PNG file while you are capturing it.

On occasion, you may need to capture only a portion of the screen. You can then use the Snipping Tool program instead of the Print Screen key. This program is a Windows 8 app. With Snipping Tool, you can capture a portion of the screen, copy it to the Clipboard, and then paste it into a document. You can also save the screen snipping in various graphic file formats.

In addition, you can capture the screen or a portion of the screen from within the Office 2013 applications using the Clipping Tool. For example, in OneNote, you can use the Clipping Tool to capture information you would like to reference from a website or other document.

Skills You Learn

1 Take a screenshot
2 Use the Snipping Tool
3 Use the Clipping Tool

Files You Need
For these skills, you do not need any student data files.

What You Create
For these skills, you capture an image of your entire desktop and paste it in a WordPad document. You also capture an image of the Taskbar on your desktop and add it to your study notes in OneNote. You then use the Clipping Tool in OneNote to capture information from a website.

Start Screen Screenshot

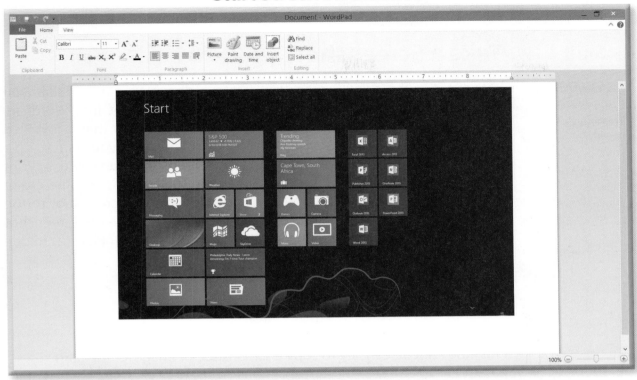

Taskbar Screenshot Pasted into OneNote

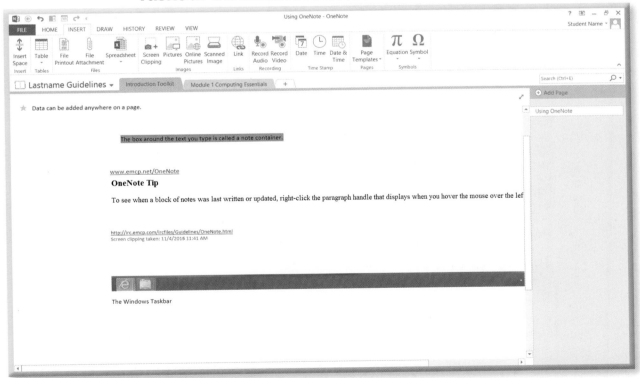

Introduction

Skill 1

Take a Screenshot

 I_C4_S01

You can use the Print Screen key to take a screenshot of your entire screen. This key is located in the top right area of your keyboard. When you press the Print Screen key, the image of your current screen is copied to a temporary storage area called the *Clipboard*. You can then paste the screenshot into a document. In this skill, you paste a screenshot into WordPad. WordPad is an app that is installed with Windows 8. If you want to save the screenshot, press Win + Print Screen. This will capture the entire screen, copy the screenshot to the Clipboard, and save the screenshot as a PNG file in your Pictures folder.

Steps

Tip On a laptop, you may need to hold down the Fn key while you press the Print Screen key.

Tip The Windows Clipboard will store only the most recent image captured.

1 Press the Windows key to display the Start screen.

2 Press the Print Screen key to copy a screenshot, or image, of the Start screen.

3 Press Win + C to display the Charms bar.

4 Click the Search charm.

5 Type WordPad in the search box.

6 Click *WordPad* in the Apps results list.

7 Click the File tab.

8 Click the *Page setup* option.

Taking It Further

Using the Paint Program If you want to edit a screenshot, you can open or paste the screenshot in an image editing program such as Paint. Like WordPad, Paint is a Windows 8 app. To start Paint, press Win + C, click the Search charm, type *Paint* in the search box, and then click *Paint* in the Apps results list.

You can use the tools in the Paint program to add callouts, erase or crop part of the screenshot, rotate the screenshot, and resize the screenshot. You can also add and edit the screenshot colors. You can choose to save the screenshot from within Paint as a PNG, JPG, BMP, or TIF file.

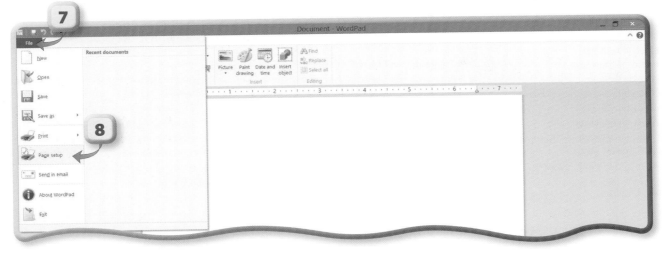

More

Introduction

Introduction

Tip Landscape orientation makes the width of the page longer than the height and is a better fit for most screenshots.

Tip Make sure to click the Paste button rather than the Paste button arrow.

9 Click the *Landscape* option in the *Orientation* section of the Page Setup dialog box.

10 Click OK to close the Page Setup dialog box.

11 Click the Paste button in the Clipboard group of the HOME tab to paste the screenshot of your Start screen into the document.

12 Close WordPad without saving.

13 Press the Windows key to display the Start screen.

14 Hold down the Windows key and then press the Print Screen key. Notice that the screen dims to show that the screenshot has been taken.

15 Use the Search charm to open Paint. *HINT: See steps 3–4 if you need a reminder on how to use the Search charm to open an application.*

16 Click the File tab and then click the *Open* option.

Tip Screenshots are named *Screenshot (1)*, *Screenshot (2)*, and so forth.

17 Browse to **Screenshot (1).png** inside the Screenshots folder, which is inside your Pictures folder.

Tip The view you see when browsing for files will vary depending on your Windows configuration. It may not exactly match the view shown for step 17 on the opposite page.

18 Double-click the screenshot file to open it in Paint.

19 Close Paint without saving.

Tip You have several options for sharing a screenshot. You can print it and share the hard copy. If you want to share an electronic copy, you can share the screenshot file as an email attachment or upload it to a web page. In addition, you can save the document you pasted it into and then send it as an email attachment.

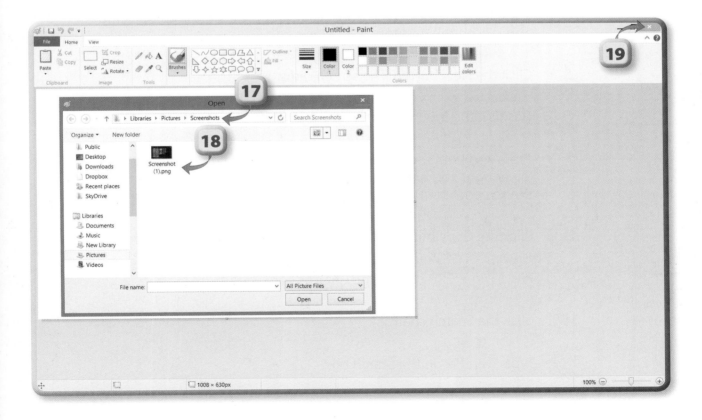

Introduction

Skill 2

Use the Snipping Tool

Video   I_C4_S02

In Skill 1, you learned to take a screenshot of the entire desktop by pressing the Print Screen key. If you want to capture only a portion of the screen instead of the entire desktop, you can use the Snipping Tool. The Snipping Tool is a Windows 8 app. After you take a screenshot with the Snipping Tool, you can copy it to the Clipboard and then paste it into a document. You can also save the file and insert it into a document or send it as an email attachment.

Steps

1 From the Start screen, press Win + C to display the Charms bar.

2 Click the Search charm.

3 Type Snipping in the search box.

4 Click *Snipping Tool* in the Apps results list. The Snipping Tool window appears on the desktop.

5 Click the New button. The screen dims.

6 Position the mouse pointer on the top left corner of the Taskbar.

▶**Tip** If you are not happy with the screenshot, click the New button to start over.

7 Press and hold the left mouse button and then drag your mouse to the lower right corner of the Taskbar. Release the left mouse button to display the screenshot in the Snipping Tool window.

8 *Another Way*
As an alternative to copying and pasting the screenshot, you can save the screenshot as a graphic file and then insert it in a document.

8 Click the Copy button to copy the screenshot to the Clipboard.

9 Press Win + C to display the Charms bar.

10 Click the Search charm.

11 Type WordPad in the search box.

12 Click *WordPad* in the Apps results list.

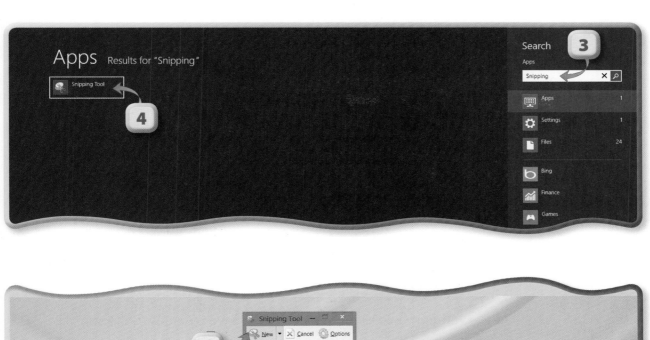

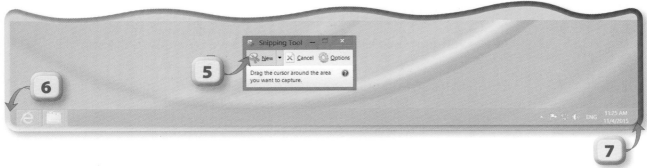

More

Introduction

13 Click the Paste button in the Clipboard group on the HOME tab to paste the Taskbar screenshot into the document.

14 Press the Enter key and then type This screenshot of the Taskbar was created using the Snipping Tool.

▶**Tip** You have several options for sharing a snipped screen. You can print it and share the hard copy. If you want to share an electronic copy, you can save the image as a graphic file from within the Snipping Tool and then share the graphic file as an email attachment or upload it to a web page.

15 Close the WordPad document.

16 Click the Don't Save button to close the WordPad window without saving the document.

17 Click the Close button in the upper right corner of the Snipping Tool window.

18 In the warning box asking if you want to save changes to the snip, click No.

▶**Tip** You do not need to save the snipped image to WordPad before saving it to OneNote.

19 Start OneNote and open your Lastname Guidelines notebook if it is not already open. **HINT:** *See steps 1–4 and 9–12 for instructions on searching for and opening an app.*

20 Click the Introduction Toolkit tab. **NOTE:** *You created this tab in Chapter 3, Skill 1 of this module.*

21 Click in a blank area of the page and then click the Paste button in the Clipboard group on the HOME tab to paste the screenshot of the Taskbar onto the OneNote page.

22 Type The Windows Taskbar. (Do not type the period.)

23 Close OneNote.

Taking It Further

Learning More about the Snipping Tool   When you capture screenshots with the Snipping Tool, you can save them in a variety of common graphic file formats, including JPG, PNG, and GIF. If you save your screenshot, you will be able to use it again later. You can also annotate screenshots in the Snipping Tool by clicking the Pen button on the toolbar and then writing on or around the screenshot. If you make a mistake, click the Eraser button and erase your mistake.

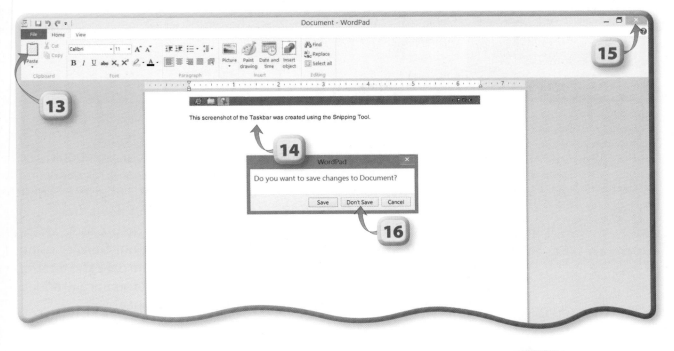

This screenshot of the Taskbar was created using the Snipping Tool.

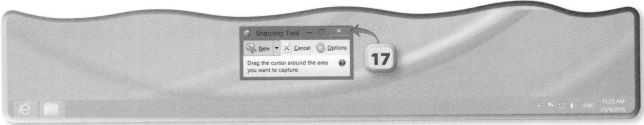

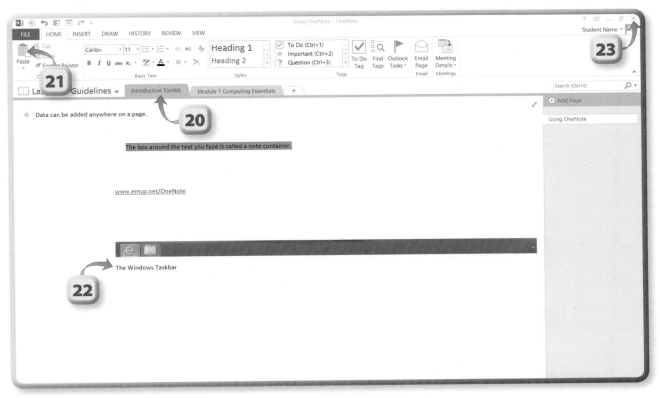

Introduction

Skill 3

Use the Clipping Tool

Video   I_C4_S03

Screenshots and screen clippings can also be captured within the Microsoft Office 2013 applications using the OneNote Clipping Tool. After you open this tool, it will be available to all other Office 2013 applications. The Clipping Tool works like the Snipping Tool, allowing you to copy portions of your window to save as image files and paste into documents. For example, you can use the Clipping Tool to take a picture of your screen and insert it into a page in your notebook. The Clipping Tool is useful for capturing information that might change, such as a breaking news story, and for copying from web pages whose formatting might not transfer using copy and paste. The date and time of the capture are automatically added to the note container.

Steps

1 Open your Guidelines OneNote notebook. **NOTE:** *You created this notebook in Chapter 3, Skill 1 of this module.*

2 Click the Introduction Toolkit tab, if it is not already selected. **NOTE:** *You also created this tab in Chapter 3, Skill 1 of this module.*

3 Click the www.emcp.net/OneNote link to display the web page in your browser window.

4 Click the OneNote button on the Taskbar.

5 Click a blank area of the page.

6 Click the INSERT tab.

7 Click the Screen Clipping button in the Images group. The web page is displayed.

8 Position the mouse pointer in the top left of the title *OneNote Tip*.

9 Press and hold the left mouse button and then drag your mouse to the bottom right corner of the *OneNote Tip* title.

10 Release the left mouse button to display the screenshot in OneNote. Notice that the source, date, and time are added to the note container.

11 Close OneNote.

▶**Tip** In Excel, Outlook, and Word, you access the Clipping Tool by clicking the Screenshot button in the Illustrations group on the INSERT tab and then clicking the *Screen Clipping* option.

▶**Tip** In PowerPoint, you access the Clipping tool by clicking the Screenshot button in the Images group on the INSERT tab and then clicking the *Screen Clipping* option.

▶**Tip** If the Clipping Tool is not available in Excel, Outlook, Word, or PowerPoint, open OneNote. The Clipping Tool will then stay open even after you close OneNote.

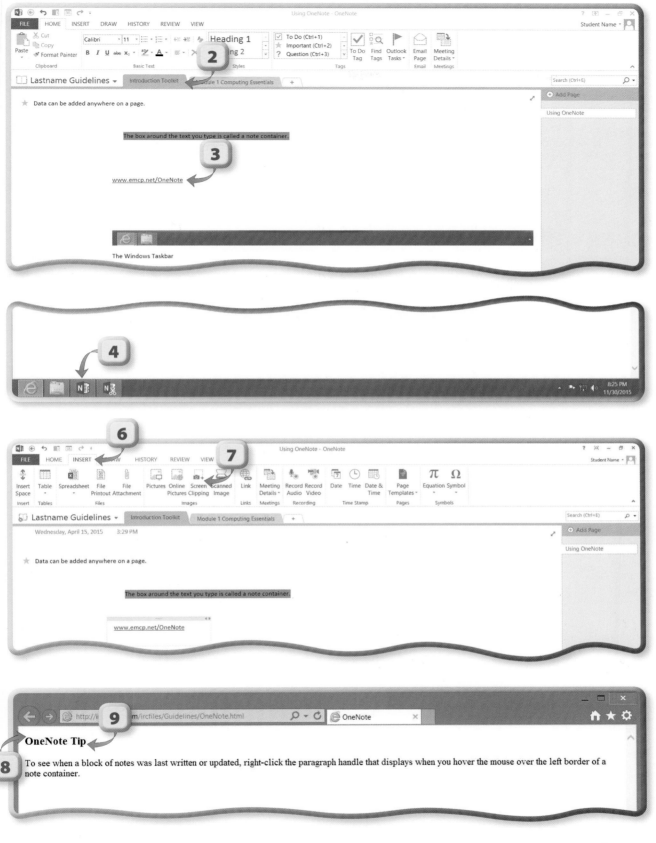

More

Introduction

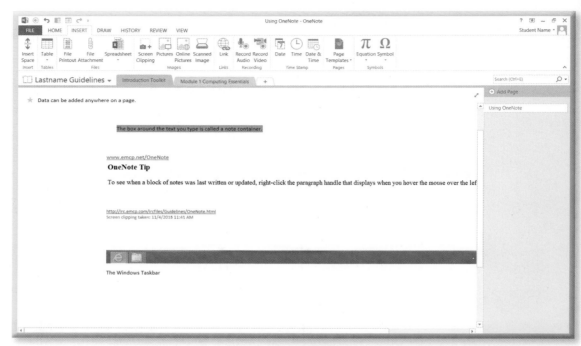

Completed Skill 3

MODULE 1

Computing Essentials

What Is a Computer System and How Does It Work?

How Do Operating Systems Software and Applications Software Differ?

This module provides a brief overview of fundamental computing concepts, including the components of a computer system, the methods computers use to process data, the elements of a computer network, and the two major types of software.

Step-by-step activities are not included with these concepts. Instead, you are encouraged to explore your own computer system to identify the hardware and software components described in this module. Doing so will give you an understanding of how your computer works, which will help you as you work through this text.

What Is a Computer System

A computer system is made up of a central processing unit (CPU) and any attached equipment, or *hardware*. The hardware and *software* (set of instructions that tell the computer what to do) in a computer system work together to turn data into information through a process called the *information processing cycle*. All computing devices—including desktop computers and mobile devices such as tablets, laptops, ultrabooks, and smartphones—use a basic information processing cycle, which follows these steps:

1 The user enters data using an input device such as a keyboard or touch screen.

2 The CPU processes the data into information and stores it in the internal memory.

3 Information is sent to the computer's screen or another output device such as a printer.

4 Information is stored on a storage medium such as a flash drive, a hard disk, or an online cloud server.

Computer System Hardware

The illustration below shows a typical desktop computer system with the hardware responsible for carrying out the four parts of the information processing cycle.

Input devices. You use hardware items, such as a keyboard, mouse, touch screen, microphone, or web cam, to enter commands and data into your computer.

Processing component. The CPU performs the mathematical operations and coordinates the functions of the computer system. The CPU is typically a microprocessor. It is located on the motherboard, the main circuit board of the computer. The physical location of the motherboard varies, depending on the type of computer. For example, in a laptop, the CPU may be in the lower half. In a desktop computer, the CPU may be in a tower.

Output devices. The job of output devices is to convert information from your computer into a usable form such as visual (printout, monitor), audio (speakers), or to send it to a storage medium in digital format (hard drive, CD/DVD drive, online cloud server).

Storage devices. You use storage devices for saving data that you want to use again. Storage media, ranging from your computer hard disk to removable storage such as a DVD or flash drive, vary in the amount of data they can store. Cloud storage has become a popular option because limited quantities are offered for free and you can access the data from any computing device with an Internet connection.

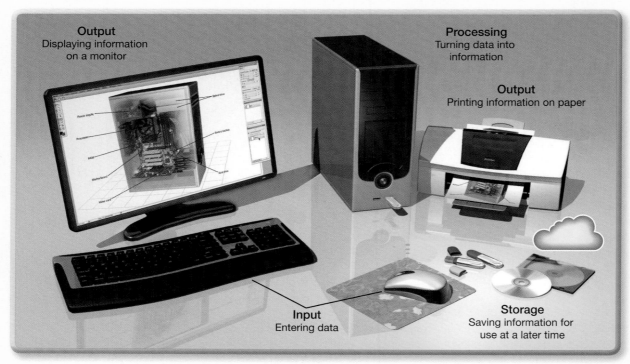

Output
Displaying information on a monitor

Processing
Turning data into information

Output
Printing information on paper

Input
Entering data

Storage
Saving information for use at a later time

and How Does It Work?

The Motherboard

The main circuit board in a computer is called the motherboard and its importance in the system deserves special attention. The motherboard is a thin sheet of fiberglass or other material with electrical pathways that connect these key components of the information processing cycle:

- microprocessor/CPU
- memory
- expansion slots for holding expansion cards

The illustration below shows these motherboard components, along with other necessary elements, including a power supply and ports for "plugging in" external hardware, such as a keyboard, mouse, and printer.

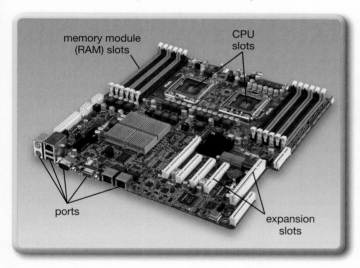

Microprocessor. The CPU of your computer is a microprocessor or *processor* located on the motherboard. It is a thin wafer or chip containing an integrated circuit that processes your requests. Some computers have several processors.

Memory. Your computer has two kinds of memory, which are located on tiny silicon chips etched with electrical circuits: (1) permanent memory, called read-only memory, or ROM, which contains start-up instructions and other permanent instructions; (2) temporary memory, called random access memory, or RAM, which holds data while your computer is on. When you close a program the RAM is made available for another use, but to completely erase the RAM you have to restart or turn off your computer.

Expansion slots. You can add expansion cards to your motherboard to add capabilities such as increased processing power and enhanced video and audio.

A Computer Network

Computers can be linked together in a network. A *network* allows the linked computers to share files, software, and resources, such as a printer. Two key types of networks are local area networks (LANs), which connect nearby computers within a home or business, and wide area networks (WANs), which connect distant computers, such as those among a company's branch offices around the country. The Internet is the largest of all WANs. Devices that make up a basic network include:

Individual computing devices. You can connect various computing devices to each other and to the Internet via a network. Networks require a communications medium, such as a wireless signal or a cable.

Modem. A modem is the hardware that sends and receives data to or from a transmission source, such as a phone or cable line. Types of modems typically used in homes and small offices include cable, DSL, and satellite.

Network adapter. A network adapter enables your computer to connect to a wired or wireless network. Wired computers typically support Ethernet standards while wireless computers support Wi-Fi standards. A network interface card (NIC) is one type of network adapter your computer can contain.

Wireless access point. Wireless access points and routers relay data among devices on a network. A wireless access point and a router can be two separate devices or combined into one device.

Bluetooth. Your computing devices may use Bluetooth technology to communicate short distances without wires. Bluetooth can connect a hands-free headset, a wireless keyboard, and sync devices, such as your smartphone with your computer.

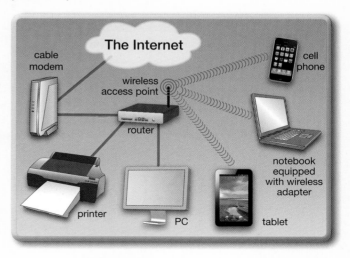

Software is the set of instructions that tells your computer what to do. Your computer has two basic types of software: its operating system and its applications. Microsoft Windows, Apple's OS X, and Linux are examples of operating systems. Word, Excel, OneNote, and the other programs in the Microsoft Office 2013 Suite are examples of applications.

Operating Systems Software

The most important piece of software used on a computer system is its operating system, or OS. When you turn on the computer, it performs a power-on self-test (POST) to check that the hardware is working properly. Then it loads the OS into memory. The OS performs several key functions:

- It manages the operations of the CPU and the computer's hardware devices.

- It provides a user interface that allows a person to interact with the computer.

- It supports operations initiated from within application programs, such as opening and closing programs and saving and printing documents.

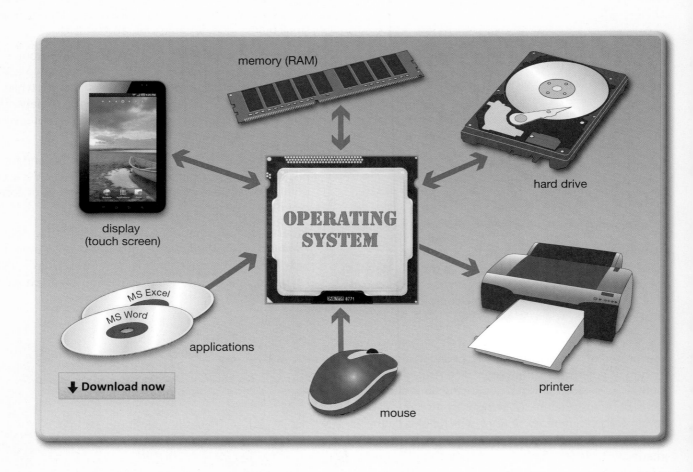

memory (RAM)

display (touch screen)

MS Excel

MS Word

applications

↓ Download now

OPERATING SYSTEM

hard drive

printer

mouse

Applications Software

Applications software is the group of programs you use to get your computer-based projects done. Applications include spreadsheets that perform numeric calculations, word processors that create text-based documents, presentation software that creates slide shows, and database software that sorts and organizes huge amounts of data. But there are many more, including games, tax preparation, Web design, desktop publishing, graphic editing, and audio and video programs. All of these applications enhance your experience using the computer and provide many tools for completing personal, academic, and work projects.

Some applications are designed to run on a particular computing device, such as a gaming device. Other applications are designed to run on a specific operating system. For example, Microsoft Office for Mac is a version of the Office suite that runs on Apple's OS X.

There are also an endless amount of small applications, or *apps*, available for a variety of computing devices including smartphones and tablets. Many of these apps are written to perform a specific single task, such as to display current headlines, and can be downloaded for free. The app pictured below displays the weather for a particular city.

MODULE 2

Microsoft Windows 8

 Chapter 2, Skill 2 of this module teaches you how to copy the module's folder of files to your hard disk, flash drive, SkyDrive, or other storage medium. No files are required for Chapter 1.

Guidelines for Using the

Windows 8 is an operating system. Your computer must have an operating system installed before it can function and before you can install other application programs, such as Microsoft Word.

The operating system performs basic tasks, including recognizing input from the keyboard and the mouse (or from the touch screen), sending output to the monitor, keeping track of saved files and folders, and controlling disk drives and printers.

Understanding How Windows Interacts with Applications

Apps is the name Windows 8 gives to programs. An app, such as Microsoft Word, interacts with the operating system to execute many of its commands, including opening and saving a file. Even when you click your mouse or tap your touch screen to select a command in Word, the operating system is what recognizes the input from the mouse or touchpad and communicates that information to the app. Similarly, when you print a document, the app interacts with the operating system in order to communicate with the printer.

The drawing below illustrates the relationships among the user, the apps, the operating system, and the computer hardware.

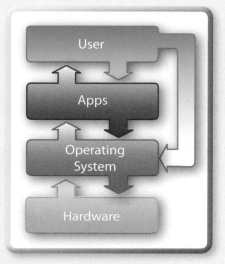

Getting Started with Windows

Have you ever wondered how Windows got its name? Microsoft chose the term *windows* to describe the graphical user interface (GUI) that it developed for use on personal computers. Earlier operating systems had used word-based commands. With Windows (as with Apple's Mac OS that came before it), users worked within a window-like frame that included pull-down menus, icons, and dialog boxes. All of these features were designed to create a simple way for users to interact with computers.

Windows 8 has dramatically changed its look and functionality. The Start button has been replaced by the Start screen. The icons present in earlier versions of Windows have been replaced by tiles. Instead of clicking Start to locate applications, documents, games, and so on, you can simply go to the Start screen and begin typing the name of what you need. The new user interface is touch-friendly, so anyone who has worked with a smartphone or tablet will feel right at home. The more traditional desktop user interface is also available, right from the Start screen.

Managing Files and Folders

Much of the work you do on a computer involves creating a document or some other kind of file that you want to save for reference or for later use. Your computer's operating system provides the tools for organizing files into folders and for copying, moving, or deleting files and folders. Learning how to manage files and folders is a critical skill in using computers successfully.

As you progress through this textbook, you will use Windows 8 commands to copy module folders from the Student Resources disc to your storage medium. The first page of each module displays information about the files needed along with a reminder to copy that

Power of Windows

module's folder of files (if required). As you work on a module, you save your files to that same folder on your storage medium so you can find them easily.

Files are named to indicate the module, the chapter (when chapters are present), and the skill. For example, the file M2-C2-S8-RecycleBin.docx is a file that is created or opened in Module 2, Chapter 2, Skill 8. The file M4-S2-Sales.xlsx is a file that is created or opened in Module 4, Skill 2. Note that because Module 4 does not contain separate chapters, its file names do not include a chapter number. The first screen capture at the right shows how the folders copied to a flash drive (identified as *Removable Disk* in the Address Bar) might be displayed.

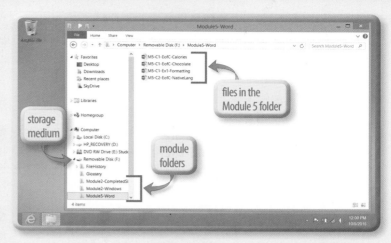

Changing Settings and Using Accessories

Windows 8 offers a Control Panel component where you can add or remove printers and other hardware devices. You can also change the screen resolution, change the date and time settings, and uninstall programs. If you have visual or hearing impairments, you can request that Windows suggest the best settings choices. You simply answer a few questions and Windows makes recommendations. The second screen capture at the right shows some of the settings choices offered on the Personalization screen of the Control Panel.

You can access computer settings in two different ways in Windows 8: (1) Using a mouse, point to the upper-right corner of the screen until the Charms bar is visible and then click the Settings charm. (If you are using a tablet, swipe in from the right edge and then tap Settings.) (2) On the Start screen, right-click in any blank area, click the All apps icon, locate the Windows System group, and then click *Control Panel*.

With a Windows 8 installation, several handy utility programs are installed and stored in the Windows Accessories group, as shown in the third screen capture above. Notepad and WordPad, for example, perform basic word processing functions. With the Snipping Tool, you can create screen captures (images) of parts of a screen. Paint allows you to create or edit various kinds of images. With Sticky Notes, you can place brief reminders on the desktop.

Using a Touch Screen

Smartphones, tablets, and some personal computers have touch screens, which can be manipulated using your fingers or a stylus. Windows 8 supports interactions with these screens. Touch screens are able to detect a touch or tap, and other movements, as well as the amount of pressure applied. Key touch screen interactions include these:

Tap. Tap the screen once. This is similar to clicking with a mouse.

Press and hold. Press on the screen for a couple of seconds. This is similar to right-clicking with a mouse.

Pinch. Touch the screen with two or more fingers spread apart and move them toward one another. This is similar to zooming in with a mouse; it makes the text or image smaller.

Stretch. Touch the screen with two or more fingers close together and move them apart. This is similar to zooming out with a mouse. It makes the text or image larger.

Rotate. Touch the screen with two or more fingers and turn your hand. This will rotate the text or image in the direction of your hand movement. ***NOTE:*** *Not all items can be rotated.*

Slide. Touch the screen and drag to the left, right, up, or down. This is like scrolling with a mouse.

Move. Press an image or text area and drag it from one part of the screen to another. This is similar to the hand option that you find in e-reader applications.

Swipe. Use a quick, short movement to swipe in from the edge of the screen. Swiping does different things on different areas of the screen, depending on the program you are in. For example, when you swipe in from the right edge in Windows 8, the Charms bar displays.

Touch screens have both advantages and disadvantages. For example, you have to be physically close to a touch screen in order to use it. In addition, if using a finger and not a stylus, a touch screen is often not as accurate as using a mouse. An advantage of a touch screen is that clicks are much faster. Another advantage is that it takes up less room and is more portable, as you will not need a keyboard or mouse.

This textbook uses the desktop (mouse-based) interface. If you have a touch screen, experiment with the interactions described above and adapt them to the instructions.

Chapter 1

Navigating around Windows

Windows 8 is the latest Microsoft Windows operating system. Operating system software is run automatically when the computer is turned on. It is used to control processing and peripherals (such as printers), running applications, and controlling input and output, among other tasks. Every computer must have an operating system installed in order to function.

When you purchase a computer, it usually comes with an operating system already installed. Once you begin using your computer, most of the work of the operating system occurs "behind the scenes," so most users are unaware of its role. However, understanding what an operating system does, and learning to use some of the Windows 8 features, will help you become a more productive and efficient computer user.

The Windows 8 user interface represents a significant change from the desktop of previous versions of Windows. The Windows 8 Start screen provides a central "jumping-off" point from which you can perform a variety of tasks, such watching a video, emailing a friend, and checking the local weather.

Skills You Learn

1. Start and sign in to Windows
2. Open and close apps with tiles
3. Open and close apps without tiles
4. Explore the desktop
5. Work with tools on the Taskbar
6. Open and close programs
7. Manipulate windows
8. Move among open windows
9. Work with menus, toolbars, and ribbons
10. Use keyboard shortcuts
11. Make selections in dialog boxes
12. Shut down or put Windows to sleep

Files You Need

For these skills, you do not need any student data files.

What You Create

In this chapter, you gain an understanding of what an operating system does and learn how to use some of the Windows 8 tools and features. You work with tiles, tabs, buttons, menus, options, and links. You become familiar with the ribbon interface in File Explorer. You explore different ways to switch between one app (program) and another. You practice using the Start screen to begin many activities, and learn how to switch back and forth between the Start screen and the desktop. You discover how to use the Charms bar to access common features such as Settings and Search.

Windows

Skill 1

Start and Sign In to Windows

Video M2_C1_S01

When you turn on a Windows-based computer, the operating system starts automatically. If separate users have been set up for the computer, a screen may display where you can click your user account to sign in, entering a password if required. If only one user is set up on the computer and that user has no password, the Windows 8 Start screen appears when the computer is turned on. On the Windows 8 Start screen, you can accomplish many of the things you could do by clicking the Start button in previous versions of Windows. For example, you can access a list of all the programs installed on your computer by displaying the Charms bar and clicking the Search charm, or by opening the Apps screen. The Start screen also displays tiles that you can click to access applications and perform tasks such as opening a website.

Steps

1 Turn on your computer. The Windows Lock screen displays. (If the Start screen displays, skip to Step 4.)

2 Press any key or click anywhere in the Lock screen to go to the Sign-in screen. If your user account does not display, click the Switch user button to view the available user accounts. Click your user account.

Tip Passwords in Windows 8 are case-sensitive, meaning that the computer "sees" an uppercase *A* and a lowercase *a* as different characters.

3 Type your password in the text box below your user account name. Press Enter or click the Submit button at the right of the text box. Windows 8 with the Start screen displays. **Note:** *Check with your instructor if you have problems signing in.*

4 *Shortcut*
Display Charms Bar
Win + C

4 Move the mouse pointer to the upper right corner of the screen. (You may need to actually move the pointer off the screen.) The Charms bar appears.

4 *Another Way*
You also can display the Charms bar by moving the mouse to the lower right corner of the screen.

5 Move the pointer down and click the Settings charm to open the Settings pane. Notice that the Settings pane allows you to perform tasks such as modifying the volume.

6 Position the mouse pointer in a blank area of the Start screen and click. The Settings pane disappears.

7 Click your account picture in the upper right corner of the Start screen to open a drop-down menu. This is where you go to change your account picture, lock your computer, sign out, or switch user accounts. Click in a blank area of the Start screen to close the drop-down menu.

More

8 Right-click (click the right mouse button) in a blank area of the Start screen to open the Windows toolbar.

9 Click the All apps icon in the Windows toolbar to display the Apps screen. The Apps screen lists all the applications stored on the computer. Notice that some apps are grouped by type—for example, Microsoft Office 2013 apps are all listed together.

10 Right-click in a blank area of the Apps screen.

11 Click the All apps icon to return to the Start screen. Leave the Start screen displayed. You will continue exploring Windows 8 in the next skill.

Windows

Windows

Open and Close Apps with Tiles

 Video M2_C1_S02

The Windows 8 Start screen makes it easy to open apps and switch between open apps. App commands are hidden until you need them and can easily be accessed by using the mouse pointer or a keyboard.

Depending on screen resolution, you can also "snap an app" to the left or right side of the screen. To snap an app, you must be working on a computer with a screen resolution of at least 1366 x 768.

Steps

▶**Tip** The home page can be set by the user, so it will vary. Setting up a home page is covered in Module 3, Skill 7.

▶**Tip** When you open the Weather app, if you see a dialog box asking you to allow locations services, click Allow.

▶**Tip** When you open the Weather app, if you see a dialog box asking for your location, type your location and then click Add.

1 From the Start screen, click the Internet Explorer tile. The Internet Explorer window opens and its home page appears.

2 Press the Windows key (⊞) to return to the Start screen.

3 Click the Weather tile to open the Weather app in a new window. Use the Windows key to return to the Start screen.

4 Click the News tile to open the News app in another new window.

5 Move the mouse pointer to the upper left corner of the screen. A thumbnail for the last app you had open (Weather) appears.

6 Click the Weather thumbnail to return to the Weather app. Move the mouse pointer away from the thumbnail to stay on the Weather window.

7 Move the mouse pointer to the upper left corner of the screen and then move it down the left edge of the screen until you see the thumbnails for Internet Explorer, News, and Desktop. Move the mouse below the desktop thumbnail to force the thumbnail pane to stay open.

8 Move the mouse pointer outside the thumbnail pane to close the pane.

9 Repeat Step 7 to reopen the thumbnail pane.

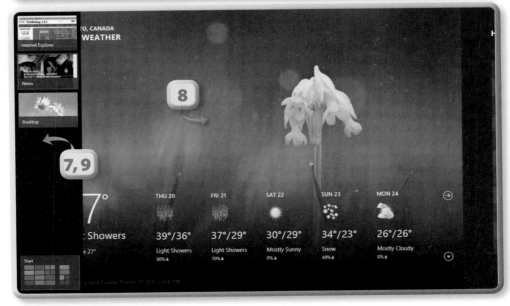

More

10 *Shortcut*

Switch between Apps
Win + Tab

11–12 *Shortcut*

Close an App
Alt + F4

11–12 *Another Way*

Right-click an app in the
thumbnail pane and then
click *Close*.

10 Click the Internet Explorer thumbnail to switch to that app.

11 Move the mouse pointer up to the top of the Internet Explorer window until the pointer changes to a hand.

12 Click your mouse button and drag down until the Internet Explorer window restores down (becomes smaller). Continue dragging down until the Internet Explorer window drops off the bottom of the screen and then release the mouse button to close the app and return to the Start screen.

13 Using the technique in Steps 11 and 12, close the Weather and News apps.

Taking It Further

Snapping an App   If your screen resolution is at least 1366 x 768, you can use a feature called *Snap* to dock an application window on the left or right side of your screen. Try this with the Weather and News apps. From the Start screen, click the Weather tile to open the Weather app. Return to the Start screen and open the News app. Move the mouse to the top edge of the News window until the mouse pointer turns into a hand and then click and drag the window to the left or right edge of the screen until it collapses. Open the collapsed window by double-clicking the vertical ellipses ⋮ on its right edge.

Taking It Further

Using Tabbed Browsing   Some apps, like Internet Explorer, offer tabbed browsing. All open tabs display in a thumbnail view at the top of the screen when you right-click in a blank area of the screen. To navigate to an open tab, click its thumbnail. To close an open tab, click the Close button on the thumbnail.

Windows

Skill 3

Open and Close Apps without Tiles

Video **M2_C1_S03**

You can locate an app quickly from the Windows Start screen and open it from the Apps screen without clicking any tiles. Powerful search techniques are built right into the Windows 8 interface. From any window, open the Charms bar and then click the Search charm to perform a search for a particular app. Alternatively, from the Start screen, simply start typing, and the Search pane and Apps results list will open automatically. To browse a list of all the programs installed on your computer, open the Apps screen using the All apps icon on the Windows toolbar.

Steps

▶**Tip** You can also display the Charms bar by pointing to the lower right corner of the Start screen.

1-2 *Shortcut*

Open Search Pane
Win + F

▶**Tip** When you are searching for an app, click *Apps* in the Search pane if it is not already selected.

▶**Tip** Paint allows you to save pictures in many popular formats, including PNG, JPEG, and BMP.

1 Open the Start screen and move the mouse pointer to the upper right corner of the screen to display the Charms bar.

2 Click the Search charm to open the Search pane.

3 Type word in the search box. In the Apps results list, you will see any programs beginning with *word* or *Word*—for example, Word 2013 and WordPad.

4 Click *WordPad* in the Apps results list to open that application.

5 Press the Windows key to return to the Start screen.

6 From the Start screen, begin to type paint. The Search pane opens and *paint* appears in the search box.

7 Click *Paint* in the Apps results list to start the application.

8 Press the Windows key to return to the Start screen.

9 Right-click in a blank area of the screen and then click the All apps icon on the Windows toolbar.

 More

Windows

10 Click *File Explorer* in the Windows System group on the Apps screen.

11 Click the Paint button on the Windows Taskbar.

12 Click the Close button in the Paint window.

13 Right-click the WordPad button on the Taskbar and then click *Close window*.

14 Use the technique described in Step 13 to close File Explorer.

Taking It Further

Comparing Apps in the Windows 8 User Interface versus the Desktop Interface   The new Windows 8 user interface (UI) was inspired by the Windows Phone interface and supports touch control. This new interface, sometimes referred to as the Modern UI, is seen on the Windows 8 Start screen, where apps are represented by tiles that you tap or click to open. Windows 8 apps give you a different experience depending on whether they are opened from the Start screen or the desktop. When opened from the Start screen, the content is displayed in a full screen, with features and tools hidden until you need them. To access these hidden options, all you need to do is right-click or double-tap in a blank area of the screen. When you do this in the new Windows 8 UI Internet Explorer, for example, a section featuring the address bar and other tools appears at the bottom of the screen, while one showing tabs appears at the top. Microsoft has made it easy to find new Windows 8 apps: from the Start screen, simply click or tap the Store tile to open the Windows Store.

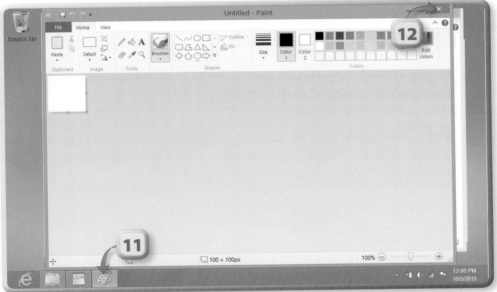

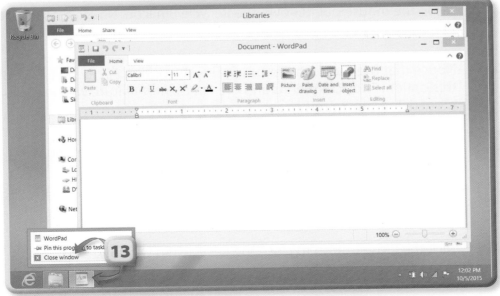

Windows

Chapter 1

Skill 4

Video M2_C1_S04

Explore the Desktop

The desktop in Windows 8 offers quick access to the Recycle Bin, the Taskbar with buttons for frequently used apps such as Internet Explorer and File Explorer, and several icons for notification features such as the Action Center, network connection, and speaker volume. The desktop can be accessed easily from the Start screen.

Steps

1 Shortcut
Display Desktop
Win + D

▶**Tip** Laptop computers have a touchpad, which can be used instead of a mouse. Drag your finger on the touchpad to move the mouse pointer.

▶**Tip** If your computer has a battery, you will see the Battery icon in the notifications area.

1 From the Start screen, click the Desktop tile.

2 Move the mouse pointer to the lower left corner of the screen until the Start thumbnail appears.

3 Click the Start thumbnail to return to the Start screen and then click the Desktop tile to return to the desktop.

4 Move the mouse pointer across the Taskbar to the icons on the right. This is the notification area. It displays the status of system functions such as speakers, network connections, and clock.

5 Move the mouse pointer to the upper right corner of the screen to display the Charms bar.

6 Move the mouse pointer away from the Charms bar to hide the bar.

7 Move the mouse pointer over the Recycle Bin icon. Notice that the icon is highlighted with a transparent box. Right-click the Recycle Bin icon.

▶**Tip** Permanently delete the contents of the Recycle Bin by clicking *Empty Recycle Bin* in the Recycle Bin shortcut menu.

▶**Tip** If you have not deleted anything yet, you will see the message *This folder is empty* in the Recycle Bin window.

▶**Tip** You can retrieve files or folders from the Recycle Bin until you permanently delete them.

8 Notice that the shortcut menu contains the option *Pin to Start*. Do not click this option. Shortcut menus and the Pin to Start feature will be explored in more detail later in this chapter.

9 Click in a blank area of the desktop to close the shortcut menu.

10 Double-click the Recycle Bin icon. The Recycle Bin window opens, displaying a list of files and folders you have deleted.

11 Click the Close button to close the Recycle Bin window.

Windows

Work with Tools on the Taskbar

Video M2_C1_S05

The Taskbar along the bottom of the desktop contains buttons that are pinned to the Taskbar and buttons for apps that are currently open on your computer. A pinned button is always displayed on the Taskbar, whether the app is open or not. Clicking a pinned button opens the app. Clicking a button for an open app displays the app window. The Taskbar also contains the notification area, located at the far right. Icons here show the status of certain system features, such as the Action Center. The Action Center is a single area that displays important messages about security and maintenance settings.

Steps

▶ **Tip** You can toggle between the Start screen and the desktop by pressing the Windows key.

1 Press the Windows key to open the Start screen.

2 Click the Desktop tile to open the desktop.

▶ **Tip** To pin an open program to the Taskbar, right-click its button on the Taskbar and then click *Pin this program to taskbar*.

3 Note the Taskbar across the bottom of the desktop. Click the pinned File Explorer button in the task buttons area on the Taskbar to open the File Explorer window and view your Libraries. (Libraries are discussed in Chapter 2.)

4 Click the Close button in the Libraries window.

5 Click the Speaker icon in the notification area on the Taskbar to display the speaker volume controls.

6 Click the speaker volume control lever, hold down the mouse button, drag the lever to the mid-point mark on the bar (*50*), and then release the mouse button to set the volume level there.

▶ **Tip** You may not be able to view, open, or modify the Action Center and Calendar (or other Windows tools) in public labs.

7 Click the Action Center icon (shaped like a small pennant) in the notification area on the Taskbar.

8 Review the information in the Action Center by clicking the Open Action Center link.

9 Close the Action Center window by clicking the Close button.

▶ **Tip** To change the date and time, click the Change date and time settings link.

10 Click the current time and date in the Taskbar to display the calendar and clock.

11 Click a blank area of the desktop to close the calendar and clock.

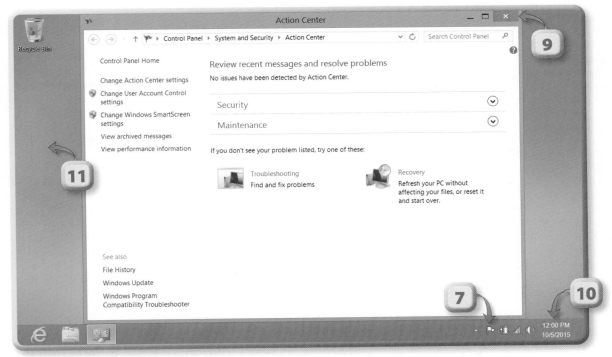

Taking It Further

Changing Notification Area Icons You can add as many icons as you like to the notification area of the Taskbar. To avoid clutter, display only those icons you want visible at all times. Keep the rest of the icons in the overflow area, which you can display by clicking the Show Hidden Icons button at the left of the Action Center icon.

Windows

Open and Close Programs

Video M2_C1_S06

The Start screen offers a couple of ways to open programs or applications. Frequently used programs are likely to be displayed as tiles on the Start screen. To access other programs, you can right-click in a blank area of the Start screen and then click the All apps icon in the Windows toolbar to view tiles for the programs installed on the computer. When the desktop is displayed, you can start a program by clicking the app's button on the Taskbar. A program opens in an application window. Close a program by clicking the Close button (X) in the upper right corner of the window.

Steps

1 Shortcut

Display Start Screen
Windows key

▶**Tip** If you don't see the Word 2013 tile on the Start screen, you will need to either scroll, open All apps and locate Word 2013, display the Charms bar and then click the Search charm, or type the app name to search for it.

▶**Tip** If the Word 2013 tile is not displayed on the Start screen, right-click in a blank area of the screen, click the All apps icon in the Windows toolbar, right-click *Word 2013* in the Microsoft Office 2013 group on the Apps screen, and click the Pin to Start icon in the toolbar.

▶**Tip** The live preview feature enables you to take a quick look at other open windows without clicking away from the window in which you are currently working.

1 Open the Start screen and click the Word 2013 tile to start the Word 2013 application and display the Word 2013 button in the Windows Taskbar.

2 Click the Internet Explorer button on the Taskbar. Internet Explorer starts and its home page displays.

3 Right-click in a blank area of the Taskbar and then click *Show the desktop* to display the desktop.

4 Move the pointer over the Word button on the Taskbar to display a live preview thumbnail of the open Word window just above the Taskbar.

5 Click the thumbnail to open the Word window.

6 Click the Close button to close Word 2013 and return to the desktop.

7 Hover the pointer over the Internet Explorer button on the Taskbar to display the live preview thumbnail.

8 Hover the mouse pointer over the thumbnail until the Close button displays in the top right corner. Click the Close button to close Internet Explorer and return to the desktop.

Taking It Further

Using Jump Lists   Jump Lists display recent documents, tasks, or commands for a particular application. You can open a Jump List from the Taskbar. For example, right-click the Internet Explorer button on the Taskbar to display a list of frequently visited websites. Or right-click the Outlook button on the Taskbar to display a list of Outlook tasks, such as *New Contact*. Open a Jump List item by clicking it.

Windows

Skill 7

Video ▶ M2_C1_S07

Manipulate Windows

In this skill, you learn techniques for manipulating windows while on the desktop, including minimizing, maximizing, restoring, resizing, and moving windows. You will find these techniques useful when working with more than one window. For example, when you minimize a window, it is reduced to a button on the Taskbar. You can then work on other tasks without having to close the first program or file. Maximizing a window increases the window to full-screen size so you can focus on that file or program. You can size and move windows that are not maximized so you can view other open windows at the same time.

Steps

1 From the Start screen, click the Desktop tile and then click the Internet Explorer button on the Taskbar. The Internet Explorer window opens and the home page displays.

2 Click the Minimize button to reduce the window to a button on the Taskbar.

3 Click the Internet Explorer button on the Taskbar to redisplay the window.

4 If the window does not currently fill the entire screen, click the Maximize button to enlarge the window size. The Maximize button turns into a Restore Down button when the window fills the entire screen.

5 Click the Restore Down button to reduce the size of the window.

6 Click the Title bar and hold down the mouse button while you drag to the right to move the window.

7 Place your mouse pointer on the right window border so that the pointer changes to a two-headed arrow. Reduce the size of the window by clicking the window border and dragging to the left.

8 Place your mouse pointer on the bottom border of the window so that the pointer changes to a two-headed arrow. Reduce the size of the window by clicking the window border and dragging upward.

9 Click the Maximize button so that the window fills the screen.

10 Click the Close button to close the window.

▶ **Tip** If more than one Internet Explorer window is open, hovering over or clicking the Internet Explorer button will provide live preview thumbnails of these windows. Hover the mouse over the thumbnail for the window you wish to maximize and then click.

▶ **Tip** Any window that is not maximized can be moved.

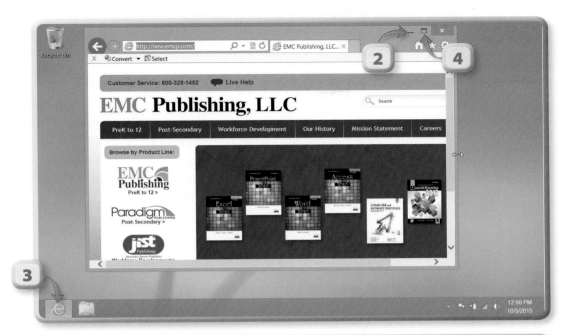

Taking It Further

Switching between Windows in the Windows User Interface   The way you switch between open windows is different in the Windows user interface (UI). From any open window, press Ctrl + Alt + Tab to see a bar displaying thumbnails of all the open windows on your computer. Hover your mouse pointer over each thumbnail to see the full open window displayed behind the thumbnail bar. Click a thumbnail to stay on a window and close the thumbnail bar.

Windows

Move among Open Windows

Video   M2_C1_S08 ▶

Windows 8 lets you have multiple windows open at the same time and move among them. This flexibility is referred to as *multitasking*. Knowing the techniques available for moving among open windows can help you to manage your workload more efficiently. In this skill, you will move among open windows on the desktop.

Steps

1 Shortcut
Display Desktop
Win + D

▶**Tip** The home page in a browser can be set by the user, so the home page that displays in Step 1 will vary.

▶**Tip** The cascade arrangement only works with windows that are not minimized.

▶**Tip** Press Alt + Tab and then continue holding down Alt while repeatedly pressing Tab to move from window to window. Release the Alt key when the window you want to work in is highlighted. Pressing Alt + Tab provides access to all open windows, including those opened in the desktop interface and Windows user interface.

1 From the desktop, click the Internet Explorer button on the Taskbar. The Internet Explorer window opens and the home page displays.

2 Click the File Explorer button on the Taskbar to display your Libraries.

3 Right-click in a blank area of the Taskbar to display the shortcut menu.

4 Click *Cascade windows* to display the Internet Explorer and Libraries windows in a cascade arrangement.

5 Right-click in a blank area of the Taskbar to display the shortcut menu.

6 Click *Show windows side by side* to display the windows in a side-by-side arrangement.

7 Click the Maximize button in the Internet Explorer window.

8 Click the Close button to close the Internet Explorer window.

9 Right-click the File Explorer button on the Taskbar to display the shortcut menu.

10 Click *Close window* to close the Libraries window.

Taking It Further

Shaking Windows   Windows 8 includes a variety of features for manipulating windows. One such feature is called *Shake*. To experiment with the Shake feature, open at least three windows and use the Restore Down button to reduce the size of all three windows. Click one of the windows and then drag that window from side to side quickly. All of the open windows minimize except the one you are "shaking." This feature provides a quick way to minimize multiple windows.

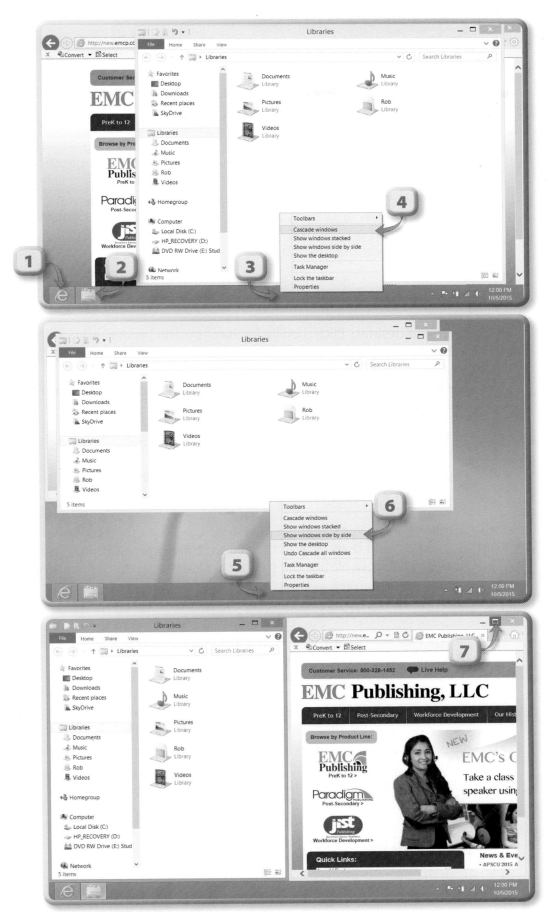

Windows

Work with Menus, Toolbars, and Ribbons

Video M2_C1_S09

In Windows 8 and other applications, you work with a variety of menus, toolbars, and ribbons. Menus display lists of options and can be accessed in various ways—such as by right-clicking an item or clicking a down-pointing arrow on a button. Toolbars contain a variety of command buttons for an application and are typically found near the top or bottom of an application window. The ribbon interface is opened from tabs across the top of most Windows-based apps and displays groups of buttons and options.

Steps

Tip When you click a button that contains a small arrow, a drop-down list appears.

1 From the desktop, click the File Explorer button on the Taskbar. The Libraries window opens. Notice the ribbon along the top of the window.

2 Click the View tab in the ribbon and then click the Sort by button to see its drop-down list.

3 Click the Close button to close the Libraries window.

4 Another Way
Open the Start screen by clicking in the lower left corner of the screen, pressing the Windows key, or pressing Ctrl + Esc.

4 Open the Start screen by pointing to the upper right corner to display the Charms bar and then clicking the Start charm.

Tip Notepad is a text editing program that comes with the Windows operating system.

5 Display the Charms bar again, click the Search charm, type notepad in the search box, and then click *Notepad* from the Apps results list to open the Notepad window. Notice the toolbar across the top of the window.

Tip Skill 11 of this chapter introduces dialog boxes.

6 Click the File button to display the File menu.

Tip Most options have default settings that can be changed in a dialog box.

7 Notice that some File menu options end with ellipses (…). Ellipses signify that a dialog box opens when the option is selected. Click *Open* to display the Open dialog box and then click the Cancel button.

8 Click the Format button to display the Format menu.

Tip A check mark indicates that the feature toggles on and off when you click it.

9 If there is not a check mark next to *Word Wrap*, click the *Word Wrap* option. (If there is a check mark, indicating that the feature is active, click in the Notepad window to close the menu.)

10 Shortcut
Close an Open Menu
Esc

10 Click the Format button. Notice that *Word Wrap* has a check mark beside it, indicating that the option has been turned on.

11 Click the Close button to close the Notepad window.

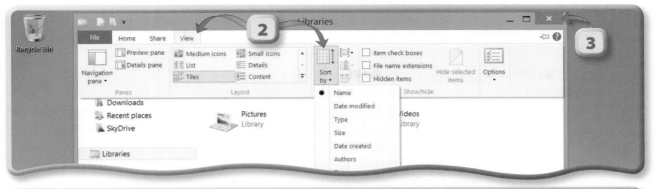

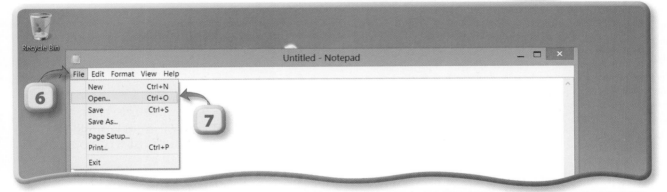

Taking It Further

Using Toolbars Toolbars are found in many Windows apps. Certain toolbars are turned on by default and others can be turned on by the user. Right-click a toolbar to see the other available toolbars you can display. Check marks display next to the names of the toolbars that are turned on and displayed.

Windows

Use Keyboard Shortcuts

Throughout the skills in this chapter, the steps have described how to use the mouse to select commands. Keyboard shortcuts provide an alternative way to get the same things done. Keyboard shortcuts are combinations of keys that you press to perform a task, such as copying text. Because your hand does not have to move from the keyboard to the mouse to perform these shortcuts, you may find them easier to use. Most programs also provide accelerator keys. If you press the Alt key, certain letters in the menu items are underlined. Press the key that corresponds to the underlined letter to select that menu item.

Steps

1 *Shortcut*

Open Search Pane
Win + Q

1 From the desktop, display the Charms bar, click the Search charm, type notepad in the search box, and then click *Notepad* in the Apps results list to open the Notepad window.

2 Press the Alt key to activate the menu bar. Each menu item contains an underlined letter.

▶**Tip** The accelerator keys are underlined after you press the Alt key.

3 Press the F key to display the File menu or press another accelerator key, such as V, to display a different menu.

▶**Tip** Many keyboard shortcuts, such as Alt + F4, perform the same function in all Office applications. For example, pressing Alt + F4 will close a Word window and it will also close an Excel window.

4 Press Alt + F4 to close the Notepad window.

5 Display the Charms bar, click the Search charm, type help in the search box, and then click *Help and Support* in the Apps results list to display the Windows Help and Support window.

▶**Tip** The F1 key is used to display the Help menu in the Windows desktop and in many other programs.

6 Press the Tab key. Notice that the cursor is now in the search box. Press Tab two more times. Notice that *Help home* is now selected. A different command or link in the Help window is highlighted each time you press Tab.

▶**Tip** Press Enter to select a highlighted command, link, or menu item.

7 Press Alt + F4 to close the Windows Help and Support window.

Taking It Further

Trying More Keyboard Shortcuts
Windows allows you to use many other keyboard shortcuts. Try these.
Win + C (Display the Charms bar)
Win + I (Open the Settings pane)

Win + X (Open a shortcut menu for accessing File Explorer, Search, Desktop, and more)
Ctrl + Alt + Del (Lock the computer, switch users, sign out, or access the Task Manager)

Taking It Further

Memorizing Your Favorite Keyboard Shortcuts   Memorizing common keyboard shortcuts can save you time and increase your productivity. For example, many Office users prefer using Ctrl + C and Ctrl + V to copy and paste information rather than selecting commands from a shortcut menu or from the ribbon. To learn more, display the Windows Help and Support window and type *keyboard shortcuts* in the search box. After pressing Enter, click one of the result links to research keyboard shortcuts that could help you become more efficient.

Windows

Video ▶ M2_C1_S11

Make Selections in Dialog Boxes

You can interact with Windows and other applications by using settings in dialog boxes. Dialog boxes allow you to specify details for a setting or to make choices about how an application performs a procedure. For example, you can interact with the Print dialog box to select a printer, designate which pages to print, and choose the number of copies to print. In this skill, you become familiar with common dialog box features by using the Notepad application that is built into Windows. Common dialog box features include check boxes, option buttons, list boxes, and boxes where you can select a value, such as the number of copies to print.

Steps

▶**Tip** Move your mouse pointer to the upper right corner of the screen to display the Charms bar, click the Search charm, type *notepad* in the search box, and click *Notepad* in the Apps results list.

1 From the desktop, open Notepad.

2 Type your first name.

3 Click the Format button to display the Format menu.

4 Click *Font* to display the Font dialog box.

5 Click *18* in the *Size* list box.

6 Click *Bold* in the *Font style* list box.

▶**Tip** In Microsoft Office programs, font formatting is applied only to selected text.

7 Click OK. Your first name is now displayed in a larger font size and in bold text. Everything you type will display in this font size and style until you reset those settings in the Font dialog box. Every new or old text file opened in Notepad will also display using these settings. Font settings are stored in the Notepad application and not with the file.

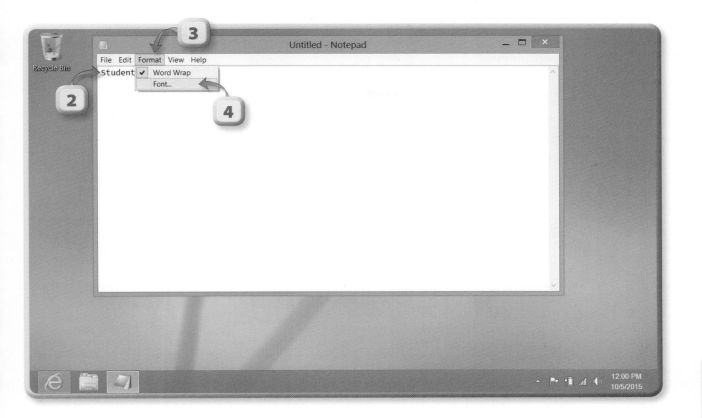

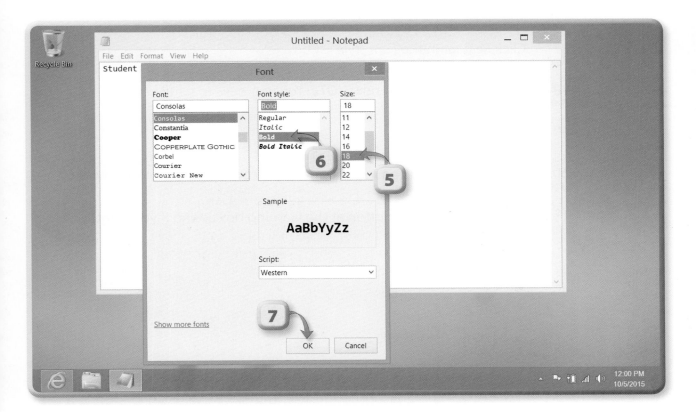

More

8   Click the File button to display the File menu.

9   Click *Print* to display the Print dialog box.

10   Click the *Print to file* check box to insert a check mark.

11   Click the up arrow next to the *Number of copies* measurement box to increase the number of copies. The number increases with each click.

12   Click the down arrow next to the *Number of copies* measurement box to decrease the number of copies. The number decreases with each click.

13   Double-click the number in the *Number of copies* measurement box to select it and then type 5.

14   Click the Cancel button to close the dialog box without printing.

15   Click the Format button to display the Format menu.

16   Click *Font* to display the Font dialog box.

17   Click *Regular* in the *Font style* list box.

18   Click *11* in the *Size* list box. **NOTE:** *You may need to scroll to see* 11.

19   Click OK.

20   Click the Close button in the upper right corner of the Notepad window.

21   Click the Don't Save button at the warning box asking if you want to save changes.

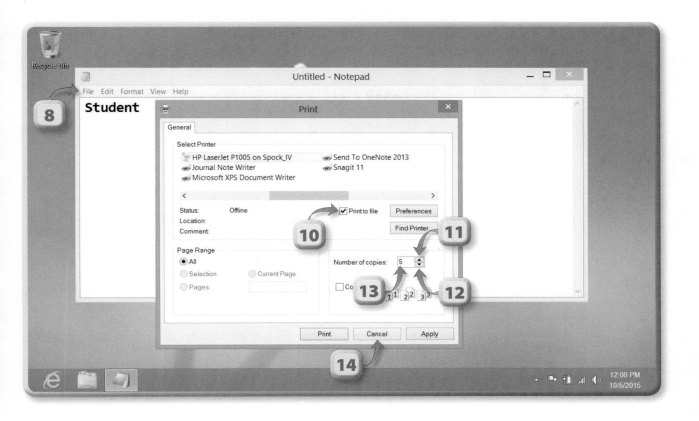

Windows

Chapter 1

Skill 12

Shut Down or Put Windows to Sleep

Video M2_C1_S12

When you are finished working on your computer, you can choose from a variety of settings. You can put your computer to sleep, which saves power without requiring you to close all of your files and shut down your system. You can lock your computer, which hides the desktop and requires you to enter a password to unlock the computer if your account is password protected. You can also log off or switch users if more than one user has an account on your computer. Or, if you prefer, you can shut down the computer completely.

Steps

▶ **Tip** You can display the Charms bar from the desktop, the Start screen, or any open app.

1 Shortcut
Open Settings Pane
Win + I

▶ **Tip** Depending on your computer settings, you may not see the *Sleep* option.

▶ **Tip** If the computer has been sleeping for an extended time, you may need to press the Power button to wake up the computer.

▶ **Tip** If you are working on a school computer, follow your school's procedure to sign in using your user name and password. See Skill 1 for a review.

▶ **Tip** You can lock your computer at any time by clicking your user name from the Start screen and then choosing *Lock*, or by pressing Win + L.

▶ **Tip** If you are working in a computer lab, be sure to close all open files and remove your storage medium before leaving the lab.

1 From the desktop, display the Charms bar and then click the Settings charm to open the Settings pane.

2 Click the Power button and then click *Sleep*. The screen goes black and the computer starts to go to sleep.

3 Wait 30 seconds or more so the computer can go completely to sleep, and then press Enter to wake up the computer and display the Lock screen.

4 Press any key to display the Sign-in screen.

5 Type your password in the *Password* text box and then press Enter to unlock the system.

6 If the Start screen is not displayed, press the Windows key to display the Start screen.

7 Click your user name and then click *Sign out*.

8 Press the Enter key to display the Sign-in screen. Click the Power button and then click *Shut down*.

Taking It Further

Restarting versus Shutting Down
Sometimes your computer stops working or freezes and you need to restart it. You can restart the computer by pressing Ctrl + Alt + Delete or by selecting *Restart* from the Power icon in the Settings panel on the Charms bar (if available). *Restart*, sometimes called *reboot*, closes Windows, powers off, and then repowers the computer and reopens Windows. *Shut down* closes Windows and powers off the computer. Be sure you have saved and closed all files prior to restarting or shutting down the computer.

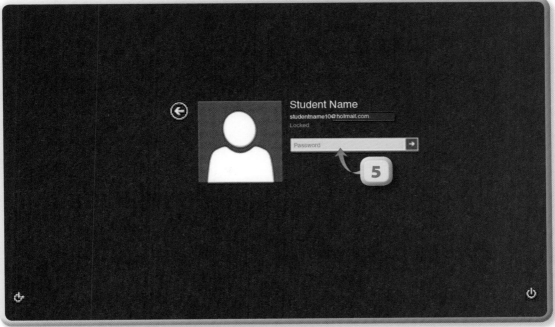

Chapter 2

Managing Files and Folders

A *file* is a collection of data that is stored on a hard drive or other storage medium. Everything that a computer does is based on data stored in files. Files can be stored on any storage medium, including a hard drive, a removable USB flash drive, a server, a CD or DVD, and in the cloud.

File names have two parts: a descriptive name you assign, such as *Resume*, and a file extension automatically assigned by the application when you save the file. For example, Excel workbook files have an .xlsx extension, PowerPoint presentation files have a .pptx extension, Access database files have an .accdb extension, and Word documents have a .docx extension. An extension indicates the file type and is used by the operating system to recognize which application to use to open the file.

Using the context-sensitive ribbons in the File Explorer window, you can copy, rename, organize, delete, and search for files. Files deleted from the hard drive are sent to the Recycle Bin where they are held for a time, permanently deleted, or restored to their original location on the computer. Files can also be compressed to reduce the file size, making it easier to email the files or transfer them to another computer. Files from various folders can be placed together into a Library, a logical grouping that helps you work with related sets of files. By default, Windows contains four libraries: Documents, Music, Pictures, and Videos.

Skills You Learn

1   Use File Explorer
2   Copy a folder from the Student Resources disc
3   Create a folder
4   Rename files and folders
5   Compress and extract files
6   Search for files
7   Delete files and folders
8   Use the Recycle Bin

Files You Need
For these skills, you need the following student data file.

M2-C2-S8-RecycleBin.docx

What You Create
In this chapter, you learn to manage the files and folders on your computer. You start to create a folder structure on your removable USB flash drive that reflects the modules in this textbook by copying a folder from the Student Resources disc. As you work through this module and the other modules in the textbook, you will use this folder structure to organize your files.

Windows

Use File Explorer

Video M2_C2_S01

File Explorer is the file management interface in Windows 8. A File Explorer window lets you view the folders and files in a selected storage location, such as your hard drive, DVD drive, server, SkyDrive, or USB flash drive. Features of a File Explorer window include a Navigation pane, an Address bar, a toolbar, a ribbon, a search box, a Details pane, and a Preview pane.

Steps

1 Another Way
Type *explorer* from the Start screen and then click *File Explorer* in the Apps results list.

▶**Tip** Libraries are a structure for organizing and managing your files in Windows 8. They are similar to folders, but different in that a library gathers together files that may be stored in several locations on your computer.

1 With the desktop displayed, click the File Explorer button on the Taskbar to display the File Explorer window.

2 Double-click *Pictures* in the *Libraries* section of the Navigation pane.

3 Notice that the path in the Address bar changes to show that you are viewing the Pictures library.

4 Notice that the Status bar shows how many items are in the Pictures library and how many locations are included in that library.

5 Click *Desktop* in the *Favorites* section of the Navigation pane to display desktop files and folders.

6 Click the Back button to redisplay the Pictures library.

7 Close the File Explorer window.

Taking It Further

Using the Preview and Details Views
Windows 8 allows you to see a preview or details of a folder or file without actually opening it. For example, open File Explorer, open a folder, and click a file to select it. Click *Preview pane* in the Panes group on the View tab to see a thumbnail image of the file. Click *Preview pane* again when you no longer wish to display the Preview pane. Click *Details pane* to see a thumbnail image plus key properties of the file. You will find shortcut buttons to these views in the lower right corner of the File Explorer window:

Taking It Further

Browsing a Location   When a File Explorer window opens, the Address bar displays the current location. The path to reach the current location is shown on the Address bar as links with arrows between them, for example, <u>Libraries</u> ▶ <u>Pictures</u>. You can jump to a location by clicking its name in the Address bar or you can jump to other locations in the path by clicking the arrow to the right of a link. For example, clicking the arrow to the right of *Libraries* displays a menu that lists all of the available libraries. Click a library in the displayed menu to jump to that location.

Windows

Skill 2

Copy a Folder from the Student Resources Disc

Video ▶ M2_C2_S02

Some of the work you do in this course involves opening student data files. These files are organized by module in folders on the Student Resources disc. The first page of each module in this book provides (when necessary) instructions for copying the folder you need from the disc to your storage medium. In this skill, you practice this procedure using a USB flash drive. (Note that the Student Resources disc is a read-only disc. Files can be copied from it, but they cannot be copied to it or removed from it.)

Steps

▶**Tip** If you do not have a CD/DVD drive on your computer, you can download the student data files from www. ParadigmCollege.net/ Guidelines13.

▶**Tip** If you are not using a USB flash drive and are working in a computer lab, ask your instructor where you should save your files.

▶**Tip** Files can be copied to SkyDrive instead of your USB flash drive. The procedure for using SkyDrive is explained in the Introduction (Your Digital Toolkit), Chapter 2.

▶**Tip** Your computer may display the removable disk storage location with a name such as *Removable Disk, USB Disk,* or *External Disk.* Or, if you've renamed your disk, it will display that name.

1 Insert the Student Resources disc into the CD/DVD drive. If an AutoPlay window displays, click the Close button.

2 Insert your USB flash drive into an available USB port. If an AutoPlay window displays, click the Close button.

3 If the desktop is not displayed, press Win + D to open your desktop.

4 Click the File Explorer button on the Taskbar to open the File Explorer window. This window displays all of the storage locations on your computer.

5 Right-click the disk drive in the Navigation pane, which displays as *Guidelines13-StudentResources*, and then click *Open in new window*.

6 Click the *Module2-Windows* folder in the File List pane.

7 Click the Home tab.

8 Click the Copy button in the Clipboard group.

9 Close the Guidelines13-StudentResources window.

10 In the File Explorer window that is still open, click your USB drive (*Removable Disk*) in *Computer* section in the Navigation pane.

11 Click the Paste button in the Clipboard group on the Home tab. The Module2-Windows folder appears as a folder in your USB drive.

12 Close the File Explorer window.

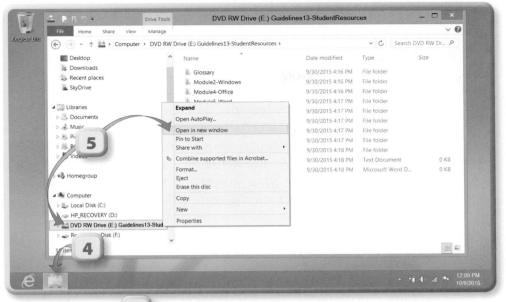

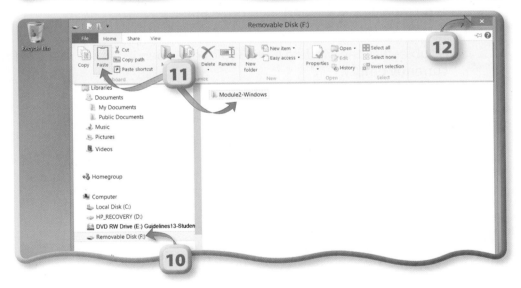

Taking It Further

Copying Folders Another Way Folders can also be moved and copied using the drag-and-drop method. One easy way to do this is to open two File Explorer windows and arrange them so that both are visible on the screen. You can then drag a folder from one window to the other. This method will either copy or move the folder, depending on the destination location. If you drag the folder to a different disk location, the folder will be copied. If the new folder location is on the same disk, the folder will be moved.

Windows

Video M2_C2_S03

Create a Folder

Just as you store printed documents that relate to each other in a single manila folder, you can store related computer files in virtual folders. For example, you might want to make a folder called *Job* *Search* to store your resume, cover letters, and portfolio documents. You can create a folder in a File Explorer window. Once you create the folder, you can save or move files to the folder.

Steps

1. With your USB flash drive inserted and the desktop displayed, click the File Explorer button on the Taskbar.

2. Double-click *Computer* in the Navigation pane and then click the removable disk drive name to see the list of files or folders saved on your USB flash drive.

3. Click the New Folder button in the New group on the Home tab to create a new folder.

4. Type Module2-Skill3 and then press Enter.

5. Double-click the Module2-Skill3 folder to open it. Notice that the folder is currently empty.

6. Click the Back button.

7. Close the File Explorer window.

Taking It Further

Creating a New Library By default, Windows has four predefined libraries (Music, Pictures, Documents, and Video). You can create additional libraries from the File Explorer window by clicking the Home tab. Click New item in the New group, and then click *Library*. A new library appears with its name open for editing. Type a unique name for your library. Remember, a library is different from a folder in that it is a place to compile like types of files. You can optimize the library and manage the type of folders that are included using the Library Tools Manage ribbon.

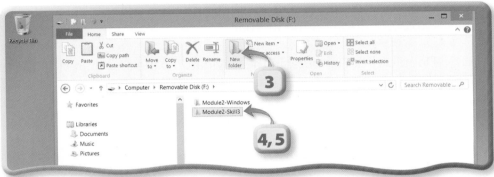

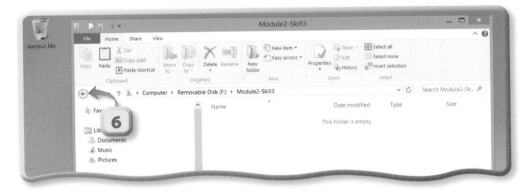

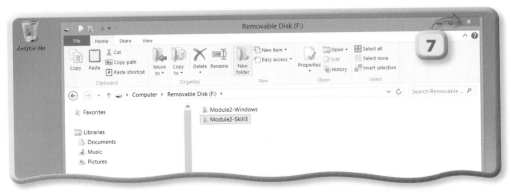

Windows

> Skill 4

Video ▶ M2_C2_S04

Rename Files and Folders

You may need to rename a file or folder after you create it. File and folder names can be up to 255 characters in length and can include spaces. Certain characters, including \ / : * ? " < > |, cannot be used in file and folder names. File names have an extension, such as .docx, which the computer program adds automatically when the file is saved. You should not change the file extension when you rename a file because the extension tells the computer which application to use to open the file.

Steps

1 With your USB flash drive inserted and the desktop displayed, click the File Explorer button on the Taskbar.

2 Double-click *Computer* in the Navigaton pane and then click the removable disk drive name to see the list of files or folders saved on your USB flash drive.

3 Right-click the *Module2-Skill3* folder to display the shortcut menu.

4 Click *Rename*. At this point the folder name becomes available for editing.

④ *Shortcut*
Rename
F2

▶*Tip* If you make a mistake when renaming a file you can click the Undo button on the Quick Access toolbar. If you do not see the Undo button, click the Customize Quick Access Toolbar button arrow and then click *Undo* to place a check mark beside this option.

5 Type Module2-Practice and then press Enter. The Module2-Skill3 folder is renamed *Module2-Practice*.

6 Make sure that the Module2-Practice folder is selected and then click the Home tab.

7 Click the Rename button in the Organize group to make the folder name available for editing.

8 Type Module2-CompletedSkills and then press Enter. The Module2-Practice folder is renamed *Module2-CompletedSkills*.

9 Close the File Explorer window.

Taking It Further

Displaying File Extensions In a default File Explorer window, file extensions are not displayed. If you prefer to have Windows display file extensions, click the View tab in a File Explorer window and then click the *File name extensions* check box in the Show/hide group to insert a check mark.

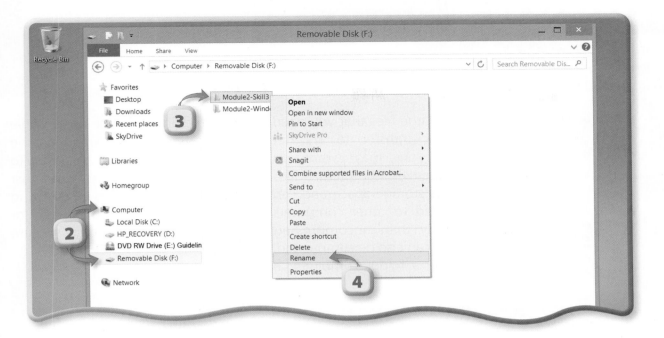

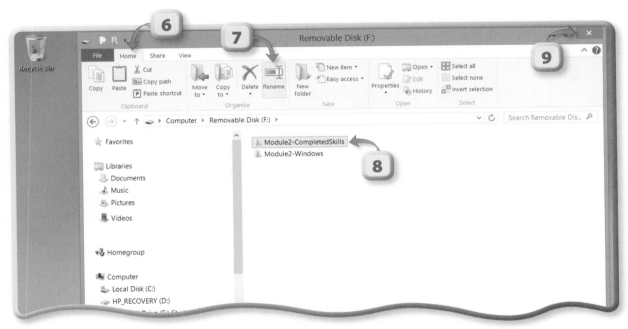

Taking It Further

Renaming Multiple Files If you want to rename a series of files, such as photo files from a digital camera, you can do so quickly if you use a specific prefix to name each of the files. For example, you could use the prefix *photo* to rename a batch of files *photo(1).jpg*, *photo(2).jpg*, *photo(3).jpg*, *photo(4).jpg*, and so forth. To do so, in a File Explorer window, hold down the Ctrl key and click each file you want to rename. Press the F2 key, type the prefix you will use to rename the files, and then press Enter. The computer automatically adds the parenthetical numbers after your prefix to differentiate the files.

Windows

Video M2_C2_S05

Compress and Extract Files

If you have large files that you need to email or transfer to another computer, you may want to compress the files. Compressed files take up less storage space and can be transferred to other computers more quickly than uncompressed files. Folders can also be compressed. Compressing a folder combines all of the files in the folder into a single file that is smaller in size than the total of the individual file sizes. To edit a compressed file, you must first extract the files. Extracting essentially reverses the process, or decompresses the file, once you are ready to use it.

Steps

1 With your USB flash drive inserted and the desktop displayed, click the File Explorer button on the Taskbar.

2 Double-click *Computer* in the Navigation pane and then click the removable disk drive name.

3 Right-click the Module2-Windows folder in the File List pane.

> ▶**Tip** Be aware that you will probably hear two different terms, *compressed* and *zipped*, used to describe such files.

4 At the shortcut menu, point to *Send to* and then click *Compressed (zipped) folder*.

5 The compressed folder appears with a folder icon with a zipper image on it. Press Enter to accept the default name for the new folder.

> ▶**Tip** If WinZip is installed on the computer, the icon will be the WinZip "folder in vise" icon rather than a folder with a zipper on it.

6 Double-click the compressed *Module2-Windows* folder.

7 Click the Compressed Folder Tools Extract tab to open the Extract Compressed (Zipped) Folders dialog box.

8 Click the Extract all button and then click the Browse button.

> ▶**Tip** Many compressed files have a .zip extension. Others have an .rar extension or other special extension, depending on the compression application used.

9 In the Select a destination dialog box, browse to the *Module2-CompletedSkills* folder on your USB flash drive and click it.

10 Click OK to close the Select a destination dialog box.

11 Click the Extract button in the Extract Compressed (Zipped) Folders dialog box. The uncompressed folder opens in a new window.

12 Close the two open windows.

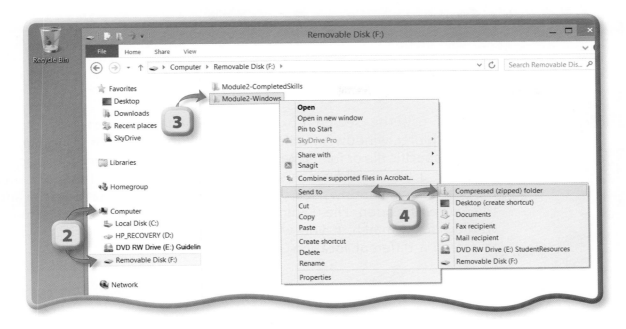

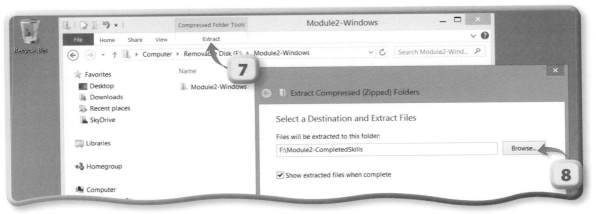

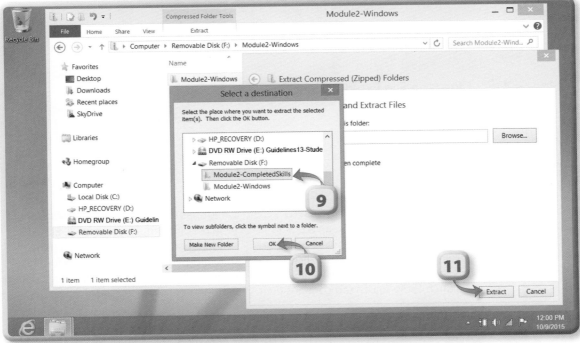

Windows

Search for Files

You can use the search box in a File Explorer window to quickly locate a specific file or folder. When you type a file or folder name in the search box, Windows searches the currently open File Explorer window for a match. If you want to search a different location, use the Navigation pane to change the search location. For example, to search your USB flash drive, click *Removable Disk* in the *Computer* section in the Navigation pane and then type the file or folder name in the search box.

Steps

1 With your USB flash drive inserted and the desktop displayed, click the File Explorer button on the Taskbar.

2 Double-click *Computer* in the Navigation pane and then click the removable disk drive name.

3 Click in the search box and type Module2. Search results display in the File List pane, indicating that there are four occurrences of *Module2*.

4 Click the Clear button next to the search box.

5 In the search box, type *.zip. The Search feature finds one zipped file and lists it in the search results.

6 Click the Clear button next to the search box.

7 Close the File Explorer window.

▶**Tip** The * is a wildcard that can be used to specify any combination of characters. In this case, you are searching for all files with a .zip file extension because * tells the computer to retrieve files with any name appearing to the left of the .zip extension.

Taking It Further

Repeating a Search and Using Search Filters When you click in a search box in a File Explorer window, previous searches are displayed in a drop-down list. Click a previous search to repeat it. The Refine group on the Search Tools Search tab contains filter categories that you can use to refine your search. For example, you can click the Date modified button and then click a date or date range to narrow the search for files or folders that were saved on a specific date or within a specific date range.

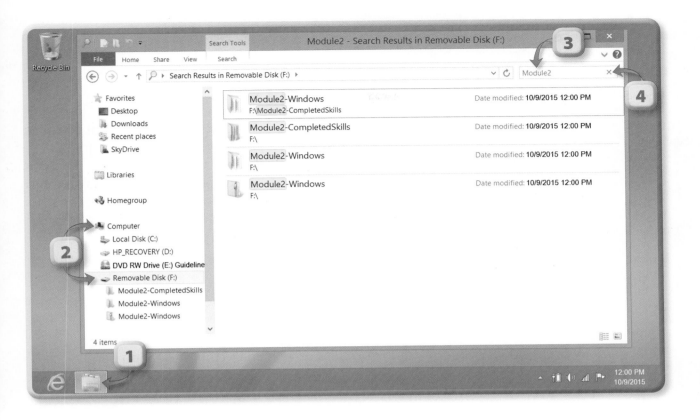

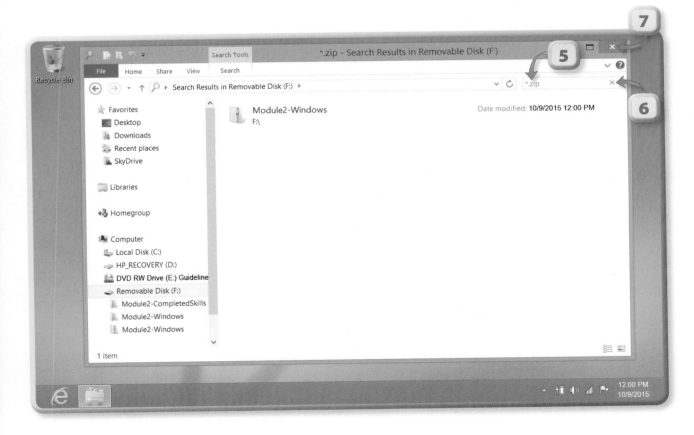

Windows

Windows

Chapter 2

Skill 7

Video M2_C2_S07

Delete Files and Folders

If you have files that you no longer need on your computer, you should delete them. Regularly deleting such files will help keep your files organized and free up disk space. You can also delete folders. When you delete a folder, all of the files and folders within that folder are deleted with it. Be sure to look within all subfolders to remind yourself of the complete contents before deleting the outer folder.

Steps

1. With your USB flash drive inserted and the desktop displayed, click the File Explorer button on the Taskbar.

2. Double-click the removable disk drive name in the Navigation pane.

3 *Another Way*
Click the file and then press the Delete key.

3. Right-click the zipped *Module2-Windows* folder in the File List pane to display a shortcut menu.

4. Click *Delete*.

5. At the warning dialog box, click Yes. The Module2-Windows file is deleted.

6. Double-click the *Module2-CompletedSkills* folder in the File List pane. The contents of the Module2-CompletedSkills folder are displayed.

7. Right-click the *Module2-Windows* folder.

8. Click *Delete*.

9. Click Yes to delete the folder.

10. Close the File Explorer window.

Taking It Further

Deleting Multiple Files If you want to delete a series of files listed one after the other, select those adjacent files by clicking the first file and then holding down the Shift key while clicking the last file. Select nonadjacent files by clicking the first file and then holding down the Ctrl key while clicking the other files. Once you've selected several files, click the Delete button in the Organize group on the Home tab. Alternatively, once you have selected the files, you can press the Delete key to delete those files.

Windows

Use the Recycle Bin

Video   M2_C2_S08

In Windows 8, when you delete a file from the hard drive, it does not, in fact, get deleted. Instead, it is moved to the Recycle Bin, which is a temporary holding area. The Recycle Bin protects you from accidental loss of files by giving you a chance to change your mind and restore a deleted file. When you are absolutely sure your deleted files are no longer needed, you can empty the Recycle Bin. The Recycle Bin stores deleted files until it runs out of storage space, at which point it will start deleting files, beginning with the files that have been in the bin the longest. When you delete a file or folder that is saved on a removable disk, it is not sent to the Recycle Bin—it is permanently deleted.

Steps

1. With your USB flash drive inserted and your desktop displayed, click the File Explorer button on the Taskbar.

2. Double-click *Computer* in the Navigation pane and then click the removable disk drive name.

3. Double-click the *Module2-Windows* folder in the File List pane.

4. If necessary, size and move the *Module2-Windows* window so that you can see the Recycle Bin and part of the desktop on the left of your computer screen.

5. Click **M2-C2-S8-RecycleBin** and drag the file onto your desktop.

6. Right-click **M2-C2-S8-RecycleBin** on the desktop and then click *Delete* at the shortcut menu. A warning dialog box displays.

7. At the warning dialog box, click Yes to send the file to the Recycle Bin.

8. Double-click the Recycle Bin icon to open the Recycle Bin window.

9. Click **M2-C2-S8-RecycleBin** in the Recycle Bin window.

10. Click the Recycle Bin Tools Manage tab and then click the Restore the selected items button in the Restore group. Notice that the file is restored to its previous location on your desktop.

11. Close the Recycle Bin window.

12. Close the File Explorer window. Repeat Steps 6 and 7 to delete the file again.

13. Eject the Student Resources disc and your USB flash drive from the computer.

▶**Tip** Dragging a file from a USB flash drive onto the desktop copies the file; the file is not removed from the folder.

▶**Tip** You may not be permitted to save files to the desktop in a public lab.

▶**Tip** If no warning dialog box appears when you click *Delete*, double-click the Recycle Bin icon, click the Manage tab, click the Recycle Bin properties button in the Manage group, click *Display delete confirmation dialog* check box to insert a check mark and then click OK.

▶**Tip** The Recycle Bin displays on the desktop by default. If the icon is not on your desktop, right-click the desktop, click *Personalize*, click *Change desktop icons*, and then click the *Recycle Bin* check box to insert a check mark. You may not be able to personalize the desktop in a public lab.

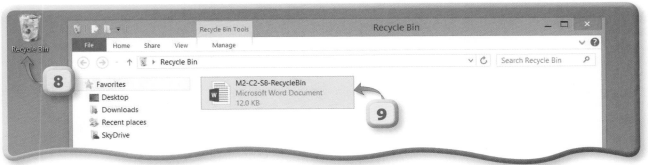

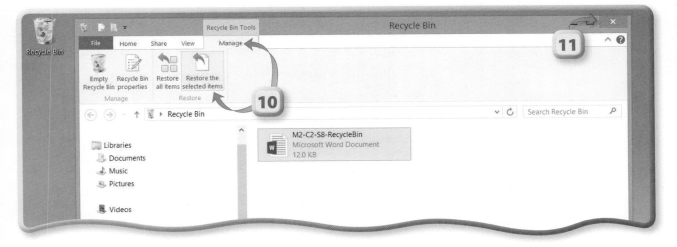

Taking It Further

Adjusting the Recycle Bin Properties

The maximum storage size of the Recycle Bin can be adjusted by right-clicking the Recycle Bin icon, clicking *Properties*, then entering a different number in the *Maximum size (MB)* box. You can also turn off the Recycle Bin (although doing so is not recommended) by selecting the option *Don't move files to the Recycle Bin. Remove files immediately when deleted.*

Windows

Working with Windows Settings, Accessories, Security, and Help

Typically, when you purchase a computer, Windows has already been installed for you. Therefore, many of its settings are the default settings applied during the installation process. You can, however, change many of the Windows 8 settings in order to personalize your computer. You can access and adjust most system settings for your computer through PC settings.

Clicking the Settings charm opens the Settings pane, where you can perform basic tasks such as modifying screen brightness, adjusting speaker volume, and changing the way Windows notifications are delivered to you. Clicking the *Change PC settings* option opens a screen where you can access groups of computer settings, including the *Personalize* group, which allows you to modify the Lock screen, Start screen, or your account picture; the *Search* group, which allows you to control search history and specify what apps are searched; and the *General* group, which allows you to set the date and time zone.

In this chapter, along with exploring PC settings and Control Panel settings, you become familiar with many useful programs that are included as Windows Accessories, such as the Calculator and Sticky Notes. You also learn how to use Windows Help.

Skills You Learn

1 Move, size, and group Start screen tiles
2 Modify the appearance of the Start screen and desktop
3 Explore Instant Search and modify search settings
4 Modify general settings
5 Review network settings
6 Modify sound, brightness, and notification settings
7 Explore accessibility options
8 Use Windows Accessories
9 Review security, maintenance, and update settings
10 Use Windows Help

Files You Need
For these skills, you do not need any student data files.

What You Create
On school computers, you may not be allowed to see, review, or make certain system and other key changes. While you can explore many of the settings, you may not be able to change them. Depending on the configuration of your school's computer labs, you may not have access to some of the settings covered in this chapter. However, you can use the knowledge in this chapter to change settings on your home or business computer.

Windows

Skill 1

Video ▶ M2_C3_S01

Move, Size, and Group Start Screen Tiles

In Windows 8, the Start button seen in earlier versions of Windows has been replaced by the Start screen. The Start screen displays tiles similar to those found on some smartphones and other mobile devices. Live tiles can display current information, such as the weather conditions for your location. Tiles can be added to or removed from the Start screen (for instance, when you install or uninstall a program). All tiles, whether large or small, can be moved, resized, and grouped. You can see groupings on the App screen, which you access from the Start screen. Windows groups tiles automatically; for example, it creates groups called *Microsoft Office* and *Windows Accessories*. You may, however, group tiles yourself; for example, you could group together all apps that perform similar functions, like Notepad, WordPad, and Word.

Steps

Move and Size Tiles

1 Open the Start screen. Notice the various large and small tiles, such as Weather (a large, live tile) and Internet Explorer (a small, static tile).

2 Click the Weather tile and hold down the mouse button.

3 Move the mouse. Notice that the Weather tile becomes transparent and moves with your mouse, while all other tiles get slightly smaller.

4 Drag the Weather tile to the top left corner of the first group on the Start screen and then release the mouse button. The Weather tile now sits at the beginning of the first row of tiles on your screen.

Taking It Further

Working with Live Tiles The Windows 8 Start screen displays tiles that you click to open applications. Some of these tiles are live, which means that they display real-time content from the Internet. You can turn a live tile into a static tile by right-clicking it and then clicking the Turn live tile off icon on the Windows toolbar. To turn a static tile into a live tile, right-click the tile and look at the toolbar. If you see the Turn live tile on icon, click it. If you do not see that icon, the live feature is not available for that tile. The Windows toolbar also offers icons for other tile options, such as Unpin from Start, Uninstall, and Smaller/Larger. You can tailor content in some live tiles to suit your needs. For example, if the live Weather tile does not show your location, click it to display the Weather screen, right-click anywhere on the screen, and then click the Places button in the bar at the top of the screen. Click the + button, type your location in the *Enter Location* text box, and then click the Add button. Right-click the new tile showing your location, click the Set as default icon on the Windows toolbar, and then press the Windows button to return to the Start screen and see the live Weather tile displaying weather for your location.

More

5 Right-click the News tile and then click the Smaller icon on the Toolbar to make the tile smaller.

6 Right-click the News tile and then click the Larger icon in the Toolbar to make the tile larger again.

7 Click the Turn live tile off icon on the Toolbar to change the image displayed on the News tile into an icon instead of real-time news.

Creating and Working with Grouped Tiles

8 Make sure you are at the Start screen.

9 Click the Finance tile and hold the mouse button down.

10 While holding the mouse button down, drag the Finance tile all the way to the right side of the screen until it crosses the second thick border. Release the mouse button.

11 Repeat Steps 9 and 10 with the News tile. You have now created a new group with two tiles in it.

12 Click the Semantic Zoom button to zoom out so you can see all the major tiles on the Start screen, including the new group you just created. Notice that the first group of default tiles is outlined with a white border.

13 Click in a blank area of the new group you created in Steps 9–11. The Start screen scrolls to display the new group.

14 Scroll left to see the other groups of tiles.

Taking It Further

Naming Groups of Tiles   In this skill, you learned how to create a group of tiles and move between groups of tiles. Naming groups of tiles can make them easier to locate when you have many different tiles and groups. To name a group of tiles, from the Start screen, click the Semantic Zoom button to zoom out, right-click one of the tiles in the group, click the Name group icon on the Windows toolbar, type the name in the *Name this group of tiles* text box, and then click the Name button. You might want to try this with the new group you created in Steps 9–11 of this skill.

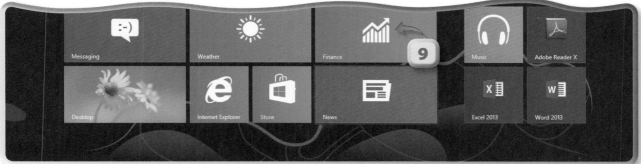

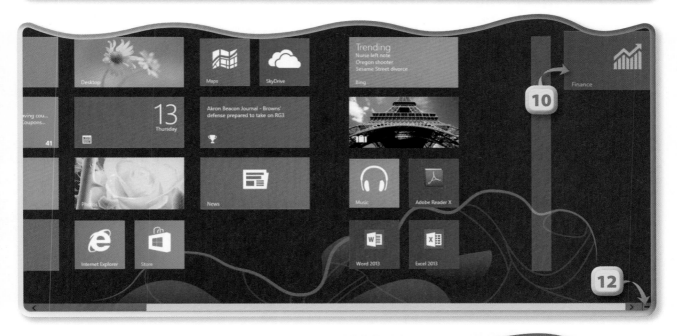

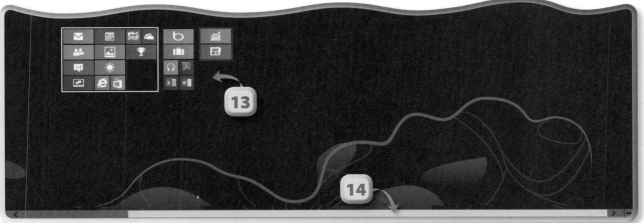

Windows

Windows

Modify the Appearance of the Start Screen and Desktop

Video ▶ M2_C3_S02

Windows 8 has a default appearance and color scheme for the Start screen. This means that it applies a specific background image and colors to the screen. It also has a default appearance and color scheme for the desktop—which means that it applies specific colors to the window borders and screen backgrounds. You can choose a new theme to completely change the color scheme and other design elements, or you can change a single design element—such as the Start screen background pattern (called a *tattoo*).

Steps

Change the Start Screen Appearance

▶**Tip** You can display the Charms bar from any screen by pointing to the top right corner of the screen.

1 Display the Charms bar and then click the Settings charm.

2 Click *Change PC settings* in the Settings pane.

3 Click *Personalize* in the left pane of the PC settings screen.

4 Click the *Start screen* option in the right pane to change the Start screen tattoo (background).

5 Click one of the tattoo thumbnails located below the Start screen preview to choose a new background.

▶**Tip** You can click a palette color button instead of dragging the color slider.

6 Drag the color slider below the Start screen preview to choose a different palette for the Start screen background.

7 Shortcut
Close Window
Alt + F4

7 Drag the PC settings screen to the bottom of your computer screen until it disappears. This closes the PC settings screen.

Taking It Further

Changing Your Account Picture Your account picture appears on the Start screen. You can change it from the PC settings screen by clicking *Personalize*, clicking *Account picture*, and then browsing for a new image or clicking the Camera button to take a picture of yourself to use as your new account picture. You can also access the *Account picture* options by clicking your user name on the Start screen and then clicking *Change account picture*.

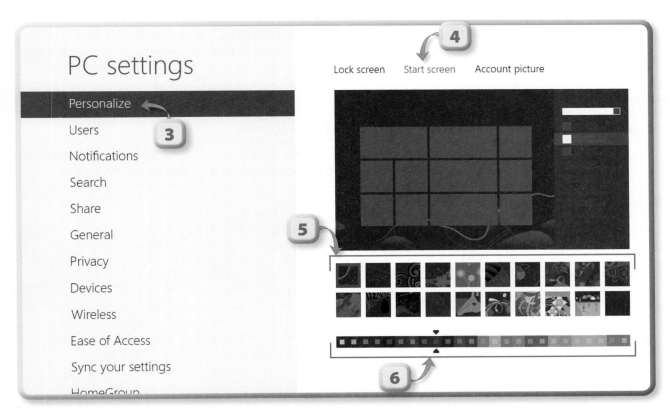

Change the Desktop Appearance

8, 9 *Another Way*
From the Start screen, type *personalization* and then click *Personalization* in the Apps results list.

8 From the Start screen, click the Desktop tile.

9 Right-click anywhere in the desktop and then click *Personalize* at the shortcut menu.

10 In the Personalization window, click a new theme (e.g., Flowers) from the *Windows Default Themes* section or from the *High Contrast Themes* section.

11 Click *Desktop Background* to change just that one component of the theme.

12 In the Desktop Background window, click the *Picture location* option box arrow and then select an option (e.g., *Windows Desktop Backgrounds*) from the drop-down list.

13 Click a background thumbnail (e.g., the first Flowers thumbnail) to select that background image.

14 Click the Save changes button to accept the new background image.

15 Click *Screen Saver* in the Personalization window.

▶**Tip** *3D Text* and some other screen savers allow you to make additional changes (such as changing the custom text to your name) by clicking the Settings button.

16 In the Screen Saver Settings dialog box, click the *Screen saver* option box arrow and then select a screen saver image (e.g., *3D Text*) from the drop-down list.

17 Click the OK button to accept your changes.

18 Click the Close button on the Personalization window to return to the desktop.

Taking It Further

Saving and Deleting a Theme   Once you have gone through the effort to change a Windows theme, you can save all of your modifications as a new theme. Open the Personalization window and click the Save theme link in the *My Themes* section of the gallery. Type a name for your new theme in the Save Theme As pop-up box. Click the Save button. The new theme will appear under *My Themes*. To delete a theme, right-click it and then click *Delete theme*. Click *Yes* in the Delete File pop-up box. **NOTE:** *You cannot delete a theme that is in use. If you want to delete the current theme, you must first apply a different theme.*

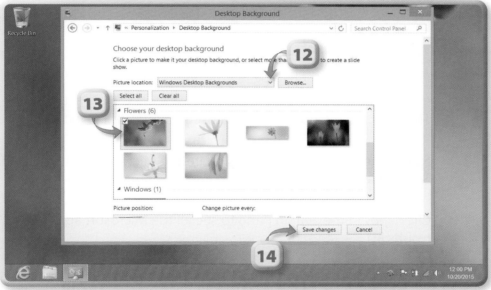

Windows

Windows

Video   M2_C3_S03

Explore Instant Search and Modify Search Settings

Instant Search allows you to search for apps, settings, or files from the Start screen simply by beginning to type the name of an app or a file. The Search pane allows you to filter the search results by categories, and the Apps screen displays the filtered results. Windows indexes certain locations (e.g., your libraries) by default to make searches fast and convenient. How you search, and the locations that are searched, can be modified in several ways. For example, you can search only for apps, add indexing locations to where Windows searches, or have Windows emphasize locations you search most often.

Steps

Explore Instant Search

1 From the Start screen, type microsoft.

2 The Search pane opens with your search term displayed in the search box.

3 Notice the categories of results related to Microsoft that are listed in the Search pane.

4 Click *Apps* in the Search pane to see all the Microsoft apps in the Apps results list.

5 Click in a blank area of the Apps screen to close the Search pane. Press the Windows key to return to the Start screen.

▶ **Tip** Your results may look different than the results on the opposite page because your computer likely has different content.

▶ **Tip** The numbers that appear beside *Apps, Settings*, and *Files* after you have searched represent how many matches were found for your search term in each respective category.

Taking It Further

Extending Your Search to the Internet   Windows automatically passes your search term to the Bing search engine in Internet Explorer. If Bing locates results on the Web, you will see the Internet Explorer icon in the Search pane. When you click the icon, Internet Explorer opens and you will see a list of search results in Bing.

Taking It Further

Exploring the Search Feature with Windows 8 Apps In earlier versions of Windows, searching was sometimes a slow process, and it could be an inconvenient one. Windows 8 has improved the search process by integrating results from some of the new Windows 8 apps. Once one of these apps is launched, search results continue to show in that app. To try this out, press Win + Q to open the Search pane. Type the stock exchange symbol for the company Research in Motion Ltd in the search box: *RIMM*. Click the *Finance* option below the Search box to open the Windows 8 Finance app. In a few seconds, Research in Motion's current stock results are displayed in the app. Now clear the search (by pointing to the search box until you see a black *X* and then clicking the *X*). When you see the prompt *Company name/Symbol* in the search box, type *IBM* to see a list of options for the company IBM below the search box. Click one of those options to display that information in the Finance app.

More

Windows

Modify Search Settings

▶Tip Open the Charms bar, click the Settings charm, and then click *Change PC settings*.

6 From the Start screen, open the PC settings screen to change the settings Windows uses for searches.

7 Click the *Search* option in the left pane.

8 By default, Windows places the apps you search most at the top of the search list. In the right pane, move the slider under *Show the apps I search most often at the top* all the way to the left to turn this feature off.

9 By default, Windows also saves searches for future suggestions. Move the slider under *Let Windows save my searches as future search suggestions* all the way to the left to turn this feature off.

▶Tip Press the Windows button to return to the Start screen.

▶Tip Changes in your search results will vary depending on the contents of your computer and your search history. For example, you may see a change in the number of files found or in the order of items in Apps results list.

10 Return to the Start screen.

11 From the Start screen, type microsoft. Note any differences between the results of this search and the results of your search in Step 1.

12 Return to the PC settings screen, click *Search*, and move the two sliders you changed in Steps 8 and 9 back to the right, so both are turned on.

▶Tip To access the PC settings screen, move the cursor to the upper left corner of the screen and drag down. Click on the correct tile.

13 Drag the PC settings screen to the bottom of your computer screen until it disappears to close the PC settings screen.

13 *Shortcut*

Close Window
Alt + F4

Taking It Further

Additional Search Settings You may wish to clear the existing search history periodically. To do this, click the Delete history button in the *Search history* section of the PC settings screen. You can also speed up searches by reducing the number of apps that Windows searches. For example, if you normally do not use a certain app (such as the Finance app) listed in the *Use these apps to search* section, move its slider all the way to the left to turn the app off in Windows searches.

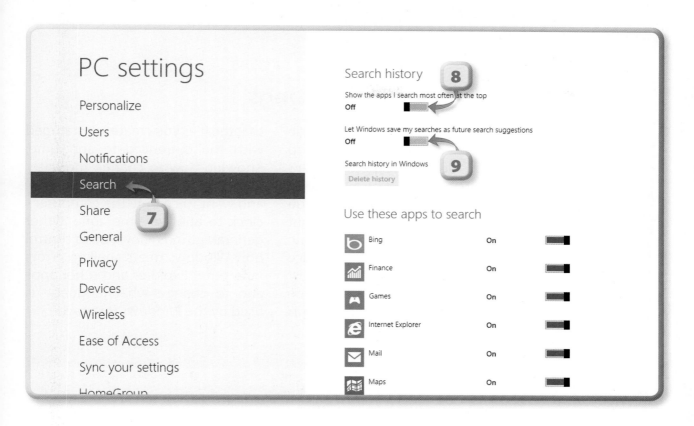

Windows

Modify General Settings

Video M2_C3_S04

Windows' general settings include date, time, spelling, language, and more. By default, your computer's date and time are set by a Windows date/time server. Additionally, if you live in an area that uses daylight saving time, Windows will update your computer's time settings twice a year for you. Your computer must have the correct date and time settings for several reasons. One is that the files you create are stamped with the current date and time. Knowing how to change the date/time settings is helpful if you travel and want to change the computer's clock to another time zone. Other general settings allow you to control how Windows treats spelling errors in Internet Explorer and other apps and to change what language is used by the Windows interface.

Steps

1 *Shortcut*

Open Settings Pane
Win + I

4-6 *Another Way*

From the desktop, click the time and date displayed on the Taskbar and then click the *Change date and time settings* option to modify the time zone and daylight saving time settings.

▶ **Tip** You may find that Autocorrect is a great help or a great nuisance. For example, if you commonly use specialized legal terms, it may repeatedly change those terms to incorrect words.

▶ **Tip** Click Win + Q to open the Search pane, type *language* in the search box, and then click *Settings* in the Search pane. All language setting options are now listed in the *Settings* results list.

▶ **Tip** Move your mouse pointer to the right edge of the pane to display the scroll bar.

1 From the Start screen, display the Charms bar and then click the Settings charm.

2 Click *Change PC settings* in the Settings pane.

3 Click *General* in the left pane of the PC settings screen.

4 Click the down-pointing arrow beside the displayed time zone to show the list of available time zones.

5 Scroll up or down and click your time zone—for example, *(UTC -0 5:00) Eastern Time (US & Canada)*—if it is not already selected.

6 If the region you live in uses daylight saving time, drag the slider below *Adjust for daylight saving time automatically* all the way to the right to turn on this option. If your region does not use daylight saving time, drag the slider all the way to the left to turn it off.

7 In the *Spelling* section, drag the slider below *Autocorrect misspelled words* all the way to the right to on this option.

8 Scroll down to the *Language* section of the right pane and click *Language preferences*.

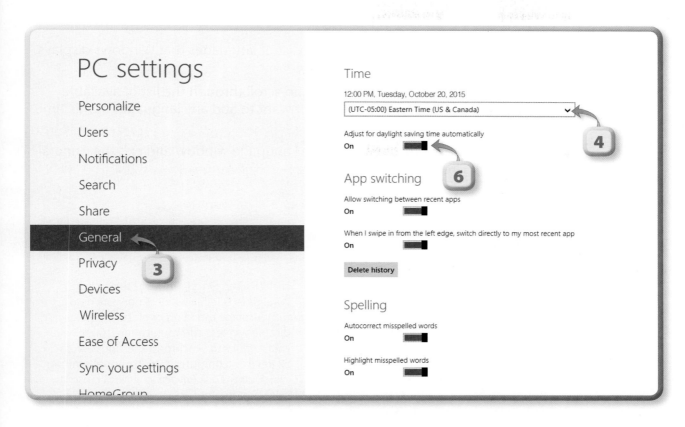

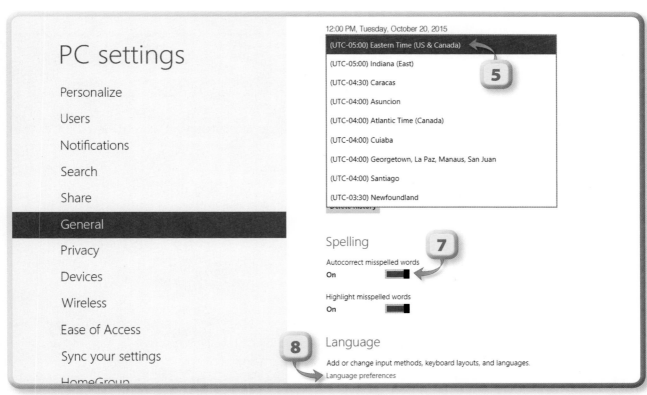

Windows

9 In the Language window, view the list of languages that Windows displays.

10 Click the Add a language button and scroll through the list of available languages. Click Cancel. You do not want to add any languages at this time.

11 Click the Close button to close the Language window and exit the General Settings screen.

Taking It Further

Modifying Other PC Settings The PC settings screen allows you to modify numerous settings in addition to the general settings explored in this skill. For example, if you click *Notifications* in the left pane, you can change which apps show notifications. (See Chapter 1 of this module for more information on notifications.) If you want to see which devices (such as a printer and a mouse) are currently connected to or recognized by Windows, or add a device, click *Devices*. On a laptop or tablet, click *Wireless* to select a wireless network or *to* turn Airplane mode on or off to enable or disable wireless communications. Click *Sync your settings* to synchronize settings across all devices (computer, tablet, phone) running Windows 8. Click *Privacy* to view Microsoft's privacy statement and to control the way Microsoft and apps collect information from you and your computer.

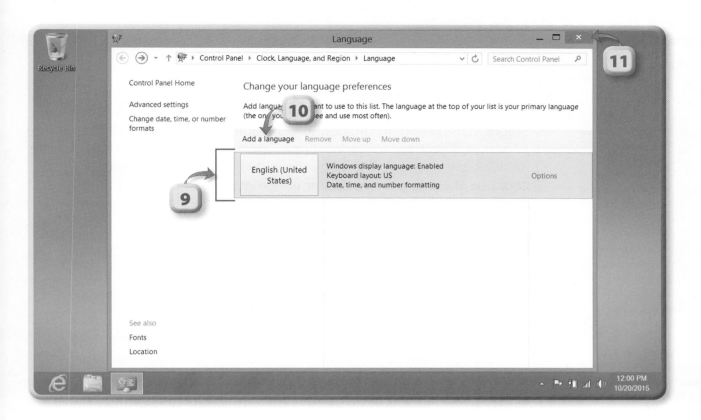

Windows

Review Network Settings

 M2_C3_S05

Before completing its installation, Windows 8 will try to connect to an available network. The network could be the one your computer is hard-wired to (through a network cable plugged into the appropriate port) or a wireless network. This skill discusses networks, including network settings, sharing, and troubleshooting.

Steps

1 Shortcut
Open Settings Pane
Win + I

1-2 Another Way
To access the Networks pane from the desktop, click the Networks icon in the notification area of the Taskbar.

▶**Tip** Clicking the Network icon will show you all wireless networks within range of your computer. Observe the number of bars in the signal strength icon (the more bars, the stronger the signal).

1 Use the Charms bar to open the Settings pane.

2 Click the network icon in the system-wide settings area. **NOTE:** *Network names are all different; you should see the name of your own network here.*

3 In the Networks pane, click the network to which you are connected. Depending on the type of connection you have, you may or may not see information about your network.

4 Click in a blank area of the Start screen to close the Networks task pane.

5 Type control panel and then click *Control Panel* in the Apps results list.

6 In the Control Panel window, click the <u>Network and Internet</u> link.

7 In the Network and Internet window, click the <u>Network and Sharing Center</u> link.

8 Click the link to your network beside *Connections* in the *View your active networks* section. The network connection status dialog box opens, showing you information about connectivity.

9 Close the network connection status dialog box.

10 In the *Change your networking settings* section of the Network and Sharing Center window, click the <u>Troubleshoot problems</u> link to see issues that Windows 8 can assist in solving.

11 Click the Back arrow to return to the Network and Sharing Center window.

12 Click the Close button to close the Network and Sharing Center window.

Taking It Further

Understanding Network Security Settings   In the Networks pane, when you hover the mouse pointer over a network name, you may see a ScreenTip. The ScreenTip will show you the network's security protocol (e.g., *WPA-PSK*) and type (e.g., *802.11g*). The WPA (Wi-Fi Protected Access) security protocol was developed to protect computers using wireless access to the Internet. The numbers and letters used in the type refer to the method of transmission. If you are using a Wi-Fi connection, such as for a notebook computer, you will see a Disconnect button when you click the network name. When you click that button you will disconnect from the network.

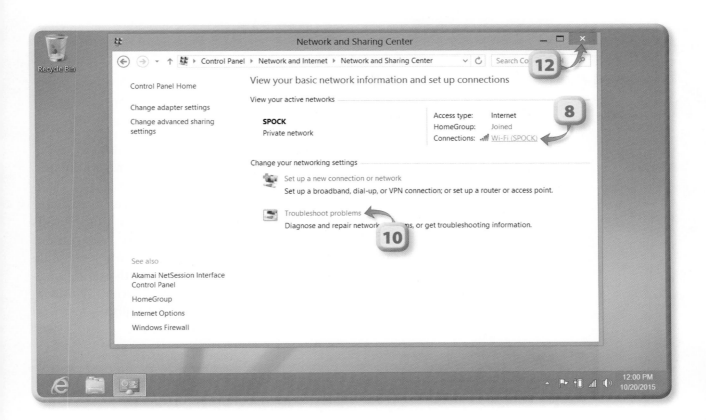

Windows

Windows

Skill 6

Modify Sound, Brightness, and Notification Settings

Video M2_C3_S06

Windows 8 has default settings that control how loud your computer's speakers are, how bright your monitor is, and more. Like most other components of Windows 8, you can control or customize these settings. For example, to save battery power (on a laptop) or the life of your monitor, you can fine-tune your computer's power settings. In addition, Windows 8 shows notifications about what is new, what updates it recommends or needs, and potential problems that need troubleshooting. You can turn these notifications off for various periods of time. You may wish to turn them off if they are distracting, or while you are updating antivirus or anti-spyware software (when Windows might constantly remind you these items need attention).

Steps

1 Shortcut
Open Settings Pane
Win + I

1-2 Another Way
To access volume controls from the desktop, click the Speakers icon in the notification area of the Taskbar.

1 Display the Charms bar and then click the Settings charm.

2 Click the Speakers icon in the Settings pane to open the volume control box.

3 Drag the slider up to increase the speaker volume. When you release the slider, the speaker will play a tone at the volume indicated and the volume control box will automatically close.

4 Click the Speakers icon to open the volume control box and then drag the slider down to decrease the speaker volume.

5 Click the Speakers icon to open the volume control box and then click the Mute Speakers button to turn off all system sounds.

6 Open the volume control box and click the Mute Speakers button again to turn on all system sounds.

Windows

▶**Tip** The Brightness icon is generally available on laptop and other portable computers. It may not be available on a desktop computer. If the Brightness icon is unavailable, you can adjust your monitor's brightness using controls on the monitor.

▶**Tip** On laptops and other portable computers, you can extend the time between battery charges by decreasing the brightness.

▶**Tip** The three power options are discussed in Chapter 1 of this module.

7 Click the Brightness icon in the Settings pane to open the brightness slider. You can drag the slider up to increase your monitor's screen brightness or down to decrease its brightness.

8 Click the Notifications icon. Choose *Hide for 1 hour* from the shortcut menu. Notice that a small clock appears on the Notifications icon. Click the Notifications icon again to turn off the 1-hour delay.

9 Click the Power icon to open a menu listing three power options available to you: *Sleep, Shut down*, and *Restart*. Click the Power icon again to close the shortcut menu.

10 Click in a blank area of the Start screen to close the Settings pane.

Taking It Further

Understanding Notifications   The Action Center icon (looks like a flag) is located on the desktop in the notification area of the Windows Taskbar. When Windows has a new message for you, it will "flag" you in this area. The kinds of things Windows will notify you about include updates to its operating system, security issues (e.g., Windows Firewall may have been turned off), and possible updates for installed hardware or software.

If the Action Center icon has a red X on it, an important issue, such as your computer's antivirus protection, needs attention. Less urgent issues are "yellow" issues. With these, you will see no change to the Action Center icon flag, but if you hover on the flag you will see a ScreenTip indicating that you have one or more messages. Yellow issues are those that may, for instance, help your PC run more smoothly.

Taking It Further

Saving Power Brightness and other settings affect the amount of power your computer uses. To control your computer's power consumption, you can change your computer's power plan. Open the Control Panel, click the <u>Hardware and Sound</u> link, and then click the <u>Power Options</u> link. Choose one of the power plans: the *Balanced (recommended)* option or the *Power save* option. You can customize either plan by clicking the *Change plan settings* option to adjust brightness and other elements.

Windows

Explore Accessibility Options

Video M2_C3_S07

Each time you begin a new Windows 8 session, accessibility options are available: look for the Ease of Access button ♿ in the lower left corner of the Sign-in screen. One accessibility tool, the Magnifier, can be used to zoom in on any area of the screen or on the whole screen, making items easier to read. Accessibility options offer over a dozen ways to customize your PC experience. You can alter the screen contrast, change the thickness of the cursor, turn a screen reader on to read text aloud, or even make the mouse easier to use. In addition, you can have Windows 8 recommend accessibility settings that will make your PC easier to use.

Steps

Use the Magnifier

1 From the desktop, click Internet Explorer in the Taskbar to open the browser.

2 Type www.emcp.com in the Address bar and press Enter.

3 *Shortcut*
Activate Magnifier
Win + Shift + +

▶**Tip** Point to the lower right corner of the screen to open the Charms bar and then click the Search charm.

3 Display the Charms bar, click the Search charm, type magnifier in the search box, and then click *Magnifier* in the Apps results list to open the Magnifier toolbar. Wait a second or two until the Magnifier toolbar changes to a magnifying glass icon.

4 *Another Way*
The amount of magnification can also be adjusted using the Options button on the Magnification toolbar.

4 Move your mouse pointer to the top right corner of the web page, the lower right corner, and finally the lower left corner. Notice that the magnifying glass icon follows your mouse pointer. the lower left corner of the page.

5 Hover over the magnifying glass icon until you see a double right arrow (>>) and then click the magnifying glass icon to reopen the Magnifier toolbar.

6 Click the + button to increase the magnification to 300%.

7 Click the - button to decrease the magnification to 100%.

8 Close the Magnifier toolbar.

9 Close Internet Explorer.

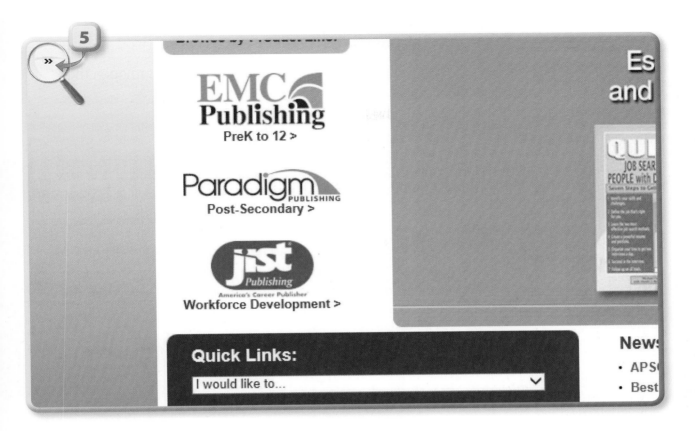

More

Chapter 3 Working with Windows Settings, Accessories, Security, and Help   **151**

Review Ease of Access Settings

10 *Another Way*

If you opened Internet Explorer from the Start screen, you can also open the Settings pane from the Start screen.

10 *Shortcut*

Open Settings Pane
Win + I

10 Open the Settings pane and then click *Change PC settings* to open the PC settings screen.

11 Click the *Ease of Access* option in the left pane.

12 In the right pane, drag the slider for the *High contrast* option all the way to the right to enable that setting. After a few seconds, you will see the screen in high contrast.

13 Drag the slider all the way to the left to return to the default setting.

▶**Tip** The *Make everything on your screen bigger* option is not available on all computers.

14 If the *Make everything on your screen bigger* option is available, drag the slider all the way to the right to enable that setting.

15 Drag the slider all the way to the left to return to the default setting.

16 Click the *Cursor thickness* option box arrow.

17 Select *3* in the option list to make the cursor thicker—and thus more noticeable.

18 Select *1* to return the cursor to its default thickness.

19 Drag the PC settings screen off the bottom of your computer screen to close the PC settings screen.

Taking It Further

Reviewing Other Accessibility Settings
The PC settings screen allows you to quickly change two other accessibility settings. (1) In the *Show notifications for* drop-down list, you can select the length of time that notifications display. (2) You can click the *Pressing Windows + Volume Up will turn on* option box arrow to choose what happens when you press the Windows key and the Volume Up key at the same time. For example, you can have Windows show you an on-screen keyboard. *NOTE:* Not all keyboards have a Volume Up button.

Windows

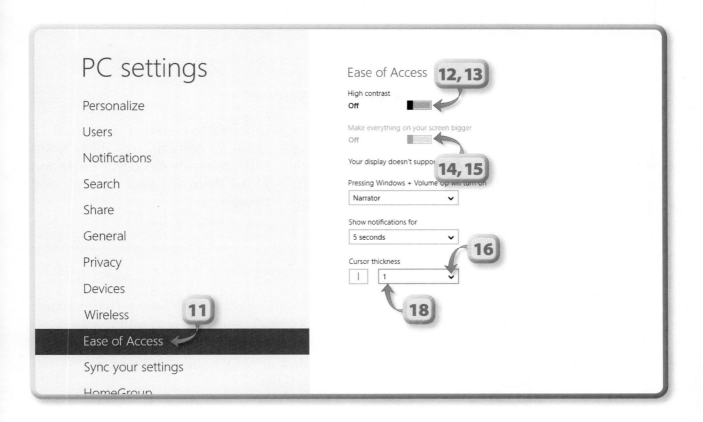

Taking It Further

Exploring the Ease of Access Center
The Ease of Access Center acts as a one-stop shopping place for changing accessibility options. To reach the Ease of Access Center, open the Control Panel, click *Ease of Access*, and then click *Ease of Access Center*. To hear audio descriptions of your choices, mark the *Always read this section* check box. Scroll down to the *Explore all settings* section, where you will find other ways to make the computer easier to see as well as options for making the mouse and keyboard easier to use. There are many more options in the Ease of Access Center. Spend a few minutes exploring them.

Windows

Windows

Use Windows Accessories

Video M2_C3_S08

Windows 8 comes with handy utility programs that are located in the Windows Accessories group. These include Calculator (used to perform calculations), Notepad (used to type unformatted text), Paint (used to create or edit images), Sticky Notes (used to create electronic notes and paste them on your screen), and many more.

Steps

Use Calculator

▶**Tip** To open any app from the Start screen, type the name of the app (e.g., *Calculator*) and then click the name of the app in the Apps results list.

1 From the Start screen, display the Charms bar, click the Search charm, type cal in the search box, and then click *Calculator* in the Apps results list.

1 Shortcut
Open Search Pane
Win + Q

2 Click buttons in the Calculator window or press numeric keys on the keyboard to multiply 11 by 13.

▶**Tip** Use the asterisk (*) for the multiplication symbol in calculations.

3 Click the Edit button on the Calculator toolbar and then click *Copy*.

▶**Tip** The Calculator view can be changed to Scientific to provide access to mathematical functions like *sin* and *cos*.

4 Close the Calculator program.

Use Notepad

5 Display the Charms bar, click the Search charm, type notepad in the search box, and then click *Notepad* in the Apps results list.

6 In Notepad, type The amount owed is $.

7 Shortcut
Paste
Ctrl + V

7 Click the Edit button on the Notepad toolbar and then click *Paste* to paste the result from the Calculator into the Notepad. Type a period.

8 Close Notepad. Click *Don't Save* in the Notepad dialog box.

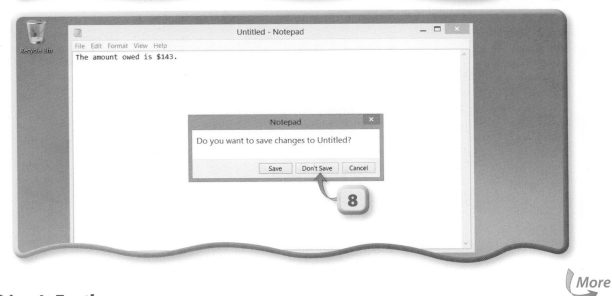

More

Taking It Further

Exploring Windows Accessories There are many more Windows accessories than the ones covered in this skill. From the Start screen, right-click to display the Taskbar, click the All apps icon, drag to the right to display the Windows Accessories group, and scroll through the list of accessories to see what is available. For example, Character Map is useful for inserting accented characters such as é or special symbols like € (the symbol for euros) when working in Notepad or Mail. Sound Recorder works with your computer's microphone to record your voice, and the resulting file is saved as a Windows Media audio file. Windows Media Player plays music and movie files and allows you to hear or view content from the Web. WordPad is used to create simple text documents with basic formatting. The Snipping Tool is used to take a picture (or capture) of all or any part of your screen. You can copy or cut and then paste the result, or save the result in any number of graphic formats (such as .jpg and .png).

Windows

Use Paint

8 Display the Charms bar, click the Search charm, type paint in the search box, and then click *Paint* in the Apps results list.

9 On the Home tab, click the *Rounded rectangle* option in the Shapes group.

10 Draw a rectangle that is 85 x 65 pixels on the canvas.

11 Click the Text button in the Tools group.

12 Click in the center of the rounded rectangle and type the first letter of your name.

13 Close Paint, saving your new image on your desktop by typing My Logo in the *File name* text box.

Tip As you draw a shape, the size in pixels (abbreviated *px*) displays in the Status bar at the bottom of the Paint window.

Use Sticky Notes

14 Display the Charms bar, click the Search charm, type sticky in the search box, and then click *Sticky Notes* in the Apps results list.

15 Type October 22, 2015, press Enter, and then type 1. Study for test.

16 Click anywhere on the desktop to leave the Sticky Note in place while you work in other apps.

17 Click the *X* on the Sticky Note and then click Yes in the warning box to delete the note.

Windows

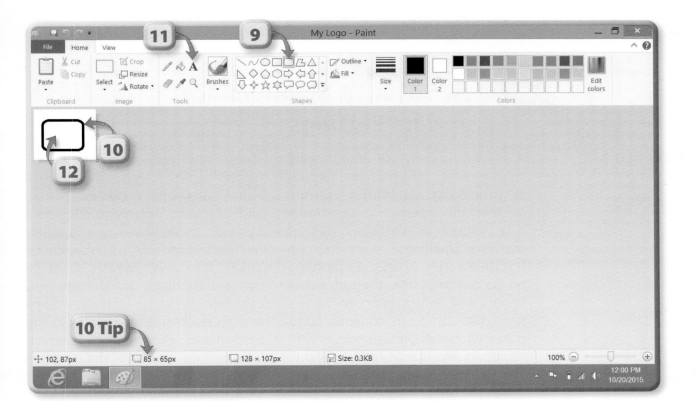

Windows

Windows

Review Security, Maintenance, and Update Settings

Video M2_C3_S09

A firewall is software or hardware that checks information coming to your computer from a network such as the Internet to determine if a hacker or certain types of malware (malicious software) are trying to gain access. Depending on its settings, the firewall either blocks the information or allows it to pass through to your computer. Windows Firewall comes with Windows and is enabled by default. You can check the Windows Firewall status and settings in the Action Center or through the Control Panel. Microsoft Windows Update allows you to download the latest updates to Windows 8 and other Microsoft products (such as Office 2013). Windows Update is set to run automatically by default. You can check Windows Update settings and review installed updates in the System and Security window, which is accessed through the Control Panel.

Steps

▶Tip You may need special user permission to open some of the security features described in this skill.

Review Security Settings

1 Display the Charms bar, click the Search charm, type action center in the search box, click the *Settings* option under the search box, and then click *Action Center* in the Apps results list.

2 In the right pane of the Action Center, click the *Security* arrow to show details about various security settings. Notice the status of each setting, such as Network firewall, Windows Update, Virus protection, and several others (scroll down to see them all).

3 If your spyware or virus protection is out of date, click the Update now button to let Windows check for and install updates.

4 Scroll down to the *Windows SmartScreen* subsection and then click the <u>Change settings</u> link.

5 In the Windows SmartScreen dialog box, notice that the default setting is *Get administrator approval before running an unrecognized app from the Internet (recommended)*.

6 Click the Cancel button to close the Windows SmartScreen dialog box.

7 Scroll back up to the *Security* arrow and click it to collapse the details section.

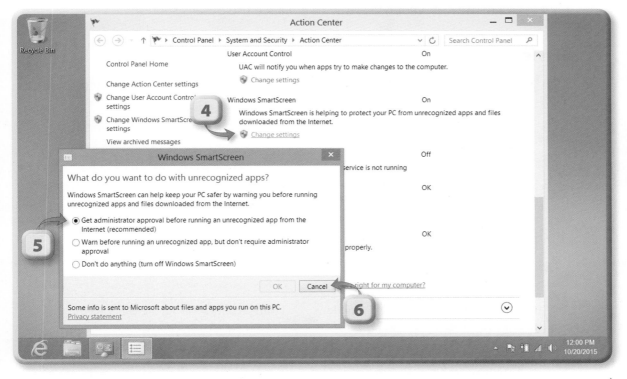

More

Taking It Further

Updating Spyware or Virus Protection When you check your Security settings in the Action Center, if you see that your spyware or virus protection is out of date, click the Update now button to let Windows check for and install updates.

Review Maintenance Settings

8 Continue scrolling down the Action Center window until you see the *Maintenance* section.

9 Click the *Maintenance* arrow to show the status of various items Windows checks regularly.

10 In the *Automatic Maintenance* section, notice the last time an Automatic Maintenance scan was run. If you see the message *Maintenance in progress*, Windows is currently running a maintenance scan, and you should skip to Step 12.

11 Click the <u>Start maintenance</u> link under *Automatic Maintenance*.

12 Note that while a maintenance scan is in progress, the link under *Automatic Maintenance* says <u>Stop maintenance</u>, and a clock appears on the Action Center flag on the taskbar. Windows will continue to run its maintenance routine, reporting on problems it encounters, until the scan is complete.

13 Click the *Maintenance* arrow to collapse the details section.

Review Update Settings

14 Click the *Windows Update* option in the *See also* section of the Action Center.

15 Confirm that your computer is set to allow Windows to install updates automatically.

16 Close the Windows Update window.

▶**Tip** Use the <u>Change settings</u> link to control the update schedule for your computer.

Taking It Further

Reviewing Windows Updates   Windows Updates automatically checks for updates on a number of items, including Windows Defender, Internet Explorer, and Windows 8 itself. Updates are either Recommended or Important. Recommended updates include those related to applications and devices, like software drivers for your mouse or keyboard. Important updates include those concerned with security and with the Windows 8 operating system. To review the update history for your computer, open the Control Panel, click <u>System and Security</u>, click *Windows Update*, and then click the <u>View update history</u> link. In the View Update History window, review the name of the update, its status (Succeeded or Failed), its level of importance, and the date it was installed.

Windows

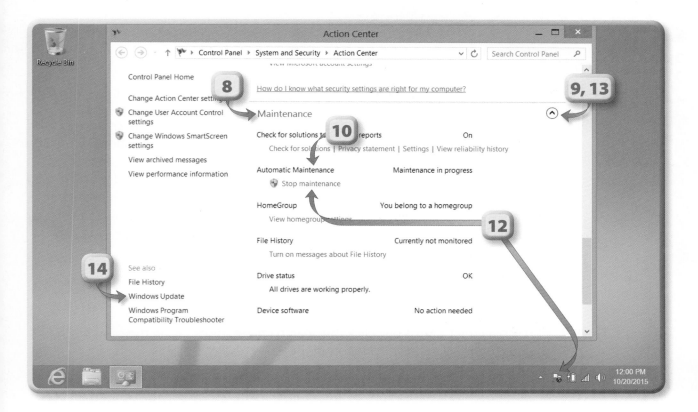

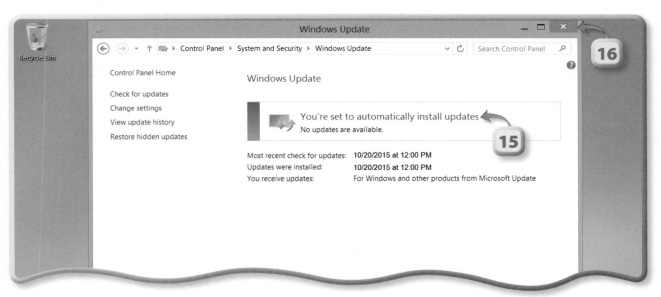

Taking It Further

Troubleshooting You may experience a problem with your computer that Windows does not list in the Action Center. For example, your computer may seem to be running sluggishly. To check for information on such problems, click the Troubleshooting link at the bottom of the Action Center window.

Windows

Skill 10

Video M2_C3_S10

Use Windows Help

Windows 8 has many more features, tools, settings, and accessories than this textbook covers. The Windows Help and Support system can help you explore or troubleshoot those on your own. This system uses help files that are stored on your computer and online to find answers to your questions. From the main Windows Help and Support window, you can choose the way you wish to get help. For example, you can choose to browse topics or search for an answer.

Steps

1 Display the Charms bar, click the Search charm, type help in the search box, and then click *Help and Support* in the Apps results list.

2 In the Windows Help and Support window, click the <u>Get started</u> link.

3 Look at the list of help topics and then click the <u>Get to know Windows</u> link.

4 Scroll through the topics and read the *Connected to the cloud* topic.

5 Click the Back arrow to return to the Get started page.

6 Click the Back arrow again to return to the Help home page.

▶ **Tip** Online content may change from time to time. You may not see the topic discussed and illustrated in this skill. If that is the case, choose any topic that interests you and follow the steps using it as an example.

Taking It Further

Getting the Most Current Help and Support Information If you have a live Internet connection, you can get the newest help and support topics and the latest versions of existing topics. To be sure that you see the most current information, click the down-pointing arrow next to *Online Help* at the bottom left corner of the Windows Help and Support window and make sure the *Get Online Help* option is selected.

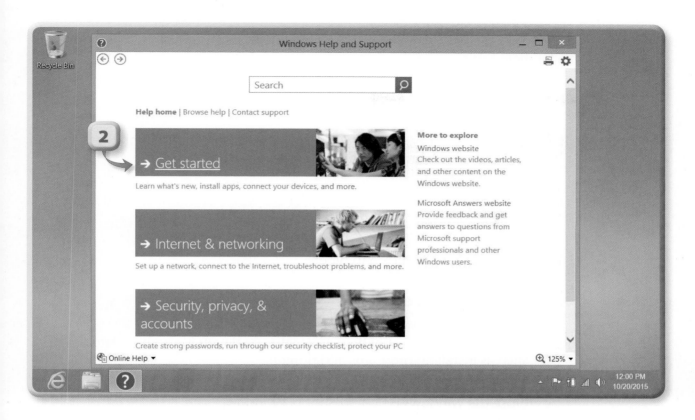

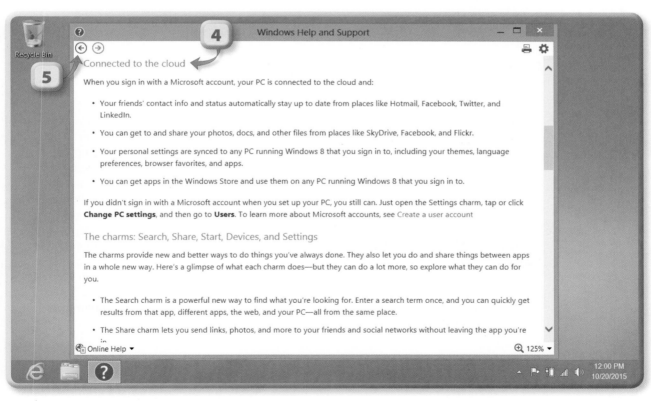

More

Windows

7 Click the Browse help link to see brief descriptions and links to Windows help topics.

8 Click the Help home link to return to the Help home page.

9 Click the Security, privacy, & accounts link to read information that can help you keep your computer safe.

10 Scroll down and click the Why use Windows Defender? link. Read the information under that topic.

11 Click in the search box and type install fonts.

12 Click the Search button.

13 Scroll through the list of help topics that deal with fonts and related topics, such as installing programs and printers.

14 Close the Windows Help and Support window.

Taking It Further

Getting More Support If you cannot find the answer you are looking for in the Windows Help and Support system, you have several options. (1) In the Windows Help and Support window, click the Help home link and then click the Windows website URL to open the Windows 8 main information page in Internet Explorer. Alternatively, click the Microsoft Community website URL to open the Microsoft Community forum page for Windows 8. Scroll through a list of answered questions and click on a topic (these change frequently). You can also click in the Find answers or Ask a question search box, type a topic or a question (for example, install fonts), and then press Enter. (2) In the Windows Help and Support window, click the Contact support link. There you'll find several options to explore, including the option to access the Windows 8 forum. (3) In the Windows Help and Support window, type remote assistance in the search box and then click the Remote Desktop Connections: Frequently asked questions link. Here you can learn about how to allow someone else to access your computer remotely over the Internet and help you fix a problem. You will also find a link to the Microsoft Answers website, which is an online community of experts.

Windows

Module 2 Project

Project 1

Skills   **CH1:** Start and sign in to Windows; open and close apps without tiles; explore the desktop; manipulate windows; move among open windows; work with menus, toolbars, and ribbons
CH2: Use File Explorer; copy a folder from the Student Resources disc; create a folder

Scenario   You will be creating files and modifying student data files throughout the course. This project helps you create an organized folder structure on your USB flash drive, SkyDrive, or local hard disk for your work for all *Guidelines* data files and solutions.

During this exercise, you will create new folders for some chapters and copy folders and files from the *Guidelines for Microsoft Office 2013* Student Resources disc for other chapters. At the conclusion of the assignment, you will have an appropriate folder/file structure that can be used for organizing your skills activities and end-of-chapter and end-of-module work.

Steps

1 Insert the Student Resources disc that accompanies the *Guidelines for Microsoft Office 2013* textbook in your CD/DVD drive. **HINT:** *If the AutoPlay window appears, click the Close button.*

2 Prepare your storage medium:
   a. If you will be saving your files to a USB flash drive:
      i. Insert your USB flash drive into any available USB port. **HINT:** *If the AutoPlay window appears, click the Close button.*
      ii. Open File Explorer, select *Computer* in the Navigation pane, and select your USB flash drive.
   b. If you will be saving your files to SkyDrive, sign in to your SkyDrive account. **HINT:** *For more information refer to the Introduction, Chapter 2, "Working with SkyDrive."*
   c. If you will be saving your files to your local hard disk, open File Explorer and browse to the Documents folder.

3 Create a folder on your storage medium and name it Guidelines2013.

4 Create a folder within the Guidelines2013 folder and name it Module1-ComputingEssentials. The *Guidelines* textbook does not provide any files to place into this folder or instructions to save files for this module. You will use this folder only if your instructor provides assignments that create saved files for this module.

5 Open File Explorer, *Computer*, select the CD/DVD drive, and then copy the following folders from the Student Resources disc to the Guidelines2013 folder on your storage medium:
   a. Module0-Toolkit
   b. Module2-Windows
   c. Module3-Internet
   d. Module4-Office
   e. Module5-Word
   f. Module6-Excel
   g. Module7-Access
   h. Module8-PowerPoint
   i. Module9-Integrating

6 Create *Completed* folders for each module; these will be used to store all finished skills and end-of-chapter/end-of-module work. To create these folders, you will open each module folder and then create a new subfolder named ModuleX-Completed (where *X* represents a corresponding number 0–9.)
   EXAMPLE 1
   For Module 5, open the Module5-Word folder and create a new subfolder named **Module5-Completed**.
   EXAMPLE 2
   For Module 8, open the Module8-PowerPoint folder and create a new subfolder named **Module8-Completed**.

When you are done, each module folder (0–9) should contain a ModuleX-Completed folder. See the image labeled Completed Step 6 for an example showing the Module4-Completed subfolder within the Guidelines2013/Module4-Office folder on your hard disk.

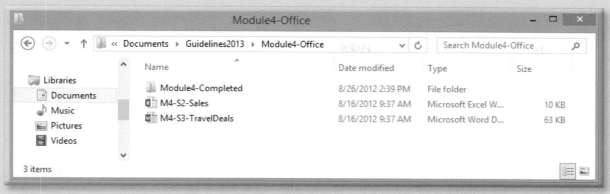

Completed Step 6

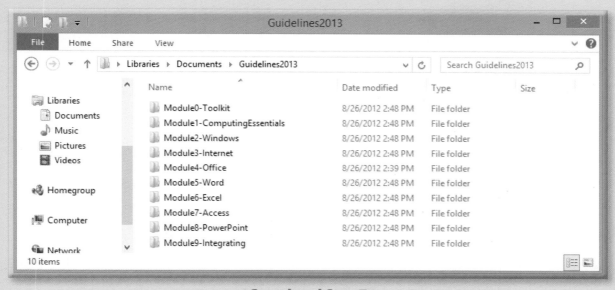

Completed Step 7

7 Arrange the window displaying the Guidelines2013 folder on your storage medium so that all the module folders appear in the window (Module0-Toolkit through Module9-Integrating), as shown in the image labeled Completed Step 7. You may need to resize the window.

8 Take a screenshot.

9 Open WordPad and enter your first and last names on the first line and today's date on the second line. Press Enter twice.

10 Paste the screenshot from Step 8 into WordPad.

11 Press Enter twice.

12 Return to your computer window and open the Module7-Access folder. Arrange the files in the window so the Module7-Completed folder and all student data files appear. (The student data files were copied from the Student Resources

disc when you copied the Module7-Access folder.) You may need to resize the window.

13 Take a screenshot. It will look similar to the Completed Step 13 image on the next page.

14 Paste the screenshot from Step 13 into WordPad below the prior screenshot and the two blank lines that were inserted in Step 11.

15 Save the WordPad file that contains the pasted screenshots, using the name **Lastname-M2-EOM-Windows**, in the Module2-Completed folder within the Module2-Windows folder. Replace the word *Lastname* in the file name with your last name. **HINT:** *Click the File tab and then click Save. Use your Windows skills to navigate to the correct folder. Enter the file name and press Save.*

16 Print or submit this file as instructed.

Completed Step 13

Student Name

Current Date

Completed Project 1

MODULE 3

Internet Basics

Skills You Learn

1 Explore Microsoft Internet Explorer 10 in the Windows 8 desktop interface
2 Explore Microsoft Internet Explorer 10 in the Windows 8 user interface
3 Explore the Mozilla Firefox interface
4 Explore the Google Chrome interface
5 Navigate among web pages
6 Use tabbed browsing
7 Set up a home page
8 Follow links and history
9 Save sites as Favorites/Bookmarks
10 Download files
11 Print a web page
12 Use search engines

Files You Need

For these skills, you do not need any student data files.

What You Create

In this module, you learn to use three of the most popular web browsers—Microsoft Internet Explorer (IE), Mozilla Firefox, and Google Chrome—to quickly navigate among web pages and become familiar with tabbed browsing. You learn how to designate a home page that displays every time you start your browser and how to save or bookmark sites that you would like to return to later. You learn to download files and print a web page. You also learn tips for specifying search criteria to find information on the Internet.

 Before beginning the module, copy the Module3-Internet folder from the Student Resources disc to your storage medium. The copied folder will become the working folder for this module.

Guidelines for Using

The Internet is the largest computer network in the world. You can use the Internet to communicate and share data with others all over the world.

In order to access and connect to the Internet, you need the following:

- a computer, tablet, smartphone, or other Internet-capable device
- a hotspot that provides free Internet access or an account with an Internet service provider (ISP) and related communications hardware such as a DSL modem or cable modem
- a wireless network card or an Ethernet card in your computer to support connectivity
- a web browser

Internet Service Provider

An Internet service provider (ISP) is a company that provides access to the Internet through one or more servers, which are large, powerful computers. ISPs usually charge a monthly fee. The ISP provides connection instructions and may provide you with necessary equipment, such as a cable modem or router. The ISP may also provide email accounts and other services. If you use a school computer or connect to the school's network, you will use the school's ISP and should ask your instructor how to connect to the Internet. You can also connect at a WiFi hotspot, which is a location that offers wireless Internet, often without a fee. Hotspots are found at many colleges and some retail locations.

Connection Options

The way you connect to the Internet varies according to the kind of Internet connection you have. The illustration below shows types of connections and the essential equipment required for each type.

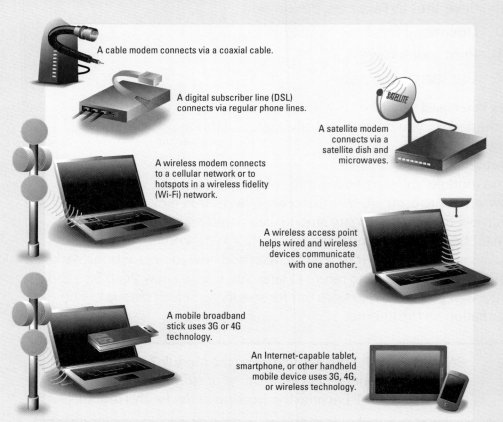

A cable modem connects via a coaxial cable.

A digital subscriber line (DSL) connects via regular phone lines.

A wireless modem connects to a cellular network or to hotspots in a wireless fidelity (Wi-Fi) network.

A satellite modem connects via a satellite dish and microwaves.

A wireless access point helps wired and wireless devices communicate with one another.

A mobile broadband stick uses 3G or 4G technology.

An Internet-capable tablet, smartphone, or other handheld mobile device uses 3G, 4G, or wireless technology.

the Internet

Web Browsers

A web browser is a software program that allows you to locate and view web pages. The term *web page* refers to a single page or document, whereas *website* refers to all of the web pages that make up a site.

Most browsers have similar interfaces and features, so browser choice is usually a matter of individual preference. Browser usage statistics vary, depending on the information source, but a recent estimate states that Mozilla Firefox has approximately 23% of the market and Chrome, approximately 28%. Internet Explorer receives approximately 27%. Other popular browsers include Safari and Opera. Portable devices, such as your cell phone, use mobile browsers. Shown below are screen captures of the National Park Service's website, accessed using Internet Explorer, Mozilla Firefox, and Google Chrome. Notice the similar features, including the Address/Location bar (where you type the address of a website).

Internet Explorer Browser

Mozilla Firefox Browser

Google Chrome Browser

Internet Basics

Module 3

Skill 1

Video M3_C1_S01

Explore Microsoft Internet Explorer 10 in the Windows 8 Desktop Interface

Internet Explorer is a web browser developed by Microsoft and included with the Windows operating system. There are two ways to run Internet Explorer 10. It can be run as a standard Windows application in desktop mode and it can also be run as an app designed for touch screens in the Windows 8 user interface (UI). Internet Explorer's desktop mode interface has several toolbars, including the Menu bar, the Command bar, and the Address bar (where you can type a web address). In this skill, you become familiar with Internet Explorer using the desktop mode interface. You also display and locate information on a web page, access commands and settings, and browse Internet Explorer Help.

Steps

▶ **Tip** Depending on your system configuration, the steps to start Internet Explorer in the desktop interface may vary.

1 Click the Desktop tile in the Start screen.

2 Click the Internet Explorer button, located on the Windows Taskbar, to start Internet Explorer.

3 Click the Address bar to select the text, type www.loc.gov, and then press Enter to display the home page for the Library of Congress.

4 If the Command bar is not displayed, right-click an empty area of the toolbar and select *Command bar*.

5 Click the Page button on the Command bar.

7 *Shortcut*

Increase text size
Ctrl + Shift + +

6 Click *Text size*.

▶ **Tip** To decrease text size, click the Page button on the Command bar, click *Text size*, and then click *Smaller*. Alternatively, you can press Crtl + -.

7 Click *Larger* to increase the size of the text and images in the web page.

▶ **Tip** To make everything (including images) larger on the page, click the Page button on the Command bar, click *Zoom*, and then select a zoom setting.

8 Click the Help button on the Command bar.

9 *Shortcut*

Internet Explorer Help
F1

9 Click *Internet Explorer Help* to display the help page for Internet Explorer 10.

▶**Tip** Click the links to various topics on the help page to learn more about IE 10.

10 Scroll to browse the help information.

11 Click the Close button to close the Help window.

12 *Another Way*

Right-click the title bar and select *Menu bar*.

12 Return to the Library of Congress window and press the Alt key to display the Menu bar, if it is not already displayed.

▶**Tip** The Alt key toggles the Menu bar on and off.

13 Click Edit on the Menu bar.

14 *Shortcut*

Open the *Find* text box
Ctrl + F

14 Click *Find on this page*.

▶**Tip** Click the Next button in the Find bar to find the next occurrence of the search text.

15 Type History in the *Find* text box.

▶**Tip** Website content changes frequently, so the number of matches you find may vary from the number shown in the screenshot on the opposite page.

16 All occurrences of *History* are highlighted on the web page and the Find toolbar indicates the number of matches.

17 Click the Close button to close the Find toolbar.

18 Click the Close button to close the browser window.

Taking It Further

Using the Refresh and Stop Buttons
Many websites, such as newspaper websites, refresh or update their site content on a regular basis. Some websites do so automatically, but others require action on your part. To refresh website content, click the Refresh button (↻), located to the right of the Address bar. Or you can simply press the F5 key. If you start to load a website and change your mind, or if the website is taking a long time to load, you can stop the loading process by clicking the Stop button (✕). The Stop button is displayed in place of the Refresh button when a website is loading. You can also stop the loading process by pressing the Esc key.

Internet Basics

Internet Basics

Internet Basics

Explore Microsoft Internet Explorer 10 in the Windows 8 User Interface

Video M3_C1_S02

In Skill 1, you explored the Internet Explorer interface in desktop mode. In this skill, you will explore Internet Explorer when it is run as a Windows 8 app designed for touch screens. Even though this version is designed for touch screens, it also works with a keyboard and a mouse. Windows 8 UI, Explorer's interface, runs in full-screen view with the Navigation bar at the bottom of the screen. The Navigation bar contains the Address bar, where you can type a Web address. It also contains several buttons including the Back, Refresh/Stop, Page Tools, and Pin to Start button. A Charms bar is displayed on the right side of the screen and is used to change settings, search the Web, and print a web page. This skill will explain how to use this app with a keyboard and a mouse as well as with a touch screen.

▶ **Tip** IE 10 will open in the Windows 8 user interface only if you have it set as your default browser. If it opens in the desktop interface, close the browser to return to the Start screen, type *Default Programs*, click *Default Programs* in the Apps results list, click the *Set your default programs* option, click *Internet Explorer* in the list of programs, click *Set this program as default*, and then click OK.

▶ **Tip** If the Address bar does not appear when you open IE, right-click the screen to display it.

▶ **Tip** When you type a URL, navigation tiles of frequently visited web pages are displayed. Tap or click a navigation tile to go to that web page.

▶ **Tip** The tab switcher will display open web pages and contains a New Tab button and a Tab Tools button.

▶ **Tip** The Charms bar contains Search, Settings, Share, and Devices charms.

9 *Shortcut*

Increase text and image size
Ctrl + Shift + +
Decrease text and image size
Ctrl + -

Steps

1. Click the Internet Explorer tile in the Start screen.

2. Click in the Address bar to select the text, type www.loc.gov, and then press Enter to display the home page for the Library of Congress.

3. Click anywhere in the web page to remove the Navigation bar.

4. Right-click anywhere in the web page to redisplay the Navigation bar and to display the tab switcher.

5. Click in the web page to remove the Navigation bar and the tab switcher.

6. Press Win + C to display the Charms bar.

7. Click the Settings charm.

8. Click *Internet Options*.

9. Click the Zoom bar to increase the text and image size on the web page and then use the Zoom bar to restore the zoom to 100%.

10. Click in the web page to remove the Internet Explorer Settings pane.

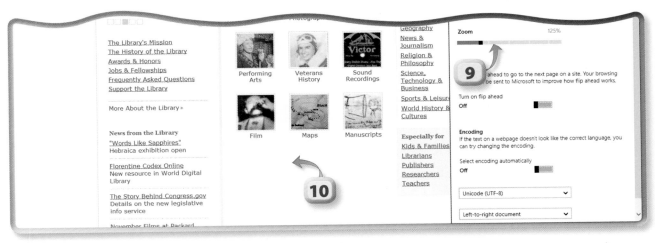

More

11 Right-click anywhere in the web page to redisplay the Navigation bar.

12 Click the Page tools button on the Navigation bar.

13 Click *Find on page*.

14 Type History in the *Find* text box.

15 All occurrences of *History* are highlighted in the web page and the Find toolbar displays the number of matches.

16 Click the Close button to close the Find toolbar.

17 Press Win + C to display the Charms bar.

18 Click the Start charm to return to the Start screen.

Taking It Further

Using a Touch Screen   Navigating Internet Explorer 10 on a touch screen is quite different from using a keyboard and mouse. Instead of clicking the mouse, you tap the screen with your finger. The Navigation bar is displayed by swiping your finger in from the bottom of the screen and the Charms bar is displayed by swiping your finger in from the right side of the screen. To increase the size of the text or an image, use two fingers to point to the text or image and then spread the two fingers apart. To decrease the size of the text or image, touch the screen with two fingers spread apart and then pull them together.

Internet Basics

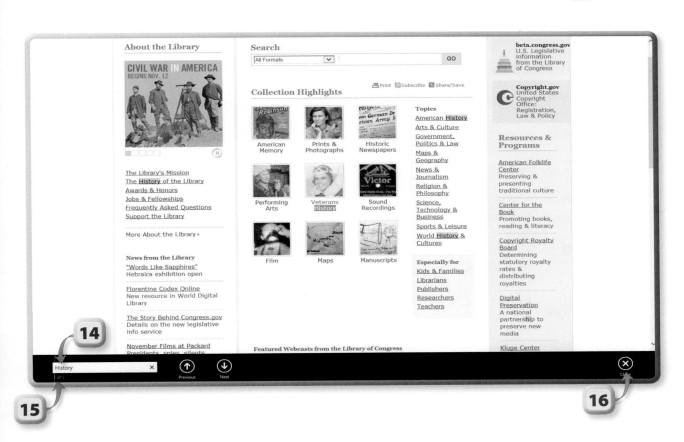

Internet Basics

Internet Basics

Skill 3

Video M3_C1_S03

Explore the Mozilla Firefox Interface

Firefox is a web browser developed by Mozilla. A free download is available from www.mozilla.com. Firefox's interface includes the Menu and Navigation bars. The Navigation bar contains the Location bar, where you type a web address, and the navigation buttons. The Status bar is located along the bottom of the Firefox window and displays information, such as a URL when you hover over a link. In this skill, you become familiar with the interface, display and locate information on a web page, use the Menu bar to access commands and settings, and browse Help.

Steps

▶Tip Depending on your system configuration, the steps to start Firefox may vary.

2 *Shortcut*
Select the URL in the Location bar
Ctrl + L

▶Tip Use the Menu bar to access Firefox commands and settings. If the Menu bar is not available, activate it by pressing the Alt key. You can force the Menu bar to remain visible by clicking View, selecting *Toolbars*, and selecting *Menu Bar*.

4–5 *Shortcut*
Increase text and image size
Ctrl + Shift + +
Decrease text and image size
Ctrl + -

▶Tip Use the Down Arrow key, the wheel on your mouse, or the vertical scroll bar to scroll down the Firefox Help window.

▶Tip Tabs are discussed further in Skill 6.

▶Tip Click the Next button in the Find bar to find the next occurrence of the search text.

1 From the Start screen, type Mozilla Firefox and then click *Mozilla Firefox* in the Apps results list.

2 Select the text in the Location bar, type www.loc.gov, and then press Enter to display the home page for the Library of Congress.

3 Press the Alt key to display the Menu bar if it is not already displayed and then click View on the Menu bar.

4 Click *Zoom* and then click *Zoom In* to increase the text and image size.

5 Click *Zoom* and then click *Zoom Out* to decrease the text and image size.

6 Press the Alt key and then click Help on the Menu bar.

7 Click *Firefox Help*. The Firefox Help web page displays in a new tab.

8 Scroll to browse the help information. The search box, where you type keywords to find help on a specific topic, is also available on this page.

9 Hover over a help topic link and notice that the URL for the link appears in the Status bar.

10 Press the Close Tab button to close the Firefox Help tab.

11 Click the Alt key and then click Edit on the Menu bar.

12 Click *Find*. The Find bar is displayed at the bottom of the window.

13 Type History in the *Find* text box and then click the Highlight all button. All occurrences of *History* are highlighted on the web page.

14 Click the Close button to close the *Find* text box.

15 Click the Close button to close the browser window.

Internet Basics

Skill 4

Explore the Google Chrome Interface

Video M3_C1_S04

Chrome is a web browser developed by Google and is available as a free download from www.google.com. Chrome's interface includes the toolbar, which contains the Address bar where you can type a web address and the buttons that you use to navigate websites. The Status bar is located along the bottom of the Chrome window and displays alerts about current activities, such as progress in downloading a file. In this skill, you become familiar with Chrome's user interface. You also display and locate information on a web page, use the browser toolbar to access commands and settings and browse Chrome Help.

Steps

1 From the Start screen, type Chrome and then click *Chrome* in the Apps results list.

2 Select the text in the browser toolbar, type www.loc.gov, and then press Enter to display the home page for the Library of Congress.

2 *Shortcut*
Select the URL in the Location bar
Ctrl + L

3 Click the Customize and Control button on the browser toolbar.

4 Click the zoom in button (+) to increase the text and image size.

4 *Shortcut*
Increase Text and image Size
Ctrl + Shift + +

5 Click the zoom out button (-) to decrease the text and image size.

5 *Shortcut*
Decrease Text and image Size
Ctrl + -

6 *Shortcut*
Chrome Help
F1

6 Click *Help* in the Customize and Control menu.

7 Scroll to browse the help information. The search box, where you type keywords to find help on a specific topic, is also available on this page.

▶ *Tip* Use the down arrow key, the wheel on your mouse, or the vertical scroll bar to scroll down the Chrome Help window

8 Click the Close Tab button to close the Chrome Help tab.

▶ *Tip* Tabs are discussed further in Skill 6.

9 Click the Customize and Control button on the browser toolbar.

10 *Shortcut*
Open the Find bar
Ctrl + F

10 Click *Find*. The Find bar is displayed at the top of the window.

11 Type History in the *Find* text box. All occurrences of *History* are highlighted on the web page.

▶ *Tip* Click the Next button in the Find bar to find the next occurrence of the search text.

12 Click the Close button to close the *Find* text box.

13 Click the Close button to close the browser window.

Internet Basics

Module 3

Skill 5

Navigate among Web Pages

Video M3_C1_S05

A Uniform Resource Locator (URL) specifies the address of a web page on the Internet. You can go to a particular web page by typing a URL, such as www.emcp.com, in the Address or Location bar of a web browser. Web pages contain links which can be clicked to display another web page. Links are usually underlined but may also take other forms, including buttons or images. You can click the Back and Forward buttons on the browser's interface to navigate through web pages you have already visited. Click the Home button on the browser's interface to display the Home page, which is the page that displays when you start the web browser.

Steps

▶ *Tip* When you enter a URL for a site (such as www.fsa.usda.gov), the page that appears is that website's home page.

▶ *Tip* The top-level domain specifies the type of website. For example, *.com* indicates it is a business, *.gov* indicates it is a government site, and *.edu* indicates it is an educational institution.

1 Start Internet Explorer in desktop mode.

2 Select the URL in the Address bar, type www.fsa.usda.gov, and then press Enter to display the home page for the United States Department of Agriculture (USDA) Farm Service Agency (FSA).

3 Click the Aerial Photography link to open a new browser window containing the USDA Aerial Photography Field Office (APFO) home page.

4 Click the About APFO button.

5 Click the Back button to return to the APFO home page.

6 Click the Close button to close the browser tab containing the APFO home page.

7 Click the Close button to close the browser window.

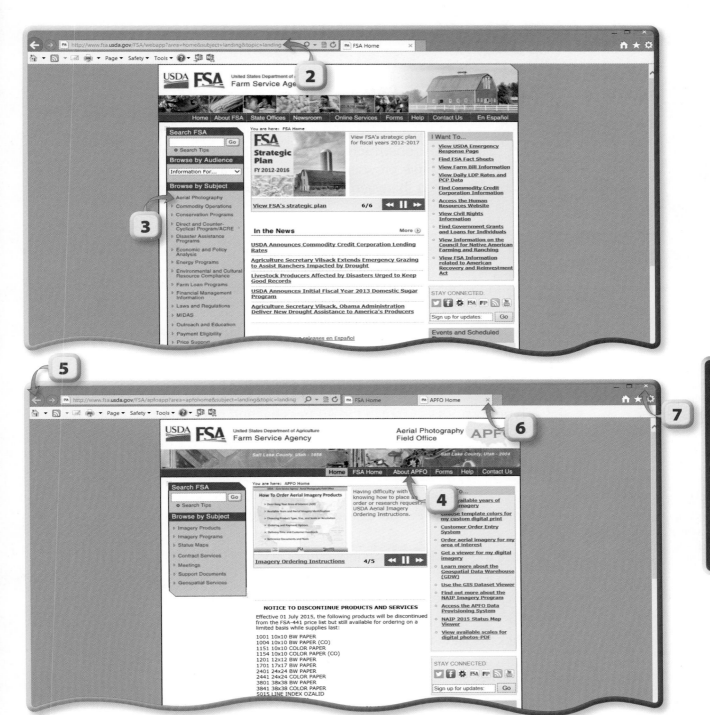

Taking It Further

The Safari Browser The Safari browser is installed with the Mac OS X and iOS operating systems, although there is also a version that can be downloaded for the Microsoft Windows operating system. A recent estimate states Safari has approximately 14% of the web browser market. However, use of the Safari browser is increasing because it runs on the iPhone and the iPad, both of which are popular devices.

Internet Basics

Use Tabbed Browsing

Video M3_C1_S06

Tabbed browsing is a browser feature that allows you to open more than one website in a single browser window. You can switch between websites by clicking the tab you want to view. When a new tab is opened, you can type a web address in the Address/Location bar to open another site.

Steps

1 Start Internet Explorer in desktop mode.

2 Type www.emcp.com in the Address bar and press Enter.

3 *Shortcut*
New Tab (IE, Firefox, and Chrome)
Ctrl + T

3 Click the New Tab button.

4 Type www.google.com in the Address bar and press Enter to display the Google home page in the new tab.

5 Right-click the Images link on the Google web page.

6 *Shortcut*
Open in New Tab
Press Ctrl while clicking a link.

6 Select *Open in new tab* to open the Google Images web page in a new tab.

7 Click the EMC Publishing tab to display it.

▶**Tip** To move between open tabs, press Ctrl + Tab.

8 Click the Close Tab button to close the EMC Publishing tab.

9 Click the New Tab button.

▶**Tip** If you have changed the new tab page to your home page, type *about:tabs* in the Address bar to see the new tab page with the Reopen closed tabs link.

10 Click the Reopen closed tabs link.

11 Click the EMC Publishing LLC | Welcome to EMC link.

▶**Tip** When you close Firefox, a prompt may ask if you want to save your tabs for the next time you start Firefox. Click Save and Quit to save them or click Quit to close without saving them.

12 Click the Close button and then click the Close all tabs button in the Internet Explorer dialog box to close the browser window.

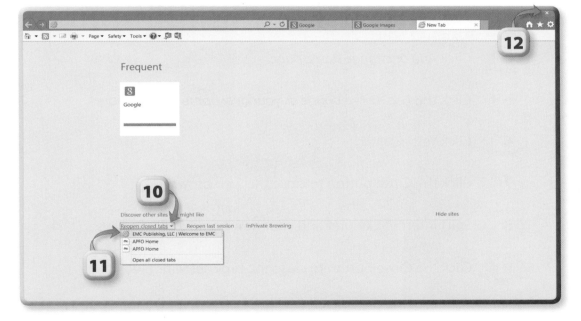

Taking It Further

Exploring New Tab Options Internet Explorer allows you to browse the Web without leaving a history trail. Simply click Safety on the Command bar and select *InPrivate Browsing*. This opens a new browser window that displays the InPrivate indicator to the left of the search box. Each new tab that you open inside this browser window will also display the InPrivate indicator. To end InPrivate browsing, close the new browser window and all its tabs. Access private browsing in Firefox by clicking Tools on the Menu bar and then selecting *Start Private Browsing*. For Chrome, click the Customize and Control button and then select *New incognito window*.

Internet Basics

Video ▶ M3_C1_S07

Set Up a Home Page

When you start your web browser, the page you see is called the browser's home page. This page also displays when you click the Home button in your web browser. Therefore, you probably want your home page to be a web page that you visit often. For example, your home page might be your company's website or one of your favorite news and information sites. In this skill, you set the home page for your browser.

Steps

1 Start Internet Explorer in desktop mode.

2 Type www.emcp.com in the Address bar and press Enter.

3 Click the Home button arrow on the Command bar.

4 Click *Add or change home page*.

5 Click the *Use this webpage as your only home page* option.

6 Click Yes.

7 Click the Close button to close the web browser.

8 Start Internet Explorer and your new home page displays.

9 Click the Close button to close the browser window.

2 *Another Way*

Depending on your IE settings, if you completed Skill 6 the IE window may display an EMCP icon. You can click this icon to open the EMC Publishing web page.

▶ *Tip* If you are using this skill to change the home page on your personal or home computer, rather than entering www.emcp.com, navigate to the web page that you plan to use as your home page.

▶ *Tip* To set up a home page in Firefox, display the website you want as your home page, press the web page icon that displays at the left of the web address in the Location bar, and then drag it to the Home button. Click Yes in the Set Home Page window.

7 *Shortcut*

Close Browser
Alt + F4

▶ *Tip* You can open your favorite pages every time you start Chrome. Click the Customize and Control button and select *Settings*. In the *On startup* section, select *Open a specific page or set of pages* and then click the Set page link to set your preferences.

Taking It Further

Choosing Multiple Home Pages Do you find it impossible to decide on just one home page? You may maintain more than one home page by having a set of two or more tabs display when you start your browser. To create a set of tabs in Internet Explorer, navigate to the selected web page, click the arrow next to the Home button, and then click *Add or change home page*. Next, click the *Add this webpage to your home page tabs* option. Repeat these steps for each page you want to add to your home page tab set.

Taking It Further

Understanding Portals You are probably familiar with the websites Yahoo!, MSN, and AOL. These websites can be classified as Web portals. A Web portal displays a variety of information, such as the weather, stock quotes, news headlines, and a search engine all on one page. Web portals are a good choice for a home page because a variety of information collected from various sources is available all on one page.

Internet Basics

Skill 8

Follow Links and History

Video ► M3_C1_S08

As you browse the Web, Internet Explorer stores information about the websites you visit. Having this information stored on your computer can be helpful. It can improve your web browsing speed and also can help you to find sites you have already visited, without requiring you to remember and type their URLs. In Internet Explorer, previously visited sites are displayed in the Address bar and you can also access them through the History tab in the Favorites Center.

Steps

▶ **Tip** When you type the first few letters of a web address in the Address/Location bar, Internet Explorer and Firefox display a list of previously entered web addresses that begin with those letters. Click one and press Enter to go to it.

▶ **Tip** In Chrome, you can type keywords in the Address bar and the browser will make suggestions based not only on your previously visited URLs, but also on similar web page titles.

6 *Another Way*

Press the Alt key to display the Menu bar, click View, select *Explorer bars*, and then select *History*. You will need to click the Close button to close the Favorites Center if you open it this way.

1 Start Internet Explorer in desktop mode.

2 Type www.nps.gov in the Address bar and press Enter to display the National Park Service website.

3 Type www.usda.gov in the Address bar and press Enter to display the United States Department of Agriculture home page.

4 Click the Show Address bar Autocomplete arrow at the end of the Address bar to display a list of web addresses that you have previously typed into the Address bar.

5 Click *http://www.nps.gov/*. The National Park Service website displays without your having to retype the web address.

6 Click the View favorites, feeds, and history button and then select the History tab. You will now see the Favorites Center with the History tab selected.

7 Click *Today* to display the websites you visited today.

8 Click the usda (www.usda.gov) folder and then the U.S. Department of Agriculture link to redisplay the USDA home page.

9 Click the Close button to close the browser window and all tabs.

Taking It Further

Changing History Duration By default, Internet Explorer keeps a 20-day history of the web pages you have visited. After 20 days, it automatically deletes those history entries. To change the number of days that Internet Explorer keeps your web page history, click Tools in the Menu bar and then click *Internet options*. In the Internet Options dialog box, click the General tab and then click the Settings button in the *Browsing history* section. On the History tab of the Website Data Settings dialog box, specify the number of days you prefer. If you do not want a web page history kept, set the number of days to *0*. Click OK to close the Website Data Settings dialog box. Click OK to close the Internet Options dialog box.

Internet Basics

Module 3

Skill 9

Video ▶ M3_C1_S09

Save Sites as Favorites/Bookmarks

Internet Explorer *favorites* are links that you save to websites you visit frequently. Firefox has a similar feature but refers to these favorite sites as *bookmarks*. In Internet Explorer, when you add a website to your Favorites bar, you can then go to that site by simply clicking its name, instead of having to type its web address. If you add a large number of favorites or bookmarks, you can organize them within folders to easily find the site you need.

Steps

1 Start Internet Explorer in desktop mode.

2 Type www.weather.gov in the Address bar and press Enter to display the website for the NOAA National Weather Service.

3 Click the View favorites, feeds, and history button and then click the Favorites tab if it is not already selected. You will now see the Favorites Center.

4 Click the Add to favorites button and a dialog box displays.

5 Replace the selected text in the *Name* box by typing NOAA National Weather Service. (Do not type the period.)

6 Click the Add button to add this site to your Favorites list.

7 Type www.nps.gov in the Address bar and press Enter to display the website for the U.S. National Park Service.

8 Click the View favorites, feeds, and history button.

9 Click the NOAA National Weather Service link in the Favorites list to redisplay the National Weather Service page.

10 Click the Close button to close the browser window.

4 *Shortcut*

Add a Favorite
Ctrl + D

▶ *Tip* Click the New Folder button to create a new folder within your Favorites folder. You can create new folders, as needed, to organize your favorites.

▶ *Tip* In Firefox, click Bookmarks and then click *Bookmark This Page* to add a bookmark. Click the Done button. For Chrome, select the Bookmark icon (shaped like a star) at the right of the Address bar.

▶ *Tip* To view suggestions for other websites based on the web page you are currently viewing, click the Suggested Sites button at the bottom of the Favorites Center. You may need to click Turn on Suggested Sites first.

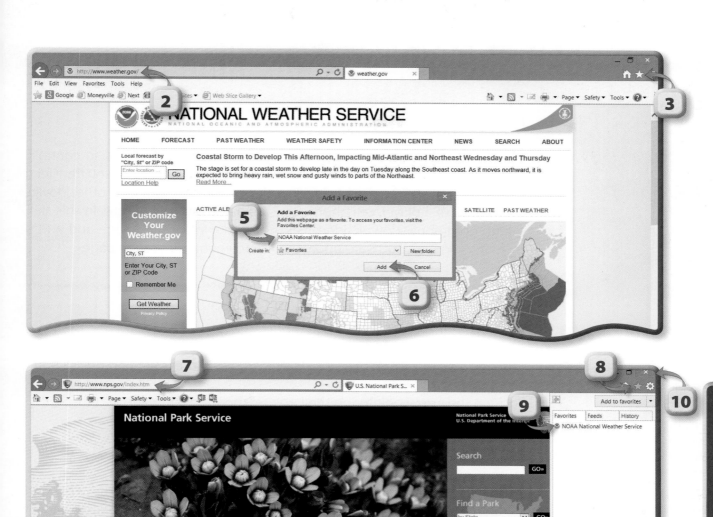

Taking It Further

Cleaning Out Your Favorites After a while your favorites or bookmarks list can get kind of long, making it hard to find what you need. (A long list defeats the whole purpose of easy-to-find favorites!) Periodically review and delete listed sites that you no longer visit very often. To do so in Internet Explorer, go to the Favorites Center and select the Favorites tab. Right-click the item you wish to remove, and click the *Delete* option from the shortcut menu.

Internet Basics

Video ▶ M3_C1_S10

Download Files

When you download a file, you transfer it from the Internet to your computer or another digital device, such as an MP3 player, cell phone, or tablet. Commonly downloaded files include programs, software updates, images, and music files. In contrast, when you upload a file, you transfer it from your computer or other device to a site on the Internet. In this skill, you download an image and a PDF document from a web page.

Steps

▶ **Tip** When you download a file, you take a risk that the file will contain a virus or a program that can damage your computer or your stored information. Be sure to install and use an antivirus program and only download files from sites you trust.

▶ **Tip** The Pictures library is the default location for saving images in Explorer. The default location for Firefox and Chrome is the Downloads folder. The default download location may have been redefined in your school.

▶ **Tip** Copyright laws protect much of the information on the Internet. Before using files you have downloaded from the Internet, check the source site for restrictions.

1 Start Internet Explorer in desktop mode.

2 Type www.emcp.net/guidelines13/M3S10 in the Address bar and press Enter.

3 Position the arrow pointer on the large textbook cover image and then right-click to display a menu.

4 Click *Save picture as* to display the Save Picture dialog box.

5 Click Save to save the image to your Pictures library and accept the assigned file name and file type. **NOTE:** *If you want to, you can change the name and type before saving the document.*

6 Click the <u>View Contents Listing (PDF)</u> link to open the Contents page for your textbook. Click *Open* if a bar appears asking if you want to open or save the file. Whether the page opens in a browser window or in Adobe Reader or Acrobat depends on your Adobe Reader or Acrobat settings. The page will only open if Adobe Reader or Acrobat is installed on your computer.

7 Click the Close button to close the tab or window containing the PDF.

8 Click the Close button to close the browser window.

Taking It Further

Installing Adobe Reader Adobe Reader is free software that is used to view PDF files. PDF is a file format that keeps all document formatting regardless of what application it was created in. It is a good file format to save a file if you are going to share the file because the person viewing the file only has to have Adobe Reader installed and not the software that the document was created in. To get and install Adobe Reader, go to get.adobe.com/reader/ and click the Download now button. If you have certain security settings in place, you may first have to agree to install an ActiveX Control on your computer or give Windows permission to download the software. Once you have cleared those security hurdles, you can begin the download and install process.

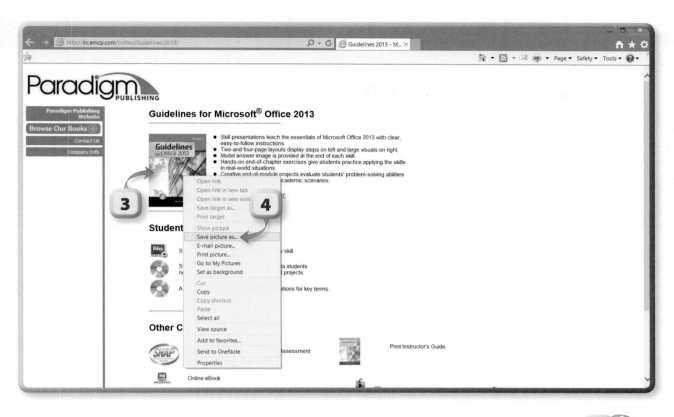

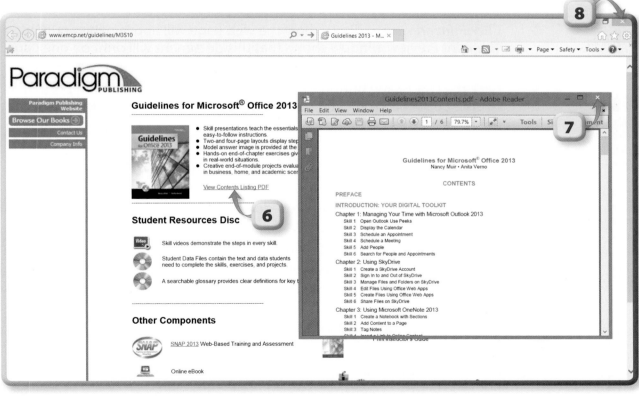

Internet Basics

Internet Basics

Module 3

Skill 11

Print a Web Page

Video M3_C1_S11

You may want to print the information you find on a web page. Keep in mind that your web page may render differently on your screen than on paper. So it is usually a good idea to preview the document before you print it. Previewing will show you exactly what the printed document will look like and how many pages are required for the printout. You can then adjust the page orientation, scaling, and margins, if necessary, in the Print Preview window before you click Print.

Steps

1 Start Internet Explorer in desktop mode.

2 Type www.fueleconomy.gov in the Address bar and press Enter.

3 Click the Print button arrow on the Command bar.

4 Click *Print preview* to display how the web page will appear when printed. The Print Preview window shows that this document will print on one page.

5 Click the Landscape button to change the page orientation from portrait to landscape format. The Print Preview window shows that this document will now print on two pages.

6 Click the *Show multiple pages* drop-down arrow and select *2 Page View*.

7 Click the *Show multiple pages* drop-down arrow again and select *1 Page View*.

8 Drag the bottom horizontal Adjust margin marker (an up-and-down-pointing arrow with a horizontal line in the middle) up slightly to divide page 1 and page 2 at an appropriate location.

9 Click the Print Document button.

10 In the Print dialog box, either click Print or click Cancel if you do not want to print the page.

11 Click the Close button to close the Print Preview window and then click the Close button to close the browser window.

4 *Another Way*
Press the Alt key to display the Menu bar, click the File tab, and then click *Print preview*.

▶**Tip** In Firefox, click the Firefox button, click *Print*, and then click *Print Preview* to display the Print Preview window. In Chrome, click the Customize and Control button and then Print. Chrome automatically displays the Preview screen when printing.

▶**Tip** In Internet Explorer, by default, the Print Size is set to *Shrink To Fit*. Stretch or shrink the page size by clicking the Change Print Size drop-down arrow and selecting a percentage. In Firefox you can change the percentage using the Scale drop-down menu.

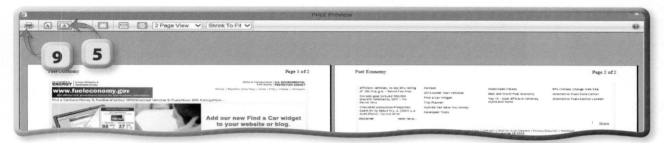

Taking It Further

Adding Headers and Footers to Printed Web Pages Place additional information at the top and bottom of your web page printouts by using headers and footers. For example, add the current date or time, page numbers, the window title, or the web page address in a header or footer. In Internet Explorer, you can add a header or footer in the Print Preview window by clicking the Page Setup button to display the Page Setup dialog box. Click the buttons in the *Headers and Footers* section and then click the items you want to print in the header and footer areas of the page. In Firefox, click *Print Preview* in the Firefox drop-down menu and then click the Page Setup button. In the Page Setup dialog box, select the Margins & Header/Footer tab. For Chrome, Click *Print* in the Customize and Control menu. Use the Margins and Options settings to make adjustments.

Internet Basics

Video ▶ M3_C1_S12

Use Search Engines

A search engine finds information on the Web by looking through web pages for words or phrases that you specify and then returning a list of matches. Search engines include Google (www.google.com), Yahoo! (www.yahoo.com), Bing (www.bing .com), and Ask (www.ask.com). To search for information in a search engine, type your search criteria in the search box and then press the Enter key or click the Search button. Most search engines include tools to help you specify search criteria in order to narrow your search.

Steps

1 Start Internet Explorer in desktop mode.

2 Click in the Address bar, type www.bing.com, and then press Enter to display the Bing home page.

3 Click in the search box and type new york city attractions.

4 Click the Search button (or press Enter) to display the search results.

5 Click a link that interests you and read the information at that site.

6 Click in the Address bar, type www.google.com, and then click the Search button (or press Enter) to display the Google home page.

7 Click the Images link.

8 Click in the search box and type red roses.

9 Click the Search button. The search results display web pages that contain images of red roses.

10 Click the Close button to close the browser window.

▶**Tip** IE, Firefox, and Chrome all display suggestions as you type words into the search box. Click a suggestion to start the search without having to type the rest of the word or phrase.

▶**Tip** In Firefox, the default search engine is listed in the search box to the right of the Location bar. You can change the default search engine by clicking the down arrow to the right of the search engine icon and then choosing your preferred search engine from the drop-down list. In Chrome, you can change the default search engine by clicking the Customize and Control button, selecting *Settings*, and making your choice in the *Search* section.

Taking It Further

Using Advanced Search   Because the Internet contains such a large quantity of information, you may sometimes have difficulty finding exactly what you want. To help you search more successfully, most search engines offer an <u>Advanced Search</u> link with options for narrowing your search. Google allows you to use Advanced Search to display options such as "none of these words." To access Advanced Search, you first need to perform a basic search. When the results are displayed, scroll to the bottom of the page and click the <u>Advanced search</u> link. Advanced Search empowers you with many options, including specifying that your search take place within a particular site or domain, such as at the site youtube.com or at sites ending with the domain destination .gov.

Internet Basics

Internet Basics

Tasks Summary

Task	Toolbar or Location	Option	Shortcut
Internet Explorer			
Open help	Menu bar	Help, Internet Explorer Help	F1
	Command bar		
Close browser	Menu bar	File, Exit	Alt + F4
Refresh screen	Menu bar	View, Refresh	F5
	To right of Address bar		
Open search box	Menu bar	Edit, Find on this page	Ctrl + F
Zoom in	Menu bar	View, Zoom, Zoom in	Ctrl + Shift + +
Zoom out	Menu bar	View, Zoom, Zoom out	Ctrl + -
Print	Menu bar	File, Print	Ctrl + P
	Command bar		
Select URL	Menu bar	File, Open	Ctrl + O
	Command bar		Ctrl + L
Open history tab	To right of most recently opened tab		Ctrl + Shift + H
Open new tab	Menu bar	File, New tab	Ctrl + T
	To right of most recently opened tab		
Add favorite/bookmark	Menu bar	Favorites, Add to favorites	Ctrl + D
	To right of most recently opened tab		
Mozilla Firefox			
Open help	Menu bar	Help, Firefox Help	
Close browser	Menu bar	File, Exit	Alt + F4
Refresh screen	To right of Location bar		F5
Open search box	Menu bar	Edit, Find	Ctrl + F

Task	Toolbar or Location	Option	Shortcut
Mozilla Firefox (continued)			
Zoom in	Menu bar	View, Zoom, Zoom In	Ctrl + Shift + +
Zoom out	Menu bar	View, Zoom, Zoom Out	Ctrl + -
Print	Menu bar	File, Print	Ctrl + P
Select URL	Location bar		Ctrl + L
Open history tab	Menu bar	History, Show All History	Ctrl + H
Open new tab	Menu bar	File, New tab	Ctrl + T
	To right of most recently opened tab	+	
Add favorite/bookmark	Menu bar	Bookmarks, Bookmark This Page	Ctrl + D
	To right of Location bar	☆ Bookmarks	
Google Chrome			
Open help	Customize and Control button	Help	F1
Close browser	Customize and Control button	Exit	Alt + F4
Refresh screen	To left of Address bar	⟳	F5
Open search box	Customize and Control button	Find	Ctrl + F
Zoom in	Customize and Control button	Zoom, +	Ctrl + Shift + +
Zoom out	Customize and Control button	Zoom, -	Ctrl + -
Print	Customize and Control button	Print	Ctrl + P
Select URL	Address bar		Ctrl + L
Open history tab	Customize and Control button	History	Ctrl + H
Open new tab	Customize and Control button	New tab	Ctrl + T
	To right of most recently opened tab	▢	
Add favorite/bookmark	To right of Address bar	☆	Ctrl + D

Module 3 Projects

Project 1

Skills Explore Microsoft Internet Explorer 10 in the Windows 8 desktop interface, explore Microsoft Internet Explorer 10 in the Windows 8 user interface, explore the Mozilla Firefox interface, explore the Google Chrome interface, use tabbed browsing, and use search engines

Scenario You have been using google.com as your primary search engine for the past year. A few of your friends are trying to convince you to use different search engines. To find out if there are differences among the search engines, you will enter the exact same search terms in three different search engines and compare the results. You will search for *Chocolate Museum*.

Steps

1 Browse to the Module 3 folder for completed work on your flash drive, SkyDrive, or other storage media. This folder was created when you completed Module 2 Windows Project 1. The folder is named **Guidelines2013\Module3-Internet\Module3-Completed**.

2 Open WordPad.

3 Change the left and right margins to 0.5 inch if they are not already set at that. ***HINT***: *Select the File tab and then click* Page setup. *If both margins are already set to 0.5 inch, click Cancel. If you need to change the margins, select the text in the* Margins Left *text box and type* 0.5". *Then select the text in the* Margins Right *text box and type* 0.5". *Click OK.*

4 Open the document **M3-EOM-P1-SearchEngine.rtf** from within WordPad.

5 Save the WordPad file using the name **Lastname-M3-EOM-P1-SearchEngine.rtf** in the Module3-Completed folder within the Module3-Internet folder. ***HINT***: *Select the File tab and then click Save As and Rich Text document. Use your Windows skills to navigate to your working drive and the correct folder. Enter the file name Lastname-M3-EOM-P1-SearchEngine.rtf and press Save.*

6 Enter your name and the date where indicated in the WordPad document.

7 Select any three search engines from the list below. If your favorite search engine is not on the list, ask your instructor if you can use it as one of your choices.
   a. www.google.com
   b. www.bing.com
   c. www.yahoo.com
   d. www.duckduckgo.com
   e. www.ask.com
   f. www.aolsearch.com

8 Enter the names and URLs for the three search engines you have chosen into the appropriate table cells in the document.

9 Open the Internet Explorer 10, Mozilla FireFox, or Google Chrome browser.

10 Enter the URL for the first selected search engine into the Address/Location bar.

11 Search for *Chocolate Museum*.

12 In the Search 1 column in the WordPad document, record the titles and URLs for the first 10 links that appear, in the order of appearance. If there are fewer than 10 links on page 1, you will need to navigate to page 2. ***NOTE***: *Sponsor links may appear at the top of the search results. Do not record sponsor links if they appear.*

13 Save the updated WordPad file. ***HINT***: *Select the File tab and then click Save.*

14 Return to the browser window, add a tab, and enter the URL for the second selected search engine into the Address/Location bar in the new tab.

15 Search for *Chocolate Museum*

16 In the Search 2 column of the WordPad document, record the titles and URLs for the first 10 links that appear, in the order of appearance. If there are fewer than 10 links on page 1 you will need to navigate to page 2. ***NOTE***: *Sponsor links may appear at the top of the search results. Do not record sponsor links if they appear.*

17 Save the updated WordPad file.

18 Return to the browser window, add a third tab, and enter the URL for the third selected search engine into the Address/Location bar in the new tab.

19 Search for *Chocolate Museum*.

20 In the Search 3 column of the WordPad document, record the titles and URLs for the first 10 links that appear, in the order of appearance. If there are fewer than 10 links on page 1 you will need to navigate to page 2. **NOTE**: *Sponsor links may appear at the top of the search results. Do not record sponsor links if they appear.*

21 Save the updated WordPad file.

22 Analyze the list of links in the table. Do the same links appear when using different search engines? Do the links appear in the same order in different search engines? Use the space provided in the WordPad document to explain your findings in one well-written paragraph.

23 Save the updated WordPad file.

24 Print or submit this file as instructed.

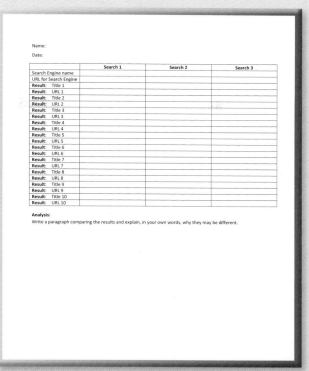

M3-EOM-P1-SearchEngine.rtf

Project 2

Skills Explore Microsoft Internet Explorer 10 in the Windows 8 desktop interface, explore Microsoft Internet Explorer 10 in the Windows 8 user interface, explore the Mozilla Firefox interface, explore the Google Chrome interface, navigate among web pages, use search engines, use tabbed browsing, follow links and history, and save sites as Favorites/Bookmarks

Scenario You are interested in finding out if there is information about you on the Internet. Searching the Web for information about yourself is called a *vanity search*. Perform a vanity search by first searching for your name in the format *Firstname Lastname* and then searching again in the format *Lastname Firstname*. Participate in a class discussion that addresses the following questions: Are the results of both searches the same? Why or why not? Is it important that the information about you is accurate? Why or why not?

Steps

1 Open the Internet Explorer 10, Mozilla Firefox, or Google Chrome browser

2 Enter the URL for a search engine of your choice.

3 Search for your name in the format *Firstname Lastname*.

4 Follow the links to determine the accuracy of the information. You may want to bookmark a few pages so you can return to them during the class discussion.

5 Open a new tab in your browser.

6 Enter the URL for a search engine of your choice.

7 Search for your name in the format *Lastname Firstname*.

8 Follow the links to determine the accuracy of the information. You may want to bookmark a few pages so you can return to them during the class discussion.

9 Review the results showing in the two tabs and determine if the results displayed from the two searches are the same sites and in the same order. Write a few notes about the similarities and differences between the searches and the accuracy of the information found so you are prepared for the class discussion.

10 Participate in the class discussion or submit your findings as directed by your instructor.

MODULE 4

Microsoft Office 2013 Suite Overview

Skills You Learn

1. Create a file and display the backstage area
2. Open and save a file
3. Understand the ribbon
4. Navigate within a file
5. Use Find and Replace
6. Use Undo and Redo
7. Change views and zoom percentage
8. Check spelling and grammar
9. Use formatting tools
10. Print a file
11. Use Help

Files You Need

For these skills, you need the following student data files.

> M4-S2-Sales.xlsx
>
> M4-S3-TravelDeals.docx

What You Create

In this module, you edit a travel agency flyer by using features common across several applications. When learning to open and save files, you work with an Excel sales workbook. You also learn to add images and illustrations to a document, giving it a professional look.

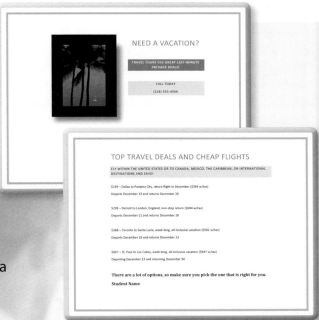

Travel Deals Flyer

 Before beginning the module skills, copy the Module4-Office folder from the Student Resources disc to your storage medium. The copied folder will become the working folder for this module.

Guidelines for Understanding

The Microsoft Office 2013 suite is made up of several applications. Earlier in this book, you learned to use Outlook to manage your schedule and people and OneNote to create a digital notebook. Other applications in the Office suite include:

- 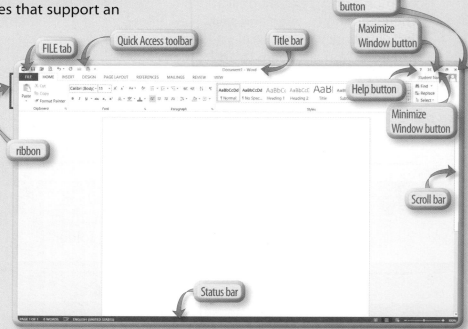 **Access 2013**   Use this database application to store and organize large amounts of data. For example, all the bits of information a company gathers about its customers and suppliers can be stored in a database. You can query a database to find specific information, such as all customers who live in a certain city. You can also produce reports from the data.

- **Excel 2013**   Use this spreadsheet application to enter numbers or other data into a grid of rows and columns. Once data is entered, Excel can perform automatic calculations, such as adding numbers to get a total. Excel can also create graphs from the data. Organizations and individuals use spreadsheets to track inventory, manage budgets, balance checkbooks, and create income statements.

- **PowerPoint 2013**   Use this presentation application to create slides that support an oral presentation. The slides help the audience follow and understand the key points of the presentation. Photos and charts in the slides can add visual interest.

- **Word 2013**   Use this document application to produce professional-looking documents, including letters, resumes, reports, and much more.

Even though each application in the Office suite is designed to perform a specific task, all applications have some common interface elements and commands. Learning about the shared features of the applications—their common "look and feel"—reduces the time you need to master the entire Office suite.

Shared Interface Elements

Each Office application interface includes the Quick Access Toolbar and the ribbon. The Quick Access Toolbar allows you to add icons for the actions you use often, such as undoing a change and saving a file. You can place your own choices on this toolbar for most-often-used commands. The ribbon is the main interface feature. The FILE tab on the ribbon displays the backstage area, which includes file management options, such as opening, printing, and saving. The ribbon offers other tabs and groups of commands that are related to each other—for example, the VIEW tab allows you to change the zoom and decide how to view multiple windows. Some of the common interface elements are shown in the image below.

Close Window button

Maximize Window button

Quick Access toolbar

Title bar

FILE tab

Help button

Minimize Window button

ribbon

Scroll bar

Status bar

Office Suite Basics

Shared Commands

In the Print backstage area, many of the commands are the same for Excel, Word, and PowerPoint. Compare the screens below for similarities.

Becoming familiar with common interface elements and commands now, before starting the skills in the Word, Excel, Access, and PowerPoint modules, will speed up your learning in each application.

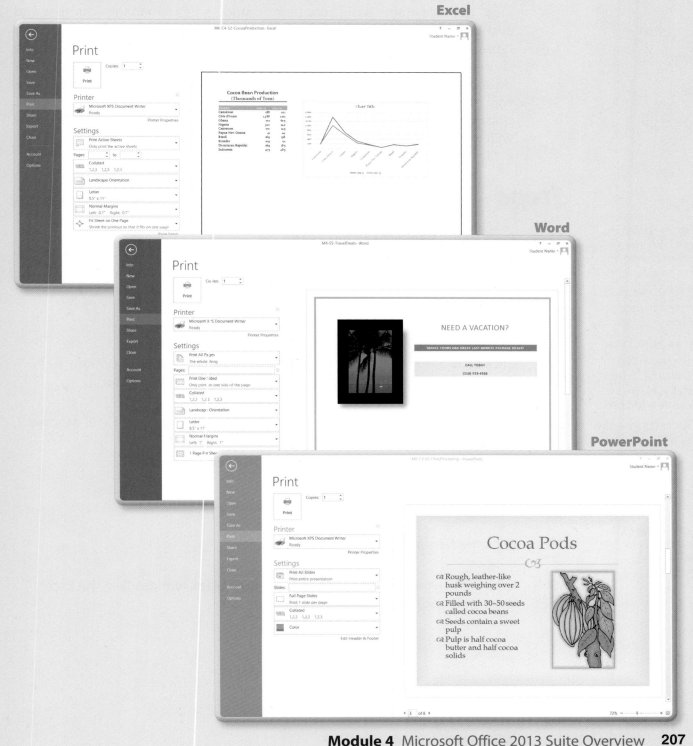

Microsoft Office

Video ▶ M4_C0_S01

Create a File and Display the Backstage Area

When you open an Office application, such as Excel or Word, you have various templates to choose from. Templates are predesigned files that contain basic content and layout information for specific types of documents, such as brochures, newsletters, budgets, and presentations. Templates are a quick way to create a professional-looking document. In the template list, you will also find options for creating a file from a blank slate, such as a blank workbook in Excel and a blank document in Word.

When you are working in an application, you will use the backstage area to manage your files and perform file tasks such as saving or printing. In all of the programs, the backstage area contains a set of commands—Info, New, Open, Save, Save As, Print, Share, and Export. Two other items display below the commands—Account and Options.

Steps

▶**Tip** See Module 2, Chapter 1, Skill 3 for illustrations showing the Charms bar and Search pane.

1-3 *Another Way*
From the Start screen, type *Excel*.

1-4 *Another Way*
You may have an Excel 2013 tile on the Start screen. If you do, you can click this tile to start Excel.

▶**Tip** The Title bar displays the file and program name.

6 *Shortcut*
Open New Document, Workbook, or Presentation Ctrl + N

▶**Tip** Each application in the Office suite has a different colored backstage area. Excel's color is green.

1 Press Win + C to display the Charms bar.

2 Click the Search charm.

3 Type Excel in the search box.

4 Click *Excel 2013* in the Apps results list to open Excel and see options for creating a blank workbook or a workbook based on a template.

5 Click *Blank workbook* to create a new blank workbook in the Excel window.

6 *Book1 - Excel* displays in the Title bar of the new blank workbook.

7 Click the FILE tab to view the backstage area.

8 Click the *New* option.

9 Click *Blank workbook* to create another new blank workbook in the Excel window. *Book2 - Excel* displays in the Title bar.

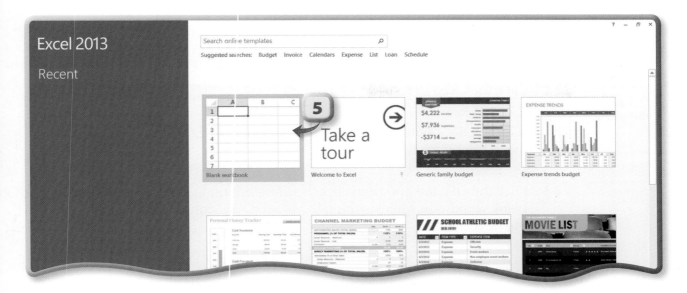

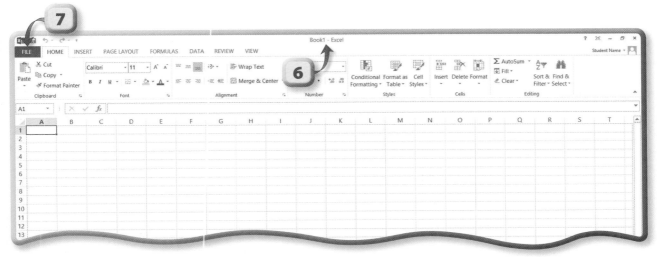

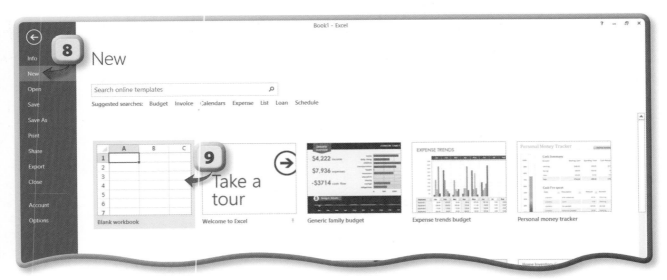

More

10 Click the Close button to close the unsaved Book2 blank workbook while keeping Excel open. Book2 closes and Book1 displays.

11 Click the FILE tab to view the backstage area.

12 Click the Back button to display the blank Book1 Excel workbook and to make the HOME tab active.

13 Click the FILE tab and then click the *Close* option to close the unsaved Book1 blank workbook while keeping Excel open. You continue to work in Excel in the next skill.

Taking It Further

Customizing the Quick Access Toolbar   The applications in the Office suite have a Quick Access toolbar in the top left corner of the window. The standard buttons on the Quick Access toolbar include Save, Undo, and Redo. You can customize the toolbar by clicking the Customize Quick Access Toolbar button and selecting from the options in the drop-down list. If you want more commands organized by the tab of the ribbon on which they reside, click *More Commands* to see additional options. Adding buttons to the Quick Access toolbar is just one example of the many ways you can customize the Office applications to help you do your work more efficiently.

Microsoft Office

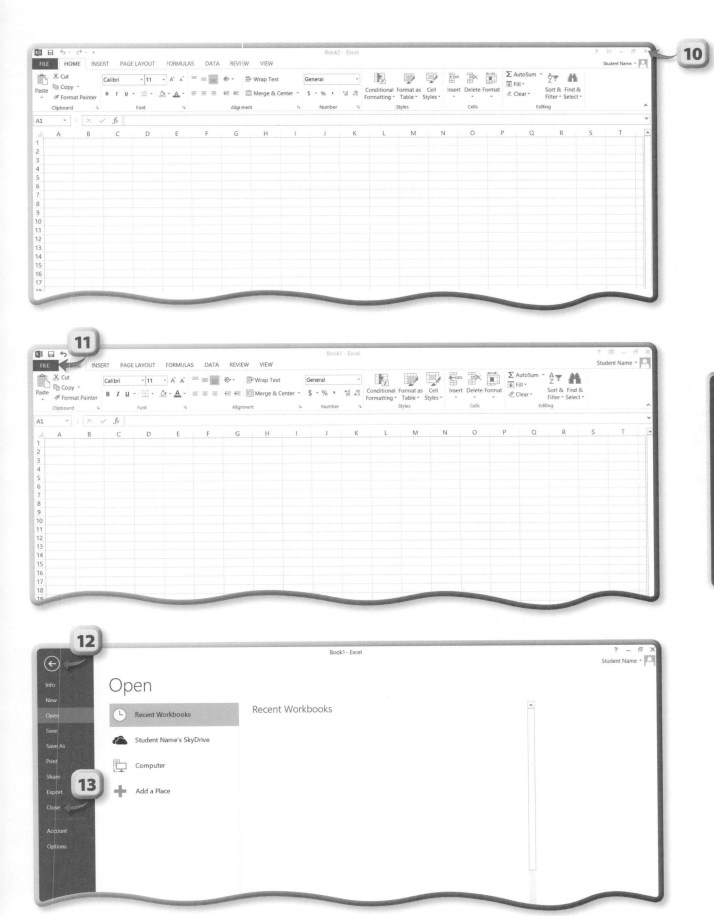

Microsoft Office

Open and Save a File

 Video   M4_C0_S02

As you saw in the previous skill, files can be created by selecting a blank workbook or from a template available in the backstage area. You can also find the commands for saving a file and opening an existing file in the backstage area. When you save a file, save it to the storage media you have been instructed to use, such as the computer's hard disk, your SkyDrive account, a CD or DVD, a flash drive, or a network drive. You can also save the file in any one of a variety of file formats.

Steps

▶**Tip** If Excel is not already open, start Excel.

1 With the Excel window active, click the FILE tab.

2 **Shortcut**
Open a Document, Workbook, or Presentation
Ctrl + O

2 Click the *Open* option.

3 Navigate to the student data file named **M4-S2-Sales.xlsx** in your Module 4 working folder. Click the file name to select it.

▶**Tip** Module 2, Chapter 2 provides instruction in file management.

4 With the **M4-S2-Sales.xlsx** file selected in the *File name* text box in the Open dialog box, click the Open button. The selected file appears in your Excel window.

5 Click the FILE tab.

6 **Shortcut**
Save As
F12

6 Click the *Save As* option.

Taking It Further

Using Save As in Access   The Save As function requires additional steps in Access. From an open Access file, click the FILE tab and then click the *Save As* option. In the Save As backstage area, click Save Database As, click Access Database, and then click the Save As button. Enter the new file name and then click the Save button.

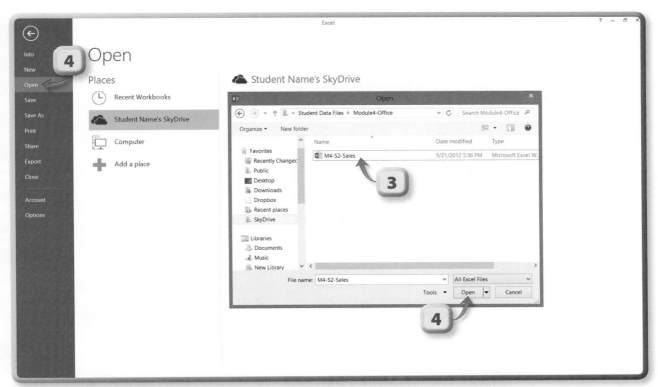

More

Microsoft Office

7 Click the *Current Folder* option.

8 In the *File name* text box, type Lastname-M4-S2-Sales, but replace *Lastname* with your last name. Be sure to save the file to your Module 4 working folder on your storage medium.

9 Click the Save button.

10 Click the FILE tab.

11 Click the *Close* option to close the file.

12 Click the Close button to close Excel.

Taking It Further

Saving Files in Alternative Formats

By default, documents, workbooks, presentations, and databases are saved as files in their native format: .docx in Word, .xlsx in Excel, .pptx in PowerPoint, and .accdb in Access. However, you can save files in an alternative format, such as PDF, by selecting a different format from the *Save as type* drop-down list in the Save As dialog box. PDF is the format used by a document reader program called Adobe Reader, which can be downloaded free from www.adobe.com and which allows users without the original software to view a file with formatting intact. You can also save files in an alternative format by clicking the FILE tab, clicking the *Export* option, and then selecting one of the options listed in the backstage area.

Microsoft Office

Microsoft Office

Video M4_C0_S03

Understand the Ribbon

The ribbon is an interface element that is displayed in the application window. It is designed to help you quickly find the commands that you need to complete a task. The ribbon is organized into a series of tabs. Each tab relates to a type of activity, such as inserting objects or formatting the visual or text elements on a page. In a tab, commands are organized in logical groups. For example, the Bold, Italic, and Font Color buttons are in the Font group on the HOME tab. To help reduce screen clutter, some tabs, known as contextual tabs, are shown only when you select certain types of objects such as tables or pictures. The PICTURE TOOLS FORMAT tab is an example of a contextual tab.

Steps

1 Open the Word student data file named **M4-S3-TravelDeals.docx** and, if you have not already done so, save the file to your Module 4 working folder on your storage medium.

▶**Tip** When a Word, Excel, or PowerPoint file opens, the HOME tab is active.

2 Click the INSERT tab on the ribbon.

3 Click the picture in the document. The PICTURE TOOLS FORMAT tab appears on the ribbon when the picture is selected.

4 Click the PICTURE TOOLS FORMAT tab to view the four groups that contain the picture editing commands: Adjust, Picture Styles, Arrange, and Size.

5 *Shortcut*
Collapse the Ribbon
Ctrl + F1

5 Click the Collapse the Ribbon button to minimize the ribbon and display only the ribbon's tabs.

▶**Tip** When the ribbon is collapsed, you can still access commands by clicking a tab. The ribbon automatically collapses after the command is selected.

6 Double-click the PICTURE TOOLS FORMAT tab to redisplay the entire ribbon.

6 *Another Way*
Click the PICTURE TOOLS FORMAT tab and then click the Pin the ribbon button (looks like a stick pin).

7 If you are not continuing on to the next skill, close the document and Word by clicking the Close button.

▶**Tip** Any tab can be double-clicked to redisplay the ribbon.

Taking It Further

7 *Shortcut*
Close the Application
Alt + F4

Using the Keyboard with Ribbon Tabs
Office 2013 provides keyboard access keys for the ribbon so you can quickly perform tasks without using the mouse. When you press the Alt key when a ribbon is pinned in any of the Office 2013 applications, letters—called KeyTips—are displayed on each tab. Depending on which letter you press, you may be shown additional KeyTips. For example, if the HOME tab is the active tab and you press N, the INSERT tab displays along with the KeyTips for the groups on that tab. Press the letter of the task you want to complete. To cancel the action and hide the KeyTips, press the Alt key.

Microsoft Office

Video M4_C0_S04

Navigate within a File

Many files you create in each of the Office applications will be more than one page long. Your monitor is a fixed size and may not be able to display the contents of the entire file at once. To navigate, it helps to know how to scroll. Scrolling helps you quickly find information or reach a specific location in the file so that you can then make edits or apply additional formatting. You can use both the keyboard and the mouse to navigate to specific locations in a file.

Steps

2 **Shortcut**
Move Insertion Point to
Top of File
Ctrl + Home

▶**Tip** When you open
a Word document,
the insertion point
is automatically at
the beginning of the
document.

▶**Tip** Your keyboard
may not look exactly the
same as the keyboard
shown. Certain keys may
be in different locations.

▶**Tip** Scrolling does not
move the insertion point.

▶**Tip** If your mouse has
a scroll wheel, you can
roll the wheel to scroll
through the document.

1 If it is not already open, open the student data file named **M4-S3-TravelDeals.docx**, the file used in Skill 3.

2 Click immediately in front of the title *NEED A VACATION?* to move the insertion point to the beginning of the document.

3 Press the Page Down key on the keyboard. The insertion point moves to display within the title *TOP TRAVEL DEALS AND CHEAP FLIGHTS* on page 2.

4 Press the Home key. The insertion point moves to the start of the title line on page 2.

5 Press the End key. The insertion point moves to the end of the title line.

6 Position the mouse pointer on the down scroll arrow on the vertical scroll bar. Click the down scroll arrow several times, until you see the top few lines of the second page of the document.

7 Press the Down Arrow key twice. The insertion point moves down two lines.

8 Drag the scroll bar upwards to the top of page 1. The insertion point remains on page 2.

Taking It Further

Navigating on a Touch Screen To place the insertion point, tap the appropriate location in the file. To scroll in a document, touch the document and then slide it up and down with your finger. To hide the ribbon, tap the Ribbon Display Options button on the title bar and then tap *Auto-hide Ribbon*. To redisplay the ribbon, tap the Ribbon Display Options button and then tap *Show Tabs and Commands*.

Taking It Further

Navigating with Keyboard Shortcuts

You can use key combinations to move the insertion point to a specific location in a file. Press Ctrl + Home to move to the start of a document in Word. In Excel, press Ctrl + Home to move to the first cell in the worksheet. Press Ctrl + End to move to the end of a document in Word or to the last cell in a worksheet in Excel. Press the F5 key in Word to display the Find and Replace dialog box with the Go To tab selected. Pressing F5 in Excel will open the Go To dialog box. In Word, you can type a page number in the Go To dialog box to move the insertion point to a specific page, and in Excel you can type a cell address to move quickly to that cell.

Microsoft Office

Skill 5

Use Find and Replace

Video M4_C0_S05

The Find feature enables you to search for specific characters or formatting. When the Find feature locates items that match your search terms, the results are displayed in the Navigation pane.

Similarly, the Find and Replace feature allows you to search for specific characters or formatting and replace them with other characters or formatting.

Steps

1 If it is not already open, open the student data file named **M4-S3-TravelDeals.docx** and save the file as **M4-S5-TravelDeals**. Be sure to save the file to your Module 4 working folder on your storage medium.

2 Shortcut
Find
Ctrl + F

2 Click the Find button in the Editing group on the HOME tab.

3 Type September in the Navigation pane search box. Matches are highlighted in the document and listed in the Navigation pane.

4 Click the Close button in the upper right corner of the Navigation pane.

5 Shortcut
Move to Top of Document
Ctrl + Home

5 Scroll to the top of the document and click at the beginning of the line containing the title *NEED A VACATION?* You decide to update the flyer by replacing all occurrences of *September* with *December*.

6 Click the Replace button in the Editing group. This opens the Find and Replace dialog box. *September* appears in the *Find what* text box.

7 Type December in the *Replace with* text box.

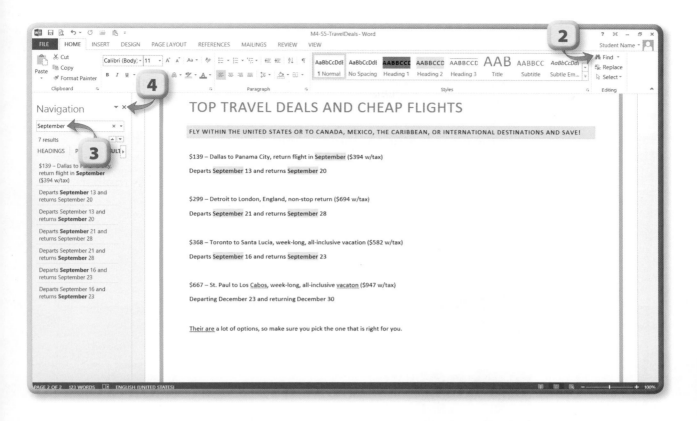

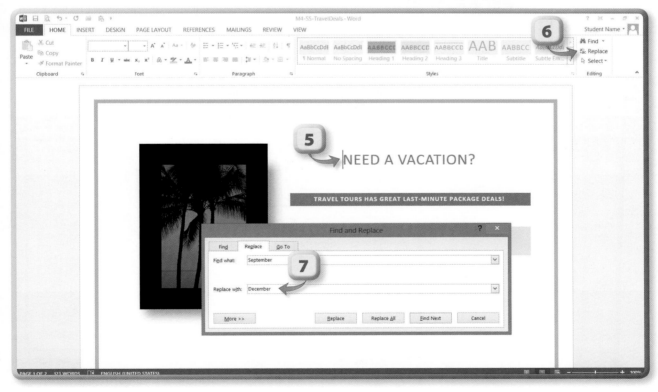

Tip Clicking the Replace button will make one change at a time. Clicking the Replace All button changes all occurrences.

8 Click the Replace All button.

9 Click OK in the dialog box that indicates that seven replacements have been made.

10 Click the Close button to close the Find and Replace dialog box.

11 Save the file by clicking the Save button on the Quick Access toolbar.

NEED A VACATION?

TRAVEL TOURS HAS GREAT LAST-MINUTE PACKAGE DEALS!

CALL TODAY
(218) 555-4566

TOP TRAVEL DEALS AND CHEAP FLIGHTS

FLY WITHIN THE UNITED STATES OR TO CANADA, MEXICO, THE CARIBBEAN, OR INTERNATIONAL DESTINATIONS AND SAVE!

$139 – Dallas to Panama City, return flight in December ($394 w/tax)
Departs December 13 and returns December 20

$299 – Detroit to London, England, non-stop return ($694 w/tax)
Departs December 21 and returns December 28

$368 – Toronto to Santa Lucia, week-long, all-inclusive vacation ($582 w/tax)
Departs December 16 and returns December 23

$667 – St. Paul to Los Cabos, week-long, all-inclusive vacaton ($947 w/tax)
Departing December 23 and returning December 30

Their are a lot of options, so make sure you pick the one that is right for you.

Completed Skill 5

Microsoft Office

Taking It Further

Finding with Narrower Limits   Click the More button in the Find and Replace dialog box to display additional search options. Select the *Match case* option to locate text with the same capitalization as that of the search text. For example, if the *Match case* option is selected, a search for *January* will not find *JANUARY*. Select *Find whole words only* to locate text that entirely matches the search text. For example, a search for *every* will not find *everyone*. Use the Format button in the Find and Replace dialog box to search for formatting, such as a specific font.

Microsoft Office

Module 4

Skill 6

Video M4_CO_S06

Use Undo and Redo

Have you ever deleted text and then changed your mind? Fortunately, you can restore the text you deleted during your current work session by clicking the Undo button on the Quick Access toolbar. The Undo button reverses the last action you performed, including formatting, deletions, insertions, and so on. You can even undo several actions at a time by clicking the arrow on the Undo button and selecting the actions you want to delete. If you want to restore the last Undo performed, click the Redo button (which looks like a half-circle arrow pointing up and to the right). The Redo button is available only after you have clicked Undo. After you click the Redo button, it changes to the Repeat button (which looks like a full-circle arrow). The Repeat button is available after every action except Undo. Use the Repeat button to perform the same action again.

Steps

1 If it is not already open, open **M4-S5-TravelDeals.docx**, the file you saved in the previous skill. Save the file as **M4-S6-TravelDeals**.

▶**Tip** Double-click to select an entire word. Triple-click to select an entire paragraph.

2 Double-click in the word *Need* in the heading on the first page of the document.

3 Click the Cut button in the Clipboard group on the HOME tab. This removes the word *Need*.

4 Shortcut
Undo
Ctrl + Z

4 Click the Undo button on the Quick Access toolbar. The last action is reversed so that *Need* reappears in the heading of the document.

▶**Tip** Clicking the Undo button changes the Repeat button to the Redo button. Clicking the Redo button reverses the last change you made.

5 Press the End key to move the insertion point to the end of the heading.

6 Type ?. (Do not type the period.)

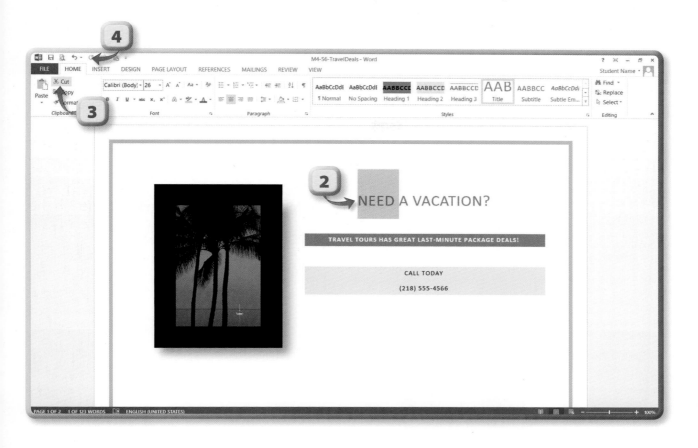

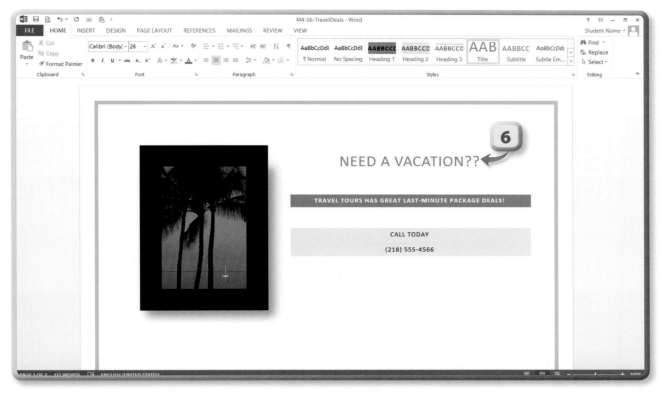

More

▶**Tip** The Redo button displays after you perform an Undo. Otherwise you will see the Repeat button in the same location.

▶**Tip** You can undo two actions at once by selecting the second item on the Undo list, three actions by selecting the third, and so on.

▶**Tip** The default number of available undos varies in each Office application and can be changed if needed.

Microsoft Office

7 Click the Repeat button on the Quick Access toolbar to insert a third *?* at the end of the heading.

8 Click the Undo button to remove the third *?* at the end of the heading.

9 Click the Undo button arrow.

10 In the drop-down list, click the option *Typing* "?". This leaves just one *?* in the document.

11 Save the file by clicking the Save button on the Quick Access toolbar.

NEED A VACATION?

TRAVEL TOURS HAS GREAT LAST-MINUTE PACKAGE DEALS!

CALL TODAY
(218) 555-4566

TOP TRAVEL DEALS AND CHEAP FLIGHTS

FLY WITHIN THE UNITED STATES OR TO CANADA, MEXICO, THE CARIBBEAN, OR INTERNATIONAL DESTINATIONS AND SAVE!

$139 – Dallas to Panama City, return flight in December ($394 w/tax)
Departs December 13 and returns December 20

$299 – Detroit to London, England, non-stop return ($694 w/tax)
Departs December 21 and returns December 28

$368 – Toronto to Santa Lucia, week-long, all-inclusive vacation ($582 w/tax)
Departs December 16 and returns December 23

$667 – St. Paul to Los Cabos, week-long, all-inclusive vacaton ($947 w/tax)
Departing December 23 and returning December 30

Their are a lot of options, so make sure you pick the one that is right for you.

Completed Skill 6

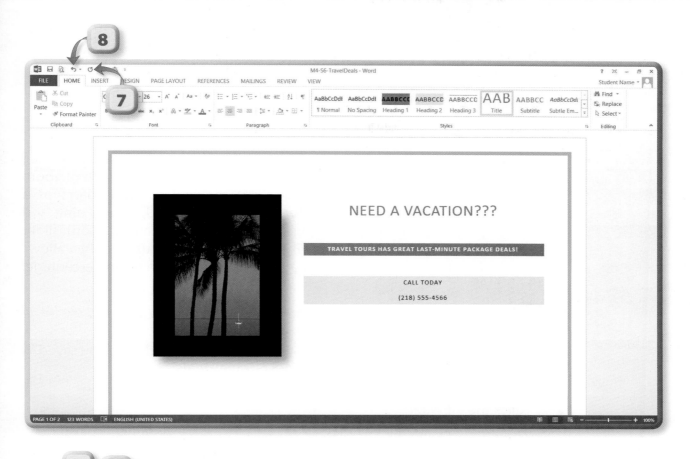

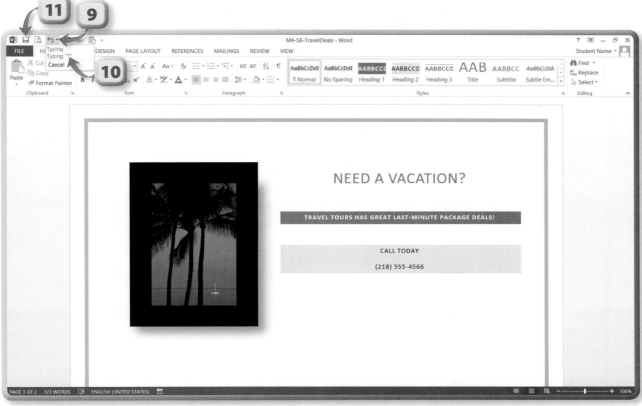

Microsoft Office

 Video   M4_C0_S07

Change Views and Zoom Percentage

The VIEW tab in Excel, PowerPoint, and Word contains buttons for changing the view of the open file. You will also find buttons for changing the zoom percentage while you are viewing a file. By default, a new, blank file opens at 100% of its normal size. However, you may want to zoom in or zoom out to view different parts of a document. Excel, PowerPoint, and Word also contain a Zoom slider bar on the Status bar that allows you to adjust the zoom percentage.

Steps

1 If it is not already open, open **M4-S6-TravelDeals.docx**, the file you saved in the previous skill. Save the file as **M4-S7-TravelDeals**.

2 Click the VIEW tab.

3 Click the Multiple Pages button in the Zoom group.

4 Click the One Page button in the Zoom group.

5 Click the Zoom button in the Zoom group to open the Zoom dialog box.

6 Click the *75%* option in the *Zoom to* section of the dialog box.

7 Click OK.

8 Drag the Zoom slider bar on the Status bar to *100%*.

Taking It Further

Experimenting with Views   Additional information about views is presented later in the book, but you can experiment now with the different views by clicking the various view options. For example, in Word, click the Web Layout button in the Views group on the VIEW tab to view the document as a web page. In Word, you can also click the Read Mode button to view the document in a full screen, which maximizes the screen space available and makes a document easier to read. In Excel, click the Page Layout button in the Workbook Views group on the VIEW tab to view the worksheet as a printed page. In PowerPoint, click the Notes Page button in the Presentation Views group on the VIEW tab to view and edit the speaker notes.

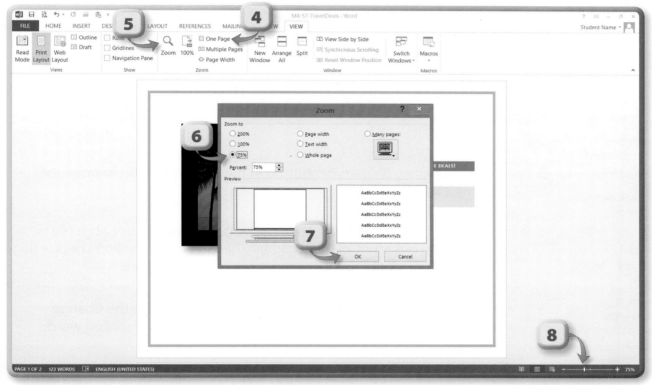

Taking It Further

Using Full Screen Mode   To view a file in a full screen when you are in Read Mode, click the Full Screen Mode button ⊞ in the upper right corner of the file window. This mode gives you more of a full screen than minimizing the ribbon, because no tabs are displayed. To redisplay the ribbon, click ⋯ and then click the Exit Full Screen Mode button ⊞.

Microsoft Office

Microsoft Office

Video M4_CO_S08

Check Spelling and Grammar

The Office applications include a spelling checker that verifies that words are correctly spelled by comparing them to a built-in dictionary. In Word and PowerPoint, if a word is spelled incorrectly or is not in the dictionary file, a red wavy line appears below it. A blue wavy line indicates a possible grammatical error. In Excel and Access, the checker looks for spelling errors only, and the spelling check is not automatic. You can start it by clicking the Spelling button, which is in the Proofing group on the REVIEW tab in Excel and in the Records group on the HOME tab in Access. Because of the limitations of the spelling checker, you should always carefully proofread your files.

Steps

1 If it is not already open, open **M4-S7-TravelDeals.docx**, the file you saved in the previous skill. Save the file as **M4-S8-TravelDeals**.

2-7 *Another Way*
You can manually check the spelling and grammar by right-clicking a word with a red or blue wavy line and select the correct replacement from the pop-up menu.

2 Click the REVIEW tab.

3 *Shortcut*
Spelling & Grammar
F7

3 Click the Spelling & Grammar button in the Proofing group to open the Spelling pane.

4 The spelling checker indicates that *Cabos* is misspelled. Los Cabos is a proper name but is not in the dictionary file, so Word's spelling checker flags it as an error. Click the Ignore button to skip over this word.

▶ *Tip* When the spelling checker presents several suggestions, select the correct choice in the list box in the Spelling pane before clicking the Change button.

5 At the screen showing the misspelled word *vacaton*, click the Change button to replace the misspelled word with the correctly spelled word, *vacation*.

6 When the checker identifies the possible grammatical error of using *Their are* rather than *There are*, click the Change button to correct the problem.

7 Click OK when prompted that the spelling and grammar check is complete.

8 Save the file by clicking the Save button on the Quick Access toolbar.

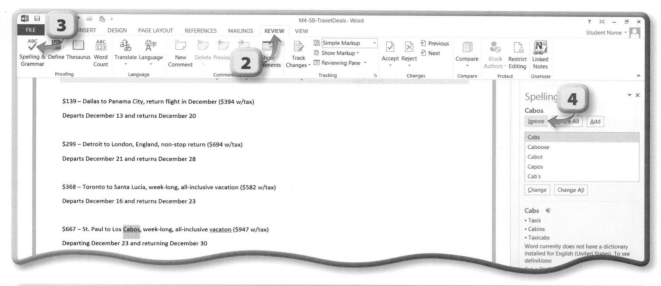

$139 – Dallas to Panama City, return flight in December ($394 w/tax)

Departs December 13 and returns December 20

$299 – Detroit to London, England, non-stop return ($694 w/tax)

Departs December 21 and returns December 28

$368 – Toronto to Santa Lucia, week-long, all-inclusive vacation ($582 w/tax)

Departs December 16 and returns December 23

$667 – St. Paul to Los Cabos, week-long, all-inclusive vacaton ($947 w/tax)

Departing December 23 and returning December 30

Completed Skill 8

Microsoft Office

Skill 9

Video ▸ M4_C0_S09

Use Formatting Tools

The way text appears on a page is called its *format*. The Font group on the HOME tab in Excel, PowerPoint, and Word and the Text Formatting group in Access contain many of the same formatting buttons, such as Bold, Italic, Underline, Font, and Font Size. These buttons can all be used to apply character formatting. To apply formatting to existing text, you need to select the text first. You can also select formatting options and then enter new text that will automatically be formatted based on the selections.

Steps

1 If is not already open, open **M4-S8-TravelDeals.docx**, the file you saved in the previous skill. Save the file as **M4-S9-TravelDeals**.

▸**Tip** Triple-clicking selects a whole paragraph of text.

2 At the bottom of page 2, triple-click the last line of text (begins *There are a lot of options*).

3 Click the HOME tab.

▸**Tip** The default font used by all of the Office applications is Calibri.

4 Click the Font button arrow in the Font group.

▸**Tip** Fonts in the *All Fonts* section of the gallery are listed in alphabetical order.

5 Click *Cambria* in the *Theme Fonts* section of the drop-down gallery.

6 Click the Bold button in the Font group on the HOME tab.

6 *Shortcut*

Apply Bold Formatting
Ctrl + B

7 Click the Font Size button arrow in the Font group.

7-8 *Another Way*

Select the number in the *Font Size* text box and type *14*.

8 Click *14* in the drop-down gallery.

9 Click at the end of the last line of text, press Enter, and type your name on a new line.

10 Save the file.

Taking It Further

Using Other Formatting Buttons Other Font group buttons are available, such as the Increase Font Size and Decrease Font Size buttons, with which you can quickly increase or decrease the text size. You can change the color of your text with the Font Color button. The Italic button applies italic formatting and the Underline button applies underlining to the selected text. If you apply formatting and then decide to remove it, click the Clear Formatting button.

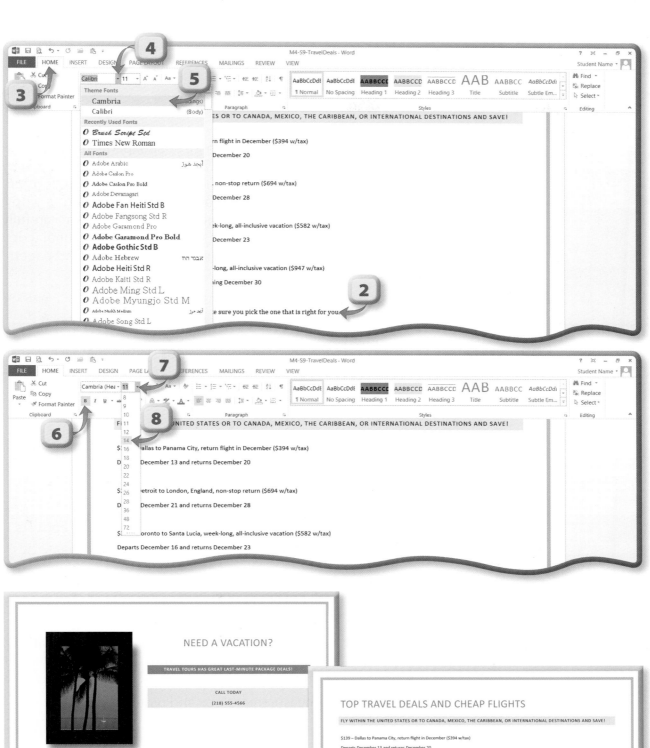

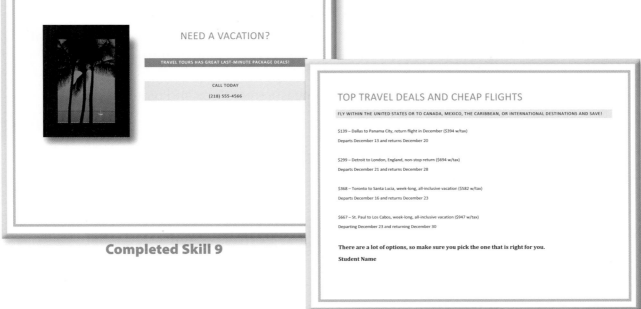

Completed Skill 9

Microsoft Office

Video   M4_C0_S10

Print a File

Print settings are accessed from the Print backstage area. The Print backstage area displays a preview of what your printed file will look like and also lets you change print options, such as the number of copies to print, page orientation, page size, and page margins. You can also zoom in on the preview image to make sure all settings are correct prior to printing a copy. Previewing your document carefully and printing only the final copy saves you time, money, and paper.

Steps

1 If it is not already open, open the student data file named **M4-S9-TravelDeals.docx**, the file you saved in the previous skill. Save the file as **Lastname-M4-S10-TravelDeals**, but replace *Lastname* with your last name. Be sure to save the file to the Module 4 working folder on your storage medium.

2 Place the insertion point at the beginning of the document.

3 Click the FILE tab.

4 *Shortcut*
Print
Ctrl + P

4 Click the *Print* option. A preview of the first page of the document appears in the preview area.

▶**Tip** To go back to your file and make changes before you print it, click the Back button in the upper left corner of the window.

5 Click the Next Page button at the bottom of the window to preview page 2 of the document.

6 Click the up-pointing arrow at the right side of the *Copies* measurement box. The number of copies to be printed changes from *1* to *2*.

7 Select the number in *Copies* measurement box and type 1.

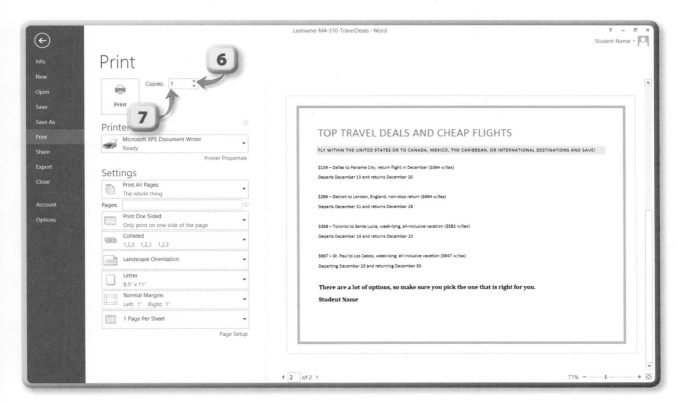

8 Click *Normal Margins* in the *Settings* category.

9 Click *Wide* in the drop-down list.

10 Verify that your instructor would like you to submit a printed copy of the document. Click the Print button if you need a printout. **NOTE:** *If you do not need a printed copy and do not click the Print button, skip Step 11 and go directly to Step 12.*

11 Click the FILE tab to return to the Print backstage area.

12 Click the *Save* option.

13 Click the Close button.

Completed Skill 10

Microsoft Office

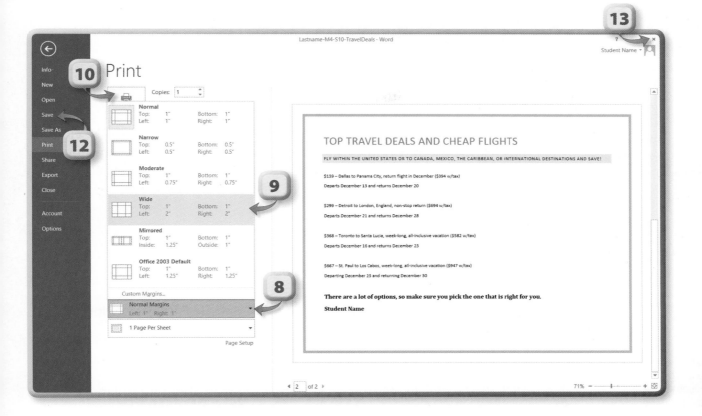

Taking It Further

Experimenting with Print Settings
When you change a print setting in the Print backstage area, the preview adjusts to show you what impact the change you have chosen will have on the printed file. Try changing the paper size, the page orientation (e.g., portrait versus landscape), and the margins. Click the Print All Pages button arrow to explore options for printing selected pages when you don't need

to print the entire document. Click the Print One Sided button to see an option for printing on both sides of the paper manually if your printer cannot perform that function automatically. You can also click the <u>Printer Properties</u> link to display printer options, such as the type of paper (e.g., plain paper or photo paper), print quality (e.g., draft or high), and color options (e.g., sepia or grayscale).

Microsoft Office

Use Help

Video M4_C0_S11

Each Microsoft Office application has its own Help window. The Help window functions similarly to a web browser. You can click links to view Help topics and use Navigation buttons to move among previously visited pages. You can also search for specific keywords.

Steps

2 *Shortcut*

Help
F1

▶**Tip** You can print Help topics by clicking the Print button on the Help window toolbar.

1 Start Excel and create a blank workbook.

2 Click the Microsoft Excel Help button to display the Excel Help window.

3 Click the <u>Formulas</u> link in the *Popular searches* section.

4 Click the <u>Overview of formulas</u> link and then read about formulas.

5 Click the Back button to return to the previous page.

6 Click the Home button to go to the initial Help window.

7 Type conditional formatting in the search box near the top of the window and then press Enter.

8 Click a link to read information about conditional formatting.

9 Click the Close button to close the Help window.

10 Close Excel.

Taking It Further

Taking Advantage of the Office.com Website If you have an Internet connection, the Help window provides links to the Office .com website where you will find additional support and links to images and templates. You can also find and download royalty-free clip art at the Office.com site by clicking the Online Pictures button in the Illustrations group on the INSERT tab and typing search criteria in the *Office.com Clip Art* text box.

Templates are also accessible by clicking the FILE tab, clicking the *New* option, and then typing search criteria in the *Search online templates* text box. **NOTE:** *Microsoft places certain restrictions on the use of templates, images, and other elements available from Office.com. To see the terms of use, go to office.microsoft.com, click the* <u>Legal</u> *link at the bottom of the page, and read the Microsoft Services Agreement.*

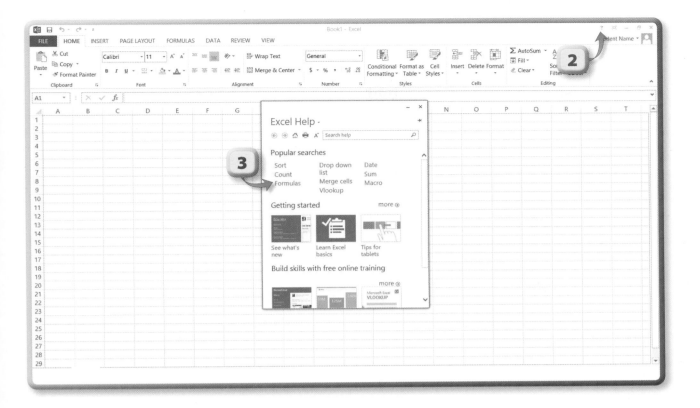

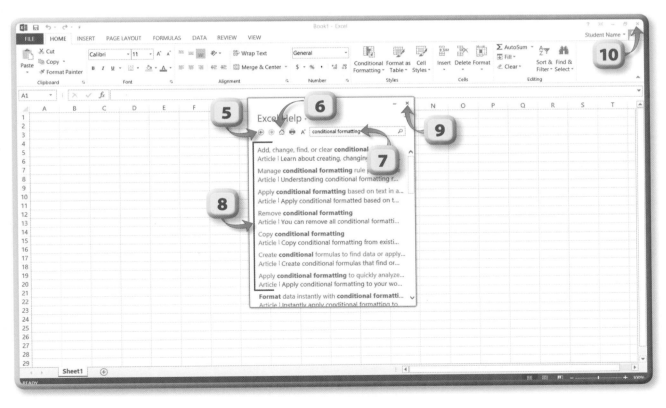

MODULE 5

Microsoft Word 2013

Before beginning the module skills, copy the
Module5–Word folder from the Student Resources
disc to your storage medium. The copied folder
will become the working folder for this module.

Guidelines for Planning and

Using Word, you can create a variety of documents, such as business letters, reports, and recipe cards, as shown in these examples.

Business Letter

Report

You can also use pre-designed documents called *templates* to create common marketing and business documents such as agendas, brochures, expense reports, and flyers.

Recipe Card

Creating Word Documents

Whatever type of document you create, taking the time to plan your message will help ensure clear and effective communication. Planning involves deciding on a purpose, identifying your audience, selecting the topic, and choosing a format.

Your purpose, or reason for writing, might be to make a point, to inform, to convince others to believe as you do, or to entertain. Making sure you know your goal helps you decide what to say as you begin to write.

Your "audience" is the person or group of people you expect to read what you write. The more you know about your audience, the better you can target your message.

Often, the type of document you are creating and the features available in Word help shape your decisions about how much to write and how to present it. For example, if you are writing a memo to a group of museum volunteers about an exhibit work schedule, you are likely to keep the memo short and visually attractive while making sure the information can be read quickly and easily. Word offers features to help you achieve that goal, as shown below.

Insert graphics to add visual interest to Word documents.

Format and align text to get your message across.

Use features such as tables and bulleted or numbered lists to organize data.

MEMORANDUM

To: Chocolate in the Media Volunteers:
Randy, Sarah, Troy, Carol, Heather, Rob, Ty, Annie

From: Helen Starkey

Date: October 19, 2015

Re: Opening Weekend Work Schedule

Here's the final work schedule for the opening of this exhibit on the weekend of November 14.

Volunteer Name	Assignment	Day	Hours
Randy O'Hara	TV show viewing room	Saturday	10-5
		Sunday	10-2
Sarah Marchand	Music station	Saturday	10-2
Troy Butler	TV show viewing room	Sunday	2-5
Carol Wang	Movie viewing room	Saturday & Sunday	10-2
Heather Menendez	Music station	Sunday	10-2
Rob Clifford	Music station	Saturday & Sunday	2-5
Ty Parks	Movie viewing room	Saturday & Sunday	2-5
Annie Suddahara	Backup for all areas	Saturday & Sunday	2-5

Thanks for your help with the exhibit!

Chapter 1

Creating Documents

In Word, you can start from scratch with a blank document, open existing documents, or open documents based on templates (predesigned documents). In this chapter you practice a combination of these three methods.

With a document open, the next logical step is to enter and edit text. (These actions are the digital equivalent of scribbling text on a piece of paper, crossing out what you do not like, and adding more words as needed.) Word offers tools that help you enter text, select text and make changes to it, and move or copy text from one place to another in that document.

If you are not a spelling expert, you will appreciate the spelling checker feature, which can spell *Mississippi* even if you can't. You can also change various properties of your document pages, such as the margins (these determine the width of the white space bordering your text) and where breaks occur between one page and another, such as between the title page and the first page of a report.

Skills You Learn

1   Enter and edit text
2   Use cut, copy, and paste
3   Perform a spelling and grammar check
4   Create a document based on a template
5   Use the Show/Hide ¶ feature
6   Indent and add tabs using the ruler
7   Set margins
8   Insert a page break
9   Insert headers and footers

Files You Need
For these skills, you need the following student data files.

M5-C1-S6-FundraisingLtr.docx

M5-C1-S9-FundraisingLtr.docx

What You Create

You work for The Chocolate Museum, a nonprofit organization that provides educational exhibits and information on the history of chocolate and its role in world cultures. The Museum contains a small gift shop and various exhibits and is supported by paid memberships and donations. Through this and the next several modules of this book, you create and edit a variety of files that can help the Museum raise funds, launch exhibits, track exhibit and gift store costs, organize membership lists, and educate visitors.

In this chapter, you create a simple fundraising letter acknowledging a contribution that has been made to the Museum as part of its 2015 fund drive.

Fundraising Letter

October 16, 2015

Helen Starkey
The Chocolate Museum
2541 Jardine Street
Boston, MA 02115

Mr. Arthur Renfrew
98 Elm Street
Brookline, MA 02116

Dear Mr. Renfrew:

Thank you for your recent contribution to the museum of $500 and your ongoing support of our mission. Your contribution will help us to continue programs that educate, entertain, and help the chocolate industry to improve its products and practices.

For example, did you know that growers of cacao beans who subscribe to fair trade practices guarantee not only the quality of their products, but also that they do not support child labor or slavery in their businesses? Also, many chocolate manufacturers use additives such as wax in making their chocolate, reducing the amount of valuable anti-oxidants that their products provide. Educating the public about issues such as these helps to make the chocolate industry a thriving and responsible part of our world.

According to "A Taste of Slavery," by Sudarsan Raghavan and Sumana Chatterjee, Knight Ridder Newspapers, June 24, 2001:

> There may be a hidden ingredient in the chocolate cake you baked, the candy bars your children sold for their school fundraiser, or that fudge ripple ice cream cone you enjoyed on Saturday afternoon.

> Forty-three percent of the world's cocoa beans, the raw material in chocolate, come from small, scattered farms in this poor West African country. And on some of the farms, the hot, hard work of clearing the fields and harvesting the fruit is done by boys who were sold or tricked into slavery. Most of them are between the ages of 12 and 16. Some are as young as 9.

In addition to helping us educate the public and support a responsible industry, you are helping to support some fun and entertaining exhibits. This year we are introducing three new exhibits to our museum: Chocolate and the Aztec Culture; Chocolate in Art, Movies, and Music; and Chocolate Tasting Parties: Hosting Your Own Chocolate Fest!

Mr. Arthur Renfrew   Page 2

Here is a summary of our donations for the last three years showing how our support is growing:

Year	Total Donations
2014	$100,789.00
2013	$97,988.00
2012	$89,322.00

We hope to see you in the museum during the year. You'll be receiving a brochure with our exhibit list, dates of new exhibit opening parties, and other fun events your contribution and membership give you access to. Please let us know if you have suggestions for new programs that you feel could enrich our community and the world of chocolate.

Thank you for your ongoing support of our mission.

Sincerely yours,

Helen Starkey
Development Director

Helen Starkey   1/3/2013

Word

Video M5_C1_S01

Enter and Edit Text

In Module 4 you learned how to create and save new documents in any Office application. In this skill, you open Word and begin to type text into a new, blank Word document. Once you enter text, you can then perform basic edits to it, such as adding new text, deleting text you no longer need, and correcting errors.

Steps

Tip To open Word, click the Word 2013 tile on the Start screen or press Win + C, click the Search charm, type *Word* in the search box, and then click *Word 2013* in the Apps results list.

Tip Click the *SkyDrive* option if your student data files are saved in your SkyDrive account.

5 *Another Way* Note that Word suggests the current date as you type. When it does this, you can press Enter to insert the date rather than typing the rest of it.

Tip Pressing Shift + Enter inserts a soft return, which moves the insertion point to the next line without creating a new paragraph and maintains the line spacing that appears within the paragraph.

Tip Note that you only need to press the Enter key at the end of a paragraph or after an entry in a list. Within paragraphs, Word wraps your text to a new line automatically.

1 Open Word and then click *Blank document* on the opening screen.

2 Click the FILE tab and then click the *Save* option to open the Save As backstage area.

3 Click the *Computer* option in the middle panel and then browse to the Module 5 working folder you created on your storage medium.

4 Type the file name M5-C1-S1-FundraisingLtr and then click the Save button.

5 Type the current date and press Enter twice.

6 Type your name, press Shift + Enter, and then type the following text:

The Chocolate Museum [**Shift + Enter**]

2551 Jardine Drive [**Shift + Enter**]

Boston, MA 02115 [**Shift + Enter**]

(617) 555-9890

7 Press the Enter key twice and then type the text provided for you at the top of the next page. (Type it exactly as written, pressing Enter only where specified—if there are mistakes, you will correct them later!)

8 Click in the second line of the first address, to the right of the word *Drive*. A blinking cursor appears indicating the insertion point (the place where you are currently working in the document).

Mrs. Agatha Kimbell [Shift + Enter]

22 Oak Lane [Shift + Enter]

Watertown, MA 02118 [Enter twice]

Dear Mrs. Kimbell: [Enter]

Thank you for your recent contribution to the museum of $500 and your ongoing support of our mission. [Enter]

For example, did you know that growers of cacao beans who subscribe to fair trade practices guarantee not only the quality of their products, but also that they do not support child labor or slavery in their businesses? Also, many chocolate manufacturers use additives such as wax in making their chocolate, reducing the amount of valuable anti oxidants that their products provide. Educating the public about issues such as these helps to make the chocolate industry a thriving And and responsible part of our world. [Enter]

Your contribution will help us to continue programs that educate, entertain, and help the chocolate industry to improve it's products and practices. [Enter]

Sincerely yours, [Enter twice]

[Your name] [Shift + Enter]

Development Director

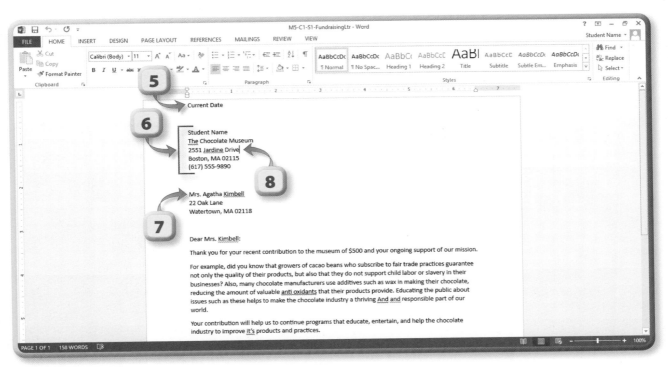

More

Tip The Delete key deletes the character to the right of the insertion point. The Backspace key deletes the character to the left of the insertion point.

Tip If you accidentally delete something and want to restore it, click the Undo button on the Quick Access toolbar or press Ctrl + Z.

Tip It is a good idea to save your files frequently so you do not lose valuable work. For more detailed steps for saving a file, see Module 4, Skill 2.

9. Press the Backspace key five times, noticing that the letters to the left of the cursor are being deleted one at a time.

10. Type the word Street.

11. You made a mistake in the street number (*2551*). To fix it, click between the two 5s in that number and then type 4. Press the Delete key to delete the number 5 to the right of the insertion point. The address should now read *2541*.

12. Click the Save button on the Quick Access toolbar to save the file.

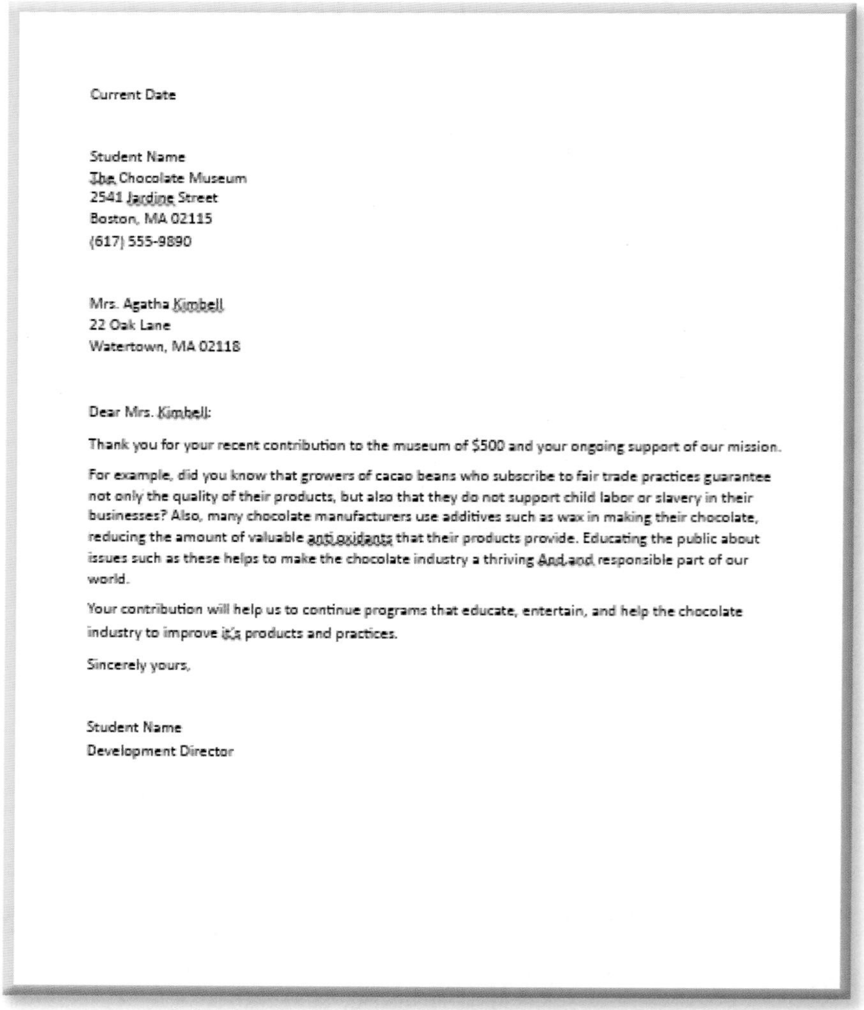

Current Date

Student Name
The Chocolate Museum
2541 Jardine Street
Boston, MA 02115
(617) 555-9890

Mrs. Agatha Kimbell
22 Oak Lane
Watertown, MA 02118

Dear Mrs. Kimbell:

Thank you for your recent contribution to the museum of $500 and your ongoing support of our mission.

For example, did you know that growers of cacao beans who subscribe to fair trade practices guarantee not only the quality of their products, but also that they do not support child labor or slavery in their businesses? Also, many chocolate manufacturers use additives such as wax in making their chocolate, reducing the amount of valuable anti oxidants that their products provide. Educating the public about issues such as these helps to make the chocolate industry a thriving And and responsible part of our world.

Your contribution will help us to continue programs that educate, entertain, and help the chocolate industry to improve it's products and practices.

Sincerely yours,

Student Name
Development Director

Completed Skill 1

Word

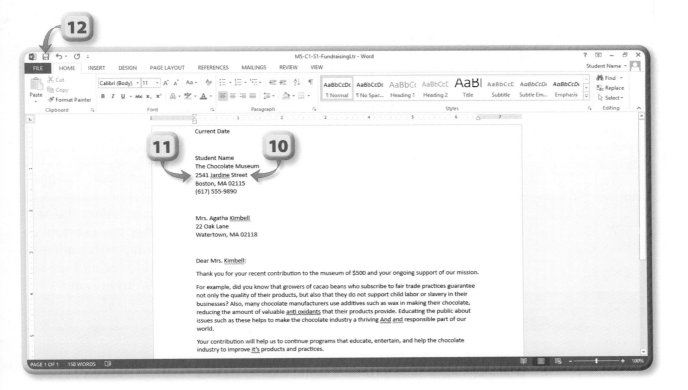

Taking It Further

Interpreting Those Wavy Underlines

This Word feature calls your attention to potentially misspelled words or possible errors in grammar or formatting. Red wavy lines under text, as under the word *Jardine* in the address you entered, flag spelling problems. Blue wavy lines note possible formatting inconsistencies or grammar errors. Because the spelling feature is based on a stored dictionary of words, proper names or names of streets or cities may be flagged as incorrect. Jardine is the correct name of the street, so you can ignore the red wavy line in this case. To find and resolve all possible problems and learn how to add words like *Jardine* to the dictionary, check out Skill 3.

Word

Skill 2

Video M5_C1_S02

Use Cut, Copy, and Paste

Beyond simple text editing such as deleting and adding text, you might also need to take a sentence or block of text from one place in a document and move it or copy it to another location. For example, you might decide that a paragraph on the first page of a letter really works better on the second page. Or you might want to copy the opening sentence of the letter, place the copy at the end of the letter, and edit it slightly to summarize the letter's purpose. To perform these tasks, select the text and then use either the Cut tool or the Copy tool, along with the Paste tool. These tools are located on the HOME tab of the Word ribbon.

Steps

1 If it is not already open, open **M5-C1-S1-FundraisingLtr.docx**, the file you saved in the previous skill, and save the file as **M5-C1-S2-FundraisingLtr**. Be sure to save the file in your Module 5 working folder on your storage medium.

2 Place your mouse pointer in the margin to the left of the second paragraph, which begins with the words *For example....* The cursor changes from a line to an arrow.

Tip Single-clicking in the selection area at the left of a Word document selects a single line of text, double-clicking in the same area selects the whole paragraph, and triple-clicking selects all of the text in the document.

3 Double-click to select the entire paragraph.

4 Click the Cut button in the Clipboard group on the HOME tab. The text is cut from the document.

5 Click just to the left of the *S* in the word *Sincerely* in the signature block at the end of the document (but do not select the word).

Tip Be sure to click the Paste button, not the Paste button arrow.

6 Click the Paste button in the Clipboard group on the HOME tab. The paragraph now appears at the indicated location.

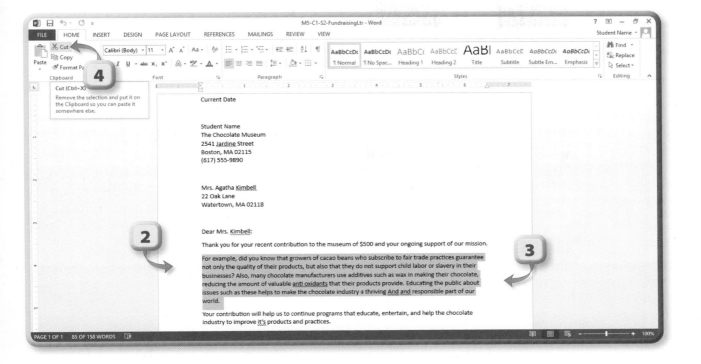

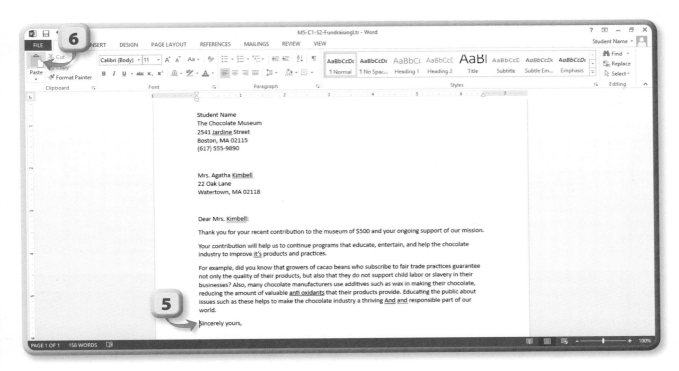

Tip To quickly select a word, hover the mouse pointer over the word and double-click. To select a paragraph, hover your mouse pointer over the paragraph and triple-click. See Skill 1 for a reminder of other simple editing techniques using the Backspace and Delete keys.

7 Select the first sentence in the body of the letter, which begins with the words *Thank you for your....*

8 Click the Copy button in the Clipboard group on the HOME tab.

9 Click to the left of the word *Sincerely* and then click the Paste button.

10 A copy of the first sentence in the letter now appears at the new location. Using any of the editing methods from the previous skill, edit the copied sentence to read *Thank you again for your ongoing support of our mission.*

11 Shortcut
Save a Document
Ctrl + S

11 Save the file.

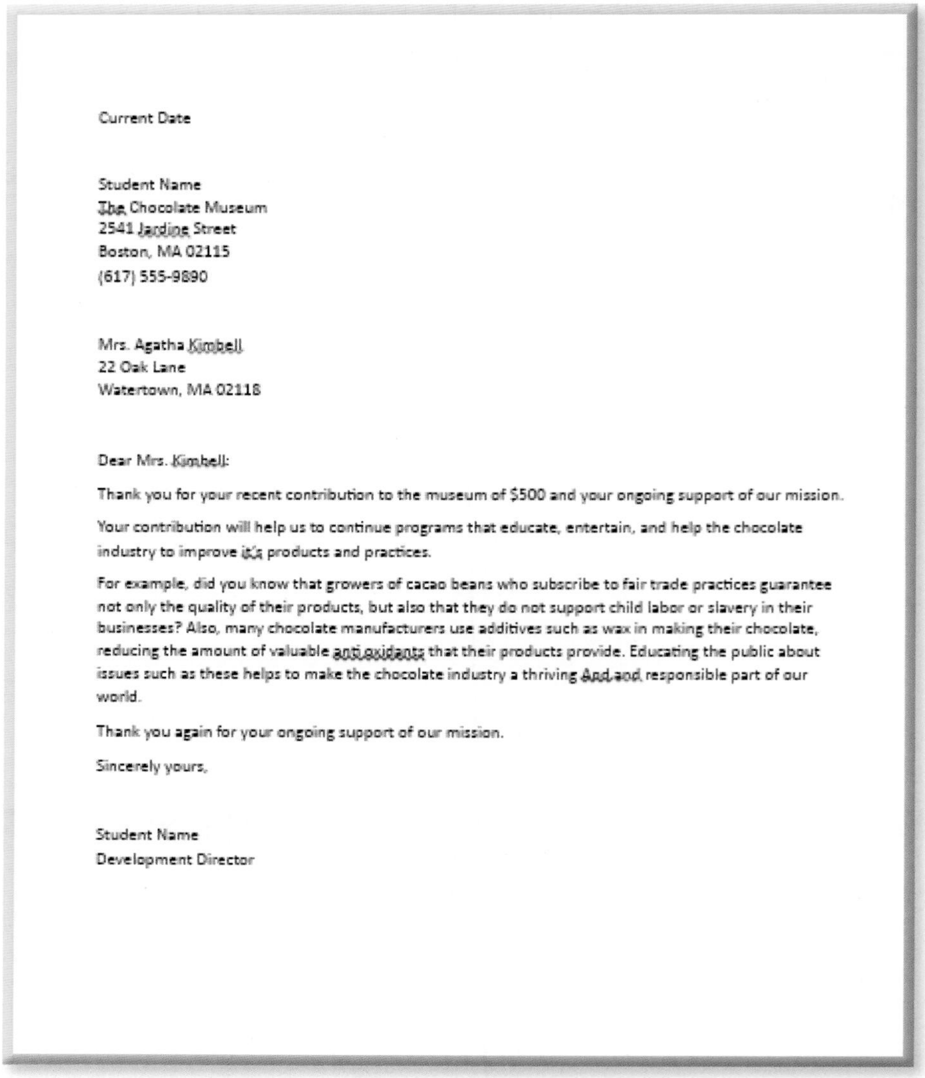

Current Date

Student Name
The Chocolate Museum
2541 Jardine Street
Boston, MA 02115
(617) 555-9890

Mrs. Agatha Kimbell
22 Oak Lane
Watertown, MA 02118

Dear Mrs. Kimbell:

Thank you for your recent contribution to the museum of $500 and your ongoing support of our mission.

Your contribution will help us to continue programs that educate, entertain, and help the chocolate industry to improve it's products and practices.

For example, did you know that growers of cacao beans who subscribe to fair trade practices guarantee not only the quality of their products, but also that they do not support child labor or slavery in their businesses? Also, many chocolate manufacturers use additives such as wax in making their chocolate, reducing the amount of valuable anti oxidants that their products provide. Educating the public about issues such as these helps to make the chocolate industry a thriving And and responsible part of our world.

Thank you again for your ongoing support of our mission.

Sincerely yours,

Student Name
Development Director

Completed Skill 2

Word

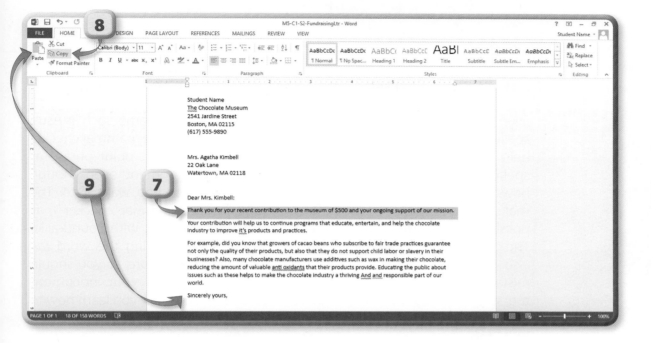

Taking It Further

Using the Clipboard   When you cut or copy text, it is placed on the Clipboard, a holding area for cut or copied text or objects such as pictures. You can click in any document and use the Paste tool to place an item on the Clipboard immediately after cutting or copying it. You can paste that item as many times as you want, until you cut or copy another item to the Clipboard. If you want to paste an item that was previously copied to the Clipboard, click the dialog box launcher in the Clipboard group on the HOME tab to display the Clipboard pane. Note that the Clipboard is cleared when you save your document and exit Word.

Word

Word

Video M5_C1_S03

Perform a Spelling and Grammar Check

Even if you are a good speller, Word's spelling and grammar checker can help you to catch typos and other spelling-based mistakes. Knowing how to use this important tool ensures that your documents are correct and polished to create the best impression. The spelling and grammar checker also checks for common grammar mistakes. You can choose to make the suggested corrections or ignore them. But remember that this feature isn't foolproof. For example, the spelling checker might flag a correctly spelled company name, such as Asus, as incorrect, and the grammar checker might flag a bullet point phrase as a sentence fragment even though it reads just as you want it to. The spelling and grammar checker may also miss mistakes with sound-alike words, such as using the word *fair* when you meant *fare*, so you should always proofread your document carefully. In this skill, you learn how to use the spelling and grammar checker and how to make appropriate choices for changes.

Steps

1 If it is not already open, open **M5-C1-S2-FundraisingLtr.docx**, the file you saved in the previous skill, and save the file as **M5-C1-S3-FundraisingLtr**.

2 Click in front of the first line of text (*Current Date*) to place your cursor at the start of the document, and then click the REVIEW tab.

▶ **Tip** When should you click Ignore and when should you click Ignore All? If you use a term, such as a company's name, several times in a document, choose Ignore All. If there is only one instance of a misspelling or misuse—say you are quoting someone who said *ain't*, but you do not want that word anywhere else in your document—choose Ignore.

3 Click the Spelling & Grammar button in the Proofing group. This opens the Spelling pane or Grammar pane. If the spelling checker suggests a change in the spelling of your name in the document, click the Ignore All button.

4 The spelling checker identifies *Jardine* as a misspelled word. Since *Jardine* is spelled correctly, click the Ignore All button.

5 The grammar checker highlights the return address block and suggests that the *The* in *The Chocolate Museum* should not be capitalized. Since *The* is part of the museum's name and is correct as typed, click the Ignore button.

6 The spelling of *Kimbell* is also correct, so click the Ignore All button.

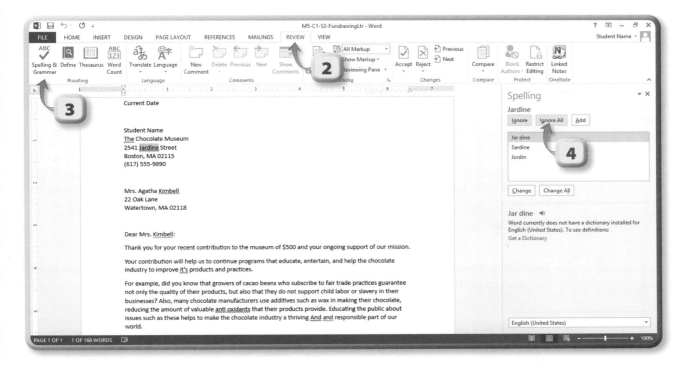

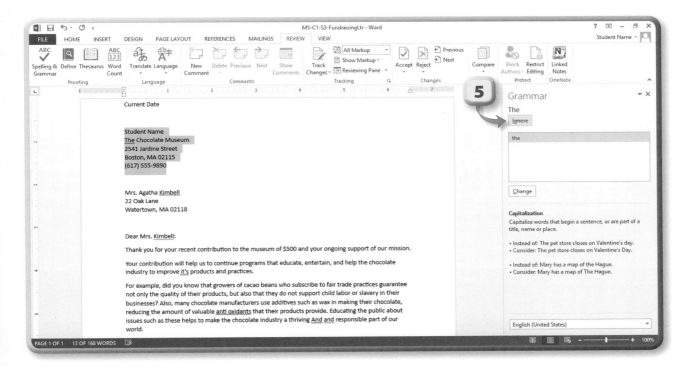

Tip The difference between Change and Change All is similar to that between Ignore and Ignore All. Clicking Change will change one particular instance of a spelling error; clicking Change All will change all instances of the misspelling in the document.

7 The next flagged word is a grammar error: you entered *it's* instead of *its*. Click the Change button to change *it's* to the suggested form of the word.

8 Click the Change button again to change *anti oxidants* to *anti-oxidants*.

9 The next flagged error is a repeated word error: you have an extra *and* in your sentence. Click the Delete button to correct the error.

10 The checker now highlights the sentence that begins *Educating the public* and suggests changing *And* to *and*. Click the Change button to accept the recommended change.

11 When the checker is finished, a dialog box appears, stating that the spelling and grammar check is complete. Click OK to close it.

12 Save the file.

Tip Printing files is covered in Module 4, Skill 10.

13 Print a hard copy or submit the file as directed by your instructor.

14 Close the file. If you have any other Word files open, also close them.

Current Date

Student Name
The Chocolate Museum
2541 Jardine Street
Boston, MA 02115
(617) 555-9890

Mrs. Agatha Kimbell
22 Oak Lane
Watertown, MA 02118

Dear Mrs. Kimbell:

Thank you for your recent contribution to the museum of $500 and your ongoing support of our mission.

Your contribution will help us to continue programs that educate, entertain, and help the chocolate industry to improve its products and practices.

For example, did you know that growers of cacao beans who subscribe to fair trade practices guarantee not only the quality of their products, but also that they do not support child labor or slavery in their businesses? Also, many chocolate manufacturers use additives such as wax in making their chocolate, reducing the amount of valuable anti-oxidants that their products provide. Educating the public about issues such as these helps to make the chocolate industry a thriving and responsible part of our world.

Thank you again for your ongoing support of our mission.

Sincerely yours,

Student Name
Development Director

Completed Skill 3

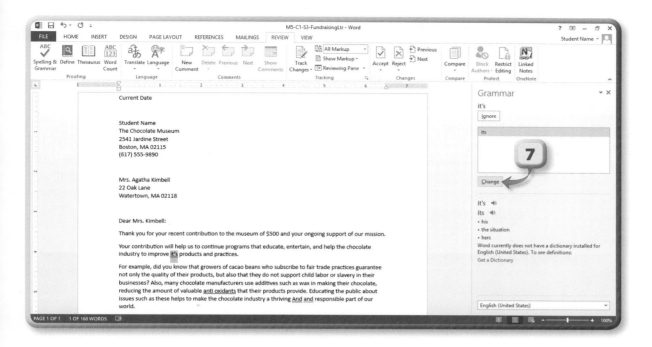

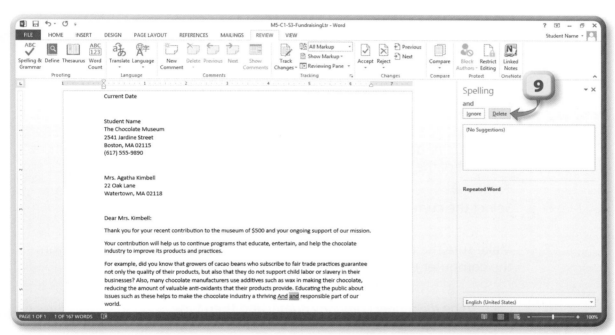

Taking It Further

Adding a Word to Your Dictionary
While performing a spelling check, you may encounter a word you know to be correct, but that keeps getting flagged by Word because it is not in the built-in dictionary. In that situation, you can save yourself the time spent checking the word again and again in each spelling check by adding it to your dictionary. While performing a spelling check, simply click the Add button in the Spelling pane when the word is challenged and you will never have to verify it again.

Word

Video M5_C1_S04

Create a Document Based on a Template

You can begin a document in a blank document and then apply formatting and add graphical elements to make it look more appealing. However, a handy shortcut to achieve a more professional-looking document is to open a predesigned document based on a template. Several such templates come built into Office 2013, and in this skill, you learn how to locate one and use it to create a fundraising letter.

Steps

▶ **Tip** If you already have a Word document open, click the FILE tab to open the backstage area and then click the *New* option to search for templates.

▶ **Tip** Word templates you locate online are downloaded when you select them. An Internet connection is required to download a template.

▶ **Tip** Note that the template includes text formatting such as a specific font, font formatting (such as bold), and font size, as well as graphical elements. Choose a template that provides a look that matches your organization's style or the tone of your content.

▶ **Tip** The phrase *[Compatibility Mode]* in the Title bar (above the ribbon) indicates that the file was created in an earlier version of Word. The Letter (Equity theme) template was created in Word 2010.

1 Open Word.

2 Click the <u>Letters</u> link in the *Suggested searches* list on the Word opening page.

3 Locate and click the *Letter (Equity theme)* option. **HINT:** *If you have trouble locating the template, type* Letter (Equity theme) *in the search box and then press Enter.*

4 Click the Create button to download the template.

5 Click *[Pick the date]* and then click the down-pointing arrow that appears at the right of the field.

6 Select the current date on the drop-down calendar.

7 Make sure the name on the next line is your name. (Word takes this from the computer user's name. If it is not correct, you can change it.)

8 Click *[Type the sender company name]* and then type The Chocolate Museum.

9 Click *[Type the sender company address],* type 2541 Jardine Street, press Enter, and then type Boston, MA 02115.

10 Click *[Type the recipient name]* and then type Mr. Arthur Renfrew.

11 Click *[Type the recipient address],* type 98 Elm Street, press Enter, and then type Brookline, MA 02116.

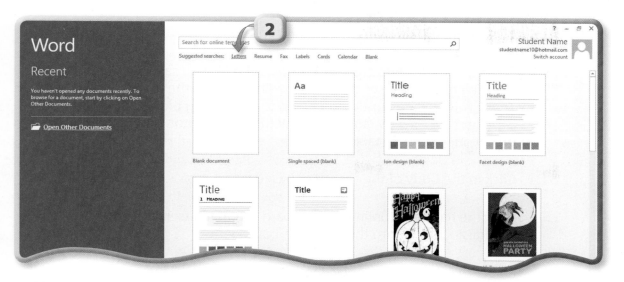

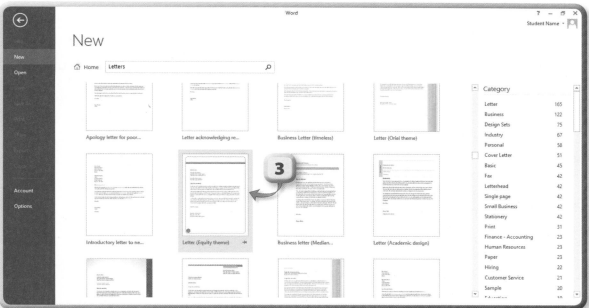

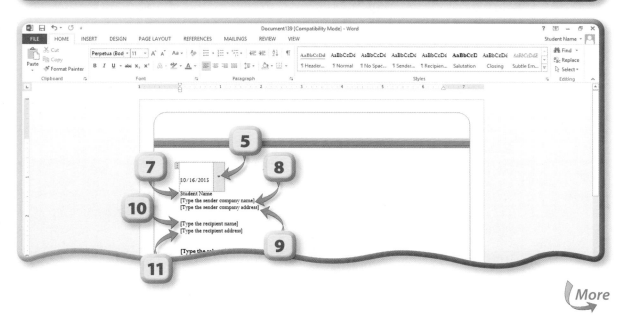

12 Click **[Type the salutation]** and then type Dear Mr. Renfrew:.

13 Open **M5-C1-S3-FundraisingLtr.docx**, the file you saved in the previous skill. Select the body of the letter, beginning with the first line (starts with *Thank you for*) and continuing down to the closing block that ends with *Development Director*, and then click the Copy button in the Clipboard group on the HOME tab.

▶ **Tip** Text can be entered directly into the body of the template-based letter.

14 Click in the body of the template-based letter.

15 Click the Paste button in the Clipboard group to insert the body of your fundraising letter into the template-based letter.

16 Select the closing block placeholders and all text below the pasted text.

17 Press the Delete key to delete the text selected in Step 16.

▶ **Tip** When you upgrade a document to the newest file format, some minor format changes may appear. After you upgrade a document, check the formatting to be sure it looks the way you want it to.

18 Save the file as **Lastname-M5-C1-S4-TemplateFundraisingLtr**, but replace *Lastname* with your last name. If you see a dialog box that says *Your document will be upgraded to the newest file format*, click OK. Be sure to save the file in your Module 5 working folder on your storage medium.

19 Print a hard copy or submit the file as directed by your instructor.

20 Close **M5-C1-S3-FundraisingLtr.docx** and **Lastname-M5-C1-S4-TemplateFundraisingLtr.docx**.

Completed Skill 4

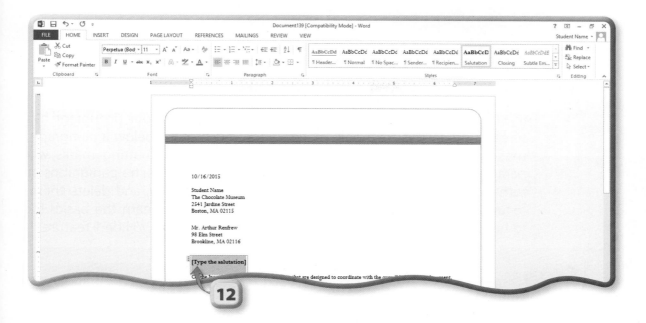

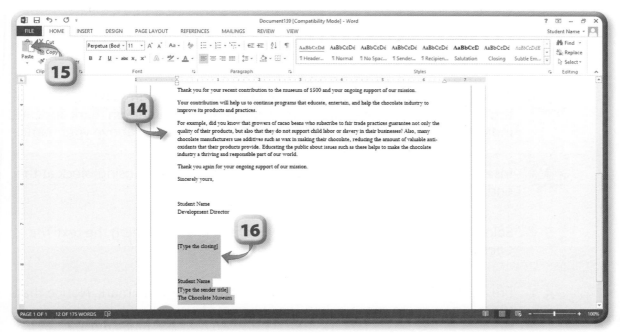

Taking It Further

Creating Your Own Template If you have created a document that you consider a good starting point for other documents of the same type, why not create your own template? You can do this by saving your original file using *Word Template* as the *Save as type* option in the Save As dialog box. Then, when starting a new document, click the FILE tab, the *New* option, and then the *Personal* option. Locate your template file and click it. A new file opens, based on the template layout and ready for your changes. The file can be saved in the same manner as any other Word document. Using this method, you can reuse the text, formatting, and graphics that you applied to the first file. You will save time and add consistency to your documents.

Word

Use the Show/Hide ¶ Feature

Video M5_C1_S05

In the student data files and screenshots in this textbook, marks that indicate formatting such as paragraphs, lines, and spaces, are turned off, or hidden. You may want to turn on these marks, or show them, to help you fix formatting problems.

For example, if your document has too much space below a paragraph, showing the formatting marks will allow you to see extra paragraphs or lines, select them, and delete them. In this skill, you learn the basics for using Word's Show/Hide ¶ feature.

Steps

1 Open **M5-C1-S3-FundraisingLtr.docx**, the file you saved in Skill 3.

2 Click the Show/Hide ¶ button in the Paragraph group on the HOME tab. Notice that this turns on (shows) the formatting marks in the document.

3 Click just to the left of your first name in the sender's address block at the top of the letter and then press Enter. Notice that a paragraph mark appears, indicating that you have inserted a new, blank paragraph above your name.

4 Insert another blank paragraph above your name in the closing block at the end of the letter.

5 Select the line break mark ↵ at the end of the line containing the text *The Chocolate Museum* in the sender's block.

▶**Tip** In Chapter 2, Skill 5, you will learn how to set paragraph and line spacing.

6 Press Enter to change the line break mark to a paragraph mark. Notice that there is now more space below *The Chocolate Museum*.

▶**Tip** Paragraphs and lines may have the same spacing or different spacing, depending on the settings in your document. If the spacing between paragraphs and lines does not look the way you expect it to and you are having trouble fixing it, try turning on formatting marks and making sure you have used line and paragraph spaces correctly.

7 Press the Backspace key to remove the paragraph mark you inserted in Step 6, and press Shift + Enter to restore the line break mark.

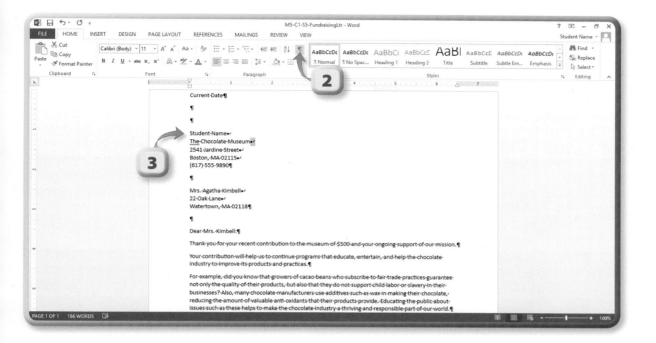

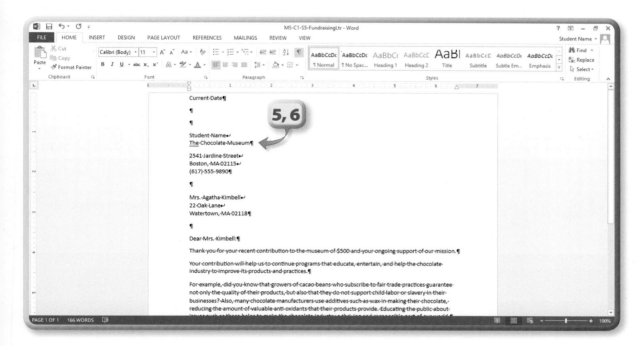

More

8 Click just to the left of the *E* in the sentence that begins *Educating the public* in the third paragraph of the body of the letter. Press the spacebar to add a space between the sentences.

9 Backspace to remove the space you just inserted.

10 Click the Show/Hide ¶ button again to see how your document looks without the formatting marks displayed.

11 Close the file without saving your changes.

▶ *Tip* Standard practice in word processing is to insert only one space between sentences. Be careful not to double-space between sentences in your documents.

Word

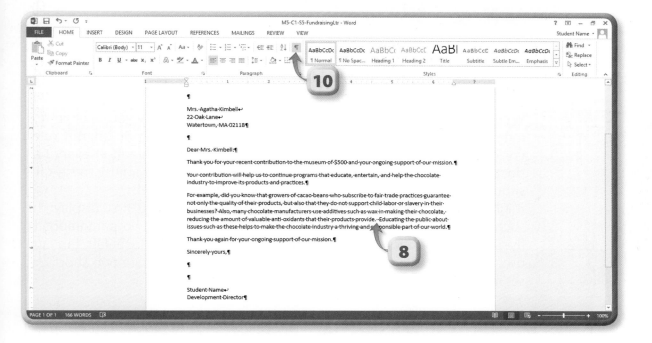

Taking It Further

Saving Paper   Have you ever printed a document and ended up with an unexpected blank page at the end? This commonly happens when the document contains extra paragraphs or lines at the end of the last page. Use the Show/Hide ¶ feature to look for blank paragraphs and lines at the end of your document—and then delete them to save paper!

Word

Video M5_C1_S06

Indent and Add Tabs Using the Ruler

In certain situations, you may want to indent a block of text in a document. For example, according to standard document formats, a long quote should always be indented. Or you might want to set off a block of text, such as a product guarantee in a flyer, to call attention to it. You can use the ruler in Word to indent text, set margins (discussed in Skill 7), and set tabs. Tabs allow you to align text using a specific spot on the ruler. Tabs are set by default at every half inch, but you can adjust these tabs or set additional tabs.

In this skill, you first display the ruler and indent two paragraphs of text. You then add a left tab and decimal tab to create two short lists of data.

Steps

Indent Paragraphs of Text

1 Open the student data file named **M5-C1-S6-FundraisingLtr.docx** and, if you have not already done so, save the file in your Module 5 working folder on your storage medium.

2 If the ruler is displayed, skip to Step 4. If the ruler is not displayed, click the VIEW tab.

3 In the Show group, click the *Ruler* check box to insert a check mark.

4 Select the fourth and fifth paragraphs of the body of the letter, beginning with *There may be a hidden ingredient…* and ending with *…as young as 9.* **HINT:** *You may need to scroll down to get to these paragraphs.*

5 On the ruler, drag the Left Indent indicator one-half inch to the right so that it rests at the one-half-inch mark on the ruler and then release the mouse button.

Set a Left Tab and a Decimal Tab

6 Click at the end of the next paragraph, after the words *Chocolate Fest!*, and then press Enter.

7 Type the text Here is a summary of our donations for the last three years showing how our support is growing: and then press Enter.

▶**Tip** To see how items on your page line up, you can display gridlines on your page, which is like placing a sheet of transparent graph paper on top of your document. Click the VIEW tab and then click the *Gridlines* check box to insert a check mark.

5 *Another Way* Click the Increase Indent button in the Paragraph group on the HOME tab.

▶**Tip** To drag an item successfully, you must press the left mouse button and hold it down while you move the mouse along. When you release the mouse button, you stop dragging the item.

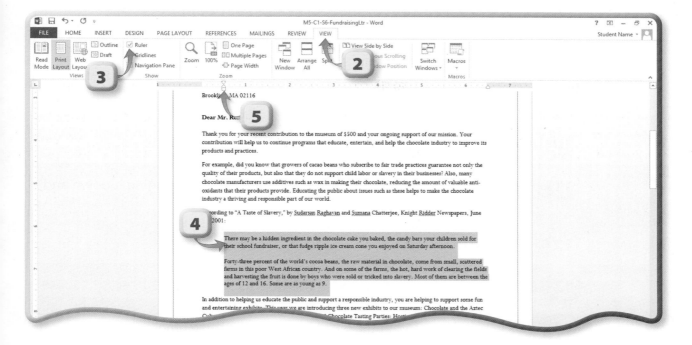

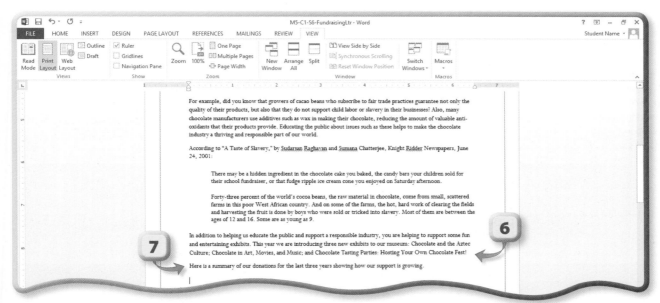

More

Taking It Further

Indenting the First Line in Paragraphs
In the letter example used in this chapter, you use a block style, which does not require the first line of each paragraph to be indented. Other document formats may require you to indent the first line of each paragraph. To do so, open the Paragraph dialog box by clicking the dialog box launcher in the Paragraph group on the HOME tab. Adjust the measurement for the left indentation, choose *First Line* from the *Special* drop-down list, and then click OK to save the changes.

8 Click the 2-inch mark and the 3.5-inch mark on the ruler. These actions place two left tabs and remove any default tabs to the left of them on the ruler for the currently selected line.

9 Press the Tab key and then type Year.

10 Press Tab again, type Total Donations, and then press Enter.

11 Remove the left tab symbol at the 3.5-inch mark by dragging it down and off the ruler.

12 Click the HOME tab.

13 Click the Show/Hide ¶ button in the Paragraph group.

▶**Tip** Left, right, and center tabs tell Word to place the left edge, right edge, or center of the text you enter at the tab location. Decimal tabs are used for columns of numbers —they tell Word to place the decimal point at the specified tab location, thereby vertically aligning those numbers.

14 Click the tab selector at the left side of the ruler three times until the ScreenTip reads *Decimal Tab* when you hover your mouse over the tab selector.

15 Click the 4-inch mark on the ruler to place a decimal tab at that point.

16 Type the following three lines, pressing Tab once before typing each year, pressing Tab once before adding each dollar amount, and pressing Enter after typing the first two dollar amounts. Do not press Enter after typing the last dollar amount. Notice the tab mark (right-arrow) that displays each time you press Tab.

2014 $100,789.00

2013 $97,988.00

2012 $89,322.00

17 Click the Show/Hide ¶ button to hide these and other formatting marks.

18 Save the file.

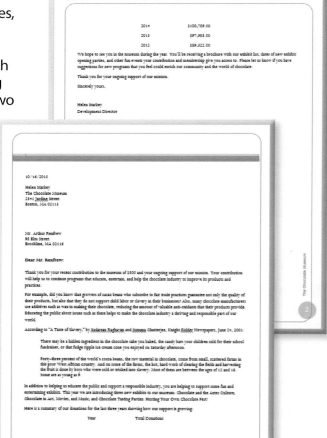

Completed Skill 6

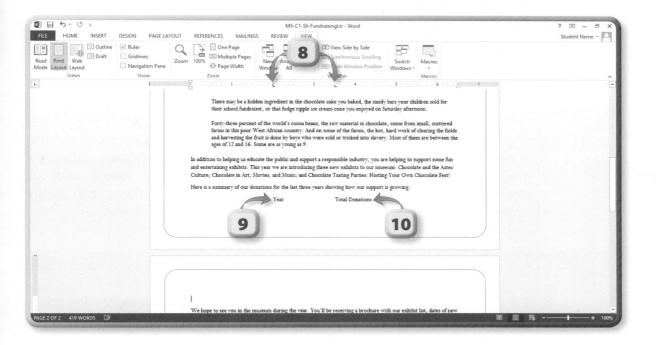

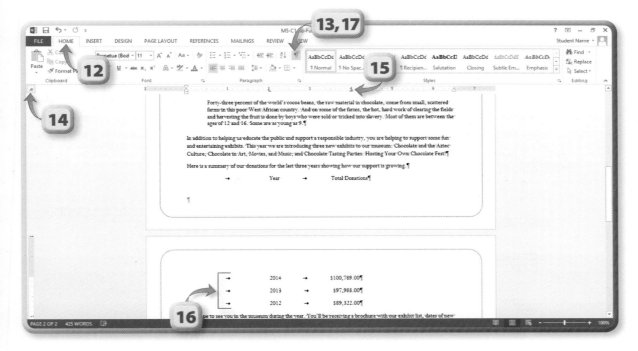

Taking It Further

Adding Tabs to Existing Text If you have already typed a list using existing tabs and decide you would like to change those tabs—for example, because your columns of text seem too close together to be easily read—you can. Select all the text whose tab settings you wish to change. To move a tab, drag the tab symbol to the new location on the ruler. To remove a tab, drag the tab marker off the ruler. To insert a new tab for the selected text, follow the method outlined in this skill.

Word

Skill 7

Video ▶ M5_C1_S07

Set Margins

Margins are the areas of white space that surround the text on your page. A document's margins are located at the top, bottom, left, and right. The preset margins for Word documents work in most cases, but you might choose to use narrower margins to fit more text on a page or use a wider top margin to accommodate the letterhead on corporate stationery, for example. Preset margin settings are available, and you can easily apply them to any document.

Steps

1 If it is not already open, open **M5-C1-S6-FundraisingLtr.docx**, the file you saved in the previous skill, and save the file as **M5-C1-S7-FundraisingLtr**.

2 Click the PAGE LAYOUT tab.

3 Click the Margins button in the Page Setup group.

4 In the drop-down gallery that appears, click the *Moderate* option. This action creates narrower margins on the left and right of the letter.

5 Save the file.

4 *Another Way*
You can also adjust the top, bottom, and side margins in your document by using the vertical or horizontal ruler. Hover your mouse over the area of the ruler where the dark gray and light gray areas meet, until the margin label appears. Drag to the right or left to adjust the margin size on the ruler across the top of the page. Drag up or down to adjust margins on the ruler along the left side of the page.

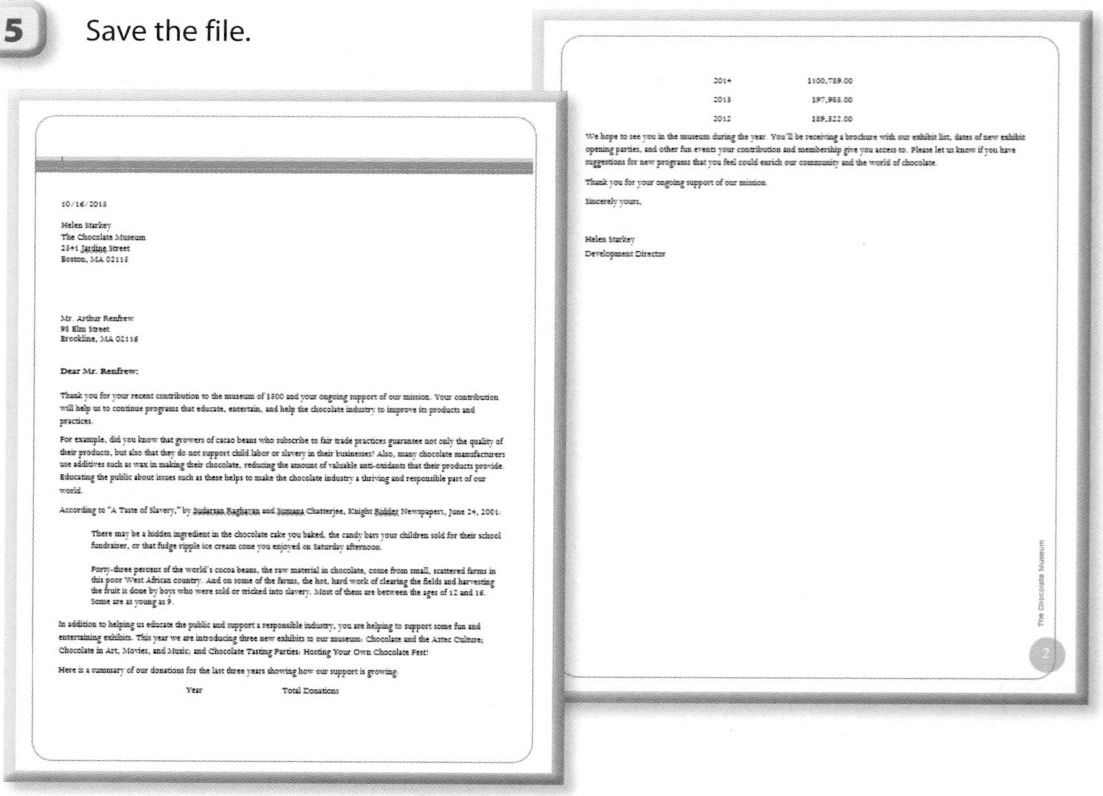

Completed Skill 7

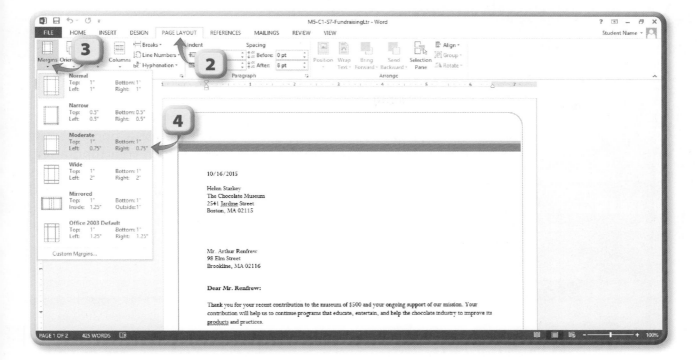

Taking It Further

Creating Custom Margins You can use the *Custom Margins* option to create margins to accommodate any document. To do so, display the PAGE LAYOUT tab, click the Margins button in the Page Setup group, and then click *Custom Margins*. The Page Setup dialog box appears with the Margins tab selected. Use the arrows in the measurement boxes (*Top*, *Bottom*, *Left*, and *Right*) to set a custom number for each margin. The gutter options are used to set space in a bound document, such as a book. In most books, there is a wider margin on the right side of the left pages and on the left side of the right pages to accommodate the fold, or binding, of the book.

Word

Word

Video M5_C1_S08

Insert a Page Break

When you are working in a document, you may find that the automatic page breaks that Word inserts do not work for you. For example, you might find that a paragraph breaks across a page so that a single line of text or a single row in a list is left dangling. Or you might want a new section of a report or new chapter of a book to start on a new page. In your fundraising letter, for example, the page breaks in the middle of the short tabbed list, making it hard to follow. You can solve this by inserting a manual page break.

Steps

1 If it is not already open, open **M5-C1-S7-FundraisingLtr.docx**, the file you saved in the previous skill, and save the file as **Lastname-M5-C1-S8-FundraisingLtr**, but replace *Lastname* with your last name. Be sure to save the file in your Module 5 working folder on your storage medium.

2 Click the Show/Hide ¶ button in the Paragraph group on the HOME tab.

3 Click at the start of the paragraph that begins with the text *Here is a summary of our donations*.

4 *Shortcut*
Insert Page Break
Ctrl + Enter

▶**Tip** If you insert a page break in the wrong place, you may delete it by using either the Backspace key (with the insertion point placed just after the page break) or the Delete key (with the insertion point placed just before the page break).

4 Click the INSERT tab.

5 Click the Page Break button in the Pages group to insert a page break.

6 Notice the page break mark that appears where you inserted the page break.

7 Click the Show/Hide ¶ button in the Paragraph group on the HOME tab to hide the page break mark and other formatting marks.

8 Save the file.

9 Print a hard copy or submit the file as directed by your instructor.

10 Close the file.

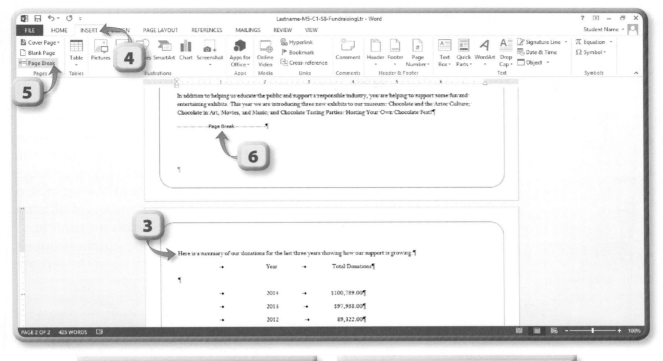

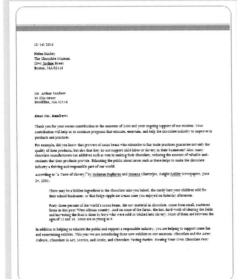
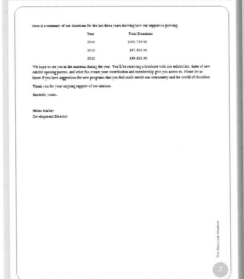

Completed Skill 8

Taking It Further

Using Page Breaks Effectively Page breaks should be used sparingly. If you place breaks throughout a long document, and then edit it by deleting or adding text, the page breaks may not make sense anymore. For example, say you are working on a 20-page report instead of the 2-page letter in this skill. If you place a page break at the end of each page, and then add a large block of text to page 1, you may need to adjust the page breaks on each of the 20 pages in the report. While you are writing and revising a document, use page breaks only in situations where you truly have to start a new page—for example, to separate the cover page of a report from the first page, the end of a chapter from the start of the next chapter, or the last page of your report from the first page of its index. When you know your document is essentially final, you might use page breaks to adjust awkward breaks between pages or to remove breaks that split tables or lists, as you did in this skill.

Word

Skill 9

Insert Headers and Footers

Video M5_C1_S09

▶

If you want text or graphics to appear at the top or bottom of most of the pages in a document, you can add them in either the header (top) or footer (bottom) areas. Word makes it easy to add text, such as your company name or logo, document identifier, page number, or date, to a document. You can also choose not to have your header or footer appear on the first page of your document—for example, on the cover sheet of a report. You can place different header or footer content on odd and even pages, or place the page numbers in different locations, as is often true for a book, where page numbers appear opposite each other in the left and right corners.

Steps

1 Open the student data file named **M5-C1-S9-FundraisingLtr.docx** and save the file as **Lastname-M5-C1-S9-FundraisingLtr**, but replace *Lastname* with your last name. Be sure to save the file in your Module 5 working folder on your storage medium.

2 Click the INSERT tab.

3 Click the Header button in the Header & Footer group and then click the *Blank (Three Columns)* option.

4 Click the *[Type here]* placeholder in the left margin of the header and then type Mr. Arthur Renfrew.

5 Click the *[Type here]* placeholder in the center of the header and then press the Delete key to remove it.

6 Click the *[Type here]* placeholder on the far right of the header and then type Page followed by a space.

▶ **Tip** The advantage of using buttons like Page Number and Date & Time to insert text in your header or footer is that they automatically update. So whenever you print the letter, the current date appears, and however many pages you add to your document, each is numbered correctly.

7 Click the Page Number button in the Header & Footer group on the HEADER & FOOTER TOOLS DESIGN tab.

8 At the drop-down list, point to the *Current Position* option and then click *Plain Number*. A page number is inserted on the right side of the header after the word *Page*.

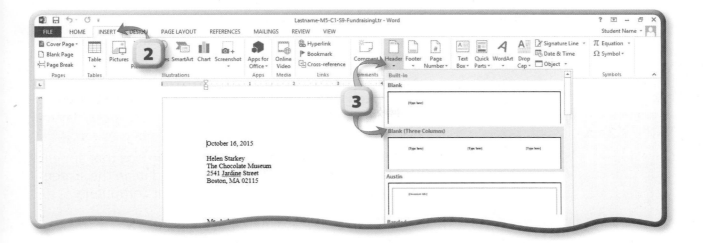

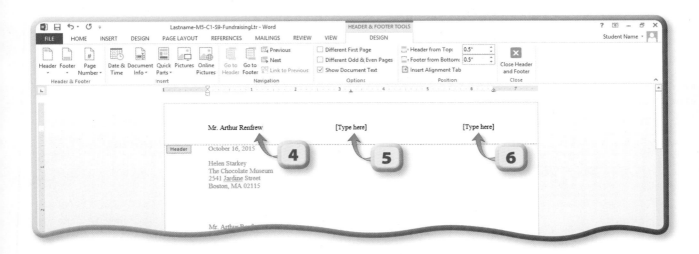

Word

9 Click in the footer area of the page (you may need to scroll down to locate it), type Helen Starkey, and then press the Tab key to move the cursor to the center of the footer.

10 Click the Date & Time button in the Insert group on the HEADER & FOOTER TOOLS DESIGN tab.

11 Choose the first available format from the list in the dialog box that appears and then click OK. (The date inserted will not match the date in the screen capture but will match the current date according to your computer's calendar.)

12 Click the *Different First Page* check box in the Options group on the HEADER & FOOTER TOOLS DESIGN tab to insert a check mark. The text is removed from the header and footer on the first page of the document.

13 Click the Close Header and Footer button.

14 Save the file.

15 Print a hard copy or submit the file as directed by your instructor.

16 Close the file.

 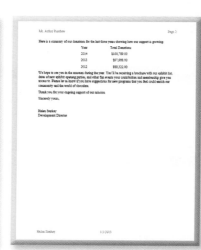

Completed Skill 9

Taking It Further

Inserting Document Properties in a Header/Footer If you click the Quick Parts button in the Insert group on the HEADER & FOOTER TOOLS DESIGN tab and choose *Document Property*, a drop-down list of possible properties appears. This list gives you a handy way to quickly insert fields for information, such as the author or company, drawn from the document properties. You can review the document properties by clicking the FILE tab. Document properties are listed on the right of the Info pane. You can edit some of these properties, but others are automatically generated (such as the date last modified).

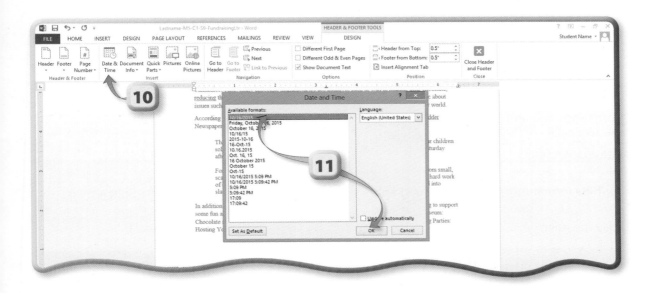

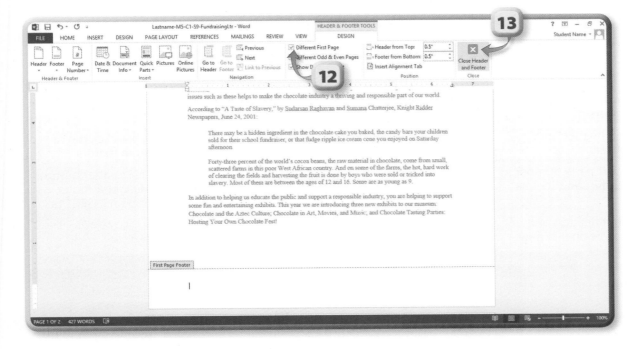

Word

Tasks Summary

Task	Ribbon Tab, Group	Button, Option	Shortcut, Alternative
Delete text			Backspace or Delete
Select a word			Double-click
Select a paragraph			Triple-click
Cut text	HOME, Clipboard		Ctrl + X
Copy text	HOME, Clipboard		Ctrl + C
Paste text	HOME, Clipboard		Ctrl + V
Perform a spelling and grammar check	REVIEW, Proofing		F7
Create a new, blank document	FILE, *New*		Ctrl + N
Show/hide formatting marks	HOME, Paragraph		Ctrl + Shift + *
Display the ruler	VIEW, Show		
Indent a block of text	HOME, Paragraph		Ruler
Set tabs	HOME, Paragraph		Ruler
Set margins	PAGE LAYOUT, Page Setup		Ruler
Insert page break	INSERT, Pages		Ctrl + Enter
Insert headers and footers	INSERT, Header & Footer		
Edit headers and footers	INSERT, Header & Footer		Double-click top or bottom margin
Insert page number in headers and footers	HEADER & FOOTER TOOLS DESIGN, Header & Footer		Page Number button in Header & footer group on INSERT tab
Omit headers and footers on first page	HEADER & FOOTER TOOLS DESIGN, Options	*Different First Page* check box	

Features Review

Select the best answer from the choices given.

1 When you open Word, it displays
   a. the last document you worked on.
   b. a pane of available templates.
   c. a blank document.
   d. the Open dialog box.

2 The Save command is accessed via which tab?
   a. HOME
   b. VIEW
   c. PAGE LAYOUT
   d. FILE

3 Pressing the Delete key deletes what text?
   a. to the right of the insertion point
   b. to the left of the insertion point
   c. the last word you entered
   d. the first word of the currently selected paragraph

4 When you cut text, what happens to it?
   a. It is removed from its current location and is placed on the Clipboard.
   b. It remains in its current location and is also placed on the Clipboard.
   c. It is deleted and irretrievable.
   d. It is placed in the Recycle Bin.

5 Which of the following statements about the spelling and grammar checker is *not* correct?
   a. It may flag a word that is correctly spelled because the word does not exist in the dictionary.
   b. It may flag a correctly spelled word that is not the correct word choice for the sentence.
   c. It looks for both grammar and spelling errors.
   d. It is launched by clicking the Spelling & Grammar button on the HOME tab.

6 You initiate a spelling check from which tab?
   a. HOME
   b. REFERENCES
   c. REVIEW
   d. PAGE LAYOUT

7 Templates may contain settings for
   a. the buttons available on the ribbon.
   b. text formatting and graphics.
   c. the location for storing the file.
   d. the maximum number of pages in the document.

8 You can set tabs in your document using which Word feature?
   a. the VIEW tab
   b. options accessed through the FILE menu
   c. Word Styles
   d. the ruler

9 Margins
   a. are special header/footer sections where you can enter text that is to appear on the top and bottom of every page.
   b. are automatically adjusted to fit the text on one page.
   c. are adjustable so you can fit more or less text on a page.
   d. justify the text on a page.

10 Headers and footers provide a way for you to
    a. add a footnote to a page.
    b. insert text you'd like to appear on every page in the document.
    c. set tabs.
    d. add white space to the edges of your document.

Hands-On Skills Review

Exercise **Check Spelling and Grammar and Proofread an Instruction Guide**

Skills   Enter and edit text and perform a spelling and grammar check

Scenario   Update a Word document to be used as part of an instruction guide for purchasing a computer. Use the spelling and grammar checker to correct the paragraph and then proofread for errors that are not caught by the spelling and grammar check feature.

Steps

1   Open the student data file named **M5-C1-ExA-ComputerPurchase.docx** and save the file as **Lastname-M5-C1-ExA-ComputerPurchase**, but replace *Lastname* with your last name.

2   Type your name, a comma, and the current date on the first line of the document and then press Enter.

3   Use the spelling and grammar checker to correct the errors in the text.

4   Proofread the document to be sure it is correct. You will find errors that were not flagged by the spelling and grammar checker.

5   Make any additional corrections to errors that you find.

6   Save and close the file.

7   Print a hard copy or submit the file as directed by your instructor.

Student Name, Current Date

Before purchasing a computer, take some time to consider how you wish to use your computer. This will help you decide if a portable computer is needed. Then investigate the various types of software that can be used for your purposes. Check the specification for the software and make a list of minimum and recommended hardware. Then it's time to consider your computer choices. Visit some online sites and review their computer sales. Compare the processor type and speed, the amount of RAM, and the size of the hard drive, as well as additional features you might find useful. Check the hardware specifications against the list for the software you plan to use. When you are comfortable that you are looking at computers that meet your needs, you will be able to make an informed purchase decision.

Completed Exercise A

Exercise B Download and Modify a Memo Template

Skills   Enter and edit text, perform a spelling and grammar check, and create a document based on a template

Scenario   Jane Doe, your supervisor at Premiere Cell Phones, Inc., has asked you to send a memo to John Smith and Sasha Jenish requesting a meeting to discuss the pricing of cell phones manufactured by your company. Ms. Doe would like you to copy her supervisor, Pamen Loosh. Download a memo template and modify it with the necessary information.

Steps

1 Download the Memo (Professional design) template. You will need to search for the template using the phrase *professional memo*. **Hint:** *In the New backstage area, type* professional memo *in the search box and press Enter.*

2 In the company name placeholder, type Premier Cell Phones.

3 For *To*, type John Smith, press Enter, type Sasha Jenish, and press Enter. For *From*, type your name. For *cc*, type Pamen Loosh. For *Date*, click the *Date* option box arrow and select *Today* to automatically show the current date. For *Re*, type Pricing of Phones.

4 Replace *[Type memo here]* with Meeting called by Jane Doe, CFO. Press Enter.

5 Enter the paragraph below, which is also shown in the finished sample.
   Please mark your schedule to attend a meeting on Wed March 17 at 2:00 PM in Conference Room

A to discuss the selling price of our cell phones. The cost of our materials has risen dramatically over the past three months, necessitating a price increase to our vendors. It is imperative that we find ways to hold the increase to a minimum. Please respond with your intention to attend.

6 Use the spelling and grammar checker to locate and correct errors. Proofread the document to be sure it is correct.

7 Use Save As to save the file with the name **Lastname-M5-C1-ExB-Memo**, but replace *Lastname* with your last name. A dialog box advising that *Your document will be upgraded to the newest file format* may display. Click OK to upgrade the memo to the newest file format before saving.

8 Print a hard copy or submit the file as directed by your instructor.

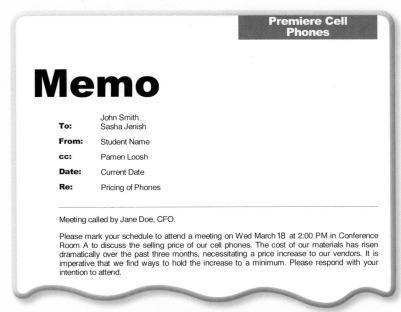

Completed Exercise B

Exercise **C** **Change Document Properties and Insert Elements into a Story**

Skills Enter and edit text; use cut, copy, and paste; use the Show/Hide ¶ feature; indent and add tabs using the ruler; set margins; insert a page break; and insert headers and footers

Scenario Your friend told you a story about her missing chocolate bars. You write the story and decide to submit it to a local publication that prints amusing tales. You have reviewed the submission guidelines and need to make some changes to your document for it to be acceptable for submission.

Steps

1 Open the student data file named **M5-C1-ExC-Chocolate.docx** and save the file as **Lastname-M5-C1-ExC-Chocolate**, but replace *Lastname* with your last name.

2 Turn on Show/Hide ¶ to display formatting marks, and insert a page break at the end of the document.

3 Select the text on the first page of the document (including the final paragraph symbol but excluding the Page Break indicator), copy it, and then paste it on the empty second page. You should now have two identical pages in this document. **NOTE:** *If you have a third, blank page, you may have copied the page break. Position the insertion point at the end of the document and backspace until you have only two pages.*

4 Add a header to the document that includes your name in the left margin and the current date in the right margin. **HINT:** *Click the INSERT tab, Click the Header button, and then click the Blank (Three Columns) option. Use the left and right placeholders and delete the one in the center.*

5 Add a footer that places the page number in the center of the footer.

6 Change the margins to 1 inch on the top and bottom and 2 inches on the left and right.

NOTE: *Perform all editing in Steps 7, 8, and 9 on Page 2 of the document.*

7 Replace the words *My brother* and *My sister* with the names of your brother and sister. If you do not have a brother or sister, use the names of friends.

8 Select those lines in the middle of the document that represent the responses of your family members to your questioning (the lines beginning with *Mom* and ending with *Who me?*) and set a left tab at 1.5 inches. **HINT:** *You may need to make the ruler visible.*

9 Indent the first line of the two paragraphs by one-half inch. **HINT:** *See* Taking It Further *in Skill 6.*

10 Save and close the file.

11 Print a hard copy or submit the file as directed by your instructor.

Student Name   Current Date

I Want Chocolate!

Last night after dinner I decided to enjoy a piece of chocolate. But when
I went to my secret chocolate hiding place, I found out it was empty! I
was sure I had at least 3 candy bars hidden away. Someone had found
my stash. I asked each member of my family if they had eaten my
chocolate bars. Here are the answers they provided:

Mom   No.

Dad   No.

My brother   Why would I have your chocolate?

My sister   No, but can I have a candy bar if you find them?

Grandmother   No, but here's $5.00 so you can buy more.

Grandfather   Who me?

I thanked my Grandmother and went to the store to purchase more
candy bars. I ate one on the way home and hid the others in a new
secret hiding place. Later that night, the mystery of the disappearing
chocolate was solved. I found the wrappers from one of my candy bars.
It was hiding under my Grandfather's pillow!

1

Student Name   Current Date

I Want Chocolate!

Last night after dinner I decided to enjoy a piece of chocolate.
But when I went to my secret chocolate hiding place, I found out it was
empty! I was sure I had at least 3 candy bars hidden away. Someone had
found my stash. I asked each member of my family if they had eaten my
chocolate bars. Here are the answers they provided:

Mom   No.

Dad   No.

Brother Name   Why would I have your chocolate?

Sister Name   No, but can I have a candy bar if you find them?

Grandmother   No, but here's $5.00 so you can buy more.

Grandfather   Who me?

I thanked my Grandmother and went to the store to purchase
more candy bars. I ate one on the way home and hid the others in a
new secret hiding place. Later that night, the mystery of the
disappearing chocolate was solved. I found the wrappers from one of
my candy bars. It was hiding under my Grandfather's pillow!

2

Completed Exercise C

Chapter 2

Formatting Documents

In Chapter 1 you learned about creating documents, entering and editing text, and working with page layout in Word. In this chapter you will learn how to format text so that it is attractive and easy to read. Formatting involves working with fonts and effects, such as bold, italic, and underlining. Word offers some nice shortcuts in the form of styles, which are formatting settings grouped together so that you can apply the group of settings with a single step. World also includes the Format Painter, which allows you to copy formats from one section of text to another. These tools are all accessible on the HOME tab. On the DESIGN tab, Word groups some formatting tools together in themes. Themes use unique sets of colors, fonts, and effects to make it even easier for you to give your documents a consistent look and feel.

Formatting tools enable you to organize text by aligning it on the page or putting it into bulleted or numbered lists. You can call attention to the elements of your text and help your readers find their way through the document when you organize and arrange your text and add useful spaces within it.

When writing reports or research papers, it is important that you include the appropriate citations for the sources you have used to create your document. Word offers tools to help you cite sources properly using accepted, professional styles for endnotes, citations, and works cited pages.

Skills You Learn

1 Change font and font size
2 Use formatting tools
3 Apply styles
4 Align text
5 Format paragraph and line spacing
6 Create bulleted or numbered lists
7 Copy formatting with Format Painter
8 Insert a footnote
9 Insert citations using professional styles
10 Create a Works Cited page
11 Format text in columns

Files You Need
For these skills, you need the following student data files.

M5-C2-S1-MayanCulture.docx

M5-C2-S8-MayanCulture.docx

What You Create

A large part of The Chocolate Museum's mission is to educate the public about the role of chocolate in societies throughout recorded history. You have been asked to write a short report on chocolate's role in the Mayan society, a group of sovereign states with a common culture, which was located primarily in southern Mexico and on the Yucatan Peninsula. Chocolate had a role in the economy, mythology, and religious rites of this society. Your report will be available to visitors in a special display in the lobby of the Museum, so you want to make it both informative and attractive.

In this chapter, you work with Word formatting tools to refine the report's appearance and with references tools to make sure that all sources are accurately credited.

Report on Mayan Culture

Origins of Chocolate in Mayan Culture

Report from The Chocolate Museum, Posted February 24, 2015

Introduction
Key Points

- Cacao was an important crop and cultural influence in the Mayan culture
- The Mayan culture began cultivating cocoa over 2,500 years ago
- Chocolate became a major force in Mayan society
- In the heyday of Mayan society cacao beans were an important commodity

Cacao was an important crop and cultural influence in the Mayan culture, a Central American society with a rich heritage of early written language, art, architecture, and astronomical systems. This culture is thought to have peaked between 250 AD and 900 AD. Its demise was largely brought about by the arrival of Spanish explorers in the seventeenth century.

Cacao's popularity followed this timeline:

1. Traces of chocolate found in Mayan pots dating from 600 BC.
2. Cacao and hot water brewed by Mayans and Aztecs in Pre-Columbian era.
3. Cortez brings hot chocolate back to Spain in 1527.
4. European courts develop passion for chocolate drinks in seventeenth and eighteenth centuries.
5. 1825 Van Houten of Holland discovers how to degrease chocolate, spreading its popularity.

Cacao Varieties
The Mayan culture began cultivating cocoa over 2,500 years ago. Criollo cacao came from Central America, and evolved separately from the cacao in the Amazon River basin that belong to the Forastero variety. Criollo cacao trees are still found in the Lacadonia rainforest.[1]

Criollo cacao is a wild variety that is genetically distinct from the other varieties of cacao found throughout Central and South America.

---

[1] The Lacadonia rainforest is located in the eastern part of the state of Chiapas, Mexico.

Chocolate through History
One of the Mayan myths of creation tells of a woman who stroked a head impaled on a cacao tree and then magically became impregnated. She escaped to earth to avoid her father's wrath and gave birth to twins, the ancestors of the Mayan culture.

Chocolate was a major force in Mayan society. Pottery cups unearthed in the nineteenth century are called *chocolateros* by local Indians and were possibly used in ceremonial events. These cups include hollow handles, which were used to blow into a chocolate drink to create foam, a practice especially associated with Mayans (see *Figure 1.1*).

Figure 1.1: A Mayan pottery cup known as a "chocolatero."

Traces of chocolate drinks found on Mayan pottery were analyzed and the contents suggest that Mayans also added honey and pepper to their drinks. (Trivedi)

Chocolate and the Mayan Economy
In the heyday of Mayan society, cacao beans were an important commodity used in trade among the Mayans and with other societies. For example, a record from 1530 notes the purchase of a rabbit and some turkey eggs for 10 cacao beans. However, the value of cacao declined over the years, according to the Museum of San Cristobal. In 1535, 200 beans were worth one real (a unit of currency). By 1720, according to Robert Miller, "one real would be worth only 15 beans." (Miller)

Works Cited
Miller, Robert J. *The Mayan Empire*. New York: Cultural Exchange, 1998.

Trivedi, Bijal P. "Ancient Chocolate Found in a Mayan Teapot." *National Geographic Today* (2012): 24–30. Electronic.

Word

Video ▶ M5_C2_S01

Change Font and Font Size

Fonts are character sets for the text you type. Using them effectively can add visual appeal to your documents. Word comes with many built-in fonts that you can apply to some or to all of the text in your document. Some font families, such as Arial, come in several variations—in this case, Arial, Arial Bold, and Arial Narrow. You can also modify the font size to add emphasis or increase readability.

Steps

1 Open the student data file named **M5-C2-S1-MayanCulture.docx**, and if you have not already done so, save the file in your Module 5 working folder on your storage medium.

2 Select the words *The Chocolate Museum* in the second line. (Do not select the comma.)

3 In the Font group on the HOME tab, click the Font button arrow and then click *Arial* in the *All Fonts* section of the drop-down list.

4 With *The Chocolate Museum* still selected, click the Font Size button arrow and then click *14* in the drop-down list.

5 Scroll down to the second page of the document and select the words *Figure 1.1* that appear below the photo.

6 In the Font group, click the Font button arrow and then click *Arial* in the *Recently Used Fonts* section of the drop-down list.

7 Click the Save button on the Quick Access toolbar to save the file.

4 *Another Way*
Click in the *Font Size* text box and type the number of the font size you want.

▶ *Tip* From the Font dialog box, you can make multiple changes to font formatting (including font style, font size, and font effects). Open the Font dialog box by clicking the dialog box launcher in the bottom right corner of the Font group on the HOME tab.

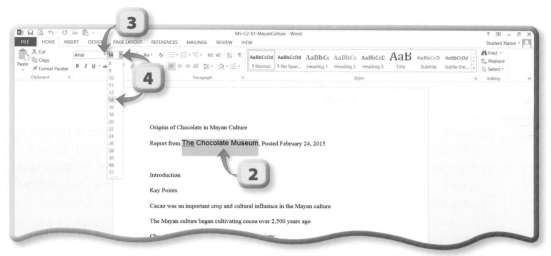

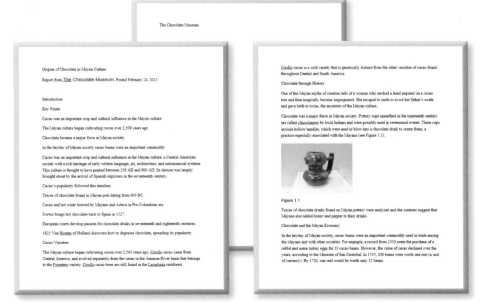

Completed Skill 1

Word

Chapter 2

Skill 2

Use Formatting Tools

Video M5_C2_S02

There are several ways you can format text beyond choosing the font and font size. You can apply effects such as bold, italic, underlining, and color. Bold and italics add emphasis. Italics are widely used for book and movie titles. Underlining is frequently used to indicate URLs. You can also change the font color to add visual interest and emphasize the tone of your document. Choose only a few font colors and select colors that either blend or contrast with each other. Keep in mind how your document will be viewed. If it will be viewed on-screen or printed on a color printer, emphasizing with color will work well. If it will be printed in black and white, using font colors will not help the look of your document.

Steps

1 If it is not already open, open **M5-C2-S1-MayanCulture.docx**, the file you saved in the previous skill, and save the file as **M5-C2-S2-MayanCulture**.

2 Select the fourth line of text, *Key Points*.

3 Shortcut
Underline Text
Ctrl + U

3 Click the Underline button in the Font group on the HOME tab.

4 Select the text *The Chocolate Museum* in the second line. (Do not select the comma after *Museum*.)

▶**Tip** More color options are available by selecting the Colors button on the DESIGN tab. You can also create and save custom themes by selecting the *Customize Colors* option.

5 Click the Font Color button arrow in the Font group and then select *Tan, Background 2, Darker 50%* from the color palette that appears.

6 Scroll down to the second page of the document and select the words *Figure 1.1* that appear below the photo.

7 Shortcut
Bold Text
Ctrl + B

7 Click the Bold button in the Font group.

8 Select the text *Figure 1.1* inside the parentheses at the end of the paragraph just above the photo.

9 Shortcut
Italicize Text
Ctrl + I

9 Click the Italic button in the Font group.

10 Save the file.

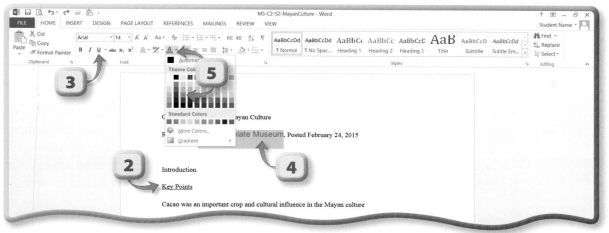

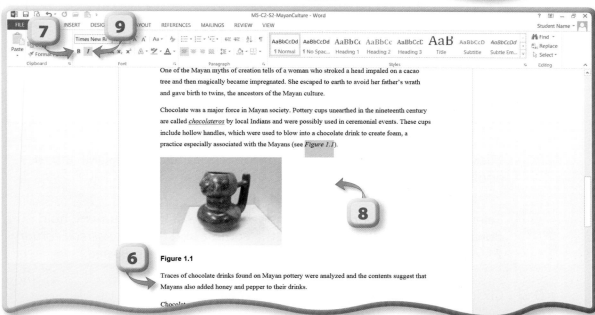

Figure 1.1

Traces of chocolate drinks found on Mayan pottery were analyzed and the contents suggest that Mayans also added honey and pepper to their drinks.

Completed Skill 2

Word

Video ▶ M5_C2_S03

Apply Styles

Styles are built-in groups of formatting settings that you can apply to text with one action rather than having to perform multiple, separate formatting actions. Styles are useful for creating headings in your documents or for formatting your company name in a unique way. You can even create and save your own styles for use in all documents.

Steps

1 If it is not already open, open **M5-C2-S2-MayanCulture.docx**, the file you saved in the previous skill, and save the file as **M5-C2-S3-MayanCulture**.

2 Click anywhere in the document heading *Origins of Chocolate in Mayan Culture*.

3 Click the *Heading 1* style option in the Styles group on the HOME tab to apply the style.

4 Select the words *Report from* on the second line of the document, hold down the Ctrl key, and then select the comma and the text *Posted February 24, 2015*. (Be sure to include the comma before the word *Posted*.)

5 Click the *Heading 2* option in the Styles gallery.

6 Apply the Heading 1 style to the following lines of text: *Introduction*, *Cacao Varieties*, *Chocolate through History*, and *Chocolate and the Mayan Economy*.

7 Save the file.

▶**Tip** If you don't see the style you want, click the More button in the bottom right corner of the Styles gallery to display all styles.

▶**Tip** To quickly apply a style to several areas of the document, select the first area of text, press and hold down Ctrl while you select the others, and then apply the style to all selected text with one click.

Taking It Further

Using Style Sets You can quickly change the appearance of your document by applying a style set. Style sets are predesigned sets of font and paragraph properties. To apply a style set, click a style set in the Document Formatting group on the DESIGN tab. You can also create your own style set by formatting a document and then clicking the More button in the Document Formatting gallery. In the list of links at the bottom, click *Save as New Style Set*, give the style a name, and then click the OK button.

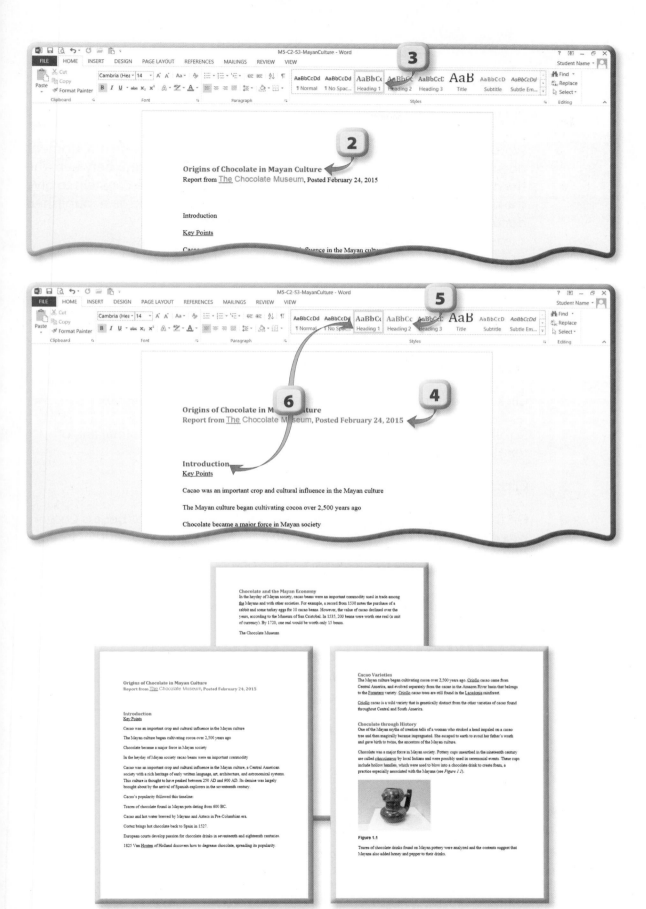

Completed Skill 3

Word

Skill 4

Video M5_C2_S04

Align Text

Word allows you to align text in your document in four ways relative to the margins that are set: at the left, at the right, in the center, or justified. A document's default alignment is at the left margin. Document titles are often centered. Justified alignment spreads the text out between the two margins, which can help to give your text the look of a published book or magazine.

Steps

1 If it is not already open, open **M5-C2-S3-MayanCulture.docx**, the file you saved in the previous skill, and save the file as **M5-C2-S4-MayanCulture**.

2 Select the first two lines of text in the document.

3 Click the Center button in the Paragraph group on the HOME tab.

4 Scroll to the end of the document and click anywhere in the final line of text, *The Chocolate Museum*.

5 Click the Center button.

6 On the first page of the document, select the paragraph that begins *Cacao was an important crop* (not the first line after *Key Points*), press and hold down the Ctrl key, and then select the text paragraphs that start with the following phrases:

> *The Mayan culture began cultivating cocoa*
> *Criollo cacao is a wild variety*
> *One of the Mayan myths of creation*
> *Chocolate was a major force in Mayan*
> *Traces of chocolate drinks found on Mayan pottery*
> *In the heyday of Mayan society*

7 Click the Justify button in the Paragraph group on the HOME tab.

8 Save the file.

3 Shortcut
Center Text
Ctrl + E

▶ **Tip** Use the single down arrow near the bottom of the scroll bar to navigate through the document.

▶ **Tip** Triple-click to select a paragraph.

▶ **Tip** To see more than one page at the same time in your Word window, click the Multiple Pages button in the Zoom group on the VIEW tab.

7 Shortcut
Justify Text
Ctrl + J

Taking It Further

Formatting with Tabs You can only apply one alignment setting to a paragraph. For example, you cannot align your address at the left and your phone number at the right on the same line at the top of your resume. Instead, left align the text and set a right tab at the right margin. Enter the address, press the Tab key, and then enter the phone number.

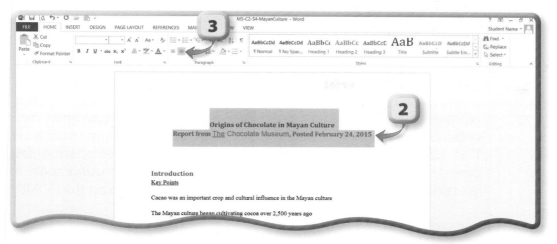

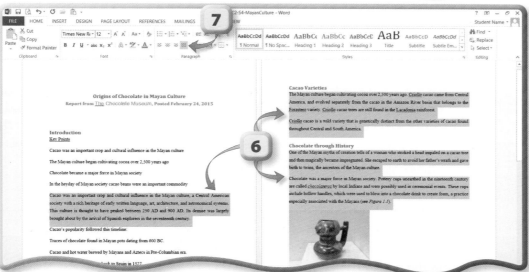

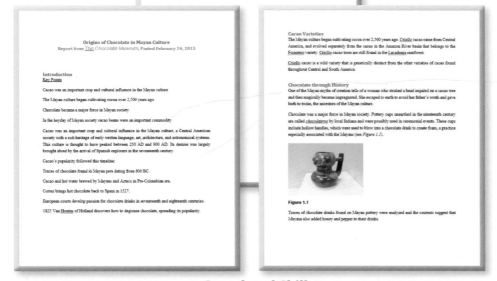

Completed Skill 4

Word

Chapter 2

Skill 5

Video ▶ **M5_C2_S05**

Format Paragraph and Line Spacing

Word enables you to adjust spacing between the lines of a paragraph. The amount of white space you provide between lines can affect the readability of your document. It can also provide a visual break between the paragraphs in your text. You can apply preset spacing settings to selected text using tools in the Paragraph group on the HOME tab.

Steps

1 If it is not already open, open **M5-C2-S4-MayanCulture.docx**, the file you saved in the previous skill, and save the file as **M5-C2-S5-MayanCulture**.

2 On the first page of the document, select the paragraph that begins *Cacao was an important crop* (not the first line after *Key Points*), press and hold down the Ctrl key, and then select the text paragraphs that start with the following phrases:

> *The Mayan culture began cultivating cocoa*
> *Criollo cacao is a wild variety*
> *One of the Mayan myths of creation*
> *Chocolate was a major force in Mayan*
> *Traces of chocolate drinks found on Mayan pottery*
> *In the heyday of Mayan society*

3 Another Way
Open the Paragraph dialog box by clicking the dialog box launcher in the Paragraph group on the HOME tab. In the *Spacing* section, click the arrow next to the *At* text box and then select *1.15* from the drop-down list. Click OK.

3 With the paragraphs still selected, click the Line and Paragraph Spacing button in the Paragraph group on the HOME tab and then click *1.15* in the drop-down list.

4 Select the first two lines of the document (the title and subtitle).

5 Click the dialog box launcher ⬚ in the bottom right corner of the Paragraph group.

6 Another Way
Type a value in the *After* measurement box.

6 In the Paragraph dialog box that appears, click the up-pointing arrow at the right side of the *After* measurement box in the *Spacing* section until *12 pt* displays.

7 Click OK to close the dialog box. Extra space has been added after the selected paragraphs.

8 Save the file.

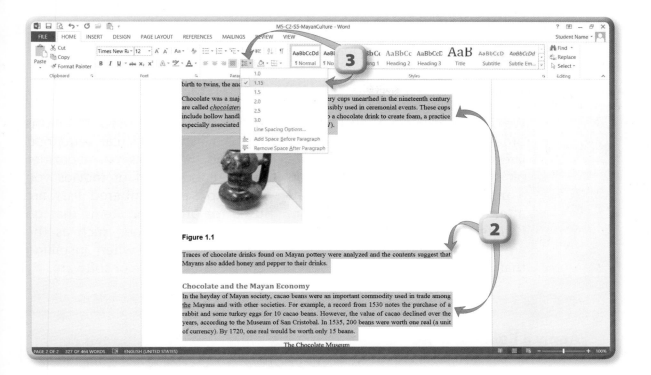

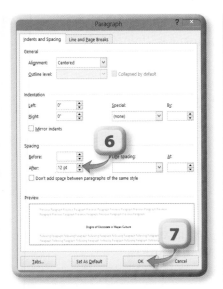

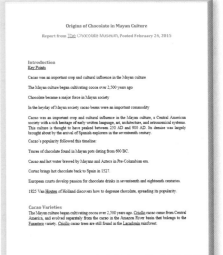

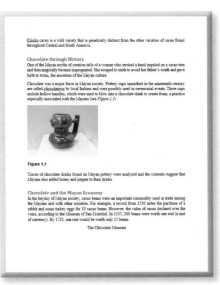

Completed Skill 5

Taking It Further

Formatting Line Spacing   You can further customize line spacing by using the *Before* measurement box in the *Spacing* section in the Paragraph dialog box. By changing the value in this measurement box, you can set how much space appears before a paragraph as well as within or after a paragraph.

Word

Video M5_C2_S06

Create Bulleted or Numbered Lists

We all make lists that help us organize the information in our lives. In documents, lists help to set off similar items, indicate steps in a procedure, or draw the reader's attention to certain information. Bulleted lists and numbered lists are two common types of lists that are easy to set up in Word.

Bulleted lists are used for items that have no particular sequence, such as the books or magazines on your bookshelf or movies you want to see. Numbered lists are used for organizing items that go in a particular order, such as the steps you follow when installing computer hardware or software.

Steps

Apply a Bulleted Style

1 If it is not already open, open **M5-C2-S5-MayanCulture.docx**, the file you saved in the previous skill, and save the file as **M5-C2-S6-MayanCulture**.

2 Select the four lines under the underlined heading *Key Points* on the first page.

3 Click the Bullets button in the Paragraph group on the HOME tab.

Apply a Numbered Style

4 Select the five lines after the paragraph that reads *Cacao's popularity followed this timeline*.

5 Click the Numbering button in the Paragraph group on the HOME tab. The default numbered list style is applied to the selected steps.

6 Save the file.

2 *Another Way* Click at the beginning of the first line of text to be selected, press and hold the Shift key, and then click at the end of the last line to make the selection.

▶**Tip** Clicking the Bullets button applies the default bullet style at the beginning of each selected paragraph. You can choose different bulleted list styles, such as square or diamond shapes rather than circles, by clicking the Bullets button arrow.

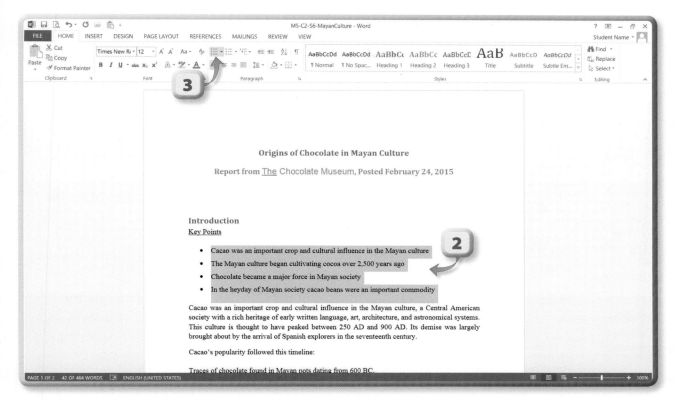

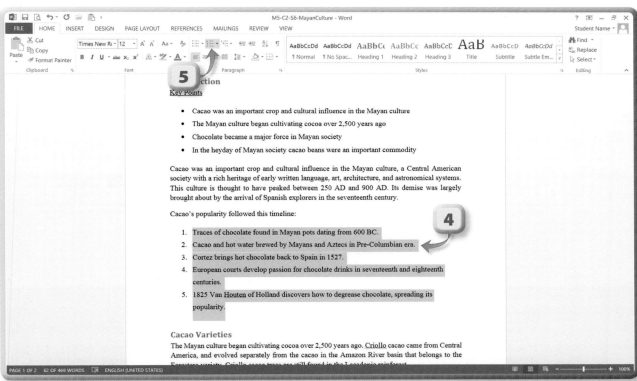

Tip As is true for bullets, you can choose different styles for numbered lists by clicking the Numbering button arrow. You might prefer using letters rather than numbers or choose Roman numerals over Arabic numerals.

Tip Click the Font button in the Define New Bullet dialog box to format the appearance of the bullets themselves, such as changing their font, font size, and font color, or applying bold, italic, or underline effects.

12 Another Way
Click a symbol instead of entering its character code.

Apply a Custom Bullet Style

7 Select the bulleted text under the *Key Points* heading on the first page of the document.

8 Click the Bullets button arrow.

9 In the drop-down gallery that appears, click *Define New Bullet*.

10 Click the Symbol button in the Define New Bullet dialog box to open the Symbol dialog box.

11 Click the *Font* option box arrow, scroll down the list, and then select *Wingdings*.

12 Select the number that appears in the *Character code* text box and then type 175.

13 Click OK to close the Symbol dialog box.

14 Click OK to close the Define New Bullet dialog box and apply the new bullet style.

15 Save the file.

Origins of Chocolate in Mayan Culture

Report from The Chocolate Museum, Posted February 24, 2015

Introduction
Key Points

* Cacao was an important crop and cultural influence in the Mayan culture
* The Mayan culture began cultivating cocoa over 2,500 years ago
* Chocolate became a major force in Mayan society
* In the heyday of Mayan society cacao beans were an important commodity

Cacao was an important crop and cultural influence in the Mayan culture, a Central American society with a rich heritage of early written language, art, architecture, and astronomical systems. This culture is thought to have peaked between 250 AD and 900 AD. Its demise was largely brought about by the arrival of Spanish explorers in the seventeenth century.

Cacao's popularity followed this timeline:

1. Traces of chocolate found in Mayan pots dating from 600 BC.
2. Cacao and hot water brewed by Mayans and Aztecs in Pre-Columbian era.
3. Cortez brings hot chocolate back to Spain in 1527.
4. European courts develop passion for chocolate drinks in seventeenth and eighteenth centuries.
5. 1825 Van Houten of Holland discovers how to degrease chocolate, spreading its popularity.

Cacao Varieties
The Mayan culture began cultivating cocoa over 2,500 years ago. Criollo cacao came from Central America, and evolved separately from the cacao in the Amazon River basin that belongs to the Forastero variety. Criollo cacao trees are still found in the Lacadonia rainforest.

Criollo cacao is a wild variety that is genetically distinct from the other varieties of cacao found throughout Central and South America.

Chocolate through History
One of the Mayan myths of creation tells of a woman who stroked a head impaled on a cacao tree and then magically became impregnated. She escaped to earth to avoid her father's wrath and gave birth to twins, the ancestors of the Mayan culture.

Chocolate was a major force in Mayan society. Pottery cups unearthed in the nineteenth century are called *chocolateros* by local Indians and were possibly used in ceremonial events. These cups include hollow handles, which were used to blow into a chocolate drink to create foam, a practice especially associated with the Mayans (see *Figure 1.1*).

Figure 1.1

Traces of chocolate drinks found on Mayan pottery were analyzed and the contents suggest that Mayans also added honey and pepper to their drinks.

Chocolate and the Mayan Economy
In the heyday of Mayan society, cacao beans were an important commodity used in trade among the Mayans and with other societies. For example, a record from 1530 notes the purchase of a rabbit and some turkey eggs for 10 cacao beans. However, the value of cacao declined over the years, according to the Museum of San Cristobal. In 1535, 200 beans were worth one real (a unit of currency). By 1720, one real would be worth only 15 beans.

The Chocolate Museum

Completed Skill 6

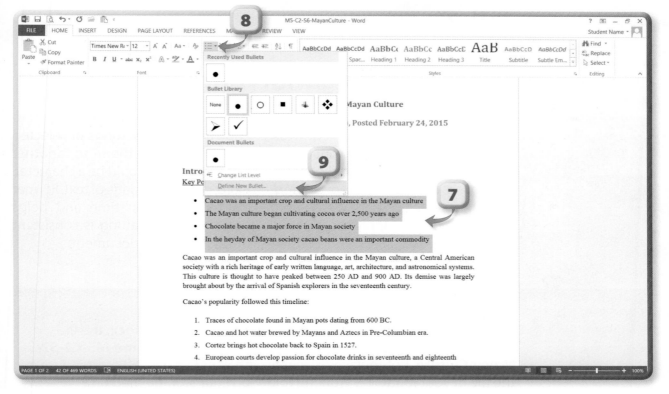

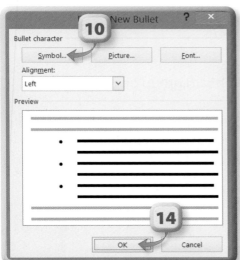

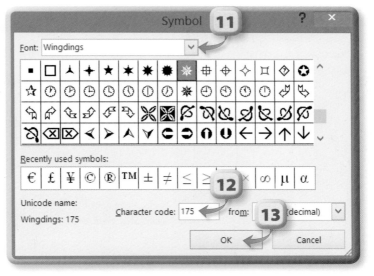

Taking It Further

Creating Lists with Multiple Levels

To create a multilevel numbered or bulleted list, place your cursor just before the item you want to move to a new level. Use the Increase Indent and Decrease Indent buttons in the Paragraph group on the HOME tab to move the item lower or to higher or lower levels in the list. You can also use the keyboard to change the levels of list items. Press the Tab key and the item indents one level. If you type text and then press Enter, the cursor automatically moves to the start of a new line at the same indent level. Press Shift + Tab to move an item up one level. Using these methods, you can modify any numbered or bulleted list to contain multiple levels.

Word

Video M5_C2_S07

Copy Formatting with Format Painter

Once you have formatted some of the text in your document—for example, by applying a font style, adding settings such as bold or italic, modifying the text color, or setting the line spacing and paragraph indents—you can apply those same settings to other text using Format Painter. Format Painter allows you to copy the format settings of selected text and apply them to another selection, which could be a character, word, or an entire page of text. Format Painter saves you time and helps ensure that formatting is consistent throughout your document.

Steps

1 If it is not already open, open **M5-C2-S6-MayanCulture.docx**, the file you saved in the previous skill, and save the file as **Lastname-M5-C2-S7-MayanCulture**, but replace *Lastname* with your last name. Be sure to save the file in your Module 5 working folder on your storage medium.

2 Click anywhere in the phrase *The Chocolate Museum* in the report subheading on page 1.

3 Click the Format Painter button in the Clipboard group on the HOME tab.

3 *Shortcut*
Activate Format Painter
Ctrl + Shift + C

▶*Tip* Use Format Painter to copy formats from one drawn shape, such as a box or circle, to another.

4 Scroll to the bottom of the document and select the last line, *The Chocolate Museum*. Note that the formatting is copied to the destination text.

5 Save and close the file.

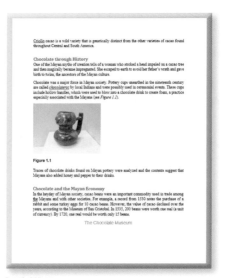

Completed Skill 7

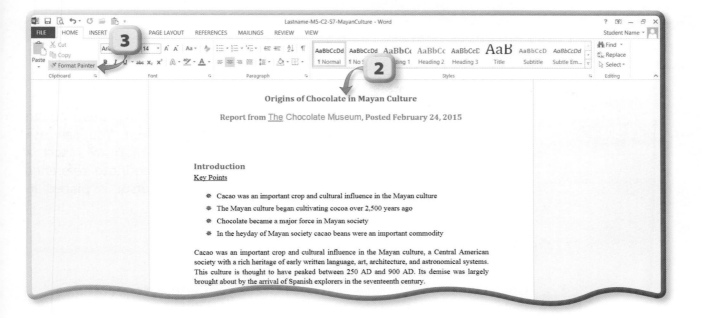

Taking It Further

Using Format Painter Multiple Times

You can use Format Painter to copy formatting to more than one place in your document. In Step 3 of Skill 7, double-click the Format Painter button and then apply the format to as many paragraphs, words, or phrases as you like. When you are done, click the Format Painter button again, or press the Esc key on your keyboard to deactivate Format Painter.

Word

Video ▶ M5_C2_S08

Insert a Footnote

Reports and research papers include footnotes or endnotes to document sources and add information about subjects mentioned in the text. Footnotes place information at the bottom of a page, in contrast with endnotes which place them at the end of a document. You can use the REFERENCES tab to insert a footnote or an endnote reference wherever your cursor is placed in your document.

Steps

1 Open the student data file named **C1-S8-MayanCulture.docx** and, if you have not already done so, save the file in your Module 5 working folder on your storage medium.

2 Click after the period that follows the words *Lacadonia rainforest* at the end of the first paragraph under the heading *Cacao Varieties*.

3 Click the REFERENCES tab.

4 Click the Insert Footnote button in the Footnotes group. A footnote reference number is inserted and the footnote opens for editing at the bottom of the page.

4 *Shortcut*
Insert a Footnote
Alt + Ctrl + F

▶**Tip** If you prefer to place your notes at the end of the document rather than at the bottom of each page, use endnotes instead of footnotes. Insert an endnote by clicking the Insert Endnote button in the Footnotes group on the REFERENCES tab or by pressing Alt + Ctrl + D.

5 Type the following footnote text: The Lacadonia rainforest is located in the eastern part of the state of Chiapas, Mexico.

6 Save the file.

Completed Skill 8

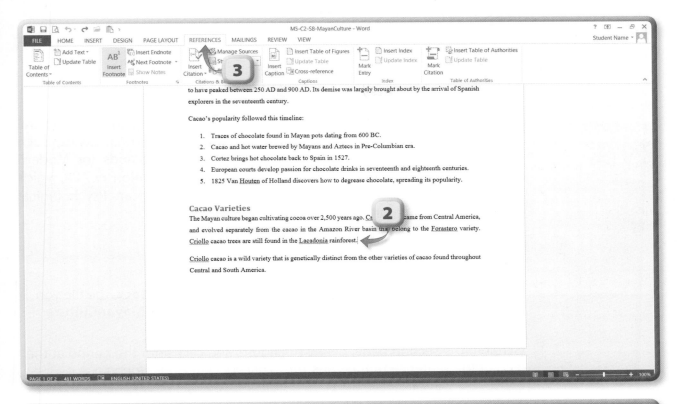

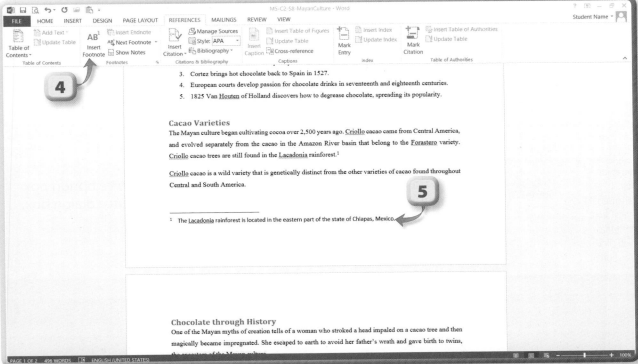

Taking It Further

Navigating Footnotes and Endnotes

To locate footnotes or endnotes in a document, you can use the Next Footnote button on the REFERENCES tab. When you click this button, you can use the options *Next Footnote*, *Previous Footnote*, *Next Endnote*, or *Previous Endnote* to navigate among your footnotes and endnotes.

Word

Video ▶ M5_C2_S09

Insert Citations Using Professional Styles

Citations give appropriate credit to sources you have quoted or taken information from when creating a document. You can use Word's Citation feature to create sources and insert their information within your text according to one of several accepted professional styles, such as MLA, which stands for Modern Language Association, or APA, which stands for American Psychological Association.

Steps

1 If it is not already open, open **M5-C2-S8-MayanCulture.docx**, the file you saved in the previous skill, and save the file as **M5-C2-S9-MayanCulture**.

2 Scroll to the second page, below the figure, and click after the period at the end of the sentence that begins *Traces of chocolate drinks found*.

3 In the Citations & Bibliography group on the REFERENCES tab, click the *Style* option box arrow and then click *MLA Seventh Edition* in the drop-down list. This option applies the Modern Languages Association professional style for citations.

4 Click the Insert Citation button in the Citations & Bibliography group.

5 Click *Add New Source* in the drop-down list.

▶**Tip** Once you enter information about a resource, you can insert it again by choosing it from the drop-down list that appears when you click the Insert Citation button.

6 Make sure that *Journal Article* is selected in the *Type of Source* option box and then type the following information in the Create Source dialog box.

Author	Trivedi, Bijal P.
Title	Ancient Chocolate Found in a Mayan Teapot
Journal Name	National Geographic Today
Year	2012
Pages	24-30
Medium	Electronic

7 Click OK to insert the citation.

Figure 1.1: A Mayan pottery cup known as a "_____."

Traces of chocolate drinks found on Mayan pottery were analyzed and the contents suggest that Mayans also added honey and pepper to their drinks.

Chocolate and the Mayan Economy

In the heyday of Mayan society, cacao beans were an important commodity used in trade among the Mayans and with other societies. For example, a record from 1530 notes the purchase of a rabbit and some turkey eggs for 10 cacao beans. However, the value of cacao declined over the years, according to the Museum of San Cristobal. In 1535, 200 beans were worth one real (a unit of currency). By 1720, according to Robert Miller, "one real would be worth only 15 beans."

More

8 Click after the final closing quotation mark of the document, located at the end of the last sentence of the paragraph that begins *In the heyday of Mayan society*.

9 Click the Insert Citation button in the Citations & Bibliography group on the REFERENCES tab and then click *Miller, Robert J.*, a source that already exists for the document. This action inserts the citation for the source into the document.

10 Save the file.

Chocolate through History
One of the Mayan myths of creation tells of a woman who stroked a head impaled on a cacao tree and then magically became impregnated. She escaped to earth to avoid her father's wrath and gave birth to twins, the ancestors of the Mayan culture.

Chocolate was a major force in Mayan society. Pottery cups unearthed in the nineteenth century are called *chocolateros* by local Indians and were possibly used in ceremonial events. These cups include hollow handles, which were used to blow into a chocolate drink to create foam, a practice especially associated with Mayans (see *Figure 1.1*).

Figure 1.1: A Mayan pottery cup known as a "chocolatero."

Traces of chocolate drinks found on Mayan pottery were analyzed and the contents suggest that Mayans also added honey and pepper to their drinks. (Trivedi)

Chocolate and the Mayan Economy
In the heyday of Mayan society, cacao beans were an important commodity used in trade among the Mayans and with other societies. For example, a record from 1530 notes the purchase of a rabbit and some turkey eggs for 10 cacao beans. However, the value of cacao declined over the years, according to the Museum of San Cristobal. In 1535, 200 beans were worth one real (a unit of currency). By 1720, according to Robert Miller, "one real would be worth only 15 beans." (Miller)

Origins of Chocolate in Mayan Culture

Report from The Chocolate Museum, Posted February 24, 2015

Introduction
Key Points

* Cacao was an important crop and cultural influence in the Mayan culture
* The Mayan culture began cultivating cocoa over 2,500 years ago
* Chocolate became a major force in Mayan society
* In the heyday of Mayan society cacao beans were an important commodity

Cacao was an important crop and cultural influence in the Mayan culture, a Central American society with a rich heritage of early written language, art, architecture, and astronomical systems. This culture is thought to have peaked between 250 AD and 900 AD. Its demise was largely brought about by the arrival of Spanish explorers in the seventeenth century.

Cacao's popularity followed this timeline:

1. Traces of chocolate found in Mayan pots dating from 600 BC.
2. Cacao and hot water brewed by Mayans and Aztecs in Pre-Columbian era.
3. Cortez brings hot chocolate back to Spain in 1527.
4. European courts develop passion for chocolate drinks in seventeenth and eighteenth centuries.
5. 1825 Van Houten of Holland discovers how to degrease chocolate, spreading its popularity.

Cacao Varieties
The Mayan culture began cultivating cocoa over 2,500 years ago. Criollo cacao came from Central America, and evolved separately from the cacao in the Amazon River basin that belong to the Forastero variety. Criollo cacao trees are still found in the Lacadonia rainforest.[1]

Criollo cacao is a wild variety that is genetically distinct from the other varieties of cacao found throughout Central and South America.

---
[1] The Lacadonia rainforest is located in the eastern part of the state of Chiapas, Mexico.

Completed Skill 9

Traces of chocolate drinks found on Mayan pottery were analyzed and the contents suggest that Mayans also added honey and pepper to their drinks. (Trivedi)

Chocolate and the Mayan Economy

In the heyday of Mayan society, cacao beans were an important commodity used in trade among the Mayans and with other societies. For example, a record from 1530 notes the purchase of a rabbit and some turkey eggs for 10 cacao beans. However, the value of cacao declined over the years, according to the Museum of San Cristobal. In 1535, 200 beans were worth one real (a unit of currency). By 1720, according to Robert Miller, "one real would be worth only 15 beans." (Miller)

Taking It Further

Editing Sources   Once you have entered source information, you may change it by clicking the Manage Sources button in the Citations & Bibliography group on the REFERENCES tab. Clicking this button opens the Source Manager dialog box. In this dialog box you can browse for sources you have saved; preview the styles, such as MLA and APA; and add, edit, or delete sources.

Word

Video ▶ M5_C2_S10

Create a Works Cited Page

Once you have inserted citations in your document, you can create a works cited page to appear at the end of your document and give detailed information about your quoted sources. Adding citations and a works cited page ensures that you have given appropriate credit and avoided plagiarizing another individual's work. This helps your document to be viewed as authoritative and complete.

Steps

1 If it is not already open, open **M5-C2-S9-MayanCulture.docx**, the file you saved in the previous skill, and save the file as **M5-C2-S10-MayanCulture**.

2 Place your cursor at the end of the document, after *(Miller)*.

3 Press Enter.

4 Type Works Cited.

5 Click *Heading 1* in the Styles group on the HOME tab to apply the Heading 1 style to the title and then press Enter.

6 Click the REFERENCES tab.

7 Click the Bibliography button in the Citations & Bibliography group and then click *Insert Bibliography* in the drop-down list that appears. This action inserts the cited works under the *Works Cited* heading.

8 Save the file.

▶**Tip** MLA style requires the works cited list to appear on its own page at the end of the document. To insert a page break, press Ctrl + Enter instead of Enter. Ask your instructor which style he or she prefers.

▶**Tip** Traditionally, a bibliography lists all sources you used as research materials when creating your document, while a works cited page lists only those sources you cited plus particularly relevant works you consulted but did not cite.

Taking It Further

Selecting Citation Styles   The format of citations vary based on the professional standard for publication. Three of the most commonly used standards are MLA (Modern Languages Association), most commonly used in English and humanities publications; APA (American Psychological Association), most commonly used in scientific publications; and Chicago, based on *The Chicago Manual of Style*. Ask your instructor which standard he or she prefers.

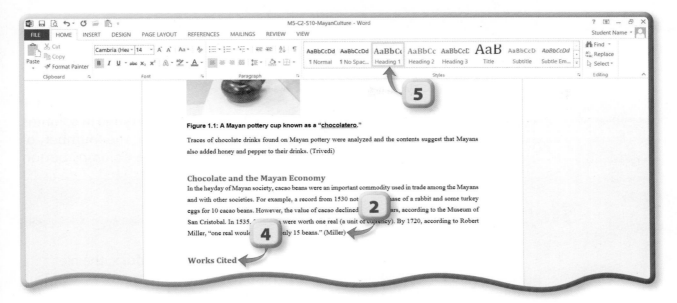

Figure 1.1: A Mayan pottery cup known as a "chocolatero."

Traces of chocolate drinks found on Mayan pottery were analyzed and the contents suggest that Mayans also added honey and pepper to their drinks. (Trivedi)

Chocolate and the Mayan Economy

In the heyday of Mayan society, cacao beans were an important commodity used in trade among the Mayans and with other societies. For example, a record from 1530 not ___ ___ase of a rabbit and some turkey eggs for 10 cacao beans. However, the value of cacao declined ___ ars, according to the Museum of San Cristobal. In 1535, ___ were worth one real (a unit of currency). By 1720, according to Robert Miller, "one real would ___ only 15 beans." (Miller)

Works Cited

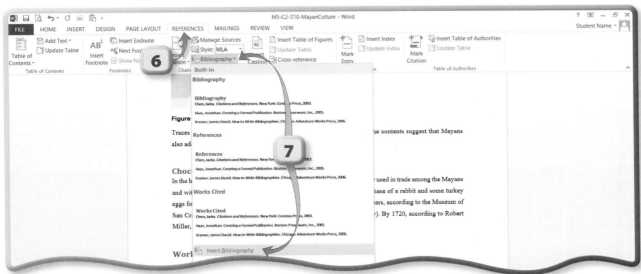

Built-In

Bibliography

Bibliography

Chen, Jacky. *Citations and References*. New York: Contoso Press, 2003.

Haas, Jonathan. *Creating a Formal Publication*. Boston: Proseware, Inc., 2005.

Kramer, James David. *How to Write Bibliographies*. Chicago: Adventure Works Press, 2006.

References

References

Chen, Jacky. *Citations and References*. New York: ___ ___ 2003.

Haas, Jonathan. *Creating a Formal Publication*. Boston: ___ eware, Inc., 2005.

Kramer, James David. *How to Write Bibliographies*. Chicago: Adventure Works Press, 2006.

Works Cited

Works Cited

Chen, Jacky. *Citations and References*. New York: Contoso Press, 2003.

Haas, Jonathan. *Creating a Formal Publication*. Boston: Proseware, Inc., 2005.

Kramer, James David. *How to Write Bibliographies*. Chicago: Adventure Works Press, 2006.

Insert Bibliography

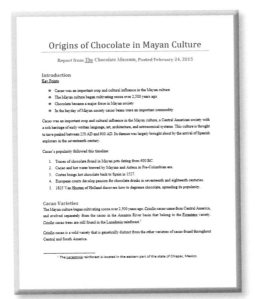

Origins of Chocolate in Mayan Culture

Report from The Chocolate Museum, Posted February 24, 2015

Introduction

Key Points

- Cacao was an important crop and cultural influence in the Mayan culture
- The Mayan culture began cultivating cocoa over 2,500 years ago
- Chocolate became a major force in Mayan society
- In the heyday of Mayan society cacao beans were an important commodity

Cacao was an important crop and cultural influence in the Mayan culture, a Central American society with a rich heritage of early written language, art, architecture, and astronomical systems. This culture is thought to have peaked between 250 AD and 900 AD. Its demise was largely brought about by the arrival of Spanish explorers in the seventeenth century.

Cacao's popularity followed this timeline:

1. Traces of chocolate found in Mayan pots dating from 600 BC.
2. Cacao and hot water brewed by Mayans and Aztecs in Pre-Columbian era.
3. Cortez brings hot chocolate back to Spain in 1527.
4. European courts develop passion for chocolate drinks in seventeenth and eighteenth centuries.
5. 1825 Van Houten of Holland discovers how to degrease chocolate, spreading its popularity.

Cacao Varieties

The Mayan culture began cultivating cocoa over 2,500 years ago. Criollo cacao came from Central America, and evolved separately from the cacao in the Amazon River basin that belong to the Forastero variety. Criollo cacao trees are still found in the Lacadonia rainforest.[1]

Criollo cacao is a wild variety that is genetically distinct from the other varieties of cacao found throughout Central and South America.

---

[1] The Lacadonia rainforest is located in the eastern part of the state of Chiapas, Mexico.

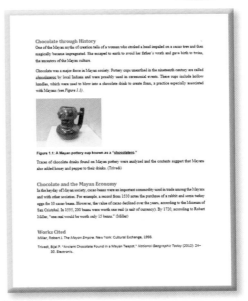

Chocolate through History

One of the Mayan myths of creation tells of a woman who stroked a head impaled on a cacao tree and then magically became impregnated. She escaped to earth to avoid her father's wrath and gave birth to twins, the ancestors of the Mayan culture.

Chocolate was a major force in Mayan society. Pottery cups unearthed in the nineteenth century are called *chocolateros* by local Indians and were possibly used in ceremonial events. These cups include hollow handles, which were used to blow into a chocolate drink to create foam, a practice especially associated with Mayans (see *Figure 1.1*).

Figure 1.1: A Mayan pottery cup known as a "chocolatero."

Traces of chocolate drinks found on Mayan pottery were analyzed and the contents suggest that Mayans also added honey and pepper to their drinks. (Trivedi)

Chocolate and the Mayan Economy

In the heyday of Mayan society, cacao beans were an important commodity used in trade among the Mayans and with other societies. For example, a record from 1530 notes the purchase of a rabbit and some turkey eggs for 10 cacao beans. However, the value of cacao declined over the years, according to the Museum of San Cristobal. In 1535, 200 beans were worth one real (a unit of currency). By 1720, according to Robert Miller, "one real would be worth only 15 beans." (Miller)

Works Cited

Miller, Robert J. *The Mayan Empire*. New York: Cultural Exchange, 1998.

Trivedi, Bijal P. "Ancient Chocolate Found in a Mayan Teapot." *National Geographic Today* (2012): 24–30. Electronic.

Completed Skill 10

Word

Video M5_C2_S11

Format Text in Columns

Using columns in a document can help save space or set off text or lists in an interesting or helpful way. To create columns, simply select the text you want to arrange in columns and then specify the number of columns using the Columns button drop-down list.

Steps

1 If it is not already open, open **M5-C2-S10-MayanCulture.docx**, the file you saved in the previous skill, and save the file as **Lastname-M5-C2-S11-MayanCulture**, but replace *Lastname* with your last name. Be sure to save the file in your Module 5 working folder on your storage medium.

2 Select the four bullets under the heading *Key Points*.

3 Click the PAGE LAYOUT tab.

4 Click the Columns button in the Page Setup group.

5 Click *Two* in the drop-down list.

6 Save and close the file.

▶**Tip** If you need more than three columns, click the *More Columns* option in the drop-down list and adjust the settings in the Columns dialog box.

Taking It Further

More Options for Formatting Columns
If you wish to have two columns of unequal width, you have two options for creating them. First, when selecting the style of column, you can choose the *Left* or *Right* style options in the Columns dialog box. *Left* makes the left column smaller; *Right* makes the right column smaller. If these options do not suit your needs, consider using a table to organize text instead. Tables give you great flexibility in creating columns of varying widths. If you like, you can even remove the border lines around the table, which results in a layout that looks more like columns than like a table. See Chapter 3 for more about creating tables.

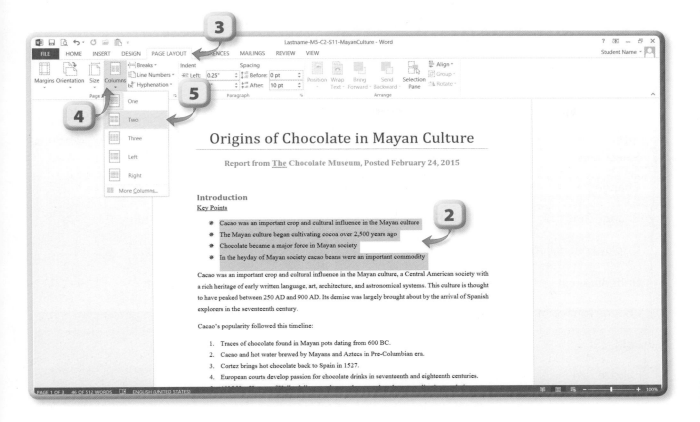

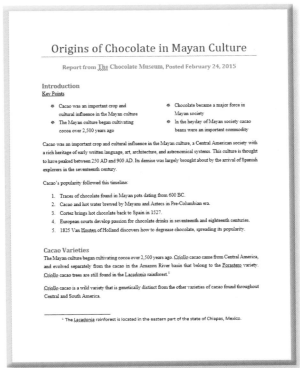

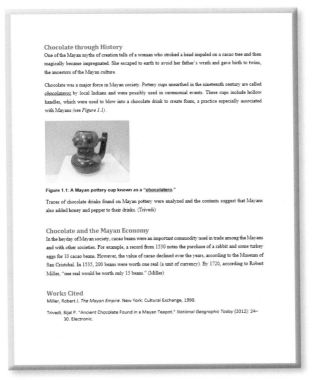

Completed Skill 11

Word

Word

Chapter 2 Assessments

Tasks Summary

Task	Ribbon Tab, Group	Button, Option	Shortcut, Alternative
Select text	HOME, Editing	Select ▾	Selection bar
Change font	HOME, Font	Times New Ro ▾	Ctrl + Shift + F
Change font size	HOME, Font	12 ▾	Ctrl + Shift + P
Display Font dialog box	HOME, Font	⌐	Ctrl + D
Underline text	HOME, Font	U ▾	Ctrl + U
Change font color	HOME, Font	A ▾	
Bold text	HOME, Font	B	Ctrl + B
Italicize text	HOME, Font	I	Ctrl + I
Apply styles	HOME, Styles	Styles Gallery	
Align text left	HOME, Paragraph	≡	Ctrl + L
Align text right	HOME, Paragraph	≡	Ctrl + R
Align text center	HOME, Paragraph	≡	Ctrl + E
Align text justified	HOME, Paragraph	≡	Ctrl + J
Change line spacing	HOME, Paragraph	↕≡ ▾	
Format text as bulleted list	HOME, Paragraph	☰ ▾	
Format text as numbered list	HOME, Paragraph	☰ ▾	
Define custom bullet	HOME, Paragraph	☰ ▾	
Copy formatting	HOME, Clipboard	🖌	Ctrl + Shift + C
Insert footnote	REFERENCES, Footnotes	AB¹	Alt + Ctrl + D
Choose citation style	REFERENCES, Citations & Bibliography	Style: APA ▾	
Insert citation	REFERENCES, Citations & Bibliography	⌐	
Create a works cited page	REFERENCES, Citations & Bibliography	Bibliography ▾	
Format text in columns	PAGE LAYOUT, Page Setup	▤	

Features Review

Select the best answer from the choices given.

1 Fonts are
   a. effects such as bold and underline.
   b. character sets for type.
   c. either italic or bold.
   d. the way Word formats text.

2 Heading 1 is a
   a. font.
   b. template.
   c. style.
   d. reference.

3 Left, center, right, and justify are examples of
   a. tabs.
   b. alignments.
   c. margins.
   d. headers and footers.

4 Paragraph settings are found on this tab.
   a. INSERT
   b. HOME
   c. FILE
   d. VIEW

5 Bullets are typically used for a list of items
   a. that has no sequence.
   b. that has a particular sequence.

6 Format Painter is used to
   a. copy text.
   b. format pictures.
   c. copy formatting from one section of the document to another.
   d. duplicate headings across pages.

7 Endnotes place information
   a. at the bottom of the page.
   b. at the end of the document.
   c. in a footer.
   d. in a header.

8 One common professional style used in documents is
   a. MLB.
   b. MLA.
   c. ABA.
   d. Illinois.

9 A works cited page helps to ensure that you
   a. provide appropriate credit to your sources.
   b. have plagiarized the cited work.
   c. have included endnotes in your document.
   d. have followed appropriate style guidelines.

10 To create columns from existing text you must
   a. set tabs.
   b. click the Columns button and then select text.
   c. first select text and then click the Columns button.
   d. change margins.

Hands-On Skills Review

Exercise **A** **Format a Document about Formatting**

Grade It

Skills Change font and font size, use formatting tools, align text, format paragraph and line spacing, copy formatting with Format Painter, and format text in columns

Scenario Use various formatting tools to add emphasis and highlight important information in this document that describes Word formatting features.

Steps

1 Open the student data file named **M5-C2-ExA-Formatting.docx** and save the file as **Lastname-M5-C2-ExA-Formatting**, but replace *Lastname* with your last name.

2 Add a header to the document that includes your name at the left margin and the current date at the right margin.

3 Add a footer to the document, placing the page number in the center.

4 Remove the first-line indentation from all paragraphs beginning with *Using Microsoft Word* and ending with *even more useful*. **HINT:** *Click the dialog box launcher in the Paragraph group on the HOME tab. In the Indentation section, click the* Special *option box arrow and select* (none). *Click OK.*

5 Add 10 point spacing after each paragraph. **HINT:** *Select all text in the document from* Format It! *through* even more useful. *and then apply the spacing.*

6 Justify the document body. **HINT:** *Select all text in the document from* Format It! *through* even more useful. *and then change the alignment.*

7 Place the names of the tabs on the Microsoft Word ribbon (from *FILE* to *VIEW*) into two columns of equal size. **HINT:** *Turn on Show/Hide ¶ to be sure you only select the tab names and their paragraph symbols.*

8 Set the line spacing for all paragraphs beginning with *Using Microsoft Word* and ending with *even more useful* to 1.15.

9 Change the font of the title (*Format It!*) to Script MT Bold and set the font size to 22 points.

10 Italicize all instances of *Microsoft Word, Word,* or *Word's.* **HINT:** *Italicize the first occurrence. Double-click the Format Painter button and then double-click the next instance of* Word. *It automatically adopts the same formatting. Continue in this manner until you have italicized all occurrences of* Word. *Click the Format Painter button again to turn off the feature.*

11 Bold the text that begins with *Term paper* and ends with *problem.* Be sure to bold the period after the word *problem.*

12 Underline *spelling bee champ.*

13 Save and close the file.

14 Print or submit the completed document as directed by your instructor.

Student Name   Current Date

Format It!

Using *Microsoft Word* I can start with a blank document and add text and graphics to create professional letters, memos, flyers, and other publications. Often, I can save time by starting from predesigned documents called templates that are available for use with *Word.* For example, if I open a letter template, the letter is already formatted for me. All I need to do is to put the correct text in the appropriate location. *Word* even offers tools that help me enter and edit text, move or copy text from one place in a document to another, and format the text to make it look exactly the way I like.

Since I'm not a <u>spelling bee champ</u>, I really appreciate the spelling check feature of *Word.* I even taught it to spell my name! **Term paper assigned? No problem.** I can use special reference tools to make it easy to enter citations, endnotes, footnotes, and works cited.

There are several tabs in *Word,* which help me utilize *Word's* capabilities. Most tabs change the ribbon content and are organized to help me perform tasks I know, and to easily learn and try new tasks. The tabs are:

FILE	REFERENCES
HOME	MAILINGS
INSERT	REVIEW
DESIGN	VIEW
PAGE LAYOUT	

The capabilities of Word are impressive. I'm ready to learn how to make *Word* even more useful.

1

Completed Exercise A

Exercise B Format an Exercise List

Skills Change font and font size, use formatting tools, align text, create bulleted or numbered lists, and copy formatting with Format Painter

Scenario You have been given a paragraph listing a variety of exercise options and the calories you will burn if you take part in them. In this format, it is difficult to focus on the calories burned by each activity. Separate the activities and create a bulleted list for easier reading.

Steps

1 Open the student data file named **M5-C2-ExB-Calories.docx** and save the file as **Lastname-M5-C2-ExB-Calories**, but replace *Lastname* with your last name.

2 Add a header to the document that includes your name at the left margin and the current date at the right margin.

3 Add a footer to the document, placing the page number in the center.

4 Turn on Show/Hide ¶ to display formatting marks, and then separate each statement into a list item. **HINT:** *To create the list, you can delete the spaces between statements and then press Enter to place each statement on its own line.* **ANOTHER WAY:** *Use Find and Replace: select the text beginning with* After *and ending with* Fun, *search for* . , *and replace with the paragraph mark (found in the* Replace *Special drop-down list).*

5 Add bullets to all the activities, beginning with *After 30 minutes of cross-country skiing and ending with Dancing for 30 minutes burns 150 calories.* Change the bullets to check marks and the font of all bulleted items to 16-point Calibri.

6 Change the font and size of the title *Burning Calories* to 28-point Lucida Sans and center the text.

7 Use Format Painter to apply the title's formatting to the final sentence of the document, which begins *Find something.* Italicize the last sentence.

8 Save and close the file.

9 Print or submit the completed document as directed by your instructor.

Burning Calories

✓ After 30 minutes of cross-country skiing, you burn up that plate of spaghetti with meat sauce and Parmesan cheese—about 450 calories.
✓ Thirty minutes on an indoor skiing machine offer the same benefits as cross-country skiing—about 450 calories.
✓ Walking at around 4 miles per hour for 30 minutes burns 180 calories.
✓ Playing active, competitive tennis for 30 minutes burns 270 calories.
✓ Vacuuming the house for 30 minutes burns 90 calories.
✓ Running 30 minutes burns 300 calories.
✓ Playing a twosome for golf burns 80 calories.
✓ Weeding the garden for 30 minutes burns 150 calories.
✓ Inline skating or roller skating at a moderate pace for 30 minutes burns 210 calories.
✓ Dancing 30 minutes burns 150 calories.

Find something you enjoy doing and have fun!

1

Completed Exercise B

Exercise **C** **Format a Report**

Skills   Change font and font size, use formatting tools, align text, format paragraph and line spacing, insert citations using professional styles, and create a works cited page

Scenario   Format a term paper so it is ready for submission. The research has already been done, and your instructor provided the following formatting guidelines:

Font: Arial 12 pt
Spacing: double
Alignment: left
Paragraph First line indentation: 0.5"
Header: your last name, a space, and the page number in upper-right corner
References: *MLA Seventh Edition* parenthetical citations
Works cited page: required

Skills

1   Open the student data file **M5-C2-ExC-NativeLang.docx**, and save the file as **Lastname-M5-C2-ExC-NativeLang**, but replace *Lastname* with your last name.

2   Change the font and size for the entire document to 12-point Arial.

3   Remove all blank lines between paragraphs. Set line spacing to double for the document. ***HINT:*** *Click the Show/Hide ¶ button to turn on the display of formatting marks, delete each extra paragraph mark, and click the Show/Hide ¶ button again.*

4   Highlight the body of the document, from *In the essay* to *approach to instruction*, and set paragraph indents and alignment as directed in the Scenario above.

5   At the top of page 1, replace the following:
    a. *Professor Name* with the name of your instructor.
    b. *Course Name* with the name of your course.
    c. *Current Date* with today's date written in the format d Month yyyy (e.g., 5 March 2015).

6   Enter your name in parentheses next to the author's name, *Nancy Robinson*. ***NOTE:*** *Nancy Robinson is the author of this paper. By enclosing your name in parentheses in this exercise, you are indicating that you modified the paper. When you write your own paper using MLA Seventh Edition, you will type your own name as author and will not enclose it in parentheses.*

7   Center the title *An Argument for Using Native Language in the Classroom*.

8   Add a one-field header that contains your last name followed by a space and the page number. ***HINT:*** *Enter your last name, a space, and*

then the page number. Make sure there is a blank line as the second line of the header. Right-align the header. The header font and size should be the same as in the rest of the document (12-point Arial).

9   Set the reference style to *MLA Seventh Edition*.

10 Add the following sources.

Type of Source	Web site
Author	Cummings, Jim
Name of Web Page	Bilingual Children's Mother Tongue: Why Is It Important for Education?
Year	2003
Year Accessed	2012
Month Accessed	May
Day Accessed	4
Medium	Web

Type of Source	Journal Article
Author	Dahlberg, Joan S.
Title	Pros and Cons of the English-Only (EO) Classroom
Journal Name	ESL Journal 29.2
Year	2006
Pages	10-15
Medium	Print

Type of Source	Journal Article
Author	Leonard, Martin; Rivera, Hector
Title	Language Skills and Achievement in the Content Areas

Journal Name	English Teachers Journal 65
Year	2010
Pages	211-15
Medium	Print

Type of Source	*Conference Proceedings*
Author	Tan, Amy
Title	Mother Tongue
Pages	1208-14
Year	2008
Conference Publication Name	Mirrors & Windows: Connecting with Literature, American Tradition
City	St. Paul, MN
Publisher	EMC Publishing
Medium	Print

Type of Source	*Web site*
Name of Web Page	Teacher Talk
Year	2007
Year Accessed	2012
Month Accessed	May
Day Accessed	4
Medium	Web

11 After entering the data shown above for the Teacher Talk website, insert a check mark in the *Show All Bibliography Fields* check box and enter the following additional information.

Editor   Walsh, Debbie

12 Enter the citations in the indicated locations using the Insert Citation tool. Be sure to delete the citation markers. Each citation marker begins and ends with **.

13 Position the cursor at the end of the document and add a page break. ***HINT:*** *Click the Page Break button in the Pages group on the INSERT tab.*

14 Use the Bibliography tool to create a works cited page. Do not modify the format of the works cited page. ***HINT:*** *Select the* Works Cited *option from the Bibliography drop-down list on the REFERENCES tab.*

15 Save and close the file.

16 Print or submit the document as directed by your instructor.

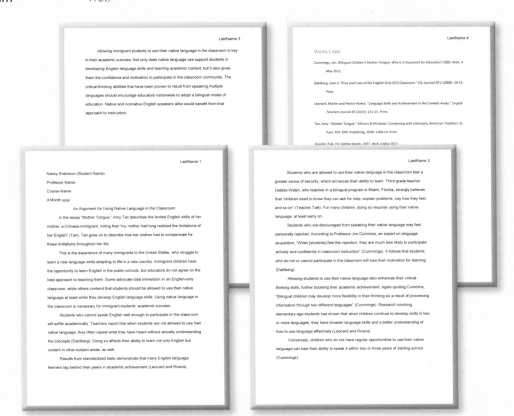

Completed Exercise C

Chapter 3

Working with Tables and Objects

There are several features in Word that help you organize information and add visual appeal to your documents. Tables organize information into rows and columns, allowing you to convey a great deal of data in a small, neat space. You can also insert visual objects, including photos, illustrations, and shapes to better illustrate a point or make your document more attractive. In this chapter you learn how to build tables and insert and manipulate objects.

Skills You Learn

1   Create tables
2   Convert text to tables
3   Change page orientation
4   Insert a row in a table
5   Merge rows or columns in a table
6   Format tables
7   Insert shapes
8   Insert objects and images
9   Resize objects
10 Rotate objects

Files You Need
For these skills, you need the following student data files.

M5-C3-S1-HCRecipe.docx

M5-C3-S3-HCRecipe.docx

M5-C3-S7-HCRecipe.docx

What You Create

You are helping to organize an open house to celebrate The Chocolate Museum's 10th year in operation. The Museum will give each guest a small tote bag containing a pad and pen stamped with the Museum's logo, a bar of chocolate from a local chocolate company, and a recipe for Mexican Hot Chocolate. Your boss has asked you to create the recipe document, including a table of ingredients, fun illustrations and pictures of hot chocolate, and recipe instructions.

In this chapter you build the recipe in Word using Word's table and column features to organize the recipe contents and then add a shape and a picture for visual interest.

Hot Chocolate Recipe

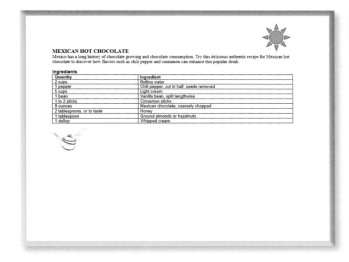

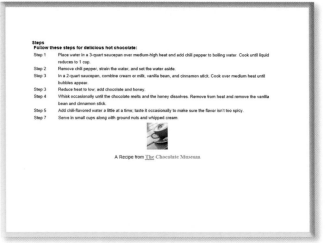

Word

Video M5_C3_S01

Create Tables

Tables use columns and rows to help organize sets of information and show relationships among separate pieces of information. For example, imagine a table used to compare the nutritional information for types of snacks. The first column of the table lists the name of each snack. The second column lists the number of calories in each snack. The third column lists the number of carbohydrates in each snack. The fourth column lists the quantity of fat in each snack. By reading down the table's columns you could compare the nutritional ingredients of each type of snack, and you might use that information to help you select which snack to eat. In this skill, you create a table that lists the amount of each recipe ingredient in the first column and the type of ingredient in the second column.

Steps

1 Open the student data file named **M5-C3-S1-HCRecipe.docx**, and if you have not already done so, save the file in your Module 5 working folder on your storage medium.

2 Click in the blank line between the words *Ingredients* and *Steps*.

3 Click the INSERT tab.

4 Click the Table button in the Tables group.

5 Click *Insert Table*.

5 *Another Way*
Click and drag over the boxes in the Table button drop-down menu to insert a table containing up to eight rows and up to ten columns.

6 At the Insert Table dialog box that appears, type 2 in the *Number of columns* field and 9 in the *Number of rows* field.

6 *Another Way*
Click the arrows to the right of each of the measurement boxes to change the number of rows and columns.

7 Click OK.

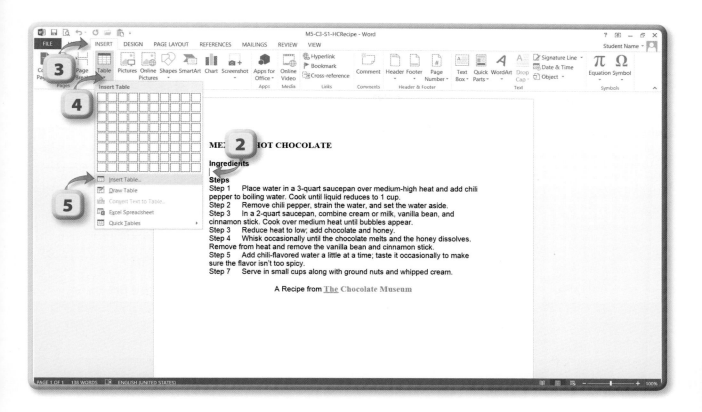

MEXI**2** HOT CHOCOLATE

Ingredients

Steps
Step 1   Place water in a 3-quart saucepan over medium-high heat and add chili pepper to boiling water. Cook until liquid reduces to 1 cup.
Step 2   Remove chili pepper, strain the water, and set the water aside.
Step 3   In a 2-quart saucepan, combine cream or milk, vanilla bean, and cinnamon stick. Cook over medium heat until bubbles appear.
Step 3   Reduce heat to low; add chocolate and honey.
Step 4   Whisk occasionally until the chocolate melts and the honey dissolves. Remove from heat and remove the vanilla bean and cinnamon stick.
Step 5   Add chili-flavored water a little at a time; taste it occasionally to make sure the flavor isn't too spicy.
Step 7   Serve in small cups along with ground nuts and whipped cream.

A Recipe from The Chocolate Museum

More

8 Click in the cells of the table and enter the following text:

2 cups	Boiling water
1 pepper	Chili pepper, cut in half, seeds removed
5 cups	Light cream
1 bean	Vanilla bean, split lengthwise
1 to 2 sticks	Cinnamon sticks
8 ounces	Mexican chocolate, coarsely chopped
2 tablespoons, or to taste	Honey
1 tablespoon	Ground almonds or hazelnuts
1 dollop	Whipped cream

9 Click the Save button in the Quick Access toolbar to save the file.

MEXICAN HOT CHOCOLATE

Ingredients

2 cups	Boiling water
1 pepper	Chili pepper, cut in half, seeds removed
5 cups	Light cream
1 bean	Vanilla bean, split lengthwise
1 to 2 sticks	Cinnamon sticks
8 ounces	Mexican chocolate, coarsely chopped
2 tablespoons, or to taste	Honey
1 tablespoon	Ground almonds or hazelnuts
1 dollop	Whipped cream

Steps

Step 1   Place water in a 3-quart saucepan over medium-high heat and add chili pepper to boiling water. Cook until liquid reduces to 1 cup.
Step 2   Remove chili pepper, strain the water, and set the water aside.
Step 3   In a 2-quart saucepan, combine cream or milk, vanilla bean, and cinnamon stick. Cook over medium heat until bubbles appear.
Step 3   Reduce heat to low; add chocolate and honey.
Step 4   Whisk occasionally until the chocolate melts and the honey dissolves. Remove from heat and remove the vanilla bean and cinnamon stick.
Step 5   Add chili-flavored water a little at a time; taste it occasionally to make sure the flavor isn't too spicy.
Step 7   Serve in small cups along with ground nuts and whipped cream.

A Recipe from The Chocolate Museum

Completed Skill 1

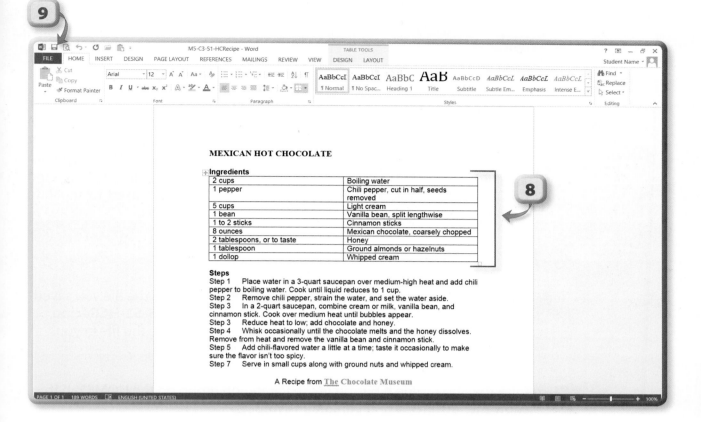

Taking It Further

Formatting Tables To save yourself some formatting time, try the Quick Tables feature. You can access Quick Tables by clicking the Table button on the INSERT tab and then clicking *Quick Tables*. Quick Tables includes common table styles that you might find useful, such as two-column lists and calendars.

Word

Video ▶ M5_C3_S02

Convert Text to Tables

If you have entered information in text form you can convert it into table form. You must provide an indicator to mark where each new column of the table should begin. Tabs are commonly used for these indicators, or separators, but you can also use commas, paragraphs, or single characters such as hyphens. Hard returns (created by pressing the Enter key) are used to separate your text into rows.

Steps

1 If it is not already open, open **M5-C3-S1-HCRecipe.docx**, the file you saved in the previous skill, and save the file as **Lastname-M5-C3-S2-HCRecipe**, but replace *Lastname* with your last name. Be sure to save the file in your Module 5 working folder on your storage medium.

2 Click the Show/Hide ¶ button in the Paragraph group on the HOME tab to show the tab arrows and paragraph symbols.

3 Select the text under the heading *Steps*, from the start of *Step 1* through the end of *Step 7*. The step list includes tabs to separate the step numbers from the step descriptions.

4 Click the INSERT tab.

5 Click the Table button.

6 Click *Convert Text to Table*.

> ▶ **Tip** Note that the *AutoFit behavior* section of the Convert Text to Table dialog box defaults to *Auto* in the *Fixed column width* option. The *Auto* setting adjusts column widths to fit the text inside them, as shown in the images on the next page.

7 In the Convert Text to Table dialog box, be sure that the *Tabs* option is selected in the *Separate text at* section.

8 Click OK.

9 Click the Show/Hide ¶ button in the Paragraph group on the HOME tab to hide the tab arrows and paragraph symbols.

10 Save and close the file.

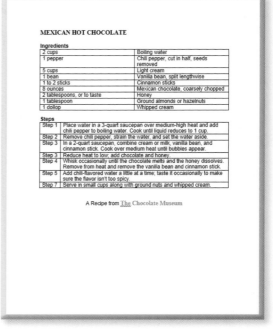

Completed Skill 2

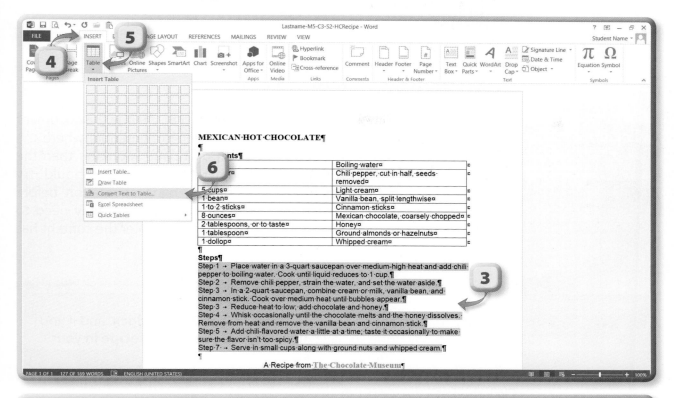

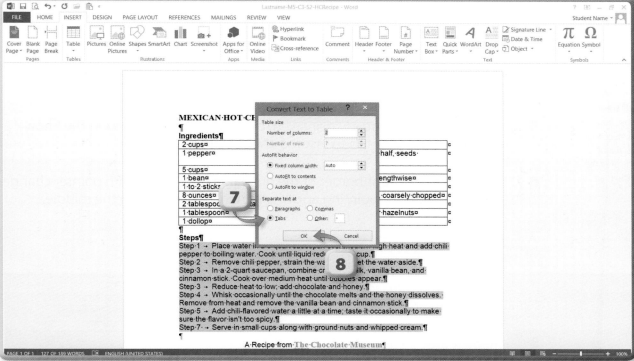

Taking It Further

Converting a Table to Text   You can also convert text in a table into plain text. Do this by selecting the desired section of the table and clicking the Convert to Text button in the Data group on the TABLE TOOLS LAYOUT tab. You then get a choice of what to use as a separator in the text (tabs, paragraphs, commas, or another symbol you indicate).

Word

Video M5_C3_S03

Change Page Orientation

Sometimes, to fit more text on a page or improve the design, you may want to change the page orientation of a document. Word offers two document orientations. By default, Word documents are set up in *portrait* orientation, where the height of a page is greater than the width. You can change the document to *landscape* orientation, where the width of a page is greater than the height. Although you should try to set the page orientation before entering content, you may need to make a change after the content has been entered.

Steps

1 Open the student data file named **M5-C3-S3-HCRecipe.docx**, and if you have not already done so, save the file as **M5-C3-S3-HCRecipe** in your Module 5 working folder.

2 Click the PAGE LAYOUT tab.

3 Click the Orientation button in the Page Setup group.

4 Click *Landscape*. The text in the document shifts to accommodate the margins of landscape orientation.

5 If the ruler is not already displayed, click the *Ruler* check box in the Show group on the VIEW tab to insert a check mark.

6 Hover over the right border of the first table until the I-beam pointer changes to a left-and-right-pointing arrow with two vertical lines in the middle.

7 Click and drag the right edge of the table to the 8.5-inch mark on the ruler to resize the table.

8 Repeat Steps 5 and 6 with the edge of the second table.

9 Save the file.

▶**Tip** Apply the desired page orientation as early as you can when creating a document so there are no surprises about how text or inserted objects, such as pictures, might shift on the page once the new margin settings are applied.

Completed Skill 3

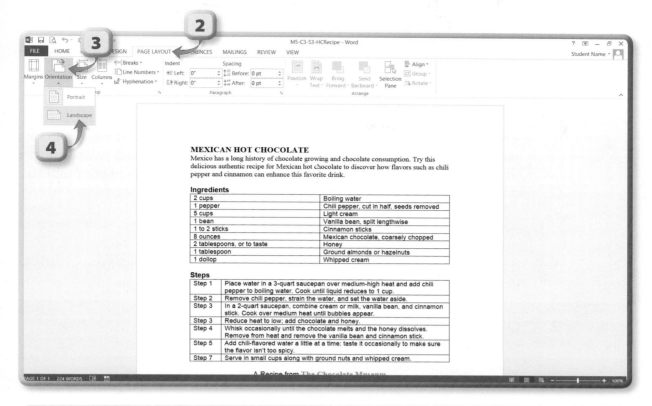

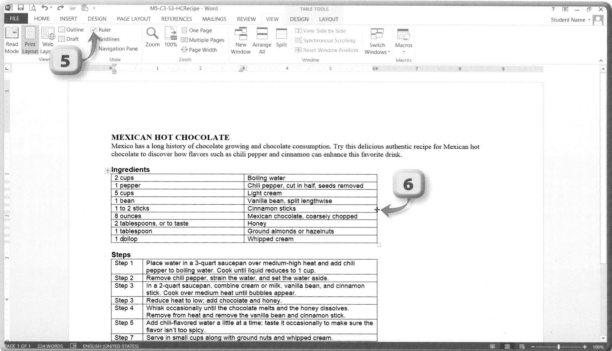

Taking It Further

Fitting Text on a Page   The standard page size for most documents is 8.5 inches x 11 inches. If a document in landscape orientation runs slightly longer than a single page, consider printing it on a larger piece of paper, such as legal paper, which is 8.5 inches x 14 inches. You can also fit more text on a page by narrowing the margins in the document. See Module 5, Chapter 1, Skill 6 for more about adjusting margins in Word.

Word

Skill 4

Video M5_C3_S04

Insert a Row in a Table

At times you will need to add more data to an existing table. To accommodate the additional data, you can easily insert new columns or rows. In this skill, you insert a heading row in one of your tables.

Steps

1 If it is not already open, open **M5-C3-S3-HCRecipe.docx**, the file you saved in the previous skill, and save the file as **M5-C3-S4-HCRecipe**.

2 Click in the first row of the first table.

3 Click the TABLE TOOLS LAYOUT tab.

> **Tip** To insert a column rather than a row, simply click in a column and then click the Insert Left or Insert Right button on the TABLE TOOLS LAYOUT tab.

4 Click the Insert Above button in the Rows & Columns group. A row is inserted above the selected row.

5 Type Quantity in the new top-left cell and Ingredient in the new top-right cell.

6 Move your mouse to the left of the first row until the pointer turns into a white arrow and then click to select the new first row.

7 Click the HOME tab.

8 Shortcut
Bold text
Ctrl + B

8 Click the Bold button in the Font group.

8 Another Way
Click the Bold button on the Mini toolbar that displays when you select the row.

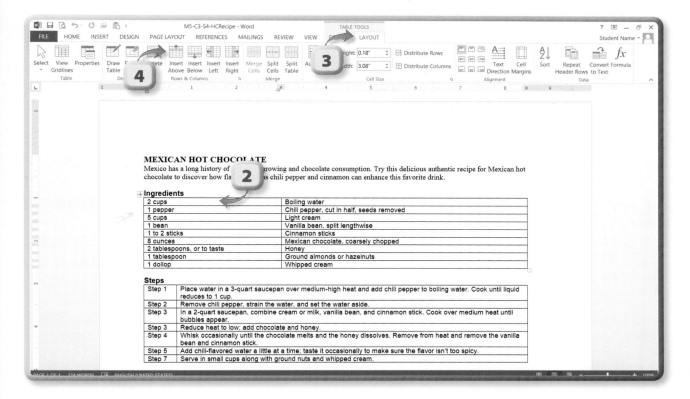

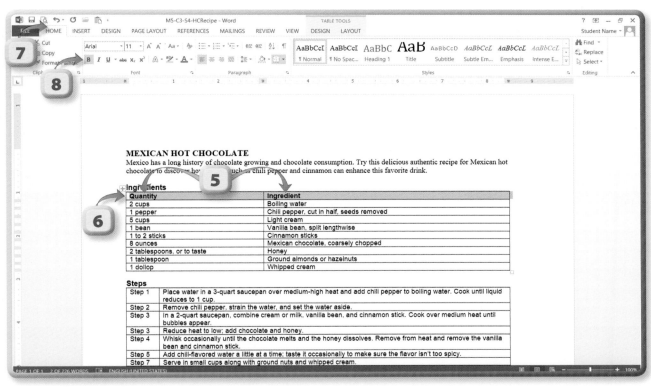

9 Click in the first cell of the second table.

10 Click the TABLE TOOLS LAYOUT tab.

11 Click the Insert Above button in the Rows & Columns group.

12 Type Follow these steps for delicious hot chocolate: in the first cell of the new row.

13 Save the file.

▶**Tip** When you insert a new column, you may find that the column width does not accommodate the data within it very well. You can resize columns by placing your cursor over a column dividing line until the cursor turns into a left-and-right-pointing arrow with two vertical lines in the middle. Click and drag the divider to the right or left to adjust column widths.

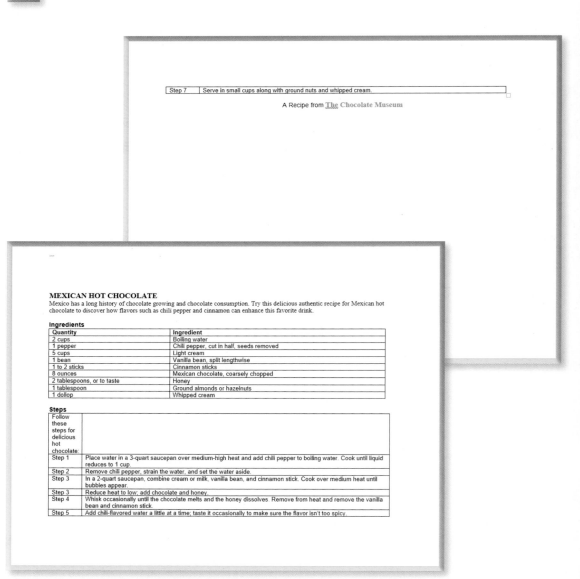

Completed Skill 4

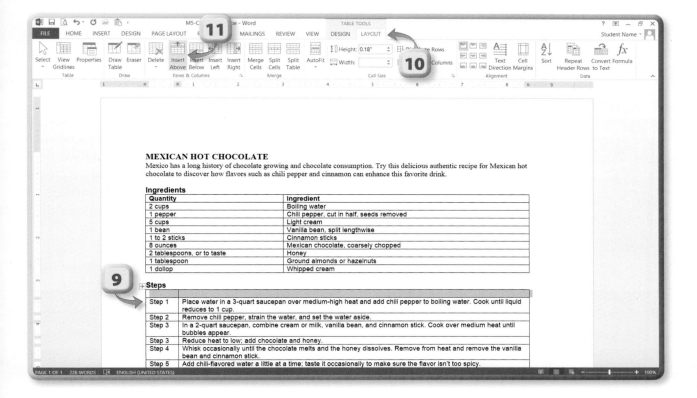

Taking It Further

Deleting Table Content If you need to delete a row or column in a table, there are a couple of ways to do so. To select a column you wish to delete, place your mouse pointer at the top of the column until the pointer turns into a solid black down-pointing arrow, click to select the column, and then drag over any additional columns to be deleted. To select a row you wish to delete, place your mouse pointer to the left of a row, click to select the row, and then drag over any additional rows to be deleted. Once you have selected the appropriate rows or columns, right-click. In the shortcut menu that appears, select either *Delete Rows* or *Delete Columns*. You can also use the Delete button on the TABLE TOOLS LAYOUT tab to perform the same action.

Word

Word

Skill 5

Video ▶ M5_C3_S05

Merge Rows or Columns in a Table

The table you have been working with in the previous skills contained a consistent sets of rows and columns. However, when organizing information in a table, you may find you need to combine rows and columns. For example, you may want to combine the cells in the top row of a table into a single cell that contains the table title, or you may want to combine several sets of cells to create blocks in a schedule. The process of combining rows or columns is called *merging*.

Steps

1 If it is not already open, open **M5-C3-S4-HCRecipe.docx**, the file you saved in the previous skill, and save the file as **M5-C3-S5-HCRecipe**.

2 Select the first row of the second table.

3 Click the TABLE TOOLS LAYOUT tab.

4 Click the Merge Cells button in the Merge group. Clicking this button merges the two selected cells.

5 With the first row still selected, click the HOME tab.

6 Click the Bold button.

7 Save the file.

▶**Tip** You can merge rows, columns, or rows and columns, based on the combination of rows and/or columns you select before clicking the Merge Cells button.

MEXICAN HOT CHOCOLATE
Mexico has a long history of chocolate growing and chocolate consumption. Try this delicious authentic recipe for Mexican hot chocolate to discover how flavors such as chili pepper and cinnamon can enhance this favorite drink.

Ingredients

Quantity	Ingredient
2 cups	Boiling water
1 pepper	Chili pepper, cut in half, seeds removed
5 cups	Light cream
1 bean	Vanilla bean, split lengthwise
1 to 2 sticks	Cinnamon sticks
8 ounces	Mexican chocolate, coarsely chopped
2 tablespoons, or to taste	Honey
1 tablespoon	Ground almonds or hazelnuts
1 dollop	Whipped cream

Steps

Follow these steps for delicious hot chocolate:	
Step 1	Place water in a 3-quart saucepan over medium-high heat and add chili pepper to boiling water. Cook until liquid reduces to 1 cup.
Step 2	Remove chili pepper, strain the water, and set the water aside.
Step 3	In a 2-quart saucepan, combine cream or milk, vanilla bean, and cinnamon stick. Cook over medium heat until bubbles appear.
Step 3	Reduce heat to low; add chocolate and honey.
Step 4	Whisk occasionally until the chocolate melts and the honey dissolves. Remove from heat and remove the vanilla bean and cinnamon stick
Step 5	Add chili-flavored water a little at a time; taste it occasionally to make sure the flavor isn't too spicy.
Step 7	Serve in small cups along with ground nuts and whipped cream.

A Recipe from The Chocolate Museum

Completed Skill 5

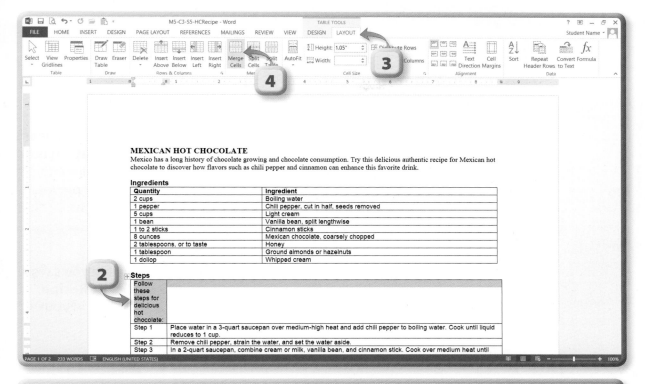

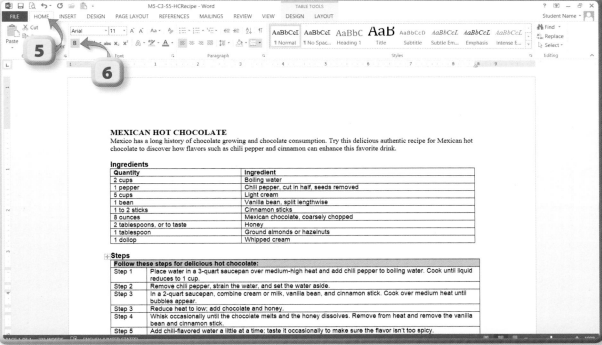

Taking It Further

Formatting with Tables Use a table and the merge function to build forms or documents such as class schedules. The following table is an example of a portion of a class schedule. Once the information is organized, you can hide the borders, if you wish.

Spring Semester	English	Monday, Wednesday; 10:00 am
	Biology	Thursday, Friday; 9:00 am
Additional Information	Syllabus will be available to students on the first day of class.	

Word

Skill 6

Format Tables

Video M5_C3_S06

A table can be formatted in a variety of ways. You can add shading or modify the thickness or color of the lines that define the table cells. You can also specify which border lines should be displayed and which should not. In this skill you learn how to alter a table so that it has no borders showing at all.

Steps

1 If it is not already open, open **M5-C3-S5-HCRecipe.docx**, the file you saved in the previous skill, and save the file as **Lastname-M5-C3-S6-HCRecipe**, but replace *Lastname* with your last name. Be sure to save the file in your Module 5 working folder on your storage medium.

2 *Another Way*
Click and drag to select all the cells of the table.

2 Click in the second table to select the table.

3 Click the table move handle (four-headed arrow).

4 Click the TABLE TOOLS DESIGN tab.

▶**Tip** Instead of using borders, you can apply shading to individual cells of your table to visually separate cell contents.

5 Click the Borders button arrow in the Borders group.

6 Click *No Border* to remove the borders from all of the cells in the table.

7 Click the HOME tab.

8 With the the contents of the second table still selected, click the Line and Paragraph Spacing button in the Paragraph group and then click *1.15*.

9 Save and close the file.

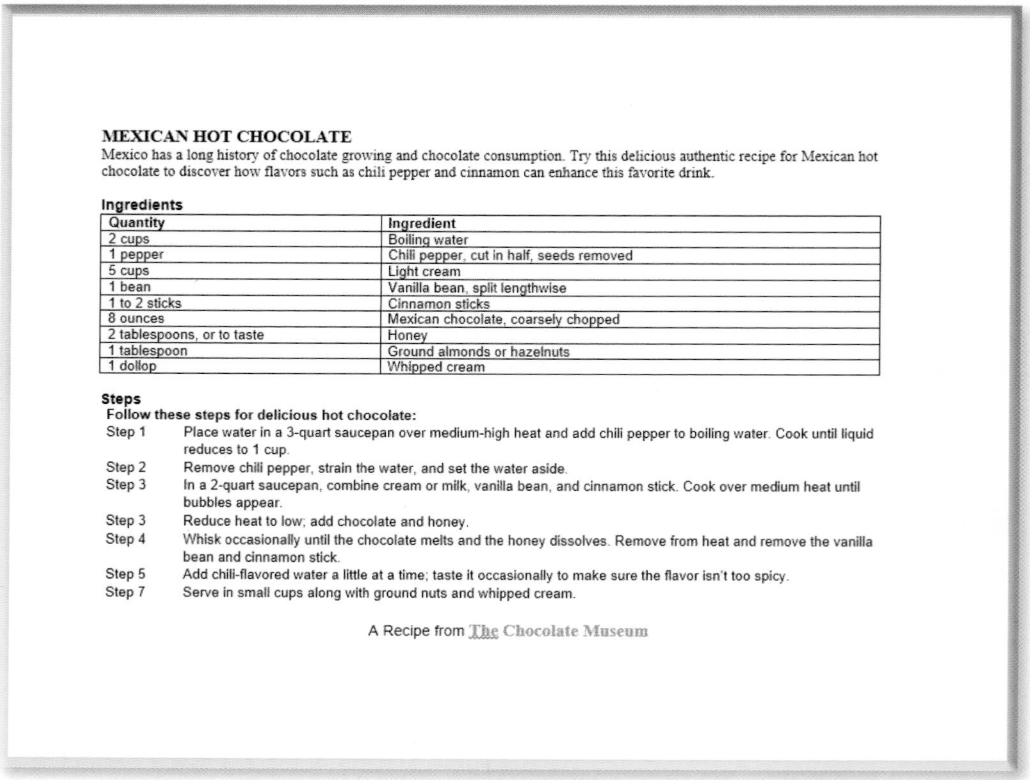

MEXICAN HOT CHOCOLATE

Mexico has a long history of chocolate growing and chocolate consumption. Try this delicious authentic recipe for Mexican hot chocolate to discover how flavors such as chili pepper and cinnamon can enhance this favorite drink.

Ingredients

Quantity	Ingredient
2 cups	Boiling water
1 pepper	Chili pepper, cut in half, seeds removed
5 cups	Light cream
1 bean	Vanilla bean, split lengthwise
1 to 2 sticks	Cinnamon sticks
8 ounces	Mexican chocolate, coarsely chopped
2 tablespoons, or to taste	Honey
1 tablespoon	Ground almonds or hazelnuts
1 dollop	Whipped cream

Steps

Follow these steps for delicious hot chocolate:

Step 1   Place water in a 3-quart saucepan over medium-high heat and add chili pepper to boiling water. Cook until liquid reduces to 1 cup.

Step 2   Remove chili pepper, strain the water, and set the water aside.

Step 3   In a 2-quart saucepan, combine cream or milk, vanilla bean, and cinnamon stick. Cook over medium heat until bubbles appear.

Step 3   Reduce heat to low; add chocolate and honey.

Step 4   Whisk occasionally until the chocolate melts and the honey dissolves. Remove from heat and remove the vanilla bean and cinnamon stick.

Step 5   Add chili-flavored water a little at a time; taste it occasionally to make sure the flavor isn't too spicy.

Step 7   Serve in small cups along with ground nuts and whipped cream.

A Recipe from The Chocolate Museum

Completed Skill 6

Word

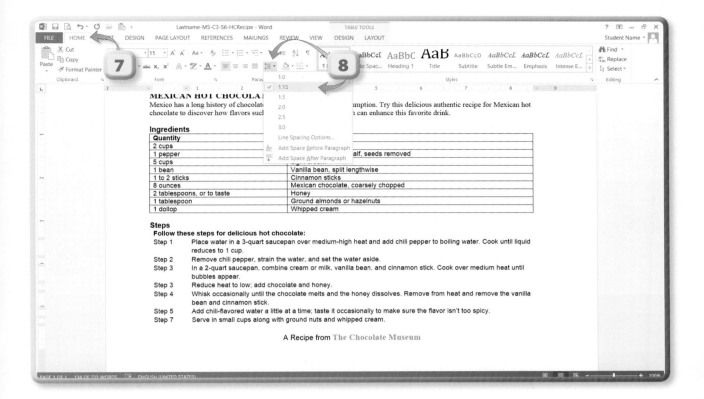

Taking It Further

Previewing the Table Styles   Table styles offer a great way to add formatting pizzazz to tables with just one click. The gallery of table styles is found on the TABLE TOOLS DESIGN tab. Experiment with table styles by clicking in a table and then moving the mouse pointer over the various style options in the Table Styles group. The *live preview* feature will show you what the style will look like. When you see one that you like, click it and the style is applied to your table, instantly!

Word

Word

Skill 7

Video M5_C3_S07

Insert Shapes

Word includes a feature called *Shapes* that lets you easily draw a variety of shapes, from lines to stars and arrows. You can use these shapes to build flow charts or simple illustrations to help you make a point or add visual appeal to a document.

Steps

1 Open the student data file named **M5-C3-S7-HCRecipe.docx**, and if you have not already done so, save the file in your Module 5 working folder on your storage medium.

2 Click the INSERT tab.

3 Click the Shapes button in the Illustrations group.

4 Click the *Sun* shape in the *Basic Shapes* section.

5 Click above the recipe title to insert a sun.

6 Select the sun and then click the DRAWING TOOLS FORMAT tab.

7 Use the *Shape Height* and *Shape Width* measurement boxes in the Size group to adjust the size until the sun is exactly 1 inch x 1 inch.

8 *Another Way*
Right-click a shape and then click *Fill* at the shortcut menu.

▶ *Tip* You can determine a color's name by hovering your mouse pointer over any color square in the Shape Fill color palette.

8 Click the Shape Fill button in the Shape Styles group.

9 Click the *Orange, Accent 6, Darker 25%* option from the color palette.

10 Drag the sun object to the top-right corner of the page, to the position shown in the Completed Skill image to the right.

11 Save the file.

Completed Skill 7

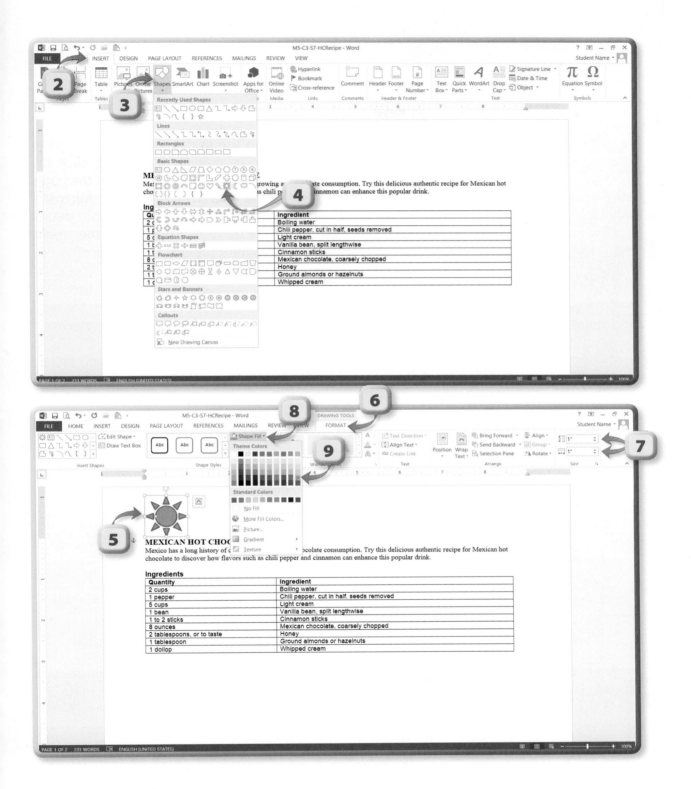

Taking It Further

Creating a Diagram If you want to draw a diagram, you can use the SmartArt feature rather than drawing individual shapes. Click the SmartArt button in the Illustrations group on the INSERT tab to access different types of diagrams, such as an organizational chart or pyramid diagram. Once you have inserted a SmartArt object, you can click in individual elements of the diagram and enter text labels.

Word

Video   M5_C3_S08
▶

Insert Objects and Images

You can insert pictures from your computer or from a variety of online sources to make your documents more interesting. You can also add audio and video clips to your document. The Office.com website contains a variety of royalty-free photos and illustrations that you can use in documents and projects. Go to *office.microsoft.com*, click the Legal link at the bottom of the page, and read Section 8 of the Microsoft Services Agreement for more details about your right to use the media content provided by Microsoft.

Steps

1 If it is not already open, open **M5-C3-S7-HCRecipe.docx**, the file you saved in the previous skill, and save the file as **M5-C3-S8-HCRecipe**.

2 Click in the blank line below the first table in the document.

3 Click the INSERT tab.

4 Click the Online Pictures button in the Illustrations group.

5 Type saucepan in the *Office.com Clip Art* search box.

6 Press Enter.

7 Click the image as shown on the opposite page.

8 Click the Insert button.

▶**Tip** Depending on the size and resolution of your monitor, you may have a different number of images in the rows than you see in the image on the opposite page.

▶**Tip** Because online content changes, you may be unable to find the exact image indicated in this skill. In that case, choose a similar image.

Taking It Further

Inserting Online Video   You can insert video from websites such as YouTube into a Word document. To insert an online video, click the Online Video button in the Media group on the INSERT tab. You can then search for online videos or paste the embed code from a website.

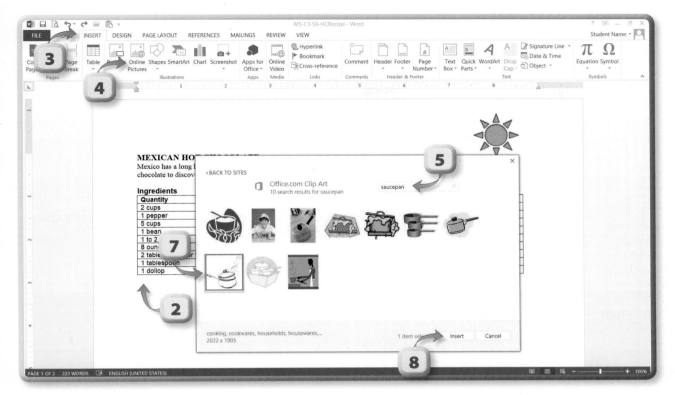

More

Taking It Further

Inserting a Screenshot You can insert a screenshot of any open window into a Word document. Start by sizing the open window and positioning the contents so they look exactly the way you want them to. In the Word document, position your cursor where you wish to insert the screenshot, click the Screenshot button in the Illustrations group on the PICTURE TOOLS FORMAT tab, and then click the correct open window in the Available Windows drop-down list. The screenshot is added to the Word document at the cursor location.

9 Scroll and then click in the blank line below the second table in the document.

10 Click the Online Pictures button in the Illustrations group on the INSERT TAB.

11 Type hot chocolate in the *Office.com Clip Art* search box.

12 Press Enter.

13 *Another Way*
If you have a photo stored on your computer that you want to insert in a document, click the Pictures button in the Illustrations group on the INSERT tab. The Insert Picture dialog box appears, allowing you to locate the picture. Click the Insert button to insert it.

13 Scroll down to find the image shown in the screen capture on the opposite page (or one that is similar) and then click the image.

14 Click the Insert button.

15 Save the file.

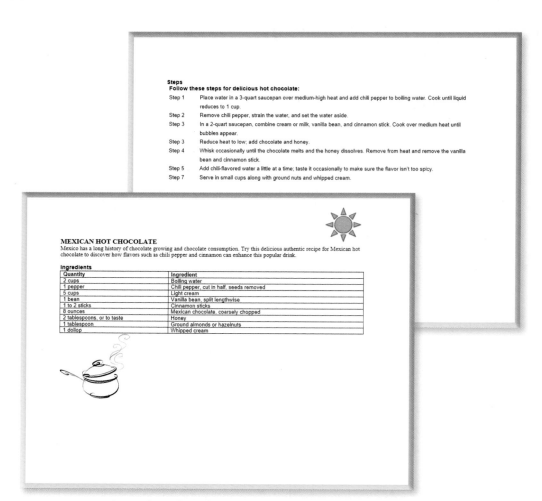

Steps
Follow these steps for delicious hot chocolate:

Step 1	Place water in a 3-quart saucepan over medium-high heat and add chili pepper to boiling water. Cook until liquid reduces to 1 cup.
Step 2	Remove chili pepper, strain the water, and set the water aside.
Step 3	In a 2-quart saucepan, combine cream or milk, vanilla bean, and cinnamon stick. Cook over medium heat until bubbles appear.
Step 3	Reduce heat to low; add chocolate and honey.
Step 4	Whisk occasionally until the chocolate melts and the honey dissolves. Remove from heat and remove the vanilla bean and cinnamon stick.
Step 5	Add chili-flavored water a little at a time; taste it occasionally to make sure the flavor isn't too spicy.
Step 7	Serve in small cups along with ground nuts and whipped cream.

MEXICAN HOT CHOCOLATE
Mexico has a long history of chocolate growing and chocolate consumption. Try this delicious authentic recipe for Mexican hot chocolate to discover how flavors such as chili pepper and cinnamon can enhance this popular drink.

Ingredients

Quantity	Ingredient
2 cups	Boiling water
1 pepper	Chili pepper, cut in half, seeds removed
5 cups	Light cream
1 bean	Vanilla bean, split lengthwise
1 to 2 sticks	Cinnamon sticks
8 ounces	Mexican chocolate, coarsely chopped
2 tablespoons, or to taste	Honey
1 tablespoon	Ground almonds or hazelnuts
1 dollop	Whipped cream

Completed Skill 8, Pages 1 and 2

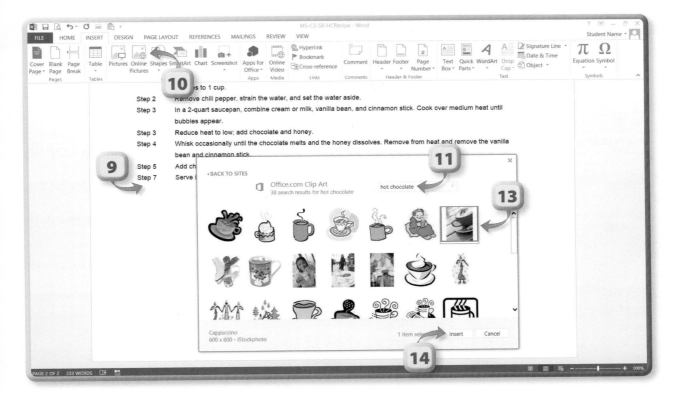

Step 2   Remove chili pepper, strain the water, and set the water aside.

Step 3   In a 2-quart saucepan, combine cream or milk, vanilla bean, and cinnamon stick. Cook over medium heat until bubbles appear.

Step 3   Reduce heat to low; add chocolate and honey.

Step 4   Whisk occasionally until the chocolate melts and the honey dissolves. Remove from heat and remove the vanilla bean and cinnamon stick.

Step 5   Add ch

Step 7   Serve

Completed Skill 8, Pages 3 and 4

Word

Video ▶ M5_C3_S09

Resize Objects

You can see from the size of the objects inserted in the previous skill that they do not always appear in a size that suits your document. You can easily resize graphic objects by using the *Shape Height* measurement box in the Size group on the PICTURE TOOLS FORMAT tab.

Steps

3-4 *Another Way*
Click the object and then drag the bottom-right corner handle to size the image proportionally. You can then refer to the *Shape Height* and *Shape Width* measurement boxes in the Size group on the PICTURE TOOLS FORMAT tab to check the actual size.

1 If it is not already open, open **M5-C3-S8-HCRecipe.docx**, the file you saved in the previous skill, and save the file as **M5-C3-S9-HCRecipe**.

2 Select the saucepan image on the first page.

3 Click the PICTURE TOOLS FORMAT tab.

4 In the Size group, change the entry in the *Shape Height* measurement box to *1"* and then press Enter. Notice that the value in the *Shape Width* measurement box adjusts to size the image proportionally.

5 Scroll to the third page of the file and select the hot chocolate image you inserted.

6 Click the PICTURE TOOLS FORMAT tab.

7 In the Size group, change the entry in the *Shape Height* measurement box to *1"* and then press Enter. Notice that the value in the *Shape Width* measurement box adjusts to size the image proportionally.

8 With the picture selected, click the Center button in the Paragraph group on the HOME tab to center the picture on the page.

9 Save the file.

Taking It Further

Wrapping Styles When you insert an object in a document, it is placed in line with the text by default. Thus, you may have text above and below the object, but not next to or behind it. To adjust how the object and text are arranged, select the picture then click the Wrap Text button in the Arrange group on the PICTURE TOOLS FORMAT tab. Text wrapping options in this drop-down menu include *Square*, *Tight*, *Through*, *Top and Bottom*, *Behind Text*, and *In Front of Text*. These options are also available from the Layout Options ▣ button that appears beside an object when you select the object.

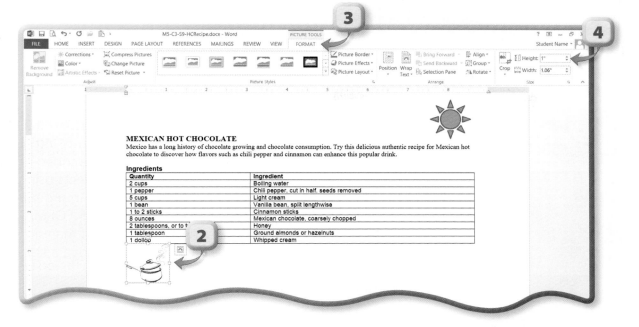

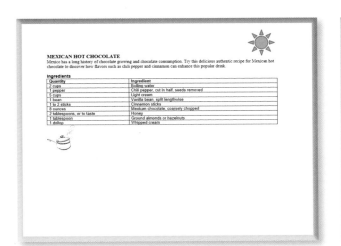

Completed Skill 9

Word

Video M5_C3_S10

Rotate Objects

Some objects contribute more clearly to your document's message if they are rotated from their original orientation, either to fit with your page design or to suggest a relationship between objects. You can also rotate an object to suggest movement. In this recipe, for example, the saucepan is inserted as if it's sitting flat on a stove. However, rotating it to bring the handle upward suggests that you are pouring the contents into cups, which is the result described in the recipe text. Rotate objects using the Rotate button in the Arrange group on the PICTURE TOOLS FORMAT tab or using the rotation handle that displays as a circle above a selected object.

Steps

1 If it is not already open, open **M5-C3-S9-HCRecipe.docx**, the file you saved in the previous skill, and save the file as **Lastname-M5-C3-S10-HCRecipe**, but replace *Lastname* with your last name. Be sure to save the file in your Module 5 working folder on your storage medium.

2 Click the saucepan image.

3 **Another Way**
Select an object and then rotate the object by dragging the rotation handle ↻ that appears above the image.

3 Click the PICTURE TOOLS FORMAT tab.

4 Click the Rotate button in the Arrange group.

5 Click *More Rotation Options*.

▶**Tip** Rotating the object may cause it to jump to the next page. You can fix or prevent this by deleting any extra spacing before the object or resizing the object to be smaller.

6 Select *20°* in the *Rotation* measurement box.

▶**Tip** You can also type in the *Rotation* measurement box. You might do that to avoid scrolling—for example, if the box displays 20° and you want to reset the rotation to 240°.

7 Click OK.

8 Save and close the file.

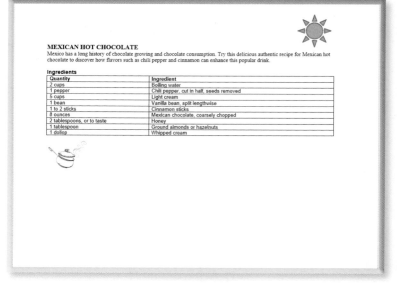

Completed Skill 10

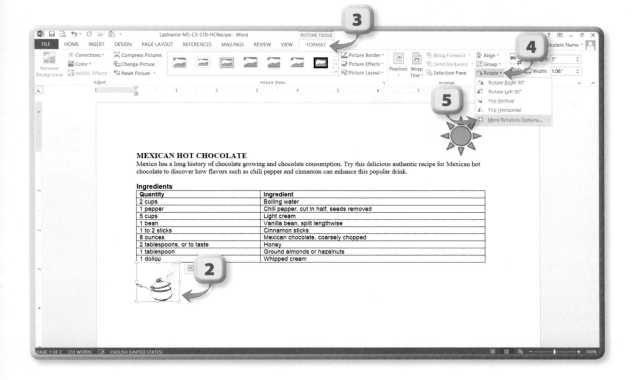

MEXICAN HOT CHOCOLATE

Mexico has a long history of chocolate growing and chocolate consumption. Try this delicious authentic recipe for Mexican hot chocolate to discover how flavors such as chili pepper and cinnamon can enhance this popular drink.

Ingredients

Quantity	Ingredient
2 cups	Boiling water
1 pepper	Chili pepper, cut in half, seeds removed
5 cups	Light cream
1 bean	Vanilla bean, split lengthwise
1 to 2 sticks	Cinnamon sticks
8 ounces	Mexican chocolate, coarsely chopped
2 tablespoons, or to taste	Honey
1 tablespoon	Ground almonds or hazelnuts
1 dollop	Whipped cream

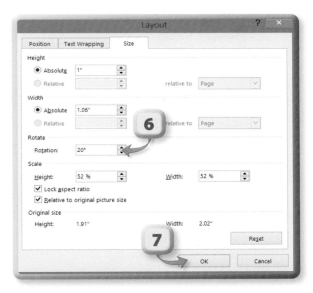

Taking It Further

Creating Word Art You can further enhance Word documents by using WordArt. Click the WordArt button in the Text group on the INSERT tab and select a WordArt style to insert a text box that reads *Your text here*. Select the placeholder text and type to customize the text. Make further formatting changes to the WordArt text by clicking options on the DRAWING TOOLS FORMAT tab, which is available when the WordArt object is active.

Word

Chapter 3 Assessments

Tasks Summary

Task	Ribbon Tab, Group	Button, Option	Shortcut, Alternative
INSERT table	INSERT, Tables		
Move to next cell			Tab
Convert selected text to table	INSERT, Tables		
Change document orientation	PAGE LAYOUT, Page Setup		
Insert rows	TABLE TOOLS LAYOUT, Rows & Columns		
Insert columns	TABLE TOOLS LAYOUT, Rows & Columns		
Merge cells	TABLE TOOLS LAYOUT		
Format cell borders	TABLE TOOLS DESIGN, Table Styles		
Insert shapes	INSERT, Illustrations		
Change shape fill	DRAWING TOOLS FORMAT, Shape Styles	Shape Fill	
Insert online picture	INSERT, Illustrations		
Insert picture from file	INSERT, Illustrations		
Resize objects	DRAWING TOOLS FORMAT, Size	*Shape Height* and *Shape Width* measurement boxes	Resizing handles
Rotate objects	DRAWING TOOLS FORMAT, Arrange	*Rotation* measurement box	Rotation handle

Features Review

Select the best answer from the choices given.

1 Tables are made up of
   a. numbered lists.
   b. bulleted lists.
   c. rows and columns.
   d. formulas.

2 The following can indicate where a new column begins when converting text to a table.
   a. tab
   b. comma
   c. hyphen
   d. tab, comma, or hyphen

3 Which orientation describes a document that is longer than it is wide?
   a. landscape
   b. portrait
   c. horizontal
   d. narrow

4 You can insert a new row above the selected row by
   a. displaying the TABLE TOOLS LAYOUT tab and clicking the Insert Above button.
   b. displaying the TABLE TOOLS LAYOUT tab and clicking the Insert Below button.
   c. pressing Ctrl + Alt + A.
   d. You can't add rows to tables after you've created them.

5 The process of combining cells in a table is called
   a. combining.
   b. mail merge.
   c. merging.
   d. collapsing.

6 A table can be made to look like columnar text by
   a. removing the cell borders.
   b. changing the font colors.
   c. modifying the line spacing.
   d. changing the paragraph spacing.

7 The Shapes button in the Illustrations group allows you to insert various shapes by
   a. choosing them from clip art.
   b. drawing them on your page.
   c. inserting pictures.
   d. copying shapes from the Internet.

8 Which of the following items *cannot* be inserted using the Illustrations group on the INSERT tab?
   a. online pictures
   b. screenshots
   c. media
   d. shapes

9 Which of the following will *not* allow you to resize a graphic?
   a. clicking the Position button on the DRAWING TOOLS FORMAT tab and then clicking the size in the drop-down list
   b. typing a number in the *Shape Height* measurement box on the DRAWING TOOLS FORMAT tab
   c. typing a number in the *Shape Width* measurement box on the DRAWING TOOLS FORMAT tab
   d. clicking and dragging the object handles

10 To keep an object proportional while resizing it, click and drag
   a. a corner handle.
   b. a side handle.
   c. a proportional handle.
   d. the center of the object.

Hands-On Skills Review

Exercise | A | Create a Party Invitation List

Skills   Create tables, change page orientation, insert a row in a table, and format tables

Scenario   You are planning a birthday party for John and inviting your family and a few close friends. You expect to send out seven invitations. Create a table to assist with tracking the responses to your invitations.

The table will have the following columns:

Name—this may be one name (Jamal Sawatdee), a couple (Rose and Jimmy Redcedar), or a family (The Stone family)

Snail Mail Address—for paper invitations

Email Address—for "Hold the Date" notices

Invited Number—how many people are invited? Using the example above, 1 for Jamal Sawatdee, 2 for the Redcedars, and 3 or more for the Stone family

RSVP Date—date when a response is received

Number Attending—how many people are planning to come? This number may differ from the number invited

Steps

1. Open **M5-C3-ExA-PartyGuests.docx**, the student data file, and save the file as **Lastname-M5-C3-ExA-PartyGuests**, but replace *Lastname* with your last name.

2. Change the page orientation to landscape and set the margins to narrow.

3. Change the font of the title *John's Birthday Party* to Calibri 18 pt and center the title.

4. On the next line, insert a table that contains six columns and eight rows (one for the header information and seven for the invitee information). The rows can be added when the table is created or as you enter data.

5. Enter the column heading information given at the beginning of this exercise. The column headings are in italics.

6. Bold all column headings.

7. Enter the following data into the columns. The semicolons in the data separate the content into columns. **HINT:** *To force the email addresses to appear as hyperlinks, use the Tab key to move from column to column.*

     Clinton, Hillary and Bill;
     864 Sunny Street,
     Chappaqua, NY 10514;
     theclintons@emcp.net;
     2 invited guests

     Franklin, Benjamin;
     56 Electric Way,
     Philadelphia, PA 19102;
     benji@emcp.net;
     1 invited guest

     Hopper, Grace and Alvin;
     12 Technology Drive,
     Richmond, VA 23219;
     debug@emcp.net;
     2 invited guests

     Maher, Bill;
     27 Hollywood Bowl,
     Los Angeles, CA 90005;
     comicbill@emcp.net;
     1 invited guest

     Nguyen, Lily;
     89 Broadway,
     Montana City, MT 59634;
     lily@emcp.net;
     1 invited guest

     Obama, Barack, Michelle, and family;
     1600 Pennsylvania Ave NW,
     Washington, DC 20500;
     firstlady@emcp.net;
     4 invited guests

     Washington, George;
     1222 Cherry Tree Lane,
     Washington, DC 20374;
     george@emcp.net;
     1 invited guest

8. Size the columns to fit the data. **HINT:** *Use the AutoFit button on the TABLE TOOLS LAYOUT tab select the AutoFit Contents option, and then then adjust the columns, if needed, to ensure the* Snail Mail Address *column uses only two lines for each invitee and all other columns use only one line per invitee.*

9 Center the headings both vertically and horizontally. **HINT:** *Use the appropriate alignment button on the TABLE TOOLS LAYOUT tab.*

10 Center the data in the *Invited Number* column.

11 Insert a page break at the end of the document.

12 Highlight the content of the title and the entire table and copy and paste the selected content below the page break. **HINT:** *You may want to turn on Show/Hide to ensure you are pasting the content just below the page break.*

13 Make the following changes to page 2 of the document. Do not modify page 1.
 a. You had an argument with Benjamin Franklin and decided he should not be invited. Delete that row from the table.
 b. Recently you became friends with the Jones family. You have decided to invite the entire family. Your invitees are arranged in alphabetical order by last name. Insert a row at the correct location and add the data for the Jones family:
 Jones Family; 1999 Pine Road, Dallas, TX 75203; momtheresa@emcp.net; 5 invited guests

14 Adjust the columns in the table on page 2, if needed, to ensure that the *Snail Mail Address* column uses only two lines per invitee and all other columns use only one line per invitee.

15 Insert a header with your name on the left and the current date on the right.

16 Insert a footer that displays the page number centered.

17 Save and close the file.

18 Print or submit the document as specified by your instructor.

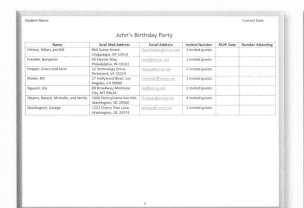

Completed Exercise A

Exercise B Creating a New Kind of "Dear John Letter"

Skills Convert text to tables, format tables, insert shapes, and resize objects

Scenario Jane has been offered a new position with additional responsibilities and a large salary increase. She had interviewed for the position several months ago, but just got the offer this morning. And the new position begins tonight! The only bad news with this job is the rather complex work schedule. Format the note Jane is leaving for her husband John to make it easy for him to follow her new work schedule.

Steps

1 Open **M5-C3-ExB-JobNote.docx**, the student data file, and save the file as **Lastname-M5-C3-ExB-JobNote**, but replace *Lastname* with your last name.

2 Add a header to the document that includes your name at the left margin.

3 Check the spelling in the document and fix all errors.

4 Replace the words *Current Date* with the date for today and format the date using the Intense Emphasis style.

5 Bold the text *My new work schedule will be:*

6 Convert the schedule (the lines beginning with the days of the week, from Sunday through Saturday) into a table. Tabs have been used to separate the day of the week and the work hours. Use AutoFit so the table appears as shown in the image of the completed exercise document.

7 Make sure there is one blank line between the table and the final paragraph that begins *It will take.* **HINT:** *Turn on Show/Hide ¶ to be sure you insert only one line at the correct location.*

8 Apply the *Intense Emphasis* style to the closing, *Love,* and *Jane.*

9 Change the font of all text in the document to 14-point Calibri.

10 Draw a heart (in the *Basic Shapes* section of the Shapes button drop-down list) that is 1.23 inches high and 2.15 inches wide. Change the fill color to red. Place the heart to the right of the closing. **HINT:** *Select the heart and use the DRAWING TOOLS FORMAT tab to adjust the size.*

11 Save and close the file.

12 Print or submit the completed document as directed by your instructor.

Completed Exercise B

Exercise Creating an Attractive Newsletter

Skills Change page orientation, insert objects and images, resize objects, and rotate objects

Scenario Open the text for the first page of a newsletter. Reformat the text so it looks similar to the final four-column newsletter shown at the end of the exercise.

Steps

1 Open **M5-C3-ExC-Newsletter.docx**, the student data file, and save the file as **Lastname-M5-C3-ExC-Newsletter**, but replace *Lastname* with your last name.

2 Change to landscape orientation.

3 Set the margins to Narrow (0.5 inch on each side).

4 Add a three-part header:
- Left: Your name
- Center: Newsletter (Change font to Copperplate Gothic Bold 22 pt.)
- Right: Winter Edition, December 28, 2015

Press enter after typing the date to add a blank line in the header.

5 Highlight the body of the newsletter and create four columns of equal width.

6 Single space the body text and change the after paragraph spacing to 6 points.

7 Bold the four headings in the newsletter and change them to small caps. **HINT:** *Use the dialog box launcher in the Font group on the HOME tab to open the Font dialog box. Click the Small caps check box to insert a check mark and then click OK. Use the Format Painter to copy the format to the remaining headings.*

8 Insert a column page break to force the heading *Discounts and More Discounts* to appear at the top of the second column. **HINT:** *Position the mouse pointer in front of the heading, click the PAGE LAYOUT tab, click the Breaks button in the Page Setup group, and then click the Column option.*

9   Move the *Red Cross Blood Drive* heading and the related text to the second column following the *Discounts and More Discounts* section. **HINT:** *Turn on Show/Hide ¶ to be sure you select only the text and place it in the correct location.*

10 If necessary, insert a column break to force the heading On This Day: to appear at the top of the third column.

11 Place a column break before *1945* so that the balance of this section moves to the fourth column.

12 Enter the following text at the bottom of the fourth column: "My New Year's resolution is to stop feeling guilty about last year's resolution." Change the font to 14-point Calibri and bold and italicize the text.

13 Insert a hard return after the 2008 entry at the end of the *On This Day* section and insert a Happy New Year online picture like the one shown in the image of the completed exercise document. Change the width of the online picture to fill the width of the column. For the online picture shown, the width is 2.13 inches.

14 Insert a text box at the bottom of the third column. **HINT:** *In the Text group on the INSERT tab, click the Text Box button and then click the Simple Text Box option.* Enter the text "If you really put a small value upon yourself, rest assured that the world will not raise your price." (Anonymous). Change the font to 16-point Calibri and italicize and center the text. Change the height of the text box to 2 inches and the width to 2.42 inches. If necessary, move the text box so it appears at the bottom of the column. **EXPERIMENT:** *Click the Shape Effects button in the Shape Styles group on the DRAWING TOOLS FORMAT tab. Select 3-D Rotation in the drop-down menu and then click the Off Axis 2 Left option in the Parallel section.* If the fourth column moves to a second page, turn on Show/Hide ¶ and delete the extra blank lines (which will now appear as paragraph symbols).

15 Enter "Blessed are we who can laugh at ourselves for we shall never cease to be amused." (Anonymous) at the bottom of column 1. Change the font to 14-point Calibri and bold and italicize the text.

16 Justify the entire document.

17 Add an underline to each year in the section *On This Day*.

18 Save and close the file.

19 Print or submit the completed document as directed by your instructor.

Completed Exercise C

Chapter 4

Finalizing and Sharing Documents

Some documents require the input of several people. Coworkers might have to give feedback on a report or project schedule prepared by another employee; your family might add names to a holiday card list generated by one member, and so on. Word makes it easy to provide that input through the tools on the REVIEW tab. These tools allow others to make changes that can be tracked and to insert comments with suggestions or questions. You can then review their suggested changes and choose which ones to accept or reject. You can also review their comments and questions and decide whether to act on them. When you're done reviewing comments, simply delete all comments and accept or reject changes and your document is final.

Word 2013 offers a new option called Simple Mode. Rather than showing you the detailed marked-up changes, the new option shows you a cleaner version of the document with edits included. Changes are shown but in a more subtle manner. Word also offers an option to lock Track Changes. You might want to use this option to make sure everyone's changes are recorded. With this option, a password is created when you turn Track Changes on and must be provided to turn Track Changes off.

How do you get your document into the hands of other people so they can begin providing you with feedback, and how do you later distribute the final version to them? Word allows you to share documents in two ways: by sending them as email attachments or by posting them to the Web in PDF format (a format that doesn't require you to have the originating software). The free, easy-to-use Adobe Reader software enables widespread use of PDF documents. Documents can also be shared using SkyDrive.

Skills You Learn

1. Turn on and lock review features
2. Send a document via email
3. Make changes and add comments
4. Accept or reject changes and review comments
5. Create a PDF document
6. Get social

What You Need
For these skills, you need the following student data files.

M5-C4-S1-WorkSchedule.docx

M5-C4-S5-WorkScheduleFinal.docx

What You Create

Today you're focusing on coordinating several volunteers who will work in a new exhibit, Chocolate in the Media, during its opening weekend at The Chocolate Museum. The exhibit presents photos and movies that feature chocolate as a major theme, such as the movie *Willy Wonka and the Chocolate Factory*. The volunteers will help make sure all the media are working correctly on this first weekend of the Museum's new exhibit.

You need to create a memo to the volunteers that includes a work schedule. To first make sure that the schedule is acceptable to all the volunteers, you send it to each of them to review, suggest changes and make comments, and return. To get the draft schedule out, you send the memo in an email and then review changes and comments that others have made so you can decide how to revise and finalize the schedule. Alternatively, you can share the schedule on SkyDrive. Once you have a final schedule, you learn how to save it as a PDF file so you can publish it to the Web and share it with anybody, whether or not they have Word on their computer.

Work Schedule Memo

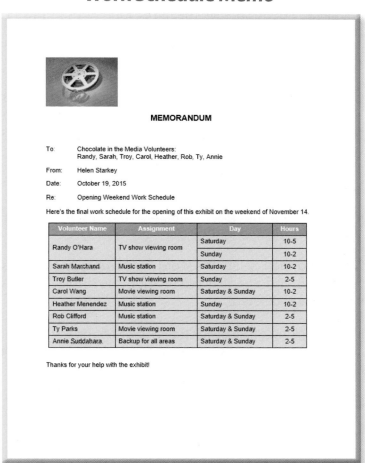

MEMORANDUM

To: Chocolate in the Media Volunteers:
        Randy, Sarah, Troy, Carol, Heather, Rob, Ty, Annie

From: Helen Starkey

Date: October 19, 2015

Re: Opening Weekend Work Schedule

Here's the final work schedule for the opening of this exhibit on the weekend of November 14.

Volunteer Name	Assignment	Day	Hours
Randy O'Hara	TV show viewing room	Saturday	10-5
		Sunday	10-2
Sarah Marchand	Music station	Saturday	10-2
Troy Butler	TV show viewing room	Sunday	2-5
Carol Wang	Movie viewing room	Saturday & Sunday	10-2
Heather Menendez	Music station	Sunday	10-2
Rob Clifford	Music station	Saturday & Sunday	2-5
Ty Parks	Movie viewing room	Saturday & Sunday	2-5
Annie Suddahara	Backup for all areas	Saturday & Sunday	2-5

Thanks for your help with the exhibit!

Word

Video ▶ M5_C4_S01

Turn On and Lock Review Features

When you are working on a document, you may want others to review it. Before you send the document out, you can turn on Word's Track Changes feature to record all changes made by the reviewers. This feature strikes a line through deleted text and applies a font color to added text so you can see what changes each person has suggested. You can lock track changes so that reviewers cannot turn the feature off. When you get the reviewed document back, you can use tools on the REVIEW tab to display various versions of the document.

Steps

1 Open the student data file named **M5-C4-S1-WorkSchedule.docx** and if you not already done so, save the file in your Module 5 working folder on your storage medium.

2 Click the REVIEW tab.

3 Click the Track Changes button arrow (not the button) in the Tracking group and then click the *Lock Tracking* option. Notice that if you turn on Lock Tracking, you have the option of setting a password. Click the Cancel button to close the dialog box without setting Lock Tracking.

▶ Tip When Track Changes is locked, reviewers cannot turn off the feature or accept or reject changes.

4 Shortcut
Track Changes
Ctrl + Shift + E

4 Click the Track Changes button (not the arrow) in the Tracking group.

▶ Tip Selecting *No Markup* displays the document as it would look with all changes accepted. *Original* shows the original document with no changes. The *All Markup* option shows all changes to formatting, as well as all deletions and additions. *Simple Markup* provides a clean view of the document and an indicator showing where a change has been made.

5 In the Tracking group, click the *Display for Review* option box arrow and then click *Simple Markup* in the drop-down list.

6 Select and then delete the word *Memorandum*. Note that the deleted text disappears and a vertical red revision line displays to the left of the line from which it was deleted.

7 In the Tracking group, click the *Display for Review* option box arrow and then click *All Markup*. Note that the revision line changes color and the deleted text changes color and has a strikethrough mark.

6 Shortcut
All Markup
Double-click the red revision line.

8 Click the Undo button on the Quick Access toolbar to undo the deletion.

9 Close the file without saving.

7 Shortcut
Undo
Ctrl + Z

Taking It Further

Using Read Mode   Use Read mode from the VIEW tab to swipe through pages horizontally as if reading a book. To zoom on a particular section, right-click.

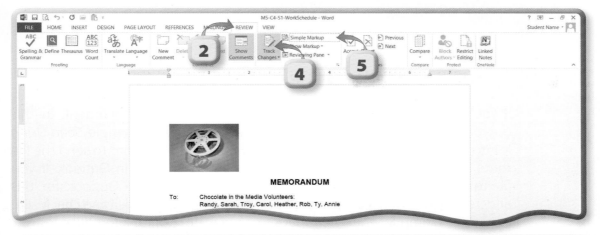

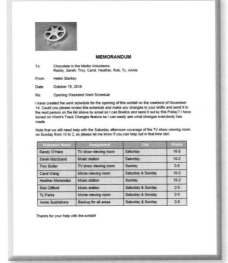

Completed Skill 1

Taking It Further

Comparing Documents The Compare feature on the REVIEW tab is useful if you want to compare two versions of a document but have not turned on Track Changes. To view the changes made to the original document, click the Compare button. You can then select two documents to compare, review the differences between them, and incorporate or reject those changes. You can also combine revisions from multiple authors into a single document using the Compare feature.

Word

Skill 2

Video ▶ M5_C4_S02

Send a Document via Email

If you want others to give feedback on your document, you have to get it into their hands. A quick and easy route is to email a copy of the Word file to them and ask them to review and return the marked-up file. You can then compile their feedback to create a final document. In this skill, you use the simple *Send Using E-mail* option in Word to send the file as an attachment in Outlook. If you are unable to use Outlook for this purpose, skip this skill and check with your instructor for alternative tasks.

Steps

1 Open the student data file named **M5-C4-S1-WorkSchedule.docx**, the file you reviewed in Skill 1.

2 Click the FILE tab.

3 Click the *Share* option.

4 Click the *Email* option in the *Share* section.

5 Click the Send as Attachment button in the *Email* section. An email form appears.

6 Enter your own email address in the *To* field.

▶ **Tip** You can also send a document as a link within an email message. The recipient clicks the link to go to the document. Using this method requires that you post the document in a shared location such as a publicly accessible website or company network.

▶ **Tip** The file name is automatically placed in the *Subject* field. Take a moment to modify the *Subject* field if the file name is not descriptive.

7 Type the following message in the body of the email: Randy, [Enter] Please review this work schedule and let me know if any of the times assigned to you will cause problems. [Enter] Helen

Completed Skill 2

8 Click the Send button.

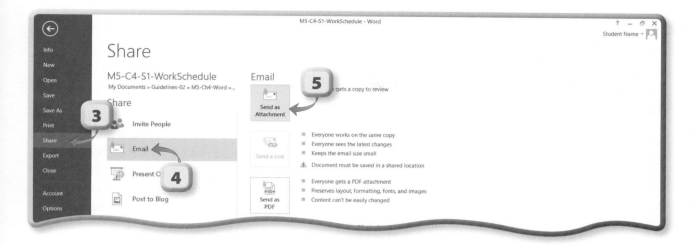

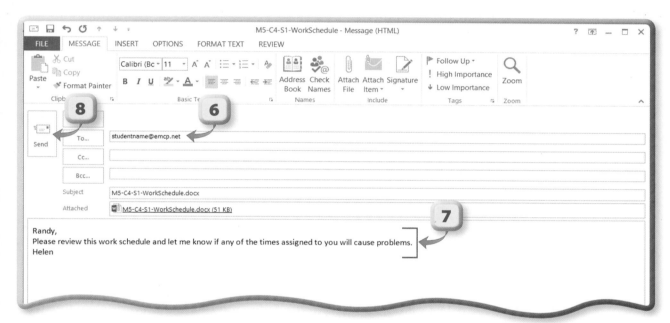

Taking It Further

Controlling the Review of the Files If you email multiple copies of a document to different people for review, you may find yourself with a "version control" issue when the many responses arrive. You may have to place each copy on your local storage medium, separately review each person's changes, and then be careful to integrate all desired changes into a single, master copy of the document. With a short document, such as our work schedule, where each person is likely to change only the small bits of content that refer to him- or herself, you may not have a major problem. However, with large documents, such as a 20-page report, filtering through several commented documents to decide upon changes and then implementing

those decisions from multiple documents into the master can be a version-management headache. In such cases, consider routing a single version of the document from person to person with direction to have the last person in the chain return the document to you. Or post one version on an online document-sharing space such as Google Drive, Dropbox, or KeepandShare.com. Many sites are free and control access to avoid version-management problems. You can also save the file to your SkyDrive account and send each reviewer a link to the document so that all the reviewers can track their changes in the same document. Skill 6 in Chapter 2 of the Introduction (Your Digital Toolkit) explains how to share files on SkyDrive.

Word

Video ▶ M5_C4_S03

Make Changes and Add Comments

When you work in a document that has Track Changes turned on, any changes you make to it are automatically recorded. Any additions or edits you make are indicated in colored text and any deletions you make are indicated with strikethroughs. Track Changes also records comments and formatting changes. You can choose to display all of these changes, some of them, or none of them, and you can display them inline, in balloons in the margin, or in a Reviewing pane. The Comments feature allows you to suggest changes rather than making them directly in the text, explain your edits, and ask questions. In this skill, you make direct changes and add comments to the document. Note that Word tracks the changes from different responders in different colors. Comments are numbered and are identified with the responders' initials.

Steps

1. If it is not already open, open **M5-C4-S1-WorkSchedule.docx**, the file you saved in Skill 1, and save the file as **M5-C4-S3-WorkSchedule**.

2. Click the REVIEW tab and then click the Track Changes button in the Tracking group.

3. Click the *Display for Review* option box arrow and then click *All Markup* in the drop-down list.

4. Select the last paragraph before the table, the one that begins *Note that we still*, and then press the Delete key.

5. Select *Randy O'Hara* in the *Volunteer Name* column of the table.

6. Change the font to Comic Sans MS.

Taking It Further

Changing Your User Name   When you hover your mouse over a change in a document that has Track Changes activated, a small box appears with details about who made the change and on what date. That user information comes from the document's properties. By default, the user name is taken from the user name you probably entered for your computer when you first set up Windows. However, you can change that name in each document if you like.

For example, you might be using a family computer and want changes tracked with your first name rather than the family name. To change the author name associated with a document, click the Change Tracking Options dialog box launcher, click the Change User Name button, enter a new user name , and then click to insert a check mark in the *Always use these values regardless of sign in to Office* check box in the Word Options dialog box that appears.

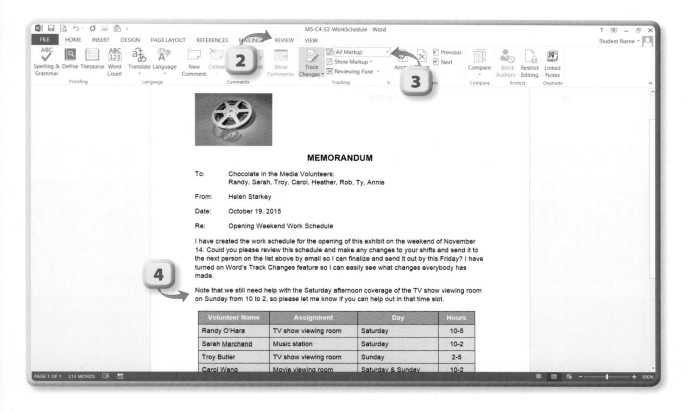

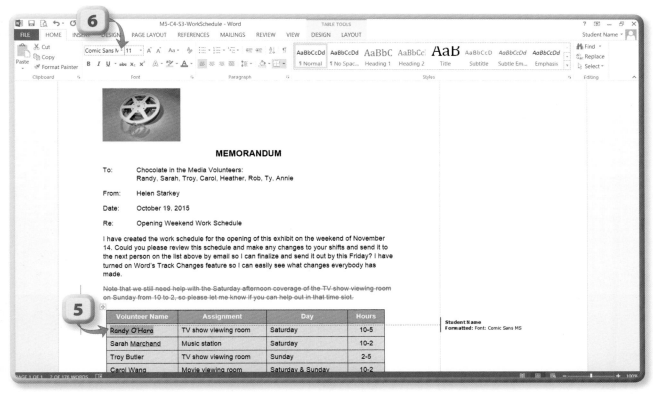

7 In the *Randy O'Hara* row, click to the right of the word *Saturday* in the *Day* column.

▶Tip Note that the reviewer's name is added to the beginning of the comment and that the time and date also appear when you hover your mouse pointer on the comment.

8 Insert a space and then type & Sunday 10-2.

9 Click the REVIEW tab.

10 Click the New Comment button in the Comments group.

▶Tip After you have read a comment and made any necessary changes or responses, you can right-click the comment and select *Mark Comment Done*.

11 In the comment balloon that appears, type I can cover the Sunday 10-2 slot so I've added that here. Randy.

12 Click the Save button on the Quick Access toolbar to save the file.

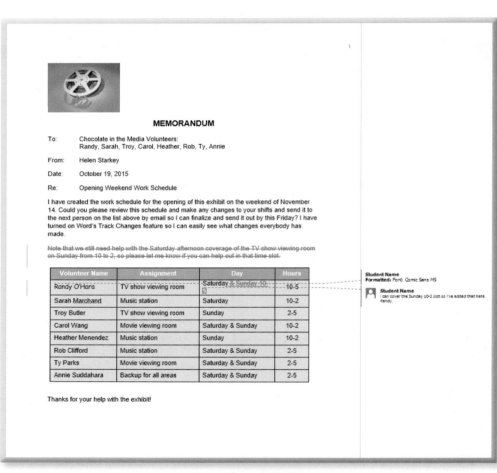

Completed Skill 3

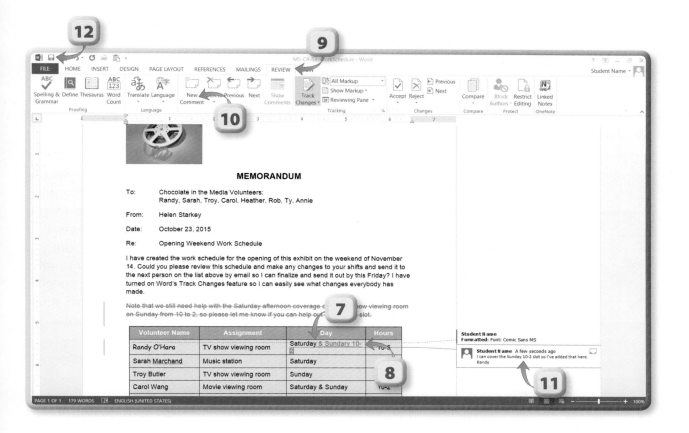

Word

Skill 4

Video ▸ M5_C4_S04

Accept or Reject Changes and Review Comments

After you have gathered feedback on your document, you must take a few more steps to finalize it. In this skill, you review everybody's changes and make choices about them. You can either accept or reject the changes one at a time or make a global decision to accept or reject *all* document changes at once. After you have acted on the suggested changes, you may have some comments remaining in the margin, because a reviewer can make changes without adding a comment and provide comments that are not connected to specific changes. As a last step, you must delete all remaining comments.

Steps

1 If it is not already open, open **M5-C4-S3-WorkSchedule.docx**, the file you saved in Skill 3, and save the file as **Lastname-M5-C4-S4-WorkSchedule**, replacing *Lastname* with your name. Be sure to save the file in your Module 5 working folder on your storage medium.

2 If it is not already active, click the REVIEW tab and set the *Display for Review* option to *All Markup*.

3 Click the Reviewing Pane button in the Tracking group. This opens the Revisions pane.

▸Tip In these steps, *Student Name* represents the user name for the document. See the Taking It Further feature in the previous skill for information about changing user names.

4 Click anywhere in the change listed under the heading *Student Name Deleted* in the Revisions pane.

5 Click the Accept button in the Changes group. This accepts the change in the file and removes the *Student Name Deleted* change from the Revisions pane.

5 *Another Way*
You can also right-click the change in the Revisions pane and choose *Accept Deletion* from the shortcut menu that appears.

6 Click anywhere in the change listed under the heading *Student Name Formatted* in the Revisions pane.

7 Click the Reject button in the Changes group to reject the change.

Taking It Further

Protecting Files   The Protect group on the REVIEW tab provides two tools for limiting what reviewers can do when looking over your documents. If you do not want reviewers to directly change your text, but do want them to make comments so that you can decide what changes to make, click the Restrict Editing button and then choose *Comments* from the drop-down list. If you want to allow some reviewers to edit the document and keep other reviewers from making any changes, use the Block Authors button.

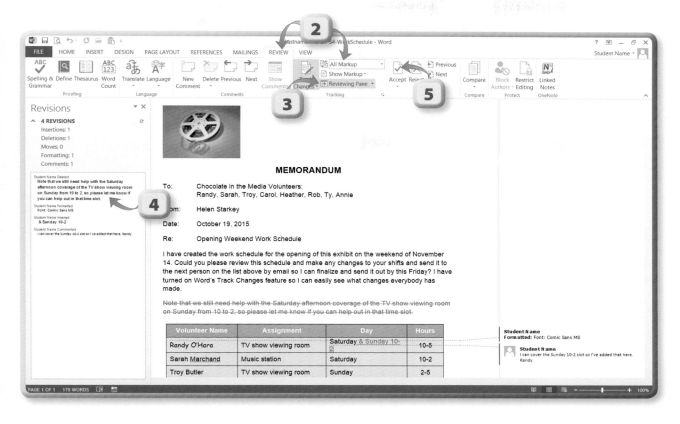

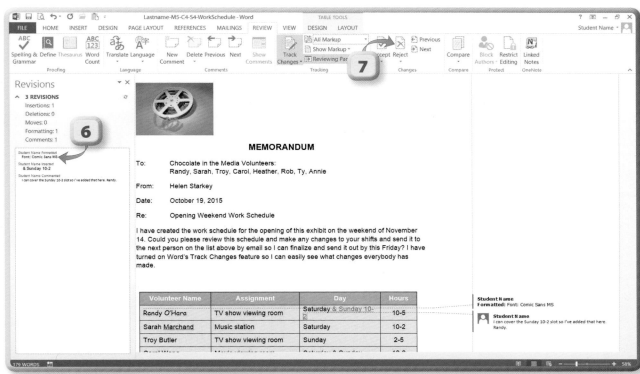

More

Tip If you want to reject or accept all changes in a document, you can use the *Accept/Reject All Changes in Document* option in the Accept or Reject button menus.

Tip If you want to delete all comments in a document, click the arrow on the Delete Comment button and then choose *Delete All Comments in Document*.

Tip Before sending out any document as final, be sure that the copy is clean by double-checking that you have accepted or rejected each change. Click the Track Changes button in the Reviewing group on the REVIEW tab to stop tracking edits to the document.

8 Click anywhere in the change listed under the heading *Student Name Inserted* in the Revisions pane.

9 Click the Accept button to accept the change and insert the text.

10 Click anywhere in the change listed under the heading *Student Name Commented* in the Revisions pane.

11 Click the Delete button in the Comments group.

12 Click the Reviewing Pane button in the Tracking group to close the Revisions pane.

13 Save and close the file.

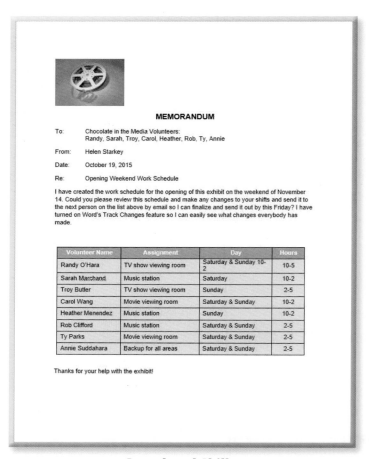

MEMORANDUM

To: Chocolate in the Media Volunteers:
         Randy, Sarah, Troy, Carol, Heather, Rob, Ty, Annie

From: Helen Starkey

Date: October 19, 2015

Re: Opening Weekend Work Schedule

I have created the work schedule for the opening of this exhibit on the weekend of November 14. Could you please review this schedule and make any changes to your shifts and send it to the next person on the list above by email so I can finalize and send it out by this Friday? I have turned on Word's Track Changes feature so I can easily see what changes everybody has made.

Volunteer Name	Assignment	Day	Hours
Randy O'Hara	TV show viewing room	Saturday & Sunday 10-2	10-5
Sarah Marchand	Music station	Saturday	10-2
Troy Butler	TV show viewing room	Sunday	2-5
Carol Wang	Movie viewing room	Saturday & Sunday	10-2
Heather Menendez	Music station	Sunday	10-2
Rob Clifford	Music station	Saturday & Sunday	2-5
Ty Parks	Movie viewing room	Saturday & Sunday	2-5
Annie Suddahara	Backup for all areas	Saturday & Sunday	2-5

Thanks for your help with the exhibit!

Completed Skill 4

Word

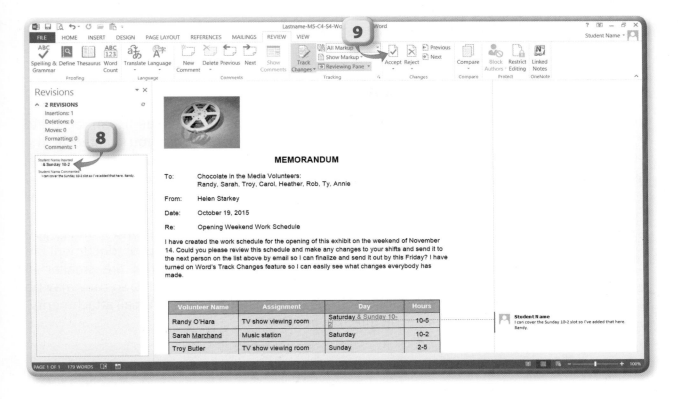

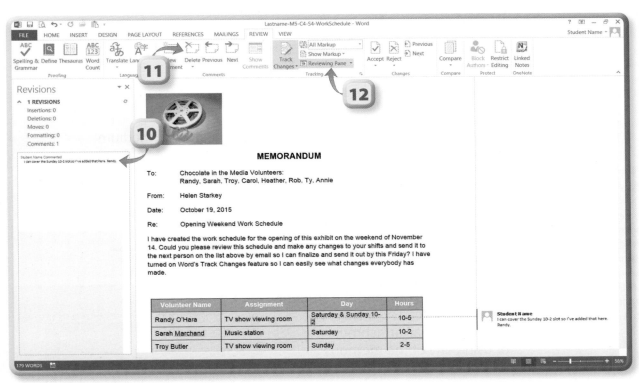

Create a PDF Document

When you are ready to share a copy of your final work schedule with others, it may be useful to save the file as a PDF file. PDF is a file format created by Adobe and is the standard for document sharing. Using the free Adobe Reader program, anybody can view a PDF file, whether or not they have Word installed on their computer. A PDF version of your document is in some ways like a picture, because what people see is an accurate image of what you created at the moment of capture. Thus, the file, or image, won't be compromised by being opened in different versions of Word, some of which may not support the fonts and features you used to create your document. In addition, PDF files are smaller in size than Word files, so they may be easier to send as email attachments.

Steps

1 Open the student data file **M5-C4-S5-WorkScheduleFinal.docx**.

2 Click the FILE tab.

3 Click the *Save as* option.

4 Locate your Module 5 working folder on your storage medium.

5 *Another Way*

Another way to save to the PDF format is to click the FILE tab and then click the *Export* option. In the Export dialog box, click *the Create PDF/XPS Document* option and then click the Create PDF/XPS button. Click the Publish button from the Publish as PDF or XPS dialog box.

▶ *Tip* To get the free Adobe Reader software used to view PDF files, go to www.adobe.com.

5 Click the *Save as type* option box arrow and then select *PDF (*.pdf)* from the drop-down list.

6 Click the Save button.

7 Close the new PDF and the student data file. You can now share the PDF as an email attachment or using any of the methods described in the next skill.

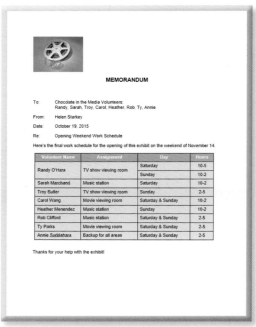

Completed Skill 5

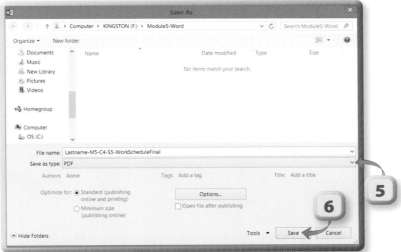

Taking It Further

Viewing and Editing PDFs   Adobe offers both the free Reader software and a more robust software program, called Acrobat, for purchase. Reader allows you to read a document in PDF format, while Acrobat allows you to edit PDF files, add comments to them, and more. For those who have Word 2013, Reader is sufficient, since Word 2013 allows you to edit PDF files. To edit a PDF in Word 2013, you must first convert the PDF to a Word document. Open a blank Word document, click the FILE tab, click the *Open* option, click the location of the PDF (e.g.,

your computer), click the Browse button, locate the PDF and select it, and then click Open. A new Word feature called PDF Reflow will convert the contents of the PDF and display them in the Word file. Make the changes you want, and then save the document as a PDF file again. ***NOTE:*** *The contents may not look exactly as they did in the PDF. For example, some fonts and art elements may not be supported by PDF Reflow. The conversion works best with documents that are mostly text.*

Word

Chapter 4

Skill 6

Video M5_C4_S06

Get Social

Sharing documents on the Web is a great way to get information out to others and receive feedback. Microsoft Office products make it easy to post files to the Web.

There are several ways to post a document on the Web using Word. Each requires that you have an online location to which you can save the document. This skill contains an overview of three methods you can access through the *Share* and *Save As* options in Word.

Steps

Save to the Cloud Using SkyDrive

▶ **Tip** Once you have added SkyDrive as a place to save, it will appear in the *Save As* options.

1 Using the SkyDrive feature of Word, you can share your documents after you have set up a Microsoft account. Once your account is established, you can upload a document file by following this command sequence: FILE tab, *Save As, Add a Place, SkyDrive*. You then sign into your Microsoft account, save your document to SkyDrive, and are ready to share a link to the document with others.

Post to Social Networks

2,3 *Another Way*
Another way to access SkyDrive and share a document is to click the FILE tab, click the *Share* option, click *Invite People*, and then click the Save to Cloud button. You can then share the document.

2 Once a file has been saved to your SkyDrive account, you can post the file to any social network sites that are connected to your Microsoft account by clicking the FILE tab, *Share*, and *Post to Social Networks*. You then click a social network, such as Facebook, to post the file to it. If your account is not connected to any social networks, click the <u>Click here to connect social networks</u> link.

Publish as a Blog Post

3 Word 2013 is set up to save files as blog postings using several popular blogging sites, including WordPress, SharePoint Blog, Blogger, Windows Live spaces, Community Server, and TypePad. Because the Web is ever-changing, additional blog sites may now be available. After you establish an account on one of these (or similar) services, you simply use this command sequence: FILE tab, *Share, Post to Blog* to post your document to a blogging site.

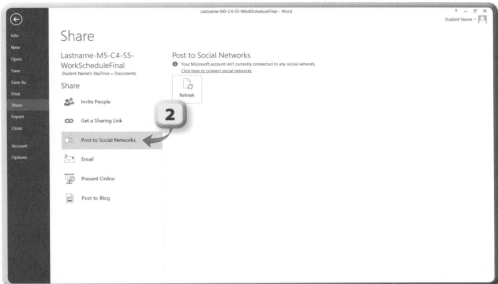

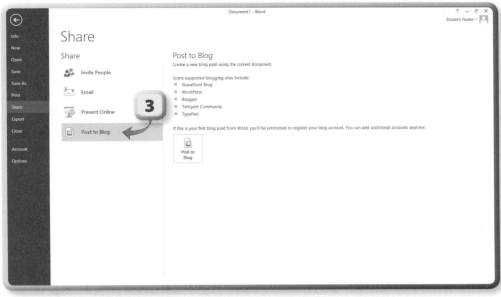

Word

Chapter 4 Assessments

Tasks Summary

Task	Ribbon Tab, Group	Button, Option	Shortcut, Alternative
Turn on/off Track Changes	REVIEW, Tracking		Ctrl + Shift + E
Display simple markup	REVIEW, Tracking	Simple Markup	
Display all markup	REVIEW, Tracking	All Markup	
Send a document via email	FILE, *Share*	*Email*	
Add comments	REVIEW, Comments		
Display Reviewing pane	REVIEW, Tracking		
Accept individual or all changes	REVIEW, Changes		
Reject individual or all changes	REVIEW, Changes		
Limit editing ability	REVIEW, Protect		
Restrict who can make changes	REVIEW, Protect		
Publish to SkyDrive	FILE, *Save As*	*Add a Place, SkyDrive*	
Post to a social network	FILE, *Share*	*Post to Social Network*	
Publish to a blog	FILE, *Share*	*Post to Blog*	
Save in PDF format	FILE, *Save As*	*PDF (*.pdf)*	

Features Review

Select the best answer from the choices given.

1 To turn on Review features in Word, click this button on the REVIEW tab.
   a. Show Markup
   b. Reviewing Pane
   c. Track Changes
   d. Review

2 Word's *Send as Email* option is set up to send an attachment via email using
   a. Internet Explorer.
   b. Yahoo! Mail.
   c. Outlook.
   d. OneNote.

3 With Track Changes turned on, Word indicates the author of each comment and edit by
   a. using different colors and commenter initials.
   b. saving the comments in separate files.
   c. using different font sizes.
   d. using the Emphasis style.

4 If the document has been edited with Track Changes turned on, you can review the edits and use the buttons in the Changes group on the REVIEW tab to either accept or _____ them.
   a. highlight
   b. bold
   c. reject
   d. refuse

5 You can share documents using this tab.
   a. REFERENCES
   b. HOME
   c. FILE
   d. MAILINGS

6 You can use the _____ software to edit PDF files.
   a. Word 2013
   b. Windows 8 Paint
   c. SkyDrive
   d. Markup 2013

7 One way to store documents in the cloud is to use
   a. a CD.
   b. SkyDrive.
   c. Outlook.
   d. a USB flash drive.

8 The Restrict Editing button on the REVIEW tab allows you to
   a. turn off the Track Changes feature.
   b. compare two documents.
   c. limit changes that reviewers can make.
   d. add comments to a document.

9 Using the Reject button on the REVIEW tab, you can choose to reject a single change or
   a. all changes.
   b. changes by a certain reviewer.
   c. formatting changes.
   d. changes made past a certain date.

10 Which of the following is *not* true of a PDF file created from a Word document?
   a. A program that allows you to view the PDF file is free.
   b. The PDF file is typically larger in size than the original Word document.
   c. The PDF file can be opened and viewed on different computers.
   d. The PDF file can be opened in Word.

Hands-On Skills Review

Exercise **A** **Have the Courage to Edit Shakespeare**

SNAP
Grade It

Skills   Turn on and lock review features, and make changes and add comments

Scenario   Shakespeare's *Macbeth* is one of the great plays of all time. In this exercise you help correct mistakes in the script. Use Track Changes on the REVIEW tab to correct the original document. Add the comments where indicated to help the average reader better understand an older version of the English language

Steps

1 Open the student data file named **M5-C4-ExA-Tragedy.docx** and save the file as **Lastname-M5-C4-ExA-Tragedy**, replacing *Lastname* with your last name.

2 Turn on Track Changes on the REVIEW tab and set Display for Review to *All Markup*.

3 Change the font for the first two lines of text in the document, *The Tragedy of Marybeth* and *By Shakespeare,* to 14-point Calibri.

4 Insert a header that contains your name on the left side and the current date on the right side.

5 Insert a footer that displays a centered page number.

6 While tracking changes, implement the following corrections to the file.
   a. In the first line, change *Marybeth* to *Macbeth*.
   b. In the second Gentlewoman line (begins *It is an*), change *15 minutes* to *a quarter of an hour*.
   c. In the third Doctor line (begins *Hark!*), change *memory* to *remembrance*.
   d. In the second Lady Macbeth line (begins *Out, damn'd spot!*), change *do it* to *do't*.
   e. In the same Lady Macbeth line, change *Fe Fie Fo Fum* to *Fie*.
   f. In the same Lady Macbeth line, insert *none can call our pow'r to* after *knows it, when*.

g. In the third Lady Macbeth line (begins *The thane of Fife*), delete *I guess I need more soap!* and the blank space that follows the exclamation point. **HINT:** *Turn on Show/Hide ¶ to confirm you have the space selected.*

h. In the third Gentlewoman line (begins *She has spoke*), select the word *spoke* and insert a comment that reads *Incorrect tense based on our current standards of English.* (Include the period when you type this comment.)

i. In the eighth Doctor line (begins *This disease is*), select the word *practise* and insert a comment that reads *Old English spelling of* practice. (Italicize the word *practice* and type the period roman, without italics.)

7 Save the document.

8 Print or submit the completed document as directed by your instructor.

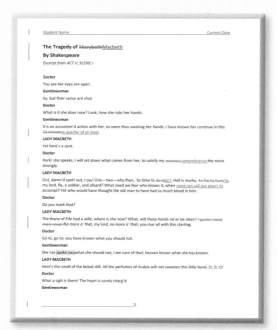

Completed Exercise A

Exercise B Revise a Poorly Edited Nursery Rhyme

Grade It

Skills Turn on and lock review features, accept or reject changes, and review comments

Scenario "Four and Twenty Blackbirds" is a nursery rhyme that is a favorite among children. They recite the words and wait for someone to pretend to "snip off" their nose.

This version of "Four and Twenty Blackbirds" has been reviewed and changes are provided that are meant to correct the errors. Unfortunately, the editor's suggestions are not all correct. Locate the real version of the nursery rhyme on the Web or use the version shown in Completed Exercise B. Compare the words in this version with the correct words. Accept or reject the editor's modifications accordingly. After acting upon the comments as needed, delete them. Do not make any other changes to the text.

Steps

1 Open the student data file named **M5-C4-ExB-NRhyme.docx** and save the file as **Lastname-M5-C4-ExB-NRhyme**, but replace *Lastname* with your last name.

2 Turn off the Track Changes feature.

3 Change the title *Four and Twenty Blackbirds* to 14-point Calibri and apply bold formatting.

4 Add a header with your name on the left side and the current date on the right side.

5 Accept or reject the changes in the student data file so that the final file matches the Completed Exercise B file displayed on the opposite page.

   a. Accept the change of *six cents* to *sixpence*.

   b. Reject the change of *sing* to *fly*.

   c. Read the comment related to the *king* to *queen* change and delete it.

   d. Reject the change of *king* to *queen*.

   e. Reject the change of *parlour* to *parlor*.

   f. Accept the change of *steak* to *bread*.

   g. Accept the change of *wash* to *clothes*.

   h. Read and delete the comment related to the last line.

6 Save the document.

7 Print or submit the completed document as directed by your instructor.

Completed Exercise B

Exercise **C** Finalize a Letter and Email It as a PDF Attachment

Skills Send a document via email and create a PDF document

Scenario Edit the letter to include the current date. Place your signature at the bottom. Create a PDF and send it to your instructor as an email attachment or as otherwise instructed.

Steps

1 Open the student data file named **M5-C4-ExC-Email.docx** and save the file as **Lastname-M5-C4-ExC-Email**, but replace *Lastname* with your last name.

2 Replace *March 12, 2015* with the current date.

3 Format the date so it is right-aligned and italicized.

4 In the closing, replace *Glenda Romero* with your name.

5 Change the font style of your name to 14-point Script MT Bold.

6 Save the document.

7 Save the document as a PDF file. Use the same name as your Word document: **Lastname-M5-C4-ExC-Email**. This file will have a .pdf extension rather than a .docx extension.

8 Share the PDF file with your instructor by sending it as an email attachment. ***NOTE:*** *Your instructor may provide different instructions for submission.*

Completed Exercise C

Module 5 Projects

Project 1

Skills   **CH1:** Enter and edit text, insert headers and footers **CH2:** Apply styles, format paragraph and line spacing, create bulleted or numbered lists, copy formatting with Format Painter, format text in columns **CH3:** Insert shapes, insert objects and images, resize objects

Scenario   You would like to enter your favorite recipe into the local cooks' competition. You decide that the recipe might be better received if the page looks inviting. Add formatting to your recipe so that the judges can't help but give it serious consideration.

Steps

1 Open the student data file named **M5-EOM-P1-TunaSalad.docx** and save the file on your student media as **Lastname-M5-EOM-P1-TunaSalad**, replacing *Lastname* with your last name.

2 Insert a header that displays your name on the left and the current date on the right.

3 Apply the Title style to *World's Best Tuna Salad*.

4 Change the layout for the ingredients list (not the subheading *Ingredients*) to two-column, single-spaced, with solid bullets. There should be five bullet points in the left column and six in the right column. If necessary, insert a column break in front of *2 stalks celery, chopped* to move it to the right column. **HINT:** *Before selecting the text, click the Show/Hide ¶ button to turn on the display of formatting characters. Be sure you do not include the paragraph mark before or after the ingredient list.*

5 The directions list should be displayed in a multi-level numbered list. Indent the content to create sublists as shown in the completed project image.

6 Add a section after the *Directions* section. With Show/Hide ¶ turned on, click on the paragraph symbol that is under numbered point 8. Press the Enter key to insert a blank line before you type the following content:

To Serve [Enter]
Line a platter with lettuce. [Enter]
Place tuna in center. [Enter]
Place tomato slices around the tuna. [Enter]
Serve with rolls, bread, or crackers.

7 Format the list under *To Serve* as a bulleted list using check marks as the bullets.

8 Search Office.com Clip Art for an image of someone mixing ingredients, by entering *mix chef* in the search text box. Select the graphic of the female chef that is shown in the completed project image. If you cannot find the exact image shown, select another appropriate graphic.

9 Size the image to a height of 2.01 inches and a width of 2.01 inches.

10 Use the PICTURE TOOLS FORMAT tab to change the Wrap Text setting to *Square* and then position the upper left corner of the female chef image horizontally at 4.5 inches to the right of the column and vertically at 3.2 inches below the margin.

11 Insert a 16-Point Star shape (*Stars and Banners* section of the Shapes button drop-down list) under the female chef image. Adjust the height and width of the image to 1 inch. Change the Shape Fill to *Orange* (in the *Standard Colors* section) and the Shape Outline to *Black, Text 1* (second option in the first row of the *Theme Colors* section). Drag the shape so it is horizontally centered under the female chef image and bottom-aligned with the last line of text.

12 Change the section subheadings (*Ingredients*, *Directions*, and *To Serve*) to 14-point Calibri and then apply bold and small caps formatting.

13 Save the document.

14 Print or submit the file as instructed.

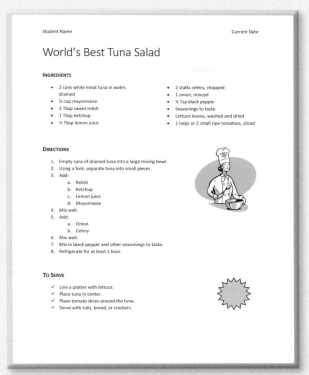

Completed Project 1

Project 2

Skills   **CH1:** Enter and edit text; use cut, copy, and paste; use the Show/Hide ¶ feature; indent and add tabs using the ruler; insert headers and footers **CH2:** Change font and font size, use formatting tools, apply styles, align text, format paragraph and line spacing **CH3:** Create tables, format tables

Scenario   You are the sales manager for a company that sells video games. You have good news to report to the president of the company. Create and format a memo that advises the president that sales are increasing and more inventory is needed.

Steps

1 Open the student data file named **M5-EOM-P2-SalesReportLtr.docx** and save the file as **Lastname-M5-EOM-P2-SalesReportLtr**, replacing *Lastname* with your last name.

2 Insert a Blank (Three Columns) header with your name on the left, *Project 2* in the center, and the current date on the right.

3 Insert a footer that includes the file name on the left. ***EXTENSION ACTIVITY:*** *Rather than type the file name, double-click the footer to make it active and then click the Quick Parts button in the Insert group on the HEADER & FOOTER TOOLS tab. From the drop-down list, click Field, select FileName from the options in the* Field names *list box, and then click OK.*

4 Select the first line, *Best Games, Inc.,* and apply the Heading 1 style.

5 Modify the three lines containing the Best Games contact information (address and phone number) as follows:
   a. Place the street address on the same line as the city, state, and zip code, separated by a comma and a single space. You now have two lines with company contact information, with the second line containing just the phone number.
   b. Apply the Subtitle style to the two lines of contact information.
   c. Single-space these lines and set the *Spacing After* option to 0.

6 Center the company name and contact information.

7 Adjust the four-line memo heading as follows:
  a. Cut and paste the lines so that they appear in the correct order: *To:, From:, Date:, Subject:*.
  b. Select the four lines and set a left tab at 1 inch.
  c. Apply bold formatting to the text *To, From, Date*, and *Subject*.
  d. Insert the current date in the *Date:* section of the memo heading.
  e. Insert your name in the *From:* section of the memo heading, replacing only the words *Student Name*.

8 Remove the extra blank line between the two paragraphs of the memo body. **HINT:** *Turn on Show/Hide ¶ and delete the second paragraph symbol after* last year *and before* To *ensure sufficient stock.*

9 Select the text *Summary of Top Sales* and change the font to 14-point Calibri. Apply bold formatting, change the font color to *Blue, Accent 1* (in the Theme Colors section of the dialog box), and center the text.

10 Insert a table on the line below *Summary of Top Sales* as follows:
  a. Insert a table that has 2 columns and 12 rows.
  b. Insert and format column headings as follows:
    i. Left column: *Name,* bold, align center left (vertical center and horizontal left)
    ii. Right column: *Release Year,* bold, align center (vertical and horizontal center)
  c. Table Data
    i. Enter the game names and years:
       Big Shock, 2007
       Call of Duty Black Ops 2, 2012
       The Elder Scrolls IV: Oblivion, 2006
       God of War, 2005
       Grand Theft Auto V, 2013
       Guitar Hero, 2005
       Halo, 2001
       Resident Evil 4, 2005
       Shadow of the Colossus, 2005
       The Sims, 2000
       World of Warcraft, 2004
    ii. Left-align the data in the *Name* column.
    iii. Center the data in the *Release Year* column.
    iv. Set the *Spacing After* option to 0 for all table rows.
  d. Size the columns to fit the contents using the AutoFit button on the TABLE TOOLS LAYOUT tab.
  e. Center the table using the Center button on the HOME tab.

11 Save the document.

12 Print or submit the file as instructed.

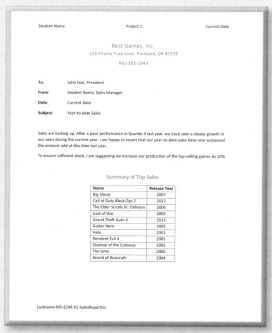

Completed Project 2

Project 3

Skills   **CH1:** Enter and edit text, perform a spelling and grammar check **CH2:** Change font and font size, use formatting tools, apply styles, align text, format paragraph and line spacing **CH3:** Insert shapes, insert objects and images, resize objects **CH4:** Turn on and lock review features, send a document via email, make changes and add comments, accept or reject changes and review comments, create a PDF document ***NOTE:*** *The skills list may vary depending upon choices made by the student.*

Scenario   Prepare a flyer about a classmate that introduces the classmate to the members of the class. To ensure the introductory content is correct, the subject of the flyer will have the opportunity to review, edit, and comment on the content of the flyer, which will be returned to you for final editing prior to submitting and sharing with your classmates.

Use at least five formatting features of Word to complete the project. For example, you may choose to change the font and font size, use formatting tools, apply styles, align text, format paragraph spacing, create a bulleted or numbered list, format text in columns, create tables, change document orientation, or insert shapes.

Steps, Part I

It is time to learn more about your classmates. Your instructor will pair you (Student 1) with another student (Student 2). Interview one another and prepare an introductory flyer that can be shared with your instructor and classmates. Student 1 interviews and creates an informative flyer about Student 2. Likewise, Student 2 interviews and creates an informative flyer about Student 1.

The flyer must include text and an image. Use at least five different formatting techniques and fill one page completely, without going over onto a second page. The flyer is to be informative and attractive. It should be ready for printing and posting of the printed copy or for conversion to PDF and electronic posting.

Some questions you may want to ask your partner to help develop content for the flyer include:
- Where were you born?
- Where do you live now?
- What are your favorite activities?
- Where do you work and what do you do at work?
- Why are you taking this class?
- What are your career goals?

When you complete the flyer, save it as **Lastname-M5-EOM-P3I-Flyer**, replacing *Lastname* with your last name. Send it as an email attachment to your partner and to your instructor.

Steps, Part II

Your partner has sent you the introductory flyer that he or she prepared. You have the opportunity to review and edit your own introduction before it is shared with the class. All changes you make in the document are to be tracked using Track Changes. You can also add comments that you believe will

be helpful to your partner as your partner makes the final modifications to the flyer. The reviewed document must contain at least two modifications to text, at least one modification to format, and at least three comments.

Save your reviewed document with the same name that your partner used to create the file in Part I, but change P3A to P3B, so the file name will be **Lastname-M5-EOM-P3II-Flyer**.

When your review is complete, send it back to your partner and your instructor as an email attachment.

Steps, Part III

The edited introductory flyer has been reviewed by its subject, Student 2, and returned to you, its creator, Student 1. Read the review comments and look over the changes suggested. Make decisions about the suggested changes by using the Accept or Reject buttons on the REVIEW tab. After you complete the review, check the document for any spelling errors. Ensure that the formatting makes the appropriate sections stand out and that the content fits on one page only. Save the completed document using the same name that your partner used when saving the edited file in Part II, but change P3B to P3C, so the file name will be **Lastname-M5-EOM-P3III-Flyer**. Create a PDF version of the flyer. Save the PDF with the same name: **Lastname-M5-EOM-P3IV-Flyer**. A .pdf extension will automatically replace the .docx extension used for Word documents.

Steps, Part IV

Share the file with your classmates via email, by posting to a course website, or as instructed.

MODULE 6

Microsoft Excel 2013

 Before beginning the module skills, copy the Module6–Excel folder from the Student Resources disc to your storage medium. The copied folder will become the working folder for this module.

Guidelines to Planning and

When you create a workbook in Excel, you should take the time to plan how you will organize the data on the worksheets. To do so, consider the source data you will use and the results you want to produce. Your plan will guide you as you enter the data on the worksheets.

For example, say you are creating a workbook of annual sales data. You have a list of four quarters of sales data and you also have a long list of products sold. You might see two arrangement options that make sense. One option is to place the data for each quarter on a separate worksheet. The other option is to create a different worksheet for each product and display each product's sales by quarter. In this example, the choice you make may depend on whether you want to emphasize the total sales of all your products for each quarter (the first option) or focus on the total sales by product (the second option).

Once you have entered and organized data on the worksheets, you can make any necessary calculations. For example, for each column of data, you can create a formula that sums the values to give you a quarterly total. And for each data row, you can create a formula that sums the results for the product in each row.

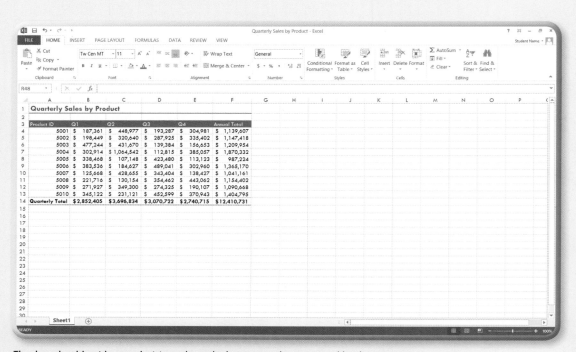

The data should guide your decisions about the best way to lay out a workbook.

Creating a Worksheet in Excel

If your worksheet includes an area where the user enters values to be calculated by Excel, position those input cells in a prominent location—usually near the top of the worksheet. Apply formatting that prompts the user for entries.

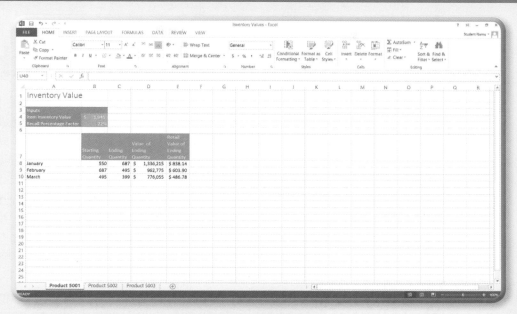

If a worksheet includes an input area, position those cells near the top of the worksheet or on a separate sheet.

In Excel, you can use business logos, shapes, and other graphics to enhance the appearance of your worksheets. Excel can also convey your worksheet data graphically in a chart. Charted data helps you spot trends and abnormalities, which can help you make better business decisions. For example, if sales for a particular product lag far behind other products' sales, a chart can help you quickly identify the trend.

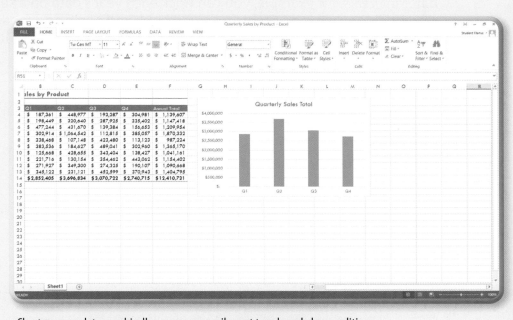

Charts convey data graphically, so you can easily spot trends and abnormalities.

When planning a worksheet, keep in mind your audience's expectations as well as industry standards. For example, in the financial industry, professionals follow accepted conventions and, in some cases, legal requirements when they design reports such as profit and loss statements, balance sheets, and loan payment tables.

Chapter 1

Creating an Excel Workbook

Excel is a spreadsheet program. Each Excel file is called a *workbook*. A workbook is divided into worksheets, and each worksheet is divided into cells so that you can organize data in a table-like format and perform calculations on that data. In this chapter, you learn how to enter data and navigate in Excel.

Excel arranges data in cells. To move from one piece of data to another, you move from cell to cell. Because you will be dealing with different types of data—numbers, text, and dates—you will learn how to enter each type of data to ensure that your calculations work. There are tools and tricks to help you out, such as automatically filling entries, quickly adding rows or columns, or checking the spelling of cell contents.

Rather than setting up each Excel spreadsheet as a single and lengthy page of data, you learn how to organize data on multiple pages, called *worksheets*, to help you group like kinds of data on their own sheets and make navigating your data easier. If you have sales data for different years, for example, you can track each year's data on a separate sheet in a single workbook. You can add sheets to a workbook and name and rename sheets as needed so that the data is easy to find and work with. Finally, you will learn how to set up and print a worksheet.

Skills You Learn

1   Understand worksheet and workbook structure
2   Use cell references
3   Enter text, values, and dates
4   Use the Auto Fill feature
5   Use the spelling checker
6   Insert and delete columns and rows
7   Work with multiple worksheets
8   Name and rename worksheets
9   Explore options for printing

Files You Need
For these skills, you do not need any student data files.

What You Create

You are continuing your work for The Chocolate Museum, a nonprofit organization that provides educational exhibits and information on the history of chocolate and its role in world cultures. The Museum must plan and budget for its exhibits and gift shop, and this planning requires tracking dates and calculating financial information. In this chapter, you produce an Excel workbook containing schedule and cost information for a new exhibit on chocolate in world cultures.

Schedule and Cost Information for the New Chocolate Museum Exhibit

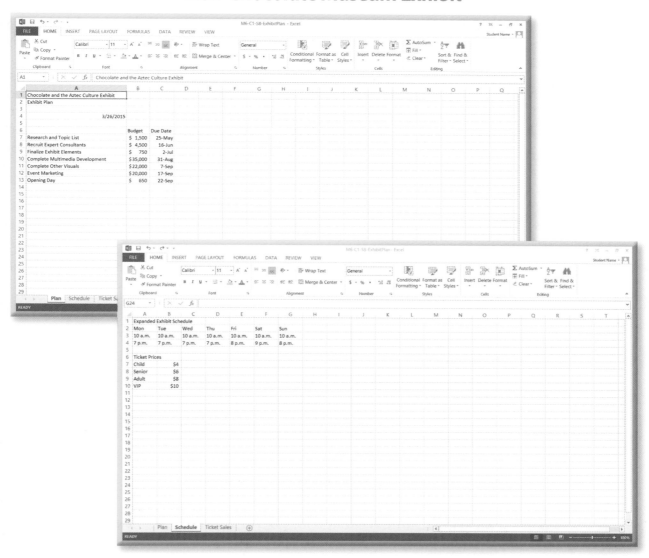

Excel

Understand Worksheet and Workbook Structure

Video ▶ M6_C1_S01

Excel files are called *workbooks*. When you start Excel, you can create a blank workbook or select a workbook template. A blank workbook contains one *worksheet*. Worksheets are like pages in a notebook. You can add worksheets, or *sheets*, to your workbook to keep your data organized.

The capital letters across the top of the worksheet are *column headings* that identify each column. The numbers down the left side are *row headings* that identify each row. The intersection of each row and column is a *cell*, into which you can type an entry. An entry can be a data value like a name, number, or date, or a formula that instructs Excel to perform a calculation. As you work, a heavy black border appears around the *active cell*. You can only make entries in the active cell.

After you have made cell entries, you can use the Formula bar located above the column headings to view and work with the entered data and modify individual cells or a range of cells.

Steps

Tip To open Excel, click the Excel 2013 tile on the Start screen or press Win + C, click the Search charm, and then type *Excel*.

1 Open the Excel application on your computer and then click *Blank workbook* in the backstage area to display a new blank workbook. Save the file as **M6-C1-S1-ExhibitPlan** in your Module 6 working folder on your storage medium.

2 Move the mouse pointer over the Formula bar. A ScreenTip that reads *Formula Bar* appears to identify that screen element.

Tip Only one sheet can be active at any given time. The active sheet is shown with its name underlined in its tab.

3 Click the New sheet button to add a worksheet (Sheet2) to the workbook and make it the active sheet.

4 Click the Sheet1 tab to make it the active sheet.

Tip The active cell is highlighted with a black border, and the cell name appears in the Name box next to the Formula bar.

5 Click in cell B3 (the cell that is in row 3 of column B), to make it the active cell. Notice that the Name box displays *B3*.

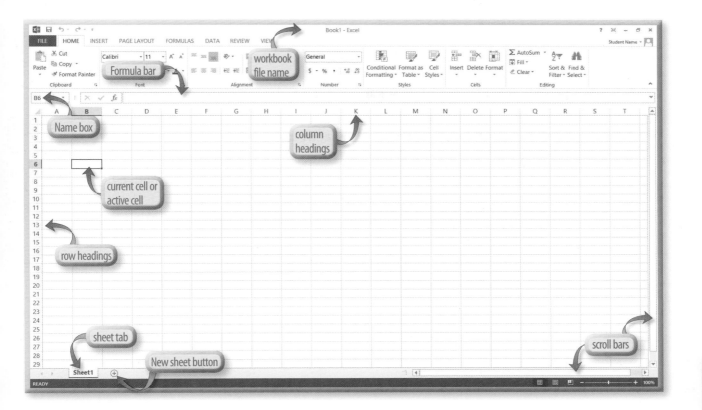

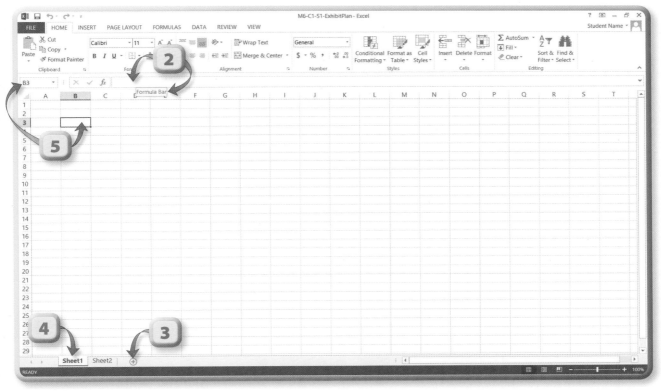

More

Tip Notice that scrolling does not change the selected cell.

6 Click the down arrow button on the vertical scroll bar to move down the page.

7 Click the up arrow button on the vertical scroll bar to move up the page.

8 *Shortcut*

Make A1 the Active Cell
Ctrl + Home

8 Click in cell A1 to make it the active cell.

Tip Click any cell that is visible on-screen to select and make it the active cell.

9 Press the Down Arrow key five times. Cell A6 is now the active cell.

11 *Another Way*

Use the Click, Shift-Click method to select a range: press the left mouse button and drag over the range or click the upper left cell and hold down Shift as you click the lower right cell.

10 Press the Right Arrow key five times. Cell F6 is now the active cell.

11 Press and hold down the Shift key and then press the Down Arrow key three times and the Right Arrow two times to select the range F6 through H9.

12 Click in cell A1 to make it the active cell.

13 Click the Save button on the Quick Access toolbar to save the file.

Taking It Further

Jumping to a Cell You can jump directly to a cell by pressing F5 or by clicking the Find & Select button in the Editing group on the HOME tab and then clicking *Go To*. Both methods open the Go To dialog box, where you can enter a cell address in the *Reference* text box and then click OK to jump to that cell.

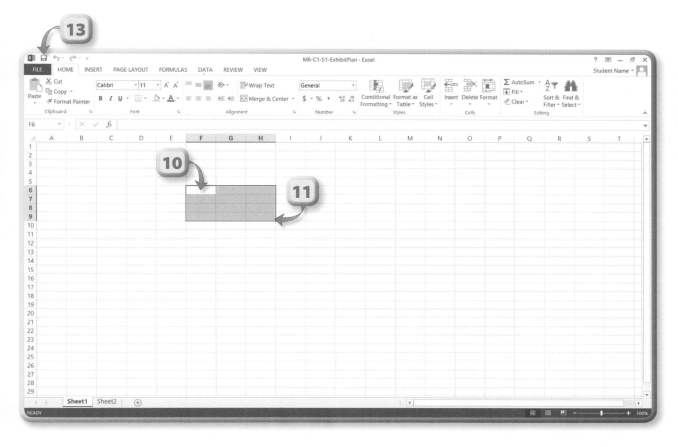

Excel

Excel

Skill 2

Video M6_C1_S02

Use Cell References

You can identify each cell by its column letter and row number, called its *cell address*, *cell reference*, or *cell name*. For example, the cell in the first column of the first row is cell A1. The cell in the eighth column of the tenth row is cell H10.

A range of cells has an address too. Identify a range by the addresses of its upper left and lower right cells, separating the addresses with a colon. For example, D5:J15 is the range that spans from cell D5 at the upper left to J15 at the lower right. A range can span a single row, such as when you select several column titles, perhaps A3:F3. A range also can fall within a single column, as in C3:C10.

You can use the Name box to the left of the Formula bar to go to a cell or range. Understanding cell and range addresses is also important when building formulas, a skill you will learn about in Module 6, Chapter 2.

Steps

Tip Sheet numbers are not reused in a workbook. If you create Sheet2 and then delete it, the next new sheet will be named Sheet3.

Tip The entire content of a data cell will display even if it is too long to fit in the cell as long as the cell immediately to the right is empty. If the cell immediately to the right contains data, the overflow cell content will be hidden.

Tip The entire contents of a cell will always display in the Formula bar.

Tip When you are selecting cells, the mouse pointer displays as a thick white plus sign.

Tip All Excel formulas begin with an equals sign.

Tip When you type a formula in Excel, you may enter letters as either capital or lowercase. The program automatically capitalizes the letters in the cell as you type.

1 If it is not already open, open **M6-C1-S1-ExhibitPlan.xlsx**, the file you saved in the previous skill, and save the file as **M6-C1-S2-ExhibitPlan**.

2 Click the Sheet2 tab to make it the active sheet.

3 Type your name in cell A1 of Sheet2 and press Enter.

4 Click in cell F6 to make it the active cell.

5 Type =A1 and press Ctrl + Enter. This action finishes entering the formula and keeps the cell active.

6 Look in the Formula bar and verify that it displays the entry you made in cell F6, while the cell itself displays the result.

7 Click in the Name box to the left of the Formula bar, which currently displays *F6*.

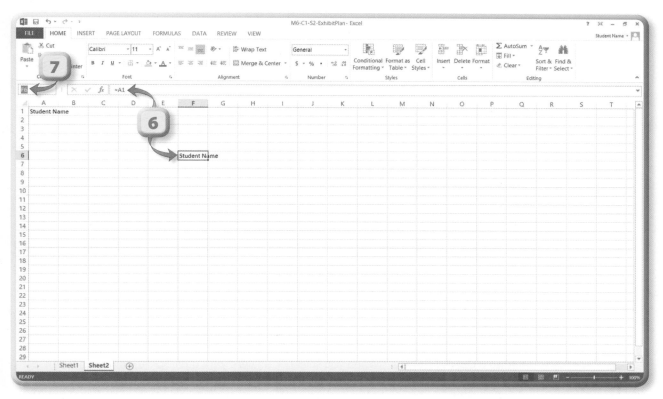

More

8 Type G7 and press Enter. Cell G7 is selected.

9 Click in the Name box to the left of the Formula bar, which currently displays *G7*.

10 Type E5:G7 and press Enter. The range of cells E5 through G7 is selected.

11 Click the Fill Color button arrow in the Font group on the HOME tab. Select *Yellow* from the *Standard Colors* section of the drop-down gallery.

12 Click in cell A1 to make it the active cell.

13 Save the file.

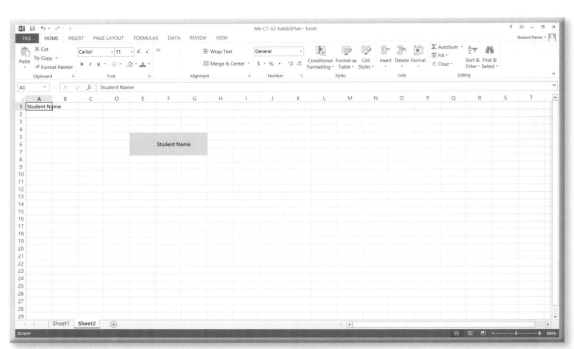

Completed Skill 2

Taking It Further

Making a Quick Analysis When you select a range of cells that contain data, the Quick Analysis button ▦ appears at the bottom right of the selected range. Click the Quick Analysis button to display a gallery where you can select from a variety of tabs to analyze your data. For example, the CHARTS tab lets you display the selected data in a chart. Another tab, FORMATTING, has options that can be used to quickly determine high and low values or highlight values greater than a specified value.

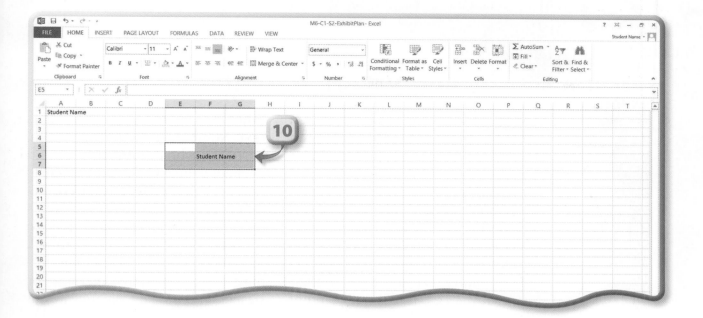

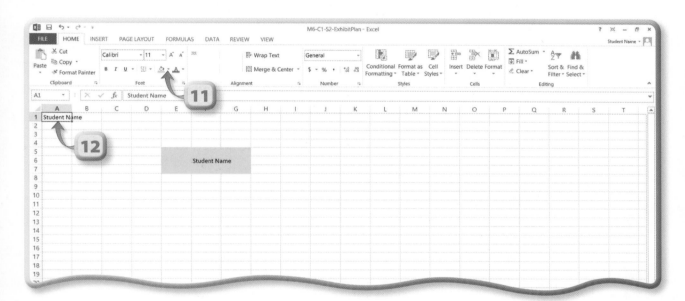

Taking It Further

Exploring a Worksheet A worksheet contains fixed number of columns and rows. The number of usable cells depends upon the amount of RAM available to your computer. Cells within a worksheet can contain numbers and dates in various formats, text, or formulas using arithmetic operators or functions. Check to see how many columns your Excel worksheet has by opening a blank workbook and then pressing End + Right Arrow. Press End + Down Arrow to see the number of rows in your worksheet.

Excel

Chapter 1

Skill 3

Enter Text, Values, and Dates

Video M6_C1_S03

Each cell in an Excel worksheet can hold a single entry. That entry can be text, a date, a value, or a formula that calculates a result.

A text entry can contain any combination of letters, numbers, or symbols that you can type on your keyboard. *Qtr 1*, *Sales*, or *Region#* are examples of text entries. By default, Excel aligns text entries at the left side of the cell. This is true even of phone numbers because they usually are entered with hyphens or other characters and are treated as text. Numbers are numeric entries, including whole numbers (15) and decimal values (2.5). You can enter numbers that have certain characteristics, such as currency symbols or a number of decimal places. Number entries are right-aligned. You enter dates in typical date formats, with hyphens (4-1-15) or slashes (4/1/15). By default, if you enter 4/1/15 or 4-1-15, Excel displays 4/1/2015 in the cell.

Steps

1 If it is not already open, open **M6-C1-S2-ExhibitPlan.xlsx**, the file you saved in the previous skill, and save the file as **M6-C1-S3-ExhibitPlan**.

2 Click the Sheet1 tab near the bottom of the screen to make it the active sheet.

3 Make cell A1 the active cell, type Chocolate and the Aztec Culture Exhibit, and then press Enter.

4 *Another Way*
Press the Down Arrow key to finish a cell entry and move one cell down, the Right or Left Arrow keys to move one column to the right or left, or the Up Arrow key to move up one row.

▶ *Tip* Excel automatically reformats the date.

4 Type Exhibit Plan in cell A2 and then press Enter twice.

5 Type 3-26-15 in cell A4 and then press Enter.

6 Make cell B6 the active cell, type Due Date, and then press Enter.

7 Make cell A7 the active cell and type the following entries exactly as shown into the range A7:A13. You will correct mistakes later!

Research [Enter]
Topic List [Enter]
Recriut Espert Consultatnts [Enter]
Finalize Exhibit Elements [Enter]
Complete Multimedia Development [Enter]
Complete Other Visuals [Enter]
Opening Day [Enter]

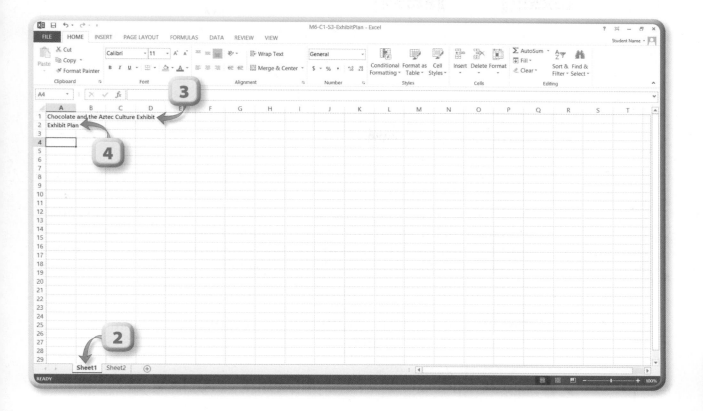

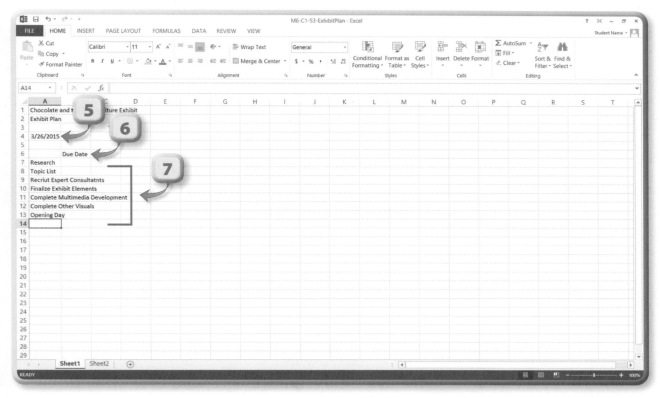

More

8 Make cell B7 the active cell and type the following entries into the range B7:B13.
5/18 [Enter]
5/25 [Enter]
6/16 [Enter]
7/2 [Enter]
8/31 [Enter]
9/7 [Enter]
9/22 [Enter]

▶ **Tip** Click a cell and look at the Formula bar to confirm that the entire entry is retained in a cell even when it is only partially displayed.

9 Notice that the date entries in column B appear to have cut off the entries in column A. The length of the entries requires that you resize column A to accommodate them. Move the mouse pointer over the divider line between the column A and column B headings until it turns into a left-and-right-pointing arrow.

10 Double-click the divider line between the column A and column B headings to resize column A.

11 Save the file.

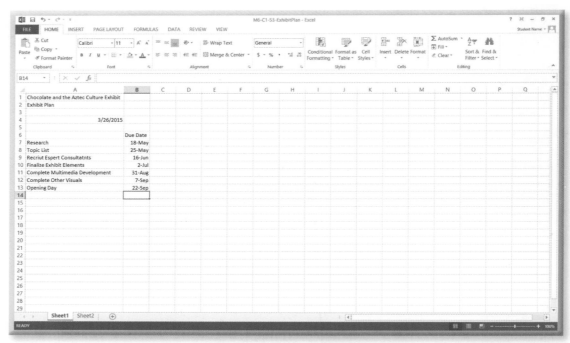

Completed Skill 3

Excel

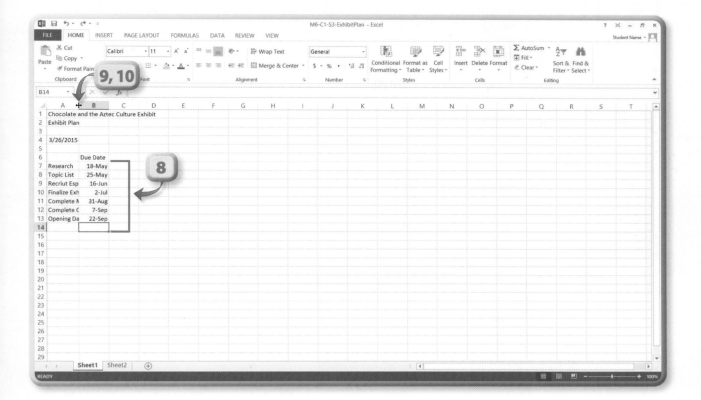

Taking It Further

Removing ### from a Cell In certain situations, such as when you enter a very large number in a cell, Excel displays a series of pound signs (###) rather than the entry itself. These signs indicate that the numeric entry is too wide to display in the cell. This feature is designed to keep readers of the data from being mislead by seeing only a portion of a number. Increase the column width for the cell contents to display properly. You will learn more about sizing cells in Chapter 3, Skill 3.

Excel

Skill 4

Video ▶ M6_C1_S04

Use the Auto Fill Feature

The Auto Fill and Flash Fill features in Excel 2013 can help you save time when entering data. *Auto Fill* enables you to either copy an entry across a row or down a column or create a *series* of entries across a row or down a column. For example, if you enter *Jan* in a cell and use the Auto Fill feature, Excel enters the following months: *Feb, Mar, Apr,* and so on. Auto Fill can also be used to fill the days of the week or common business entries such as *Qtr 1, Qtr 2,* and so on.

If you use Auto Fill to enter a number or other entry that Excel does not recognize as part of a series, Excel simply copies the entry to the area you are filling. You can create your own series by entering the first two or three values in the series and then using Auto Fill from there.

Flash Fill looks for patterns in your data and then automatically enters the rest of your data based on the pattern.

Steps

▶ **Tip** Ctrl + Enter finishes an entry without moving the cursor to another cell.

▶ **Tip** Click the Auto Fill Options button that appears after a fill if you want to change the fill. For example, you might want to fill formatting only or copy cells rather than fill a series.

1 If it is not already open, open **M6-C1-S3-ExhibitPlan.xlsx**, the file you saved in the previous skill, and save the file as **M6-C1-S4-ExhibitPlan**.

2 With Sheet1 active, make cell D16 the active cell, type Expanded Exhibit Schedule, and then press Enter.

3 Type Mon and press Ctrl + Enter.

4 Move the mouse pointer over the fill handle (which looks like a small square) in the lower right corner of the cell D17. When the mouse pointer changes to a black crosshair, press and hold down the left mouse button and then drag to the right until you see a ScreenTip that reads *Sun*.

5 Release the mouse button to finish filling the days of the week.

6 Make cell D18 the active cell, type 10 a.m., and then press Enter.

7 Drag over the range D18:J18 to select it. (Do not use the Auto Fill feature.)

8 Click the Fill button in the Editing group on the HOME tab.

9 Click the *Right* option. Excel copies the *10 a.m.* entry across the selected range.

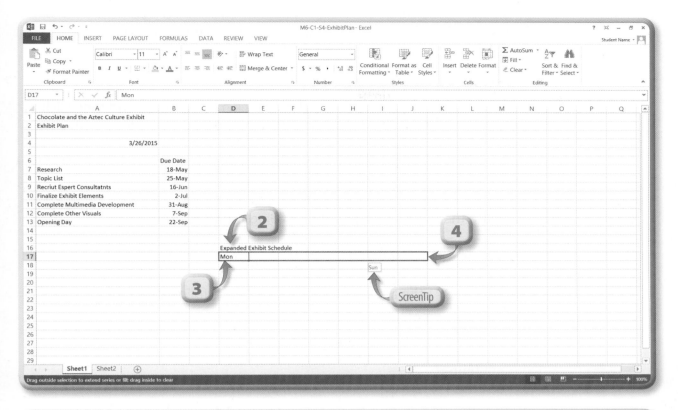

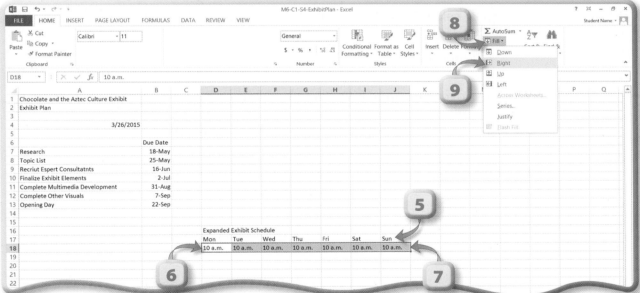

 More

Taking It Further

Using Flash Fill Flash Fill will save you time when entering data that is repeated in a pattern. For example, suppose you enter a list of employee email addresses in column A, and each email address contains the employee's last name and first initial. When you start typing employee last names in column B, Excel will recognize the pattern and fill in the remaining last names in column B.

10 Make cell D19 the active cell, type 7 p.m., and then press Enter.

11 Drag over the range D19:G19 to select it.

12 In the Editing group on the HOME tab, click the Fill button and then click *Right*. Excel copies the *7 p.m.* entry across the selected range.

13 Make cell G19 the active cell. Drag the fill handle to the right until cell I19 is selected.

▶**Tip** Excel will not fill all times correctly. For example, it fills *12 p.m.* and then *13 p.m.*, an obvious error.

14 Release the mouse button to finish filling the series from *7 p.m.* to *9 p.m.*

15 Make cell J19 the active cell, type 8 p.m., and then press Enter.

16 Make cell D21 the active cell and then type the following entries:

Ticket Prices [Enter]
Child [Enter]
Senior [Enter]
Adult [Enter]
VIP [Enter]

▶**Tip** You can type some number formats, such as dollar signs and percent signs, when entering the numbers, or you can apply number formatting later.

17 Make cell E22 the active cell and then type the following entries:

$4 [Enter]
$6 [Enter]

18 Drag over the range E22:E23 to select it.

19 Drag the fill handle down until cell E25 is selected.

20 Release the mouse button to finish filling the custom series from *$4* to *$10*.

21 Save the file.

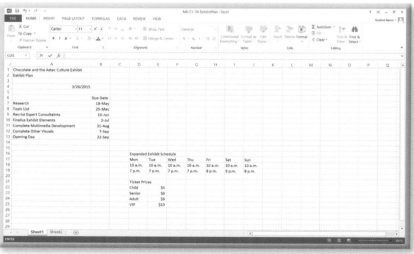

Completed Skill 4

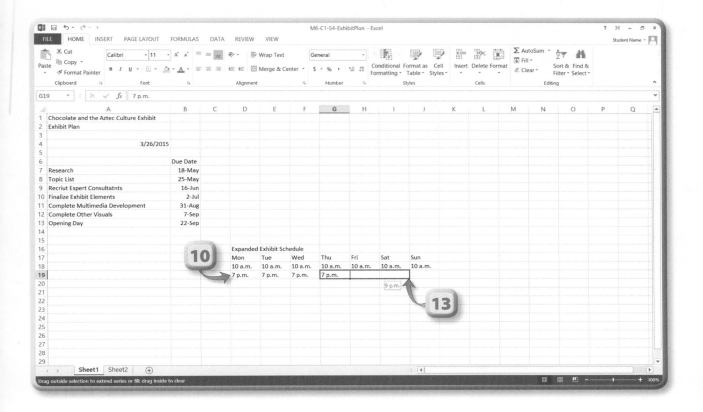

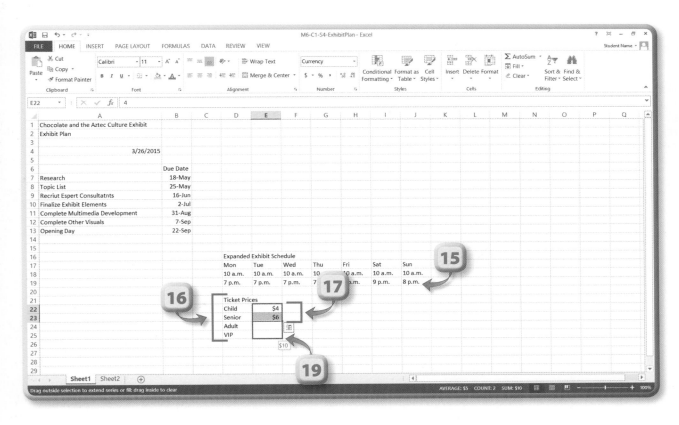

Excel

Video M6_C1_S05

Use the Spelling Checker

Spreadsheets can be filled with typos, requiring an eagle-eyed person to read closely to find and eliminate those pesky misspellings. Excel includes a feature to help you ensure that your worksheets are free of typos. The Excel spelling checker works much like the Word spelling checker, except that it opens in a dialog box instead of a pane. There is one extra caution with using this feature in Excel: the spelling checker only reviews text entries. It cannot ensure that you have entered numbers and dates correctly, so double-check your data thoroughly!

Steps

1. If it is not already open, open **M6-C1-S4-ExhibitPlan.xlsx**, the file you saved in the previous skill, and save the file as **M6-C1-S5-ExhibitPlan**.

2. With Sheet1 active, make cell A1 the active cell.

3. Click the REVIEW tab.

4. Click the Spelling button in the Proofing group.

5. The Spelling dialog box displays the first typing mistake, *Recruit*. The correct spelling is already selected in the *Suggestions* list box, so click the Change button to replace the misspelled word.

6. Click the Change button twice more to correct the next two misspellings, *Espert* and *Consultatnts*.

7. Click OK in the message box that informs you that the spelling check is complete.

8. Save the file.

3-4 *Shortcut*

Spelling Checker
F7

▶**Tip** The spelling checker starts from the current cell, and Excel displays a message when it needs to return to the beginning of the sheet.

Taking It Further

Using Auto Correct Excel can correct some misspellings for you as you type. Each of us has our own unique tendency to mistype certain words. For example, perhaps your last name is *Smith*, but you often mistype it as *Simth*. Excel cannot, by default, correct that mistake. However, you can customize the AutoCorrect feature so that the correction will be made. To do so, click the FILE tab and then click *Options*. Click *Proofing* at the left side of the Excel Options dialog box and then click the AutoCorrect Options button in the right panel. In the AutoCorrect dialog box, with the AutoCorrect tab selected, type your frequent typo (such as *Simth*) in the *Replace* text box and then type the correction (*Smith* in this instance) in the *With* text box. Click Add and then click OK twice.

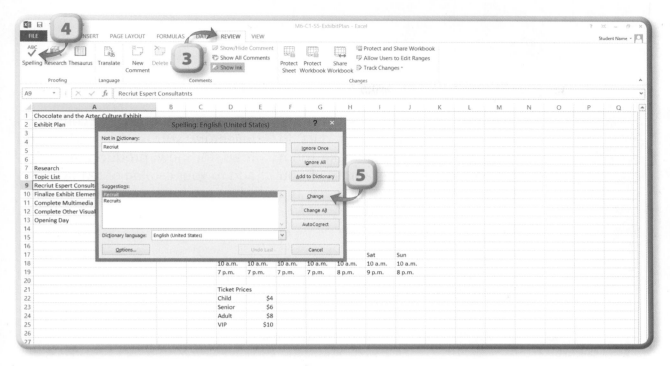

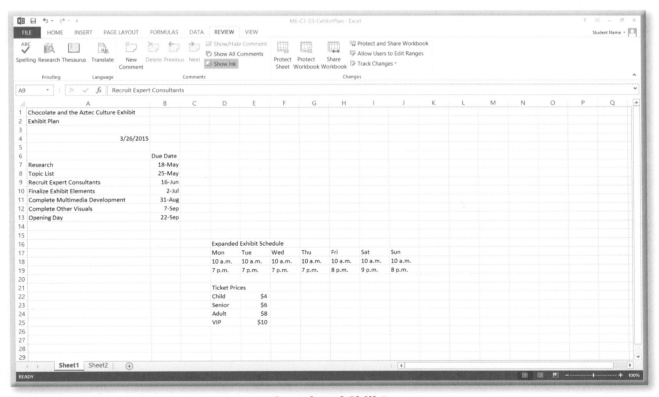

Completed Skill 5

Excel

Skill 6

Insert and Delete Columns and Rows

Video M6_C1_S06

You can insert and delete rows and columns within your data to rearrange the data or make room for new data. For example, if you created a worksheet to track the value of products in your company's inventory, you might need to add rows for new products that you add to your catalog or remove rows when products are discontinued.

Steps

1 If it is not already open, open **M6-C1-S5-ExhibitPlan.xlsx**, the file you saved in the previous skill, and save the file as **M6-C1-S6-ExhibitPlan**.

2 On Sheet1, make cell A7 the active cell.

3 Click the HOME tab.

4 Click the Delete button arrow in the Cells group.

4-5 *Another Way*
Right-click a column or row heading and use the *Delete* option.

▶ **Tip** Before deleting rows and columns, save your worksheet. Make sure to check the rows and columns before you delete them to be sure you will not be losing important data.

5 Click *Delete Sheet Rows*. Excel removes the row immediately and does not display a warning that you will be deleting the contents of the row.

6 With cell A7 still selected but now reading *Topic List*, type Research and Topic List and then press Enter to update the contents of the cell.

▶ **Tip** If you accidentally delete the wrong row or column, immediately click the Undo button on the Quick Access toolbar to restore the deleted content.

7 Make cell A12 the active cell.

8 Click the Insert button arrow in the Cells group on the HOME tab.

8-9 *Another Way*
Right-click a column or row heading and use the *Insert* option.

9 Click *Insert Sheet Rows*.

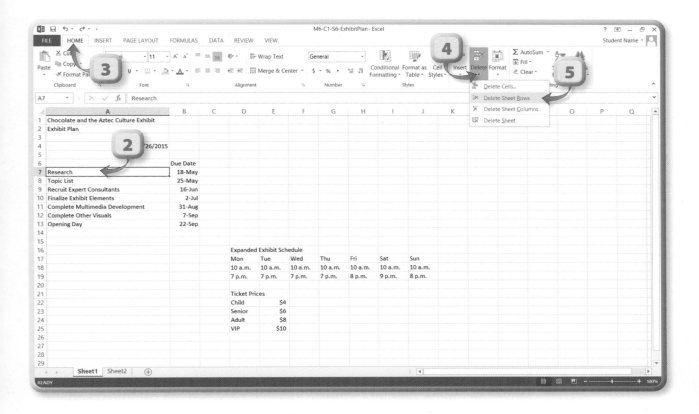

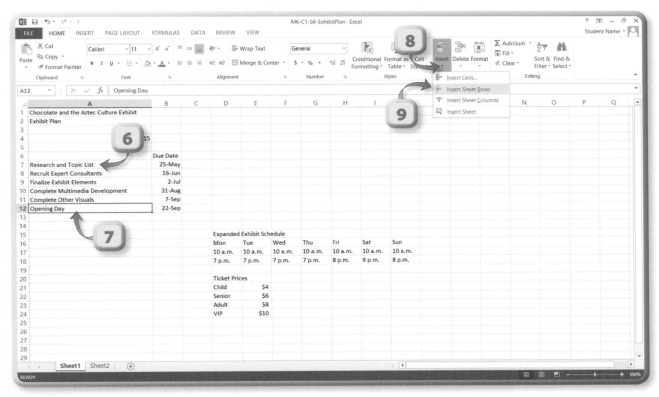

More

10 In cell A12, type Event Marketing and then press the Right Arrow key.

11 In cell B12, type 9/17 and then press Enter.

12 Right-click the column B column heading to display a shortcut menu.

13 Click *Insert*. A new column appears.

▶**Tip** Each Excel worksheet always has the same number of rows and columns. When you insert and delete rows and columns, you are simply changing where the blank rows and columns appear in the sheet.

14 Make cell B6 the active cell and then type the following entries down the column:

Budget [Enter]
$1,500 [Enter]
$4,500 [Enter]
$750 [Enter]
$35,000 [Enter]
$22,000 [Enter]
$20,000 [Enter]
$650 [Enter]

15 Move the mouse pointer to the divider line between the column B and column C headings until you see a left-and-right-pointing arrow. Double-click to resize the column.

16 Right-click the column D heading to display a shortcut menu.

17 Click *Delete*. The *Expanded Exhibit Schedule* and *Ticket Prices* tables shift to the left.

18 Save the file.

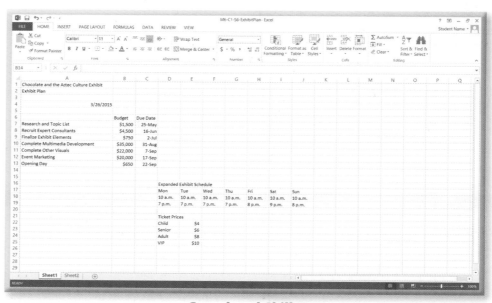

Completed Skill 6

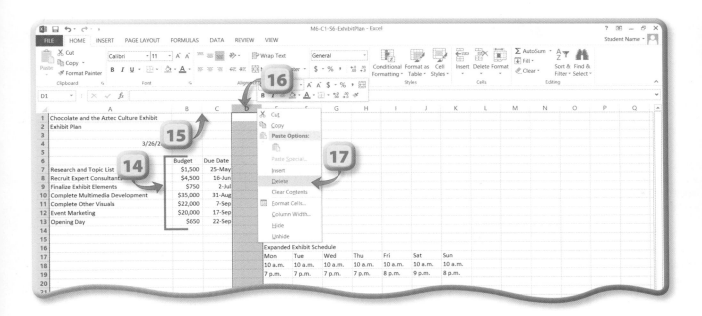

Taking It Further

Designing Worksheets Using Rows and Columns Rows and columns can play both functional and design roles in your worksheet. For example, when you perform calculations and certain other activities such as charting, you will find the actions easiest to perform when all the data is located in adjoining rows and columns.

Excel

Work with Multiple Worksheets

Video M6_C1_S07

Given the size of each worksheet, it would be possible to arrange a wide variety of different sets of data in ranges spread throughout a single sheet. However, you would have to spend a lot of time scrolling and otherwise navigating to find the section of the sheet containing the data you want to view and use. Dividing data into multiple worksheets is often more efficient for reading the data.

Each Excel workbook enables you to create multiple worksheets. If you have to track data for many stores, no problem! You can create a sheet for each one or copy an existing sheet to a new sheet for editing. You also can delete sheets with old data you no longer need. This skill offers instruction and practice for all of these options.

Steps

1 If it is not already open, open **M6-C1-S6-ExhibitPlan.xlsx**, the file you saved in the previous skill, and save the file as **M6-C1-S7-ExhibitPlan**.

2 Click the New sheet button to add Sheet3.

3 Click the Sheet2 tab, press and hold down the Ctrl key, and then click the Sheet3 tab to select Sheet2 and Sheet3.

▶Tip The Ctrl key allows you to select multiple items, including multiple worksheet tabs.

4 In the Cells group on the HOME tab, click the Delete button arrow.

4-5 *Another Way*
You can right-click a sheet tab and then click *Delete* at the shortcut menu.

5 Click *Delete Sheet*.

6 Click the Delete button in the message box warning you that sheets may contain data that will be deleted.

7 Right-click the Sheet1 sheet tab and then click *Move or Copy*.

8 Click *(move to end)* in the *Before sheet* list box in the Move or Copy dialog box.

9 Click the *Create a copy* check box to insert a check mark.

10 Click OK. The new sheet, named *Sheet1 (2)*, appears and is the active sheet.

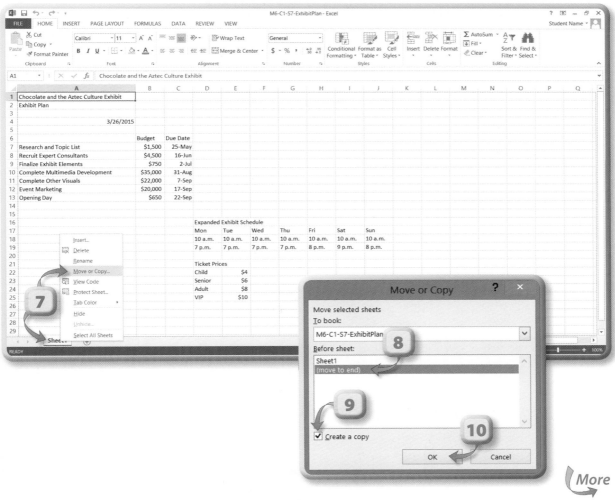

More

11 On the new sheet, point to column heading A until you see a down-pointing arrow, click and drag to the right to select columns A through C, right-click, and then click *Delete*.

12 Point to the row 1 heading until you see a right-pointing arrow, click and drag down to select rows 1 through 15, right-click, and then click *Delete*.

13 Make cell A1 the active cell.

14 Click the Sheet1 tab.

15 Click and drag over the column headings to select columns D through J, right-click, and then click *Delete*. You have separated the data you created onto two sheets.

16 Click the Sheet1 (2) sheet tab.

17 Make cell A1 the active cell.

18 Click the New sheet button. The new sheet, named *Sheet5*, appears.

19 Save the file.

Completed Skill 7, Sheet1 and Sheet1 (2)

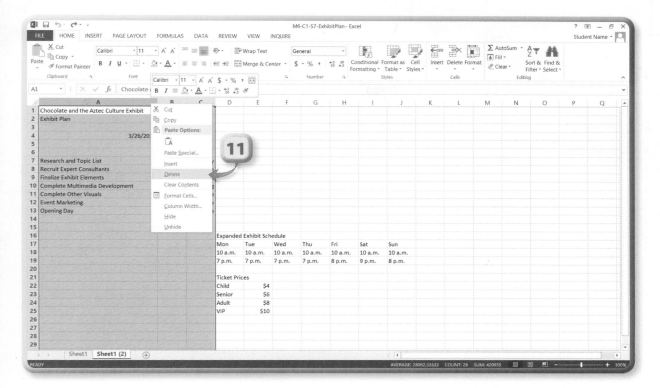

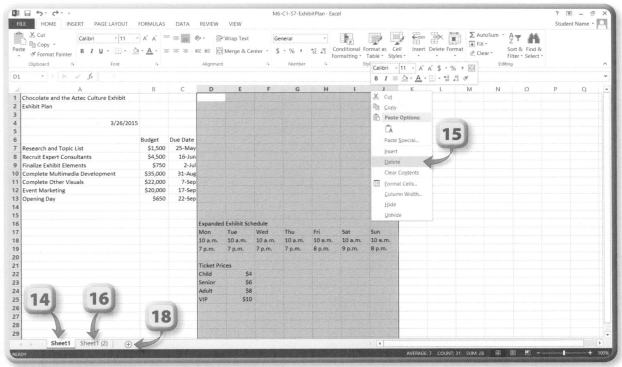

Taking It Further

Copying Data to Another Workbook

You may have noticed that the Move or Copy dialog box includes a *To book* option box. If you have another workbook open, you can select it in this option box to move or copy the specified worksheet to that workbook rather than within the current workbook. This action enables you to transfer data to other workbook files using a method that is faster than copying and pasting.

Excel

Skill 8 **Name and Rename Worksheets**

Video M6_C1_S08

If the goal of adding worksheets is to make information easier to find and identify, then "mystery" worksheet names, such as Sheet1 and Sheet2, certainly do not help. Giving each worksheet a unique name that identifies its contents makes it much easier to determine which tab to click to find the data you need.

Use the worksheet tab to rename the worksheet. A sheet name can be up to 31 characters and can contain most characters on the keyboard, including spaces. Only a handful of characters, such as / (slash), \ (backslash), * (asterisk), ' (apostrophe), and : (colon) are not allowed in worksheet names.

Steps

1. If it is not already open, open **M6-C1-S7-ExhibitPlan.xlsx**, the file you saved in the previous skill, and save the file as **M6-C1-S8-ExhibitPlan**.

2. Right-click the Sheet1 tab.

3. Click *Rename*.

4. Type Plan and press Enter.

5. Double-click the Sheet1 (2) tab, type Schedule, and then press Enter.

6. Double-click the Sheet5 tab, type Ticket Sales, and then press Enter.

7. Click the Plan tab.

8. Save the file.

Taking It Further

Color Coding Sheet Tabs   Color-coding worksheet tabs is another way to make it easier to find data in a workbook. For example, if you are tracking store profitability, you could use green tabs for all the stores making a profit and red tabs for all the stores losing money. To change the color of a sheet tab, right-click the tab, point to *Tab Color*, and then click the color you want from the palette.

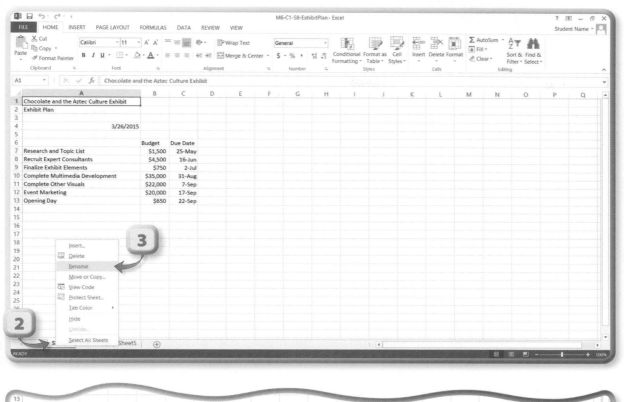

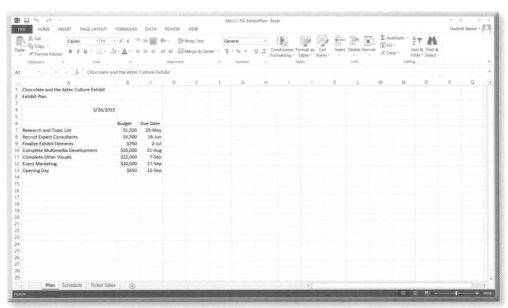

Completed Skill 8

Excel

Chapter 1

Skill 9

Video ► M6_C1_S09

Explore Options for Printing

Whenever possible, many of us try to avoid printing so that we can save paper—and trees! However, distributing printouts, or *hard copies,* is sometimes the most convenient way to collectively review information in meetings and other situations. When each person has a copy of the item being discussed, individuals can freely jump from page to page and zero in on the data they find important.

Excel offers numerous options for setting up and printing a worksheet. This skill will give you a preview of the most useful print settings.

Steps

1 If it is not already open, open **M6-C1-S8-ExhibitPlan.xlsx**, the file you saved in the previous skill, and save the file as **Lastname-M6-C1-S9-ExhibitPlan**, but replace *Lastname* with your last name. Be sure to save the file in your Module 6 working folder on your storage medium.

▶ **Tip** Click the Plan tab to make the Plan worksheet the active sheet.

2 With the Plan sheet active, drag over the range A1:B13.

3-4 *Shortcut*
Ctrl + P

3 Click the FILE tab.

4 Click the *Print* option to open the Print backstage area, which displays print settings and a preview of the printout.

5 Verify that the correct printer is selected in the *Printer* option box. Click the down-pointing arrow to display the drop-down list. Ask your instructor if more than one printer is available and you are not sure which one to choose.

▶ **Tip** You can click other options to print only the active sheets or the entire workbook.

6 Click the down-pointing arrow in the first option box in the *Settings* section and then click *Print Selection* to print only the current selection.

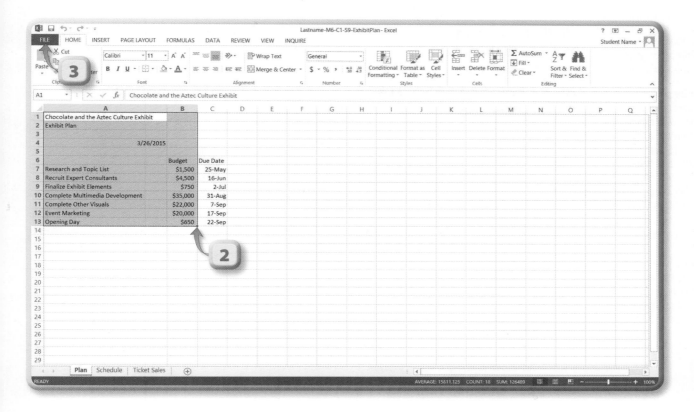

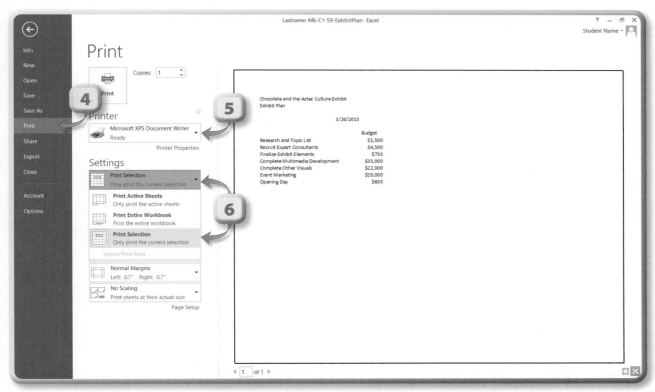

Excel

7 Another Way
Click the Page Setup button in the Print backstage area and then click *Landscape*.

▶ **Tip** The printed appearance of your worksheet can be modified using the PAGE LAYOUT tab or the Page Setup button in the Print backstage area. In addition to setting page orientation, you can add a header and footer, gridlines, and row and column headings to your printout.

▶ **Tip** If you want to adjust your printout to have all rows or columns on one page, you can use the scaling options in the last option box in the *Settings* category.

7 In the third option box in the *Settings* section, click the down-pointing arrow and then click *Landscape Orientation*.

8 If your instructor asks you to print the document, click the Print button. Otherwise, click the Back button.

9 Save and close the file.

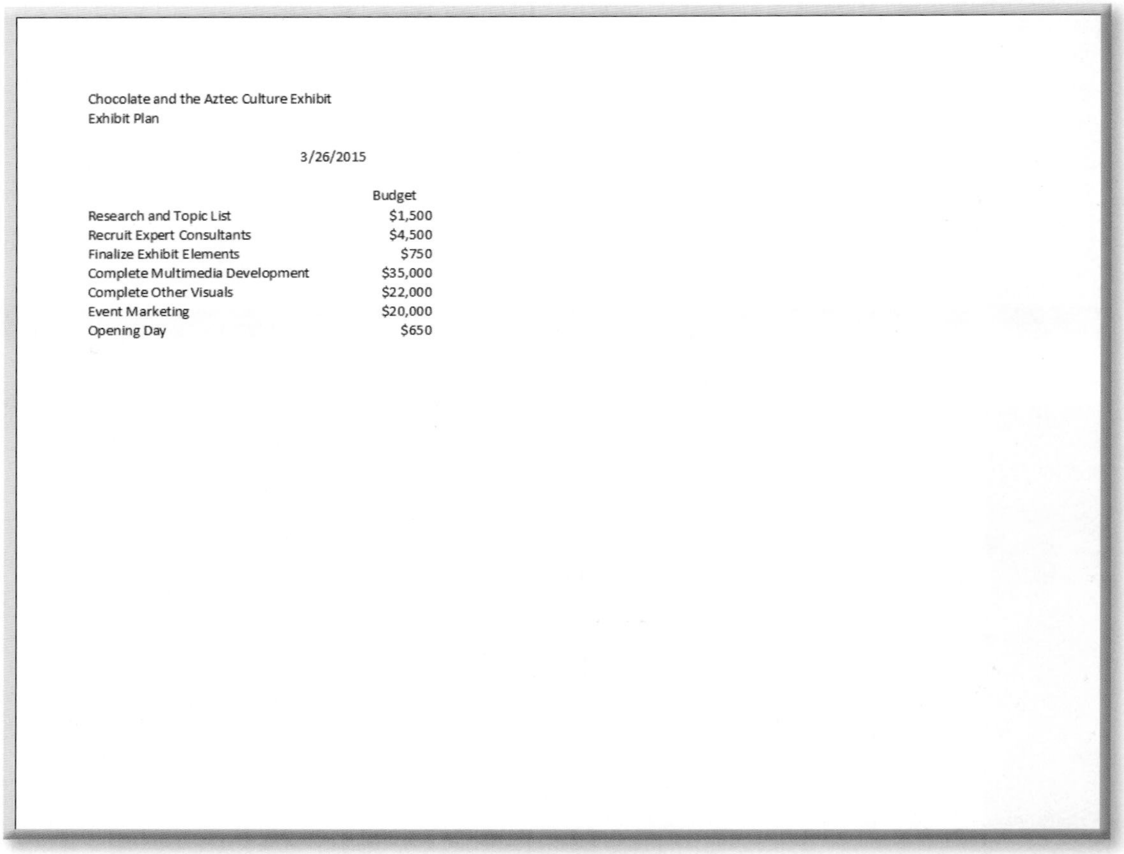

Chocolate and the Aztec Culture Exhibit
Exhibit Plan

3/26/2015

	Budget
Research and Topic List	$1,500
Recruit Expert Consultants	$4,500
Finalize Exhibit Elements	$750
Complete Multimedia Development	$35,000
Complete Other Visuals	$22,000
Event Marketing	$20,000
Opening Day	$650

Completed Skill 9

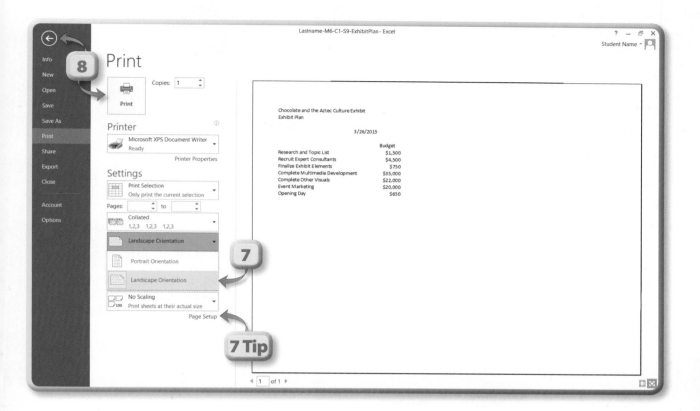

Taking It Further

Adding Headers and Footers You can add a header and a footer to an Excel worksheet to include identifying information such as the file name, your name, your company name, or page numbers on a printout. Click the INSERT tab and then click the Header & Footer button in the Text group. Type information in the placeholders that appear on the worksheet for the header or footer, or use the choices on the HEADER & FOOTER TOOLS DESIGN tab, to insert elements such as page numbers and the file name. You also can use the Header button and Footer button drop-down lists in the Header & Footer group to add predefined text to the selected header or footer area. Note that adding a header or a footer switches the workbook to Page Layout view. To return to Normal view, click in any cell, click the VIEW tab, and then click the Normal button in the Workbook Views group.

Tasks Summary

Task	Ribbon Tab, Group	Button, Option	Shortcut, Alternative
Navigate			Arrow keys, Ctrl + Home
Select sheet tab			Click tab
Enter text			Enter, Ctrl + Enter, Tab, or arrow key to finish entry
Select a range	Name box		Drag, click upper left cell and then Shift + click lower right cell, click upper left cell and then use arrow keys to extend the selection
Select an entire sheet			Ctrl + A
Fill a series or values	HOME, Editing	Fill ▾	Drag fill handle
Perform a spelling check	REVIEW, Proofing	ABC	F7
Insert a row	HOME, Cells		Right-click selected rows and click *Insert*
Insert a column	HOME, Cells		Right-click selected columns and click *Insert*
Delete a row	HOME, Cells		Right-click selected rows and click *Delete*
Delete a column	HOME, Cells		Right-click selected columns and click *Delete*
Copy a worksheet			Right-click sheet tab and click *Move or Copy*
Insert a blank worksheet	HOME, Cells		Click New sheet button
Delete a worksheet	HOME, Cells		Right-click sheet tab and click *Delete*
Rename a worksheet			Double-click sheet name and type new name. Or right-click sheet tab, click *Rename*, and type new name.
Print	FILE, *Print*	Print	Ctrl + P

Features Review

Select the best answer from the choices given.

1 Finish a cell entry by pressing
   a. Enter.
   b. Ctrl + Enter.
   c. the Right Arrow key.
   d. Enter, Ctrl + Enter, or the Right Arrow key.

2 Use this to view a different section of a worksheet without changing the active cell.
   a. ribbon
   b. scroll bar
   c. arrow key
   d. Name box

3 The column letter and row number make up the cell reference or
   a. value.
   b. range name.
   c. cell address.
   d. formula.

4 Describe a way to select a range of cells.
   a. Drag over it.
   b. Search for it.
   c. Type it in a cell.
   d. Insert dashes.

5 The _____ feature enables you to create a series of entries down a column or across a row.
   a. Copy
   b. Auto Fill
   c. Templates
   d. Clear

6 The spelling checker can find errors in these types of entries.
   a. text
   b. values
   c. dates
   d. worksheet names

7 Doing this to a row or column removes it and its contents.
   a. inserting
   b. copying
   c. deleting
   d. summing

8 An equals sign is the first item entered in a
   a. numeric entry.
   b. text entry.
   c. date entry.
   d. formula.

9 Change the _____ for a worksheet on the sheet tab to describe its contents.
   a. theme
   b. color
   c. value
   d. name

10 Click the Print button on the FILE tab to display printing choices in
   a. the Print backstage area.
   b. Print Preview view.
   c. the Print dialog box.
   d. the PAGE LAYOUT tab.

Hands-On Skills Review _____

Exercise **A** Tracking Song Purchases

Skills   Understand worksheet and workbook structure; use cell references; enter text, values, and dates; use the Auto Fill feature; insert and delete columns and rows; and explore options for printing

Scenario   You have recently begun purchasing digital songs online, and you want to create a list of your purchases. Create a new workbook and enter the initial data about your collection now.

Steps

1 Create a new, blank workbook file.

2 Save the file as **Lastname-M6-C1-ExA-Songs**, but replace *Lastname* with your last name.

3 In cell A1, type My Digital Songs.

4 In cell A2, type your name.

5 Type the following entries in cells A3:E3.

> Title
> Artist
> Format
> Price
> Date Purchased

6 Type the following entries in cells A4:E4.

> California Gurls
> Katy Perry
> MP3
> $1.29
> 3/12/2015

7 Use Auto Fill to fill the Artist entry and Format entry for rows 5 and 6 **HINT:** *Select the* Copy Cells Auto Fill *option.*

8 Add these entries where appropriate on rows 5 and 6:

Hot N Cold	$.99	3/12/2015
Waking Up in Vegas	$.99	3/13/2015

9 Insert a new column C.

10 Type Rating as the column title.

11 Type 5, 3, and 4 in the new column in rows 4, 5, and 6, respectively.

12 Change the width of columns A, B, and F to fit the contents.

13 Click the FILE tab and then click the *Print* option to see how the file will look when printed.

14 Save the workbook file.

15 Print or submit the completed workbook file as directed by your instructor.

◢	A	B	C	D	E	F
1	My Digital Songs					
2	Student Name					
3	Title	Artist	Rating	Format	Price	Date Purchased
4	California Gurls	Katy Perry	5	MP3	$1.29	3/12/2015
5	Hot N Cold	Katy Perry	3	MP3	$0.99	3/12/2015
6	Waking Up in Vegas	Katy Perry	4	MP3	$0.99	3/13/2015

Completed Exercise A

Exercise B Creating a Meal Budget

Skills Understand worksheet and workbook structure; use cell references; enter text, values, and dates; use the Auto Fill feature; insert and delete columns and rows; and explore options for printing

Scenario You sell security products for Endpoint, Inc. You will be taking a sales trip soon and need to create a report of projected expenses for your food. You have researched the cost of meals in restaurants in the area you will be visiting. Create an Excel worksheet that displays the daily cost for food while traveling.

Steps

1 Create a new, blank workbook file.

2 Save the file as **Lastname-M6-C1-ExB-FoodExpense**, but replace *Lastname* with your last name.

3 In cell A1, type Trip Meal Expenses.

4 In cell A2, type your name.

5 Type Mon for Monday in cell B3.

6 Auto Fill the entry in B3 across the row through the *Sat* value.

7 Make the following entries in cells A4:A8.

Breakfast
Snack
Lunch
Dinner
Snack

8 Make the following entries in cells B4:B8. Be sure to type the numbers exactly as shown, including the trailing zeros.

$20.00
$1.25
$25.00
$45.00
$2.50

9 Select the range B4:B8 and copy the values across the rows through column G.

10 Delete row 5, the first *Snack* row.

11 Replace the entry in cell F6 with $75.00.

12 Delete the entries in cells G5:G7.

13 Change the print orientation to landscape orientation.

14 Save the workbook file.

15 Print or submit the completed workbook file as directed by your instructor.

	A	B	C	D	E	F	G
1	Trip Meal Expenses						
2	Student Name						
3		Mon	Tue	Wed	Thu	Fri	Sat
4	Breakfast	$20.00	$20.00	$20.00	$20.00	$20.00	$20.00
5	Lunch	$25.00	$25.00	$25.00	$25.00	$25.00	
6	Dinner	$45.00	$45.00	$45.00	$45.00	$75.00	
7	Snack	$2.50	$2.50	$2.50	$2.50	$2.50	

Completed Exercise B

Exercise **Listing Birthdays**

Skills   Understand worksheet and workbook structure; use cell references; enter text, values, and dates; use the Auto Fill feature; use the spelling checker; name and rename worksheets; and explore options for printing

Scenario   Your company sends birthday cards to clients. Create a workbook file for tracking the birthday cards that need to be sent out in January.

Steps

1   Create a new, blank workbook file.

2   Save the file as **Lastname-M6-C1-ExC-BDays**, but replace *Lastname* with your last name.

3   Enter Birfhdays in cell A1. (Type exactly as written here. You will correct typos later.)

4   In cell A2, type your name.

5   Enter Janary in cell A3 and Name in cell B3.

6   Enter 1, for the first day of the month, in cell A4.

7   Use Auto Fill to fill the remaining days of the month in cells A5 through A34.

8   Type the following entries in the specified cells.

B5	June Holloway
B7	Jim Levinson
B10	Linda Lemur
B16	Rolanda James
B24	Butch Wilson
B34	Carson Myers

9   Check spelling in the worksheet, fixing only obvious errors and not changing any names.

10   Rename the current sheet as *January*.

11   Change the size of column B so that the names fit in the column.

12   Review the worksheet to ensure it looks like the completed worksheet shown.

13   Save the workbook file.

14   Print or submit the completed workbook file as directed by your instructor.

Completed Exercise C

Chapter 2

Working with Formulas and Functions

Excel offers more than the ability to simply organize data in neat rows and columns; it can also perform calculations using that data. You can use calculations to determine the payments on a new car, decide which home would be a better buy, or budget for your next family vacation. In business, Excel can be used for financial tracking, business decision making, trend analysis, and more. Excel recalculates formulas when you change the data in your worksheet. This makes it easier for you to repurpose worksheets you have created for new similar projects.

With Excel's help, you can quickly create complicated calculations, even if you are not a math lover. In this module you will learn to use simple mathematical operators, like + for addition, - for subtraction, * for multiplication, and / for division, to create formulas. You will also learn to use parentheses —(and)— to ensure that Excel performs calculations in the correct order. Excel also offers a number of shortcuts for quickly building formulas and for creating complex formulas using a calculation feature called functions.

Formulas can be copied from cell to cell and they will automatically adjust relative to the cell they are copied to. When the active cell contains a formula, you see the result of the formula in the cell but see the formula in the Formula bar.

Skills You Learn

1 Enter a formula
2 Enter a function
3 Insert a function
4 Use AutoSum
5 Use absolute and relative cell references
6 Copy and paste cell contents
7 Edit cell contents
8 Use Show Formulas

Files You Need
For these skills, you need the following student data file.

M6-C2-S1-DailySales.xlsx

What You Create

The Chocolate Museum operates a small gift shop to raise money to support the annual operating budget. The gift shop sells a variety of items, including gourmet chocolates and other chocolate foods, cooking utensils for preparing various types of chocolate dishes, chocolate recipe books, books about the history of chocolate, and other keepsake and novelty items. The Museum totals the daily sales for the gift shop on a worksheet and uses that information to double-check against the cash, check, and charge amounts collected for the day. The Museum also uses the daily data to calculate weekly totals.

In this chapter, you work on the daily sales worksheet to add the formulas and functions needed to calculate the desired results.

The Chocolate Museum Gift Shop's Daily Sales Worksheets

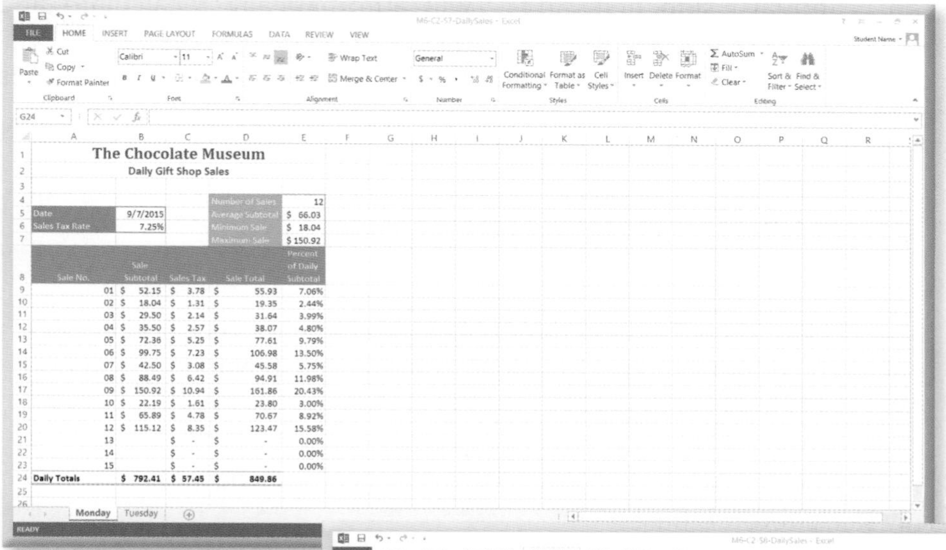

Monday Sheet

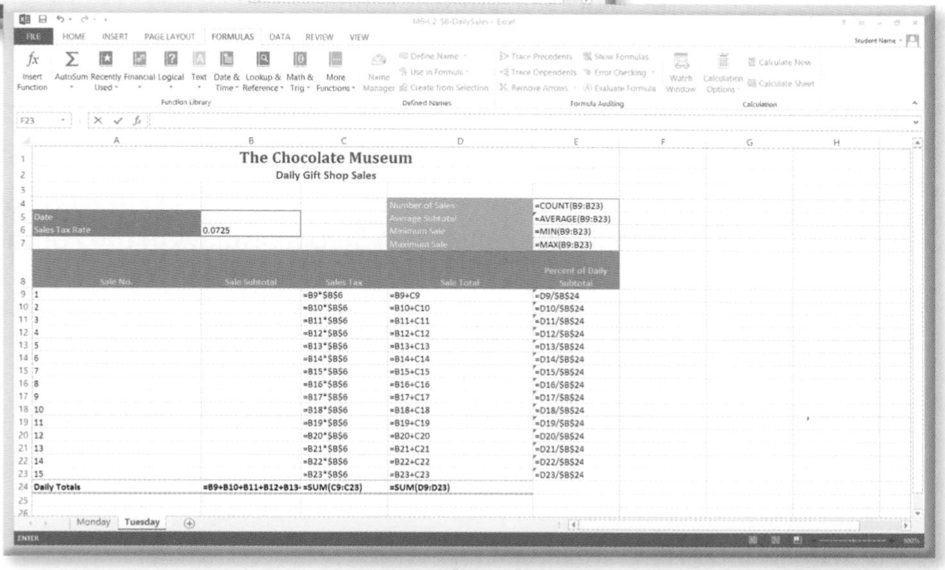

Tuesday Sheet

Excel

Chapter 2

Skill 1

Enter a Formula

 Video M6_C2_S01

In Excel, you can enter formulas directly in cells or use the Formula bar. Formulas perform calculations, the most important capability offered by Excel. There are rules for creating formulas. If you don't follow the rules, Excel indicates an error.

When you enter a formula, always type an = (equals) sign first, and then enter the rest of the formula. You can enter a number or a cell reference in a formula. For example, if you want to add the gift shop sales and the ticket sales together, you would enter the formula =C1+D1, where C1 and D1 are the cells that contain those values. When you finish entering the formula, the cell displays the calculated result. If you later update the data in any cells referenced in the formula, Excel will automatically recalculate and display the updated result.

After you have entered a formula in a cell, you can edit it.

Steps

1 Open the student data file named **M6-C2-S1-DailySales.xlsx**, and if you have not already done so, save the file in your Module 6 working folder on your storage medium.

> **Tip** The formula appears in both the Formula bar and the cell as you type it or when you later select the cell.

2 Click in cell B23 to make it the active cell. You will enter a formula to total the daily sale subtotals here.

> **Tip** You learn to use a function to simplify this formula in Skill 2.

3 Type =B8+B9+B10+B11+B12+B13+B14+B15+B16+B17+B18+B19+B20+B21+B22.

> **Tip** Pressing Ctrl + Enter enters the formula without changing the active cell.

4 Press Ctrl + Enter. The calculated value *$792.41* displays in cell B23 and the formula you entered in Step 3 displays in the Formula bar.

5 Click in cell D8 to make it the active cell.

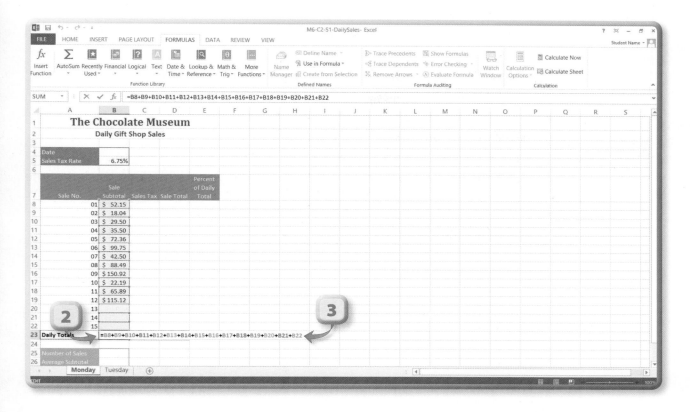

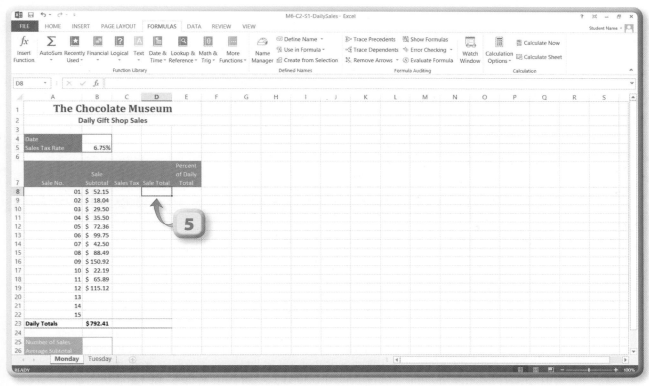

8 **Another Way**
Rather than typing a cell reference into a formula, click the cell on the worksheet to add it to the formula.

▶**Tip** Click the Formula bar Cancel button (looks like an x) to cancel the cell entry.

9 **Another Way**
Press Enter.

6 Type =B8+C8, which calculates the total for the first sale.

7 Press the Right Arrow key to enter the formula and make cell E8 the active cell.

8 Click in the Formula bar and type =D8/B23.

9 Click the Formula bar Enter button (looks like a check mark) to the left of the formula to finish entering the formula in the cell.

10 Save the file.

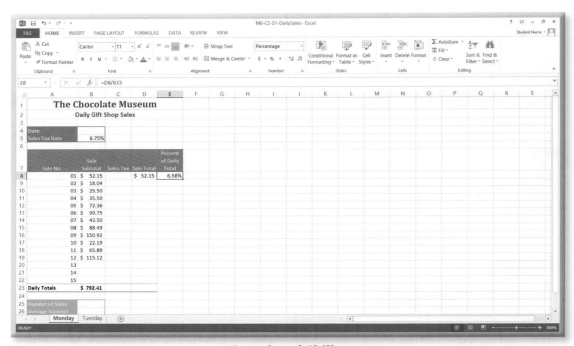

Completed Skill 1

Taking It Further

Calculating in Excel Excel follows the standard mathematical order of operations when evaluating formulas. This means that Excel performs multiplication (*) and division (/) before performing addition (+) and subtraction (-). If the operator precedence is the same, Excel calculates from left to right. Adding parentheses enables you to control the calculation order. Parentheses must be used in pairs, and you can use multiple pairs. Excel calculates from the innermost set of parentheses outward. For example, the formula =5+6*3 calculates to 23 because Excel multiplies first. In contrast, =(5+6)*3 calculates to 33 because Excel adds the values in parentheses first.

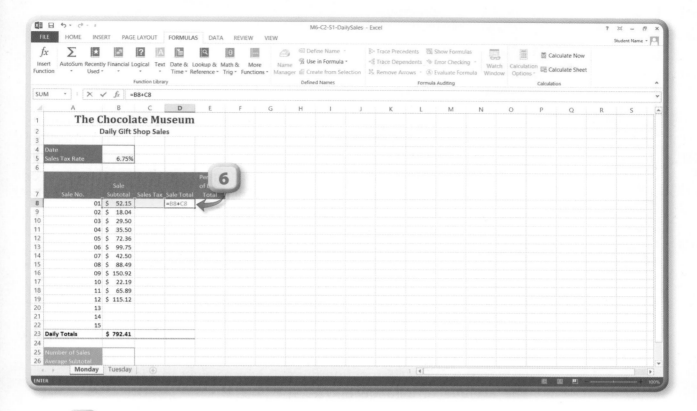

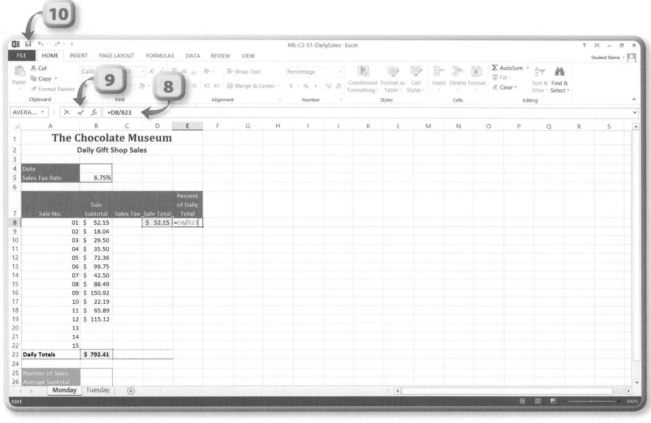

Excel

Video M6_C2_S02

Enter a Function

Excel functions simplify entry of lengthy and complicated formulas. Each function has a name and performs a predefined calculation when you include it in a formula. Excel offers dozens of functions in several different categories, such as *Math & Trig, Financial, Logical, Statistical, Lookup & Reference,* and more.

The function name typically indicates what type of calculation the function performs. For example, the SUM function sums a range of values, the AVERAGE function finds the average of a range of values,

and the COUNT function counts the number of cells in a specified range. You can use the MAX and MIN functions to find the maximum or minimum value in a range. Use the TODAY function to enter the current date, which will update each time you open the workbook.

Most functions require one or more arguments surrounded by parentheses. The arguments are the values on which the function performs its calculations. For example, the SUM function needs to know which values to add.

Steps

1 If it is not already open, open **M6-C2-S1-DailySales.xlsx**, the file you saved in the previous skill, and save the file as **M6-C2-S2-DailySales**.

2 Click in cell B4 to make it the active cell.

3 In the Formula bar, type =TODAY(). (Do not type the period.)

3 Another Way
Functions are not case-sensitive, so typing them in all lowercase letters also works.

▶**Tip** When you are typing a function, a ScreenTip appears to help you type the proper arguments.

4 Press Enter. The current date appears in cell B4.

5 Click in cell C23 to make it the active cell.

6 Type =SUM(. (Do not type the period.)

7 Drag to select the range C8:C22 to enter it in the formula.

7 Another Way
Type the range address *C8:C22.*

8 Type) to close the function argument list.

8 Another Way
This step can be skipped.

9 Click the Formula bar Enter button to the left of the formula to finish entering the formula that sums the sales tax for all the sales in the cell. (Cell C23 currently shows *$ -* because the cells in the selected range do not contain values or formulas. You will enter sales tax formulas in cells C8:C22 in Skill 5.)

9 Another Way
Press Enter.

10 Save the file.

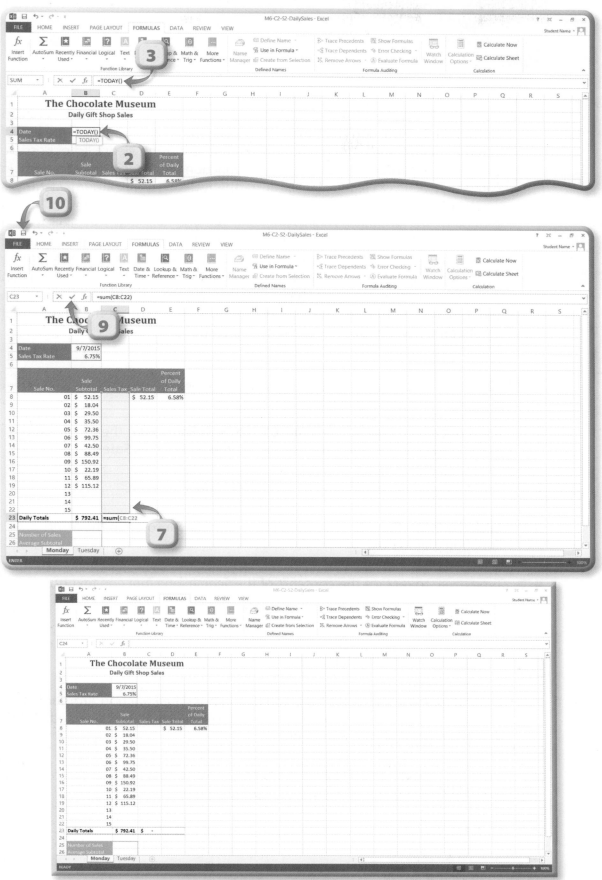

Completed Skill 2

Excel

Excel

Insert a Function

Video M6_C2_S03

You can insert a function using buttons in the Function Library group on the FORMULAS tab. Function buttons organize functions by category, such as *Financial*, *Logical*, and *Math & Trig*. There are additional groupings for *Statistical*, *Engineering*, and *Compatibility* functions. The groupings help you locate the function you need for your formula.

If you don't know the name of the function you need but know what you want it to do, you can find the function in the Insert Function dialog box. Here you can type a brief description and view a list of possible function matches. Click an item in the list to view its arguments and a description of what it does.

As you will learn in Skill 4, you can also insert a function using the AutoSum button in the Editing group on the HOME tab. You begin this skill by entering a function in cell B25 to count the day's total number of sales.

Steps

1 If it is not already open, open **M6-C2-S2-DailySales.xlsx**, the file you saved in the previous skill, and save the file as **M6-C2-S3-DailySales**.

2 Scroll down if necessary and make cell B25 the active cell.

3 Another Way
Click the Insert Function button on the FORMULAS tab.

3 Click the Insert Function button on the Formula bar to open the Insert Function dialog box.

▶**Tip** Rather than searching, you could select a category from the *Or select a category* drop-down list.

4 Type count to replace the contents of the *Search for a function* text box.

5 Another Way
Press Enter.

5 Click the Go button.

6 Confirm that *COUNT* is selected in the *Select a function* list box.

▶**Tip** The dialog box collapses automatically, but you also could use the Collapse Dialog button at the right end of the text box to collapse and expand the dialog box.

7 Click OK to close the Insert Function dialog box. The Function Arguments dialog box appears, with the contents of the *Value1* text box selected. (Each text box represents an argument.)

8 Drag over the range B8:B22 on the Monday worksheet to enter this range in the *Value1* text box.

▶**Tip** Drag the dialog box title bar to move it out of the way if it is covering the cell ranges.

9 Click OK. The counted result *12* appears in cell B25.

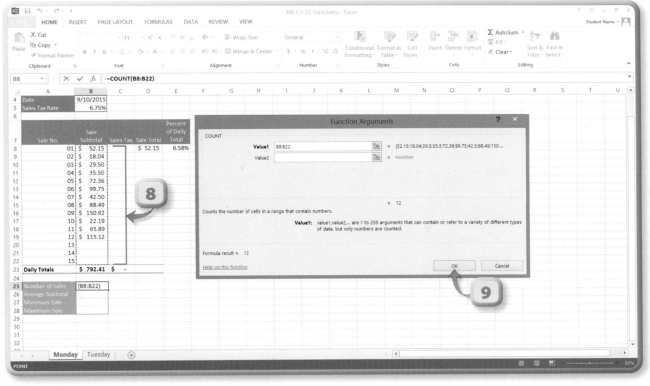

More

10 Press Down Arrow to make B26 the active cell.

11 Click the FORMULAS tab.

▶ **Tip** Click a Function button, such as Financial or Logical, in the Function Library group to see a list of functions within that category.

14 *Another Way*
Type *B8:B22* in the Number1 text box.

12 Click the More Functions button in the Function Library group.

13 Point to *Statistical* in the menu that appears and then click *AVERAGE*.

14 Drag over the range B8:B22 to enter it in the *Number1* text box in the Function Arguments dialog box.

15 Click OK. The calculated average *$66.03* appears in cell B26.

16 Press Down Arrow to make cell B27 the active cell.

17 Type =M. (Do not type the period.)

18 Double-click *MIN* in the *Formula AutoComplete* list.

19 Drag over the range B8:B22 to enter it into the formula and then type) to close the argument.

20 Press Enter. Cell B27 displays *$18.04*, the minimum value found in the range B8:B22.

21 Save the file.

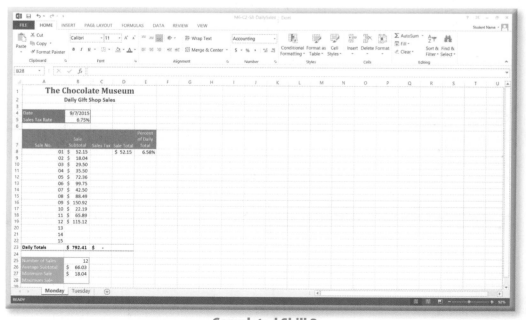

Completed Skill 3

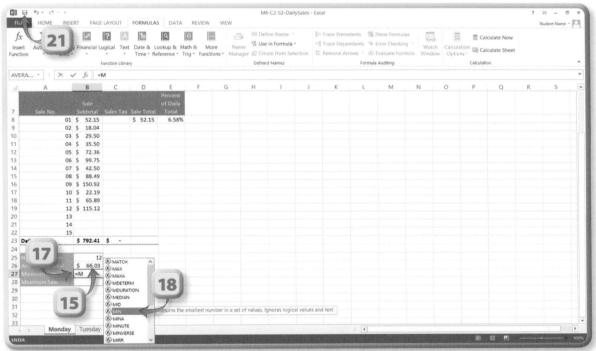

Taking It Further

Inserting Multiple Arguments More complex functions require multiple arguments. When you are typing in a function and need to include multiple arguments—such as multiple cell or range addresses or other values—add a comma between arguments. For example, the IF function is used to display one value if a condition is true and another value if false and requires multiple arguments, such as =if(A5>100,1,0).

Excel

Skill 4

Video ▸ M6_C2_S04

Use AutoSum

The AutoSum feature provides a quick way to enter commonly used functions into a formula. These functions include SUM, AVERAGE, COUNT, MIN, and MAX. To see the result of an AutoSum function without actually entering the formula into a cell, drag over a range of cells and then check the Status bar.

AutoSum functions are also available by clicking the Quick Analysis button after you have selected a range of cells. In the Quick Analysis gallery, select the TOTALS tab to display AutoSum functions. (The Quick Analysis button was described in the Taking It Further feature for Chapter 1, Skill 2.)

Steps

1. If it is not already open, open **M6-C2-S3-DailySales.xlsx**, the file you saved in the previous skill, and save the file as **M6-C2-S4-DailySales**.

2. Click the HOME tab.

3. Select the range B8:B22.

4. Observe the *AVERAGE*, *COUNT*, and *SUM* values that appear in the Status bar.

5. Make cell D23 the active cell.

6. Click the AutoSum button in the Editing group.

7. Press Enter to accept the suggested range and insert the formula in cell D23. Cell D23 displays *$52.15*, the sum of D8:D22.

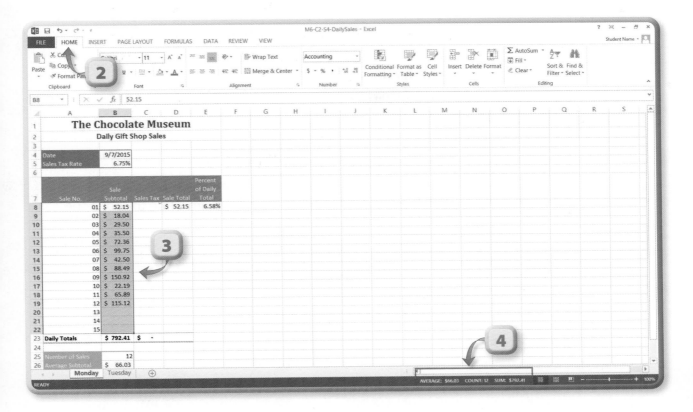

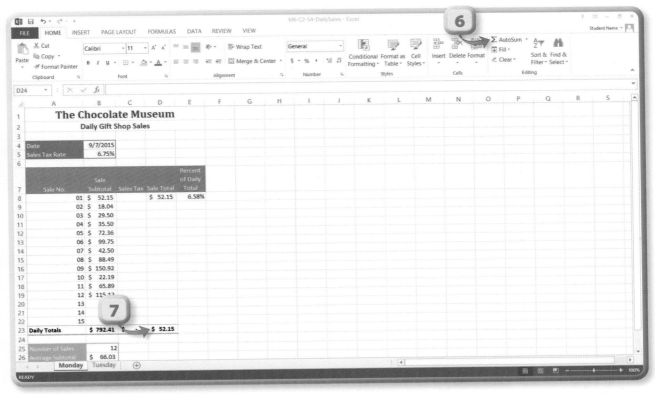

8   Scroll down, if necessary, and make cell B28 the active cell.

9   Click the AutoSum button arrow.

10   Click *Max*.

11   Drag over the range B8:B22 to enter it into the formula.

12   Press Enter. Cell B28 displays *$150.92,* the maximum value found in the specified range.

13   Save the file.

Taking It Further

Using Additional Functions   In addition to MIN, MAX, AVERAGE, SUM, COUNT, and TODAY, there are several other functions that you will find valuable as you begin exploring Excel. The IF function permits you to test a condition and perform different calculations based on the result. COUNTIF counts the number of cells that meet a specified condition. The PMT function calculates the payment amount of a loan. For example, you might use this function to determine the payments if you are planning to obtain a car loan.

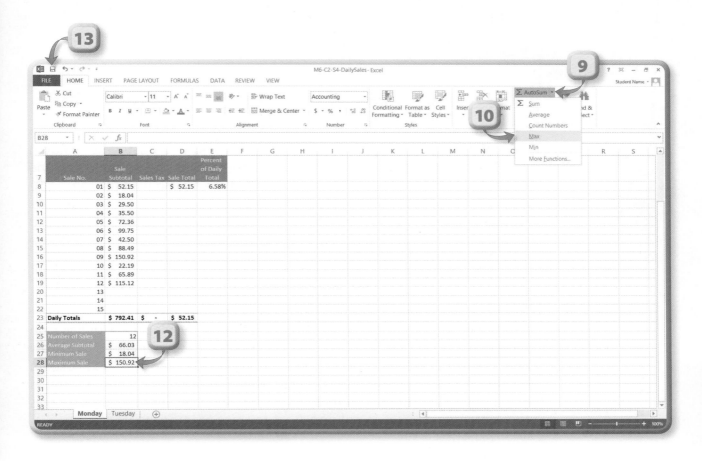

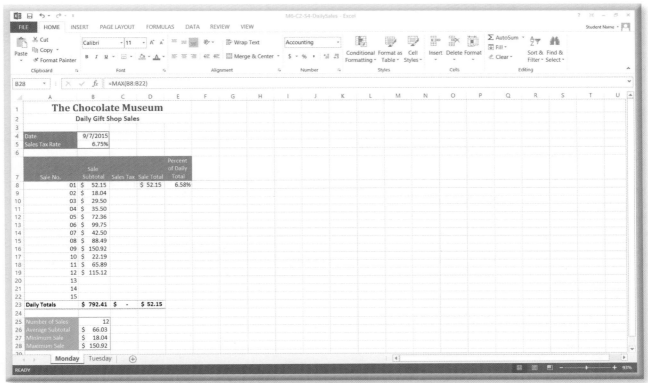

Completed Skill 4

Excel

Chapter 2

Skill 5

Video ▶ M6_C2_S05

Use Absolute and Relative Cell References

Cell references in formulas can be either relative or absolute. A relative cell reference will change if you copy or move the formula. For example, say you created a worksheet that tracks household expenses by month. In January, you entered the expenses for that month and entered a formula to total them at the bottom of column A. Now it is February. You enter the February expenses in column B, but rather than type the SUM formula again, you decide to copy it from column A. Even though the formula was originally written to reference the January expenses in column A,

copying the formula one column to the right adjusts the column references in the formula by one column, causing it to reference the February expenses. For example, =SUM(A3:A10) would change to =SUM(B3:B10) if you copied it one column to the right.

If you don't want a cell reference to change when you are copying a formula, make it an absolute reference by placing a dollar sign before the column letter and row number, for example, A5. Use an absolute reference when a formula contains a key piece of data, such as tax rate or interest rate.

Steps

1 If it is not already open, open **M6-C2-S4-DailySales.xlsx**, the file you saved in the previous skill, and save the file as **M6-C2-S5-DailySales**.

2 Make cell C8 the active cell.

3 Type =B8*B5.

4 Another Way
You also can type the dollar signs to create an absolute reference.

4 Press F4. Excel changes the formula to =B8*B5, making the second cell reference an absolute reference.

▶**Tip** The reference to cell B5 is made an absolute cell reference because the same sales tax rate applies to all of the sold items.

5 Press Ctrl + Enter to finish creating the formula with the absolute reference. Notice that the values in cells D8:E8 and C23:D23 recalculate automatically.

6 Save the file.

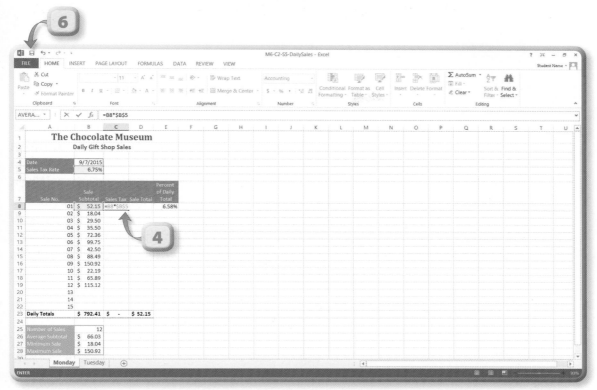

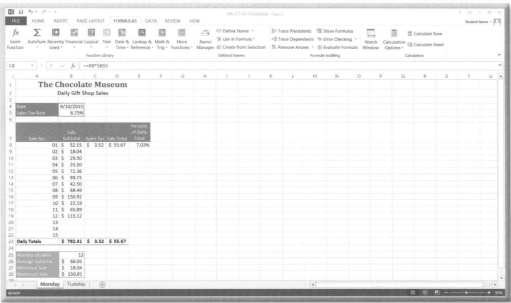

Completed Skill 5

Taking It Further

Placing Reference Data Choosing a good position for key data referenced by formulas on a worksheet can save you trouble later. If you need to change the value in one or more cells referenced in formulas throughout the worksheet, placing that information near the top of the sheet makes it more accessible. Some worksheet designers set up an input range at the top of the sheet to give the worksheet user clear direction about where to enter values. For other types of worksheets, you might want the user to be able to see the results but not the data on which those results are based. In such a case, you would place the input data far down and to the right on the sheet, or even on another worksheet in the workbook file.

Excel

Video M6_C2_S06

Copy and Paste Cell Contents

Often, a worksheet or workbook will contain cell content, such as data values and formulas, that repeats. For example, if a workbook contains budget information for two chain store locations, the budget data for each store is likely to use the same column and row headings and the same formulas.

You can save time entering duplicate data by using the Copy and Paste buttons. You also can use the Cut and Paste buttons to move data or formulas from one location on a worksheet to another. When copying cells that contain formulas, the relative cell references will adjust when the formula is pasted. However, absolute cell references will not. These will need to be changed manually.

Steps

1 If it is not already open, open **M6-C2-S5-DailySales.xlsx**, the file you saved in the previous skill, and save the file as **M6-C2-S6-DailySales**.

2 Drag to select the range C8:D8.

3 Click the Copy button in the Clipboard group on the HOME tab.

4 Make cell C9 the active cell.

5 Click the Paste button in the Clipboard group. The first relative reference in the pasted formula in cell C9 has been updated to refer to cell B9, but the absolute reference in the copied formula still refers to cell B5.

6 Make cell C10 the active cell.

7 Press Enter to paste the copied formula again.

8 With C10:D10 selected, double-click the fill handle at the lower right corner of cell D10 to use Auto Fill to copy the formulas down through cells C22:D22.

▶**Tip** Be sure to click the Copy button, not the Copy button arrow.

▶**Tip** The Office Clipboard can store up to 24 items that have been cut or copied. To open the Office Clipboard, click the Clipboard task pane launcher in the Clipboard group on the HOME tab. You can then choose items to paste.

▶**Tip** Be sure to click the Paste button, not the Paste button arrow.

▶**Tip** Click Paste if you expect to paste copied cells into more than one location. Press Enter to paste the content for a single or the final time.

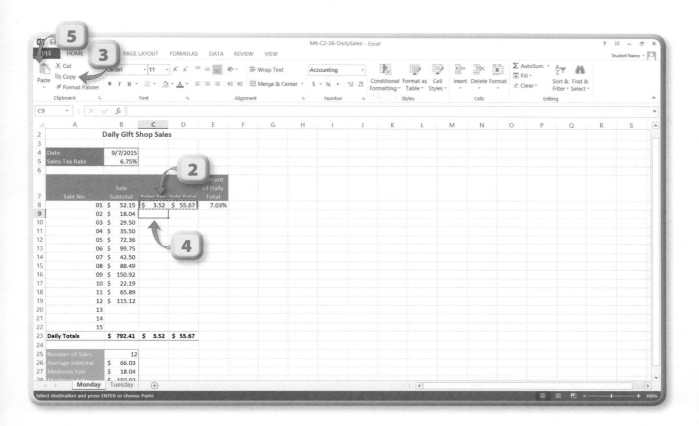

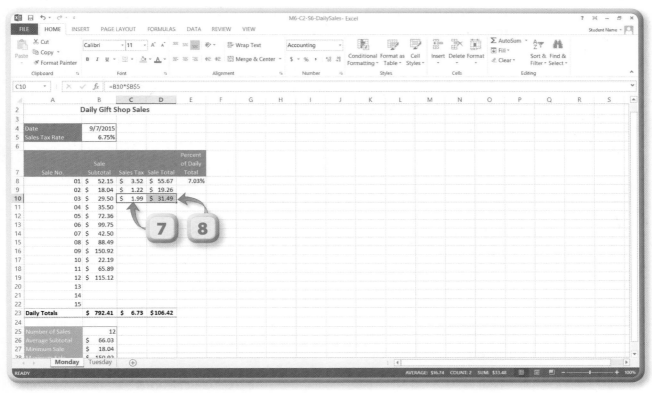

9 Make cell E8 the active cell.

10 Double-click the fill handle. A number of #DIV/0! errors appear in the range because the original formula does not have an absolute reference, but needs to. You will learn how to edit the cell to fix this issue in the next skill.

11 *Shortcut*
Undo
Ctrl + Z

11 Click the Undo button on the Quick Access tool bar.

12 Right-click the row 3 row heading.

▶ ***Tip*** Relative references adjust when you insert or delete rows or columns.

13 Click *Insert* to insert a sheet row.

14 Scroll down, if necessary, and select the range A26:B29.

15 *Shortcut*
Cut
Ctrl + X

15 Click the Cut button in the Clipboard group to cut the range from that location. A scrolling marquee appears around the selected cells.

▶ ***Tip*** Pressing Esc clears the scrolling marquee.

16 Scroll up, if necessary, and make cell D4 the active cell.

17 *Shortcut*
Paste
Ctrl + V

17 Click the Paste button in the Clipboard group. The moved selection appears in its new location. Notice that even though the formulas contain relative references to the range B9:B23, none of the results change when you move the formulas.

18 Double-click the right border of the column D column heading to AutoFit the width of the column.

19 Save the file.

Taking It Further

Using Paste Button Options   Clicking the bottom half of the Paste button (with the down arrow on it) in the Clipboard group on the HOME tab displays additional paste options, such as the Formulas button for pasting only formulas, the Transpose button for transposing (vertical to horizontal and vice versa) the location of the pasted cells, and the Paste Values button for pasting data without underlying formulas or formatting. The numerous choices here enable you to achieve outcomes not possible without the paste options. You also can access the Paste choices by clicking the Paste Options button that appears at the lower right corner of any pasted cell or range.

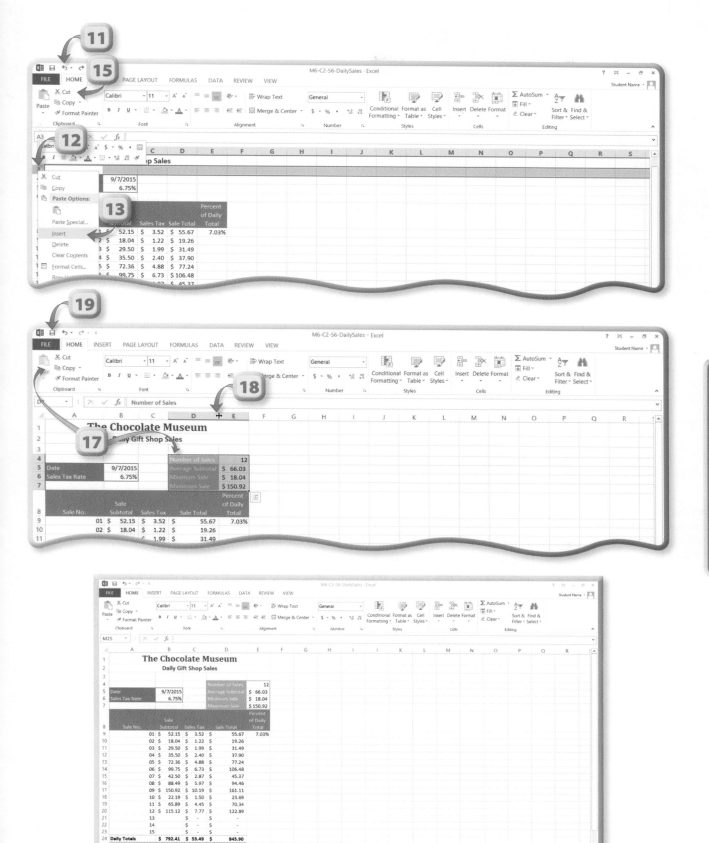

Completed Skill 6

Excel

Edit Cell Contents

Video M6_C2_S07

When you want to use different labels for data, update the data to reflect new information, or make corrections to formulas, you have to edit a cell's contents. Excel offers a number of methods for removing or changing cell contents. You can edit a cell's content directly in the cell or in the Formula bar. You can also use the Clear button in the Editing group on the HOME tab to edit a cell's contents.

Steps

1 If it is not already open, open **M6-C2-S6-DailySales.xlsx**, the file you saved in the previous skill, and save the file as **M6-C2-S7-DailySales**.

2 Make cell B6 the active cell.

3 Type 7.25 and press Enter. This number is a new sales tax rate. Notice that the values shown are automatically recalculated because of the change.

4 Double-click cell E8.

5 Change the last word in the cell from *Total* to *Subtotal* and press Enter.

6 Click in the Formula bar, which shows the formula for the active cell, E9. The D9 reference is correct, but the reference to cell B24 needs to be an absolute reference. Click in the B24 cell reference, press F4, and then press Ctrl + Enter.

7 Double-click the fill handle at the lower right corner of cell E9 to copy the formula down the column through cell E23.

8 Select the range A1:E24.

9 Click the Copy button in the Clipboard group on the HOME tab.

4 *Shortcut*
Open a Cell for Editing
F2

▶ *Tip* Changing cell contents does not change the formatting. In the Editing group on the HOME tab, click the Clear button and then select *Clear Formats* to remove cell formatting.

▶ *Tip* Pressing F2 or double-clicking in a cell puts Excel in Edit mode and displays *Edit* on the left end of the Status bar.

9 *Shortcut*
Copy
Ctrl + C

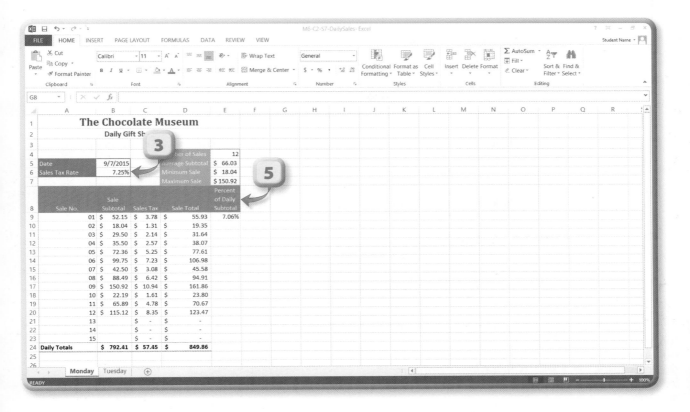

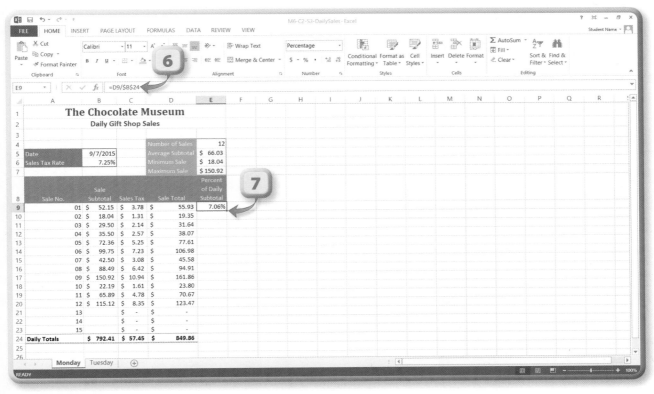

More

10 Click the Tuesday sheet tab.

11 Shortcut
Paste
Ctrl + V

11 Click the Paste button in the Clipboard group to paste the data on the Tuesday sheet.

12 Click the Paste Options button that appears at the lower right corner of the pasted range.

13 Click the Keep Source Column Widths button.

14 Make cell B5 the active cell and then press Delete.

15 Select the range B9:B20.

16, 17 *Another Way*
You also can right-click the selection and click *Clear Contents* in the shortcut menu or press Delete.

16 Click the Clear button in the Editing group on the HOME tab.

17 Click *Clear Contents*.

18 Save the file.

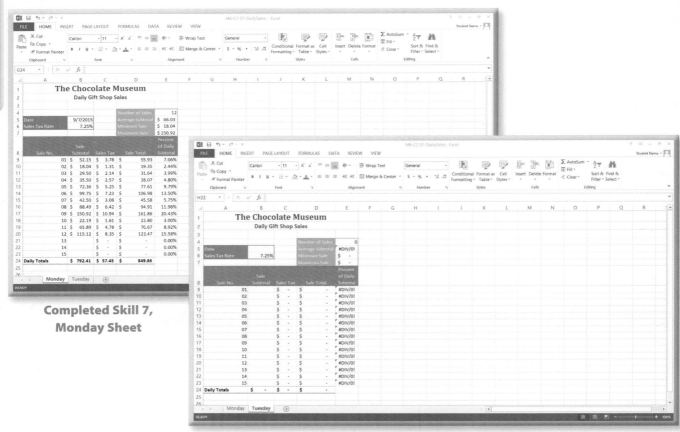

Completed Skill 7,
Monday Sheet

Completed Skill 7, Tuesday Sheet

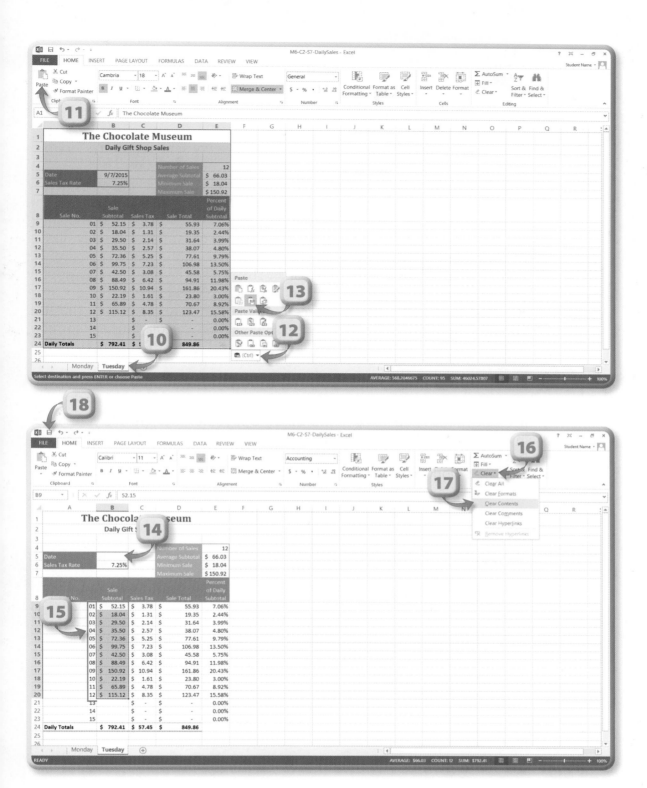

Taking It Further

Using the Clear Button Options The menu for the Clear button in the Editing group on the HOME tab offers additional choices so you can specify exactly what to clear from the selected cell or range. For example, you can take separate actions by selecting only *Clear Formats, Clear Comments,* or *Clear Hyperlinks,* or you can use *Clear All* to clear the cell contents plus any formatting and comments.

Use Show Formulas

Excel displays an error code in a cell if you have made an error when entering a formula. For example, #DIV/0 means the formula is trying to divide by 0 and #VALUE means the formula is using the wrong type of argument. However, Excel will not catch all errors. For example, if you reference the wrong column of numbers in a SUM function, Excel adds the wrong numbers. Because of this, you should always double-check your formulas.

Rather than clicking cells one by one to review their formulas in the Formula bar, you can use the Show Formulas feature to display all the formulas on the worksheet at once. This makes it easy to thoroughly review all cell references and formula structures to ensure that the worksheet calculations are correct.

Steps

1 If it is not already open, open **M6-C2-S7-DailySales.xlsx**, the file you saved in the previous skill, and save the file as **Lastname-M6-C2-S8-DailySales**, but replace *Lastname* with your last name. Be sure to save the file in your Module 6 working folder on your storage medium.

2 Click the Tuesday sheet tab, if it isn't already selected.

3 *Shortcut*
Make cell A1 active
Ctrl + Home

3 Make cell A1 the active cell.

4, 5 *Shortcut*
Show Formulas
Ctrl + `

4 Click the FORMULAS tab.

▶**Tip** Click the Show Formulas button again to hide the formulas.

5 Click the Show Formulas button in the Formula Auditing group.

6 Save and close the file.

Taking It Further

Printing a Worksheet with Formulas Shown   If you print while formulas are displayed, the formulas print but the cell contents do not. This type of printout can provide a handy reference to how the data in the sheet is constructed. In this situation, review the print preview carefully. You may need to adjust print settings, such as orientation and margins. Printouts are easier to read if gridlines and column and row headings are added. To add these options, click the PAGE LAYOUT tab and then click the *Print Gridlines* and *Print Headings* check boxes in the Sheet Options group.

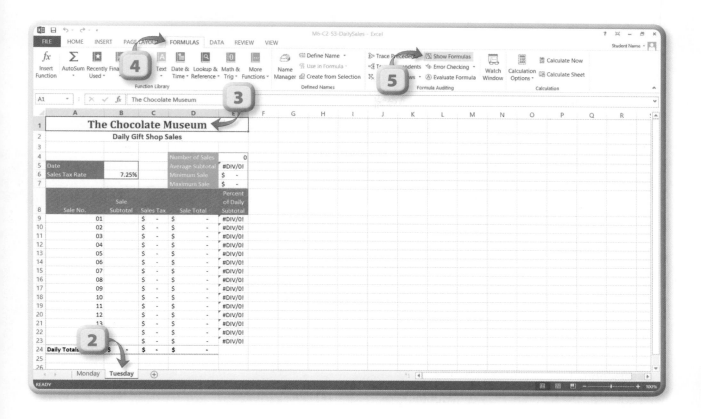

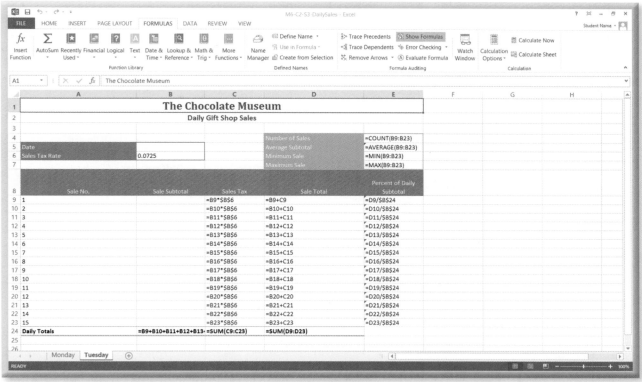

Completed Skill 8

Tasks Summary

Task	Ribbon Tab, Group	Button, Option	Shortcut, Alternative
Enter formulas			Press =, type formula, press Ctrl + Enter
Insert a function with the Insert Function dialog box	FORMULAS, Function Library	*fx* Insert Function	Click *fx* to left of formula bar
Insert a function with Function AutoComplete			Press =, type first few letters, click function, press Tab
Use AutoSum	HOME, Editing or FORMULAS, Function Library	Σ	
Copy a cell or selection	HOME, Clipboard		Ctrl + C
Cut a cell or selection	HOME, Clipboard		Ctrl + X
Paste a cell or selection	HOME, Clipboard		Ctrl + V
Toggle absolute reference when entering or editing a cell reference			F4
Delete cell contents	HOME, Editing	Clear ▾ Clear All Clear Formats Clear Contents	Delete
Enter Edit mode			Press F2, double-click cell, or click in formula bar
Show Formulas	FORMULAS, Formula Auditing	Show Formulas	Ctrl + `

Features Review

Select the best answer from the choices given.

1 Start every formula by typing this.
   a. +
   b. @
   c. =
   d. -

2 The order in which Excel calculates operators is called the
   a. order of priority.
   b. order of hierarchy.
   c. operator processing.
   d. order of operations.

3 You can enter _____ in a formula to tell Excel what to calculate.
   a. numbers
   b. cell references
   c. range references
   d. numbers, cell references, or range references

4 Cell C27 contains the value 10. What is the result when Excel evaluates the formula =2*3+C27/5?
   a. 8
   b. 5.2
   c. 10
   d. More information is needed to determine the formula result.

5 Which statement is false?
   a. Functions are grouped by category.
   b. Functions can be entered directly into a cell.
   c. Functions can be entered as the result of a search.
   d. Functions can change the format of the cell value.

6 Which formula will add the values in cells B3, C3, and D3?
   a. =B3+C3+D3
   b. =SUM(B3/C3/D3)
   c. =SUM(B3-D3)
   d. =B3+C3+D3, =SUM(B3/C3/D3), and =SUM(B3-D3)

7 Most functions require one or more _____ that specify what to calculate.
   a. lists
   b. rows
   c. arguments
   d. lists, rows, and arguments

8 The _____ group on the HOME tab contains the tools for copying and pasting.
   a. Clipboard
   b. Font
   c. Number
   d. Editing

9 When you want to have a reference remain unchanged when you copy a formula, use this type of reference.
   a. fixed
   b. absolute
   c. relative
   d. circular

10 Press the _____ key to remove the contents of a selected cell range.
   a. Backspace
   b. Tab
   c. Spacebar
   d. Delete

Hands-On Skills Review

Exercise **A** **Splitting the Bill**

SNAP
Grade It

Skills Enter a formula, enter a function, insert a function, use AutoSum, use absolute and relative cell references, and edit cell contents

Scenario You often meet with a large group of friends for lunch. One person picks up the bill and the tip at the restaurant, and then the others reimburse that person later on. You need a worksheet to calculate the correct amount for each person.

Steps

1. Open the student data file named **M6-C2-ExA-Tip.xlsx**. Save the file as **Lastname-M6-C2-ExA-Tip**, but replace *Lastname* with your last name.

2. Type your name in cell A2.

3. In cell B14, enter a formula using a function that totals the meal costs.

4. Copy the formula so that totals display in the *Tip Due* and *Total* columns.

5. In cell C6, enter a formula that calculates the percentage of the first diner's meal out of the total meal, using an absolute reference in the appropriate place. The percentage for each person is the cost of his or her meal divided by the cost of all the meals. Do not use any functions in the formula.

6. Copy the formula from cell C6 down the column for each diner. Do not copy the formula into the *Total* row.

7. In cell D6, enter a formula that calculates the first diner's share of the tip, using the *Gratuity Percentage* in cell B3 and an absolute reference where appropriate. Do not use any functions in the formula. **HINT:** *The tip is calculated by multiplying the diner's cost by the tip percentage.*

8. Copy the formula from cell D6 down the column for each diner. Do not copy the formula into the *Total* row.

9. In cell E6, enter a formula that adds the *Cost of Meal* and *Tip Due* for the first diner. Do not use any functions in the formula.

10. Copy the formula from cell E6 down the column for each diner. Do not copy the formula into the *Total* row.

11. You decide to increase the gratuity to 20%. Change the entry in cell B3 to *20%*. The other values recalculate accordingly.

12. Save the worksheet file.

13. Print or submit the completed worksheet as directed by your instructor.

	A	B	C	D	E
1	Tip Share Calculator				
2	Student Name				
3	Gratuity Percentage	20%			
4					
5		Cost of Meal	Percentage of Total	Tip Due	Total
6	Jane	$ 21.50	19.47%	$ 4.30	$ 25.80
7	Allen	$ 17.12	15.50%	$ 3.42	$ 20.54
8	Tina	$ 9.95	9.01%	$ 1.99	$ 11.94
9	Tom	$ 7.95	7.20%	$ 1.59	$ 9.54
10	Fred	$ 4.50	4.07%	$ 0.90	$ 5.40
11	Kendall	$ 16.24	14.70%	$ 3.25	$ 19.49
12	Sasha	$ 18.19	16.47%	$ 3.64	$ 21.83
13	Kiki	$ 14.99	13.57%	$ 3.00	$ 17.99
14	Total	$ 110.44		$ 22.09	$ 132.53

Completed Exercise A

Exercise B Completing an Invoice

Skills   Enter a formula, enter a function, insert a function, use AutoSum, use absolute and relative cell references, copy and paste cell contents, and edit cell contents

Scenario   You sell security products for Endpoint, Inc. You need an invoice that totals the amount due for each item purchased based on the quantity, calculates and adds tax, and then calculates the amount of tax and invoice totals. You also need a blank version of the worksheet to use as a starting point for additional invoices.

Steps

1. Open the student data file named **M6-C2-ExB-Invoice.xlsx**. Save the file as **Lastname-M6-C2-ExB-Invoice**, but replace *Lastname* with your last name.

2. Type your name in cell A3.

3. Change the entry for *Invoice Number* to *1010*.

4. Insert a function to change the entry for *Date* to the current date.

5. In cell D9, enter a formula that calculates the cost amount for the quantity purchased and then copy it through row 15. Do not use a function.

6. In cell E9, enter a formula that calculates the tax due using an absolute reference that refers to the tax rate in cell B6. Do not use a function. Copy the formula through row 15.

7. In cell F9, enter a formula that adds the amount and tax for the first item and copy it through row 15. Do not use a function.

8. Using a function, create a formula in cell E16 that calculates the total amount of tax for this order. The total should include rows 9 through 15 so that it will automatically recalculate correctly if additional items are added to the invoice at rows 13 through 15.

9. Use a function in cell F18 that calculates the invoice total for cells F9 through F15.

10. Adjust the width of column A so the contents of all cells are completely visible.

11. Add a new sheet, Sheet2, to the workbook.

12. Select the range A1:F18 on Sheet1, copy it, and then paste it to the same range on Sheet2. Use Paste options to keep the original column widths.

13. On Sheet2, clear the contents from cells B4:B5 and A9:C12 to prepare a blank invoice.

14. Rename Sheet2 Blank Invoice and Sheet1 Invoice 1010.

15. Save the workbook file.

16. Print or submit the completed workbook as directed by your instructor.

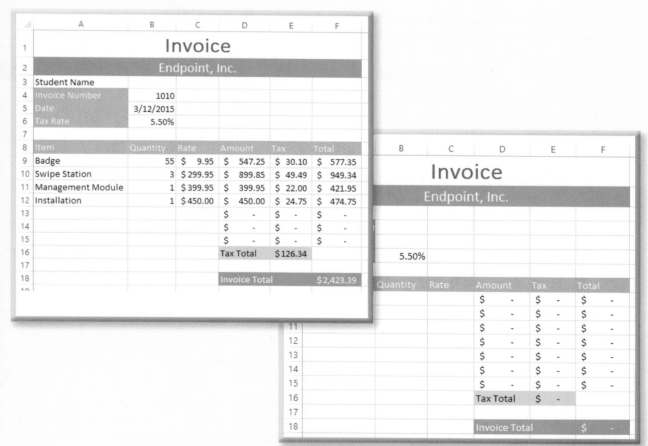

Completed Exercise B, Invoice 1010 and Blank Invoice

Exercise C Calculating Your Utility Budget

Skills   Enter a formula, insert a function, use AutoSum, use absolute and relative cell references, and copy and paste cell contents

Scenario   You keep track of your monthly utility bills and want to use that data to create a budget for next year. You expect your utility bill will be higher based on modifications to your purchase plans as well as a projected percentage increase from all suppliers. Complete the budget and review its formulas.

Steps

1   Open the student data file named **M6-C2-ExC-UtilBudget.xlsx**. Save the file as **Lastname-M6-C2-ExC-UtilBudget**, but replace *Lastname* with your last name.

2   Type your name in cell A2.

3   Using a function, calculate the monthly totals for January through December in row 9.

4   Using a function, calculate the monthly averages for January through December in row 10.

5   In the range N5:P9, use functions to find the annual *Total*, *Average*, and *Max* values for each type of utility and the total utility amount.

6   Copy the range A3:P10 and paste it at cell A14 to use the current year data as the base data for next year.

7   Change the entry in cell A14 to *Projected*.

8   Change the Water/Sewer values in the range B19:M19 to *$23.99*.

9   In cell A23, type Total Plus Increase.

10   In cell B23, enter a formula that multiplies the total from B20 by the *Increase Percentage* in cell B12. Use an absolute reference where required. Do not use a function.

11   When you finish the entry, you can see that the amount calculated is below the total, which means the formula is incorrect. The amount shown is the increase, not the new total including the increase. Edit the formula in cell B23, changing it so the formula adds the total to the increase, displaying a new total.

12   Copy the formula in cell B23 to the appropriate monthly cells in row 23.

13   In the range N23:P23, use functions to find the annual *Total*, *Average*, and *Max* values.

14   Save the workbook file.

15   Print or submit the completed workbook as directed by your instructor.

	A	B	C	D	E	F	G	H	I	J	K	L	M	N	O	P
1	**Utility Budget**															
2	Student Name															
3	**Current Year**															
4	Utility	Jan	Feb	Mar	Apr	May	Jun	Jul	Aug	Sep	Oct	Nov	Dec	Total	Average	Max
5	Mobile Phone	$ 75.50	$ 65.97	$ 72.93	$ 76.77	$ 75.50	$ 75.50	$ 98.22	$ 75.50	$ 93.09	$ 88.24	$ 101.99	$ 75.50	$ 974.71	$ 81.23	$ 101.99
6	Electricity	$ 78.22	$ 65.21	$ 56.12	$ 44.09	$ 65.09	$ 101.99	$ 121.99	$ 92.80	$ 88.55	$ 99.04	$ 115.15	$ 99.99	$ 1,028.24	$ 85.69	$ 121.99
7	Natural Gas	$ 215.09	$ 180.99	$ 176.77	$ 39.99	$ 14.90	$ 12.50	$ 10.50	$ 10.50	$ 67.04	$ 88.50	$ 97.65	$ 201.98	$ 1,116.41	$ 93.03	$ 215.09
8	Water/Sewer	$ 22.50	$ 22.50	$ 22.50	$ 22.50	$ 22.50	$ 22.50	$ 22.50	$ 22.50	$ 22.50	$ 22.50	$ 22.50	$ 22.50	$ 270.00	$ 22.50	$ 22.50
9	Total	$ 391.31	$ 334.67	$ 328.32	$ 183.35	$ 177.99	$ 212.49	$ 253.21	$ 201.30	$ 271.18	$ 298.28	$ 337.29	$ 399.97	$ 3,389.36	$ 282.45	$ 399.97
10	Average	$ 97.83	$ 83.67	$ 82.08	$ 45.84	$ 44.50	$ 53.12	$ 63.30	$ 50.33	$ 67.80	$ 74.57	$ 84.32	$ 99.99			
11																
12	Increase Percentage	5.90%														
13																
14	**Projected**															
15	Utility	Jan	Feb	Mar	Apr	May	Jun	Jul	Aug	Sep	Oct	Nov	Dec	Total	Average	Max
16	Mobile Phone	$ 75.50	$ 65.97	$ 72.93	$ 76.77	$ 75.50	$ 75.50	$ 98.22	$ 75.50	$ 93.09	$ 88.24	$ 101.99	$ 75.50	$ 974.71	$ 81.23	$ 101.99
17	Electricity	$ 78.22	$ 65.21	$ 56.12	$ 44.09	$ 65.09	$ 101.99	$ 121.99	$ 92.80	$ 88.55	$ 99.04	$ 115.15	$ 99.99	$ 1,028.24	$ 85.69	$ 121.99
18	Natural Gas	$ 215.09	$ 180.99	$ 176.77	$ 39.99	$ 14.90	$ 12.50	$ 10.50	$ 10.50	$ 67.04	$ 88.50	$ 97.65	$ 201.98	$ 1,116.41	$ 93.03	$ 215.09
19	Water/Sewer	$ 23.99	$ 23.99	$ 23.99	$ 23.99	$ 23.99	$ 23.99	$ 23.99	$ 23.99	$ 23.99	$ 23.99	$ 23.99	$ 23.99	$ 287.88	$ 23.99	$ 23.99
20	Total	$ 392.80	$ 336.16	$ 329.81	$ 184.84	$ 179.48	$ 213.98	$ 254.70	$ 202.79	$ 272.67	$ 299.77	$ 338.78	$ 401.46	$ 3,407.24	$ 283.94	$ 401.46
21	Average	$ 98.20	$ 84.04	$ 82.45	$ 46.21	$ 44.87	$ 53.50	$ 63.68	$ 50.70	$ 68.17	$ 74.94	$ 84.70	$ 100.37			
22																
23	Total Plus Increase	$ 415.98	$ 355.99	$ 349.27	$ 195.75	$ 190.07	$ 226.60	$ 269.73	$ 214.75	$ 288.76	$ 317.46	$ 358.77	$ 425.15	$ 3,608.27	$ 300.69	$ 425.15

Completed Exercise C

Chapter 3

Formatting Cells

Applying formatting to worksheet cells provides organization and context. Formatting also clarifies the meaning of the data. For example, to specify whether Excel should format a cell value as a date, currency amount, or percentage, you would apply a number format. Other formatting tools, such as those that control font and size, determine how labels and values look and align within cells. You can also change the column width and row height to ensure entries display completely and correctly.

You can use other tools to group data visually. For example, you can apply a new fill color to cells that contain the column labels in a worksheet, or add a border around a range, or even merge cells together. You learn how to use formatting to enhance a worksheet in this chapter.

Skills You Learn

1 Apply number formats
2 Work with other formatting tools
3 Adjust column width and row height
4 Fill cells with a color
5 Add borders
6 Merge cells

Files You Need
For these skills, you need the following student data file.

M6-C3-S1-MajorDonors.xlsx

What You Create

As a nonprofit organization, The Chocolate Museum accepts donations to help support their operating costs, exhibits, and educational programs. A staff member has created a worksheet to track donations made over the last few years. It is up to you to apply formatting to the worksheet.

Worksheet for Tracking Major Donors

	A	B	C		D		E	F	G	H
1					The Chocolate Museum					
2					Major Donors					
3	Updated:	Monday, March 23, 2015								
4										
5					Donation					
6	Donor ID	Donor/Organization Name	This Year		Last Year		Change in Dollars	Change in Percentage	Action Required	
7	001	Mr. and Mrs. Jeff Butler	$	1,500	$	1,250	$250	20.0%	Donation receipt	
8	002	Krell Foundation	$	1,250	$	1,500	($250)	-16.7%	Donation challenge	
9	003	Ms. Wanda Matheson	$	1,250	$	1,250	$0	0.0%	Donation receipt	
10	004	Carson Partners	$	1,750	$	1,850	($100)	-5.4%	Donation challenge	
11	005	Dr. Peter Winter	$	-	$	1,500	($1,500)	-100.0%	Reminder letter	
12	006	Mr. and Mrs. Carl Thomas	$	1,600	$	1,460	$140	9.6%	Donation receipt	
13	007	Peterson Family Foundation	$	10,000	$	7,500	$2,500	33.3%	Donation receipt	
14	008	Miss Sylvia Phillips	$	1,150	$	1,150	$0	0.0%	Donation receipt	
15	009	The Chocolatier, LLC	$	1,750	$	1,600	$150	9.4%	Donation receipt	
16	010	Positivity Center	$	2,500	$	1,500	$1,000	66.7%	Donation receipt	
17	011	Mr. and Mrs. James Lyon	$	1,000	$	500	$500	100.0%	Donation receipt	
18	012	Mr. Fred Morgan	$	1,250	$	3,250	($2,000)	-61.5%	Donation receipt	
19	Totals		$	25,000	$	24,310	$690	2.8%		
20										
21										

Excel

Apply Number Formats

Video M6_C3_S01

When you type an entry into a cell, it is automatically formatted according to the General format. When you type a date in a cell, Excel recognizes it and formats it automatically as a date. You can apply formats to add dollar signs, commas, and other characters to the cells. Applying a new format changes the display of an entry.

The number format applied to a cell holding numerical data determines how Excel displays the number. For example, applying the Accounting format to a cell places, by default, a dollar symbol ($) to the left of the value, adds a thousands separator, adds a decimal point and two places to the right of it for the "cents," and aligns the amount in the cell according to the decimal point. You can apply other formats, such as Date, Currency, or Percentage, and change number formats as needed.

Steps

1 Open the student data file named **M6-C3-S1-MajorDonors.xlsx** and, if you have not already done so, save the file in your Module 6 working folder on your storage medium.

2 Make cell B3 the active cell.

▶**Tip** When you do not include the year, Excel assumes you want the current year. Dates are stored as sequential serial numbers so they can be used in calculations.

3 Enter the date 3/23 and then press Ctrl + Enter.

4 Click the *Number Format* option box arrow in the Number group on the HOME tab.

5 Click *Long Date*. The width of column B increases automatically to accommodate the longer number format.

6 Drag to select the range C7:D19.

7 *Another Way*
Click the *Number Format* option box arrow and then click *Accounting*.

7 Click the Accounting Number Format button.

8 Click the Decrease Decimal button two times.

▶**Tip** Excel will recognize some number formats when you type symbols such as $ and %.

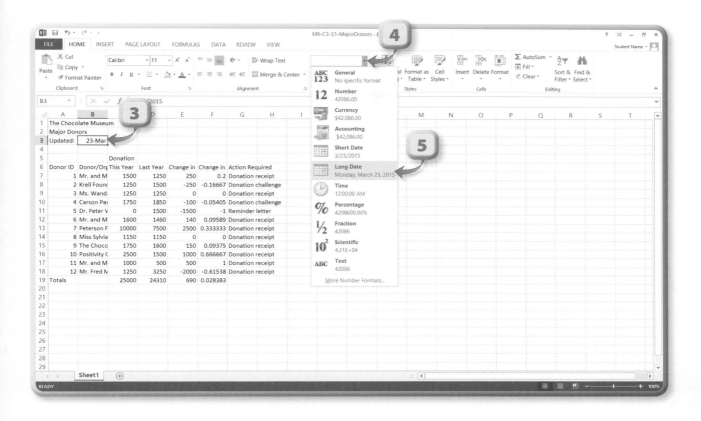

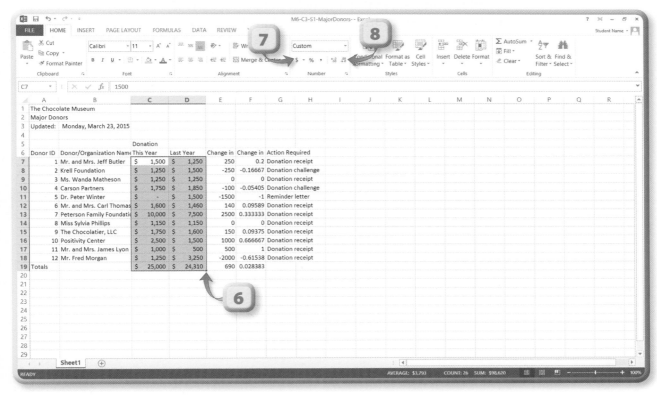

More

9 Drag to select the range E7:E19.

10 Click the *Number Format* option box arrow.

11 Click *Accounting* in the drop-down list. This format displays negative values in parentheses.

12 Click the *Number Format* option box arrow.

13 Click *Currency*. This format displays negative values with a minus sign (-).

14 Click the *Number Format* option box arrow.

15 Click *More Number Formats*. This opens the Format Cells dialog box.

16 *Another Way*
Highlight the number in the *Decimal places* measurement box and type the desired number, *0.*

16 In the Format Cells dialog box, click the down-pointing arrow at the right of the *Decimal Places* measurement box two times to change the value to *0*.

17 In the *Negative numbers* list box, click the fourth choice, which displays negative numbers in red and with parentheses. This changes the default display for currency from negative signs to red parentheses.

18 Click OK.

Excel

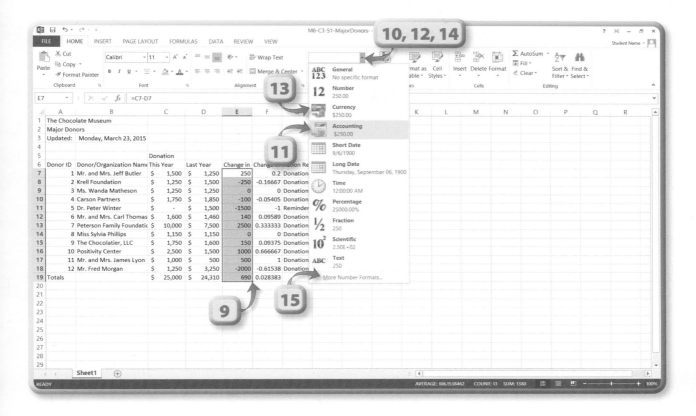

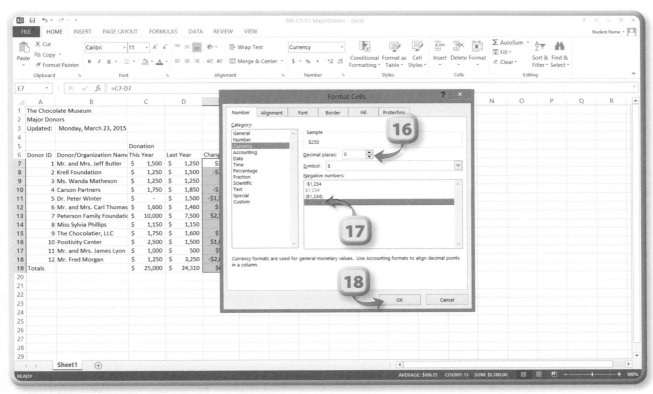

More

19 Drag to select the range F7:F19.

20 Click the Percent Style button in the Number group on the HOME tab.

21 Click the Increase Decimal button.

22 Drag to select the range A7:A18.

23 Click the Number group dialog box launcher.

▶**Tip** Steps 24–26 create and apply a custom style, something you can do if none of the existing styles and options displays a number the way you prefer.

24 In the Format Cells dialog box with the Number tab selected, click *Custom* in the *Category* list box.

25 Double-click the value that appears in the *Type* text box and then type 00#.

26 Click OK.

27 Click the Save button on the Quick Access toolbar to save the file.

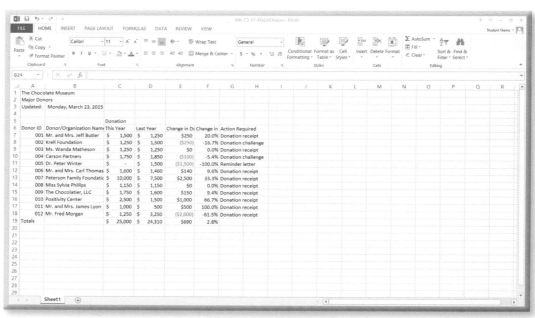

Completed Skill 1

Taking It Further

More Choices for Number Formatting

Some variations of the number formats are available as styles in the *Cell Styles* gallery. Click the HOME tab and then click the Cell Styles button in the Styles group to access the gallery. The *Number Format* section of the gallery lists the number styles you can apply. You also can click *New Cell Style* to create a custom cell style to apply to the selected cell or range.

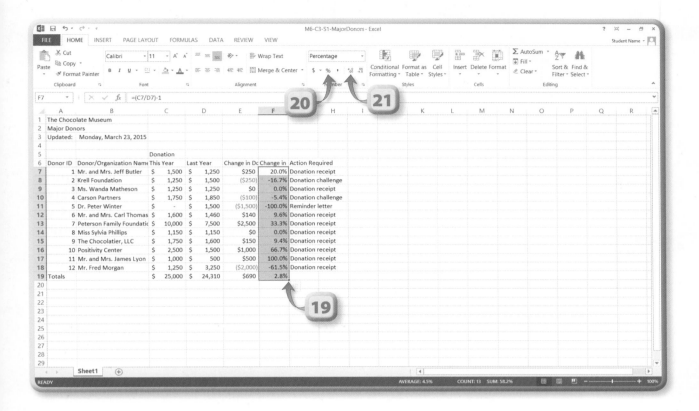

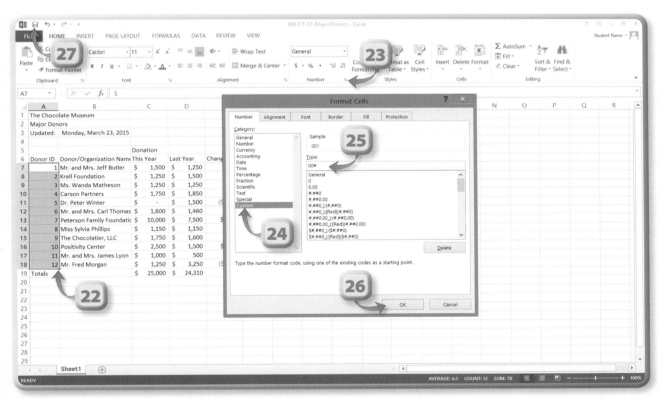

Excel

Video M6_C3_S02

Work with Other Formatting Tools

Excel lets you apply a variety of formats to cells to change the basic look of a worksheet. You can use the Increase Font Size and Decrease Font Size buttons to adjust the font size of the contents of selected cells. You can also apply bold, italic, and underlining, as well as change the color of the text and the cell background. Use the alignment tools to change the vertical and horizontal alignment of cell entries. The Cell Styles button in the Styles group on the HOME tab lets you apply several formatting settings at once.

Steps

1 If it is not already open, open **M6-C3-S1-MajorDonors.xlsx**, the file you saved in the previous skill, and save the file as **M6-C3-S2-MajorDonors**.

2 Make cell A1 the active cell.

3 Click the Cell Styles button in the Styles group on the HOME tab.

4 Click *Title* in the *Titles and Headings* section to apply the Title style to the selected cell.

5 Drag to select the range A2:B3.

6 Click the Font button arrow in the Font group.

7 Scroll down and then click *Cambria* in the drop-down gallery.

7 *Another Way*
Select the text in the Font text box and type *Cambria*.

8 Click the Increase Font Size button twice to change the font size to 14 points.

8 *Another Way*
Select the number in the Font Size text box and type *14* or click the Font Size button arrow and click *14* in the drop-down gallery.

9 Drag to select the range A5:G6.

▶**Tip** The unit of measurement for font size is the point (pt), which is equal to 1/72nd of an inch.

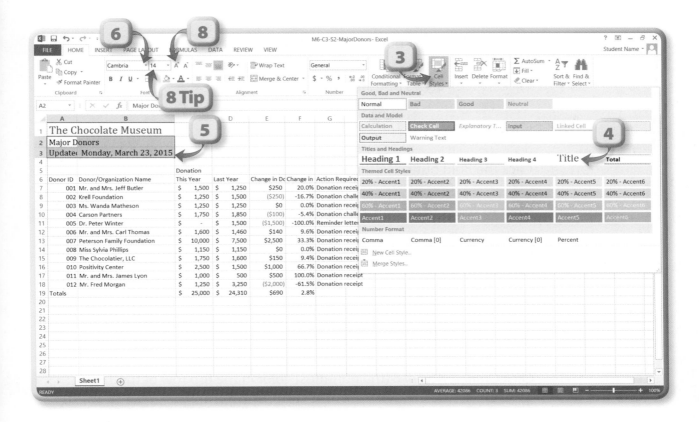

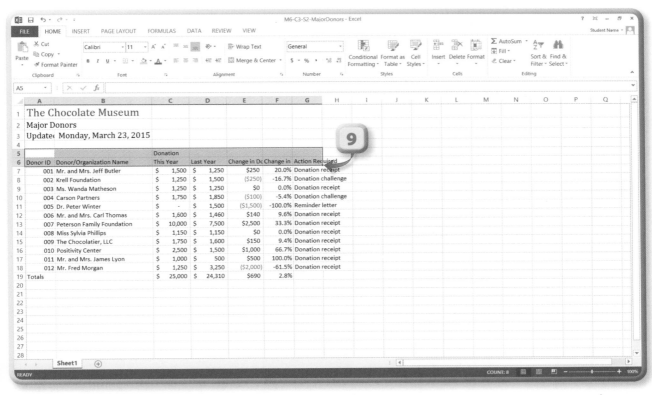

More

10 Click the Wrap Text button in the Alignment group.

11 Click the Cell Styles button in the Styles group.

12 Click *Accent2* in the *Themed Cell Styles* section.

13 Click the Bold button in the Font group.

14 Drag to select the range A19:F19.

15 Click the Italic button in the Font group.

16 Make cell G11 the active cell.

17 Click the Font Color button arrow.

18 Click *Orange, Accent 6* (the rightmost color in the top row of the *Theme Colors* section).

19 Save the file.

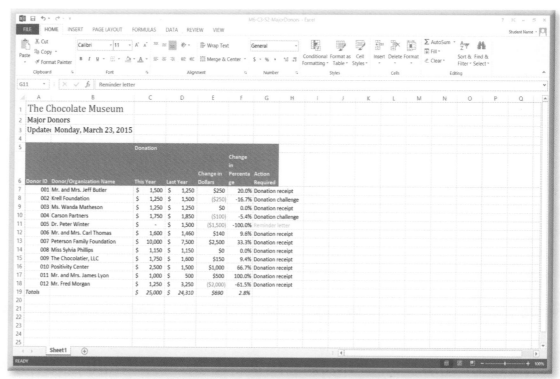

Completed Skill 2

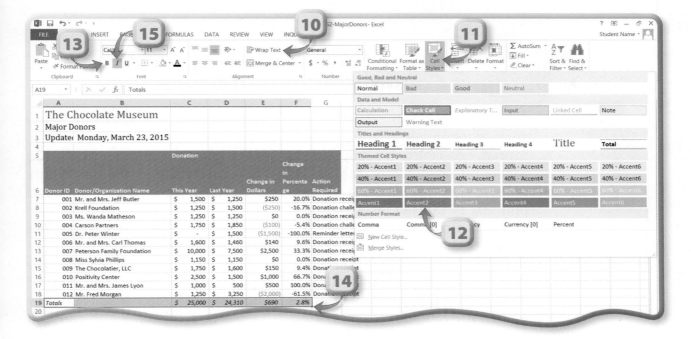

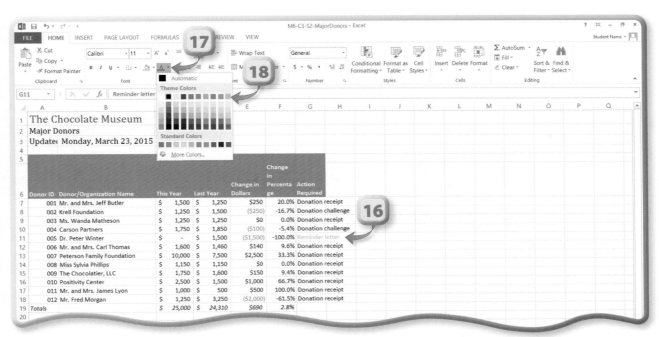

Taking It Further

Changing the Theme You can change the overall look of the worksheets in a workbook simply by changing the theme. The theme supplies the overall formatting settings for the workbook file, including the theme fonts (those used by default for that specific theme), theme colors, theme effects, and cell styles. If you have applied your own cell styles or if you have chosen a theme and decide you do not like it, you can choose another. You can do so by clicking the Themes button in the Themes group on the PAGE LAYOUT tab and then clicking the theme you want. Pointing to any theme displays a live preview of the changes it applies.

Excel

Skill 3

Adjust Column Width and Row Height

Video M6_C3_S03

When you perform some actions, such as when you change the cell format, Excel automatically widens a column or increases the height of a row. If you make a change and Excel doesn't automatically widen the column or increase the height of the row to accommodate the changed entry, you could find that some entries don't fit into their cells. If the cell to the right is empty, the long entry simply runs over, into the cell(s) to the right. But if the cell to the right is not empty and the entry is text, Excel only displays as much of the entry that fits in the cell, hiding the rest. If the entry is a number that is too long to display in the cell width, Excel displays a string of pound signs (######) to cue you that the numeric cell entry does not fit. You need to resize the column.

You may need to adjust the row height when you wrap text or increase font size. Modifying row height and column width can also help make the worksheet more readable.

Steps

1 If it is not already open, open **M6-C3-S2-MajorDonors.xlsx**, the file you saved in the previous skill, and save the file as **M6-C3-S3-MajorDonors**.

2 Make cell A1 the active cell.

3 Click the Format button in the Cells group on the HOME tab.

4 Click *Row Height* in the *Cell Size* section of the drop-down list.

5 Type 35 in the *Row height* text box.

6 Click OK to close the dialog box.

7 Click the Middle Align button in the Alignment group.

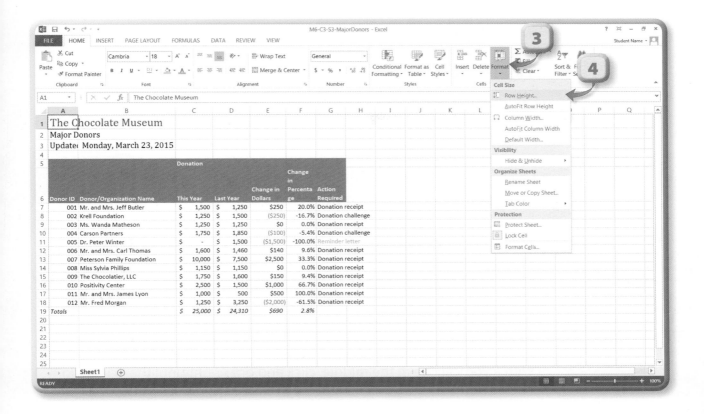

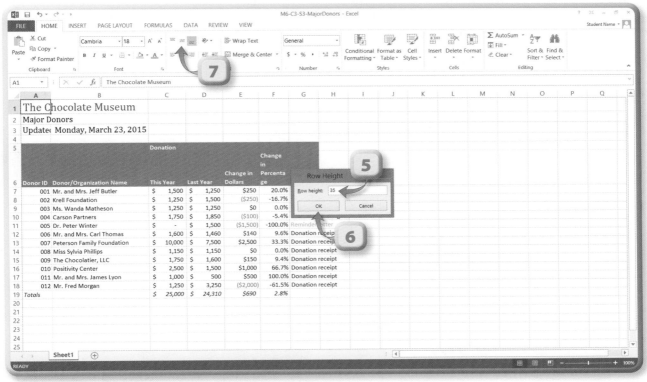

More

8 Make any cell in column F the active cell.

9 Click the Format button in the Cells group.

10 Click *Column Width* in the *Cell Size* section of the drop-down list.

11 Type 12 in the *Column width* text box.

12 Click OK to close the dialog box.

13 **Another Way**
Click the *AutoFit Column Width* option in the *Cell Size* section of the Format button drop-down list to AutoFit the column to its widest entry.

13 Move the mouse pointer over the right border of the column G column heading until the mouse pointer becomes a left-and-right-pointing arrow with a vertical line in the middle and double-click to allow Excel to AutoFit the column size.

▶**Tip** When text wrapping is applied to cells in a row, the row height does not decrease automatically to fit the text when a cell is edited. You have to manually reduce the row height to fit the text.

14 Move the mouse pointer over the right border of the column A column heading until the mouse pointer becomes a left-and-right-pointing arrow with a vertical line in the middle, click and drag right until the ScreenTip reads *Width: 11.00 (82 pixels)*, and then release the mouse button.

15 Move the mouse pointer over the bottom border of the row 6 row heading until the mouse pointer becomes an up-and-down-pointing arrow with a horizontal line in the middle and then double-click.

16 Save the file.

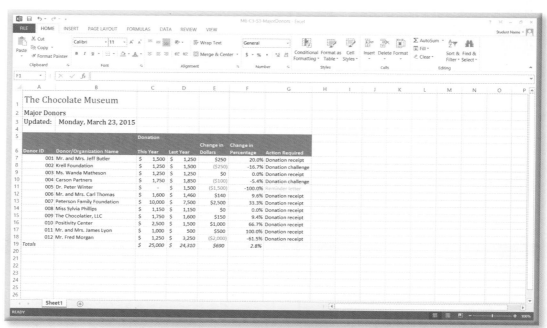

Completed Skill 3

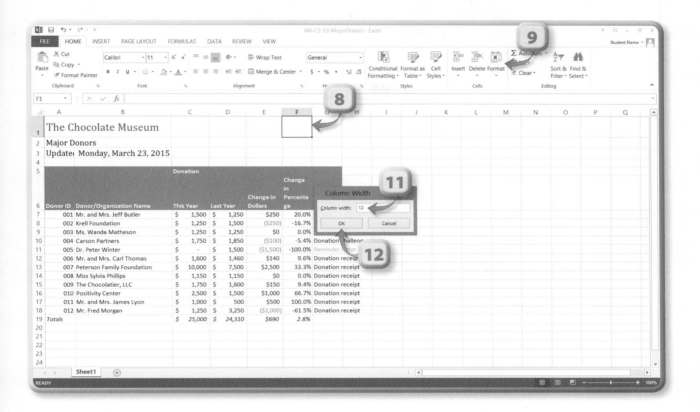

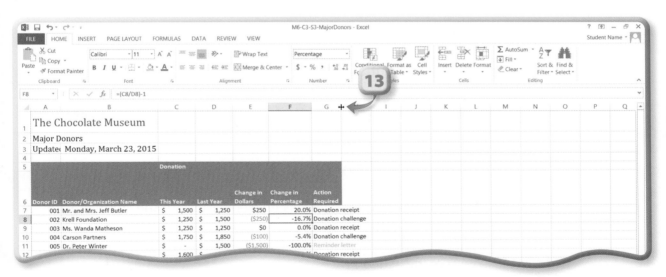

Taking It Further

Changing Column Width Default Settings

With the default Office Theme applied, the default column width is 8.43 characters and the default row height is 15 points. Changing the theme applied to the workbook may change these defaults. You can adjust the default column setting by clicking the Format button in the Cells group on the HOME tab and then clicking *Default Width* at the drop-down list. A dialog box displays in which you can enter a new standard column width for the workbook.

Excel

> Skill 4

Video   M6_C3_S04

Fill Cells with a Color

You can fill a selected cell or range with color to draw attention to it or help distinguish it from other items in a worksheet. Click the Fill Color button down arrow in the Font group on the HOME tab to display a gallery of fill colors. You can then click a color to apply it to the selection. Conveniently, the color you applied most recently appears on the button itself. Simply click the button to apply that same fill color to other selections.

Another way to apply formatting is by using the Format Painter button in the Clipboard group on the HOME tab. Make the cell with the formatting you wish to apply the active cell, click the Format Painter button, and then click the cell you wish to format.

Steps

1 If it is not already open, open **M6-C3-S3-MajorDonors.xlsx**, the file you saved in the previous skill, and save the file as **M6-C3-S4-MajorDonors**.

2 Make cell A1 the active cell.

3 Click the Fill Color button arrow in the Font group on the HOME tab.

▶ **Tip** In Step 4, the title will not be completely shaded, but you will fix this in Skill 6.

4 Click *Olive Green, Accent 3, Lighter 40%* (the fourth color from the top in the seventh column) in the *Theme Colors* section of the palette.

5 Drag to select the range A19:G19.

6 Click the Fill Color button. Excel fills the selection with the color you applied in Step 4.

7 Make cell G8 the active cell.

8 Click the Fill Color button arrow.

9 Click *Yellow* (the fourth option from the left) in the *Standard Colors* section.

10 With cell G8 the active cell, click the Format Painter button in the Clipboard group.

11 Click in cell G10. Excel fills the cell with the color you applied in Step 9.

12 Save the file.

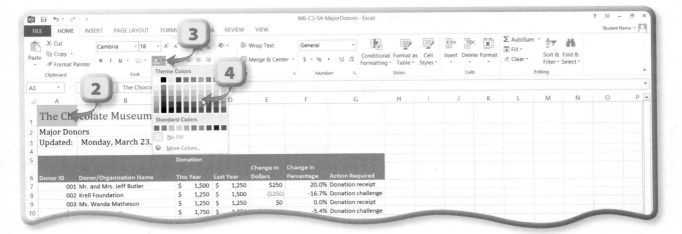

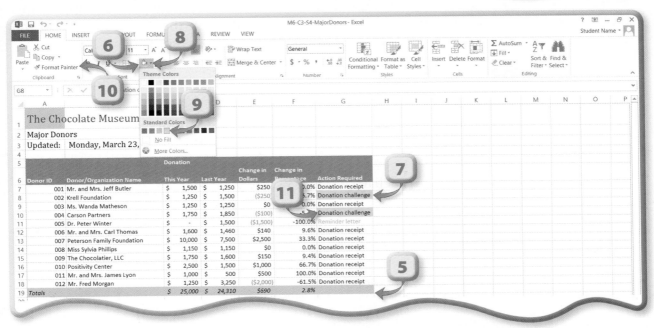

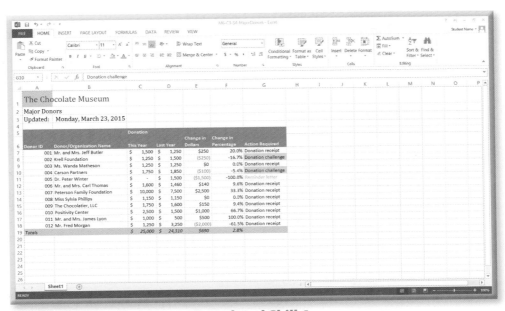

Completed Skill 4

Excel

Add Borders

Video M6_C3_S05

Applying a border around a cell or cell range in a worksheet provides another way to group or emphasize the data visually. Borders can be especially useful when you use the default print setting and print a worksheet without cell gridlines. For example, accountants often place a single border at the top and a double border at the bottom of a row presenting data totals. You also can use a border to set off a range where the user should type in data for calculations or to highlight important data or formula results. In addition, you can add borders as purely decorative elements—but make sure the border appearance fits with the other formatting that you have applied.

Steps

1 If it is not already open, open **M6-C3-S4-MajorDonors.xlsx**, the file you saved in the previous skill, and save the file as **M6-C3-S5-MajorDonors**.

2 Make cell A2 the active cell.

▶**Tip** In Step 3, you should not worry that the border does not underline all of the text in cell A2. The next skill teaches you how to address that issue.

3 Click the Borders button in the Font group on the HOME tab. Excel applies a single border to the bottom of the cell.

4 Drag to select the range A19:G19.

5 Click the Borders button arrow.

▶**Tip** In Step 3, if a border other than a bottom border appears, click the Borders button arrow and then click *Bottom Border*.

6 Click *Top and Bottom Border* in the *Borders* section of the drop-down list.

Taking It Further

Using Conditional Formatting   Use conditional formatting to change formatting based on the cell value. Start by clicking the Conditional Formatting button in the Styles group on the HOME tab. Click an option at the drop-down menu and then click additional options or enter text to specify when to apply the conditional formatting. For example, you can add a red border to all cells displaying values less than 0 by clicking *Highlight Cells Rules* and then *Less Than* to open the Less Than dialog box, and then typing *0* in the *Format cells that are LESS THAN* text box and selecting *Red Border* from the *with* drop-down menu. The available options include creating your own conditional rules and formats.

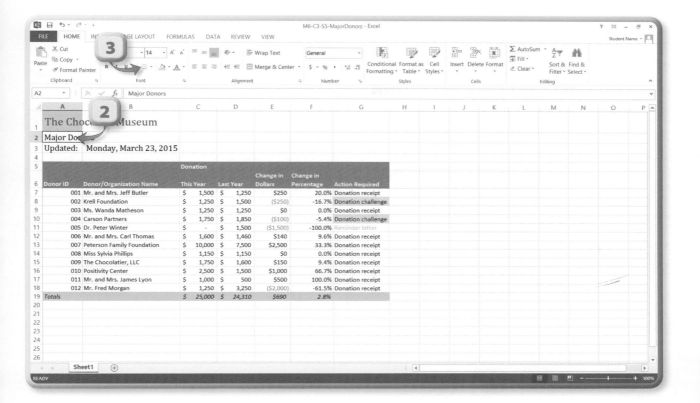

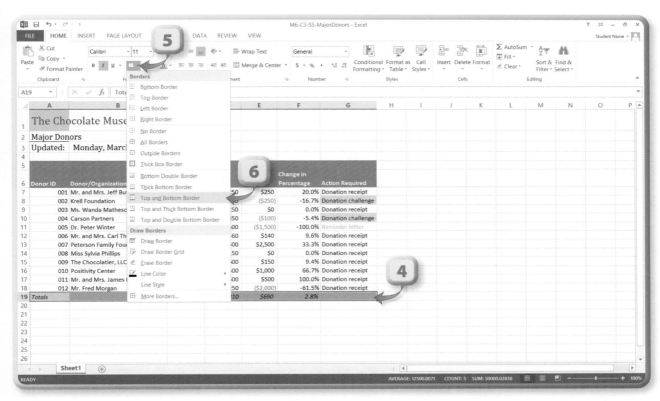

More

7 Drag to select the range A11:G11.

▶ *Tip* To select multiple cells that are next to one another, click the first cell, hold the Shift key, and then click the last cell. Release the Shift key.

▶ *Tip* To select multiple cells that are scattered around the worksheet, click the first cell, hold the Ctrl key, and then click each of the other cells. When all the cells have been clicked, release the Ctrl key.

8 Hold down the Ctrl key, drag to select the range A17:G17, and then release the Ctrl key.

9 Click the Borders button arrow.

10 Click *More Borders* in the drop-down list.

11 On the Border tab of the Format Cells dialog box, click the *Color* option box arrow.

12 Click *Purple, Accent 4* (the first color in the eighth column) in the *Theme Colors* section of the palette.

▶ *Tip* Clicking the Outline button places the border around the entire range, not around each individual cell in the range.

13 Click the Outline button in the *Presets* section.

14 Click OK.

15 Save the file.

	A	B	C	D	E	F	G	H
1	The Chocolate Museum							
2	Major Donors							
3	Updated:	Monday, March 23, 2015						
4								
5			Donation					
6	Donor ID	Donor/Organization Name	This Year	Last Year	Change in Dollars	Change in Percentage	Action Required	
7	001	Mr. and Mrs. Jeff Butler	$ 1,500	$ 1,250	$250	20.0%	Donation receipt	
8	002	Krell Foundation	$ 1,250	$ 1,500	($250)	-16.7%	Donation challenge	
9	003	Ms. Wanda Matheson	$ 1,250	$ 1,250	$0	0.0%	Donation receipt	
10	004	Carson Partners	$ 1,750	$ 1,850	($100)	-5.4%	Donation challenge	
11	005	Dr. Peter Winter	$ -	$ 1,500	($1,500)	-100.0%	Reminder letter	
12	006	Mr. and Mrs. Carl Thomas	$ 1,600	$ 1,460	$140	9.6%	Donation receipt	
13	007	Peterson Family Foundation	$ 10,000	$ 7,500	$2,500	33.3%	Donation receipt	
14	008	Miss Sylvia Phillips	$ 1,150	$ 1,150	$0	0.0%	Donation receipt	
15	009	The Chocolatier, LLC	$ 1,750	$ 1,600	$150	9.4%	Donation receipt	
16	010	Positivity Center	$ 2,500	$ 1,500	$1,000	66.7%	Donation receipt	
17	011	Mr. and Mrs. James Lyon	$ 1,000	$ 500	$500	100.0%	Donation receipt	
18	012	Mr. Fred Morgan	$ 1,250	$ 3,250	($2,000)	-61.5%	Donation receipt	
19	Totals		$ 25,000	$ 24,310	$690	2.8%		
20								
21								
22								

Completed Skill 5

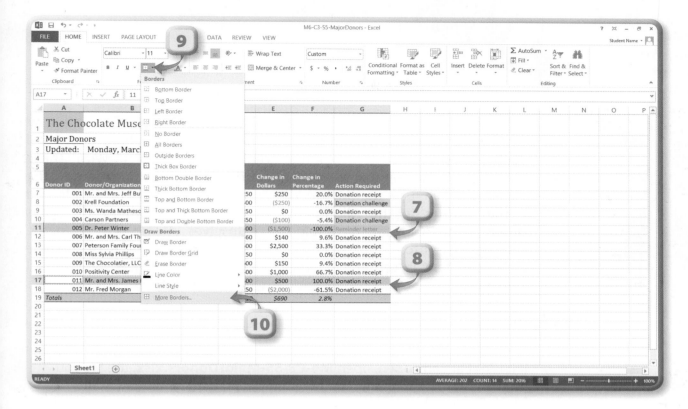

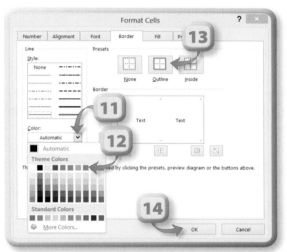

Taking It Further

More Border Options When you click *More Borders* to display the Format Cells dialog box, options in the *Style* list box enable you to choose another border weight or a different border appearance, such as dashed or dotted. Because these border styles are a bit less formal than a plain cell border or outline, you should use them sparingly, especially in business documents.

Excel

Skill 6

Video M6_C3_S06

Merge Cells

To enhance the readability of a worksheet, you might choose to center the sheet title across all the columns of data in the sheet. In Excel you can use the Merge & Center button in the Alignment group on the HOME tab to combine selected cells into a single cell. The combined text is centered in the single cell.

Click the Merge & Center button arrow to display three additional formatting options. With these options, you can merge the columns across each selected row without merging the rows themselves (*Merge Across*), merge a range into a single cell (*Merge Cells*), and unmerge a merged cell (*Unmerge Cells*).

Steps

1. If it is not already open, open **M6-C3-S5-MajorDonors.xlsx**, the file you saved in the previous skill, and save the file as **Lastname-M6-C3-S6-MajorDonors**, but replace *Lastname* with your last name. Be sure to save the file in your Module 6 working folder on your storage medium.

2. Drag to select the range C5:D5.

3. Click the Merge & Center button in the Alignment group on the HOME tab. This action merges and centers a title that is common to the two columns of data.

4. Click the Cell Styles button in the Styles group.

5. Click *60% - Accent3* in the *Themed Cell Styles* section of the gallery.

6. Drag to select the range A1:G2.

7. Click the Merge & Center button arrow in the Alignment group.

8. Click *Merge Across* in the drop-down list.

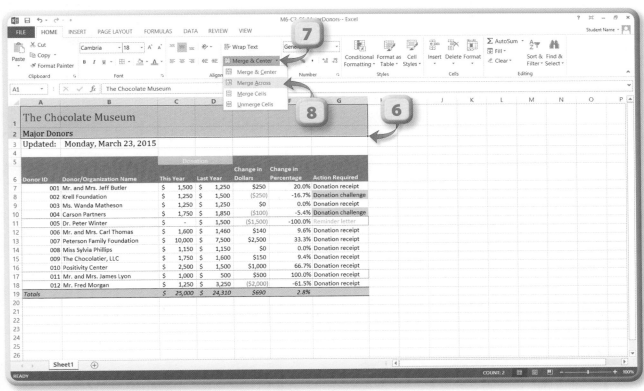

More

9 Click the Center button in the Alignment group.

10 Make cell A2 the active cell.

11 Click the Borders button arrow in the Font group.

12 Click *Bottom Border* in the *Borders* section of the drop-down list.

13 Save and close the file.

Tip The cell address listed in the Name box above the upper left corner of the worksheet is the address for the far left cell in the merged range.

Tip Be sure to check all formatting when merging and centering. In this case, merging removed the previously applied bottom border, so you must reapply the border.

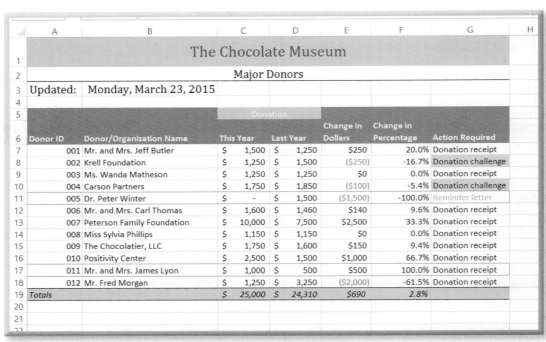

Completed Skill 6

Excel

Taking It Further

Designing Worksheets In this skill, you created a balanced appearance in the completed worksheet by using the same fill color for the top and bottom rows and limiting the number of applied formats.

Keeping your design simple and taking advantage of the color palette supplied by the theme helps you to design professional worksheets that highlight the most important data for decision making.

Excel

Tasks Summary

Task	Ribbon Tab, Group	Button, Option	Shortcut, Alternative
Choose a number format	HOME, Number	General	
Apply Accounting format	HOME, Number	$	
Apply Percent format	HOME, Number	%	
Apply Comma format	HOME, Number	,	
Increase or decrease decimal places	HOME, Number	←.0 .00 .00 →.0	
Apply a cell style	HOME, Styles		
Copy a cell style	HOME, Clipboard		
Change the font	HOME, Font	Calibri	
Change the font size	HOME, Font	11	
Increase or decrease the font size	HOME, Font	A˄ A˅	
Apply bold	HOME, Font	B	Ctrl + B
Apply italics	HOME, Font	I	Ctrl + I
Apply underline	HOME, Font	U	Ctrl + U
Change character color	HOME, Font	A	
Wrap cell entries	HOME, Alignment		Press Alt + Enter when making a cell entry to wrap lines manually
Change vertical or horizontal cell alignments	HOME, Alignment		
Change column width or row height	HOME, Cells	*Column Width* or *Row Height*	Drag or double-click the right column border or bottom row border

Task	Ribbon Tab, Group	Button, Option	Shortcut, Alternative
Fill a cell with color	HOME, Font		F2, or double-click the cell
Add borders to a cell or selection	HOME, Font		
Merge cells	HOME, Alignment		

Features Review

Select the best answer from the choices given.

1 This number format applies a currency symbol, adds two decimal places, and changes the cell's alignment.
a. Accounting
b. Number
c. Percent
d. General

2 Use the Format Painter to
a. choose a background color for a cell.
b. shrink the width of the text in a cell.
c. copy formatting from one cell to another cell.
d. copy a formula from one cell to another cell.

3 When creating a worksheet, it is good professional style to
a. make each column a different color.
b. use borders to help organize the worksheet into sections.
c. apply the Accounting format to entries that represent dates.
d. always make very wide columns.

4 If you do not modify the display of a cell, the cell entry displays using which format?
a. Accounting
b. Number
c. Currency
d. General

5 Excel stores dates as
a. labels.
b. cell references.
c. sequential serial numbers.
d. formulas.

6 Use the _____ feature to display a cell's entry on multiple lines within the cell.
a. wrap text
b. Merge & Center
c. borders
d. cell styles

7 Use the _____ feature to combine multiple cells into a single cell.
a. wrap text
b. Merge & Center
c. borders
d. cell styles

8 These may include font, border, fill, and other formatting settings.
a. wrap text
b. Merge & Center
c. borders
d. cell styles

9 Applying _____ helps set off data, which especially helps the reader if you do not print gridlines.
a. wrap text
b. Merge & Center
c. formulas
d. cell styles

10 The _____ feature helps you size a row or column automatically.
a. Format Painter
b. wrap text
c. Format Cells
d. AutoFit

Exercise **Formatting a Tip Shares Worksheet**

Skills   Apply number formats, work with other formatting tools, adjust column width and row height, fill cells with a color, and merge cells

Scenario   You are working with another tip calculation worksheet. This time, you apply formatting to make the worksheet more attractive.

Steps

1   Open the student data file named **M6-C3-ExA-Tip.xlsx** and save the file as **Lastname-M6-C3-ExA-Tip**, but replace *Lastname* with your last name.

2   Type your name in cell A2.

3   Apply the Title cell style to cell A1 and change the font color to *Green, Accent 6, Darker 25%*. Apply bold formatting to the cell.

4   Merge and center cells A1:E1.

5   Increase the font size for cells A3:B3 to 14 and apply bold formatting.

6   Apply the Percentage number format with no decimal places to the entry in cell B3.

7   Format the ranges B6:B12 and D6:D12 to use Accounting number format with two decimal places.

8   Format the range C6:C11 to use Percent Style with two decimal places.

9   Apply the Green, Accent 6, Darker 25% fill color to the range A5:E5.

10   For range A5:E5, change the font color to *White, Background 1*, apply bold formatting, and middle align and wrap the text. **HINT:** *Click the Wrap Text button in the Alignment group on the HOME tab.*

11   Autofit columns A and B.

12   Select the range A12:E12 and apply the Total cell style.

13   Format cells E6:E12 to use the Currency number format with two decimal places.

14   Apply the Green, Accent 6, Darker 25% fill color to the range A12:E12.

15   Save the file.

16   Print or submit the completed worksheet as directed by your instructor.

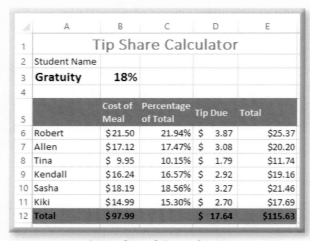

Completed Exercise A

Exercise B Formatting Stock Portfolio Information

Skills   Apply number formats, work with other formatting tools, adjust column width and row height, fill cells with a color, add borders, and merge cells

Scenario   You track a portfolio of stocks and other securities using an online service such as Yahoo! Finance. You are able to download daily quote data, but it downloads in a raw, unformatted version that makes it difficult to review. Apply formatting to make the downloaded data more attractive and useful.

Steps

1   Open the student data file named **M6-C3-ExB-Quotes.xlsx** and save the file as **Lastname-M6-C3-ExB-Quotes**, but replace *Lastname* with your last name.

2   Type your name in cell A28.

3   Delete column D, which holds time information.

4   Insert two new rows at the top of the sheet and then type Quotes in cell A1.

5   Change the font size of the text in cell A1 to 24 points and apply the Blue, Accent 1, Darker 25% font color.

6   Merge and center the contents of cells A1:G1.

7   Select the cells in the *Closing Price*, *Change*, *Low*, and *High* columns and apply the Currency format with two decimal places while displaying negative values in red with parentheses.

8   Apply a date format to the cells in the *Date* column that displays the dates in 3/14 format. **HINT:** *Use the* More Number Formats *option in the* Number Format *drop-down list to display the* Format cells dialog box. With the Date *selected in the* Catagory *list box, select* 3/14 *in the* Type *list box.*

9   Apply the Number format with the thousands separator and no decimal places to the cells in the *Volume* column. **HINT:** *Use the* More Numbers Formats *option in the* Number Format *drop-down list to display the* Format Cells dialog box. Select Number *in the* Category *list box and adjust the number of decimals and separator values as needed.*

10 Apply the Accent5 cell style to the range A3:G3, and bold, center, and wrap the text.

11 Select the range A4:G4, apply the Blue, Accent 1, Darker 25% border color, and then add a bottom border only.

12 Use the Format Painter to copy the formatting from A4:G4 to A5:G28. **HINT:** *In this case Excel copies the border formatting without changing any of the formatting you have previously applied.*

13 Change the height for row 2 to 6.00 (8 pixels), and apply the Blue, Accent 5, Lighter 60% fill color to cells A2:G2.

14 Save the file.

15 Print or submit the completed worksheet as directed by your instructor.

	A	B	C	D	E	F	G
1				Quotes			
3	Ticker	Closing Price	Date	Change	Low	High	Volume
4	AAPL	$249.64	8/20	($0.24)	$249.38	$253.92	12,819,960
5	AFL	$46.63	8/20	$0.07	$46.27	$46.82	3,538,567
6	AIBDX	$14.31	8/20	($0.03)	N/A	N/A	N/A
7	CREE	$57.93	8/20	($0.30)	$58.50	$58.99	2,817,486
8	CSCO	$22.23	8/20	$0.01	$22.19	$22.41	50,631,176
9	CSX	$49.79	8/20	($0.50)	$49.75	$50.14	2,570,915
10	DNDN	$38.22	8/20	$0.81	$37.31	$38.42	2,776,871
11	F	$11.77	8/20	($0.12)	$11.85	$11.90	48,953,016
12	GE	$15.03	8/20	($0.22)	$15.18	$15.18	62,621,528
13	GOOG	$462.02	8/20	($5.95)	$467.26	$471.59	3,746,910
14	HGT	$19.97	8/20	($0.21)	$20.22	$20.27	123,582
15	HI	$20.09	8/20	($0.05)	$20.21	$20.21	223,294
16	HRC	$33.47	8/20	($0.55)	$33.86	$33.92	492,225
17	JNK	$39.10	8/20	$0.12	$38.98	$39.10	2,469,011
18	PAYX	$25.38	8/20	$0.12	$25.23	$25.44	2,842,257
19	PFF	$39.86	8/20	($0.01)	$39.90	$39.91	889,101
20	QCOM	$38.91	8/20	$0.80	$38.24	$39.09	17,744,644
21	RMBS	$19.38	8/20	$0.63	$18.95	$19.53	1,960,981
22	SNDK	$41.50	8/20	($0.40)	$41.61	$41.85	19,264,916
23	SPH	$48.29	8/20	($0.06)	$48.59	$48.59	56,686
24	SWK	$55.05	8/20	($0.14)	$54.64	$55.22	934,075
25	TBT	$31.69	8/20	$0.07	$31.49	$31.81	10,221,104
26	TIVO	$8.69	8/20	$0.21	$8.40	$8.70	1,029,798
27	TLT	$106.04	8/20	($0.12)	$106.42	$106.83	6,652,347
28	WFC	$24.60	8/20	$0.17	$24.43	$24.71	37,754,832
29							
30	Student Name						

Completed Exercise B

SNAP Grade It

Exercise **C** Reviewing Sales Bonus Eligibility

Skills Apply number formats, work with other formatting tools, adjust column width and row height, fill cells with a color, add borders, and merge cells

Scenario You track a small sales force and are reviewing quarterly sales for the prior year. Each salesperson receives a base salary and commission. To keep the team members motivated and competitive, you offer an additional bonus based on the percentage that each sales person achieves relative to total sales. Finish your tracking worksheet by formatting it now.

Steps

1 Open the student data file named **M6-C3-ExC-Sales.xlsx** and save the file as **Lastname-M6-C3-ExC-Sales**, but replace *Lastname* with your last name.

2 Type your name in cell A3.

3 Use the PAGE LAYOUT tab to apply the Slice theme to the workbook. ***HINT:*** *Use the Themes button in the Themes group on the PAGE LAYOUT tab.*

4 Apply the Title cell style to cell A1.

5 Use *Merge Across* to merge A1:G1 and A2:G2. Do not change the new alignments.

6 Change cell A2 to the Long Date format.

7 Select the range A4:B5, apply the Dark Blue, Accent 1, Darker 25% border color, and add a Thick Box border.

8 Apply the Dark Blue, Accent 1, Lighter 80% fill color to cell B4 and apply the Dark Blue, Accent 1, Lighter 40% fill color to cell B5.

9 Format the range A7:G7 with the Accent 1 cell style, and then center and wrap the text for these cells.

10 Apply the Accounting format with no decimal places to the values for each quarter and the totals.

11 Apply the Percent number format with no decimal places to cells B4:B5.

12 Apply the Percent number format with two decimal places to the values in the *Production Percentage* column.

13 Increase the width of columns A and G so each word in the heading fits completely on one line. Then AutoFit all columns.

14 AutoFit the height of row 7.

15 Format the *Productions Percentage* column entries that meet or exceed the Bonus Level 1 percentage (cell B4) but are less than the Bonus Level 2 percentage (cell B5) with the same fill color as used for the Bonus Level 1 percentage (Dark Blue, Accent 1, Lighter 80%). ***EXTENSION ACTIVITY:*** *Use conditional formatting to create a rule for highlighting cells that are between two values.*

16 Change the page orientation to landscape.

17 Save the file.

18 Print or submit the completed file as directed by your instructor.

	A	B	C	D	E	F	G
1	Sales Review						
2						Thursday, January 1, 2015	
3	Student Name						
4	Bonus Level 1	20%					
5	Bonus Level 2	25%					
6							
7	Salesperson	Q1	Q2	Q3	Q4	Total	Production Percentage
8	Jameson	$ 440,220	$ 355,907	$ 672,001	$ 109,554	$1,577,682	17.24%
9	Parker	$ 598,033	$ 409,556	$ 342,999	$ 667,884	$2,018,472	22.06%
10	Khalil	$ 129,999	$ 794,202	$ 882,001	$ 203,229	$2,009,431	21.96%
11	Carter	$ 357,899	$ 594,009	$ 204,506	$ 662,087	$1,818,501	19.87%
12	West	$ 202,455	$ 611,770	$ 400,229	$ 511,887	$1,726,341	18.87%
13	Total	$1,728,606	$2,765,444	$2,501,736	$2,154,641	$9,150,427	

Completed Exercise C

Chapter 4

Working with Charts

If you have a lot of numbers in a worksheet, a chart can simplify your understanding of the data by showing it in a visual arrangement. When you represent the data in a chart, you can easily show patterns or trends in the data. You can create a variety of chart types in Excel, including pie, bar, and line charts.

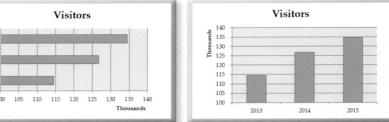

- A *pie chart* is a circular chart that is divided into parts. Each part represents a piece of the whole pie, or a percentage of the total. The example of a pie chart, *Visitors*, illustrates that out of all the visitors to The Chocolate Museum, 18% are from the local area, 64% are out-of-town visitors, and 18% are international visitors.

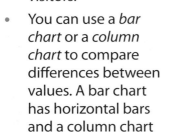
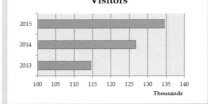

- You can use a *bar chart* or a *column chart* to compare differences between values. A bar chart has horizontal bars and a column chart has vertical bars. These examples of a bar chart (left) and a column chart (right) compare the total number of Chocolate Museum visitors by calendar year.

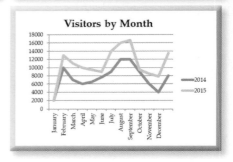

- *Line charts* illustrate changes, or trends, over time. The example of a line chart, *Visitors by Month*, shows how the number of monthly visitors to The Chocolate Museum varied through the years 2014 and 2015.

This chapter helps you understand the parts of a chart, including the parts labeled in the examples below.

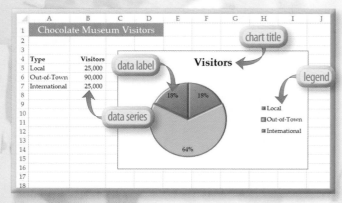

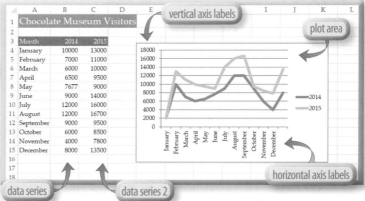

Skills You Learn

1 Create a line chart
2 Modify chart data
3 Create a column chart
4 Add and edit chart labels
5 Create a pie chart
6 Modify a pie chart

Files You Need

For these skills, you need the following student data files.

M6-C4-S1-CocoaProduction.xlsx

M6-C4-S3-CocoaProduction.xlsx

What You Create

The Chocolate Museum has a number of exhibits, including one that shows how much cocoa is produced in various countries. You prepare a pie chart and a column chart to illustrate these production levels by country. You apply a theme, add a style, and change the formatting to enhance the appearance of the charts. You also add descriptive titles so that the reader can easily understand the data represented in the charts.

*Cocoa Bean Production
by Country Line Chart*

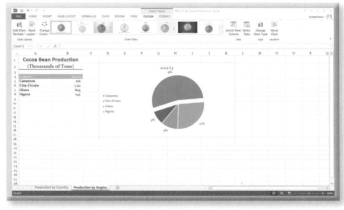

*Cocoa Bean Production
by Country Bar Chart*

*Cocoa Bean Production
by Region Pie Chart*

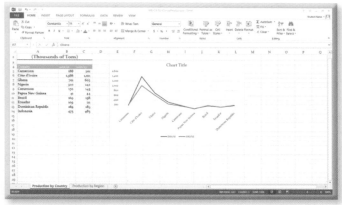

Excel

Create a Line Chart

Video   M6_C4_S01

In this skill, you create a line chart. The line chart uses two series of data from the worksheet. One data series charts the cocoa bean production for several cocoa-producing countries for the fiscal year 2011/12 and the other data series charts that production for the fiscal year 2012/13. Once you create the line chart, you move and size the chart.

Steps

▶**Tip** If you are not sure which type of chart to use, click the Recommended Charts button in the Charts group to see if Excel can help.

▶**Tip** Hover the mouse pointer over a chart option to display the name of the chart.

▶**Tip** The ScreenTip *Chart Area* indicates that the entire chart will move. To move part of a chart, hover your mouse pointer until you see a four-headed arrow and a ScreenTip for that part of the chart.

▶**Tip** The names of the countries that produce the cocoa are listed along the horizontal axis of the line chart, and the cocoa bean production amounts are listed along the vertical axis.

▶**Tip** In a line chart, the chart legend tells you which line belongs to which category of data. In this case, the legend tells you, by color, which line belongs to which fiscal year.

1 Open the student data file named **M6-C4-S1-CocoaProduction.xlsx** and, if you have not already done so, save the file in your Module 6 working folder on your storage medium.

2 In the Production by Country worksheet, select cells A4:C13.

3 Click the Insert Line Chart button in the Charts group on the INSERT tab to display a gallery of line charts.

4 Click the *Line* chart option (the first option in the *2-D Line* section) to insert a line chart in the worksheet.

5 Move the mouse pointer over the chart so the mouse pointer changes to a four-headed arrow ⁘ and the ScreenTip *Chart Area* appears. Click and drag the chart so that its upper left corner is positioned over cell E3.

6 Position the mouse pointer over the lower-right corner of the chart border so that the mouse pointer changes to a two-headed diagonal arrow (⬂). Drag down and to the right so that the bottom-right corner of the chart covers cell L19. While you drag, the two-headed diagonal arrow displays as a cross. When you release the mouse pointer, the cross turns back into the two-headed diagonal arrow.

7 Click the Save button on the Quick Access toolbar to save the file.

Taking It Further

Moving the Chart Location   By default, a chart is placed in the existing worksheet. You can move the chart to a new worksheet by first selecting the chart. When you select a chart, the CHART TOOLS DESIGN tab becomes the active tab. To move the chart, click the Move Chart button in the Location group and then select the *New sheet* option in the Move Chart dialog box. When you click OK, the chart moves to a new worksheet named *Chart1*. This option automatically adjusts the size of the chart to fill the worksheet page.

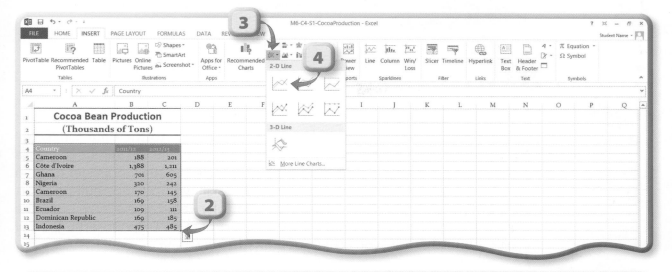

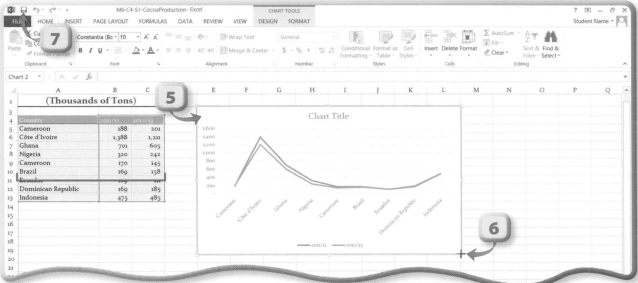

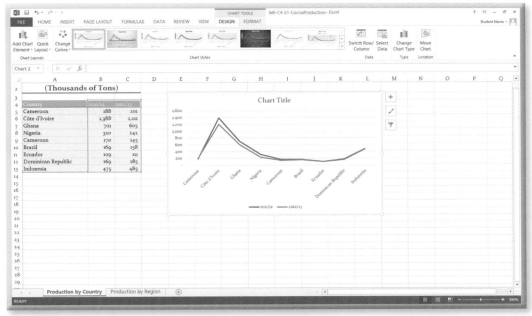

Completed Skill 1

Excel

Excel

Modify Chart Data

Video M6_C4_S02

When you select a chart, colored boxes appear around the data that you used to create the chart. Different colored boxes appear around the different parts of the chart. For example, the *data series* used to create the chart has a blue box around it. If you change a number in the data series or add another row to the data series, the chart automatically updates because it is linked to the worksheet data. In this skill, you practice editing chart data by removing a row from the chart data and then inserting a row with new data.

Steps

1 If it is not already open, open **M6-C4-S1-CocoaProduction.xlsx**, the file you saved in the previous skill, and save the file as **Lastname-M6-C4-S2-CocoaProduction**, but replace *Lastname* with your last name. Save the file in your Module 6 working folder on your storage medium.

2 **Another Way**
Click the Chart Filters button and then click to clear the *Indonesia* check box.

2 With the chart selected in the Production by Country worksheet, drag the lower-right selection handle for the blue selection box (located in the bottom right corner of cell C13) up until you have changed the range to B5:C12. The chart updates automatically and the Indonesia data is no longer included on the chart.

3 Right-click the row 10 heading.

4 Click *Insert* to insert a new row.

5 **Another Way**
Press the Tab key rather than the Right Arrow key.

▶**Tip** The line chart automatically updates to show the data you have entered in row 10 of the table.

▶**Tip** If you are using the Number, Currency, or Accounting format, you do not need to type the comma in large numbers such as 1,011. Excel will add the comma automatically.

5 Type the following entries in cells A10:C10 to add the data for that category to the chart, pressing the Right Arrow key after each entry.

A10   Papua New Guinea
B10   41
C10   44

6 Type 1011 in cell C6 and press Enter. The line chart updates automatically.

7 Save and close the file.

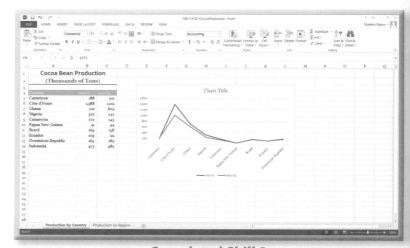

Completed Skill 2

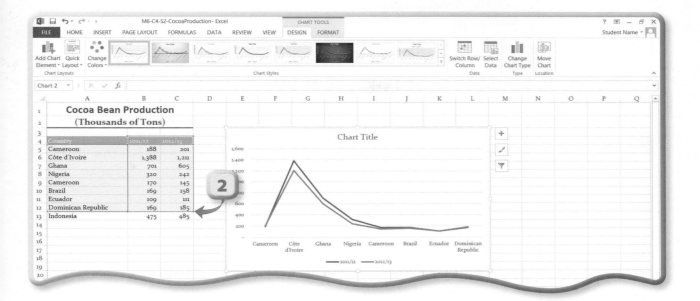

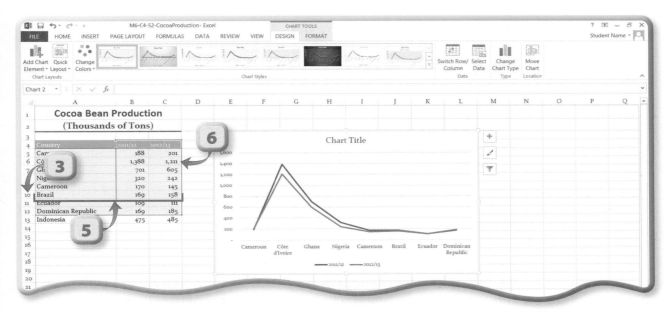

Taking It Further

Editing Chart Data Sometimes when you create a chart, the data and labels do not appear just the way you would like. You can edit the data and labels by selecting the chart and then clicking the Select Data button in the Data group on the CHART TOOLS DESIGN tab. This opens a dialog box that shows the current axis labels and legend entries. You can click the Edit button and then select the correct cells in the worksheet to change the labels or the information in the legend. You can also edit chart data by clicking the Chart Filters button and then checking or unchecking data you do not want displayed. You might want to save a separate copy of the file you used in Skill 2 and experiment with these editing tools.

Excel

 Video M6_C4_S03

Create a Column Chart

In this skill, you create a column chart. Column charts compare differences between values over time. The column chart you create shows how the cocoa production in each country increased or decreased between the 2011/12 and the 2012/13 fiscal years.

Steps

1 Open the student data file named **M6-C4-S3-CocoaProduction.xlsx** and, if you have not already done so, save the file in your Module 6 working folder on your storage medium.

2 On the Production by Country worksheet, select cells A4:C13.

3 Click the Insert Column Chart button in the Charts group on the INSERT tab to display a gallery of column chart options.

4 Click the *Clustered Column* chart option (the first option in the *2-D Column* section) to insert the column chart in the worksheet.

5 Move the mouse pointer over the chart so it changes to a four-headed arrow and then drag the chart so that its upper left corner is positioned over cell E3.

6 Position the mouse over the lower-right corner of the chart border so that the mouse pointer changes to a two-headed diagonal arrow. Drag down and to the right so that the bottom right corner of the chart covers cell L18.

7 Save the file.

Taking It Further

Changing the Chart Type   Bar charts, like column charts, can clearly show differences in charted values. You can easily change a column chart into a bar chart. To do so, select the chart and click the CHART TOOLS DESIGN tab. Click the Change Chart Type button in the Type group and then click *Bar* in the left pane. Select a bar chart option in the right pane and then click OK.

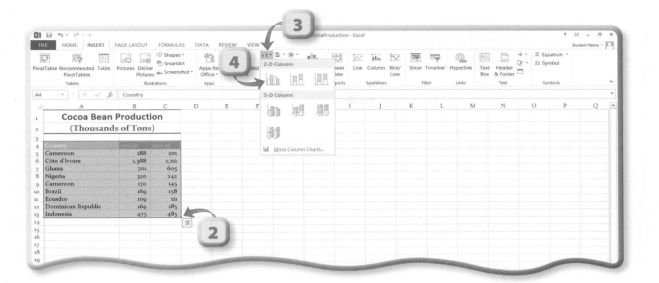

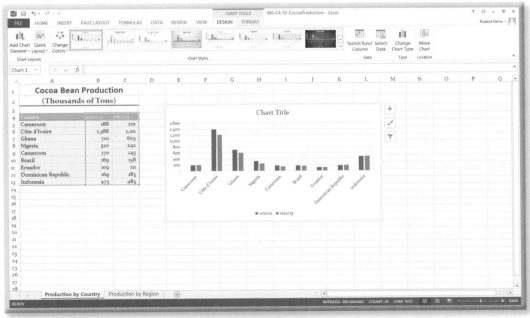

Completed Skill 3

Excel

Chapter 4

Skill 4

Video ▶ M6_C4_S04

Add and Edit Chart Labels

You can add and edit labels on a chart to make its elements easier to understand. When you create a chart, Excel adds some labels automatically, based on the data you selected to create the chart. You can edit these labels and add other labels using options on the CHART TOOLS DESIGN tab. For example, you can add individual data labels to show the quantity that a single column or pie slice represents. You can also edit the chart title and add x- and y-axis labels.

Steps

Tip You may want to use axis titles to describe what the numbers and labels along each axis represent. To add titles to the vertical or horizontal axis, click the Chart Elements button (looks like a plus sign), click *Axis Titles*, and then click the right-pointing arrow to see your options.

Tip You can place data labels in various places, such as the outside end of the data point, inside end of the data point, or centered on the data point. For some chart types, you can also select a *Best Fit* option that places the data labels where Excel determines they fit best in the chart.

Tip To hide a chart element, such as a chart title or legend, click the Chart Elements button + next to the chart and then click to clear the element check box. Also use the Chart Elements button to add, delete, or change chart elements.

1 If it is not already open, open **M6-C4-S3-CocoaProduction.xlsx**, the file you saved in the previous skill, and save the file as **M6-C4-S4-CocoaProduction**.

2 Click the chart on the Production by Country worksheet.

3 Click the Chart Title placeholder to select the placeholder.

4 Triple-click the *Chart Title* placeholder text to select it.

5 Type Cocoa Bean Production to edit the title of the chart.

6 Click the Add Chart Element button in the Chart Layouts group on the CHART TOOLS DESIGN tab.

7 Click *Data Labels* in the drop-down list.

8 Click the *Outside End* option. Notice that this action adds data labels to the outside end of the columns in the chart.

9 Enlarge the chart by dragging the lower right corner of the chart border down and to the right so that it covers cell N23.

10 Save the file.

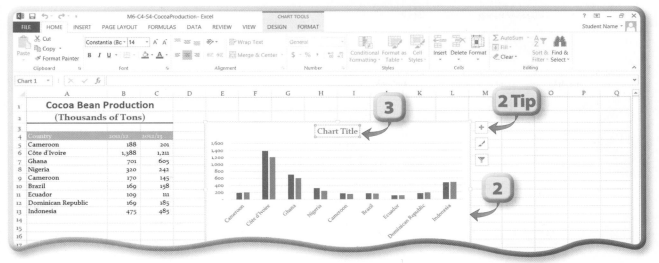

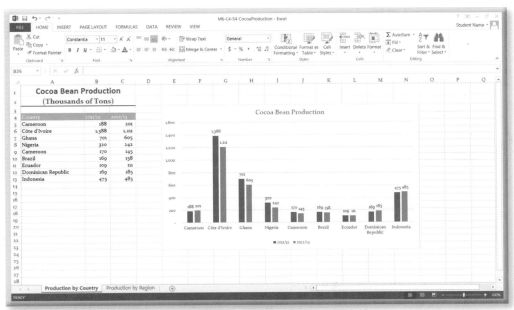

Completed Skill 4

Excel

Video ▶ M6_C4_S05

Create a Pie Chart

In this skill, you create a pie chart. A pie chart is a circular chart that is divided into parts. Each part represents a percentage of the total quantity. The pie chart you create represents the total amount of cocoa production for four countries. The pie is divided into four parts, one for each country's cocoa production. The size of each piece represents how much of the total cocoa production comes from that country.

Steps

1 If it is not already open, open **M6-C4-S4-CocoaProduction.xlsx**, the file you saved in the previous skill, and save the file as **M6-C4-S5-CocoaProduction**.

2 Click the Production by Region worksheet tab.

▶**Tip** A pie chart can contain only one data series.

3 Select cells A4:B8.

4 In the Charts group on the INSERT tab, click the Insert Pie or Doughnut Chart button to display a gallery of pie chart options.

5 Click the *Pie* chart option (the first option in the *2-D Pie* section) to insert the pie chart into the worksheet.

6 Move the mouse pointer over the chart border so it changes to a four-headed arrow and then drag the chart so that its upper left corner is positioned over cell D2.

7 Position the mouse pointer over the lower right corner of the chart border so that the mouse pointer changes to a two-headed diagonal arrow. Drag down and to the right so that the lower right corner of the chart covers cell K17.

8 Save the file.

Taking It Further

Using Quick Analysis When you select a range of cells, such as A1:K19, the Quick Analysis button ⊞ is displayed to the right of the selected range. You can use this button to create a chart from the selected range of data. Click the Quick Analysis button, click CHARTS in the drop-down gallery, hover over a chart type button to see how the selected data will appear in the chart, and then click a chart type button to apply the type to your chart.

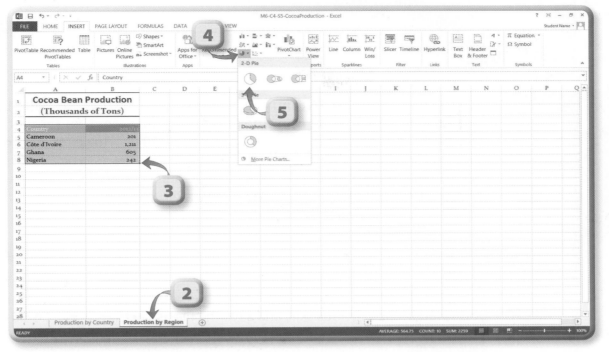

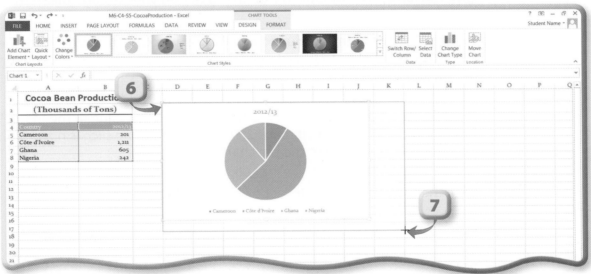

Completed Skill 5

Excel

Excel

Video M6_C4_S06

Modify a Pie Chart

You can rotate the pie chart and you can *explode* a slice away from the rest of the pie chart. An exploded slice sits outside the circle of the pie, to call attention to the content or data it represents. You can add data labels to a chart. By default, these will display as numbers without any special formatting, such as 1011. However, the data labels in pie charts typically display as a percentage, such as 80%. In this skill, you learn to display data labels as percentages.

Steps

1 If it is not already open, open **M6-C4-S5-CocoaProduction.xlsx**, the file you saved in the previous skill, and save the file as **Lastname-M6-C4-S6-CocoaProduction**, but replace *Lastname* with your last name. Be sure to save the file in your Module 6 working folder on your storage medium.

2 In the pie chart on the Production by Region worksheet, double-click the largest slice, the slice that represents *Côte d'Ivoire* cocoa bean production. This action opens the Format Data Series pane.

3 *Another Way*
Type *220* in the *Angle of first slice* text box and press Enter.

3 Drag the *Angle of first slice* slider to the right until the value in the measurement box beside it reads *220°*. The *Côte d'Ivoire* slice is now rotated 220° and sits at the top of the pie chart.

4 Click the Close button to close the Format Data Series pane.

5 Drag the *Côte d'Ivoire* pie slice up and away from the rest of the pie.

6 Click a blank area of the chart to deselect the pie piece.

7 Click the Add Chart Element button in the Chart Layouts group on the CHART TOOLS DESIGN tab.

8 Click *Data Labels* in the drop-down list.

9 Click *More Data Label Options* to display the Format Data Labels pane.

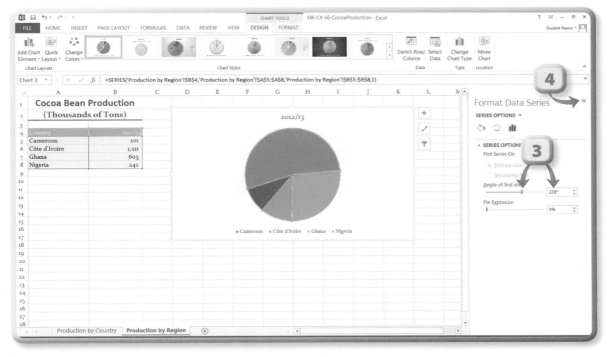

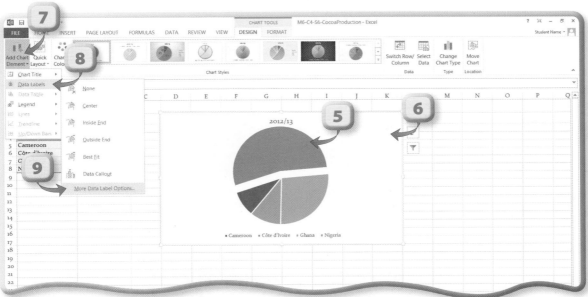

More

Taking It Further

Changing Pie Chart Themes and Styles
When you create a chart, the theme applied to the workbook file determines the chart colors. If you apply a different theme to the file, using the Theme button on the PAGE LAYOUT tab, the colors in the chart update automatically. Another way to modify the chart colors is to apply a chart style. Chart styles change the chart color, and they may

also change the chart background color and apply other effects. You can change the chart style by clicking a thumbnail from the gallery in the Chart Styles group on the CHART TOOLS DESIGN tab, or by clicking the Style and Color button ✎ next to the selected chart, clicking *Style*, and then clicking a different chart style.

10 Click the *Percentage* check box in the *Label Contains* section to insert a check mark.

11 Click the *Value* check box in the *Label Contains* section to remove the check mark.

12 Click the *Outside End* option in the *Label Position* section to place the data labels outside the slices.

13 In the Format Data Labels pane, click the LABEL OPTIONS button arrow.

14 Click *Legend* in the drop-down list.

15 Click the *Left* option in the *Legend Position* section.

16 Click the Close button to close the Format Legend pane.

17 Save and close the file.

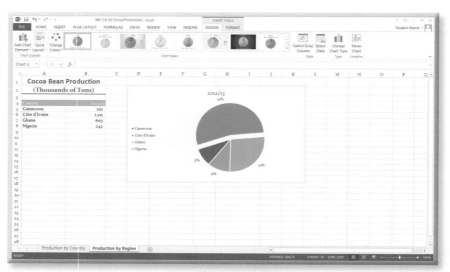

Completed Skill 6

Taking It Further

Changing the Chart Legend When the slices in a pie chart or the lines in a line chart have different colors, how do you know what the colors represent? You look at the chart legend. The chart legend tells you which piece of data each colored slice or line represents By default, Excel places the legend at the right side of the chart. You can change the position of the legend by clicking the Add Chart Element button in the CHART TOOLS DESIGN tab, clicking *Legend* in the drop-down list, and then clicking the desired position in the list of options. You can click *More Legend Options* to open the Format Legend pane with more options. You can even click *None* to remove the legend if you think the reader can easily understand the chart without it.

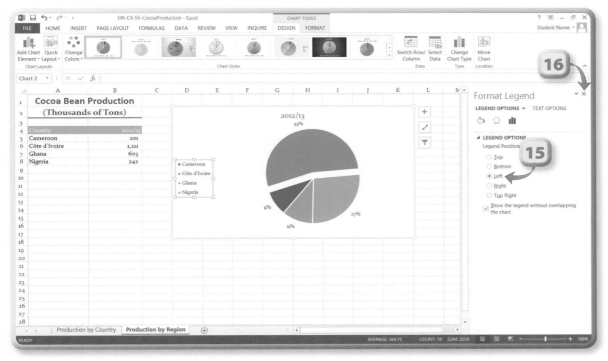

Taking It Further

Using Quick Layout If you want to quickly change the overall layout of a chart, you can click the Quick Layout button in the Chart Layouts group on the FORMAT TOOLS DESIGN tab to display a gallery of chart layouts. For example, if you want the legend under the title and percentage data labels on a pie chart, click *Layout 2*.

Tasks Summary

Task	Ribbon Tab, Group	Button, Option	Shortcut, Alternative
Insert a default column chart on the current worksheet	INSERT, Charts		Alt + F1
Insert a default column chart on a chart worksheet			F11
Insert another chart type on the current worksheet	INSERT, Charts		
Move a chart to a chart worksheet	CHART TOOLS DESIGN, Location		
Modify chart data	CHART TOOLS DESIGN, Data		Change values in charted range with keyboard
Add chart labels	CHART TOOLS DESIGN, Chart Layouts		
Change the chart legend	CHART TOOLS LAYOUT, Chart Layouts		Move or remove legend
Modify chart style	CHART TOOLS DESIGN, Chart Styles		
Change pie chart rotation			Double-click pie, use *Angle of first slice* setting
Explode a pie slice			Drag slice away from pie
Change chart theme	PAGE LAYOUT, Themes		
Change chart style	CHART TOOLS DESIGN, Chart Styles		Click Style and Color button to right of selected chart and then click *STYLE*
Change chart layout quickly	CHART TOOLS DESIGN, Chart Layouts		

Features Review

Select the best answer from the choices given.

1 Which chart type would best compare the attendance at an annual meeting for the past four years?
   a. column
   b. line
   c. pie
   d. bar

2 Which chart type would best show the average monthly rainfall for a year?
   a. bar
   b. column
   c. line
   d. pie

3 Which chart type would best show how much of a company's total salary budget was spent on each department in the company?
   a. bar
   b. column
   c. line
   d. pie

4 To select a chart,
   a. use Find.
   b. click near the border or edge within the chart.
   c. click the worksheet tab that contains the chart.
   d. scroll.

5 Name one way you can modify the lines in a line chart.
   a. Change an entry in the charted range.
   b. Click the chart and then click Bold.
   c. Change the text color of the charted range.
   d. Change the font color in the charted range.

6 A descriptive heading for a chart is a chart
   a. layout.
   b. label.
   c. legend.
   d. title.

7 You can remove a legend from a chart.
   a. True
   b. False

8 This can be added to a chart to display the value or percent for the data points.
   a. data labels
   b. a chart style
   c. a theme
   d. data labels, a chart style, or a theme

9 You can move a chart to a new worksheet in the workbook.
   a. True
   b. False

10 To explode a pie slice,
   a. select it and then drag it away from the other slices.
   b. double-click it.
   c. rotate it 220 degrees.
   d. add data labels.

Hands-On Skills Review

Exercise **Charting Budget Data**

Skills   Add and edit chart labels, create a pie chart, and modify a pie chart

Scenario   You have created a monthly budget to manage your finances. You have organized your spending into the categories rent, entertainment, food, car, and savings. Create a pie chart to show how much you are spending on each budget category.

Steps

1 Open the student data file named **M6-C4-ExA-Budget.xlsx** and save the file as **Lastname-M6-C4-ExA-Budget**, but replace *Lastname* with your last name.

2 Type your name in cell A10.

3 Create a 2-D pie chart using the data in A3:B7.

4 Add the chart title *Monthly Budget* above the chart.

5 Add data labels and display the data labels as percentages.

6 Add category labels to each slice. **HINT:** *Click the Add Chart Element button in the Chart Layouts group on the CHART TOOLS DESIGN tab, click* Data Labels, *and then click* More Data Label Options. *Click the check box* Category Name *so it contains a check mark and then click Close.*

7 Remove the legend. **HINT:** *Click the Add Chart Element button in the Chart Layouts group on the CHART TOOLS DESIGN tab, click* Legend, *and then click* None.

8 Move the chart so that its top-left corner covers cell D2.

9 Explode the *Car* slice.

10 Change the page orientation for the entire worksheet (the data and the chart) to landscape.

11 Save the file.

12 Print or submit the completed file as directed by your instructor.

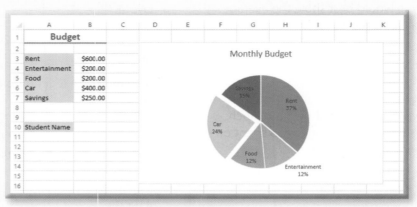

Completed Exercise A

Exercise B Comparing Temperatures

Skills Create a line chart, modify chart data, and add and edit chart labels

Scenario You are deciding where and when to go on your next vacation. You have charted the average monthly temperature in two cities to help you make your decision. You create a line chart to illustrate the differences in temperature.

Steps

1 Open the student data file named **M6-C4-ExB-Temperature.xlsx** and save the file as **Lastname-M6-C4-ExB-Temperature**, but replace *Lastname* with your last name.

2 Insert a 2-D line chart using the data in A3:C15.

3 Move the line chart to a new sheet.

4 Add the chart title *Average Monthly Temperatures* above the chart.

5 Add the title *Months* to the x axis. **HINT:** *Click the Add Chart Element button in the Chart Layouts group on the CHART TOOLS DESIGN tab, click* Axis Titles. *Click* Primary Horizontal, *and then type* Months. *Press Enter.*

6 Add the title *Temperature in Degrees* to the y axis. Use the Hint in the previous step but click *Primary Vertical*.

7 Use the CHART TOOLS DESIGN tab to change to the Style 6 chart style. **HINT:** *Chart styles are listed in numeric order in the Chart Styles group on the CHART TOOLS DESIGN tab.*

8 Save the file.

9 Print or submit the completed workbook file as directed by your instructor.

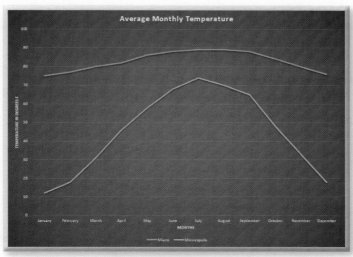

Completed Exercise B

Exercise C Charting Sales

Skills   Modify chart data, create a column chart, and add chart labels

Scenario   You manage a sales team. You have sales numbers, by employee, for the first quarter and the second quarter of this year. You create a column chart to compare sales levels among your employees.

Instructions

1   Open the student data file named **M6-C4-ExC-Sales.xlsx** and save the file as **Lastname-M6-C4-ExC-Sales**, but replace *Lastname* with your last name.

2   Select the quarterly sales data for all four salespeople along with the column titles.

3   Insert a column chart using the *3-D Clustered Column* subtype under *3-D Column* section from the gallery that appears when you insert a column chart.

4   Add *Sales Performance* as the chart title above the chart. If requested by your instructor, save the file at this point and submit it.

5   Andre Perez has left the company. Remove his sales data from the chart and the worksheet.

HINT: Change the chart data to remove Andre Perez from the column chart and then remove the data from the worksheet.

6   Change the chart type to a *Clustered Bar* in the *Bar* section.

7   Move the chart to a new sheet.

8   Save the file.

9   Print or submit the completed file as directed by your instructor.

	A	B	C
1		Employee Sales	
2			
3	Employee #	First Quarter	Second Quarter
4	Jason Ruskett	$670,000	$500,000
5	Paula Wilson	$235,000	$450,000
6	Tanisa Brown	$750,000	$800,000

Completed Exercise C Data

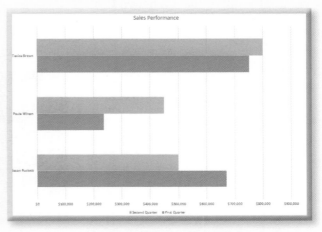

Completed Exercise C Chart

Module 6 Projects

Project 1

Skills   **CH1:** Understand worksheet and workbook structure; use cell references; enter text, values, and dates; name and rename worksheets, explore options for printing **CH2:** Enter a formula; enter a function **CH3:** Work with other formatting tools; adjust column width and row height; merge cells **CH4:** Create a column chart; add and edit chart labels

Scenario   You are working in a marketing department. You company is looking at marketing a new product internationally and you have been asked to do prepare a spreadsheet and chart that show the population in various countries.

Steps

1   Open the student data file named **M6-EOM-P1-Population.xlsx** and save the file as **Lastname-M6-EOM-P1-Population.xlsx**, but replace *Lastname* with your last name.

2   Type Population in cell A1.

3   Merge and center cells A1:B1.

4   Format cell A1 with the Heading 1 cell style.

5   Enter the following data in cells A4:B9.

Japan	126,804,433
United States	310,232,863
Mexico	112,468,855
Canada	33,759,742
France	64,057,792
Germany	82,282,988

6   In cell A11, type the label Total.

7   In cell A12, type the label Minimum.

8   In cell A13, type the label Maximum.

9   Right-align and bold the labels in A11:A13.

10 Use the appropriate function to insert the total population for the listed countries in cell B11.

11 Use the appropriate function to insert the lowest population in cell B12.

12 Use the appropriate function to insert the highest population in cell B13.

13 AutoFit both column A and column B so that they are just wide enough to display the data in the column.

14 Select cells A3:B3 and then format the cells with the Accent 1 cell style.

15 Select cells A3:B9 and then insert a 3-D Clustered Column chart.

16 Change the chart style to *Style 9*. **HINT:** *Chart styles are listed in numeric order in the Chart Styles group on the CHART TOOLS DESIGN tab. Click the More button to see a gallery of chart styles.*

17 Move the chart so that the top left corner of the chart is in cell D2.

18 Change the name of Sheet 1 to *Population*.

19 Change the page orientation for the entire worksheet (the data and the chart) to landscape.

20 Save the workbook file.

21 Print a copy of the worksheet or submit the completed file as directed by your instructor.

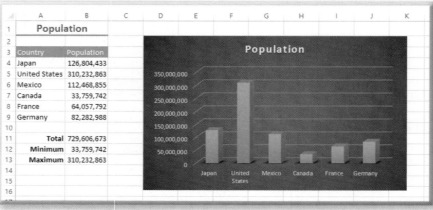

Completed Project 1

Project 2

Skills **CH1:** Understand worksheet and workbook structure; enter text, values, and dates; use the spelling checker; explore options for printing **CH3:** Apply number formats; work with other formatting tools; adjust column width and row height; merge cells **CH4:** Add and edit chart labels; create a pie chart; modify a pie chart

Scenario You manage a restaurant. You want to try and cut some of your monthly expenses. To do this you create a worksheet that displays your expenses. You then chart the information.

Steps

1 Open a blank workbook in Excel and name it **Lastname-M6-EOM-P2-Restaurant**, but replace *Lastname* with your last name.

2 Type Restaurant Expenses in cell A1.

3 Merge and center cells A1:B1.

4 Format cell A1 with the Heading 1 cell style.

5 Enter the following data in cells A3:B7.

Expense	Cost
Food	13400
Building	3500
Taxes	1890
Advertising	1450

6 You forgot to add an expense. Insert a row between row 4 and row 5 and enter the following data.

Staff	16000

7 Spell check the worksheet.

8 Format cells B4:B8 with the Currency format and two decimal places.

9 Change the width of column A and column B to 12.00 (89 pixels).

10 Select cells A3:B3 and then format the cells with the Heading 3 cell style.

11 Right-align cell B3.

12 Select cells A3:B8 and then insert a 3-D Pie chart.

13 Change the chart title from *Cost* to *Restaurant Expenses*.

14 Move the chart so that the top left corner of the chart is in cell D2.

15 Add data labels to the inside ends of the pie chart pieces. Display the data labels as percentages.

16 Type your name in cell A10.

17 Change the page orientation to landscape for the entire worksheet (the data and the chart).

18 Save the worksheet.

19 Print a copy of the worksheet or submit the completed file as directed by your instructor.

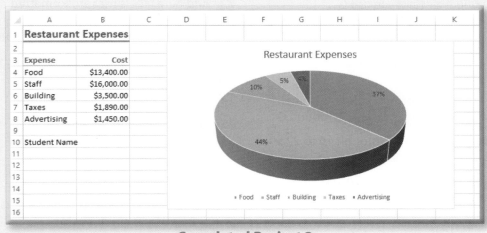

Completed Project 2

Project 3

Skills **CH1:** Understand worksheet and workbook structure; use cell references; enter text, values, and dates; use the Auto Fill feature; name and rename worksheets; explore options for printing **CH2:** Enter a formula; enter a function; insert a function; use AutoSum; use absolute and relative cell references; copy and paste cell contents **CH3:** Apply number formats; work with other formatting tools; adjust column width and row height; add borders; merge cells **CH4:** Add and edit chart labels; create a pie chart; modify a pie chart

Scenario You are in charge of calculating the payroll for the employees at Paradigm Steel. The employees receive a base salary plus commission. You need to calculate a new salary figure for all of the employees because all employees will receive a 5.25% raise.

Steps

1 Open the student data file named **M6-EOM-P3-Steel.xlsx** and save the file as **Lastname-M6-EOM-P3-Steel**, but replace *Lastname* with your last name.

2 Change the width of column A to 22.00 (159 pixels). Change the width of column B to 13.00 (96 pixels).

3 Change the width of columns C through G to 16.00 (117 pixels).

4 Type the title Commission in cell E2.

5 In cell E3, calculate the commission using a formula that multiplies projected sales by the commission rate. **HINT:** *Use an absolute reference for cell B18.* Copy the formula in cell E3 to cells E4:E12.

6 Type the title Salary in cell F2.

7 In cell F3, calculate the salary by adding the base salary and the commission. Copy the formula in cell F3 to cells F4:F12.

8 Type the title New Salary in cell G2.

9 Employees will all receive a 5.25% raise. In cell G3, calculate the new salary using the formula Salary + (Salary * 5.25%). Copy the formula in cell G3 to cells G4:G12.

10 Apply the Currency format with no decimal places to the values in columns C through G.

11 Set the height of rows 13 through 16 to 22.50 (30 pixels).

12 Right align the *Total, Average, Lowest,* and *Highest* labels and apply bold formatting.

13 Use the appropriate function to calculate the *Total, Average, Highest,* and *Lowest* values for columns C through G.

14 Merge and center cells A1:G1 and set the row height of row 1 to 48.00 (64 pixels).

15 Change the font in cell A1 to 28-point Cooper Black.

16 Set the row height of row 2 to 20.25 (27 pixels).

17 Center the column headings in row 2, change the font to 12-point Cambria, and apply bold formatting.

18 Create a thick box border around the column headings in row 2.

19 Type your name in cell A20.

20 Change the page orientation to landscape.

21 Create a 3-D pie chart of the new salary for all employees. **HINT:** *Use the Ctrl key to highlight A2:A12 and G2:G12 before creating the chart.*

22 Add data labels that are formatted as percentages and category names on the outside end of the pie pieces. Remove the legend.

23 Modify the chart title so that it reads *Employee 2015 Salaries.*

24 Rename Sheet1 as *Data.*

25 Move the location of the chart to a new sheet and name the sheet *Salary Chart.*

26 Save the workbook.

27 Print a copy of the worksheet and the chart sheet or submit the completed workbook as directed by your instructor.

	Employee	Hire Date	Base Salary	Projected Sales	Commission	Salary	New Salary
1	**Paradigm Steel Company**						
2	Employee	Hire Date	Base Salary	Projected Sales	Commission	Salary	New Salary
3	Chronowski, John	10/12/2004	$46,950	$422,165	$13,720	$60,670	$63,856
4	Mandinka Al-Jab Bar	12/14/2009	$30,250	$323,912	$10,527	$40,777	$42,918
5	McDonald Jack	10/25/2012	$29,581	$238,584	$7,754	$37,335	$39,295
6	Meeks Tyrone	6/13/2002	$42,500	$342,413	$11,128	$53,628	$56,444
7	Putin, Nikita	5/24/1997	$39,500	$750,450	$24,390	$63,890	$67,244
8	Adley, Martha	4/11/2013	$36,253	$384,616	$12,500	$48,753	$51,313
9	Damato, Michelle	5/13/2010	$37,157	$489,401	$15,906	$53,063	$55,848
10	DeJesus, Gino	2/10/2014	$44,219	$599,689	$19,490	$63,709	$67,054
11	Flynn, Georgeana	3/20/2007	$41,821	$619,984	$20,149	$61,970	$65,224
12	Frost, Leonard	11/19/2006	$41,272	$338,914	$11,015	$52,287	$55,032
13	Total		$389,503	$4,510,128	$146,579	$536,082	$564,226
14	Average		$38,950	$451,013	$14,658	$53,608	$56,423
15	Lowest		$29,581	$238,584	$7,754	$37,335	$39,295
16	Highest		$46,950	$750,450	$24,390	$63,890	$67,244
17							
18	Commission Rate	3.25%					
19							
20	Student Name						

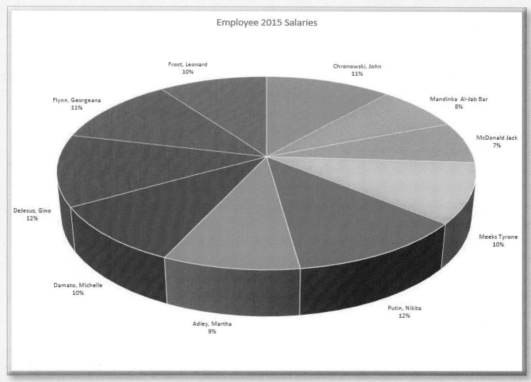

Completed Project 3

MODULE 7

Microsoft Access 2013

Before beginning the module skills, copy the Module7–Access folder from the Student Resources disc to your storage medium. The copied folder will become the working folder for this module.

You may have heard our present time referred to as the *Information Age*. Businesses, schools, and individuals rely on instant access to information and expect to have that information at their fingertips. Computers today enable you to store large amounts of data and to quickly retrieve and organize that data. Much of the information you retrieve from a computer or from a website is stored in a database.

A *database* is an organized collection of related data. A business's employee data, a store's inventory, and an airline's flight listing are all examples of data that is typically stored in a database.

Database Terminology

To understand how databases work, you need to learn some database terminology.

Database applications such as Access use an object called a *table* to enter and organize data. When you open a table in Access, the table displays in a datasheet. For example, this Products table is part of a computer store database for tracking the store's inventory and sales.

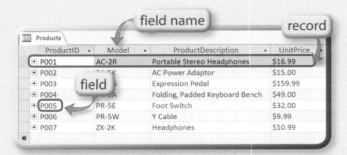

A *field* is an area of a table where a particular type of information is recorded, or a space in the database that is allocated for a particular type of data.

Each field has a *field name*, such as *Product ID*, *Model*, *ProductDescription*, or *UnitPrice*.

A collection of related fields is called a *record*. In the Products table example, all of the information supplied for one product (ID, model, description, and unit price) makes up a single record.

Access is a *relational database* application, meaning that Access creates files that use a series of related tables to organize data in the database. Each table is usually related to at least one other table by sharing a column of data. For example, assume the Products table and the Inventory table shown below are part of the same Access database. The Products table contains a ProductID field but no ProductName field. The ProductName field is stored in another table, the Inventory table. But the tables are related because both contain the ProductID column of data. This relationship allows you to access all the information for each product, regardless of where it is stored.

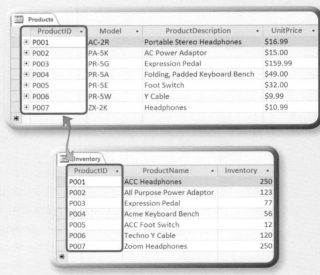

Databases and the Best Uses of Access

To enter records into a database, you can either enter the data directly into the table or fill in user-friendly forms that are designed for data entry. When you enter data in a form, that information is also entered into the corresponding table. A form for entering information about products is shown below.

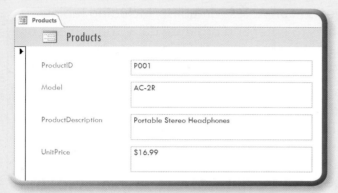

Once you have entered records into a database, you can use Access to answer queries or questions about the data. For example, you could query a computer store's database to find out which customers have ordered ACC headphones. The results of this query are shown below.

Or you could query the database to find out which products have an inventory of 100 items or fewer and may need to be reordered. The results of this query are shown below.

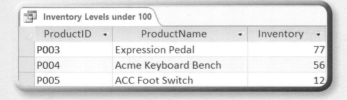

You can also generate printed reports about the stored data. You may want to put query results information in a professional-looking report, like the one shown below, that you can pass along to the supervisor who makes reordering decisions.

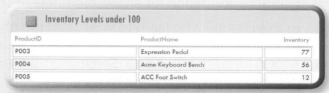

Use Access when you need to organize and store large amounts of data, such as employee or inventory records. By organizing that information in a database, you are able to quickly find the data and answers you need.

If you have a Microsoft account, you can create an Access app that can be viewed, edited, and shared on the Web. An Access app stores data in the cloud. You can use the Custom web app template that is displayed in the list of available templates when Access is started to create an Access app. Predefined tables can then be added to the app to store data.

Chapter 1

Working with Databases

The Access database application is used to manage large amounts of data, such as the contact information for all the members of The Chocolate Museum.

In this chapter, you learn to work with the objects in an Access database, including tables, forms, queries, and reports. You use Access tables to enter and organize data. You can also use Access *forms* to enter data. Some users prefer to enter records into forms instead of tables, because forms allow them to enter and view one record at a time.

Once you have entered data in a database, you can then organize the data by sorting or filtering it. *Filtering* temporarily displays only those records meeting a certain condition or conditions, such as just those members of The Chocolate Museum who live in Boston, Massachusetts. You can also run a *query* (ask a question) to locate specific information in a database. For example, you could query the database to find all Chocolate Museum members whose last name is Brown. Also, queries can be saved and run at a later time. If you need to print information from a database, you can create a *report* to present the information in a professional-looking format.

In Access, you can create a desktop database, which is saved on a storage media or you can create a custom web app, which can be accessed and shared through a web browser. In this chapter, you work with a desktop database, entering data in a table and in a form. You edit, sort, and filter data and format a datasheet. You also run a query and display a report.

Skills You Learn

1 Open and navigate a database
2 Enter data
3 Edit data
4 Sort data
5 Filter data
6 Format a datasheet
7 Use existing queries and reports

Files You Need
For these skills, you need the following student data file.

M7-C1-Members.accdb

Note: *Before you begin working with student data files for this chapter, make sure you have copied your Module7-Access folder from the Student Resources disc to your storage medium. Access database files opened directly from the Student Resources disc are read-only. You need to open all database files from your working folder on your storage medium. Steps for copying a folder from the disc are provided in Module 2, Project 1, pages 166–168.*

What You Create

The Chocolate Museum has a membership program that people can join to receive admission discounts, receive the monthly newsletter, and be among the first invited to preview new exhibits. All of the information about the Museum's membership program is stored in a database. In this chapter, you explore the objects in this database. You also add records, sort and filter data, run a query, and display a report.

Membership Program Database

Access

Chapter 1

Skill 1

Video M7_C1_S01

Open and Navigate a Database

When a database opens, you do not see a document as you do in Word or a workbook as you do in Excel. Instead, you see a Navigation pane on the left side of the window that lists the names of the objects that make up the database. This list of objects includes all tables, forms, queries, and reports that are part of the database. To open an object, you double-click the object in the Navigation pane.

Steps

> **Tip** Be sure to open all database files from your working folder on your storage medium. Access database files opened directly from the Student Resources disc are read-only. Steps on how to copy a folder from the disc are presented on pages 110–111 and 166–168 of this textbook.

> **Tip** If the Navigation pane is not open, click the Shutter Bar Open/Close button at the top of the Navigation pane.

1 Open the student data file named **M7-C1-Members.accdb** from your Module 7 working folder on your storage medium.

2 If a security warning appears immediately below the ribbon, click the Enable Content button.

3 Review the objects listed in the Navigation pane and then double-click *Member Data* in the Tables group. The table displays in a datasheet and the first record is selected.

4 Click the Next record button in the Record Navigation bar to select the second record.

5 Click the Last record button in the Record Navigation bar to select the last record in this table, record 379.

6 Click the Close button to close the table.

> **Tip** You can use the Member Data form to enter records in the Member Data table. The form contains the same fields found in the table.

7 In the Navigation pane, double-click *Member Data* in the Forms group. The form displays only one record.

8 Click the Next record button in the Record Navigation bar to display the next record.

9 Click the New (blank) record button in the Record Navigation bar to display a new blank record. However, do not enter any new data at this time.

10 Click the Close button to close the Member Data form.

Completed Skill 1

520   **Module 7** Access

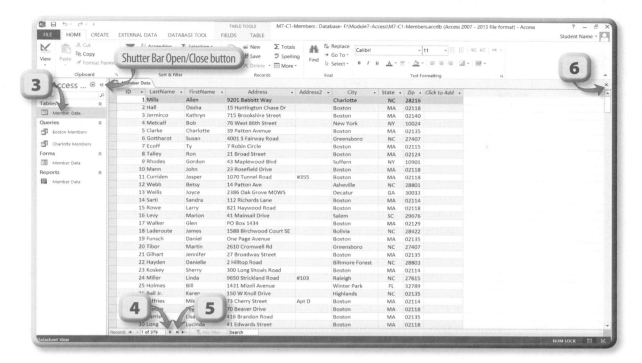

Taking It Further

Opening More Objects   You can have more than one object open at a time in Access. For example, you can open a table and then open a second table or a form. Switch between open objects by clicking the tab at the top of the object. Each tab contains the name of the object and an icon that indicates the object type. For example, notice the Member Data tabs above the table and form in the screenshots on this page. Try opening both the Member Data table and the Member Data form in the **M7-C1-Members.accdb** file and toggling between them using their tabs.

Access

Enter Data

Video M7_C1_S02

You can enter data in a table or in a form. Entering data in a table is useful for comparing records because you can see multiple records at once. However, this method can be confusing if you are entering a record with a lot of fields and you have to scroll through the fields. A form displays one record at a time. Entering data in a form is less confusing because you usually do not have to scroll a record to see all the fields, and this can help you avoid errors.

Steps

▶ **Tip** A database file may contain a huge amount of data. Instead of continually duplicating the database by saving it with a new name, users schedule regular Access file backups. You will use the same database file throughout this module. Copy M7-C1-Members.accdb from the Student Resources disc if you need to start the module again.

▶ **Tip** The *ID* field is an AutoNumber field. For such fields, the new record will automatically be assigned the next number, which is 380 in this case. Pressing the Tab key moves the insertion point to the next field.

▶ **Tip** Access automatically saves records that you enter in a table or a form, so you do not have to save before closing the table.

▶ **Tip** The data value for a field is called an *entry*.

1 With **M7-C1-Members.accdb** open, double-click *Member Data* in the Tables group in the Navigation pane.

2 Click the New (blank) record button in the Record Navigation bar.

3 Press Tab.

4 Add the following information to create a new record, pressing Tab to move to the next field:

LastName	FirstName	Address	Address2	City	State	Zip
Marks	Carol	3015 Mossdale Ave	(blank; press Tab)	Durham	NC	27707

5 Close the Member Data table.

6 In the Navigation pane, double-click *Member Data* in the Forms group.

7 Click the New (blank) record button in the Record Navigation bar.

8 Press the Tab key and then add the following information to create a new record, pressing Tab to move to the next field:

LastName	FirstName	Address	Address2	City	State	Zip
Conway	Philip	12 Church Street	Apt A	Boston	MA	02135

9 Close the Member Data form.

Completed Skill 2

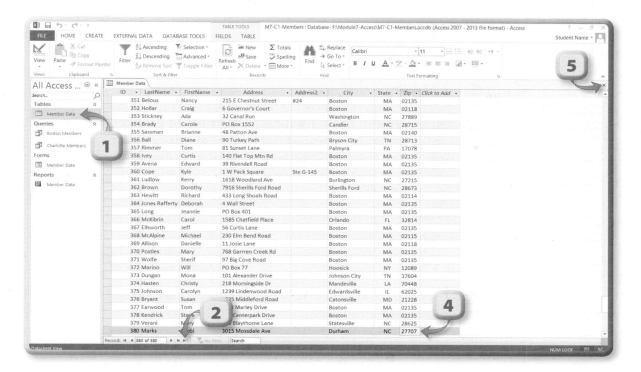

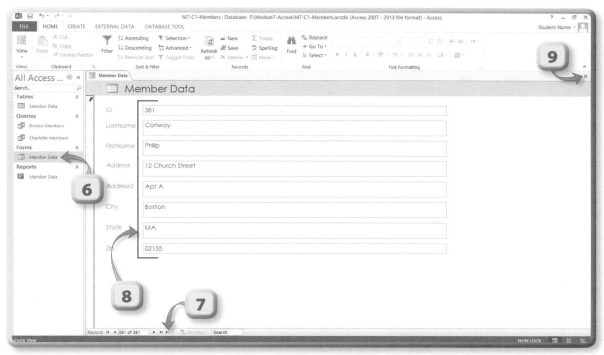

Taking It Further

Checking Spelling The information that you enter into a database must be correct so that you can run queries and reports successfully and avoid problems in the future. In addition to proofreading, use the spelling checker to check the correctness of your data. To do so, click the Spelling button on the HOME tab. If Access finds any spelling errors, it displays a dialog box you can use to correct errors.

Access

Skill 3

Edit Data

Video M7_C1_S03

A database stores a lot of information, but the information is only useful if the records in the database are kept up-to-date. For example, if a member of The Chocolate Museum changes his or her address and that informa-tion is not updated in the database, the member won't receive mailings about museum events and special offers. In this skill, you learn to edit data in a table.

Steps

1 With **M7-C1-Members.accdb** open, double-click *Member Data* in the Tables group in the Navigation pane.

2 In record 2, double-click *Dasha* in the *FirstName* column.

3 Type Darla and press the Tab key.

4 Close the Member Data table.

5 In the Navigation pane, double-click *Member Data* in the Forms group to display the form for the first record.

6 Double-click *Allen* in the *FirstName* field.

7 Type Ellen and press the Tab key.

8 Close the Member Data form.

Taking It Further

Deleting a Record   If a member, such as Mr. Saake, does not renew his membership, you need to delete the record. In such cases, locate the specific record in the table and click the record selection area, which is the gray box to the left of the record's first field. Next, click the HOME tab and click the Delete button arrow in the Records group. In the drop-down menu, click *Delete Record* and then click Yes to confirm the deletion.

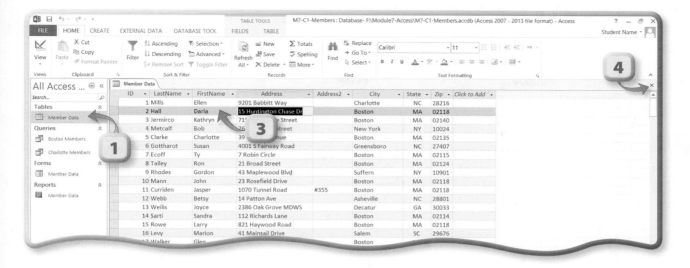

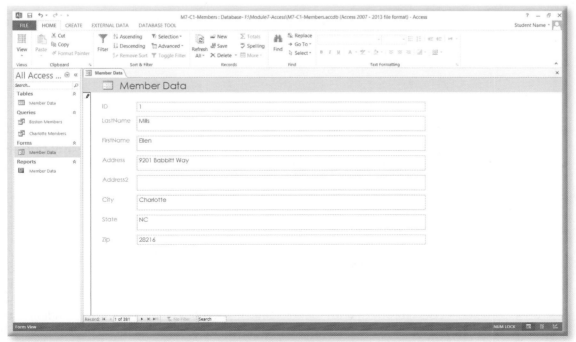

Completed Skill 3

Access

Access

Sort Data

Video ▶ M7_C1_S04

It is good practice to enter database records in the order in which you receive them. For example, you might enter the data for a new member of The Chocolate Museum on the day you receive it. However, when you are looking for specific information, you may find it helpful to sort a table by a particular column, such as *LastName*, rather than by date entered, so that you can easily find the member you are looking for. In this skill, you learn to sort the data in a table.

Steps

1 With **M7-C1-Members.accdb** open, double-click *Member Data* in the Tables group in the Navigation pane.

2 Click *Mills* in the *LastName* column of the first record.

▶**Tip** *Ascending* means to sort alphabetically, from A to Z.

3 Click the Ascending button in the Sort & Filter group on the HOME tab. The records are now sorted by last name, in alphabetical order.

3 *Another Way*
Click the drop-down arrow in the *LastName* column heading and then click *Sort A to Z.*

4 Click the Remove Sort button. The records are no longer sorted by the *LastName* column.

5 Click *Charlotte* in the *City* column of the first record.

6 Click the Ascending button to sort the records by city, in alphabetical order.

7 Click the Remove Sort button.

8 Close the Member Data table.

9 Click No in the dialog box that appears. You have not made any permanent changes to the design and do not need to save the table.

Taking It Further

Sorting a Form When you sort records in a table, the sort affects only that table. It does not affect the order of records displayed in the related form. For example, if you sort the Member Data table by the *LastName* column and then open the Member Data form, the records in the Member Data form will not be sorted by last name. However, you can sort the data in a single field in a form by clicking a field entry box and then clicking either the Ascending button or the Descending button in the Sort & Filter group on the HOME tab.

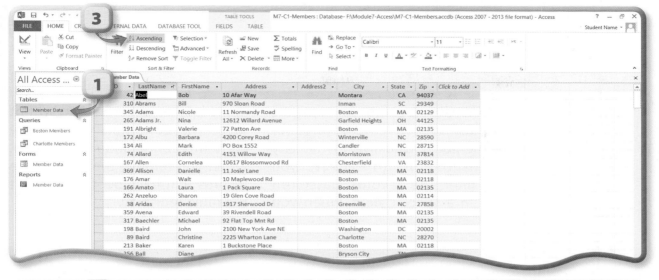

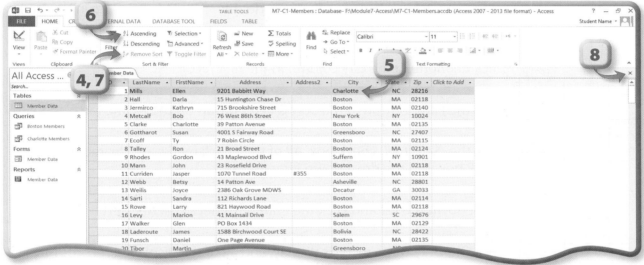

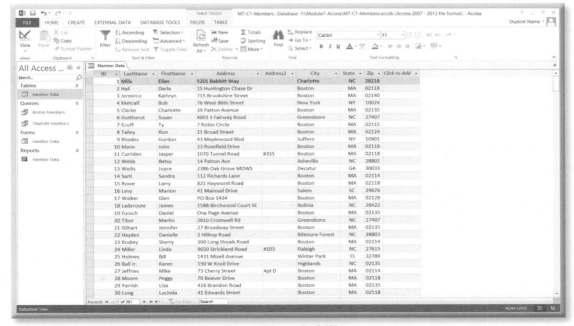

Completed Skill 4

Access

Video   M7_C1_S05

Filter Data

If you are looking for specific records, such as the records of all members who live in the city of Charlotte, North Carolina, you can filter the records based on data in a specific field. When you apply a filter, records that do not meet the condition you specify are temporarily hidden from view. When you remove the filter, those records that have been "hidden" in the table redisplay.

Steps

1 With **M7-C1-Members.accdb** open, double-click *Member Data* in the Tables group in the Navigation pane.

2 Click *Charlotte* in the *City* column in the first record.

3 Click the Filter button in the Sort & Filter group on the HOME tab.

3 *Another Way*
Click the drop-down arrow in the *City* column heading.

4 Click the *(Select All)* check box. All of the check marks are cleared from the check boxes in the drop-down filter list.

5 Scroll down the list and click the *Charlotte* check box to insert a check mark.

6 Click OK. Only three records display, and all of the displayed records have the entry *Charlotte* in the *City* column.

7 Click the Toggle Filter button to redisplay all records in the table.

8 Close the Member Data table and click No in the dialog box that appears.

Taking It Further

Learning More about Filtering Data
You can filter records based on more than one piece of information in a particular field. For example, you can filter records to find members who live in Charlotte and those who live in Boston. To do so, click both city names in the drop-down filter list. You can also filter by more than one column. For example, if you apply a filter that displays just those members living in Charlotte, you could then click in the *LastName* column and apply a second filter to display only those members having the last name *Mills* who also live in Charlotte.

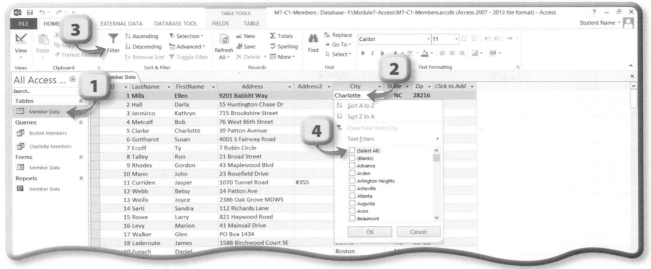

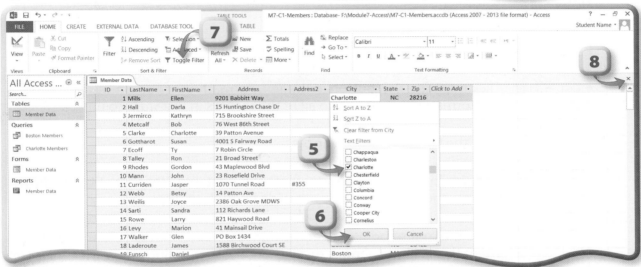

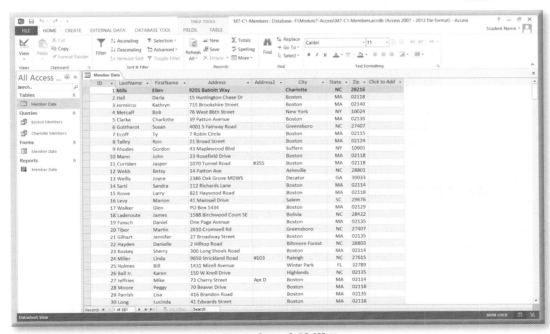

Completed Skill 5

Access

Format a Datasheet

Video M7_C1_S06

When you open a table, it displays in a datasheet. A datasheet organizes the data in rows and columns. You may want to apply formatting, such as bold and italic, or change the font size to make the datasheet easier to read. You can also align the data in a column and adjust the width of a column so that all of the data in the fields display.

Steps

1. With **M7-C1-Members.accdb** open, double-click *Member Data* in the Tables group in the Navigation pane.

2. Click the first record in the *State* column.

3. Click the Align Left button in the Text Formatting group on the HOME tab. The formatting is applied to all of the records in the *State* column.

4. Click the Font Size button arrow.

5. Click *14*. The font size changes for the entire table. Notice that the *Address* column and *Zip* column are not wide enough to display all of their data.

6. Move the mouse pointer over the right border of the *Zip* column heading. When the pointer changes to a left-and-right-pointing arrow with a vertical line in the middle (✛), double-click. The column widens to display all the data in the column.

7. Move the mouse pointer over the right border of the first *Address* column heading. When the pointer changes a left-and-right-pointing arrow with a vertical line in the middle, double-click.

8. Close the Member Data table and click Yes to save the changes to the table. The changes are permanent and will appear next time you open the table.

Taking It Further

Learning More about Formatting a Datasheet   By default, every other row in a datasheet has a different background color. You can change the background color of every second row by clicking the arrow on the Alternate Row Color button in the Text Formatting group on the HOME tab and selecting a different color. Also by default, the horizontal and vertical gridlines display. Visible gridlines help you to clearly see the borders of each cell in the datasheet. You can change the gridlines that are displayed by clicking the Gridlines button in the Text Formatting group on the HOME tab.

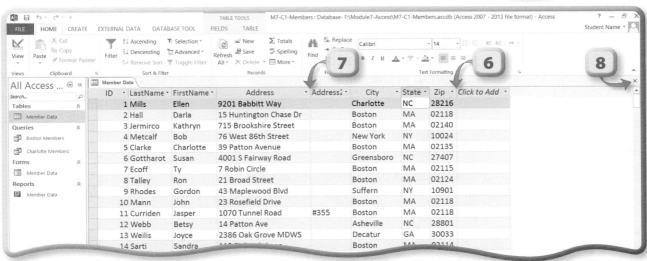

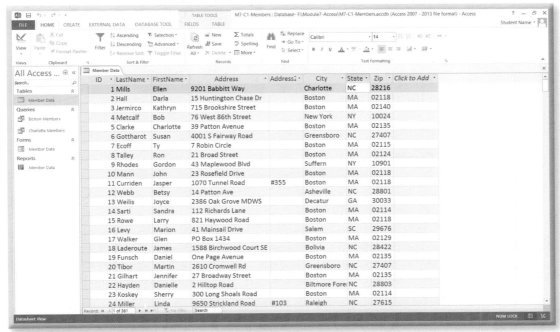

Completed Skill 6

Access

Use Existing Queries and Reports

Video M7_C1_S07

In previous skills in this chapter, you learned to use existing tables and forms to enter and edit data. In this skill, you work with two other objects: queries and reports. You create a query to find records that meet a certain condition. The records are pulled from one or more tables, in a process called *extracting*. You also run two queries that have been created for you. Lastly, you display a report that has been saved in the database. A report presents data from a combination of one or more tables and queries.

Steps

▶ **Tip** In Chapter 3, you will learn how to create a query. Creating a query differs from simply filtering records. Because a query is an Access object, it is saved with the database. As a result, once you create a query, you can run it over and over again.

1 With **M7-C1-Members.accdb** open, double-click *Charlotte Members* in the Queries group in the Navigation pane to display records for all members living in Charlotte, North Carolina.

2 Close the Charlotte Members query.

3 In the Navigation pane, double-click *Boston Members* in the Queries group to display records for all members living in Boston, Massachusetts.

4 Close the Boston Members query.

5 In the Navigation pane, double-click *Member Data* in the Reports group. The report displays records of The Chocolate Museum members.

6 Close the Member Data report.

7 Close the database.

Taking It Further

Printing an Object You can print any open objects, including tables, forms, queries, and reports. To print an active object, click the FILE tab and then click the *Print* option to open the Print backstage area. You then have three print options to choose from. You should always click *Print Preview*, the third option, to view the object before you print it. You can then use options on the PRINT PREVIEW tab to adjust settings, such as the page size or page orientation (portrait or landscape), before clicking the Print button in the Print group to print the object.

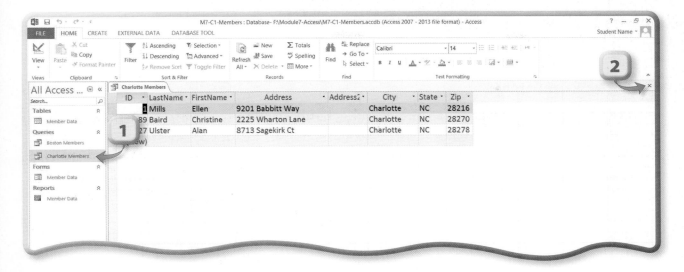

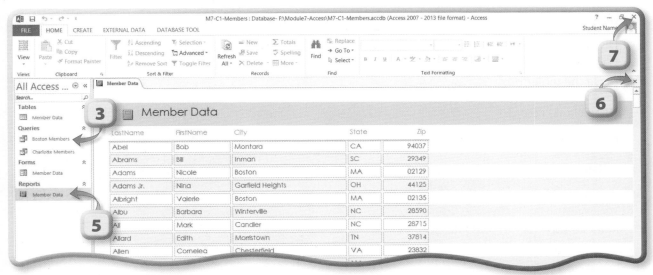

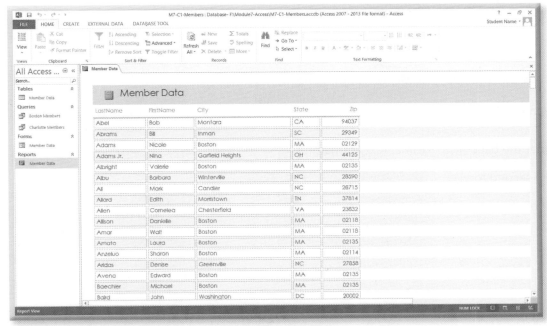

Completed Skill 7

Tasks Summary

Task	Ribbon Tab, Group	Button, Option	Shortcut, Alternative
Collapse or expand the Navigation pane		«	
Open an object			Double-click object in Navigation pane; select object in Navigation pane and press Enter
Navigate in a datasheet			Tab, Arrow Keys
Display the next record		▶	
Display the last record		▶|	
Close the table/form		×	
New (blank) record		▶*	
Check spelling	HOME, Records	✓ᴬᴮᶜ Spelling	
Delete a record	HOME, Records	✕ Delete	
Sort data	HOME, Sort & Filter	ᴬ↓ Ascending	
Remove sort	HOME, Sort & Filter	ᴬ↓ Remove Sort	
Filter data	HOME, Sort & Filter	▼	
Remove a filter	HOME, Sort & Filter	▼ Toggle Filter	
Left align text in a field	HOME, Text Formatting	≡	
Change the font size	HOME, Text Formatting	14 ▾	
Widen a column			Double-click a column border
Format the background color of every second row	HOME, Text Formatting	▦ ▾	

Features Review

Select the best answer from the choices given.

1 The Navigation pane lists all _____ in the database.
   a. records
   b. worksheets
   c. objects
   d. macros

2 You can enter data in a
   a. table and form.
   b. form and report.
   c. table and report.
   d. report and query.

3 A set of information, such as a first name or city, that is entered in a database is called a
   a. field.
   b. column.
   c. record.
   d. row.

4 A group of related fields, such as all the information about one employee, is stored in a
   a. field.
   b. column.
   c. record.
   d. row.

5 In a form, you usually see
   a. only one field.
   b. only one record.
   c. only one table.
   d. the entire database.

6 Which of the following is *not* a valid method for moving between cells in a table?
   a. Press Tab.
   b. Press the right arrow key.
   c. Click a cell.
   d. Press the Backspace key.

7 Which sort order organizes data alphabetically from A to Z?
   a. ascending
   b. descending
   c. reverse
   d. arrange

8 Which action temporarily displays records matching the criteria you specify for one or more fields?
   a. sort
   b. hide
   c. filter
   d. parse

9 The _____ group on the HOME tab has choices for formatting the datasheet.
   a. Sort & Filter
   b. Records
   c. Find
   d. Text Formatting

10 Which action closes an open object?
   a. Double-click it in the Navigation pane.
   b. Click its Close button.
   c. Click the Last record button.
   d. Click its tab and then press Enter.

Hands-On Skills Review

Exercise **Updating and Sorting a Jewelry Store Database**

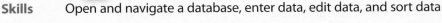

Skills   Open and navigate a database, enter data, edit data, and sort data

Grade It

Scenario   You are in charge of updating the records in a jewelry store database. You add some new items to the database and make an edit to an existing record. You also sort a datasheet to make it easier to find information in the table.

Steps

1 Open the student data file named **M7-C1-ExA-Jewelry.accdb** and save the file as **Lastname-M7-C1-ExA-Jewelry**, but replace *Lastname* with your last name. ***HINT:*** *To save an Access file using a new name, click the FILE tab,* Save As *option,* Save Database As *option,* Access Database *option, and* Save As *button.* ***NOTE:*** *If a security warning appears immediately below the ribbon, click the Enable Content button.*

2 Open the Customers table.

3 In record 3, edit the contents of the *LastName* field to *Katz* instead of *Kati*.

4 Close the Customers table.

5 Open the Products form.

6 Click the New (blank) record button in the Record Navigation bar.

7 Add the following information to create three new records:

ItemNumber	ItemDescription	Price
A682	Emerald Earrings	1795.00
D328	Diamond Necklace	2845.00
K325	Diamond Bracelet	1550.00

8 Close the Products form.

9 Open the *Orders* table.

10 Sort the Orders table by the *CustomerID* field in ascending order.

11 Save the Orders table. *HINT: Click the Save button on the Quick Access toolbar.*

12 Print the Orders table or submit the completed database as directed by your instructor.

13 Remove the sort and save the Orders table again.

14 Close the Orders table and then the database.

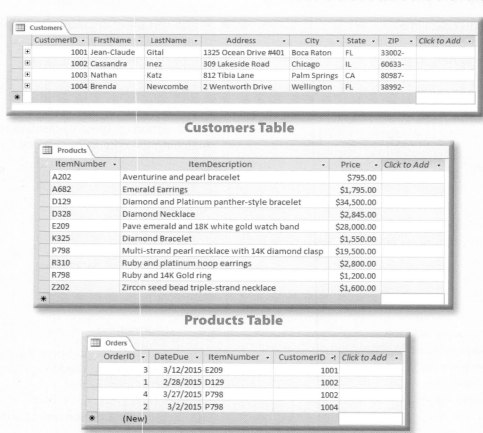

Customers Table

Products Table

Sorted Orders Table

Exercise B Filtering a Bookstore Database

Skills Open and navigate a database, filter data, and use existing queries and reports

Scenario You are the manager of a bookstore. You order books for your store from several suppliers. You have some questions about the orders you have made and so you filter the records and run existing queries to find the information that you need.

Steps

1 Open the student data file named **M7-C1-ExB-Books.accdb** and save the file as **Lastname-M7-C1-ExB-Books**, but replace *Lastname* with your last name. *HINT: To save an Access file using a new name, click the FILE tab,* Save As *option,* Save Database As *option,* Access Database *option, and Save As button.* **NOTE:** *If a security warning appears immediately below the ribbon, click the EnableContent button.*

2 Open the Tons of Books Orders query to display all of the orders from the Tons of Books supplier.

3 Close the Tons of Books Orders query.

4 Open the Book Depot Orders query to display all of the orders from the Book Depot supplier.

5 Close the Book Depot Orders query.

6 You now need to check the orders from the Books Unlimited supplier. Open the Orders table.

7 Filter the *SupplierName* column so that only the Books Unlimited records are displayed.

8 Save the Orders table. **HINT:** *Click the Save button in the Quick Access toolbar.*

9 Print the Orders table or submit the completed database as directed by your instructor.

10 Toggle the filter to turn it off and save the Orders table again.

11 Close the Orders table and then the database.

Book Depot Orders Query

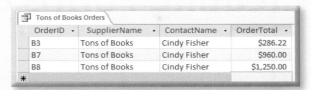

Tons of Books Orders Query

OrderID	SupplierName	OrderTotal	Click to Add
B1	Books Unlimited	$739.35	
B4	Books Unlimited	$94.10	
B9	Books Unlimited	$1,450.00	

Filtered Orders Table

Exercise C Tracking Community Volunteers

SNAP
Grade It

Skills Open and navigate a database, sort data, format a datasheet, and use existing queries and reports

Scenario You have set up a database to track student community service hours. This data is important because many students volunteer to meet graduation or financial aid requirements. You sort the data in this database, format a datasheet, and display a report.

Steps

1 Open the student data file named **M7-C1-ExC-CommunityService.accdb** and save the file as **Lastname-M7-C1-ExC-CommunityService**, but replace *Lastname* with your last name. **HINT:** *To save an Access file using a new name, click the FILE tab, Save As option, Save Database As option, Access Database option, and Save As button.* **NOTE:** *If a security warning appears immediately below the ribbon, click the Enable Content button.*

2 Open the Organizations report to display information about the community agencies at which students can volunteer.

3 Close the Organizations report.

4 Display the Volunteer Hours table.

5 Change the font size to 12 points.

6 Center the text in the fields of the *ServiceDate* column.

7 Sort the table by the *OrganizationName* column in ascending order.

8 Save the changes to the Volunteer Hours table.

9 Print the Volunteer Hours table or submit the completed document as directed by your instructor.

10 Close the Volunteer Hours table and then the database.

Organizations Report

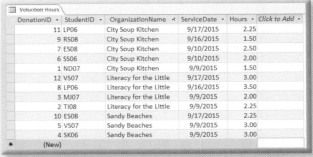

Volunteer Hours Table

Chapter 2

Creating Forms and Tables

In this chapter, you learn to create a table and a form. When you create a table, you need to give each field a name and also assign it a data type. The data type tells Access which type of data you will be storing in that field. There are a number of field types you can use, including:

- AutoNumber field— automatically stores a number that is one greater than the last number used

- Short Text field—stores characters and numbers that do not require calculations, such as names and zip codes

- Number field—stores numbers only

- Date/Time field—stores dates and times

- Currency field—stores dollar amounts

Access has several views that you use to perform different tasks. When you enter records in a table, you do so in Datasheet view. When you create a table in this chapter, you create it in Design view. To switch views, you use the View button arrow on the HOME tab.

You can enter data in a table or form. A form provides a user-friendly interface to enter data to be stored in a table. When you enter a record using a form, that record is added to the corresponding table just as if you added the record directly into the table in Datasheet view. When you use the Form button to create a form, the form initially displays in Layout view. You can edit the form in either Design or Layout view. You then must switch to Form view to add records to the underlying table.

In this chapter, you learn how to create a table and a form and you also enter data in a table and a form.

Skills You Learn

1. Create a table
2. Enter data in a table
3. Create a form
4. Enter data in a form

Files You Need
For these skills, you need the following student data file.

M7-C2-Members.accdb

What You Create

The Chocolate Museum charges an annual fee for its membership program. The standard fee is $120. Many members choose to donate additional funds to support the Museum. In this chapter, you create a table that stores data on the annual fee payments and additional donation amounts that members make to The Chocolate Museum. You also create a form so that you can easily enter records in this table.

Membership Fee and Donations Table

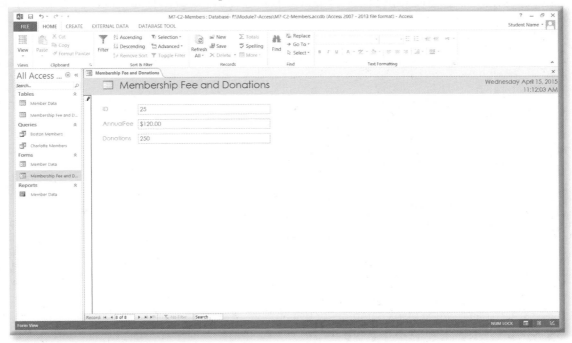

Membership Fee and Donations Form

Access

Chapter 2

Skill 1

Create a Table

Video **M7_C2_S01**

In Chapter 1, you opened a table, added a record to the table, and edited data in the table. In this skill, you add a new table to the database. This new table will store membership fee and donations data for each member of The Chocolate Museum. You create the table in Design view. You need to name each field and select a data type for each field in the table. When you save the table, Access asks you if you want to make one of the fields a primary key. You won't assign a primary key to the table you create in this skill, but you should know that a *primary key* can be assigned to one of the fields in a table, such as the member ID number, to simplify retrieval of a specific record and to make sure no two records in a table are the same. The primary key column cannot contain duplicate entries.

Steps

▶ **Tip** Be sure to open all database files from your working folder on your storage medium. Access database files opened directly from the Student Resources disc are read-only. Steps on how to copy a folder from the disc are presented on pages 110–111 and 166–168 of this textbook.

▶ **Tip** Alternatively, you can include an entry in the *Description* column, to the right of the *Data Type* column. You can use this entry to describe the contents of the field.

1 Open the student data file named **M7-C2-Members.accdb** from your storage medium.

2 If a security warning appears immediately below the ribbon, click the Enable Content button.

3 Click the CREATE tab.

4 Click the Table Design button in the Tables group so that you can create the table in Design view.

5 In the first field in the *Field Name* column, type ID and then press the Tab key.

6 In the first field in the *Data Type* column, click the drop-down arrow and then click *Number* in the drop-down list.

Taking It Further

Using Templates In this module, you open existing desktop databases and then start working in Access. To create a new database, select one of the templates that are available when you start Access. You will see templates for both desktop and web applications. For example, if you want to start with a blank database for use on your desktop, select the Blank desktop database template, or if you want to create a database that you can share online, select the Custom web app template. When you select the Custom web app template, you will also be able to add table templates to the online database.

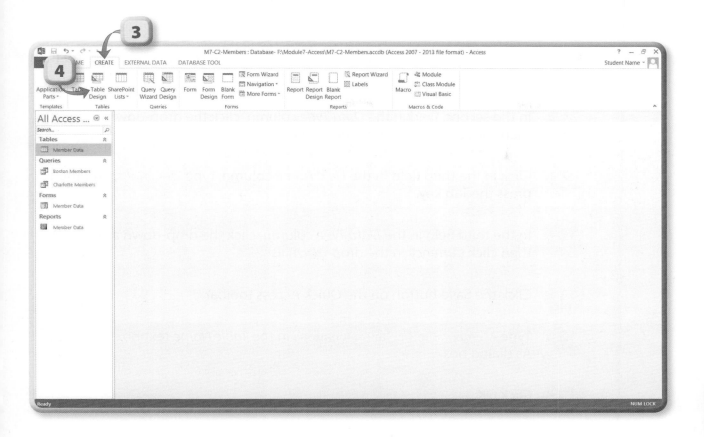

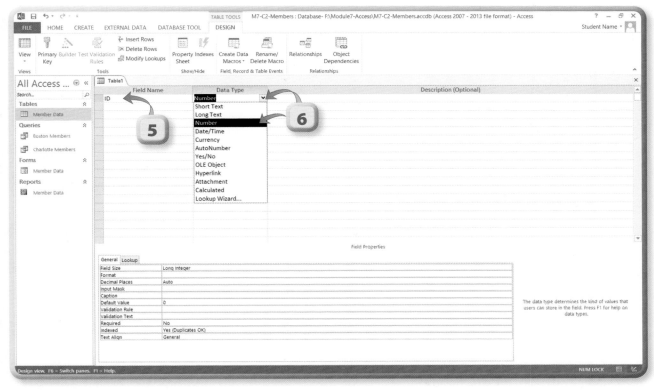

More

7   Click in the second field in the *Field Name* column, type AnnualFee, and then press the Tab key.

8   In the second field in the *Data Type* column, click the drop-down arrow and then click *Currency* in the drop-down list.

9   Click in the third field in the *Field Name* column, type Donations, and then press the Tab key.

10   In the third field in the *Data Type* column, click the drop-down arrow and then click *Currency* in the drop-down list.

11   Click the Save button on the Quick Access toolbar.

12   Type Membership Fee and Donations in the *Table Name* text box in the Save As dialog box.

13   Click OK.

14   Click No at the warning box indicating that a primary key is not selected.

15   Click Close to close the Membership Fee and Donations table.

▶ *Tip* You can assign a primary key to a field in a table to make sure no two records in a table are the same.

Taking It Further

Changing Field Size   Some field data types have a specified or a maximum field size. For example, Short Text fields can store up to 255 characters. In some situations, you might want to limit a Short Text field to fewer characters—for instance, you might want to limit fields for phone numbers or zip codes to help reduce data entry errors. To do this, you replace the *Field Size* value of *255* with another value. Change this setting in the *Field Properties* section of the Design view window. A field size cannot be set for Long Text, Date/Time, Currency, or Hyperlink fields.

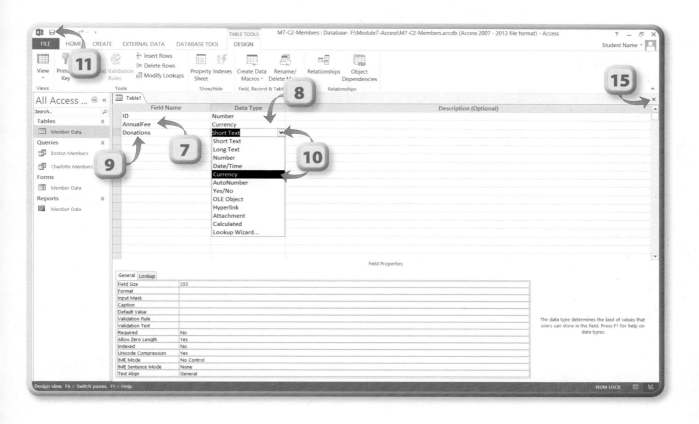

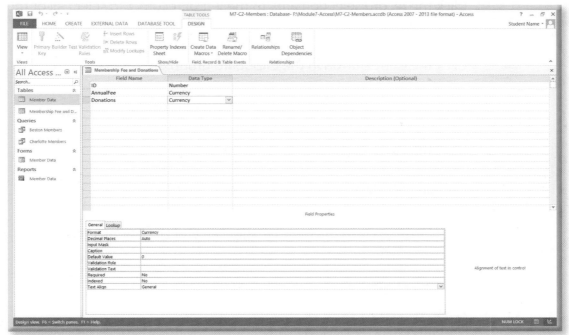

Completed Skill 1

Access

Skill 2

Enter Data in a Table

Video ▶ M7_C2_S02

In the previous skill, you created a new table. The new table is an object in the database. In this skill, you add records to the table. Typing records is one way to enter data in a table. You can also copy and paste data from other programs or databases, which saves time and also helps to prevent data entry errors. Adding records is sometimes referred to as *populating* the database.

Steps

1 With **M7-C2-Members.accdb** open, double-click *Membership Fee and Donations* in the Tables group in the Navigation pane.

▶**Tip** When you enter numbers in the *AnnualFee* and *Donations* columns, they are automatically formatted as currency to match the field type.

2 Add the following information to create a new record, using the Tab key to move between fields:

ID	AnnualFee	Donations
8	120	2000

▶**Tip** The ID number matches the member ID number in the Member Data table.

3 Click the record selection area to the left of record 1 to select all of the fields in record 1.

▶**Tip** You can use copy and paste to save time when a new record is almost identical to an existing record. After pasting, you change only the part of the record that differs. In this case, all of the record data is the same except the value in the *ID* field.

4 Click the Copy button in the Clipboard group on the HOME tab.

5 Click the record selection area to the left of record 2.

6 Click the Paste button.

7 Double-click in the *ID* field for record 2 and type 10.

4-6 *Another Way*
Use Ctrl + ' to repeat data in the same field from a previous record.

8 Click Close to close the Membership Fee and Donations table.

Taking It Further

Copying and Pasting Data Another way to populate a table is to copy existing data from a Word or Excel file into an Access table. To copy all of the data from a Word source, first separate the data by tabs or copy it from a table. Whether you copy the data from Word or Excel, the field names, data types, and data have to match the fields in the Access table. Click the record selection area for the next blank record before pasting the data. Note that you may copy and paste multiple records. Module 9 provides more information about data sharing between Office applications.

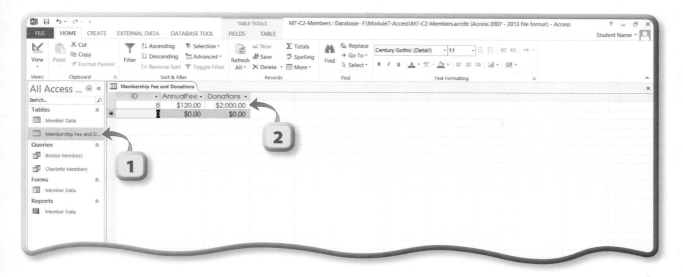

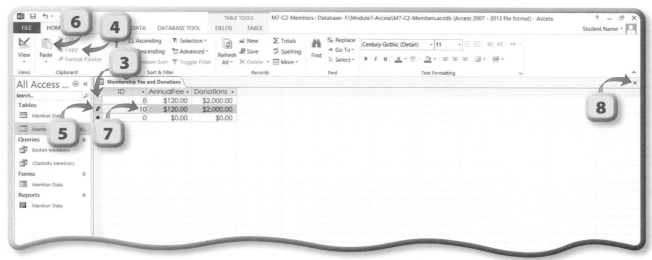

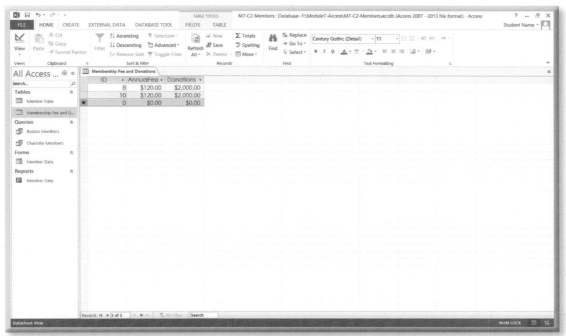

Completed Skill 2

Access

Skill 3

Video M7_C2_S03

Create a Form

A form is a database object used for entering records in a table. You can also use a form to view existing records. Most forms show only one record at a time, which provides a simple interface for entering data and helps you to avoid data entry mistakes. A new form can be based on one or more database objects. The form you create in this skill is based on a table. When you first create a new form, it displays in Layout view, where you can format it.

Steps

▶ **Tip** Single-click to make a table active so that you can create a form for the table. Double-click to open the table.

3 *Another Way*
You can also use the Form Design button to create a form. In that case, the form displays in Design view instead of in Layout view.

1 With **M7-C2-Members.accdb** open, click *Membership Fee and Donations* in the Tables group in the Navigation pane.

2 Click the CREATE tab.

3 Click the Form button in the Forms group to display a form.

4 Hover the mouse over the right border of the *ID* field until it becomes a left-and-right-pointing arrow, press the left mouse button, drag the right border to the left until the box is about half of its original size, and then release the mouse button. This action adjusts the width of all of the fields.

5 Click the Date and Time button in the Header/Footer group on the FORM LAYOUT TOOLS DESIGN tab.

6 In the Date and Time dialog box, click OK to add the date and time.

7 Click the Save button on the Quick Access toolbar.

8 Click OK to accept the form name *Membership Fee and Donations*. The form object is added to the Navigation pane.

9 Click Close to close the Membership Fee and Donations form.

Taking It Further

Changing Form Formatting and Views
When you create a form, the FORM LAYOUT TOOLS tabs are displayed on the ribbon. You can use options on the FORM LAYOUT TOOLS FORMAT tab to change the font, font size, and font style. You can use options on the FORM LAYOUT TOOLS ARRANGE tab to insert fields or alter the order of the fields.

You can use options on the FORM LAYOUT TOOLS DESIGN tab to add an image to the form or to change the form's theme. However, you cannot enter records in the form until you switch to Form view. To do so, click the View button arrow in the Views group on the FORM LAYOUT TOOLS DESIGN tab or the HOME tab, and select *Form View*.

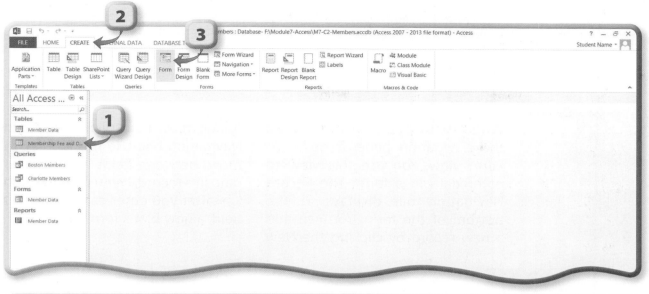

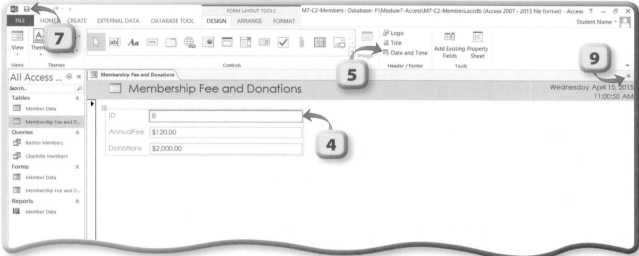

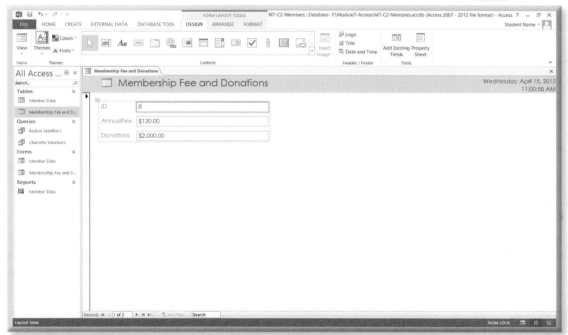

Completed Skill 3

Access

Enter Data in a Form

Video M7_C2_S04

When you open a form from the Navigation pane, it opens in Form view. You use this view to enter data in a form. The Record Navigation bar displays at the bottom of the form. You can add a new record by clicking the New (blank) record button in the Record Navigation bar. Use the Tab key to move between fields as you enter data in a record. If you press the Tab key after you enter data in the last field, a new blank form displays.

Steps

Tip If the form does not display in the Navigation pane, click the down-pointing arrow in the Navigation pane header and click *All Access Objects*.

1 With **M7-C2-Members.accdb** open, double-click *Membership Fee and Donations* in the Forms group in the Navigation pane.

2 In the Record Navigation bar, click the New (blank) record button.

3 Type 12 and press the Tab key.

4 Type 120 and press the Tab key.

5 Type 600 and press the Tab key. A new blank form displays.

6 Add these five additional records:

ID	AnnualFee	Donations
48	120	1000
17	120	2000
5	120	5000
37	120	0
25	120	250

Tip When you enter data in a form, Access saves the data automatically.

7 Click Close to close the Membership Fee and Donations form.

8 Close Access.

Taking It Further

Record Navigation Bar Counter The Record Navigation bar indicates which record is currently displayed and how many records are available for viewing—for example, *1 of 381*. If you have not filtered the table or form, the second number indicates the total number of records in the object. If you have filtered the object, the second number indicates the number of records that match your request and the Filtered icon ▼ is highlighted in the Record Navigation bar.

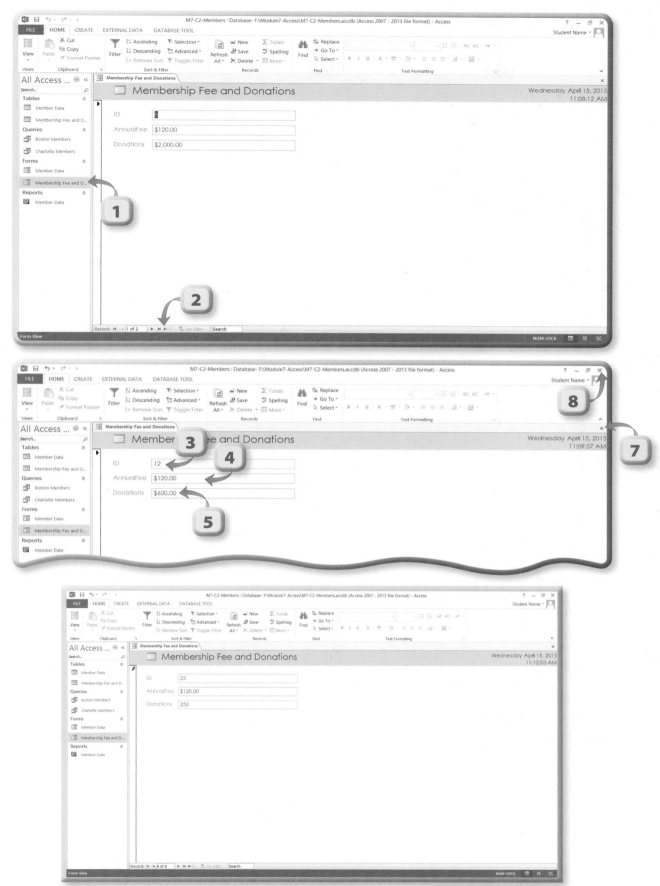

Completed Skill 4

Tasks Summary

Task	Ribbon Tab, Group	Button, Option	Shortcut, Alternative
Create a table	CREATE, Table	⊞	
Save a table		💾	Ctrl + S
Select a record			Click the record selection area.
Copy a record	HOME, Clipboard		Ctrl + C
Paste a record	HOME, Clipboard		Ctrl + V
Create a form	CREATE, Form	📇	
Add the date and time to a form	FORM LAYOUT TOOLS DESIGN, Header/Footer	🕒 Date and Time	
Change views	FORM LAYOUT TOOLS DESIGN, Views	⊟	HOME, *View*

 Features Review

Select the best answer from the choices given.

1 Which button can you use to create a table?
   a. Table Design
   b. Filter
   c. Report
   d. Form Design

2 Which field data type would you use to store a number that is one greater than the last number used?
   a. Short Text
   b. Number
   c. AutoNumber
   d. Currency

3 Which field data type would you use to store dollar amounts?
   a. Text
   b. Number
   c. AutoNumber
   d. Currency

4 Which field data type would you use to store characters and numbers that do not require calculations, such as zip codes?
   a. Short Text
   b. Number
   c. AutoNumber
   d. Currency

5 Which view do you use to enter records in a table?
   a. Design view
   b. Datasheet view
   c. Print Preview
   d. Layout view

6 Which action selects an entire record?
   a. Press the Tab key.
   b. Click the Record button.
   c. Click the first field in the record.
   d. Click the record selection area.

7 Which button creates a form and displays it in Layout view?
   a. Form
   b. Design
   c. Report
   d. Layout

8 Adding records is referred to as _____ the database.
   a. sorting
   b. populating
   c. filtering
   d. parsing

9 You can save a form by clicking the Save button on the Quick Access toolbar.
   a. True
   b. False

10 Which action copies a selected record?
   a. Click the record selection area.
   b. Click the Copy button.
   c. Click the View button.
   d. Click the Next record button.

Hands-On Skills Review

Exercise **Adding to a Jewelry Store Database**

Skills   Create a table and enter data in a table

Scenario   You are in charge of updating a jewelry store database. You need to add a new table to the existing database. The table will store information about upcoming sales events. You also need to add some data to the new table.

Steps

1 Open the student data file named **M7-C2-ExA-Jewelry.accdb** and save the file as **Lastname-M7-C2-ExA-Jewelry**, but replace *Lastname* with your last name.

2 Create a new table in Design view.

3 Add three fields to the table.

Field Name	Data Type
Event	Short Text
SaleItem	Short Text
Discount	Currency

4 Save the table, naming it *Events*. If a warning box displays, indicating a primary key is not defined, click No.

5 Close the Events table.

6 Open the Events table in Datasheet view. **HINT:** *If the Events table does not immediately appear in the Tables group in the Navigation pane, close and then reopen* **Lastname-M7-C2-ExA-Jewelry.accdb**.

7 Add the following information to create three new records.

Event	SaleItem	Discount
Fall Celebration	Diamond Bracelet	100
Winter Sale	Emerald Earrings	200
Wedding Sale	Diamond Rings	200

8 Copy record 2, Winter Sale.

9 Paste the copied data as record 4.

10 Edit the *Event* field in record 4 to read *Spring Sale* instead of *Winter Sale*.

11 Adjust the column widths in all columns (*Event*, *SaleItem*, and *Discount*) in the datasheet so that all of the data in every column is visible. **HINT:** *Use the double-click method taught in Chapter 1.*

12 Print the Events table or submit the completed database as directed by your instructor.

13 Save the database.

14 Close the Events table and then the database.

Events Table

Exercise B Making a Bookstore Database Easier to Use

Skills Create a form and enter data in a form

Scenario You are the manager of a bookstore. One of your responsibilities is to keep the bookstore's database up to date. To make data entry easier, you create a form to enter records.

Steps

1 Open the student data file named **M7-C2-ExB-Books.accdb** and save the file as **Lastname-M7-C2-ExB-Books**, but replace *Lastname* with your last name.

2 Create a form based on the Orders table. **HINT:** *See Skill 3.*

3 Modify the form to include the date and time.

4 Narrow the width of the fields in the form to about half of their original width.

5 Save the form, naming it *Orders*.

6 Close the form.

7 Open the *Orders* form and add the five records listed at the top of the next column to those that already exist in the table. **HINT:** *If the Orders form does not immediately appear in the Forms group in the Navigation pane, close and then reopen **Lastname-M7-C2-ExB-Books.accdb**.*

OrderID	SupplierName	OrderTotal
B10	Books Unlimited	560
B11	Tons of Books	1350
B12	Books Unlimited	765
B13	Book Depot	250
B14	Book Depot	375

8 Print the Orders table or submit the completed database as directed by your instructor.

9 Close the Orders table and then the database.

Orders Form with Half-Size Form Fields

OrderID	SupplierName	OrderTotal	Click to Add
B1	Books Unlimited	$739.35	
B10	Books Unlimited	$560.00	
B11	Tons of Books	$1,350.00	
B12	Books Unlimited	$765.00	
B13	Book Depot	$250.00	
B14	Book Depot	$375.00	
B2	Book Depot	$40.32	
B3	Tons of Books	$286.22	
B4	Books Unlimited	$94.10	
B5	Book Depot	$375.00	
B6	Book Depot	$2,300.00	
B7	Tons of Books	$960.00	
B8	Tons of Books	$1,250.00	
B9	Books Unlimited	$1,450.00	
*			

Orders Table

Exercise C Entering Information into the Community Volunteers Database

Skills   Create a form

Scenario   You have created a database to track student community service hours. In this exercise you create forms to make entering data in two of the tables in the database easier.

Steps

1 Open the student data file named **M7-C2-ExC-CommunityService.accdb** and save the file as **Lastname-M7-C2-ExC-CommunityService**, but replace *Lastname* with your last name.

2 Create a form based on the Volunteer Hours table. **HINT:** *See Skill 3.*

3 Narrow the width of the fields in the form to about half of their original width. **HINT:** *If you cannot see the right side of the form, place your cursor over the right border of the Navigation pane and then click and drag to the left to reduce the width of the Navigation pane while increasing the width of the Forms pane.*

4 Apply the Integral form theme. **HINT:** *See the Taking It Further box in Skill 3.*

5 Save the form, naming it *Volunteer Hours.*

6 Create a form based on the Students table.

7 Save the form, naming it *Students.*

8 Print the Volunteer Hours and Students forms or submit the completed database as directed by your instructor.

9 Close both forms and then close the database.

Volunteer Hours Form

Students Form

Working with Queries and Reports

A database may contain hundreds of records that are divided among many related tables. An easy way to find the information you are looking for is to create and run a query.

A query asks a question of the database, such as "How many members of The Chocolate Museum paid their annual fee?" or "How many members of The Chocolate Museum live in Boston?" A query shows only the data that you want to view at any given time. You can look at a limited number of fields from a single table or select fields from multiple tables to view that data together. You can even sort or filter the query results to display only a subset of the results data, arranged in the order you prefer.

You can use the information in a table or in a query to create a professional-looking report. Then you can distribute the report in printed or electronic form. When preparing a report, you have several options. You might sort or group the report or format it by changing the font or by applying a theme.

In this chapter, you learn how to create queries to find the information you are looking for within an Access database. You also learn how to create, preview, and print a report.

Skills You Learn

1. Use the Query Wizard
2. Create a query in Design view
3. Use more than one table in a query
4. Create a report
5. Preview a report

Files You Need

For these skills, you need the following student data file.

> M7-C3-Members.accdb

What You Create

You create two queries in this chapter. One query displays only certain fields from the Member Data table. Another query finds all members of The Chocolate Museum who have donated more than $500 to the Museum. You then use the second query, focused on Museum members donating over $500, to create a report that is sorted and grouped. Lastly, you preview and then print the report.

Member Last Name and Zip Query

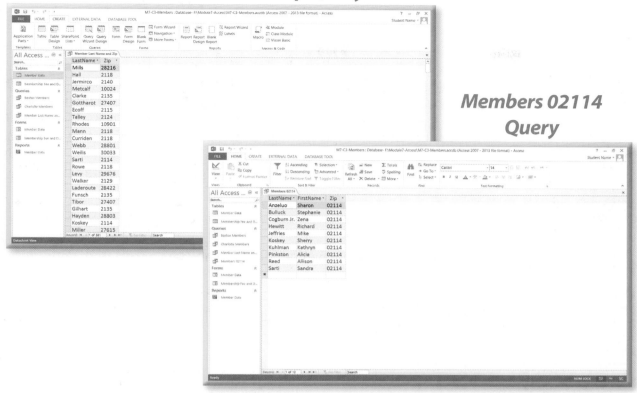

Members 02114 Query

Donations > $500 Query

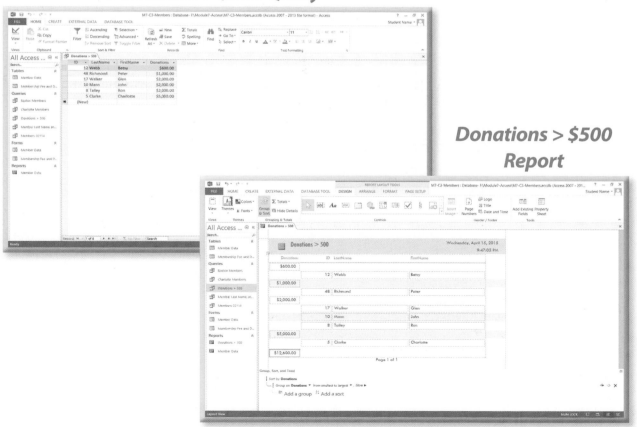

Donations > $500 Report

Access

Skill 1

Use the Query Wizard

Video M7_C3_S01

Once you have entered information into a database, you can query the database to find records that meet certain criteria. A query pulls, or *extracts*, data from one or more tables. In this skill, you use the Query Wizard to create a simple query, which displays data from fields that you pick. The simple query you create in this skill displays the *LastName* and *Zip* fields from the Member Data table.

Steps

▶Tip Be sure to open all database files from your working folder on your storage medium. Access database files opened directly from the Student Resources disc are read-only. Steps on how to copy a folder from the disc are presented on pages 110–111 and 166–168 of this textbook.

1 Open the student data file named **M7-C3-Members.accdb** from your storage medium.

2 If a security warning appears immediately below the ribbon, click the Enable Content button.

3 Click *Member Data* in the Tables group in the Navigation pane.

4 Click the CREATE tab.

5 Click the Query Wizard button in the Queries group.

6 In the New Query dialog box, click *Simple Query Wizard*, if it is not already highlighted, and then click OK.

7-8 *Another Way*
Double-click the field name *LastName*.

7 Click *LastName* in the *Available Fields* list box.

8 Click the single right arrow button (>) to add the field to the query.

▶Tip If you need to select all available fields, click the double right arrow button (>>).

9 Click *Zip* in the *Available Fields* list box.

▶Tip If you accidentally select a field you do not want, click the field name in the *Selected Fields* list box and then click the single left arrow button (<) to deselect the field.

10 Click the single right arrow button (>) to add the field to the query.

11 Click Next.

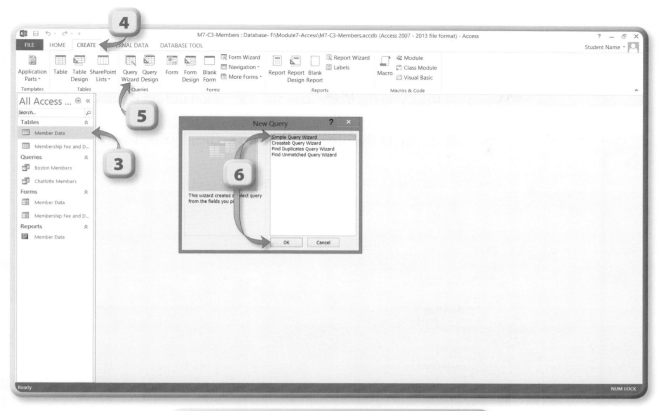

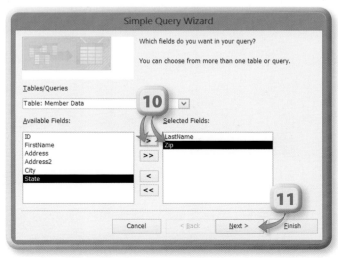

More

12 Select the text in the *What title do you want for your query?* text box and then type Member Last Name and Zip.

13 Make sure the *Open the query to view information* option is selected.

▶ **Tip** The new query now appears in the *Queries* list in the Navigation pane.

14 Click Finish to direct the query to run and to display the results.

15 Close the Member Last Name and Zip query.

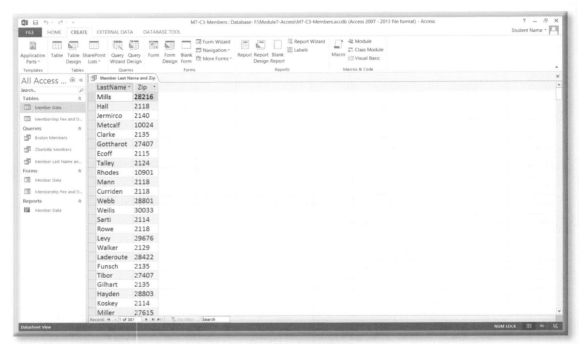

Completed Skill 1

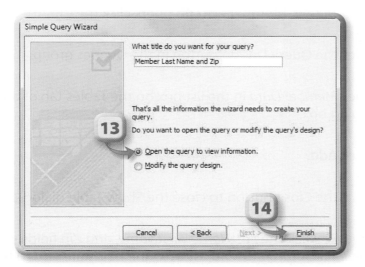

Taking It Further

Deciding whether to Query or to Filter There are important differences between running a query and simply filtering data. When you create a query, Access saves the query as an object in the database. Because the query is saved, you can run it again at a later time without having to re-create the query. Another advantage of running a query is that you can easily create a report from a query, giving you the option of presenting the query results in a professional format. In contrast, filtering displays the results temporarily. Filtering is useful when you need to see a subset of data in datasheet format, and you only need to see that subset once. For example, if you need the address of The Chocolate Museum member Cara Brown, you can filter the *LastName* column to display all members with the last name *Brown* and locate this information quickly.

Access

Create a Query in Design View

In the previous skill, you learned to create a query using the Query Wizard. You can also create a query in Design view by using the *query design grid*. When you create a query in Design view, you have more options and more control than you do with the Query Wizard. In this skill, you create a query to find all the members who live in a specific zip code. You then sort the query by last name.

Steps

1   With **M7-C3-Members.accdb** open, click the CREATE tab.

2   Click the Query Design button in the Queries group.

3   Click *Member Data* in the list box on the Tables tab of the Show Table dialog box.

4   Click Add.

5   Click the Close button to close the Show Table dialog box.

▶Tip Double-click carefully, choosing only those fields that you need for the query. You may need to scroll to see the *Zip* field.

6   Double-click the *LastName*, *FirstName*, and *Zip* fields, in that order, in the *Member Data* table field list box. The fields are added to the query design grid at the bottom of the window.

7   Click the *Sort* cell for the *LastName* field in the query design grid.

8   Click the down-pointing arrow that appears and then click *Ascending* at the drop-down list.

9   Click in the *Criteria* cell for the *Zip* field in the query design grid and type 02114.

10 *Another Way*
You can also run the query by clicking the View button. When you click the View button, you switch from Design view to Datasheet view and the query results display.

10   Click the Run button in the Results group on the QUERY TOOLS DESIGN tab to display the query results in a datasheet.

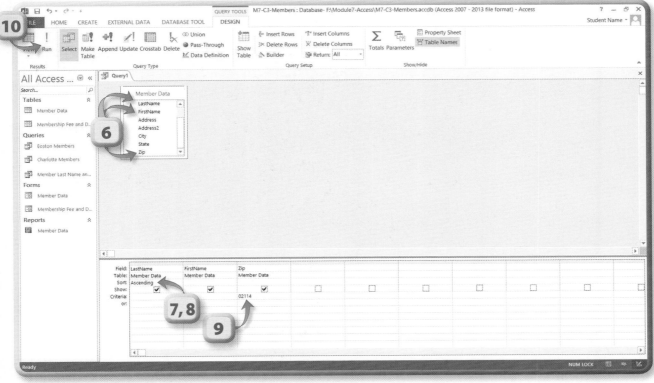

More

11 Click the Save button on the Quick Access toolbar.

12 Type Members 02114 in the *Query Name* text box in the Save As dialog box.

▶**Tip** The new query now appears in the Queries group in the Navigation pane.

13 Click OK to finish saving the query.

14 Close the Members 02114 query.

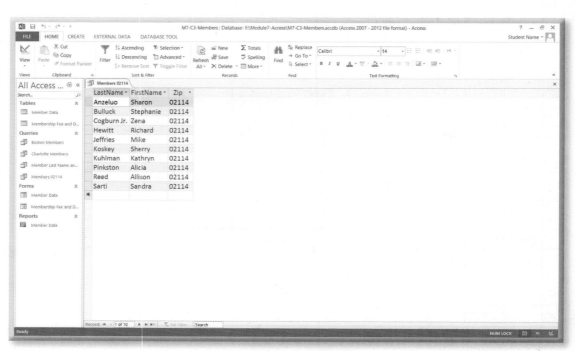

Completed Skill 2

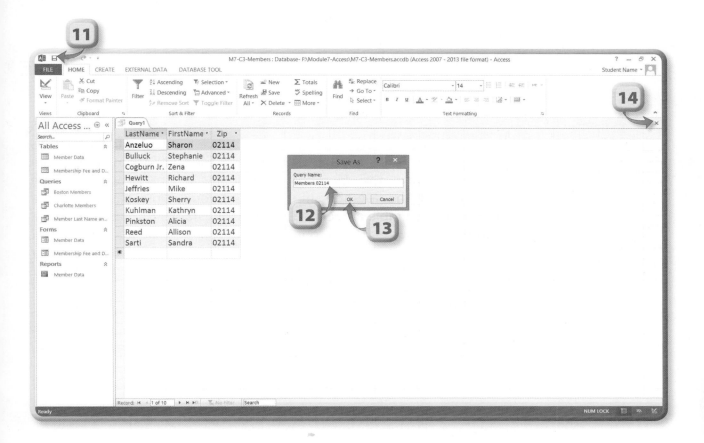

Taking It Further

Specifying Criteria In this skill, you specified the query criteria by typing in the *Criteria* cell of the *Zip* field. You can also create a query with criteria from more than one field and you can use wildcards to represent any combination of letters, numbers, and special symbols. For example, to find all members of The Chocolate Museum whose last names start with the letter *S* and who also live in Boston, you would type *Boston* in the *Criteria* row of the *City* field and then type *S** in the *Criteria* row of the *LastName* field. The * is a wildcard character.

Access

Use More Than One Table in a Query

Tables in a database can be related through a common column of data. For example, the Member Data table and the Membership Fee and Donations table are related through the *ID* column. The field in this column assigns a unique number to each Museum member. Such database design features are helpful because the tables do not need to contain a lot of duplicate data and, as a result, the database operates more efficiently. When Access tables are related, you can pull data from more than one table to create a query. In this skill, you create a query that pulls data from both the Member Data table and the Membership Fee and Donations table.

Steps

1 With **M7-C3-Members.accdb** open, click the CREATE tab.

2 Click the Query Design button in the Queries group.

3 Make sure that *Member Data* is selected in the list box on the Tables tab of the Show Table dialog box and then click Add.

4 Click *Membership Fee and Donations* on the Tables tab in the Show Table dialog box and then click Add.

> **Tip** A join line appears between the *ID* fields. (Joins are to queries what relationships are to tables: an indication of how data in two sources can be combined based on data values they have in common.)

5 Click Close to close the Show Table dialog box.

6 Double-click *ID*, *LastName*, and *FirstName*, in that order, in the *Member Data* table field list box.

> **Tip** Double-click carefully, choosing only those fields specifically needed for the query.

7 Double-click *Donations* in the *Membership Fee and Donations* table field list box.

8 Click in the *Sort* cell for the *Donations* field in the query design grid.

9 Click the down-pointing arrow that appears and then click *Ascending* in the drop-down list.

> **Tip** In addition to > (greater than), you can use other relational operators including > = (greater than or equal to), < (less than), < = (less than or equal to), = (equal to), and < > (not equal to) as search criteria.

10 Click in the *Criteria* cell for the *Donations* field and then type >500.

11 Click the Run button in the Results group on the QUERY TOOLS DESIGN tab. The query results appear in a datasheet.

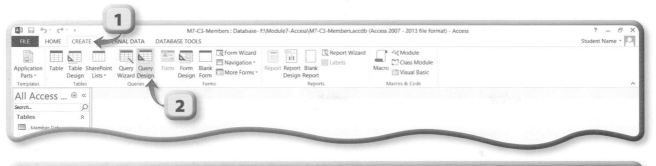

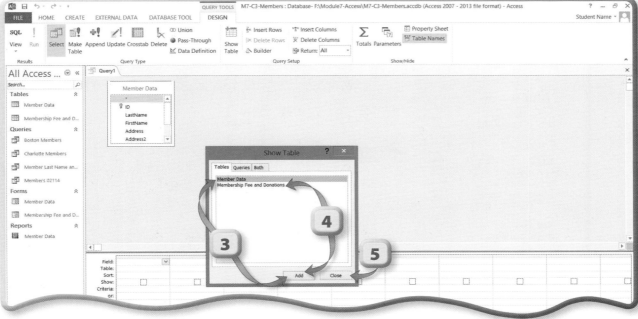

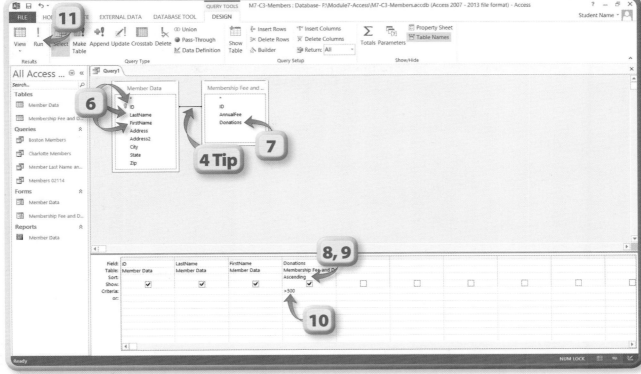

More

12 Click the Save button on the Quick Access toolbar.

13 In the Save As dialog box, select the text in the *Query Name* text box and then type Donations > $500.

14 Click OK.

15 Close the Donations > $500 query.

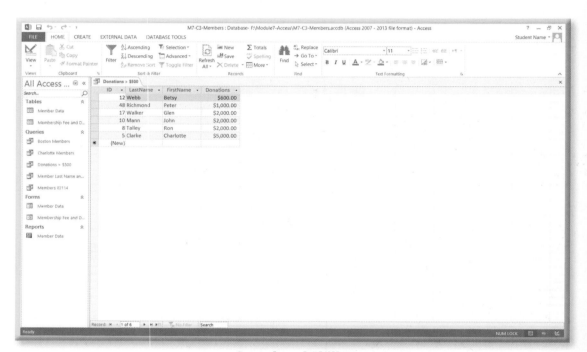

Completed Skill 3

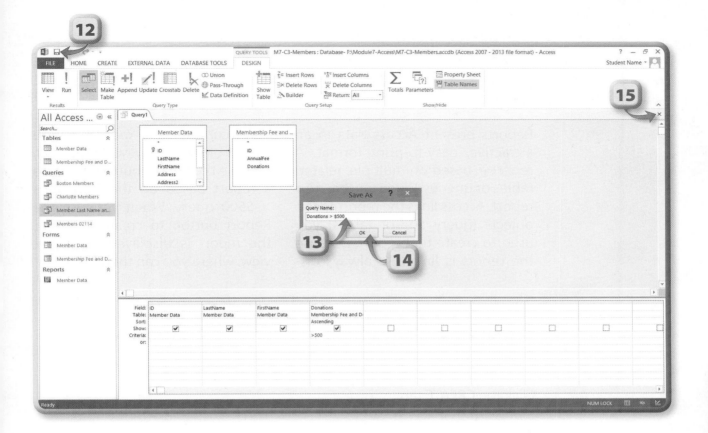

Taking It Further

Creating Table Relationships Most Access databases contain multiple tables that share data. An effective database designer avoids data redundancy (the duplication of data) by creating relationships between tables for the data fields that they share. You can define a relationship by clicking the Relationships button in the Relationships group on the DATABASE TOOLS tab and then dragging a common data field from one table to another table. To view existing table relationships, click the Relationships button and then click the All Relationships button.

Access

Video   M7_C3_S04

Create a Report

Reports present Access data in an attractive, easy-to-print format. A report is based on multiple, related tables or queries. When you create a report, Access links the report to the objects (query and/or tables) you used to create that report. Because the report is linked, it always dis-plays current data. You can create a report in several ways. In this skill, you use the Report button to create a report based on the Donations > $500 query. When you use the Report button to create a report, the report is displayed in Layout view, where you can then format it.

Steps

1   With **M7-C3-Members.accdb** open, click *Donations > $500* in the Queries group in the Navigation pane.

2   Click the CREATE tab.

Tip The REPORT LAYOUT TOOLS DESIGN tab is now the active tab.

3   Click the Report button in the Reports group to display the report in Layout view.

4   Click the Themes button in the Themes group on the REPORT LAYOUT TOOLS DESIGN tab.

5   Click *Integral* (the third theme in the first row in the *Office* section) to apply the Integral theme to the report.

6   Click the Group & Sort button in the Grouping & Totals group to display the Group, Sort, and Total pane.

7   Click the Add a sort button.

8   Select the *Donations* option to sort the report by the *Donations* column.

9   Click the *Donations Total* cell to make it active.

10   Hover the mouse pointer over the border of the cell until the pointer becomes a left-and-right-pointing arrow with a vertical line in the middle and then double-click the cell border to AutoFit the cell.

11   Click the Add a group button.

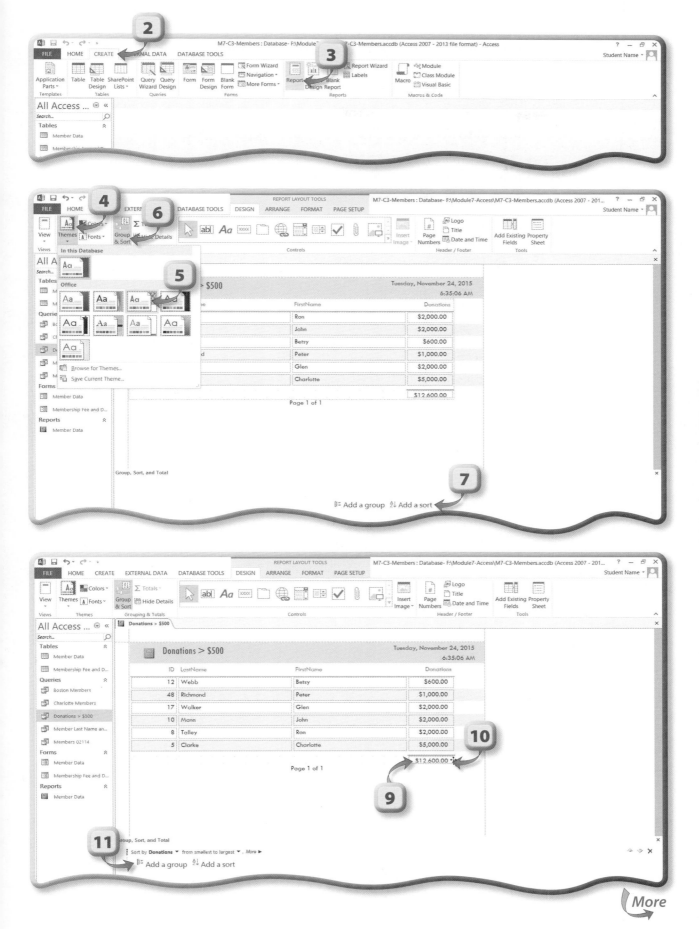

12 Click *Donations* to group the report by donation amount.

13 Click the Save button on the Quick Access toolbar.

14 Click OK to accept the *Donations > $500* report name.

15 Close the Donations > $500 report.

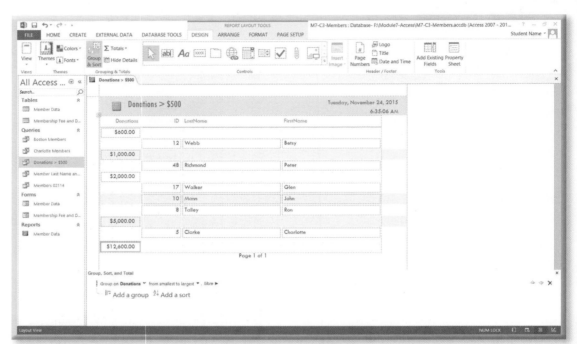

Completed Skill 4

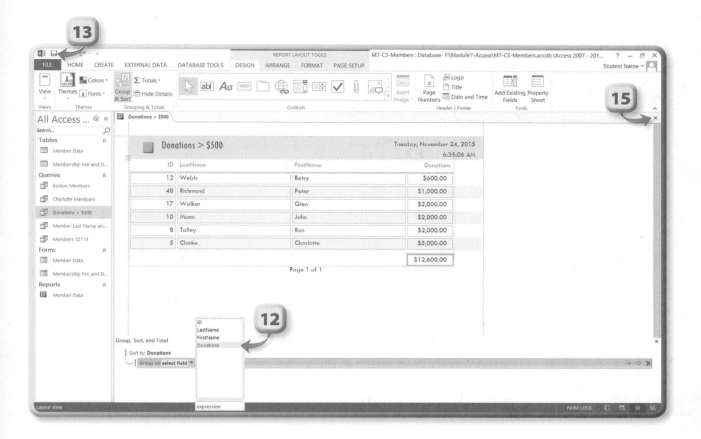

Taking It Further

Formatting a Report The REPORT LAYOUT TOOLS DESIGN tab contains options for formatting a report. For example, you can click the Logo button in the Header/Footer group to add a business logo to the report. You can also modify the title and the date and time that are displayed by default in the report. Double-click the title to modify it or click the Date and Time button in the Header/Footer group to display the date and time format options. The REPORT LAYOUT TOOLS FORMAT tab also contains options for formatting a report. You can click a cell in the report and then change options, such as the font, font size, text color, or fill color. You can also add a background image to the report. The REPORT LAYOUT TOOLS ARRANGE tab contains options for inserting rows and columns and altering the layout of the report. The REPORT LAYOUT TOOLS PAGE SETUP tab contains options for formatting the page size and the page layout.

Access

Skill 5

Preview a Report

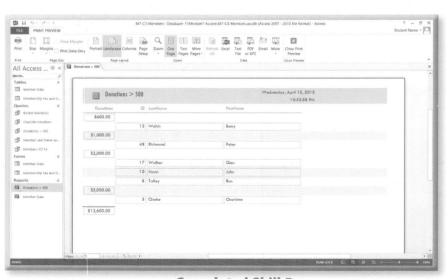

Video M7_C3_S05

Before printing a report, it is good practice to use the Print Preview feature to view what the printed copy will look like and adjust the print settings, if necessary. The PRINT PREVIEW tab in Access contains print and page layout options as well as options for exporting the report to another format, such as PDF. When you preview the report, make sure to check the presentation of the data and the page setup.

Steps

1 With **M7-C3-Members.accdb** open, double-click *Donations > $500* in the Reports group in the Navigation pane.

2 Click the View button arrow in the Views group on the HOME tab.

3 Click *Print Preview* at the drop-down list.

3 *Another Way*
Right-click a report object in the Navigation Pane and then select *Print Preview*.

4 Click the Landscape button in the Page Layout group on the PRINT PREVIEW tab to change the print orientation to landscape.

5 Click the Print button.

6 Click OK if your instructor asks you to print the report. If not, click Cancel.

7 Close the Donations > $500 report.

8 Close Access.

Completed Skill 5

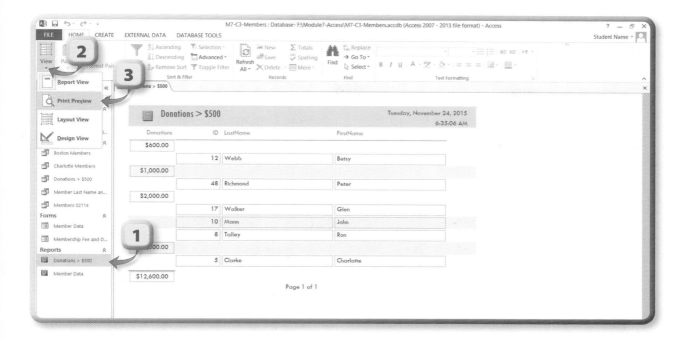

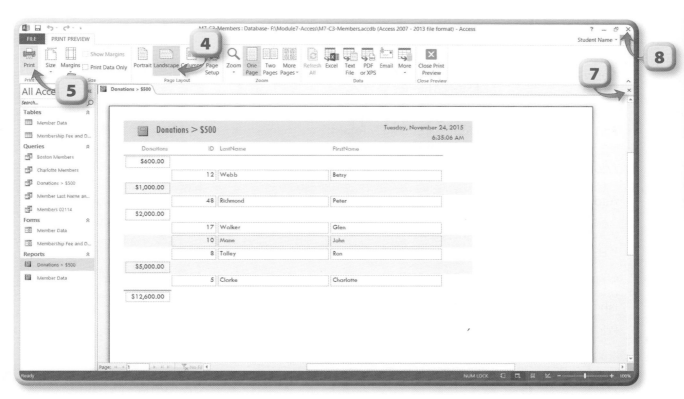

Taking It Further

Saving a Report as a PDF File   You can save an Access report in other formats. For example, you may want to save a report as a PDF file. PDF allows anybody to use a free reader program to view the report with its formatting intact, so the report looks the same on every computer. To save a report as a PDF file, click the PDF or XPS button in the Data group on the PRINT PREVIEW tab and then click the Publish button in the Publish as PDF or XPS dialog box.

Tasks Summary

Task	Ribbon Tab, Group	Button, Option	Shortcut, Alternative
Create a query using the Query Wizard	CREATE, Queries		
Create a query in Design view	CREATE, Queries		
Add a table from the Show Table dialog box		Add	
Close the Show Table dialog box		Close	
Run a query	QUERY TOOLS DESIGN, Results	!	Click the View button to switch from Design view to Datasheet view.
Create a report	CREATE, Reports		
Apply a theme to a report	REPORT LAYOUT TOOLS DESIGN, Themes		
Display the Group, Sort, and Total pane	REPORT LAYOUT TOOLS DESIGN, Grouping & Totals, Group & Sort		
Add a sort	Group, Sort, and Total pane	Add a sort	
Add a group	Group, Sort, and Total pane	Add a group	
Print Preview a report	HOME, Views		
Change the print orientation to landscape	PRINT PREVIEW, Page Layout		
Print a report	PRINT PREVIEW, Print		
Create a PDF copy of the report	PRINT PREVIEW, Data		

Features Review

Select the best answer from the choices given.

1. Which asks a question of the database?
   a. table
   b. form
   c. query
   d. report

2. When a query pulls data from one or more tables, the process that occurs is referred to as
   a. extracting data.
   b. importing data.
   c. sorting data.
   d. grouping data.

3. You can distribute a database report
   a. in printed format.
   b. in electronic format.
   c. as a PDF file.
   d. in printed format, in electronic format, and as a PDF file.

4. When you create a query using the _____ button, you select query options from a series of dialog boxes.
   a. Query Design
   b. Query Wizard
   c. Query Report
   d. Report Wizard

5. When you create a query in Design view, you use the _____ to create the query.
   a. Query Wizard dialog boxes
   b. query design grid
   c. layout design grid
   d. Print Preview window

6. When creating a query, you can only select fields from one table.
   a. True
   b. False

7. To find all records where the Amount field was less than $1000, enter _____ in the Criteria cell for the Amount field.
   a. 1000
   b. >1000
   c. <1000
   d. <>1000

8. Use the _____ button to create a report with grouped data.
   a. XPS or PDF
   b. Query
   c. Theme
   d. Group & Sort

9. Which button changes the print orientation from the default setting of portrait orientation?
   a. Group & Sort
   b. Themes
   c. Landscape
   d. Print

10. Which view do you use to change the print orientation?
    a. Form view
    b. Datasheet view
    c. Print Preview view
    d. Design view

Hands-On Skills Review

Exercise **Summarizing Store Events—Jewelry Store Database**

Grade It

Skills   Use the Query Wizard, create a report, and preview a report

Scenario   You need to find out about all upcoming sale events and review the featured sale item for each event. You query the jewelry store database to find this information.

Steps

1. Open the student data file named **M7-C3-ExA-Jewelry.accdb** and save the file as **Lastname-M7-C3-ExA-Jewelry**, but replace *Lastname* with your last name.

2. Click *Events* in the Table group in the Navigation pane.

3. Use the Query Wizard to create a simple query that lists the *Event* and the *SaleItem* fields, in that order.

4. Save the query, naming it *Events Query*.

5. Close the Events Query query.

6. Click *Events Query* in the Queries group in the Navigation pane.

7. Using the Report button, create a report based on the Events Query query. **HINT:** *If Events Query does not immediately appear in the Queries group in the Navigation pane, close and then reopen* **Lastname-M7-C3-ExA-Jewelry.accdb**.

8 Save the report, naming it *Events Query*.

9 Print the Events Query report or submit the completed database as directed by your instructor.

10 Close the Events Query report and then the database.

Events Query Query

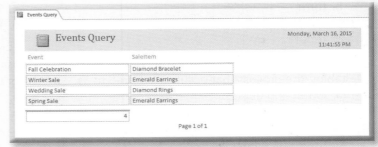

Events Query Report

Exercise B Finding Information in a Bookstore Database

Skills Create a query in Design view, use more than one table in a query, create a report, and preview a report

Scenario You are the manager of a bookstore. You need to query the database to find all orders over $500 and then create a report based on the query.

Steps

1 Open the student data file named **M7-C3-ExB-Books.accdb** and save the file as **Lastname-M7-C3-ExB-Books**, but replace *Lastname* with your last name.

2 Query the database to find all orders over $500. Add the Orders table and then the Suppliers table to create your query in Design view. The query should display the *OrderID*, *ContactName*, *SupplierName*, and *OrderTotal* fields, in the order listed.

3 Save the query, naming it *Orders over $500*, and then close the query. Run the query to confirm that it is selecting the correct records.

4 Create a report based on the Orders over $500 query. **HINT:** *If* Orders over $500 *does not immediately appear in the Queries group*

in the Navigation pane, close and then reopen **Lastname-M7-Ce-ExB-Books.accdb**.

5 Modify the report to sort by the *OrderTotal* field.

6 AutoFit the *OrderTotal Total* cell. **HINT:** *Use the double-click method described in Step 10 of Skill 4.*

7 Save the report, naming it *Orders over $500*.

8 Use the Print Preview feature to preview the report before printing it.

9 Print the Orders over $500 report or submit the completed database as directed by your instructor.

10 Close the Orders over $500 report and then the database.

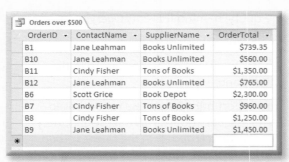

Orders over $500 Query

Orders over $500 Report

Exercise C Finding and Reporting Information from the Community Volunteers Database

Skills   Create a query in Design view, use more than one table in a query, create a report, and preview a report

Scenario   You have set up a database to track student community service hours. You first find out how many hours students are volunteering at the various organizations and then present this information in a report.

Steps

1 Open the student data file named **M7-C3-ExC-CommunityService.accdb** and save the file as **Lastname-M7-C3-ExC-CommunityService**, but replace *Lastname* with your last name.

2 Query the database to find out how many student hours are being spent at each organization. In Design view, add the Organizations table and then the Volunteer Hours table to create your query. The query should display the *OrganizationName* (from the Organizations table), *StudentID*, and *Hours* fields, in the order listed.

3 Save the query, naming it *Volunteer Hours by Organization*, and then close the query. Run the query to confirm that it is selecting the correct records.

4 Use the Report button to create a report based on the Volunteer Hours by Organization query. **HINT:** *If* Volunteer Hours by Organization *does not immediately appear in the Queries group in the Navigation pane, close and then reopen* **Lastname-M7-C3-ExC-CommunityService.accdb**.

5 Modify the report to group by the *OrganizationName* field.

6 Modify the report to sort by the *Hours* field.

7 Save the report, naming it *Volunteer Hours by Organization*.

8 Use the Print Preview feature to preview the report before printing it.

9 Print the Volunteer Hours by Organization report or submit the completed document as directed by your instructor.

10 Close the Volunteer Hours by Organization report and then the database.

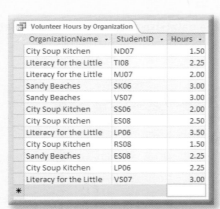

Volunteer Hours by Organization Query

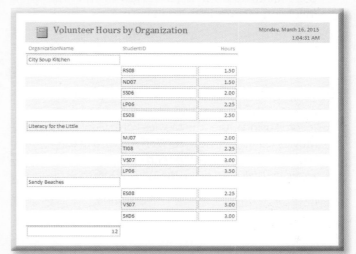

Volunteer Hours by Organization Report

Module 7 Projects

Project 1

Skills   **CH1:** Open and navigate a database, enter data **CH2:** Create a table, enter data in a table, create a form, enter data in a form **CH3:** Create a query in Design view, create a report, preview a report

Scenario   You manage a movie rental store. You have created a database to store data on each of the store's movies. You now need to create a table to store the information about each movie and then create a form to enter records in the database.

Steps

1   Open the student data file named **M7-EOM-P1-Movie.accdb** and save the file as **Lastname-M7-EOM-P1-Movie**, but replace *Lastname* with your last name.

2   Create a new table in Design view.

3   Define the table to have the following fields and data types:

Field Name	Data Type
ID	Number
Title	Short Text
Rating	Short Text

4   Save and close the table, naming it *Movies*. Do not add a primary key.

5   Use the Form button to create a form based on the Movies table.

6   Use the Date and Time button to add the date and time to the form.

7   Save the form, naming it *Movies*.

8   Use the Movies form in Form view to enter the following records in the database:

ID	Title	Rating
3155	Unstoppable	PG-13
3479	Morning Glory	PG-13

9   The movie rental store stocks many duplicate copies of the same movie. Enter the rest of the records using either the Movies Form view or the Movies Datasheet view. ***HINT:*** *If you wish to use copy and paste to save time and avoid data entry errors, you will need to use the Movies Datasheet view.*

ID	Title	Rating
3480	Morning Glory	PG-13
3455	Skyline	PG-13
3466	Skyline	PG-13
3467	Skyline	PG-13
3877	Cool It	PG
3878	Cool It	PG
3901	The Next 3 Days	PG-13

ID	Title	Rating
3902	The Next 3 Days	PG-13
4011	Red	PG-13
4012	Red	PG-13
4015	Toy Story 3	G
4016	Toy Story 3	G
4017	Toy Story 3	G

10   In Design view, create a query to find all movies rated PG-13. Display the fields *Title* and then *Rating* in your query.

11   Save the query, naming it *PG-13 Movies*.

12   Ask your instructor if you should print a copy of the query. Close the query.

13   Use the Report button to create a report based on the PG-13 Movies query.

14   Sort the report in ascending order by the *Title* field.

15   Group the report by the *Title* field.

16   Save the report, naming it *PG-13 Movies*, and then close the report..

17   Ask your instructor if you should print a copy of the report.

18   Close the database and submit the completed file as directed by your instructor.

PG-13 Movies Query

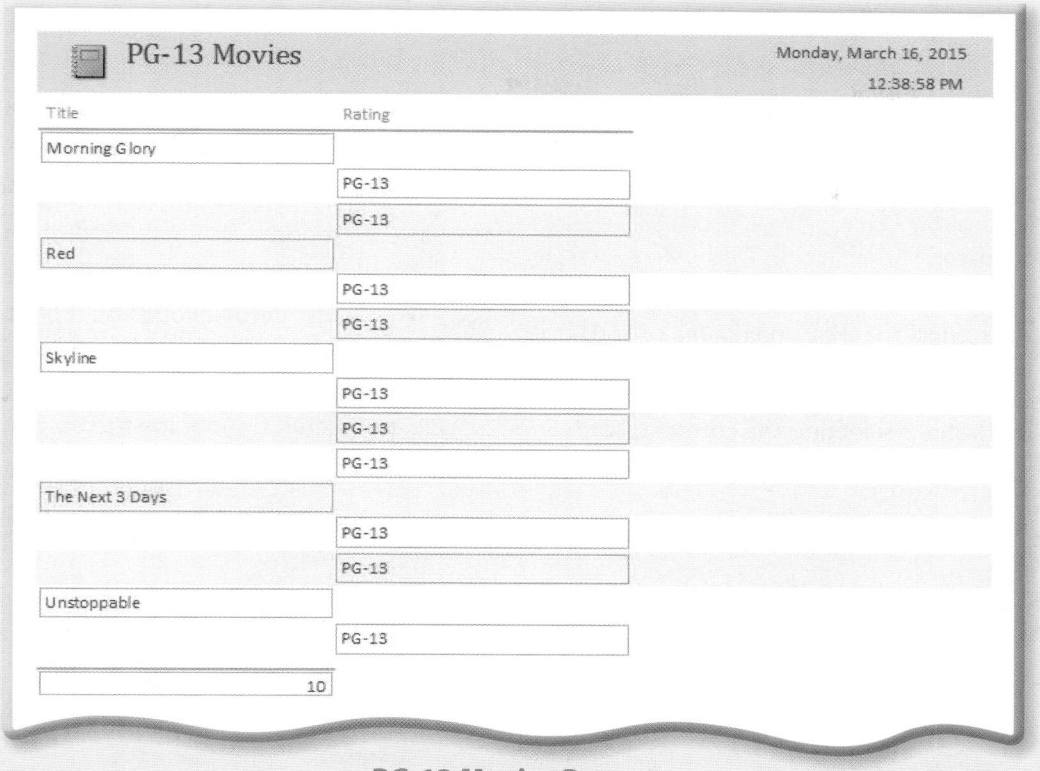

PG-13 Movies Report

Project 2

Skills **CH1:** Open and navigate a database, enter data, use existing queries and reports **CH2:** Create a table, enter data in a table, create a form, enter data in a form **CH3:** Create a query in Design view, create a report, preview a report

Scenario You run a computer-support website. Users pay either a six-month fee of $60.00 or an annual fee of $120.00 to have access to online computer help. You need to create a table in your database to store information about your subscribers.

Steps

1 Open the student data file named **M7-EOM-P2-ComputerSupport.accdb** and save the file as **Lastname-M7-EOM-P2-ComputerSupport**, but replace *Lastname* with your last name.

2 Create a new table in Design view.

3 Define the table to have the following fields and data types:

Field Name	Data Type
ID	Number
LastName	Short Text
FirstName	Short Text
JoinMonth	Short Text
Fee	Currency

4 Save the table, naming it *Customers*. Do not add a primary key. Close the table.

5 Use the Form button to create a form based on the Customers table.

6 Use the Date and Time button to add the date and time to the form.

7 In Form Layout view, press and drag the right border of each entry box to the left until the boxes are about half their original size.

8 Save the form, naming it *Customers*.

9 Use the Customers form in Form view to enter the following records in the database:

ID	LastName	FirstName	JoinMonth	Fee
5155	Mitchell	Paul	September	120.00
5167	Ableson	Michelle	October	60.00
5169	Quinn	Terry	October	60.00
5170	Samuels	Jennifer	November	60.00
5180	Watson	Robert	November	120.00
5290	Simpson	Ann	December	120.00
5400	Gregory	Michaela	December	60.00

10 Use the Query Design button to create a query of all customers that have paid a fee of $60.00. Display the *LastName*, *FirstName*, and *Fee* fields, in that order, in the query. Run the query to confirm that it is selecting the correct records.

11 Save the query, naming it *$60 Customers*, and close the query.

12 Ask your instructor if you should print a copy of the query.

13 Use the Report button to create a report based on the $60 Customers query.

14 Sort the report based on the *LastName* field.

15 Save the report, naming it *$60 Customers*, and close the report.

16 Ask your instructor if you should print a copy of the query.

17 Close the database and submit the completed file as directed by your instructor.

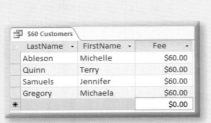

$60 Customers Query

$60 Customers Report

Project 3

Skills   **CH1:** Open and navigate a database, enter data, use existing queries and reports **CH2:** Create a table, enter data in a table, create a form, enter data in a form **CH3:** Create a query in Design view, create a report, preview a report

Scenario   You run a car rental company. You need to add a table to the database to store information about your car inventory. You then add records to the table.

Steps

1 Open the student data file named **M7-EOM-P3-Cars.accdb** and save the file as **Lastname-M7-EOM-P3-Cars**, but replace *Lastname* with your last name.

2 Create a new table in Design view.

3 Define the table to have the following fields and data types.

Field Name	Data Type
CarYear	Number
Model	Short Text
Make	Short Text
Color	Short Text
Mileage	Number

4 Save the table, naming it *Cars*. Do not add a primary key to the table. Close the table.

5 Use the Form button to create a form based on the Cars table.

6 Use the Date and Time button to add the date and time to the form.

7 In Form Layout view press and drag the right border of each entry box to the left until the boxes are about half their original size.

8 Save the form, naming it *Cars*.

9 Use the Cars form in Form view to enter the following records in the database:

CarYear	Model	Make	Color	Mileage
2012	Ford	Fiesta	Red	37295
2012	Ford	Fiesta	Blue	12000
2013	Honda	Civic	Brown	10000
2013	Honda	Civic	Black	12000
2013	Chevy	Cruze	Black	8550
2013	Chevy	Cruze	White	22000

10 Use the Query Design button to create a detail query of all 2013 cars. Display the *CarYear*, *Model*, *Make*, and *Mileage* fields, in the order listed, in the query.

11 Finish the query, naming it *2013 Cars*.

12 Ask your instructor if you should print a copy of the query.

13 Use the Report button to create a report based on the Cars table.

14 Change the report title to *Car Inventory*. **HINT:** *Double-click the title,* Cars, *to edit the report title.*

15 Sort the report based on the *Mileage* field.

16 Use the PAGE SETUP tab to change the page orientation to landscape.

17 Save the report, naming it *Car Inventory*, and close the report.

18 Ask your instructor if you should print a copy of the report.

19 Close the database and submit the completed file as directed by your instructor.

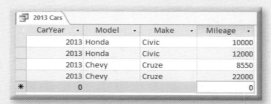

2013 Cars Query

Car Inventory Report

MODULE 8

Microsoft PowerPoint 2013

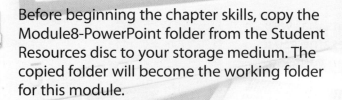

Before beginning the chapter skills, copy the Module8-PowerPoint folder from the Student Resources disc to your storage medium. The copied folder will become the working folder for this module.

Guidelines for Creating a

Before you begin to create a PowerPoint presentation, you should have a focused topic, have a clear purpose, and know who your audience will be. Ask yourself how much your audience members are likely to know about your topic, what they might do with the information, and whether they would appreciate humor, for example.

A well-organized slide show helps you lead your audience to your presentation's goal. That goal may be to get them to take an action, such as joining a group or buying something, or it may be to give them the information they need to do their job, achieve a goal, or accomplish a task.

Hand-Drawn Storyboard

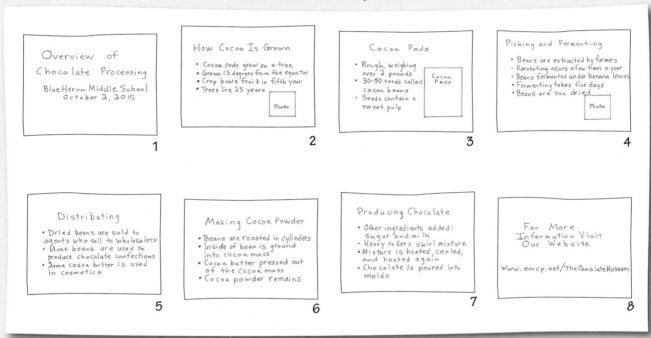

You should have a basic idea of how to organize the information in your presentation. To work out the best flow for the information, you might draw a quick storyboard (a tool used by many filmmakers), making brief notes and sketches on paper, by hand. Or you might even use PowerPoint itself to create the storyboard on slides, later refining those storyboard slides into polished content.

PowerPoint provides different layouts that you can use for different purposes. For example, use a Title Slide layout for the first slide in your show.

Title Slide Layout

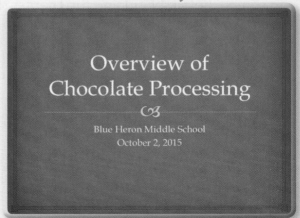

PowerPoint Presentation

Use Content layouts such as Title and Content, Two Content, and Content with Caption to provide concise bullet points or to insert graphics, videos, or photos for visual interest and richer communication.

Title and Content Layout

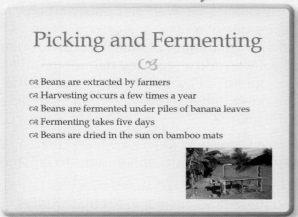

It is generally best to include no more than six bullet points per slide, and keep them brief—fitting on a single line when possible. Bullet points guide the audience through the presentation and don't need to spell out every detail. The speaker's words are the focus and should provide the full story.

While you don't want to crowd your slides with information, you also don't want to overuse graphic elements and animations. These features, used sparingly, can provide interest and entertain. But if overdone, they can distract viewers from the speaker's message (and greatly increase file size).

You can keep the look of your slides consistent by using a built-in design. If you modify the design, a good tip is to avoid using more than two fonts on a single slide and two or three fonts in the entire presentation.

Set up your slide show either to be given in person and navigated manually (reflected by the options chosen in the Set Up Show dialog box shown below) or to run automatically with saved timings and a recorded narration when there is no speaker present.

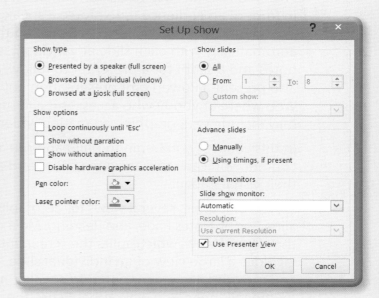

When running a show in Slide Show view, take advantage of presentation tools in the Slide Show control bar in the lower left corner of the slide. Always rehearse your show to help avoid technical problems and to make sure the show runs within your allotted time slot, allowing time for audience questions.

Slide Show View

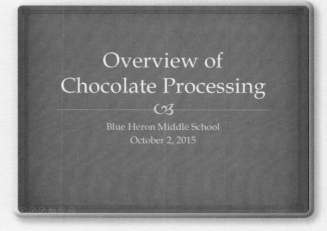

Creating a Presentation

PowerPoint is an easy-to-use presentation program for creating slide shows that can be run in front of an audience to reinforce a speaker's key points. A PowerPoint presentation can be run manually with a person advancing the slides one at a time, or it can be set up to run automatically with each slide advancing itself after a set amount of time. You can include notes and a script for a presenter to follow, and you can add a recorded narration. You can also present a PowerPoint presentation online or publish a PowerPoint slide show to the Web where anybody who accesses it can run the presentation at their convenience. Slides may include text, graphics, animation, videos, and sound.

In this chapter, you begin to build and run a simple slide show. Once you have created slide content, you can reorganize the slides and apply different layouts and designs to enhance their visual impact.

PowerPoint offers several views for accomplishing these tasks, including Normal, Outline, Slide Sorter, Notes Page, and Reading. Most of your work building a slide show is done using the Normal view, which splits the screen into three main sections, or panes. The *slide pane* includes a large view of an individual slide, the smaller *notes pane* is below the slide pane and provides an area for entering speaker notes, and the left side panel is called the *slide thumbnails pane*. You will probably use the slide thumbnails pane on a regular basis. You can click a slide thumbnail and view the corresponding slide in the larger slide pane.

In this chapter, you also work with Outline view and Slide Sorter view. When you view a presentation in Outline view, the outline pane displays the text contained on each slide in an outline or storyboard format. Slide Sorter view is the best view to use for organizing your presentation.

Skills You Learn

1 Open PowerPoint and insert a slide
2 Enter text on slides
3 Use the Outline feature
4 Add notes
5 Apply a layout
6 Apply a theme
7 Organize slides using the Slide Sorter feature

Files You Need

For these skills, you need the following student data files.

M8-C1-S4-FairTrade.pptx

M8-C1-S7-FairTrade.pptx

What You Create

The cocoa-growing industry is spread throughout several countries around the world. Because of its geographical range, the industry has varying standards for how growers get paid and how workers are treated. "Fair trade" is a term for an industry standard that requires that growers be paid fairly for what they grow and that workers are treated well.

In this chapter, you create a simple PowerPoint presentation on fair trade in the chocolate industry. Your presentation will be used to inform the public and gain funding for The Chocolate Museum. You create slides; enter text; organize the presentation; and use layouts, designs, and color schemes to add visual appeal.

Fair Trade Presentation

PowerPoint

Skill 1

Open PowerPoint and Insert a Slide

Video M8_C1_S01

When you open PowerPoint, you can create a blank presentation or select a presentation template. A blank presentation contains a single title slide and is displayed in Normal view. Most slides contain placeholders into which you can enter text. A title slide contains a title placeholder, with the text *Click to add title*, and a subtitle placeholder, with the text *Click to add subtitle*. When you insert a new slide, by default it has a Title and Content layout, which includes a title placeholder and a content placeholder. The content placeholder contains a bullet symbol and the words *Click to add text*, as well as buttons that can be clicked to add other objects, such as charts or videos, to the slide.

Steps

▶**Tip** You can access the Charms bar from any screen by moving your mouse pointer to the upper right corner of the screen.

1-4 *Another Way*
You may have a PowerPoint 2013 tile on the Start screen. If you do, you can click this tile to start PowerPoint.

1 Press Win + C to display the Charms bar.

2 Click the Search charm.

3 Type PowerPoint.

4 Click *PowerPoint 2013* in the Apps results list to display the PowerPoint landing page.

5 Click *Blank Presentation*. A blank presentation opens in Normal view with the HOME tab displayed.

6 *Shortcut*
Insert New Slide
Ctrl + M

6 *Another Way*
Right-click a thumbnail on the left side of the Normal view and choose *New Slide* from the menu that appears.

6 Click the New Slide button in the Slides group on the HOME tab. The new slide appears with a title placeholder on top and a content placeholder below.

7 Click the FILE tab.

8 Click the *Save As* option to display the Save As backstage area.

9 Browse to your Module 8 working folder on your storage medium, type M8-C1-S1-FairTrade in the *File name* text box, and then click Save.

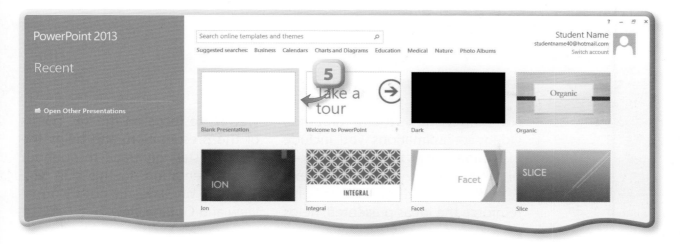

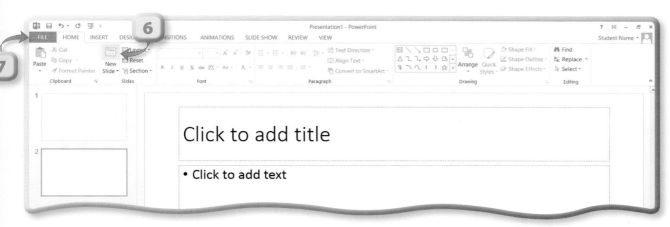

Taking It Further

Using a Template When you open PowerPoint, the page you see is sometimes referred to as a landing page. On this page, you can select from a variety of templates that are preformatted, allowing you to quickly create a professional looking presentation. If you do not see a template you want to use, you can type search criteria in the *Search online templates and themes* text box. Suggested search criteria, such as *Business and Photo Albums*, is listed under the search text box to help you find what you are looking for.

PowerPoint

Skill 2

Enter Text on Slides

Video M8_C1_S02

No matter how many graphics, videos, or animations you include in a slide show, the heart of your presentation is often the text. Text that you enter on slides helps reinforce the ideas presented, helps viewers to focus on the key points of the presentation, and helps the speaker stay on track throughout the presentation. In this skill, you add text on slides in both Normal view and Outline view.

Steps

1 If it is not already open, open **M8-C1-S1-FairTrade.pptx**, the file you saved in the previous skill, and save the file as **M8-C1-S2-FairTrade**. Be sure to save the file in your Module 8 working folder.

2 If the first slide does not already appear in the slide pane, click the first thumbnail in the slide thumbnails pane.

> **Tip** If you do not see the slide thumbnails pane in your presentation, click the VIEW tab and then click the Normal button in the Presentation Views group.

3 In the slide pane, click anywhere in the title placeholder text *Click to add title* and then type Fair Trade and Chocolate.

4 In the slide pane, click in the subtitle placeholder text *Click to add subtitle* and then type Promoting a Fair and Sustainable Industry.

5 Click Slide 2 in the slide thumbnails pane to display that slide in the slide pane.

6 In the slide pane, click in the title placeholder and type What is Fair Trade?

> **Tip** You press Enter to start a new bullet point in a content placeholder, but there is no need to press Enter in other types of placeholders. PowerPoint automatically wraps text to fit within the placeholder width, expanding its height as needed.

7 Click in the content placeholder (formatted as a bulleted list by default) and enter the following text, pressing the Enter key after each line as indicated:

Above-market prices to growers [Enter]

No slavery used in production of cocoa [Enter]

Sustainable practices [Enter]

Benefits to trading partners' communities

> **Tip** If you accidently press Enter after typing the last bullet point, press Ctrl + Z or Backspace to undo the action.

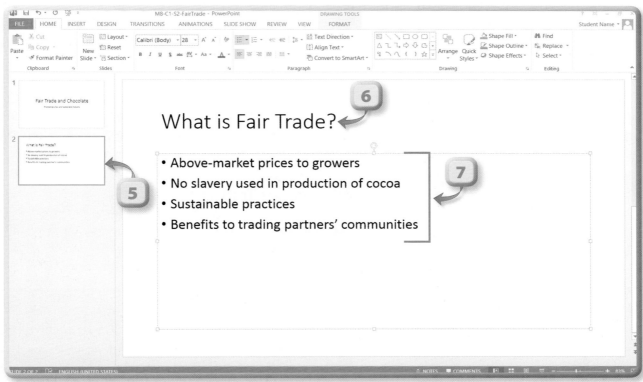

More

8 Click the FILE tab.

9 Click the *Save* option.

10 Click the SLIDE SHOW tab.

11 *Shortcut*
Start Slide Show from Beginning
F5

11 Click the From Beginning button in the Start Slide Show group. This starts the slide show and the first slide fills your screen.

12 *Another Way*
Press the Page Down key, Down Arrow key, Right Arrow key, or Enter key to advance to the next slide.

12 Click your mouse to advance to Slide 2.

13 Click your mouse to advance to the end of the presentation.

14 At the screen that reads *End of slide show, click to exit*, click your mouse once to return to Normal view.

Fair Trade and Chocolate
Promoting a Fair and Sustainable Industry

What Is Fair Trade?

- Above-market prices to growers
- No slavery used in production of cocoa
- Sustainable practices
- Benefits to trading partners' communities

Completed Skill 2

Taking It Further

Exploring PowerPoint Views You can look at your PowerPoint slides in a number of different views, including Normal, Outline, Slide Sorter, Notes Page, and Reading. Normal view is the default view and is typically where a presentation is created. Outline view is used to create an outline or storyboard for your presentation. Slide Sorter view displays all the slides in the presentation on one screen as thumbnails. This view is often used to rearrange the order of slides. Notes Page view displays the current slide with any added notes below it. You can add or edit notes in Normal view, Outline view, or Notes Page view. Reading view displays the slides in full-screen view and is often used to review a presentation. There are also three Master views, which are used to create style changes to every slide in your presentation. You can change views using buttons on the VIEW tab. You can also change to Normal, Slide Sorter, Reading, or Slide Show view by using the following buttons in the view area of the Status bar: ▣ ▦ ▥ ▼. If you do not see these buttons, right-click the Status bar and click to insert a check mark beside each of these options.

PowerPoint

PowerPoint

Skill 3

Use the Outline Feature

 Video M8_C1_S03

When you are primarily focused on adding text rather than visual elements to your presentation, using Outline view is helpful. Outline view is used to create an outline for your presentation. This feature allows you to organize your ideas, enter text, promote lines of text to a higher level, demote lines of text to a lower level, and move content around a slide or among slides. In Outline view, the highest level heading is the slide title, which marks the start of a new slide.

Steps

1 If it is not already open, open **M8-C1-S2-FairTrade.pptx**, the file you saved in the previous skill, and save the file as **Lastname-M8-C1-S3-FTTitleSlide**, but replace *Lastname* with your last name. Be sure to save the file in your Module 8 working folder on your storage medium.

2 Click the VIEW tab.

3 Click the Outline View button.

4 In Slide 2 in the outline pane, click to the right of the last bullet point, *Benefits to trading partners' communities*.

5 Press Enter. The insert point moves to a new bullet on Slide 2.

6-7 *Another Way*
Right-click the line and then click *Promote* at the shortcut menu.

6 Click the HOME tab.

7 *Shortcut*
Promote a Line
Shift + Tab

7 Click the Decrease List Level button in the Paragraph group. The line is promoted to the highest level, creating a new slide.

▶**Tip** Text typed at the highest level of the outline appears in the title placeholder in the slide pane.

8 Type The Global Nature of Chocolate Growing.

9 Press Enter. The insertion point moves to a new Slide 4.

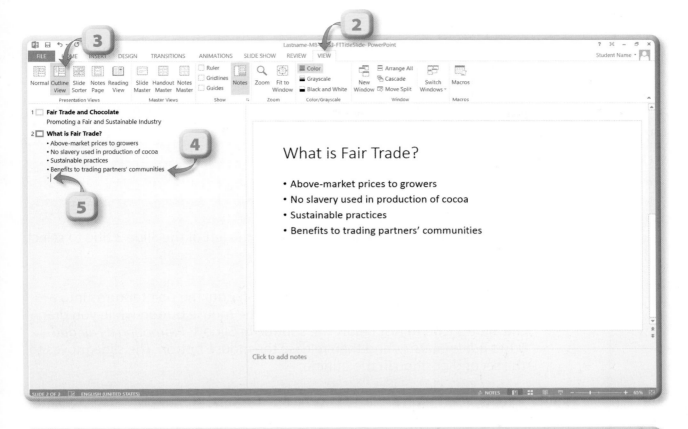

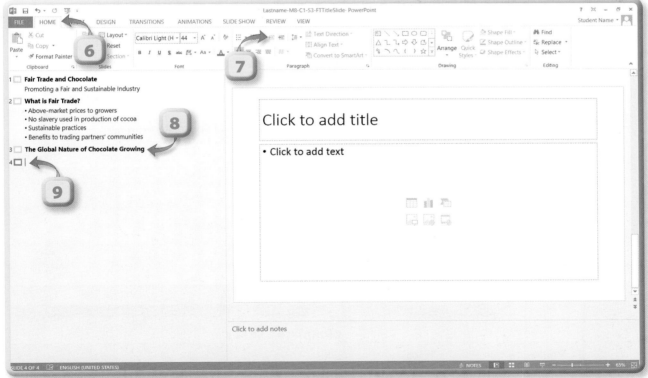

More

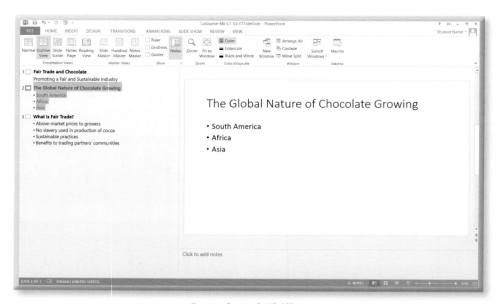 **Shortcut**
Demote a Line
Tab

▶**Tip** PowerPoint
automatically formats the
subtopics within outlines
as bulleted points.

10 Click the Increase List Level button in the Paragraph group on the HOME tab. The insertion point is demoted to a bullet point on Slide 3.

11 Type the following text, pressing Enter as indicated to create new bullet points:

South America [Enter]
Africa [Enter]
Asia

12 In the outline pane, click the slide icon to the left of the Slide 3 title to select all the text on Slide 3.

13 Move the mouse pointer over the slide icon until the pointer turns into a four-headed arrow, click and hold down the mouse button while you drag the Slide 3 icon to just below the subtitle of Slide 1, *Promoting a Fair and Sustainable Industry,* and then release the mouse button. The slide moves to the second position in the outline.

14 Save and close the file.

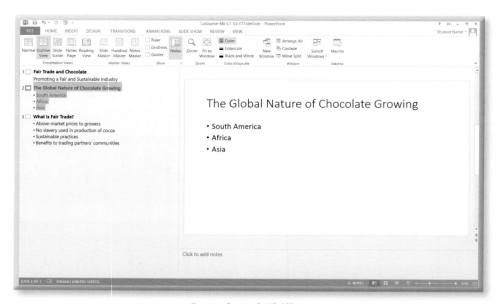

Completed Skill 3

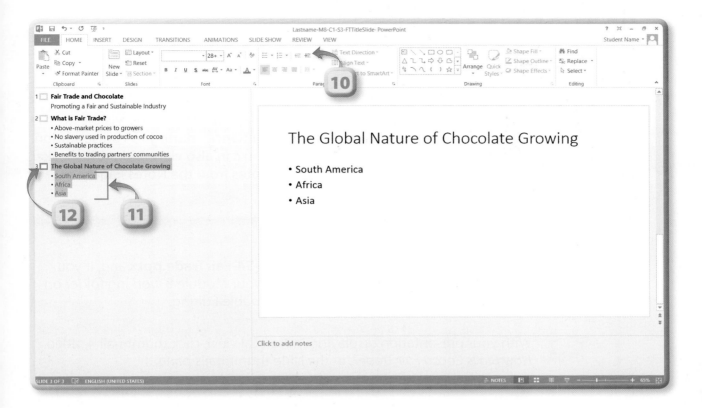

Taking It Further

Expanding and Collapsing Outlines

When you are working on a long presentation, the Expand or Collapse feature in the outline pane in Outline view can make it easier to view the slide information. This feature collapses the slide content in the outline pane, hiding subtopics from view when you double-click a slide icon. To reverse the process, double-click again and the subtopics display. You can also right-click anywhere in the outline pane in Outline view and choose *Collapse* or *Expand* from the shortcut menu that appears. You can then choose either to expand or collapse only the currently selected slide contents or to expand all or collapse all slides.

PowerPoint

Skill 4

Video ▶ M8_C1_S04

Add Notes

In the notes pane of PowerPoint's Normal, Outline, and Notes Page views, you can enter information that would be useful to a presenter but that will not be visible to the audience during a presentation. You can also view and print speaker notes from the Notes Page view.

Steps

1 Open the student data file named **M8-C1-S4-FairTrade.pptx** and, if you have not already done so, save the file in your Module 8 working folder on your storage medium. If necessary, click Enable Editing.

2 With your presentation displaying in Normal view, click thumbnail 4, titled *How Big Is Cocoa Fair Trade?*, in the slide thumbnails pane.

▶ **Tip** If the notes pane is not displayed, click the NOTES button on the Status bar.

▶ **Tip** Enlarge the notes pane when in Normal view by clicking the line dividing it from the slide pane and dragging upward.

3 Click in the notes pane (where the placeholder reads *Click to add notes*) and type the text Ten origins for cocoa include Ghana, Ecuador, Bolivia, and the Dominican Republic.

4 Click Slide 5 in the slide thumbnails pane.

5 Click in the notes pane and type The ability to track beans to their origins ensures that chocolate flavors are pure and authentic.

6 Click the Notes Page button in the Presentation Views group on the VIEW tab. This displays Slide 5 along with the associated note.

7 *Another Way*
Click the Normal button 🔲 in the view area of the Status bar.

7 Click the Normal button to return to Normal view.

8 Save the file.

Completed Skill 4

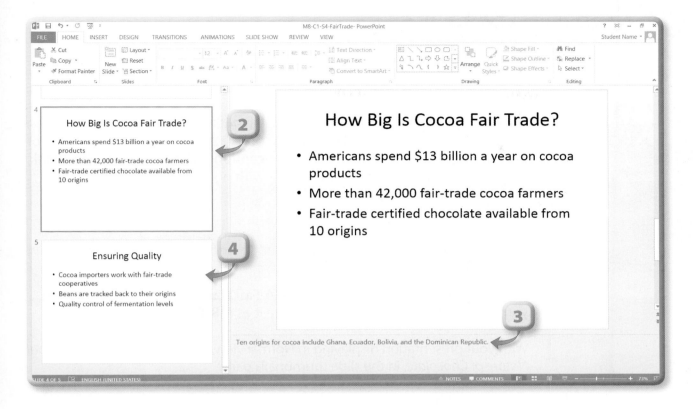

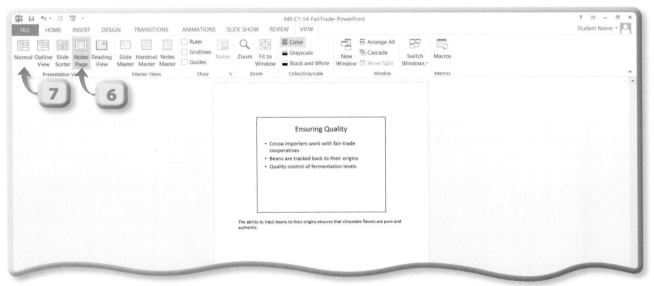

Taking It Further

Using Notes What kind of information might you include in notes? A good rule of thumb is to include only key points on your slides and place supporting points or speaker notes in the notes pane. Many presenters write out information like statistics or quotes to help them through their presentation. Other presenters write out their entire speech for each slide. You might also include links to websites or articles you have used for research in case your audience requests additional information or asks for the source of your data. Presenters using multiple screens can choose to open notes on the nonprojecting screen during the presentation.

PowerPoint

Apply a Layout

The way in which placeholders are arranged on a slide is known as a *layout*. You can apply an existing layout to a new slide or design your own layout for the material.

Layouts can include titles, subtitles, one or two content placeholders, or captions. They can even be blank, with no placeholders.

Steps

1 If it is not already open, open **M8-C1-S4-FairTrade.pptx**, the presentation you saved in the previous skill, and save it as **M8-C1-S5-FairTrade**.

2 With your presentation displaying in Normal view, click Slide 2, titled *The Global Nature of Chocolate*, in the slide thumbnails pane.

3 Click the HOME tab.

4 Click the Layout button in the Slides group.

5 Click the *Two Content* option at the drop-down gallery. This adds a content placeholder to the right side of Slide 2.

6 In the slide pane, click in the content placeholder at the right and type
Europe is the largest cocoa-processing region [Enter]
Local markets dictate taxes and currency fluctuations

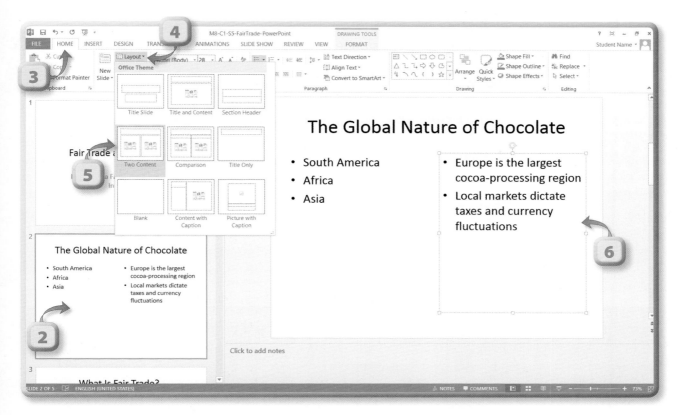

More

Taking It Further

Working with Placeholders The predefined layouts in PowerPoint contain a variety of placeholders, such as title, content, and caption. If you can't find a predefined layout that works for your slide, you can insert a text box to create a placeholder. To insert a text box, click the Text Box button in the Text group on the INSERT tab, click a blank area of the slide, and then drag to create the text box. You can then add content and drag the placeholder to an appropriate location on the slide. You can also delete a placeholder from a slide; however, blank placeholders are not visible during the viewing of a presentation. ***NOTE:*** *If you add a text box and text, the contents of the text box do not appear in Outline view.*

Tip If you click the New Slide button rather than the button arrow, a new slide is inserted with the same layout as the slide before it. Clicking the arrow on the New Slide button allows you to select from a gallery of slide layout options.

7 In the slide thumbnails pane, click Slide 5, titled *Ensuring Quality*.

8 In the Slides group on the HOME tab, click the New Slide button arrow.

9 Click the *Picture with Caption* option to insert a new Slide 6 with that layout.

10 In the slide pane, click the *Click to add title* placeholder and then type Map of global cocoa markets.

11 Save the file.

Completed Skill 5

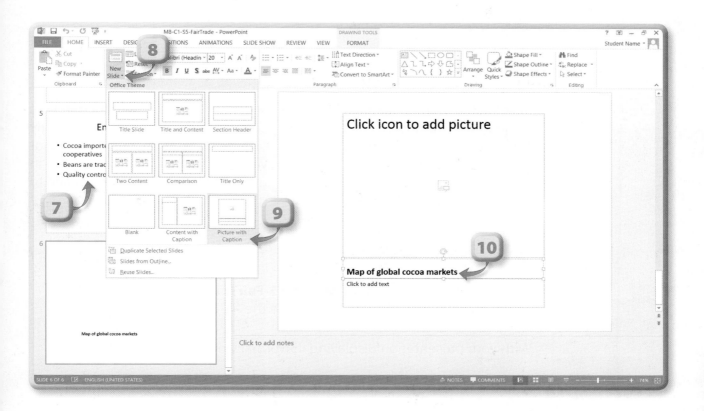

PowerPoint

PowerPoint

Video ▶ M8_C1_S06

Apply a Theme

Just as the Layout feature controls the type and number of placeholders on slides, the Themes feature controls a slide's colors, fonts, and graphical elements. You can apply a theme to all slides or to individual slides in a presentation. You can also apply more than one theme in a presentation, but do so sparingly to avoid a disconnected look. Color variations of each theme, located in the Variants group, can be applied to give the theme a different look.

Steps

1 If it is not already open, open **M8-C1-S5-FairTrade.pptx**, the presentation you saved in the previous skill, and save the file as **M8-C1-S6-FairTrade**.

2 With your presentation displaying in Normal view, click the DESIGN tab.

▶**Tip** After the first design theme (Office), the design themes are listed in alphabetical order.

3 Find the Facet design theme by hovering your mouse pointer over the themes in the Themes group. As the mouse pointer moves over a theme option, the theme's name displays and the theme is previewed on the current slide in the slide pane.

4 Click the *Facet* theme to apply it to all slides in the presentation.

5 In the Variants group, click the blue color variation of the Facet design theme.

▶**Tip** The variant color theme selected will determine the suggested theme colors. You can see the suggested colors by selecting a text box and then clicking the Font Color button in the Font group on the HOME tab.

6 In the slide thumbnails pane, click Slide 1.

7 Click the More arrow at the right side of the *Themes* gallery to display all built-in themes.

8 Right-click *Office Theme* (the first option) and then click *Apply to Selected Slides*.

9 Save and close the presentation.

Completed Skill 6

Taking It Further

Finding Themes Online   While many attractive themes are built in to PowerPoint, to give your presentation a unique look, you can find additional themes online. Go to office.microsoft.com/en-us/templates and search for PowerPoint themes to explore more options for your presentations.

PowerPoint

PowerPoint

Skill 7   **Organize Slides Using the Slide Sorter Feature**

 M8_C1_S07

The best view for reorganizing slides is Slide Sorter view. This view presents thumbnail images of your slides in rows and columns so you can view several at once and think about your options for organizing them. You can drag slides from one position to another in the Slide Sorter view and determine the best arrangement for your presentation.

Steps

1 Open the student data file named **M8-C1-S7-FairTrade.pptx** and save the file as **Lastname-M8-C1-S7-FairTrade**, but replace *Lastname* with your last name. Be sure to save the file in your Module 8 working folder on your storage medium.

2 With your presentation displaying in Normal view, click the VIEW tab.

3 Click the Slide Sorter button in the Presentation Views group.

4 Press and hold down the mouse button on Slide 9, titled *MAP OF GLOBAL COCOA MARKETS* (when selected, the slide appears with an orange border) and then drag the slide to the space between Slide 2 and Slide 3. (Slide 3 and all following slides will move to make room for Slide 9.)

5 Release the mouse button to place the slide in the new position. Notice that the slides renumber.

> **Tip** Use the Shift key to select multiple, contiguous slides. Use the Ctrl key to select noncontiguous slides.

6 Click Slide 7, press and hold down the Shift key, and then click Slide 8. Both Slides 7 and 8 are now selected.

> **Tip** Using the Shift key to select multiple slides is commonly called Click, Shift-Click.

7 Click and drag one of the selected slides to the space between Slide 3 and Slide 4 and then release the mouse button.

8 Click Slide 1 to select it.

> **Tip** You can also delete a slide or add a new slide while in Slide Sorter view. Right-click a slide and select *Delete Slide* or *New Slide*.

9 Click the HOME tab.

10 *Another Way*
Right-click the slide in the slide thumbnails pane and then click *Duplicate Slide*.

10 Click the Copy button arrow in the Clipboard group and then click *Duplicate*.

11 Click and drag the new Slide 2 to the end of the presentation and then release the mouse button.

10 *Shortcut*
Duplicate Slide
Ctrl + D

12 Save and close the file.

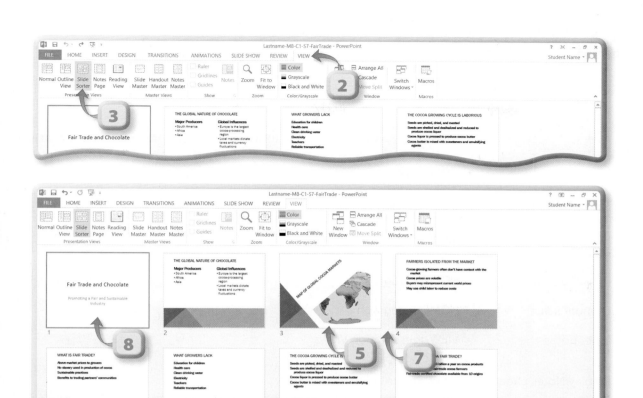

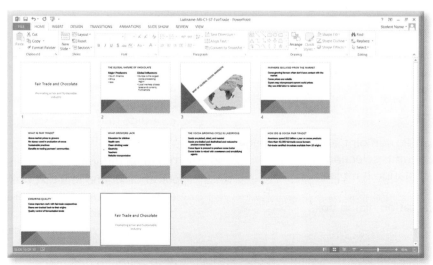

Completed Skill 7

PowerPoint

Tasks Summary

Task	Ribbon Tab, Group	Button, Option	Shortcut, Alternative
Insert a new slide	HOME, Slides		Ctrl + M
Save a presentation	Quick Access Toolbar		Ctrl + S, FILE, *Save As*
Display slide thumbnails pane	VIEW, Presentation Views		
Promote a line	HOME, Paragraph		Shift + Tab
Demote a line	HOME, Paragraph		Tab
Enter notes	VIEW, Presentation Views		
Display Notes page	VIEW, Presentation Views		
Apply a Layout	HOME, Slides		
Apply a design theme	DESIGN, Themes		
Apply a color theme variant	DESIGN, Variants		
Display Slide Sorter view	VIEW, Presentation Views		
Duplicate slides	HOME, Clipboard	Copy, *Duplicate*	Ctrl + D

Features Review

Select the best answer from the choices given.

1 To access the New Slide button, display this tab.
   a. INSERT
   b. VIEW
   c. HOME
   d. SLIDE SHOW

2 When you start PowerPoint, an opening page appears that permits selection of the
   a. Blank Presentation template.
   b. HOME tab.
   c. New Presentation dialog box.
   d. FILE tab.

3 A content placeholder is formatted to contain this by default.
   a. a numbered list
   b. clip art
   c. a slide title
   d. a bulleted list

4 The main difference between text entered in a placeholder and in a text box is that text in a
   a. text box does not appear in the outline.
   b. placeholder does not appear in the outline.
   c. text box is not automatically formatted with a font.
   d. There is no difference.

5 To enter text in a presentation, you can use the
   a. notes pane.
   b. Slide Sorter view.
   c. outline pane.
   d. notes pane, Slide Sorter view, and outline pane.

6 To demote a heading in the outline, press
   a. down arrow.
   b. Ctrl + D.
   c. Tab.
   d. Enter.

7 The notes pane appears in
   a. Slide Show view.
   b. Normal view.
   c. Slide Sorter view.
   d. Reading view.

8 Layouts can include
   a. content placeholders.
   b. title placeholders.
   c. subtitle placeholders.
   d. content, title, and subtitle placeholders.

9 Which is *not* true of themes?
   a. Themes provide colors, fonts, and graphical elements.
   b. Themes can be applied to all slides in a presentation.
   c. Only one theme can be applied to a presentation.
   d. Theme variants are available to modify the theme color scheme.

10 The best view to use to reorganize slides is the
   a. Reorganize Slides view.
   b. Normal view.
   c. Slide Sorter view.
   d. Slide Show view.

Hands-On Skills Review

Exercise **Prepare a Presentation about PowerPoint 2013**

Grade It

Skills   Open PowerPoint and insert a slide, enter text on slides, apply a layout, and organize slides using the Slide Sorter feature

Scenario   You want to revise a presentation so that it provides a few key points about PowerPoint 2013. Edit the file provided to improve the presentation.

Steps

1 Open the student data file named **M8-C1-ExA-AboutPowerPoint.pptx** and save the file as **Lastname-M8-C1-ExA-AboutPowerPoint**, but replace *Lastname* with your last name.

2 Enter your name and the current date in the subtitle placeholder on the first slide so the information appears on two separate lines.

3 At the end of the presentation, insert a new slide with a Two Content layout for the text.
   a. Type Features as the slide title.
   b. In the left column, type Objects as a first-level bullet. Under that bullet, type the following sub-bullets:
      Text
      Graphics
      Animation
      Videos
      Sound

   c. In the right column, type Views as a first-level bullet. Under that bullet, type the following sub-bullets:
      Normal
      Outline View
      Slide Sorter
      Notes Page
      Reading View

4 Review the slide order and reorganize the slides so they appear in the following sequence:
   Slide 1 *PowerPoint 2013*
   Slide 2 *Uses*
   Slide 3 *Features*
   Slide 4 *Text Is Important*

5 Save the file.

6 Preview the presentation. **HINT:** *Click the SLIDE SHOW tab and then click the From the Beginning button.*

7 Submit the completed presentation to your instructor.

Completed Exercise A

SNAP
Grade It

Exercise **B** **Prepare a Slide Show about Effective Presentations**

Skills   Enter text on slides, use the Outline feature, and apply a theme

Scenario   You are working on a presentation that will be delivered to your company's sales reps at the national sales meeting. This presentation will remind the reps how to make interesting and engaging presentations.

Steps

1   Open the student data file named **M8-C1-ExB-EffectivePresentations.pptx** and save the file as **Lastname-M8-C1-ExB-EffectivePresentations**, but replace *Lastname* with your last name.

2   Enter your name and the current date in the subtitle placeholder on the first slide so the information appears on separate lines.

3   In Slide 2, demote (increase the list level of) the four bullet points that follow the *Order the slides* bullet point and the one bullet point that follows *Storyboard*.

4   Apply the Organic theme to all slides.

5   Apply the fourth variant to all slides.

6   Save the presentation.

7   Preview the presentation.

8   Submit the completed presentation to your instructor.

Completed Exercise B

Exercise C Prepare a Slide Show about the Evolution of Phone Technology

Skills Enter text on slides, add notes, apply a theme, and organize slides using the Slide Sorter feature

Scenario You recently found an old rotary-style phone in your attic. This discovery prompted you to look at the changes in phone communications over the past years. You documented what you learned in a presentation. Finish the presentation by making it more eye-catching. Add the remaining speaker notes so you have discussion points.

Steps

1 Open the student data file named **M8-C1-ExC-PhoneChanges.pptx** and save the file as **Lastname-M8-C1-ExC-PhoneChanges**, but replace *Lastname* with your last name.

2 Enter your name and the current date in the subtitle placeholder on the first slide so the information appears on two separate lines.

3 In Slide 1, format *Phones through the Ages* to 32-point Calibri italic. **HINT:** *See Module 4, Skill 9, Use Formatting Tools, if you need a reminder of the procedure.*

4 Place the slides into the correct sequence: (1) *It's More Than Just Talk!*, (2) *Topics*, (3) *Dark Ages of Phones*, (4) *Dark Ages Start to Recede*, (5) *Heading Toward Enlightenment*, (6) *Current Age of Phones*, and (7) *Phones of the Future*.

5 Add the following bullet points to Slide 5, *Heading Toward Enlightenment:*
   Improving networks
   Smaller
   Lightweight
   One per person
   Replace land line?

6 Add the following speaker notes to Slide 3, *Dark Ages of Phones*:
   In the beginning, phones were installed in hallways in residential buildings. The phone and phone line were shared by all. Later, individual apartments and homes had a phone installed, but the phone number and the line were shared. This was called a party line. As additional phone service became available, each household had one or more individual phone lines and phone numbers.

7 Add a sentence to the end of the speaker notes for Slide 7, *Phones of the Future*:
   Let's ask the crystal ball!

8 Apply the Facet theme. Do not change the color scheme variant.

9 Save the file.

10 Preview the presentation.

11 Submit the completed presentation to your instructor.

Completed Exercise C

Chapter 2

Working with Slide Masters and Handouts

A presentation contains at least one slide master. The slide master stores details about the presentation's design theme including its slide layout and formatting. When you make a change to the slide master, that change is automatically applied to every slide in your presentation. For example, if you change the font color on the slide master, the font color will automatically change on all of the slides in your presentation. This can save you a lot of work because you only have to make the change on one slide as opposed to every slide in the presentation.

If you create a blank presentation, the Office Theme will be applied to the presentation's slide master. The Office Theme contains no background or graphics but does assign font formatting and layouts to all placeholders in the slide presentation. If you apply a different design theme, the slide master will contain the formatting and layout associated with the selected theme.

In this chapter, you will use Slide Master view to change formatting; insert a logo; and add a footer, text, and slide numbers. You will also change the formatting for a particular type of placeholder on all slides and hide master elements on individual slides.

This chapter focuses primarily on formatting slides using the slide master, but features of the handout master and notes master work similarly. In the last skill, you work with a handout master for a slide presentation and print a handout of the presentation.

Skills You Learn

1. Change formatting in Slide Master view
2. Insert a graphic in Slide Master view
3. Add a footer in a slide master
4. Hide a slide master element on a slide
5. Change the color scheme
6. Insert a header in a handout master and print a handout

Files You Need
For these skills, you need the following student data file.

M8-C2-S1-AboutChocMuseum.pptx

What You Create

You've been invited to give a talk about The Chocolate Museum at a prestigious trade show for the confection industry. Because your goal is to build awareness of your brand at the trade show, you plan to create a PowerPoint presentation including the Museum logo on every slide. You also create handouts of your presentation.

Handout of Presentation Slides

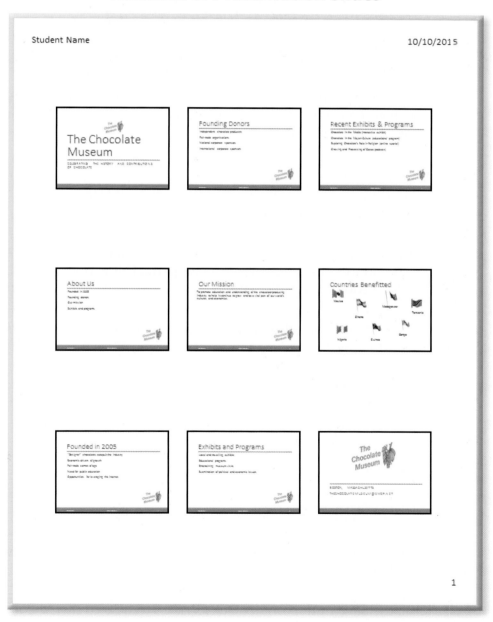

PowerPoint

Skill 1

Change Formatting in Slide Master View

 Video M8_C2_S01

If your organization asked you to use the Franklin Gothic Heavy font on all titles in company PowerPoint presentations, it would be time-consuming to format every slide title individually. You can easily format the title placeholder in the slide master just once, and the title of every slide that uses that slide master will be formatted the same way. Also, if you later need to change the slide titles to another font (perhaps someone decides the company font must be Tunga), you can use the slide master to change all title formatting with a single action.

Steps

1 Open the student data file named **M8-C2-S1-AboutChocMuseum.pptx** and, if you have not already done so, save the file in your Module 8 working folder on your storage medium.

2 Click the VIEW tab.

▶**Tip** You may need to scroll up the slide thumbnails pane to find the top slide.

3 Click the Slide Master button in the Master Views group.

▶**Tip** Hover your mouse over each slide master layout to display the name of the layout.

4 Click the top (and largest) slide layout thumbnail (Office Theme Slide Master) in the slide layout thumbnails pane. This action displays the slide master layout in the slide pane.

5 *Another Way*
Click the border of the placeholder text box to select all the text within the placeholder text box. Notice that when you click the placeholder border it changes from a broken line to a solid line.

5 Click in the title placeholder and select the placeholder text *Click to edit Master title style*.

6 Click the HOME tab.

7 Click the Font button arrow in the Font group.

6,7,8 *Another Way*
Right-click the selected text and then click *Font* at the shortcut menu. Make changes to the font in the Font dialog box.

8 Click *Franklin Gothic Heavy* in the drop-down gallery.

9 Click the SLIDE MASTER tab.

9,10 *Another Way*
Click the Normal button in the Presentation Views group on the VIEW tab to close Slide Master view and return to Normal view.

10 Click the Close Master View button to return to the previous view—in this case, Normal view.

11 Click the Save button on the Quick Access toolbar to save the file.

Completed Skill 1

PowerPoint

Skill 2

Insert a Graphic in Slide Master View

Video M8_C2_S02

Modifying global formatting is a great way to use slide masters. You can also use them to insert a graphic on all or most slides in your presentation. For example, many companies place their logo on every slide. Rather than inserting the logo on each slide individually, you can place it once in the slide master. In this skill, you place a logo on all slides that use the Title and Content layout.

Steps

Tip Chapter 3 also includes skills about using graphics in PowerPoint presentations.

1 If if is not already open, open the student data file named **M8-C2-S1-AboutChocMuseum.pptx**, the file you saved in the previous skill, and save the file as **M8-C2-S2-AboutChocMuseum**.

2 In Normal view, click the Museum logo in Slide 1 in the slide pane.

3 Shortcut
Copy
Ctrl + C

3 Click the Copy button in the Clipboard group on the HOME tab.

Tip If you want a graphic to appear on every slide in the presentation, you should place it on the uppermost slide in a slide master set, rather than on only one layout in the set.

4 Click the VIEW tab.

5 Click the Slide Master button in the Master Views group.

6 Click the third slide layout thumbnail (Title and Content Layout) in the slide layout thumbnails pane.

Tip Changes on individual slides override slide master settings.

7 Click the HOME tab.

8 Shortcut
Paste
Ctrl + V

8 Click the Paste button in the Clipboard group to paste the copied logo into the slide master.

9 Another Way
Use the arrow keys to move the selected object on the slide.

9 Hover your mouse pointer over the logo until the pointer becomes a four-headed arrow and then click and drag the pasted logo to the bottom right corner of the content placeholder of the slide in the slide pane.

Tip If the graphic is too close to the contents on any individual slide, reposition it on the slide master. You cannot access the graphic from the individual slides.

10 Click the VIEW tab.

11 Click the Normal button in the Presentation Views group. The logo appears in the bottom right corner of all slides with the Title and Content Layout (Slides 2–8).

12 Save the file.

Completed Skill 2

PowerPoint

PowerPoint

Skill 3

Add a Footer in a Slide Master

Video M8_C2_S03

Another item you might want to place on every slide is a footer containing text. Footer placeholders in the slide master can accommodate information such as your company name, the presenter's name, slide numbers, and important words such as "Confidential" or "Copyrighted." The slide master offers three footer placeholders by default.

Steps

1 If it is not already open, open **M8-C2-S2-AboutChocMuseum.pptx**, the file you saved in the previous skill, and save the file as **M8-C2-S3-AboutChocMuseum**.

2 In Normal view, click the INSERT tab.

3 Click the Header & Footer button in the Text group.

▶**Tip** Header and footer formatting that is done on the Slide tab of the Header and Footer dialog box is applied to the slide master.

4 In the Header and Footer dialog box with the Slide tab selected, click the *Date and time* check box to insert a check mark.

5 Confirm that the *Update automatically* option is selected.

▶**Tip** If you want a specific date on your slides instead of the current date, click the *Fixed* option instead of the *Update automatically* option.

6 Click the *Slide number* check box to insert a check mark.

7 Click the *Footer* check box to insert a check mark.

8 Type Copyright 2015 in the *Footer* text box.

▶**Tip** Step 9 removes the footer from all slides that use the Title layout.

9 Click the *Don't show on title slide* check box.

10 Click the Apply to All button.

11 Save the file.

Taking It Further

Customizing Slide Footers You can apply a footer to individual slides using the same process described in this skill. However, remember that one of the benefits of inserting a footer on the slide master is that you do not have to create or change each footer individually. If only a few slides require a different footer, apply the global footer to all slides, and then make footer changes on the few individual slides one by one.

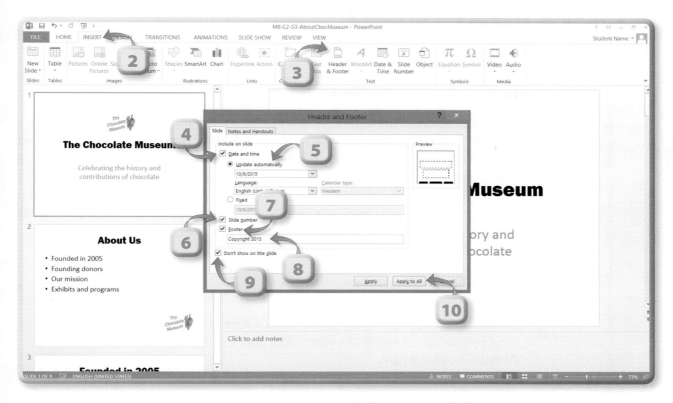

Completed Skill 3

Chapter 2 Working with Slide Masters and Handouts **619**

PowerPoint

Skill 4

Hide a Slide Master Element on a Slide

A graphic placed on a slide master cannot be moved or resized on individual slides—it takes its size and position from the master slide. Sometimes you may need to hide a master graphic on a few individual slides. Hiding might be necessary if a slide starts to look too crowded or confusing once you apply other required graphics or if you need the space to accommodate a large chart or another object that would overlap the master graphic. In such cases, you can hide master graphics on individual slides.

Steps

1 If it is not already open, open **M8-C2-S3-AboutChocMuseum.pptx**, the file you saved in the previous skill, and save the file as **M8-C2-S4-AboutChocMuseum**.

2 Another Way
Navigate to specific slides by using the scroll bar at the right side of the slide thumbnails pane. Click on the slide you want to be active.

2 In Normal view, click Slide 8 in the slide thumbnails pane.

3 Click the DESIGN tab.

4 Click the Format Background button in the Customize group to display the Format Background pane.

▶**Tip** Hiding background graphics hides all graphics on the slide master for the current slide; if you place more than one graphic there, you cannot hide each individually.

5 Click the *Hide background graphics* check box to insert a check mark. The graphic from the slide master disappears.

6 Click Close to close the Format Background pane.

7 Save the file.

Taking It Further

Inserting Graphics on Individual Slides
What if you hide the master graphic because the placement does not suit a particular slide, but you would still like to include some form of the graphic on that slide? You can insert the same graphic on the slide after hiding the master graphic. You can then move it around the slide, resize it, or even rotate it to make it work with the other slide elements. Refer to Chapter 3 for more information on working with graphics.

Completed Skill 4

PowerPoint

Skill 5

Change the Color Scheme

Video M8_C2_S05

The colors used for text, slide back-grounds, and graphical elements are preset by the theme you apply. However, once you have applied a theme, you can change its color palette to match your taste or enhance your presentation's tone or message. The background color drop-down gallery enables you to preview color schemes on your slide before you choose one. Changing the color palette on the slide master is a quick way to update your entire presentation with a coordinated, predesigned color scheme.

Steps

1 If it is not already open, open **M8-C2-S4-AboutChocMuseum.pptx**, the file you saved in the previous skill, and save the file as **M8-C2-S5-AboutChocMuseum**.

2 In Normal view, click the VIEW tab.

3 Click the Slide Master button in the Master Views group.

4 Click the top (and largest) slide layout thumbnail (Office Theme Slide Master) in the slide layout thumbnails pane.

5 Click the Themes button in the Edit Theme group.

6 Click the *Retrospect* theme.

7 Click the Colors button in the Background group to display the drop-down gallery.

8 Click the *Red* color scheme to apply it to all slides.

9 Click the Close Master View button to return to Normal view.

10 Save the file.

11 Click the SLIDE SHOW tab.

12 Click the From Beginning button in the Start Slide Show group to run the slide show.

▶ *Tip* To view the name of the currently applied color scheme, move your mouse over the Colors button. The current theme name is listed in the *Theme Colors* information box that appears.

▶ *Tip* Click *Customize Colors* to create a custom color scheme.

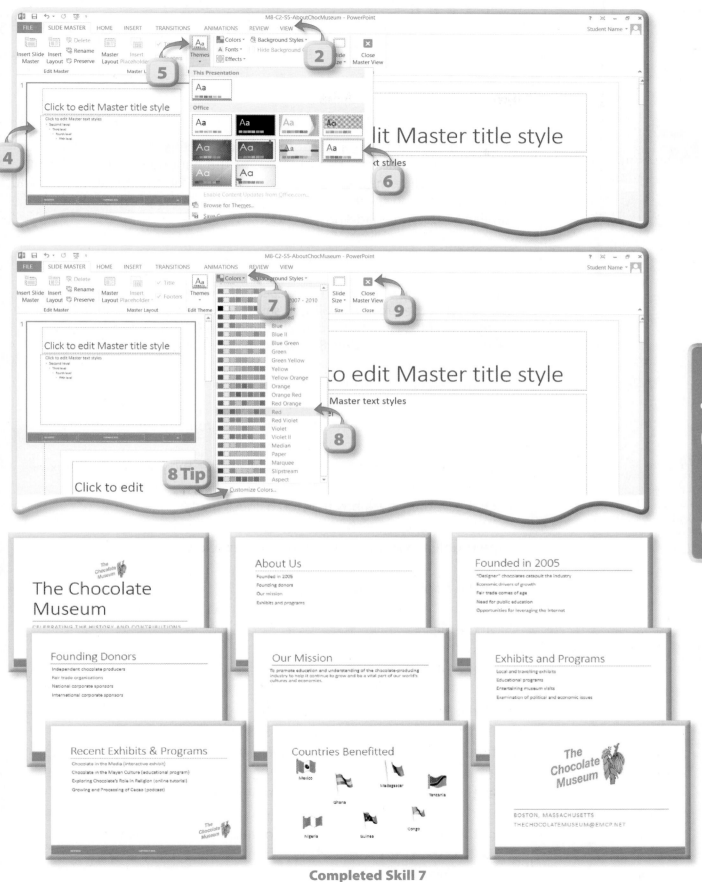

Completed Skill 7

PowerPoint

Chapter 2

Skill 6

Video M8_C2_S06

Insert a Header on the Handout Master and Print a Handout

The handout master and notes master have features similar to those of the slide master. The steps for adding text in these layouts are similar to those for adding text to slides. In this skill, you add a header to the handout master and print a handout of the presentation you created in the previous skills.

Steps

1 If it is not already open, open **M8-C2-S5-AboutChocMuseum.pptx**, the file you saved in the previous skill, and save the file as **Lastname-M8-C2-S6-AboutChocMuseum**, but replace *Lastname* with your last name. Be sure to save the file in your Module 8 working folder on your storage medium.

2 In Normal view, click the INSERT tab.

3 Click the Header & Footer button in the Text group.

4 Click the Notes and Handouts tab in the Header and Footer dialog box.

▶ Tip Header and footer formatting that is done on the Handouts tab of the Header and Footer dialog box is applied to the handout master.

5 Click the *Header* check box to insert a check mark.

6 Type your first and last names in the *Header* text box.

▶ Tip To add a footer to the handout master, in the Header and Footer dialog box, click the *Footer* check box to insert a check mark and then type your text in the *Footer* text box.

7 Click the Apply to All button.

8 Save the file.

9 Click the FILE tab.

10 Click the *Print* option.

▶ Tip Chapter 4 covers other printing options.

11 In the *Settings* category, click the *Full Page Slides* gallery.

12 Click the *9 Slides Horizontal* option in the *Handouts* section.

13 Click the Print button if your instructor tells you to print handouts.

14 Close the file.

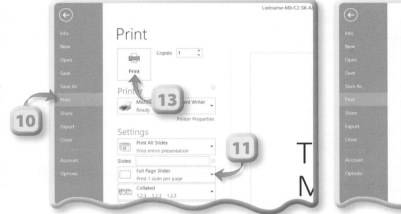

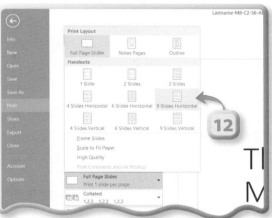

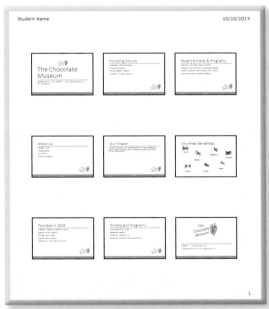

Completed Skill 6

PowerPoint

PowerPoint

Tasks Summary

Task	Ribbon Tab, Group	Button, Option	Shortcut, Alternative
Display slide master	VIEW, Master Views		
Display handout master	VIEW, Master Views		
Display notes master	VIEW, Master Views		
Insert header and footer	INSERT, Text		
Hide master graphic	DESIGN, Format Background	, *Hide background graphics*	
Print handouts	FILE, *Print*	Print	Ctrl + P

Features Review

Select the best answer from the choices given.

1 Using slide masters you can
   a. insert text or graphics once and have them appear on every slide.
   b. apply a design template to every slide.
   c. create notes for every slide in the presentation.
   d. rearrange the order of your presentation.

2 If you want a specific date placed on your slides rather than the current date, use the
   a. *Fixed* option.
   b. *Date* option.
   c. *Current* option.
   d. Slide Show view.

3 The default slide master
   a. is the first theme you create.
   b. is created by the first theme you apply.
   c. uses the Office theme.
   d. always uses a custom theme.

4 To have a graphic appear on every slide in the presentation, place it on
   a. every slide.
   b. the uppermost slide in a slide master set.
   c. every slide in a slide master set.
   d. the first slide in your presentation.

5 Typical information placed in the footer includes
   a. slide numbers.
   b. slide titles.
   c. bullet points.
   d. clip art.

6 Footers on slides have this many placeholders by default.
   a. two
   b. five
   c. three
   d. none

7 The *Hide background graphics* check box is located on the
   a. VIEW tab.
   b. INSERT tab.
   c. SLIDE SHOW tab.
   d. DESIGN tab.

8 When you are in Slide Master view you can
   a. add a theme.
   b. change the color palette.
   c. change the font for slides that use the Two Content layout.
   d. add a theme, change the color palette, and change the font for slides that use the Two Content layout.

9 The slide master has features similar to the
   a. notes master.
   b. handout master.
   c. notes master and handout master.
   d. There are no similarities between the slide master, handout master, and notes master.

10 Changes on individual slides override slide master settings.
   a. True
   b. False

Hands-On Skills Review

Exercise **A** **Promote a School's Music Program**

Skills Change formatting in Slide Master view, add a footer in a slide master, and change the color scheme

Scenario It is the end of the school year. You are meeting with parents and students who are interested in joining the school's instrumental music program for the next academic year. Update the presentation to ensure it delivers the appropriate information.

Steps

1 Open the student data file named **M8-C2-ExA-GWHSMusicProg.pptx** and save the file as **Lastname-M8-C2-ExA-GWHSMusicProg**, but replace *Lastname* with your last name.

2 Enter your name and the current date in the subtitle placeholder in Slide 1 so that they display on two separate lines.

3 Using the Title and Content layout, insert a new Slide 3 titled *Topics* that explains what you will discuss. In addition to the title, include four bulleted points on the slide:

    Musical opportunities
    School commitment
    Student commitment
    Parent commitment

4 Change the slide order to the following sequence: (1) *George Washington High School Instrumental Music Program*, (2) *Topics*, (3) *Opportunities*, (4) *School Commitment*, (5) *Student Commitment*, (6) *Parent Commitment*, (7) *Parent Commitment (Continued)*, (8) *Looking forward to a wonderfully musical year!*

5 Apply the Ion Boardroom theme to all slides. Do not select a variant.

6 Modify the slide master.
   a. Apply the Arial Narrow font style and bold formatting to the text in the title placeholder on all slides.
   b. Apply the Violet II theme color to all slides.
   c. Close Slide Master view.

7 Add to all presentation slides a three-part footer that contains the current date, the text *George Washington High School Music Program*, and the slide number. Do not show the footer on the title slide.

8 Apply the second variant for the Ion Boardroom theme to Slide 1 and Slide 8.

9 Select the final slide (Slide 8) and modify the title placeholder so that the text is centered and the font is all capital letters. Center the text in the title placeholder. **HINT:** *To modify the alignment, click the HOME tab and then click the Center button in the Paragraph group. To modify the font, click the HOME tab, click the Font dialog box launcher, click the* All Caps *check box to insert a check mark, and then click OK.*

10 Select the title slide (Slide 1) and change the font size of the text in the title placeholder to 40 points.

11 Save the presentation.

12 Preview the presentation.

13 Submit the completed presentation to your instructor.

Completed Exercise A

Exercise **B** **Enhance a Presentation**

Grade It

NOTE: *This assignment can be done immediately if you are comfortable inserting and sizing Online Pictures as directed in Module 5 (Word), Chapter 3, Skills 8 and 9. As an alternative, return to this assignment after completing Skills 1 and 2 in Module 8 (PowerPoint), Chapter 3.*

Skills Insert a graphic in Slide Master view

Scenario The presentation you completed in Exercise A for the meeting with parents and students interested in joining next year's instrumental music program looks very plain. Add interest to the presentation by inserting a graphic in the slide master so that the graphic will appear on most slides.

Steps

1 Open **Lastname-M8-C2-ExA-GWHSMusicProg .pptx**, the file you saved in the previous exercise, and save the file as **Lastname-M8-C2-ExB-GWHSMusicProg**.

2 In Slide Master view, select the Title and Content Layout slide master that is used by Slide 2 and Slides 4–7. Be sure you select the proper slide master. You will use this slide master to add an Online Picture to all Title and Content Layout slides. **HINT:** *Select the third slide in the master set.*

a. Using the Online Pictures button in the Images group on the INSERT tab, search for *high school buildings* at Office.com Clip Art and select the third school building image that appears (or an image similar to the image shown in the Completed Exercise B images below).

b. Insert the image and position it so that the lower right corner of the image fits exactly in the lower right corner of the content box placeholder. **HINT:** *The image is in the correct location when the right and lower lines that surround the image are sitting on the right and lower lines of the placeholder.*

3 Close Slide Master view and return to Normal view.

4 Save the presentation.

5 Preview the presentation and ensure the image is seen on Slide 2 and Slides 4–7.

6 Submit the completed presentation to your instructor.

Completed Exercise B

Exercise C Format Handouts for a Presentation

Grade It

Skills Insert a header in the handout master and print a handout

Scenario The presentation you completed in Exercise B for the meeting with parents and students interested in joining next year's instrumental music program is ready to present, but you want to provide printed handouts to distribute at the meeting. Add a running header and footer to the handout master and print it so you can make copies.

Steps

1 Open **Lastname-M8-C2-ExB-GWHSMusicProg .pptx**, the file you saved in the previous exercise, and save the file as **Lastname-M8-C2-ExC-GWHSMusicProg** but replace *Lastname* with your last name.

2 Insert a header in the handout master that includes your first and last names and the current date.

3 Insert a footer in the handout master that includes your instructor's name and the page number. **HINT:** *To insert a footer, follow the same*

steps as you do to insert a header, except in the Header and Footer dialog box, click the Footer *check box and type in the* Footer *text box.*

4 Save the presentation.

5 Prepare the handouts to print horizontally with six slides per page.

6 Submit the completed presentation to your instructor. Submit the printed handout if required.

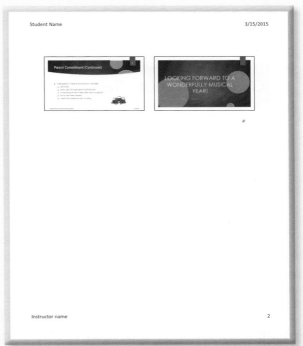

Completed Exercise C

Chapter 3

Adding Visual Elements and Sound

PowerPoint slides use words to communicate the ideas in your presentation, but visuals can help reinforce those ideas and make your slides more attractive. Visuals may include photos or illustrations, transition effects for moving from one slide to another, animated sequences that can include sound, and video clips. When you combine these elements in your presentation, you get your message across and keep your audience engaged and entertained.

Skills You Learn

1   Insert an object on a slide
2   Format a picture
3   Add transitions
4   Add sound
5   Add animations
6   Choose animation effects

Files You Need

For these skills, you need the following student data files.

M8-C3-S1-ChocProcessing.pptx

M8-C3-S1-CocoaGrowers.jpg

What You Create

Your local middle school has asked you to attend a career fair and give a presentation about how cocoa is grown and processed into chocolate. You want to create a PowerPoint presentation that uses visual and media elements, including photos, drawings, animations, and sounds, to tell the story of chocolate processing.

In this chapter, you learn how to work with visual objects in slides and perform basic formatting on those objects. You use effects to transition between slides and add animations that put slide objects in motion. You also add sounds to the objects on your slides.

How Cocoa Is Grown

- Cocoa pods grow on a tree
- Grown 15 degrees north or south of equator
- A delicate crop, bears fruit in fifth year
- A tree can live 25 years or more

animation effect applied

Overview of Chocolate Processing

Blue Heron Middle School
October 2, 2015

Cocoa Pods

illustration added and formatted

- Rough, leather-like husk weighing over 2 pounds
- Filled with 30–50 seeds called cocoa beans
- Seeds contain a sweet pulp
- Pulp is half cocoa butter and half cocoa solids

Picking and Fermenting

- Beans are extracted by farmers
- Harvesting occurs a few times a year
- Beans are fermented under piles of banana leaves
- Fermenting takes five days
- Beans are dried in the sun on bamboo mats

photo added and positioned

Distributing

- Dried beans are sold to agents who sell to wholesalers
- Most are used to produce chocolate confections
- Some cocoa butter is used in cosmetics

Making Cocoa Powder

- Beans are roasted in cylinders
- Inside of bean (nib) ground into cocoa mass
- Cocoa butter pressed out of the cocoa mass
- Cocoa powder remains

Producing Chocolate

- Other ingredients are added: sugar, milk, etc.
- Heavy rollers swirl mixture (conching)
- Mixture is heated, cooled, and then heated (tempering)
- Chocolate is poured into molds
- Used to make candies such as chocolate surrounding caramel (enrobing)

sound and animation effect applied

For More Information Visit Our Website

www.emcp.net/TheChocolateMuseum

PowerPoint

Skill 1   **Insert an Object on a Slide**

 M8_C3_S01

If a slide contains a content place-holder, you can insert objects, such as tables, charts, SmartArt graphics, online pictures, and video, by clicking one of the placeholder buttons. For example, clicking the Online Pictures button allows you to search the Office.com website for copyright-free photos and illustrations or use the search engine Bing to search the Web for images. Alternatively, you can use buttons on the INSERT tab to insert objects you have saved to your computer or storage medium, including illustrations, screenshots, photos, shapes, videos, and sounds.

Steps

Insert an Online Picture

1 Open the student data file named **M8-C3-S1-ChocProcessing.pptx** and, if you have not already done so, save the file in your Module 8 working folder on your storage medium.

2 Click Slide 3 in the slide thumbnails pane to display it in the slide pane.

3 Another Way
Click the Online Pictures button in the Images group on the INSERT tab.

3 Click the Online Pictures button in the content placeholder to display the Insert Pictures dialog box.

4 Click in the *Office.com Clip Art* search box, type cocoa pods, and then press Enter.

5 Click the cocoa pods clip art image shown in the the screenshot on the opposite page. **NOTE:** *Online pictures may change. If you are not able to find the image shown here, select a similar image. If the search term* cocoa pods *does not produce any results, try another term such as* cocoa beans.

6 Click the Insert button.

Taking It Further

Insert and Size Objects   As you learned in this skill, there are a number of different objects you can insert on a slide using options on the INSERT tab. To insert a picture from your computer or SkyDrive account, click the Pictures button. To insert a shape, such as an arrow, click the Shapes button. If you need to present data on a slide, you can insert a table using the Table button and then enter the data in the table. You can also insert SmartArt graphics, which can be used to illustrate information in the form of a diagram such as an organizational chart or a Venn diagram. Size an object by selecting it and then dragging the corner handles. You can also specify an exact size by typing or selecting a value in the *Height* and *Width* measurement boxes in the Size group on the PICTURE TOOLS FORMAT tab.

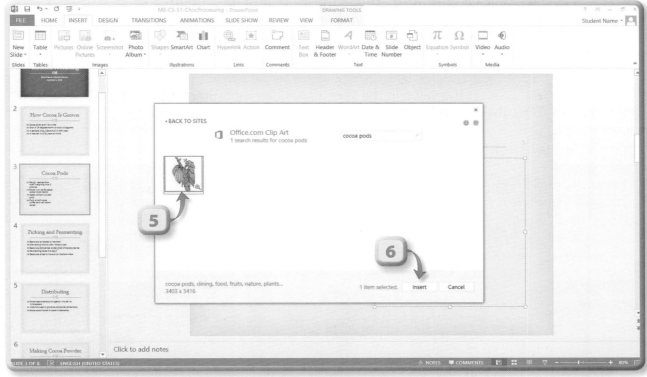

More

Taking It Further

Snap Pictures and Objects to a Grid You can align pictures and objects to a specific location on a slide using snap-to options. You first have to turn on the snap-to options by clicking the dialog box launcher in the Show group on the VIEW tab. Next, click the *Snap objects to grid* check box to have objects to snap to the closest grid intersection. You should also click *Display grid on screen* to view the grid on the slide, which is helpful when aligning pictures and objects. Once the snap-to options are turned on, you can override them by pressing the Alt key while you drag a picture or object.

Chapter 3 Adding Visual Elements and Sound **633**

Insert a Picture File

7   Click Slide 4 in the slide thumbnails pane.

8   Click the INSERT tab.

9   Click the Pictures button in the Images group.

10   In the Insert Picture dialog box, browse to the Module8-PowerPoint folder on your storage medium and then click the student data file named **M8-C3-S1-CocoaGrowers.jpg**.

11 *Another Way*
Display a layout with a content placeholder and click the Picture button.

11   Click the Insert button to place the picture on Slide 4.

▶*Tip* Steps 12–16 show how to place objects in exact locations on a slide. You can place objects in approximate locations by clicking and dragging them.

12   Click the task pane launcher in the Size group on the PICTURE TOOLS FORMAT tab to display the Format Picture pane.

13   Click *POSITION* to expand the list of position options.

14   Select the value in the *Horizontal position* measurement box, type 6.5, and then press Enter.

15   Select the value in the *Vertical position* measurement box, type 5.25, and then press Enter.

16   Click Close to close the Format Picture pane.

17   Click the Save button on the Quick Access toolbar to save the file.

 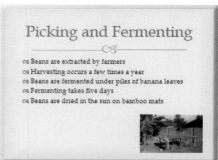

Completed Skill 1 (Slides 3 and 4)

Taking It Further

Insert Visuals in Masters   If you want to use a graphic on every slide or on most slides in a presentation, you should use the procedures in this skill to insert the image in the Slide Master view. With that method, you only have to insert the item once, and it appears on every slide. See the previous chapter for detailed information on using masters. Now that you know more about adding graphics, you may wish to repeat Skill 2 in Chapter 2 of this module.

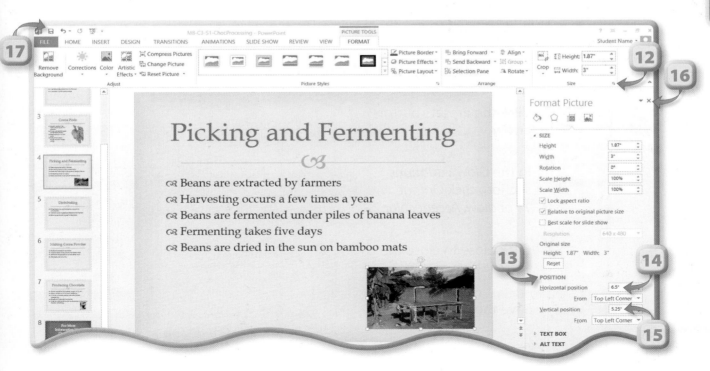

PowerPoint

Format a Picture

Video M8_C3_S02

PowerPoint provides several tools for formatting pictures, including the ability to set a border around a picture, add shadows or a glowing effect to a border, modify photo colors and brightness, and crop or resize an image. You can take advantage of these tools to give your picture a unique appearance.

Steps

1 If it is not already open, open **M8-C3-S1-ChocProcessing.pptx**, the file you saved in the previous skill, and save the file as **M8-C3-S2-ChocProcessing**.

2 Click Slide 3 in the slide thumbnails pane.

3 In Slide 3 in the slide pane, right-click the cocoa bean image and then click *Format Picture* in the shortcut menu to display the Format Picture pane.

3-9 Another Way
Click the PICTURE TOOLS FORMAT tab and use the Picture Border and Picture Effects galleries in the Picture Styles group to make the changes listed in Steps 3–9.

4 In the Format Picture pane, click the Fill & Line button.

5 Click *LINE* to expand the list of line options.

6 Click the *Solid Line* option to select it.

7 In the Format Picture pane, click the Effects button.

8 Click *GLOW* to expand the list of glow options.

9 Click the Presets button arrow.

10 In the *Glow Variations* section, click *Orange, 11 pt glow, Accent color 2*.

▶ **Tip** If you want to change the color of the image itself, click the Color button in the Adjust group and select an option from the *Recolor* drop-down list.

11 Click Close to close the Format Picture pane.

12 Save the file.

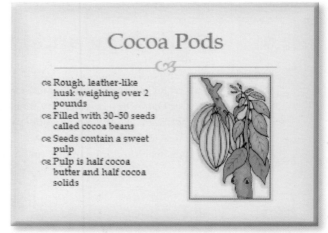

Completed Skill 2 (Slide 3)

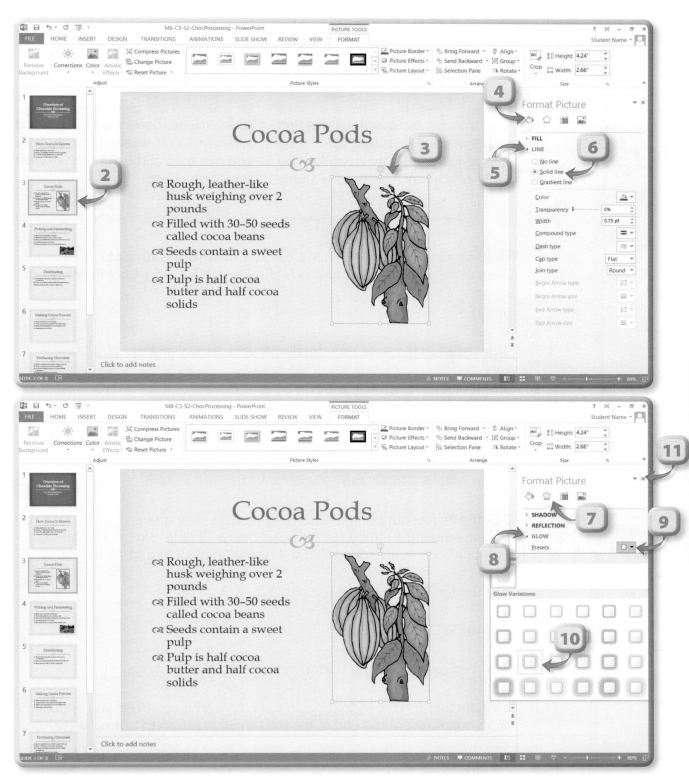

Taking It Further

Arranging Objects If you place more than one image on a slide, you can arrange objects so that one appears to be in the front with the others tucked beneath it. To create this effect, select one of the images to make it active and then click the PICTURE TOOLS FORMAT tab. In the Arrange group, use the *Bring Forward* and *Send Backward* options to change an object's position relative to the other images.

PowerPoint

Skill 3 — Add Transitions

 Video M8_C3_S03

Slide transitions are animations that occur when you move from slide to slide in Slide Show view. You can apply transition effects to a single slide, to multiple slides, or to all slides in a presentation. In addition, you can control the duration of each transition effect.

Steps

1 If it is not already open, open **M8-C3-S2-ChocProcessing.pptx**, the file you saved in the previous skill, and save the file as **M8-C3-S3-ChocProcessing**.

2 Click the HOME tab.

3 Click Slide 1 in the slide thumbnails pane to display it in the slide pane.

4-5 *Shortcut*
Select All
Ctrl + A

4 Click the Select button in the Editing group.

5 *Another Way*
Click Slide 1 in the slide thumbnails pane, press Shift, and then click the last slide.

5 Click *Select All* at the drop-down list. This action selects all of the slides in the slide thumbnails pane.

6 Click the TRANSITIONS tab.

▶ *Tip* To view more effects in the Transitions to This Slide group, click the More button ⊽ located at the right of the transitions options.

7 Click the Reveal button in the Transition to This Slide group. A small transition icon (resembling a sliding star) appears below all slide numbers in the slide thumbnails pane, indicating that the transition is applied to each slide.

8 Save the file.

9 Click the SLIDE SHOW tab.

10 Click the From Beginning button in the Start Slide Show group.

▶ *Tip* To navigate from slide to slide, click the mouse or press the Page Down, Right Arrow, Down Arrow, or Enter keys.

11 Navigate through the slide show to view the transition effects you applied. Click your mouse at the end of the slide show to return to Normal view.

Taking It Further

Removing Transitions Using too many transitions in a single presentation can be distracting for your audience. If you decide that you have too many transitions, you can remove some of them. To remove a transition, click the slide or slides where the transition is applied and then click the TRANSITIONS tab. In the Transition to This Slide group, click the None button in the Transitions gallery.

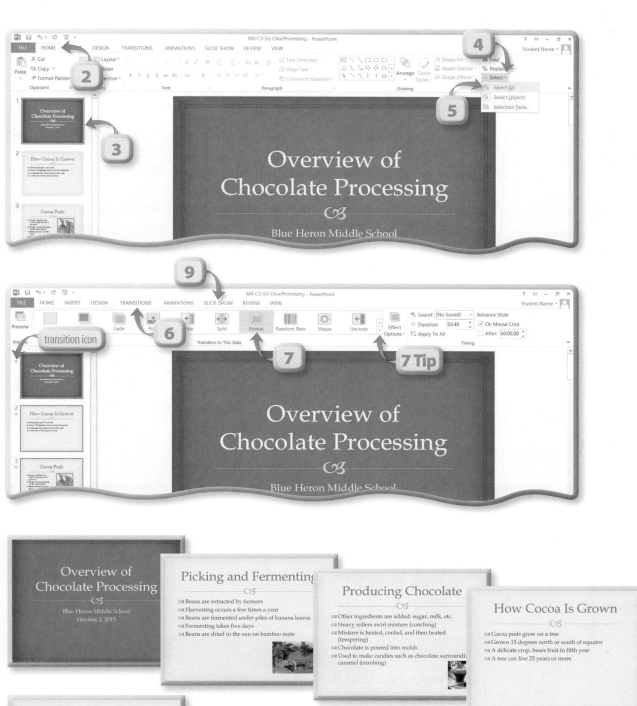

Reveal transition applied to all of the slides in this file.

Completed Skill 3 (All Slides)

PowerPoint

PowerPoint

Add Sound

Video   M8_C3_S04

Transitions can be accompanied by sounds. It is usually best to use a carefully chosen sound for only one or two transitions within a presentation. For example, if you display great sales numbers for the quarter, you might add a brief sound of applause, or if you display a slide containing a photo, you might add a camera click sound. Be careful that you do not overuse sounds. Playing a sound for every transition can annoy your audience and detract from your message. Use sounds rarely and only when they will add to or emphasize the content.

Steps

1 If it is not already open, open **M8-C3-S3-ChocProcessing.pptx**, the file you saved in the previous skill, and save the file as **M8-C3-S4-ChocProcessing**.

2 In the slide thumbnails pane, select the last slide in the presentation.

3 Click the TRANSITIONS tab.

4 In the Timing group, click the *Sound* option box arrow to display a drop-down list of sounds.

5 Click *Applause* in the drop-down list to apply this sound to the selected slide.

6 **Another Way**
Click in the *Duration* measurement box and type *3.00*.

6 Click the down arrow in the *Duration* measurement box twice to change the time to *03.00*.

7 Save the file.

8 Preview the applied sound and animation for Slide 8 by clicking the Slide Show view button at the bottom of the screen.

9 After previewing the slide, press Esc to return to Normal view.

For More Information Visit Our Website

ℭℨ

www.emcp.net/TheChocolateMuseum

The sound of applause automatically runs for 3 seconds when this slide displays.

Completed Skill 4 (Slide 8)

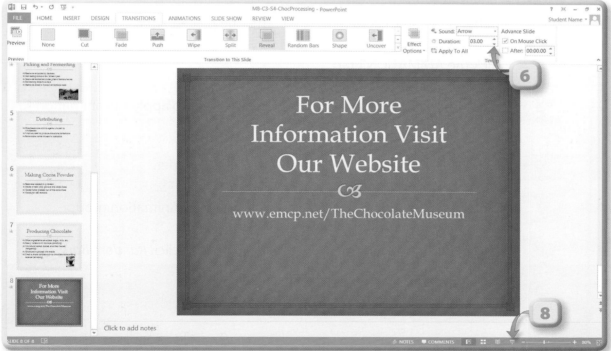

Taking It Further

Using Your Own Audio in a Presentation
You can use any audio file that you have created or downloaded in your PowerPoint presentation. Simply click the INSERT tab and then click the Audio button. Browse to locate the audio file on your computer or storage medium and insert it. A small speaker icon with a Play button appears on your slide during the slide show. Click the Play button to play the audio.

PowerPoint

Add Animations

 M8_C3_S05

Transitions apply effects when a slide appears, whereas animations apply effects when slide content appears. For example, you can animate a heading to zoom in or a picture to fade in. You can use tools on the ANIMATIONS tab or in the Animation Pane to control what causes the effect to play. For example, the effect may play when you click your mouse or when another animation starts. Animations can be applied to text or image objects.

Steps

1. If it is not already open, open **M8-C3-S4-ChocProcessing.pptx**, the file you saved in the previous skill, and save the file as **M8-C3-S5-ChocProcessing**.

2. Click Slide 1 in the slide thumbnails pane.

3. In the slide pane, click anywhere in the title placeholder.

4. Click the ANIMATIONS tab.

5. In the Animation group, click the *Float In* option to apply the animation to the title.

6. On Slide 1, click anywhere in the subtitle placeholder.

7. Click the Add Animation button in the Advanced Animation group.

8. In the *Entrance* section of the drop-down gallery, click *Random Bars*.

▶ **Tip** In a content placeholder with multiple bullet points, each bullet point is animated separately and in number order.

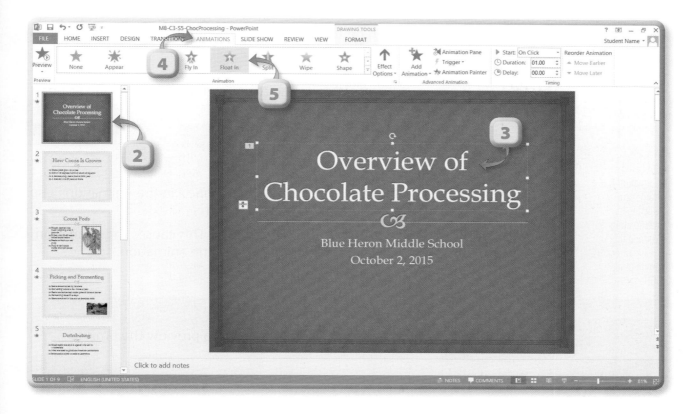

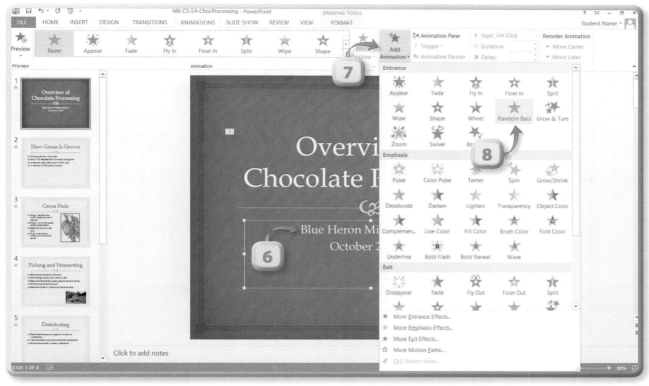

More

9 Click the Preview button on the ANIMATIONS tab to preview the animations applied to the current slide.

Tip The Animation Pane displays a summary of the animations you add to a slide.

10 Click the Animation Pane button in the Advanced Animation group to open the Animation Pane.

Tip Items that are animated are numbered in order in the Animation Pane. You can reorder an animation by selecting its summary in the Animation Pane and then clicking the Move Earlier or Move Later button in the Timing group on the ANIMATIONS tab.

11 Click *Subtitle 2* in the Animation Pane.

12 Click the down-pointing arrow at the right of *Subtitle 2* in the Animation Pane.

13 Click *Start With Previous* at the drop-down menu. This causes the animation of the subtitle to begin at the same time as the title animation.

14 Click a blank area of the Animation Pane.

Tip If the Play button in the Animation Pane says *Play Selected*, deselect the animation in the Animation Pane. When there are no animations selected, the button will read *Play All*.

15 Click the Play All button in the Animation Pane to preview the timing.

16 Close the Animation Pane.

17 Save the file.

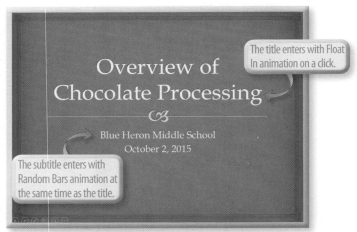

Completed Skill 5 (Slide 1)

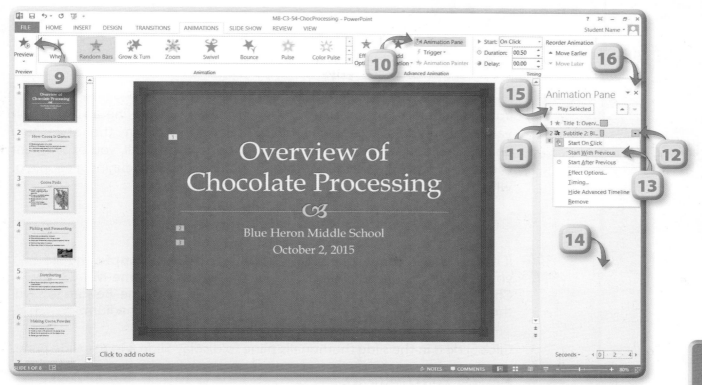

Taking It Further

More Animation Effects   If you do not find the effect you want in the Animation gallery, be sure to explore additional animation options by clicking the Add Animation button in the Advanced Animation group on the ANIMATIONS tab. This button offers additional entrance, emphasis, and exit effects, as well as motion paths. Motion path animations move an object along a path on your slide, such as around a circle or six-pointed star.

PowerPoint

Skill 6   **Choose Animation Effects**

Video   M8_C3_S06

You can refine animation styles in a variety of ways. For example, if you animate text so that it flies in, you can also choose the direction from which the text enters. The ways in which you can refine an animation style depend on the style you choose. In this skill, you experiment with adding and refining a couple of animation styles.

Steps

1   If it is not already open, open **M8-C3-S5-ChocProcessing.pptx**, the file you saved in the previous skill, and save the file as **Lastname-M8-C3-S6-ChocProcessing**, but replace *Lastname* with your last name. Be sure to save the file in your Module 8 working folder on your storage medium.

2   Click Slide 8 in the slide thumbnails pane to display Slide 8 in the slide pane.

3   Click the ANIMATIONS tab.

4   Click in the subtitle placeholder.

5   Click the *Float In* effect in the Animation group.

6   Click the Effect Options button in the Animation group.

7   Click *Float Down* in the *Direction* section.

8   Click the Preview button to view the Float Down animation.

9   Click in the subtitle placeholder.

10   Click the *Shape* option in the Animation group to apply a different animation style to the subtitle placeholder.

11   Click the Effect Options button.

12   Click *Out* in the *Direction* section.

13   Click the Preview button to view the animation.

14   Save and close the file.

> **▶ Tip** Note that each effect you choose offers appropriate options for that effect.

For More Information Visit Our Website

℃ℨ

www.emcp.net/TheChocolateMuseum

The subtitle is animated to appear using the Shape animation and grows from the center out.

Completed Skill 6

Taking It Further

Timing Animations You can change the timing of animations with the *Duration* and *Delay* measurement boxes in the Timing group on the ANIMATIONS tab. Select an object with an animation applied and use the *Duration* measurement box to set the length of time the animation should play. Use the *Delay* measurement box to set the length of delay between two animations. While you applied animation features to slides with the Title layout in Skills 5 and 6, you can also apply animations to slides with other layouts. For example, you can animate the bullet points in a slide with the Title and Content layout by having them fade in or out.

Tasks Summary

Task	Ribbon Tab, Group	Button, Option
Insert Office.com clip art	INSERT, Images	
Insert a picture	INSERT, Images	
Format a picture	PICTURE TOOLS FORMAT, Picture Styles	
Arrange objects	PICTURE TOOLS FORMAT, Arrange	
Apply a transition	TRANSITIONS, Transition to This Slide	
Add a sound	TRANSITIONS, Timing	
Set sound duration	TRANSITIONS, Timing	
Apply an animation	ANIMATIONS, Animation	
Display Animation Pane	ANIMATIONS, Advanced Animation	
Choose animation effects	ANIMATIONS, Animation	
Preview animations	ANIMATIONS, Preview	

 Features Review

Select the best answer from the choices given.

1. To add an object to a slide, you can click buttons in the content placeholder or on the
   a. PICTURE TOOLS FORMAT tab.
   b. INSERT tab.
   c. ANIMATIONS tab.
   d. SLIDE SHOW tab.

2. To select a picture from a folder on your computer or storage medium and insert it in a slide, use the _____ button.
   a. Images
   b. Online Pictures
   c. Shapes
   d. Pictures

3. To do a keyword search for a picture that is not on your computer or storage medium, click the _____ button.
   a. Images
   b. Online Pictures
   c. Shapes
   d. Pictures

4. You can format a picture by
   a. adding borders.
   b. adding special effects.
   c. changing the picture size.
   d. adding borders, adding special effects, and sizing the picture.

5 One button you can use to arrange picture objects on your slide is the _____ button.
   a. Group
   b. Bring Forward
   c. Picture Effects
   d. Text Direction

6 To enhance your slide presentation you should
   a. set the text color the same as the background color so the text is easy to read.
   b. add simple transitions and animations to help keep the audience engaged.
   c. add sounds that play repeatedly to every slide to be sure everyone is listening when you present.
   d. set the text color the same as the background color, add simple transitions and animations, and add sounds.

7 Transitions are effects that occur
   a. when you move from one slide to another.
   b. when you click an animation button.
   c. when you display bullet points on a slide.
   d. if you play several animations on one slide.

8 The length of time a sound is played
   a. is always the same as the length of the sound.
   b. can be modified by changing the duration setting.
   c. is always the same as the length of the slide show.
   d. changes depending on the transition chosen.

9 Animations affect
   a. what appears when you move from one slide to another.
   b. transition sounds.
   c. how the content of each slide appears.
   d. videos inserted into your presentation.

10 You select animation effects to apply to objects on your slide using the
   a. Transitions gallery.
   b. Design gallery.
   c. Animations gallery.
   d. Effects Options button.

Hands-On Skills Review

Exercise **Promote the Music Industry**

Skills Add transitions, add animations, and choose animation effects

Scenario Format a presentation about a possible career in the music industry. The final presentation should be enhanced with appropriate transitions and animation effects.

Steps

1 Open the student data file named **M8-C3-ExA-MusicIndustry.pptx** and save the file as **Lastname-M8-C3-ExA-MusicIndustry.pptx**, but replace *Lastname* with your last name.

2 Enter your name and the current date on two separate lines in the subtitle placeholder of Slide 1.

3 Use the Header and Footer dialog box to insert a footer containing the slide number and *The Music Industry* on all slides except the title slide.

4 Apply the Organic theme to all slides. The first color variant is selected by default. Do not change the color variant.

5 Animate the arrow shapes on Slide 6 (*Job Outlook*) as follows:
   a. To the arrow that points up, apply the Wipe animation with the From Bottom effect option. Using the Animation Pane, set the transition to *Start After Previous*.

   b. To the arrow that points down, apply the Wipe animation with the *From Top* effect option. Using the Animation Pane, set the transition to *Start After Previous*.

6 Insert the following entrance and emphasis animations using the ANIMATIONS tab. Use the Animation Pane to set each animation to start after the previous animation is done.
   a. Slide 2: *Zoom*; Effect Options: *Object Center*
   b. Slide 3: *Fade*
   c. Slide 4: *Shape*; Effect Options: *Direction = In, Shape = Plus*
   d. Slide 7: *Teeter* (Set the animation on the table.)
   e. Slide 8: *Grow/Shrink*, Effect Options: *Direction = Both, Amount = Larger*

7 Add transitions as follows:
   a. Slide 1: *Split*; Effect Options: *Vertical Out*
   b. Slides 2–8: *Push*; Effect Options: *From Right*

8 Type the following speaker notes for Slide 2. Using the skills you learned in Module 5, format the notes as a bulleted list. ***HINT:*** *Use the Bullets button in the Paragraph group on the HOME tab.*

- Musicians play musical instruments independently or in a group like a rock band, jazz band, or an orchestra.
- Singers may sing the part of a character, as in a musical.
- Directors and conductors lead instrumental and vocal groups.
- Composers create original music.
- Arrangers adapt existing music for use by specific performing groups.
- Repairers and tuners keep instruments in working order.

9 Save the presentation.

10 Preview the presentation.

11 Submit the completed presentation to your instructor.

Completed Step 8

Completed Exercise A

Exercise **B** Enhance a Car Racing Presentation

Skills   Insert an object on a slide, format a picture, add transitions, and add sound

Scenario   Add interest to a presentation about race cars by adding images, a sound, and transitions.

Steps

1 Open the student data file named **M8-C3-ExB-CarRacing.pptx** and save the file as **Lastname-M8-C3-ExB-CarRacings**, but replace *Lastname* with your last name.

2 Enter your name and the current date on two separate lines in the subtitle placeholder of Slide 1.

3 Make the following modifications to the slide master:

  a. Insert the image of the race car from **M8-C3-ExB-RaceCar1.jpg**. The image should appear on all slides, regardless of the slide layout. **HINT:** *Use the Office Theme Slide Master layout (the top layout choice).*

  b. *Size the image to a height of 1.1 inches and a width of 1.65 inches. Then move the image to the horizontal position 10.77 inches from the top left corner and to the vertical position 5.66 from the top left corner.* **HINT:** *Use the SIZE options and POSITION options in the Format Picture pane.*

  c. In Normal view, add a footer to all slides that displays the slide number. Do not show the footer on the title slide.

  d. Close Slide Master view.

4 Using the Format Background pane on the DESIGN tab, hide the **M8-C3-ExB-RaceCar1.jpg** image on Slide 6 and insert **M8-C3-ExB-RaceCar2.jpg** in the content placeholder on the right side.

5 Add transitions:

  a. Slide 2: *Doors*

  b. Slides 3–5: *Zoom*

  c. Slide 6: *Clock*

  d. Slide 7: *Vortex*

6 Using the TRANSITIONS tab, apply the camera sound to Slide 6.

7 Save the presentation.

8 Preview the presentation.

9 Submit the completed presentation to your instructor.

Completed Exercise B

Exercise C | How I Found the Perfect Gift

Skills Insert an object on a slide, format a picture, add transitions, add sound, add animations, and choose animation effects

Scenario You decide to tell your friends the story of your search for a perfect gift. Because you plan to show this presentation to your friends, you experiment to select some fun sounds and transitions, even though the combination you select might be considered "too much" for a business presentation.

Steps

1 Open the student data file named **M8-C3-ExC-BirthdayGift.pptx** and save the file as **Lastname-M8-C3-ExC-Perfume**, but replace *Lastname* with your last name.

2 Enter your name and the current date on two separate lines in the subtitle placeholder of Slide 1.

3 Type Jane's Birthday Present as the footer on all slides except the title slide.

4 Insert a picture on Slide 3 (*Idea*) to match the "man and bulb" image shown in Completed Exercise C on the opposite page. To find the image, search online at Office.com Clip Art using the keywords *idea cartoon*. Select the "man and bulb" picture. (It should be the fifth image. If you cannot locate this image, select an image that is similar.) Using the Format Picture pane, move the picture to the horizontal position 8.25 inches from the top left corner and to the vertical position 1.8 inches from the top left corner. Do not change the size of the picture.

5 On Slide 6 (*Perfect*), insert the picture of the sale bag, using the student data file named **M8-C3-ExC-Sale.jpg**, in the right column content placeholder.

6 Apply the Facet theme to all slides and select the third color variant (purple).

7 Add transitions to slides as follows:
   a. Slide 1: *Ripple*
   b. Slide 7: *Vortex*

8 Using the TRANSITIONS tab, add sounds that play during slide transitions as follows:
   a. Slide 2: *Cash register*
   b. Slide 3: *Drum roll*
   c. Slide 5: *Wind*
   d. Slide 7: *Applause*

9 Add animations to Slide 4 (*Look for the Perfect Scent*).
   a. Perfume bottle on left – *Fly In* animation and *From Left* effect option
   b. Perfume bottle on right – *Fly In* animation and *From Right* effect option
   c. Set each animation to *Start After Previous*.

10 Save the presentation.

11 Preview the presentation.

12 Submit the completed presentation to your instructor.

Completed Exercise C

Chapter 4

Completing, Running, and Sharing Your Show

After you have finished adding content to your presentation, you should perform a final spelling check to make sure that no embarrassing errors lurk in your text. You must also specify settings for how your slide show should run. These settings control how your show moves from slide to slide, either manually with a click or key press or automatically using recorded slide timings. You can also set up a show to loop continuously so that it plays over and over again.

You might want to print a copy of your slides for your own reference, print handouts for your audience, or print speaker notes to use while presenting or for reference later on. You can also use the powerful tools in PowerPoint to broadcast your presentation online where it can be viewed by others as you navigate through the slides.

Skills You Learn

1   Check spelling
2   Run a show
3   Rehearse timings
4   Set up a show
5   Print presentation notes
6   Present online

Files You Need
For these skills, you use the following student data file.

> M8-C4-S1-ChocolateInMovies.pptx

What You Create
A fun new exhibit is opening at the Museum. It focuses on the role of chocolate in the world of entertainment: movies, TV shows, and songs. You have been asked to create a short, self-running slide show highlighting the uses of chocolate in movies. The presentation is a teaser to encourage Museum visitors to step into the exhibit. Visitors can run the show at a kiosk set up in the lobby, so you need to prepare a few things ahead of time. You specify the slide show's playback settings and set timings for how long each slide is displayed.

In this chapter, you master all of these tasks, print a copy of the presentation for the exhibit director, and broadcast the presentation online.

Chocolate in Movies Presentation

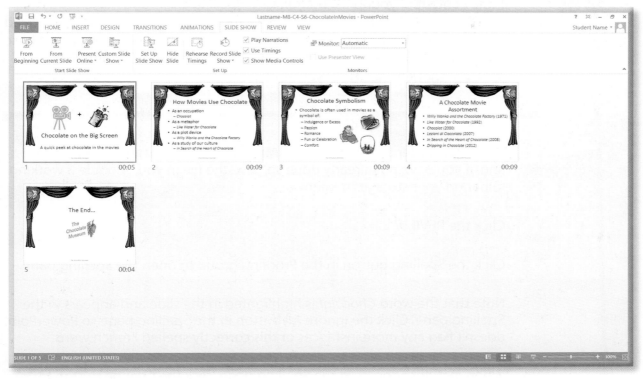

PowerPoint

Check Spelling

Video M8_C4_S01

If the content of your presentation is spelled correctly, your audience is more likely to take your message seriously. PowerPoint's built-in spelling checker can help you find spelling errors and make suggestions for correcting them, but you need to decide what to do with these recommendations.

Steps

1 Open the student data file named **M8-C4-S1-ChocolateInMovies.pptx** and, if you have not already done so, save the file in your Module 8 working folder on your storage medium.

2 Click the REVIEW tab.

3 **Shortcut**
Spelling Check
F7

3 Click the Spelling button in the Proofing group to open the Spelling pane.

▶Tip If you are certain that a word only appears once, click the Ignore button. If it is possible that a word appears more than once, click the Ignore All button.

4 Note that the word *Chocolat* is highlighted in the slide and appears in the Spelling pane. Click the Ignore All button in the Spelling pane so PowerPoint doesn't flag any more instances of this correctly spelled French word.

5 When *metafor* appears in the Spelling pane, click the Change button to replace this word with the correct spelling, *metaphor*.

6 When *Wonka* appears in the Spelling pane, click the Ignore All button.

7 When *Lezioni* appears in the Spelling pane, click the Ignore button.

8 When *Cioccolato* appears in the Spelling pane, click the Ignore button.

9 When a message appears saying the spelling check is complete, click OK.

10 Close the Spelling pane.

11 Save the file.

Completed Skill 1

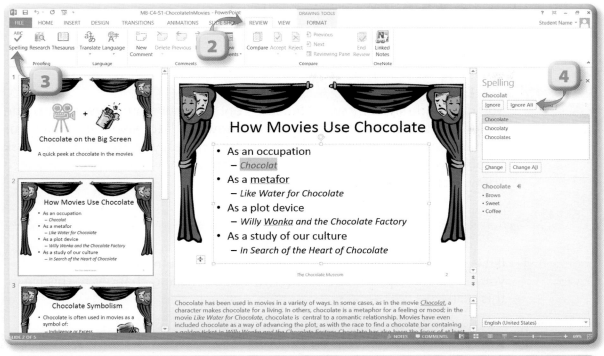

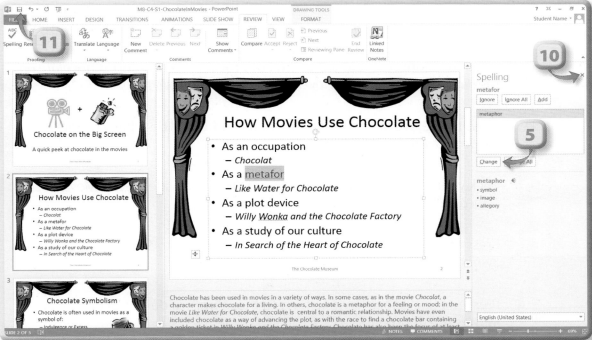

Taking It Further

Add Words to the Spelling Check Dictionary

Any word not found in the dictionary is questioned during the spelling check. If you frequently use a word that the spelling check questions, such as your company name or your last name, you can add that word to the spelling check dictionary—just click the Add button in the Spelling pane when that word is questioned during a spelling check. Once you add a word to the dictionary, it no longer appears as an error in the Spelling pane. If you later need to remove a word from the dictionary, click the FILE tab, click *Options*, click the *Proofing* option, and then click the Custom Dictionaries button.

PowerPoint

Chapter 4

Skill 2

M8_C4_S02

Run a Show

You run a slide show by switching to Slide Show view. The tools available in that view help you to navigate through your slides. Running a slide show works differently depending on whether you have set up the show to advance manually or automatically. In this skill, you work with a show set up to advance manually.

Steps

▶**Tip** If you are using an LCD display or television to show your presentation, check the device's user manual to make sure you set up the display equipment properly.

1 If it is not already open, open **M8-C4-S1-ChocolateInMovies.pptx**, the file you saved in the previous skill. You will not be making changes to this file in this skill.

2 Click the SLIDE SHOW tab.

3 Click the From Beginning button to run the slide show from the first slide.

4 *Another Way*
Next Slide
N

4 Press the Right Arrow key one time to proceed from Slide 1 (*Chocolate on the Big Screen*) to Slide 2 (*How Movies Use Chocolate*).

5 *Another Way*
Previous Slide
P

5 Press the Left Arrow key one time to move from Slide 2 back to Slide 1 (*Chocolate on the Big Screen*).

6 Click your mouse button to move from Slide 1 to Slide 2 (*How Movies Use Chocolate*).

7 *Another Way*
Advance one slide by pressing the Page Down button.

7 Press the spacebar one time to move from Slide 2 to Slide 3 (*Chocolate Symbolism*).

8 *Another Way*
Go back one slide by pressing the Page Up button.

8 Press the Backspace key one time to move from Slide 3 to Slide 2 (*How Movies Use Chocolate*).

9 Right-click in Slide 2 and then click *See All Slides* in the pop-up menu to display thumbnails of all slides in the presentation.

10 Click Slide 4 to display it in full-screen Slide Show view.

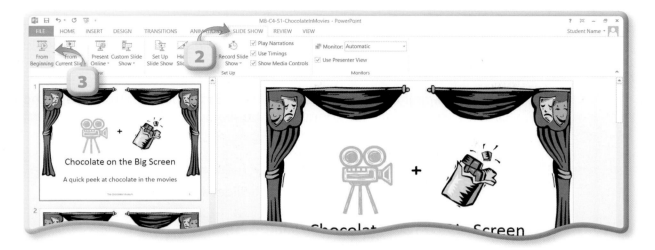

More

11 Hover your mouse pointer over the lower left corner of the slide to reveal the buttons in the Slide Show toolbar. Click the Previous ⊲ button to navigate from Slide 4 to Slide 3 (*Chocolate Symbolism*).

12 Click the Magnifying Glass ⊛ button in the Slide Show control bar and then click the word *Comfort* to zoom in on the slide.

13 Right-click once to zoom back out.

14 Click the See All Slides ⊞ button in the Slide Show toolbar.

15 Click Slide 5 to display it in Slide Show view.

16 Click the Pen ⊘ button in the Slide Show toolbar.

17 Click *Laser Pointer* in the pop-up menu.

18 Use the laser pointer to point to the cocoa pod image on Slide 5.

19 *Shortcut*
End Show
Esc

19 Right-click the current slide and then click *End Show* in the pop-up menu. This returns the presentation to Normal view.

Taking It Further

Using Presenter View   Another way to view your PowerPoint slides is in Presenter view. If you have the necessary hardware, Presenter view lets you see your notes while you are delivering your presentation. (The audience sees just the presentation, not your notes.) Access Presenter view by clicking ⊙ on the Slide Show control bar in the bottom left corner of the slide and then clicking *Show Presenter View*. In Presenter view, you have access to the Slide Show control bar, which allows you to navigate your presentation, see all your slides as thumbnails (making it easy to jump to a particular slide), zoom in on slides, and use digital tools, such as a pen, to highlight information on a slide.

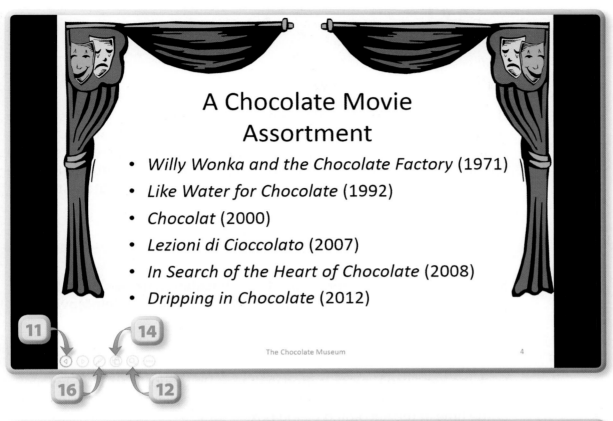

PowerPoint

Skill 3

Video M8_C4_S03

Rehearse Timings

If no speaker will be present to run a slide show, you need to record timings for how long each slide should display before advancing to the next slide. PowerPoint uses those timings to automatically advance the show. In this skill, you learn how to rehearse and save specific timings for each slide. In Skill 4, you apply settings to make the show advance automatically.

Steps

1 If it is not already open, open **M8-C4-S1-ChocolateInMovies.pptx**, the file you saved in Skill 1, and save the file as **M8-C4-S3-ChocolateInMovies**.

2 Click the SLIDE SHOW tab.

3 Click the Rehearse Timings button in the Set Up group. Read Slide 1 while the timer runs. Note how long it takes to read the slide content by looking at the time in the Recording dialog box.

4 Another Way
You can allow the timer to run and then press Enter when you wish to stop the timer.

4 Select the time in the timing measurement box (to make the timer stop running). If the timer does not show 0:00:05, type 0:00:05 and then press Enter.

▶**Tip** The idea is to provide an appropriate amount of time for the slide to display, depending on the amount of information on the slide.

5 Type 0:00:09 in the timing measurement boxes for Slides 2 through 4.

6 Type 0:00:04 in the timing measurement box for Slide 5.

▶**Tip** If you are not happy with the timings you recorded, choose No in Step 7 and they will not be saved.

7 At the warning box indicating that the total time was 0:00:36, click Yes. This opens the presentation in Normal view.

8 Click the VIEW tab and then click the Slide Sorter button in the Presentation Views group. View the assigned times for each slide in the presentation.

9 Save the file.

Taking It Further

Recording a Narration If you wish, you can record a narration to play along with your slide show. When you record a narration, you can save timings that match the length of each slide's narration. Use the Record Slide Show button in the Set Up group on the SLIDE SHOW tab to record a narration, such as the one contained in the notes pane of the movie slide show.

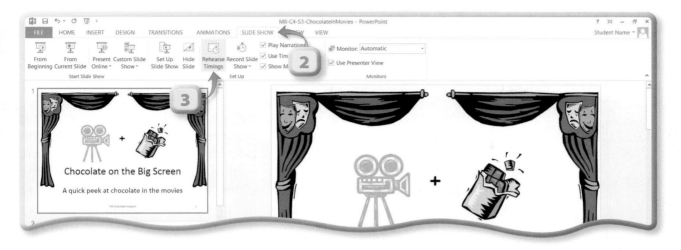

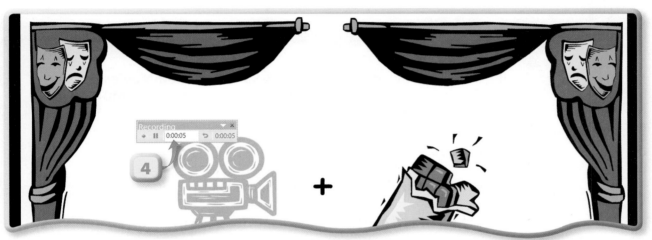

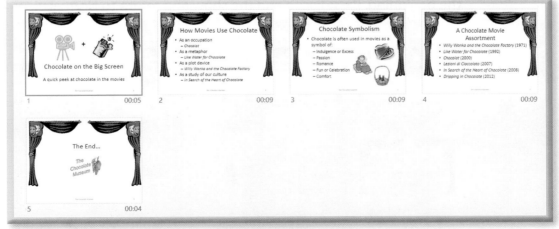

Completed Skill 3

PowerPoint

Set Up a Show

M8_C4_S04

PowerPoint provides three different playback options. One option is for a live speaker to give the presentation. With this choice, the speaker provides information and typically advances each slide when he or she is ready to go to the next topic. Another option is to allow the show to be run by a viewer using onscreen controls. The final option is to have the show run on its own, continuously looping through the slides. When you set up a show to run on its own, the timings you save determine when the show advances from one slide to another.

Steps

1 If it is not already open, open **M8-C4-S3-ChocolateInMovies.pptx**, the file you saved in the previous skill, and save the file as **M8-C4-S4-ChocolateInMovies**.

2 Click the SLIDE SHOW tab.

3 Click the Set Up Slide Show button in the Set Up group.

▶ **Tip** When you select the *Browsed at a kiosk (full screen)* setting, viewers cannot control the show.

4 Click the *Browsed at a kiosk (full screen)* option in the *Show type* section.

5 Confirm that the *Using timings, if present* option is selected in the *Advance slides* section.

6 Click OK.

7 Save the file.

8 **Shortcut**
Run Show
F5

8 Run the show and watch it advance slide by slide, and then start again at the beginning. Press Esc to end the show and return to Normal view.

Slides set to run automatically with set timings for each slide.

Completed Skill 4

Taking It Further

Creating a Custom Show   When creating a custom show, you have the option to select certain slides from a longer presentation. For example, if you have a long presentation about student government, you might want to create a shorter version containing only the slides about school administration. To create a custom show, click the SLIDE SHOW tab, click the Custom Slide Show button in the Start Slide Show group, and then click *Custom Shows* from the drop-down list to open the Custom Show dialog box. Click the New button to open the Define Custom Show dialog box. Name the custom slide show by typing the name in the *Slide show*

name text box. Choose a slide you wish to include in your show by clicking the slide number on the left. Click the Add button to move that slide to the *Slides in custom show* list. When you have added all the slides you want to include in your custom show, click OK and then click Close. Set up your custom show by clicking the Set Up Slide Show button in the Start Slide Show group to open the Set Up Show dialog box, clicking the *Custom show* option in the *Show slides* section, clicking your custom show in the drop-down list, and then clicking OK. When you run your custom slide show, you will see only the slides you selected for it.

PowerPoint

Print Presentation Notes

 **Video** M8_C4_S05

Once you have finalized your presentation, you may want to print copies of it. You can print full-page slides, print audience handouts that include any of several combinations of single or multiple slides oriented horizontally or vertically on the page (as you did in Module 8, Chapter 2, Skill 6), or print each slide with its accompanying speaker notes. In this skill, you perform the third option: printing the Notes pages.

Steps

1 If it is not already open, open **M8-C4-S4-ChocolateInMovies.pptx**, the file you saved in the previous skill. You will not be making changes to this file.

2 Click the FILE tab.

3 Click the *Print* option.

4 In the *Settings* category, click the *Full Page Slides* option.

5 In the *Print Layout* section of the drop-down list, click *Notes Pages*.

6 Click the Print button if your instructor would like a printout. The six slides in the presentation print as Notes pages on your default printer.

2 Shortcut
Print backstage area
Ctrl + P

▶**Tip** If you want to print a subset of slides, click the first setting (by default, *Print All Slides*) and choose to print the currently active slide or click *Custom Range* and enter a range of slides to print.

▶**Tip** In the *Print Layout* section, you have two other options besides *Notes Pages*: *Full Page Slides* or *Outline*. The default option is *Full Page Slides*.

▶**Tip** When you click *Full Page Slides*, the drop-down list also gives you options for printing handouts with various layouts, framing the slides, scaling the printout to fit the paper, and producing high-quality printouts.

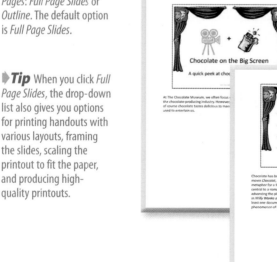

Completed Skill 5

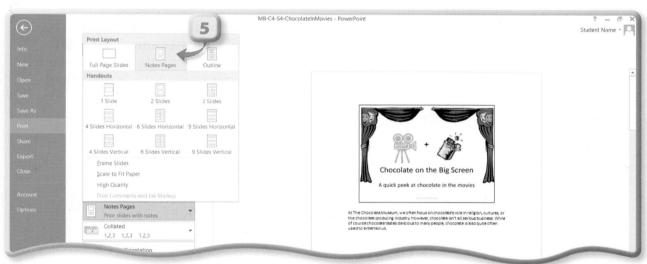

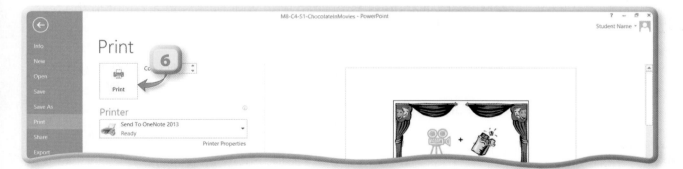

Taking It Further

Advanced Print Settings There are a few more settings you can select to affect how your document prints. For example, you can choose to collate copies so that multiple copies print as sets (rather than printing three page 1s in a stack, three page 2s in a stack, and so on). You can also choose to print in color or on both sides of the paper (which may require that you turn over the paper in your printer after printing the first side). All these options are available in the Print backstage area.

PowerPoint

Video M8_C4_S06

Present Online

PowerPoint provides a powerful feature for presenting your presentation online in real time. This feature is free and uses the Office Presentation Service, so you don't even need your own website to present online.

However, you are required to have a Microsoft account. You can use the same Microsoft account that you used to create a SkyDrive account in the Introduction (Your Digital Toolkit), Chapter 2.

Steps

1 If it is not already open, open **M8-C4-S4-ChocolateInMovies.pptx**, the file you saved in Skill 4, and save the file as **Lastname-M8-C4-S6-ChocolateInMovies**, but replace *Lastname* with your last name. Be sure to save the file in your Module 8 working folder on your storage medium.

2 Click the FILE tab.

3 Click the *Share* option.

4 Click *Present Online* in the *Share* category.

5 Click the Present Online button.

6 Enter the email address associated with your Microsoft account in the text box in the Microsoft account dialog box.

7 Enter your password in the text box in the Microsoft account dialog box.

8 Click the Sign in button.

2-5 *Another Way*
Click the SLIDE SHOW tab, click the Present Online button in the Start Slide Show group, and then click the CONNECT button in the Present Online dialog box.

▶**Tip** If you want remote users to be able to download the presentation to their computers after viewing the online presentation, click the *Enable remote viewers to download the presentation* check box in the Present Online pane, to insert a check mark.

▶**Tip** If you do not have a Microsoft account, click the <u>Sign up</u> link to sign up.

▶**Tip** If you are already signed in to your Microsoft account, you will skip Steps 6–8.

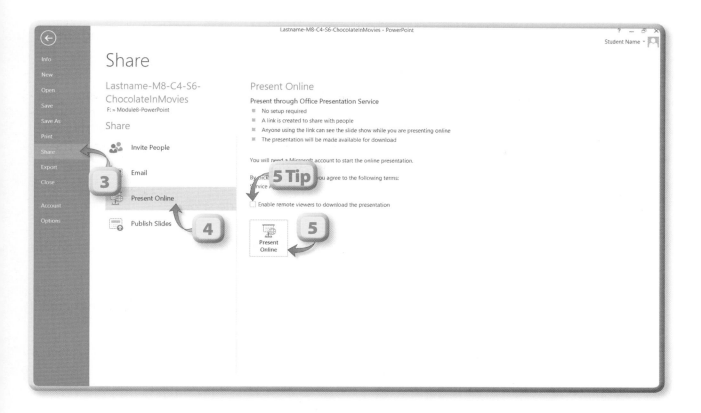

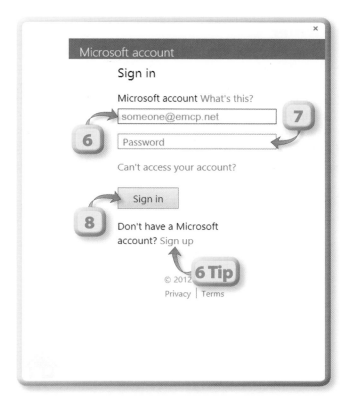

More

Tip You can provide this link to as many people as you would like to view the presentation. Don't forget to provide a presentation starting time when you pass along the URL to your attendees! They need to know when you will be running the presentation.

9 In the Present Online dialog box, click *Send in Email…* and then send the link to yourself.

10 Click the START PRESENTATION button to begin the live presentation. Individuals who have have received a link to the online presentation and have clicked that link can watch the presentation as you run it. The slides advance automatically according to the timings set in the slide show. The show continues to loop from Slide 6 back to Slide 1.

11 Press Esc when you are done watching the slide show.

12 Click the End Online Presentation button in the Present Online group on the PRESENT ONLINE tab.

13 At the warning box indicating that all remote viewers will be disconnected if you continue, click End Online Presentation.

14 Save and then close the file.

Taking It Further

Share a Presentation Using Sky Drive
You can also share a presentation by first saving it to your SkyDrive account. To save a presentation to your SkyDrive account, click the FILE tab, click *Save As*, and then select your SkyDrive account in the *Save As* list. You can then share the presentation with other people by clicking the FILE tab, clicking *Share*, and then clicking the *Invite People* option in the *Share* category. Refer to Chapter 2 in the Introduction (Your Digital Toolkit) for more information on SkyDrive.

PowerPoint

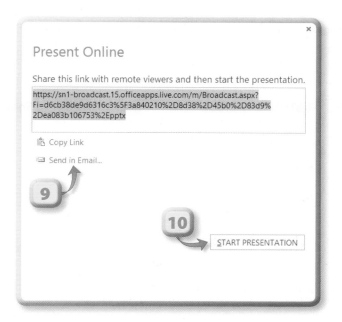

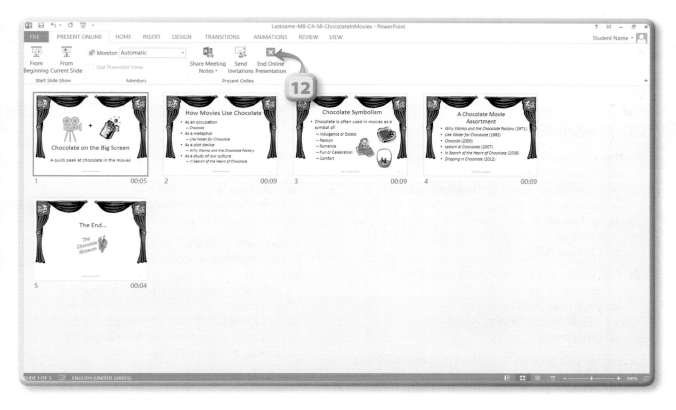

PowerPoint

Tasks Summary

Task	Ribbon Tab, Group	Button, Option	Shortcut, Alternative
Check spelling	REVIEW, Proofing	ABC ✓	F7
Set show type	SLIDE SHOW, Set Up		
Set how slides advance	SLIDE SHOW, Set Up		
Print a presentation	FILE, *Print*	Print	Ctrl + P
Rehearse timings	SLIDE SHOW, Set Up		
Run a show	SLIDE SHOW, Start Slide Show		F5
Present a presentation online	FILE, *Share*	Present Online	

Features Review

Select the best answer from the choices given.

1 If you want the spelling check feature to leave all instances of a spelling alone, choose _____ while running the spelling check.
  a. Ignore
  b. Ignore All
  c. Change
  d. Change All

2 The spelling check feature is based on
  a. an online dictionary.
  b. your past spelling choices.
  c. a built-in dictionary.
  d. Wikipedia.

3 Before you give an in-person presentation to a large group, you must
  a. obtain a copyright for the materials.
  b. connect display equipment to your computer.
  c. save a backup copy.
  d. add timings.

4 One way to manually advance from one slide to the next is to
  a. click the left mouse button.
  b. press Backspace.
  c. press Esc.
  d. click the left mouse button, press Backspace, or press Esc.

5 Pressing the P key while running a slide show
  a. ends the show.
  b. takes you to the next slide.
  c. takes you to the previous slide.
  d. restarts the show.

6 If you want your slide presentation to run continuously at a professional trade show, you must
  a. rehearse your presentation timings in advance.
  b. uncheck *Use timings if present*.
  c. log in to your Windows Live account.
  d. create a custom show.

7 The *Slide Show type* option that is typically used to advance manually from slide to slide during a meeting is
  a. *Browsed by an individual (window)*.
  b. *Browsed at a kiosk (full screen)*.
  c. *Presented by a speaker (full screen)*.
  d. *Loop continuously until 'Esc'*.

8 In PowerPoint you can print
  a. full-page slides.
  b. handouts.
  c. notes.
  d. full-page slides, handouts, and notes.

9 When you choose to print handouts, you can set
   a. how many slides to print on each page.
   b. whether to include icons for sounds.
   c. whether to include images on the printout.
   d. the number of slides per page and whether to include images on the printout.

10 Before you print a presentation, you should
   a. run a spelling check.
   b. change the design.
   c. back up the file.
   d. record a narration.

Hands-On Skills Review

Exercise **A** **Complete an Animal Shelter Presentation**

Skills   Check spelling and run a show

SNAP
Grade It

Scenario   You are completing a presentation about pet adoption. As one of the final steps in your preparation, review the content for spelling errors.

Steps

1 Open the student data file named **M8-C4-ExA-Pets.pptx** and save the file as **Lastname-M8-C4-ExA-Pets**, but replace *Lastname* with your last name.

2 Enter your name and the current date in the subtitle placeholder on two separate lines on the title slide (Slide 1). If necessary, move an image so your entire name and the date are visible.

3 Use the Header and Footer dialog box to insert a footer on all of the slides displaying *Helping Shelters* and the slide number. Do not show the footer on the title slide.

4 Check the spelling of the slide content and correct any errors you find. Check your corrections aginst the Completed Excercise A slides shown below.

5 Save the file.

6 Preview the presentation.

7 Submit the completed presentation to your instructor.

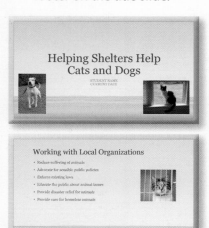

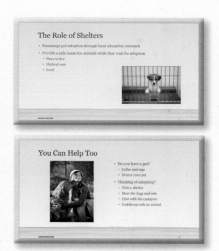

Completed Exercise A

Exercise **B** | **Print Animal Shelter Presentation Handouts and Notes Pages**

Skills   Print presentation notes

Scenario   You are preparing to deliver your presentation about pet adoption. Print handouts for the audience and print notes pages that you can use as a guide while presenting.

Steps

1 Open **Lastname-M8-C4-ExA-Pets.pptx**, the file you saved in the previous exercise, and save the file as **Lastname-M8-C4-ExB-Pets**, but replace *Lastname* with your last name.

2 Add a header and a footer to the notes and handouts pages. Insert your name and the date in the header and the page number in the footer.

3 Save the file.

4 Print one set of handouts of all of the slides in the presentation using three slides per page. **HINT:** *Select* 3 Slides *under* Handouts *in the* Settings *area of the Print menu.*

5 Print one set of the notes pages of all of the slides in the presentation to use as talking points during delivery of the presentation.

6 Submit both sets of printouts to your instructor.

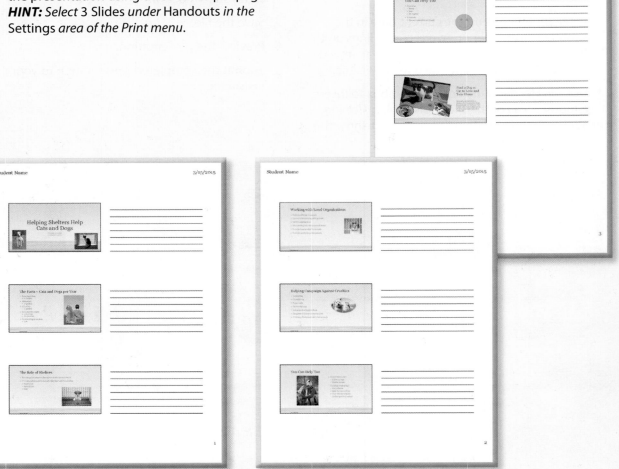

Completed Exercise B (Step 4)

Completed Exercise B (Step 5)

Exercise **C** **Broadcast an Animal Shelter Presentation**

Skills   Run a show, rehearse timings, set up a show, and present online

Scenario   Your presentation was popular, and the audience enjoyed hearing about pets and adoption. A local shelter has asked if they can have a copy of the presentation to share with visitors. You decide to set timings so the slide show progresses without a speaker present.

Steps

1   Open **Lastname-M8-C4-ExB-Pets.pptx**, the file you saved in the previous exercise, and save the file as **Lastname-M8-C4-ExC-Pets**, but replace *Lastname* with your last name.

2   Complete one of the following:
   a.   Set the timings for the slides in the presentation as follows:

Slide 1	*Helping Shelters Help Cats and Dogs*	0:00:03
Slide 2	*The Facts*	0:00:08
Slide 3	*The Role of Shelters*	0:00:07
Slide 4	*Working with Local Organizations*	0:00:07
Slide 5	*Helping Campaign Against Cruelties*	0:00:08
Slide 6	*You Can Help Too*	0:00:09
Slide 7	*You Can Help Too*	0:00:07
Slide 8	*Find a Dog or Cat*	0:00:15

   b.   Add customized timings to all slides in the presentation using the Rehearse Timings button on the SLIDE SHOW tab. ***HINT:*** *It is difficult to determine how long each slide should appear. To achieve realistic timings, read every line on the slide slowly, as if you are seeing it for the first time, spend a moment looking at each of the images on the slide, and then move to the next slide.*

   c.   ***Extension activity:*** Record a narration of the slide's notes and set the timing to match the length of the narration. ***HINT:*** *Review the Taking It Further: Recording a Narration feature in Skill 3. Find a quiet place to record the narration. Ask for a microphone if necessary. Speak slowly and give the viewer enough time to look at the slide images before moving to the next slide.*

3   Set up the slide show to play automatically when browsed at a kiosk.

4   Save the file.

5   Preview the presentation.

6   Submit the completed presentation to your instructor.

7   If possible, present the slide show online using the Office Presentation Service. Ask your instructor where to send the email link.

Completed Exercise C

Module 8 Projects

Project 1

Skills **CH1:** Add notes, apply a theme **CH2:** Change formatting in Slide Master view, insert a graphic in Slide Master view, insert a footer in a slide master, insert a header in a handout master and print a handout **CH3:** Insert an object on a slide, format a picture, add transitions **CH4:** Run a show, print presentation notes

Scenario You just returned from a great trip to New York City, where you visited many attractions. The school glee club is considering a trip to NYC for a singing competition. You decide to share your experience with them using a PowerPoint presentation. Be sure to add graphics and interest to the presentation and then print handouts, three slides per page, so club members can take notes while you discuss your trip.

Steps

1 Open the student data file named **M8-EOM-P1-NYC.pptx**, and save the file as **Lastname-M8-EOM-P1-NYC**, but replace *Lastname* with your last name.

2 Add four pictures to the slides as described below, using the image files provided:
   a. Add **M8-EOM-P1-img1.jpg** to the left content area of the Statue of Liberty slide (Slide 3).
   b. Add **M8-EOM-P1-img2.jpg** to the right content area of the Empire State Building slide (Slide 4).
   c. Add **M8-EOM-P1-img3.jpg** to the Central Park slide (Slide 5). Change the size of the image to 3.19 inches high and 4.82 inches wide. Place the image in the lower right corner of the content area at the horizontal position 7.6 inches from the top left corner and the vertical position 3.57 inches from the top left corner.
   d. Add **M8-EOM-P1-img4.jpg** to the content area of the final slide (Slide 6).

3 Open Slide Master view and change the title font for the slides to Broadway. ***HINT:*** *Select the top slide in the slides pane and click in the title placeholder before changing the font.*

4 Add a footer to all slides that displays the current date, *New York City*, and the slide number.

5 Add a header and a footer to the Notes and Handouts pages. Enter your name and the date in the header. Enter *New York City* and the page number in the footer.

6 In Normal view, apply the Retrospect theme to all slides and select the fourth color variant (gray).

7 Apply the Checkerboard transition with the From Left effect option to Slide 2.

8 Apply the Blinds transition with the Vertical effect option to Slide 6.

9 Enter these speaker notes for Slide 2:

There is a lot to see and do when you visit NYC. Spend some time visiting the landmark buildings. Sit and relax in Central Park. See world-famous museums. Take in a Broadway show. The list is practically endless. A few landmarks are highlighted in this presentation.

10 Print handouts for your audience, three per page. ***HINT:*** *Open the Print backstage area. In the* Settings *section, click the* Full Page Slides *down-pointing arrow and then click* 3 Slides *in the* Handouts *section.*

11 Print the Notes page for Slide 2.

12 Save the file.

13 Preview the presentation.

14 Submit the completed file, the handouts, and the Notes page to your instructor.

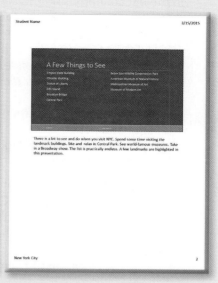

Completed Project 1

Project 2

Skills   **CH1:** Apply a theme **CH2:** Change formatting in Slide Master view, insert a graphic in Slide Master view **CH3:** Insert an object on a slide, format a picture, add transitions, add animations, choose animation effects **CH4:** Run a show, present online

Scenario   Your neighbor's son is learning arithmetic and needs some help. Create an arithmetic flash card tutorial using PowerPoint. Make it interesting and fun as well as educational so that he practices often.

Steps

1 Open the student data file named **M8-EOM-P2-FlashCards.pptx**, and save the file as **Lastname-M8-EOM-P2-FlashCards.pptx**, but replace *Lastname* with your last name.

2 Enter your name and the current date in the subtitle placeholder on two separate lines.

3 Display Slide Master view and click the Comparison layout.

4 Modify the Comparison layout by performing Steps a through d (listed below) for both the left and the right content placeholders. You can do so by selecting the content placeholders in both the left and right columns of the slide and performing the steps just once, or by selecting the content placeholders one at a time and performing Steps a through d for each column separately. ***HINT:*** *To select both content placeholders, click one, hold down the Shift key while you click the other, and then release the Shift key. This selects both content placeholders.*

a. Turn off bullets. ***HINT:*** *Click the Bullets button in the Paragraph group on the HOME tab.*

b. Center the text.

c. Vertically center the text. ***HINT:*** *Click the Align Text button in the Paragraph group on the HOME tab and then click the* Middle *option.*

d. Change the font size to 40 points.

5 Select the caption placeholders above both the left and right columns of the slide. You can perform Steps a and b (listed below) twice, once for each caption placeholder or, if you wish to perform the steps only once, use the Click, Shift-Click method (click one placeholder, hold down the Shift key while you click the other, and then release the Shift key).

a. Center the text.

b. Change the text to all uppercase letters. ***HINT:*** *Click the Change Case button arrow in the Font group on the HOME tab and then click the* UPPERCASE *option.*

6. Click the caption and content placeholders in the left column using the Click, Shift-Click method, and then make the following changes using the Drawing group on the DRAWING TOOLS FORMAT tab. **HINT:** *With the Click, Shift-Click method, you click in a slide element, press the Shift key, then click other slide elements while holding the Shift key.*
   a. Apply the Black, Text 1 theme color to the shape outline.
   b. Apply the Blue, Accent 5, Lighter 40% theme color to the shape fill.

7. Select the caption and content placeholders in the right column using the Click, Shift-Click method, and then make the following changes using the Drawing group on the DRAWING TOOLS FORMAT tab:
   a. Apply the Black, Text 1 theme color to the shape outline.
   b. Apply the Green, Accent 6, Darker 25% theme color to the shape fill.

8. Return to Normal view.

9. Add the Smiley Face shape to the final slide (Slide 7) and change the size of the image to 3.5 inches high and 3.5 inches wide. Place the face at the horizontal position 8.0 inches from the top left corner and the vertical position 2.25 inches from the top left corner. Fill the shape using Orange, Accent 2, and set the shape outline to Blue-Gray, Text 2.

10. Add transitions as follows:
    a. Slide 1: *Fade*; Effect Option: *Smoothly*
    b. Slides 2–6: *Push*; Effect Option: *From Right*
    c. Slide 7: *Shape*; Effect Option: *Circle*

11. Add animations as follows:
    a. Open Slide Master view.
    b. Select the Comparison layout. **HINT:** *This is the same layout that you modified in the first few steps of this assignment.*
    c. Select the caption and content placeholders in the right column using the Click, Shift-Click method.
    d. Apply the Appear animation and the As One Object effect option.
    e. Return to Normal view.

12. Apply the Wisp theme to the title slide and the final slide (Slides 1 and 7).

13. Save the file.

14. Preview the presentation.

15. Submit the completed file to your instructor.

16. If possible, present the slide show online using the Office Presentation Service. Ask your instructor where to send the email link.

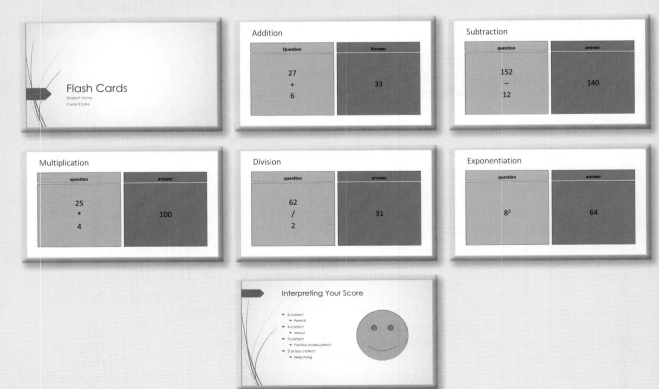

Completed Project 2

Project 3

Skills   **CH1:** Open PowerPoint and insert a slide, enter text on slides, add notes, apply a layout, apply a theme **CH2:** Change formatting in Slide Master view, insert a footer in a slide master **CH3:** Insert an object on a slide, format a picture, add transitions, add sound, add animations, choose animation effects **CH4:** Check spelling, run a show, rehearse timings, set up a show, print presentation notes, present online

Scenario   Create an engaging and informative presentation about your home—real or imaginary. The presentation should provide detail about the place where you live or where you wish you lived.

Steps

1 Create a new PowerPoint file and save the file as **Lastname-M8-EOM-P3-Home.pptx**, but replace *Lastname* with your last name.

2 Create the presentation according to the following specifications:
   - Include at least five, but not more than eight, slides.
   - At least three slides should contain online pictures or your own photos. Include the source of each image in the Notes section of the slide it appears on.
   - Use the Title Slide layout on Slide 1 and use two additional layouts on other slides.
   - Use one or more design themes.
   - Apply at least two different transitions to two or more slides.
   - Apply one appropriate sound to play during a transition.
   - Animate the images and/or text on two or more slides.
   - Add a footer to all slides except the title slide that includes the date, your name, and the slide number.
   - Make a modification to the title font on the master slide that will affect all slides.
   - Include speaker notes that can be used to deliver the presentation.
   - Set timings that are appropriate for individuals viewing the slide show without a speaker (*Extension activity: Add both narration and timings.*)

3 Ensure your slides are set to advance using the timings you have added.

4 Check your spelling in the slides and the notes.

5 Ask your instructor whether you will be sharing the presentation online or delivering it in class. If you are to deliver the presentation in class, make any required adjustments so the slides advance manually.

6 Save the file.

7 Preview the presentation.

8 Submit the completed file to your instructor.

MODULE 9

Integrating Word, Excel, Access, and PowerPoint

Skills You Learn

1 Export a Word outline to PowerPoint
2 Insert an Excel chart in Word
3 Create an Access table from Excel data

Files You Need

For these skills, you need the following student data files.

M9-S1-BusinessPlan.docx
M9-S2-Letter.docx
M9-S2-Chart.xlsx
M9-S3-Inventory.xlsx
M9-S3-Chocolate.accdb

What You Create

In this module, you export a Word outline of a business plan into PowerPoint to create a new presentation. You then enhance a business letter by inserting an Excel chart into a Word document. You also copy Excel data into an Access table.

Fundraising Totals Letter

Business Plan Presentation

Chocolate Inventory Database

 Before beginning the module skills, copy the Module9-Integrating folder from the Student Resources disc to your storage medium. The copied folder will become the working folder for this module.

Guidelines for Integrating

A key advantage in using the Office 2013 suite is that you can integrate data between the application programs. *Integrating* means that you bring together two or more different application files. First you create a document or file in the Office application that best suits the data. That application is called the *source* program. Then you copy or export that file or its data to one of the other applications, called the *destination* program. For example, if you needed to create an inventory chart, you would use Excel as shown in the screen at the right.

Source Program: Excel

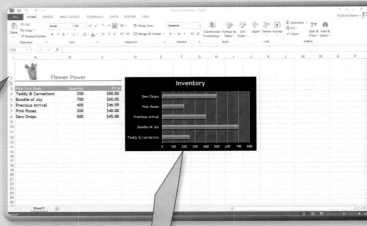

Destination Program: Word

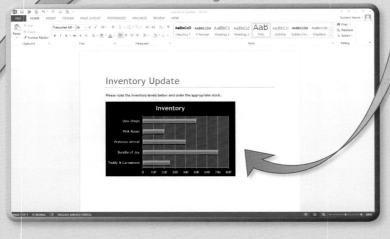

You could then insert that Excel chart in a Word document to help get your message across.

Destination Program: Access

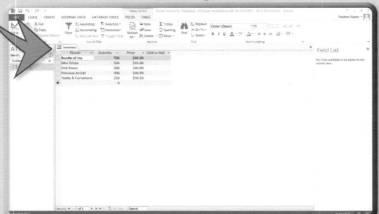

You could also copy the Excel chart data into an Access table to create new database records.

Content between Programs

As another example, if you need to create a PowerPoint presentation and you already have the information for the slide show typed as an outline in a Word document, you don't need to retype the text into PowerPoint. Instead, you simply export, or copy, the Word outline into a blank PowerPoint presentation as shown below.

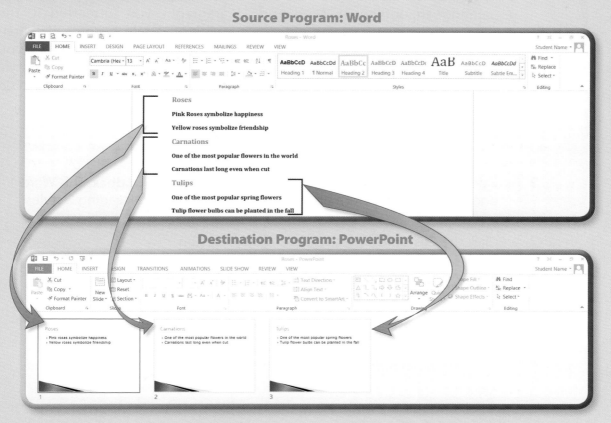

Source Program: Word

Destination Program: PowerPoint

When you integrate data or objects from one application into another, you can choose between two methods: (1) copying and pasting or (2) embedding or linking the data or object. Copying and pasting works well for single-use situations, such as the above example of copying the Word outline into PowerPoint. However, embedding or linking works well for situations in which you might continue to use the source and destination files separately as well as together.

Embedding and linking are notably different. When you *embed* an object, such as an Excel chart in a Word document, the chart becomes a separate object in the Word document. Any changes you make to the chart in the source Excel workbook will not affect the embedded chart in the Word document.

In contrast, if you *link* the chart, it then resides, or has its home, in the Excel workbook. Then, even though you can see that linked chart in the Word document, that chart is not a separate object. Because it is a linked object, when you change the chart in the Excel workbook, it will automatically be updated in the Word document. The embed option and the link option both have an advantage over copying and pasting, because you can edit an embedded or a linked object using the tools of the source program.

Integrating Word, Excel, Access, and PowerPoint

Module 9

Skill 1

Video ▶ M9_C0_S01

Export a Word Outline to PowerPoint

Some people prefer to plan their PowerPoint presentations by creating an outline in Word and then exporting that content to PowerPoint to work on slide design. PowerPoint creates new slides based on the heading styles that you used in the Word outline. PowerPoint creates slide titles from text that you formatted with the Heading 1 style. Paragraphs you formatted in the Heading 2 style become the first-level bulleted text. Paragraphs you formatted in the Heading 3 style become the second-level bulleted text, and so on.

Steps

1 Open the student data file named **M9-S1-BusinessPlan.docx**. This Word document has been formatted with the Heading 1 and Heading 2 styles.

2 Click the Customize Quick Access Toolbar button.

3 Click *More Commands* at the drop-down list.

4 Click the *Choose commands from* option box arrow.

▶**Tip** The commands are listed in alphabetical order.

5 Click *All Commands*.

6 *Another Way*
Scroll through the list box, click the command, and then click the Add button.

6 Scroll through the list box and then double-click *Send to Microsoft PowerPoint*.

7 Click OK.

▶**Tip** Your Quick Access toolbar may have different buttons than the ones shown in the image on the opposite page. If you are unsure which button to use, hover the mouse pointer over each button until you locate the one with the Tooltip that reads *Send to Microsoft PowerPoint*.

8 Click the Send to Microsoft PowerPoint button on the Quick Access toolbar. PowerPoint opens and displays the presentation in Normal view.

9 Save the PowerPoint presentation as **Lastname-M9-S1-BusinessPlan**, but replace *Lastname* with your last name. Save the file in your Module 9 working folder on your storage medium.

▶**Tip** You are saving the file in PowerPoint and the file has a .pptx extension, even though the initial data came from a Word file, with a .docx extension.

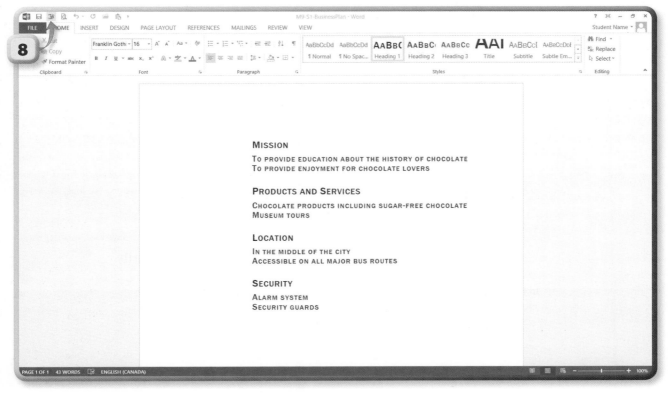

More

10 Close PowerPoint.

11 In the Word window, right-click the Send to Microsoft PowerPoint button on the Quick Access toolbar.

12 Click *Remove from Quick Access Toolbar.*

13 Close Word without saving the document.

Taking It Further

Exporting a PowerPoint Presentation to Word   You can also export a PowerPoint presentation to Word. You may want to do this so that you can use Word's features to customize your handout formatting. Another reason might be to use the contents of your presentation as the basis for a report or other document. To send presentation data to Word, click the FILE tab, click the *Export* option, click *Create Handouts,* and then click the Create Handouts button. In the Send To Microsoft Word dialog box that displays, click a layout option and then click OK.

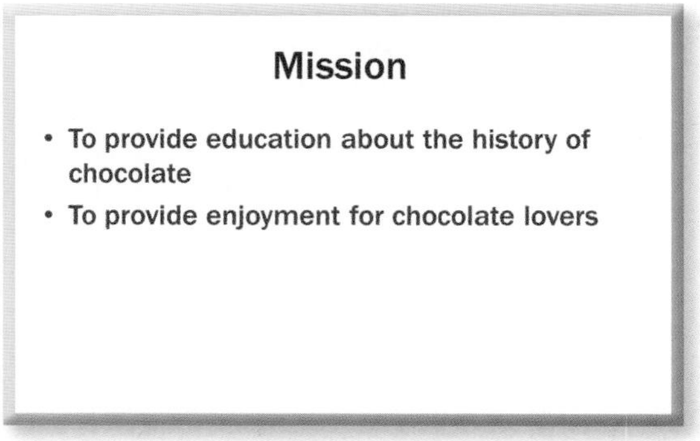

Mission

- To provide education about the history of chocolate
- To provide enjoyment for chocolate lovers

Slide 1

Products and Services

- Chocolate products including sugar-free chocolate
- Museum tours

Slide 2

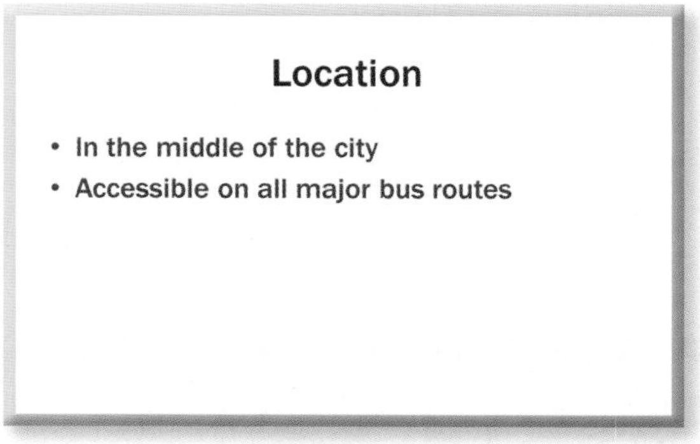

Location

- In the middle of the city
- Accessible on all major bus routes

Slide 3

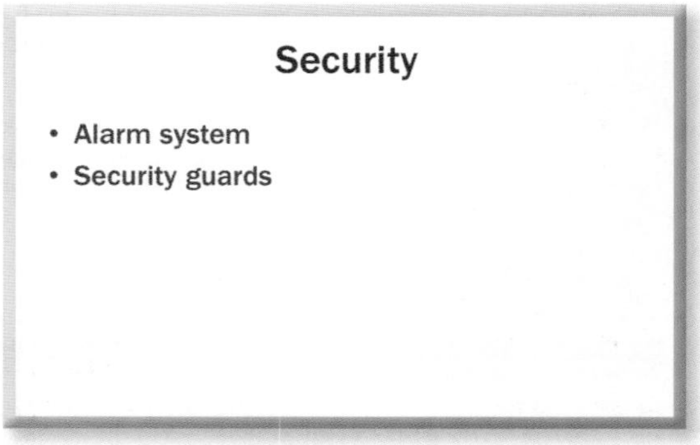

Security

- Alarm system
- Security guards

Slide 4

Completed Skill 1

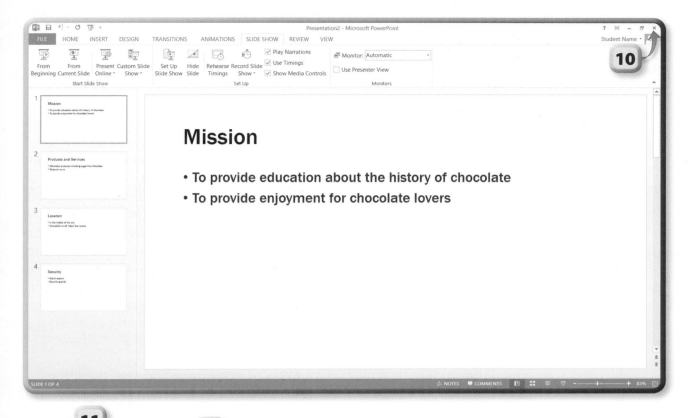

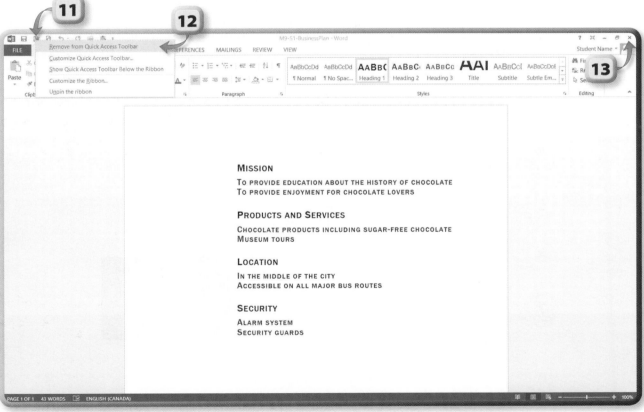

Integrating Word, Excel, Access, and PowerPoint

Skill 2

Video M9_C0_S02

Insert an Excel Chart in Word

You can copy an Excel chart to a Word document. When you do so, you have the option to link the chart. When you link the chart, you will be able to edit the object in Excel (called the *source program*) even though the chart is in a Word document. If you change the chart in Excel, the chart will also be updated in Word (called the *destination program*) if the Word file is open on the same computer when the Excel file is edited. In other words, if you edit a linked chart with both the source and destination files open on the same computer at the same time, you will always have an up-to-date chart. **NOTE:** *If you edit data in Excel, you may need to click the Refresh Data button in the Data group on the CHART TOOLS DESIGN tab for the edits to appear in the linked Word chart.*

Steps

1 Open the student data file named **M9-S2-Letter.docx** and save the file as **Lastname-M9-S2-Letter**, but replace *Lastname* with your last name. Be sure to save the file in your Module 9 working folder on your storage medium.

2 Press Ctrl + End to move the insertion point to the end of the document. **NOTE:** *This step ensures that the chart from Excel will be inserted in the correct position in the Word document.*

3 Open the student data file named **M9-S2-Chart.xlsx** and, if you have not already done so, save the file to your Module 9 working folder.

4 Click a blank area of the chart to select the chart.

5 *Shortcut*
Copy
Ctrl + C

5 Click the Copy button in the Clipboard group on the HOME tab.

▶**Tip** You can see the linked object (chart) in the Word document, but the object itself is located in its original Excel file.

6 Click the Word button on the Taskbar.

▶**Tip** Click Use Destination Theme & Link Data button to link the chart and change the chart formatting to match the formatting in the document.

7 Click the Paste button arrow in the Clipboard group on the HOME tab.

8 Click the Keep Source Formatting & Link Data button (the fourth button under *Paste Options*).

9 Save the Word document.

10 Close Word and Excel.

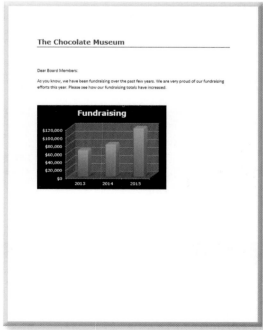

Completed Skill 2

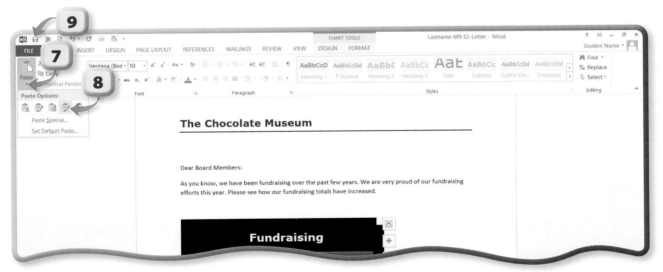

Taking It Further

Editing and Formatting a Linked Chart in Word In Word, click a linked chart to display the CHART TOOLS DESIGN and LAYOUT tabs. You can use options on these tabs to edit and format the linked chart without having to leave Word. For example, to edit the chart data, click the CHART TOOLS DESIGN tab and then click the Edit Data button. To change the chart style, click the CHART TOOLS DESIGN tab and then select a chart style from the Chart Styles gallery. The CHART TOOLS FORMAT tab includes options for changing shape styles and WordArt styles. You can also use the Layout Options, Chart Elements, Chart Styles, and Chart Filters buttons that appear next to a selected chart to format and edit a linked chart.

Integrating Word, Excel, Access, and PowerPoint

Module 9

Skill 3

Video   M9_C0_S03

Create an Access Table from Excel Data

Add new records to an Access table by directly typing them in or by copying the information from a Word file or an Excel file. In this skill, you learn to add records to an Access table by copying them from an existing Excel file. Copying existing data can help you avoid mistakes that can sometimes occur when retyping data.

Steps

Tip Be sure to open the database file from your working folder on your storage medium, not directly from the Student Resources disc.

1 Open the student data file named **M9-S3-Chocolate.accdb** and save the file as **Lastname-M9-S3-Chocolate**, but replace *Lastname* with your last name. Be sure to save the file in your Module 9 working folder on your storage medium.

2 If a security warning appears immediately below the ribbon, click the Enable Content button.

3 Open the Chocolate table. The table currently does not contain any records.

4 Open the student data file named **M9-S3-Inventory.xlsx**. The worksheet provides an inventory of chocolate products.

5 Select cells A1:C12.

6 *Shortcut*
Copy
Ctrl + C

6 Click the Copy button in the Clipboard group on the HOME tab.

7 Click the Access button on the Taskbar.

8 Click the Paste button arrow in the Clipboard group on the HOME tab.

Tip You select the *Paste Append* option because you are adding records to an existing table.

9 Click *Paste Append* at the drop-down list.

10 At the warning box asking if you are sure you want to paste the 11 records, click Yes.

11 Print the Chocolate table or submit the Access file as directed by your instructor.

12 Close Access and Excel.

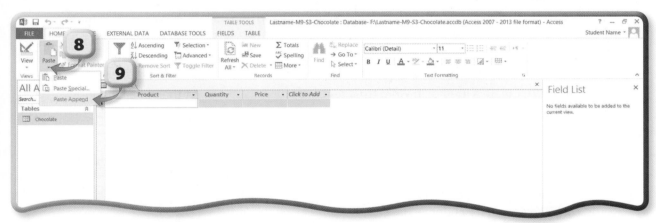

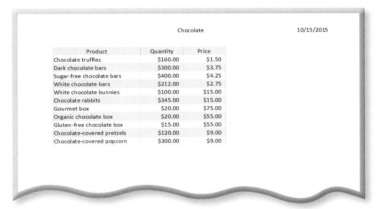

Completed Skill 3

Taking It Further

Importing Excel Data Another way to enter data into an Access table is to import the data from an existing Excel file. When you import data, the file is converted for use by the destination application. To import an Excel file, click the EXTERNAL DATA tab in Access and then click the Excel button in the Import & Link group. You can then select the Excel file and specify other import options in the Import Spreadsheet Wizard dialog box.

Module 9 Project

Project 1 ─────────────────────────────

Skills Skills used will vary depending upon choices you make. Requirements include web research; use of OneNote, Word, Excel, Access, and PowerPoint; and integration of OneNote with Access, Access with Word, and Excel with Word.

Scenario Your school's Travel Club is sponsoring a trip to the Galápagos Islands to study birds. You volunteer to assist with the computing functions necessary to advertise the trip and monitor the pretrip activities. You have agreed to do the following:

- **Part I:** Use a web browser to research some of the endemic birds that live on the Galápagos Islands.
- **Part II:** Create an Access database that includes basic facts about birds endemic to the Galápagos Islands.
- **Part III:** Create a flyer (using Word) describing the trip and inviting all interested students and their families to an upcoming meeting of the Travel Club.
- **Part IV:** Create a PowerPoint presentation for the meeting of the Travel Club.
- **Part V:** Create a sample budget (in Excel) for students to use in planning their trip expenses.
- **Part VI:** Create a memo (in Word) that reminds students to submit their initial deposit.
- **Part VII:** Submit the files to your instructor.

Steps, Part I

Use a web browser to research some of the endemic birds that live on the Galápagos Islands.

1. In your web browser, enter appropriate search words. **HINT:** *You might try* Endemic birds of the Galápagos Islands.

2. Select 10 birds for further study. At a minimum, find out each bird's common name, scientific name, and habitat, and record the URL where you found the information. Whenever possible, also locate an image of the bird.

3. Copy the relevant information into OneNote.

Steps, Part II

Create an Access database of birds endemic to the Galápagos Islands.

1. Open a new, blank database and name it **Lastname-M9-EOM-P1-Galapagos.accdb**.

2. Create a table in the database and name the table *Birds*.

3. The table will contain the following information:
   a. Common name
   b. Scientific name
   c. Habitat
   d. Source (URL)
   e. Image of bird (optional)

4. Using the results of your research, enter the data for at least 10 different types of birds.

Steps, Part III

Create a flyer about the trip to be distributed to all students. The flyer should be attractive and should encourage students to attend the upcoming Travel Club meeting. It must include the following items.

1. Start with a new, blank Word document.

2. Type information about the trip and the upcoming Travel Club meeting. Include the common names of birds, source URLs, and images (where appropriate) copied from the Access table. **NOTE:** *Extend what you learned in Skills 2 and 3 of this module to copy the Access table and insert it into the Word document.*

3. Don't forget to include the trip dates and the date, time, and location for the meeting. The departure date for the trip is four months from today and the trip will last 14 days. The first Travel Club meeting about the trip will be exactly one month from today.

4. Lay out the flyer in an interesting way with all the information on one page. Use the page space appropriately and completely, making sure the content does not flow onto a second page.

5. Include at least two different images that are not from the Access table. Place the images appropriately to enhance the readability of the flyer.

6. Use two or more fonts, colors, and styles.

7 Use various font sizes to encourage everyone to read the entire flyer.

8 Insert a footer that includes your name and the current date.

9 Save the flyer with the name **Lastname-M9-EOM-P1-Galapagos.docx**.

Steps, Part IV

Create a PowerPoint presentation to be shown at the Travel Club meeting. It must contain the following items.

1 Start with a new, blank PowerPoint file.

2 Include seven to nine slides in the presentation.

3 Use the Title Slide layout for the first slide.

4 For the slides following the title slide:
   a. Use at least two different slide layouts.
   b. In at least four slides, insert one or more images; each image should include a caption that indicates its source.
   c. Include text on every slide.
   d. Include transitions between at least two slides; use at least two different transitions in the presentation.
   e. In three slides, animate one or more objects. The animations are to start on a mouse-click since the presentation will be delivered by a facilitator.

5 On the final slide, list all the sources you used while researching and creating your presentation.

6 Insert a footer on every slide except the title slide that includes the date, your name, and the slide number.

7 Apply a theme to the presentation.

8 Include speaker notes that you will use to deliver the presentation at the Travel Club meeting.

9 Save the presentation with the name **Lastname-M9-EOM-P1-Galapagos.pptx**.

Steps, Part V

Create a sample budget in Excel for students to use in planning their trip expenses.

1 Research the cost for a flight to the Galápagos Islands and a cruise upon arrival. The following costs are applicable. You may modify these cost categories as appropriate.
   a. Flight
   b. Cruise
   c. Food
   d. Transfers
   e. Activities, including entrance fees if appropriate
   f. Souvenirs
   g. Clothing

2 Enter the headings and the data into an Excel worksheet.

3 Calculate totals using a function.

4 Include a payment schedule.
   a. List three installments.
      i. Installment 1: $250 deposit to reserve your place
      ii. Installment 2: 50% of the balance
      iii. Installment 3: balance
   b. Be sure to use absolute references when calculating the installments.

5 Format the worksheet using appropriate number formats.

6 Size the columns and rows and add color, borders, and other visual formatting to make the worksheet easier to read.

7 On a separate worksheet in the same workbook, create a pie chart that compares the various costs.
   a. Add a title to the chart.
   b. Remove the legend and label the slices of the pie with the cost type and the percent.

8 Name the worksheets containing the data and the pie chart.

9 Add a footer to both the data worksheet and the pie chart worksheet; in the footer, include your name and the current date.

10 Save the Excel workbook as **Lastname-M9-EOM-P1-Galapagos.xlsx**.

Steps, Part VI

Create a memo in Word that will be emailed to students interested in participating in the trip.

1 Use a memo template provided by Word.

2 Replace the template placeholders with appropriate text.

3 Write a paragraph thanking the student for his or her interest and summarizing the costs of the trip. Copy the budget from the Excel workbook into the body of the memo. Include a reminder that the first payment (deposit) is due immediately. ***NOTE:*** *Extend what you learned in Skills 2 and 3 of this module to copy the budget from the Excel worksheet and paste it into the Word document.*

4 Add a footer that includes your name and the current date.

5 Save the Word document as **Lastname-M9-EOM-P1-GalapagosMemo.docx**.

6 Save the memo as a PDF with the name **Lastname-M9-EOM-P1-GalapagosMemo.pdf** so it is ready to be distributed electronically to all interested students.

Steps, Part VII

Submit the following six files to your instructor.

1 **Lastname-M9-EOM-P1-Galapagos.accdb**

2 **Lastname-M9-EOM-P1-Galapagos.docx**

3 **Lastname-M9-EOM-P1-Galapagos.pptx**

4 **Lastname-M9-EOM-P1-Galapagos.xlsx**

5 **Lastname-M9-EOM-P1-GalapagosMemo.docx**

6 **Lastname-M9-EOM-P1-GalapagosMemo.pdf**

GLOSSARY

.accdb the file format for an Access 2013 document

.docx the file format for a Word 2013 document

.pptx the file format for a PowerPoint 2013 document

.xlsx the file format for an Excel 2013 document

absolute reference a cell reference in which the row and column letter do not change when you fill or copy the formula; a dollar sign precedes the column letter and row number (A1)

accelerator keys a feature that allows you to select menu items by pressing the Alt key and a designated letter

Accept a button on the REVIEW tab of Word; allows you to accept some or all changes made by reviewers

Access the Microsoft Office database application

accessibility options tools that provide more than a dozen ways to customize your PC experience and make it easier to use

Accounting a number format that displays the value in a cell by placing the dollar symbol ($) or another currency symbol at the left edge of the cell, using a thousands separator, including two decimal places, and aligning cell amounts by decimal point; places negative numbers in parentheses

Action Center an icon on the Taskbar that displays important messages about security and maintenance settings

active cell the cell that the user has selected by clicking it or navigating to it using another method, such as the keyboard; also known as the *current cell*

Address bar the location in Internet Explorer and Chrome browser windows where you type a web address

Adobe Acrobat a document-sharing software program used to view and make edits to PDF files

Adobe Reader free software used to view PDF files

advance to use any one of various methods, such as clicking the mouse or pressing the Right Arrow key, to move to the next slide in a presentation while in Slide Show view

align a paragraph formatting feature that sets the text relative to the left and right margins of the document; alignment options are left, right, center, or justify (which spreads the text across the line from the left margin to the right resulting in an even right margin)

All Markup a Track Changes feature in Word that shows all changes to formatting as well as all content deletions and additions to a document

animation a sequence of visual effects that influences how content appears on the currently displayed slide; can be applied to text or graphical objects

animation effects movement effects, such as flying in or spinning, that you can apply to animations

Animation Pane the pane you can display using a button on the Animations tab; allows you to locate, apply, and control animations

antivirus software software that can be installed to protect your computer from viruses

applications software the group of programs you use to complete computer-based projects; includes spreadsheet programs to perform calculations, word processors to create text-based documents, games, and drawing programs, among others

appointment an activity that you schedule in an electronic calendar (such as the one in Outlook) with starting and ending times

apps small applications that are available for a variety of computing devices such as smartphones and tablets; also the name Windows 8 gives to programs such as Microsoft Word

argument the values used by a function when performing a calculation; functions can have required or optional arguments; arguments include numeric values, dates, text, and cell references and ranges

Arrange a group containing options (including *Send Backward* and *Bring Forward*) used to control the order of stacked items on a slide

ascending a sort order that sorts data alphabetically from A to Z or from the smallest value to the largest value

Auto Fill an Excel feature used to copy an entry or fill a series across a row or down a column

AutoFit a setting in the Convert Text to Table process that creates a flexible column width for each column in the table, based on each column's contents

AutoNumber a data type that automatically stores a number that is one greater than the last number used

AutoSum an Excel feature that provides a quick way to insert commonly used functions into a formula; functions that can be inserted include SUM, AVERAGE, COUNT, MIN, and MAX

backstage area an interface element in all Office programs; contains a variety of options and commands that allow you to manage your files and perform tasks such as saving and printing

bar chart a chart that is used to compare differences between values; has horizontal bars in Excel

Block Authors a tool in the Protect group of the REVIEW tab on the Word ribbon that allows you to block reviewers from making any changes to your document

Bluetooth technology used to communicate over short distances without wires

bookmarks a feature in Firefox and Chrome that allows you to save links to websites that you visit frequently

border an outline around a certain area; used to group or emphasize data

Brightness a monitor setting that can be adjusted in Windows 8; also a feature used to control the amount of light in photos in a presentation or document

bulleted list a list format used for items without a set order or sequence

Calculator a Windows 8 accessory program used to perform calculations

Calendar an Outlook scheduling tool that can keep track of appointments, create reminders about events, and schedule meetings

cell the intersection of a row and a column in a worksheet; a location for entering data

cell address a combination of a column heading letter and a row heading number, such as A1; uniquely identifies a cell location; also known as a *cell name* or *cell reference*

cell name (see *cell address*)

cell reference (see *cell address*)

cell styles predefined formats that you can apply to a cell to change the font, size, color, border, and number format all at once

central processing unit (CPU) the part of the computer that performs mathematical operations and coordinates the functions of the computer system; typically a microprocessor located on the motherboard

Charms bar a bar on the right side of the Windows screen; contains charms used to search for files, display the Start screen, and change system settings

chart title a chart element that describes the contents of the chart

citations notes that give credit to sources of information used in a document

clip art a collection of graphical objects, including illustrations, photos, videos, and sounds; can be inserted in a PowerPoint presentation, a Word document, or an Excel spreadsheet

Clipboard a holding area for cut/copied text or objects; items in the Clipboard are available to be pasted into a file

Collapse a feature that hides all subtopics in the outline pane when working in Outline view in PowerPoint

color scheme the colors used for text, slide backgrounds, and graphical elements on a slide

color theme variant determines the color theme used for the presentation design

column chart a chart that is used to compare differences between values; has vertical bars in Excel

column heading capital letters across the top of a worksheet that are used to identify a particular column

columns Word feature that lets you divide portions of a document into one or more vertical sections

Command bar the location in Internet Explorer where you can access commands and settings

comment a reviewing feature in Word you can use to suggest changes rather than making them directly in the text

Compare a Word feature that shows the differences between two documents

compress a process used to reduce the size of a file; creates one file from one or more files or folders to facilitate sharing

contextual tab a tab that is displayed on the ribbon when a certain object, such as a picture or table, is selected

Control Panel provides the ability to access and adjust most system settings for your computer

copy to place a duplicate of a selected portion of text or object on the Clipboard so that the duplicated item can be pasted into other locations

criteria one or more conditions that must be met for a record to be selected in Access

crop to remove areas of a graphical object, such as a photo

Currency in Excel, a number format that displays the value in a cell by placing the dollar symbol ($; or other currency symbol) next to the left-most number, using a thousands separator, including two decimal places, and aligning cell amounts by decimal point; offers options for how negative numbers are displayed; in Access, a data type used to store amounts using a dollar sign, comma separator, and 2 decimal places

current cell (see *active cell*)

cursor a blinking symbol that indicates the current insertion point in the document

Custom Show a feature that allows you to define a subset of slides in a PowerPoint file for running as a variation on the longer slide show

cut to remove a selection of text or an object from its current location and place it on the Clipboard so that it can be pasted into a different location

data label a chart element that tells the exact value or percentage that each pie slice, bar, or line represents

data redundancy the duplication of data; data redundancy should be avoided

data series data used to create a chart

datasheet the view in which a table is displayed when it is first opened; organizes data in rows and columns

Datasheet view the view used to enter records in a table in Access

date code a serial number used to store a date in Excel so that Excel can perform calculations using dates

Date/Time an Access data type that stores dates and/or times; dates are stored as sequential numbers and can be used to do date-based arithmetic, such as finding the number of days between two dates

Design view the view used to design a table in Access; field name, data type, and other properties are specified in Design view

desktop a screen in Windows 8 that offers quick access to areas and settings such as the Recycle Bin, the Taskbar, network connections, and speaker volume

destination refers to the document or file into which copied information is pasted, embedded, or linked

Details view SkyDrive and File Explorer view that displays information about files such as the date the file was created and the file size

dialog boxes provide a way to interact with Windows and other applications; used to specify details for a setting or to make choices about how an application performs a procedure

download the process of transferring a file from a remote location (such as the Internet) to a local device (such as your computer, tablet, cell phone, or MP3 player)

Ease of Access button click to view accessibility options for Windows 8

embedded data data that is not connected to the source data but that can be edited using the tools of the source program

endnote used in reports and research papers to document or cite the source of information or to add additional information or comments; placed at the end of a document

entry the data value for a field in Access or a cell in Excel

error code a code, such as #DIV/0, that displays in a cell when you make an error while entering a formula in Excel

Excel the Microsoft Office spreadsheet application

Expand feature that displays all subtopics in the outline pane when working in Outline view in PowerPoint

expansion slots used to insert expansion cards to your motherboard to add capabilities such as increased processing power and enhanced video and audio

explode to move a pie slice away from the rest of the pie chart to draw attention to that particular slice

export saving or sending a file in a format that another application can use

extract a process in which a compressed file or folder is decompressed; in Access, the process of pulling data from one or more tables

favorites an Internet Explorer feature that allows you to save links to the websites you visit frequently

field an area of an Access table where a particular type of information is recorded, or a space in an Access database that is allocated for a particular type of data

field size the maximum number of characters you can enter in a field in Access

file a collection of data that is stored on a hard drive or other storage medium

File Explorer the file management interface in Windows 8

file extension a set of characters, such as *.docx*, that is automatically added to a file name by an application; tells the operating system which program to use to open the file

filter in Access or Excel, used to temporarily display only those records or cells that meet a certain condition or conditions

Find a Microsoft Office feature that allows you to search for specific characters or formatting

Find and Replace a Microsoft Office feature that allows you to search for specific characters or formatting and replace them with other characters or formatting

Firefox a web browser application developed by Mozilla

firewall software or hardware that checks data coming to your computer from the Internet or a network and blocks transmissions that are not secure

Flash Fill an Excel feature that looks for patterns in data and then automatically enters the rest of the data based on the pattern

folder a way to store and organize a group of related files

font character sets for text that control the shape of the characters and add visual appeal to the text

font effects used to add emphasis or set text apart; bold, italic, and underlining are common font effects

font family a group of fonts that all share the same name, such as Arial, and come in several variations, such as Arial Bold and Arial Narrow

footer the area at the bottom of a page or slide that you can use to insert text or graphics, such as the date or a company logo, that are to appear on every page or slide in the document or presentation

footnote used in reports and research papers to document or cite the source of information or to add additional information or comments; placed at the bottom of the page

form a database object that provides access to data; usually allows you to view or edit only one record at a time

Form view the view used to add or edit a record using a form object

format the way a document, presentation, text, or an object appears

Format Painter a tool that allows you to copy formatting from one set of text to another

formula text entered in a cell to perform a calculation; always begins with an equal sign (=) and can include cell references, values, and functions

Formula bar the area immediately above the column headings; used to view and edit the contents of the active cell

function a predefined calculation that can be inserted into a formula in Excel

General default format for a cell entry in Excel

Glow an effect you can apply to make the edges of an object appear to glow

gridlines intersecting vertical and horizontal guidelines you can display to help you see how objects and text are aligned on a page or slide

group a way to organize an Access report by causing specified fields with the same value to be grouped together

handles small boxes at the corners and sides of selected objects that you can drag to resize an object

handout a printed version of a PowerPoint presentation

handout master the view used to format and arrange the contents of printed handouts of presentation slides

hard copy a printed copy

hard return pressing Enter to begin a new paragraph

hardware the physical parts of a computer

header the area at the top of a document page or slide that you can use to insert text, such as the document title, or graphics that are to appear on every page or slide in the document or presentation

Help a Microsoft Office feature that allows you to search and browse for information about Office application features

Hide background graphics an option you can apply to an individual slide to hide graphics included on the slide master

Highlighter a PowerPoint tool that can be used in Slide Show view to highlight text on a slide

history a list of previously visited websites stored in a browser

home page the first page that displays when you visit a website; also the page that displays when you open your browser

horizontal axis the axis along the bottom of a bar, column, or line chart; runs between the left and right areas of the chart

import the process of converting data for use by the destination application

indent to move text a certain amount of space from the left or right margins; indent settings can be applied to the first line in a paragraph or to an entire paragraph or document

information processing cycle hardware and software working together to turn data into information; the four parts of the information processing cycle are input, process, output, and storage

InPrivate Browsing an Internet Explorer feature (called Private Browsing in Firefox and New incognito window in Chrome) that automatically clears your website history when you close the browser window

input device a device, such as a mouse, keyboard, microphone, webcam, or touch screen, that allows you to communicate commands and enter data into your computer

insertion point the active place in the document where whatever you type or insert next will appear

Instant Search a Windows 8 feature that allows you to search for apps, settings, or files from the Start screen

integrating bringing together two or more different Office application files by copying, pasting, embedding, or linking data or objects

Internet a worldwide network; the physical infrastructure that allows worldwide communication between computing devices; the world's largest wide area network (WAN)

Internet Explorer a web browser application developed by Microsoft

Internet Service Provider (ISP) a company that provides access to the Internet and related services

Jump lists a list that can be opened from the Windows 8 Taskbar; displays recent documents, tasks, or commands for a particular application

keyboard shortcuts keyboard combinations, such as Ctrl + Home, that perform actions such as moving the insertion point to a specific location in a document or cutting or pasting text

landscape a page orientation that turns the page sideways so that the width is longer than the length

layout the arrangement of placeholder elements in a slide

Layout view the view used to apply formatting to a form in Access

legend a chart element that describes what each pie slice, bar, or line represents

Library a logical grouping that helps you work with related sets of files; by default, Windows contains four libraries: Documents, Music, Pictures, and Videos; libraries are similar to folders but are able to gather files stored in several locations on your computer

line chart a chart that is used to illustrate changes or trends over time

link a component on a web page, image, button, or text that can be clicked to open another web page or file; also, in Access, data that is connected to the source data will automatically update if the source data is changed

list level the level that a line of text occupies in an outline hierarchy

live tiles tiles on the Windows 8 Start screen that can display current information

local area network (LAN) a type of network that connects nearby computers within a home or business

Location bar the location in the Firefox browser window where you can type a web address

Lock Tracking a Word feature that lets you use a password to control when track changes is turned off

Long date a date that displays in a spelled-out format such as *Sunday, January 8, 2015*

loop to automate a slide presentation to run continuously

malware malicious software

margins the areas of white space at the top, bottom, left, and right of a document

maximizing a window increases the window to a full-screen size

meeting request an appointment that is sent to other people and can include the meeting's location and associated information, such as the meeting's topic and goals

memory stores programs and data currently in use; may be permanent (as with read-only memory or ROM) and contain instructions for the operating systems; can also be temporary (as with random access memory or RAM), holding data in memory while the computer is on, losing the data when it is turned off or when the computer is restarted

menus used in Windows 8 and other applications to display a list of commands

merge the process of combining multiple table cells into a single cell

microprocessor the central processing unit is a microprocessor containing an integrated circuit and is located on the motherboard; the CPU processes your requests

Microsoft account an account that allows you to sign in to Microsoft services, including Hotmail and SkyDrive

Microsoft Office 2013 suite a package of Microsoft Office applications

minimizing a window reduces the window to a button on the Taskbar

modem the hardware that sends and receives data to or from a transmission source, such as a phone or cable line; types of modems include cable, DSL, and wireless

motherboard the main circuit board in the computer; composed of a thin sheet of fiberglass or other material with electrical pathways that connect key components of hardware, including the microprocessor/CPU, memory, and expansion slots

Motion Path a feature of animations that lets you control the movements of an object around a slide during an animation

move a technique used on a touch screen in which the user presses an image or text area and drags it from one part of the screen to another; also to cut a selection or object from its current location and then paste it in a different destination location

multi-level list a bulleted or numbered list with more than one indent level

multitasking working with more than one window at the same time

Name box displays the cell address of the active cell; used to navigate to a specific cell or cell range

narration a recorded audio track saved with a PowerPoint presentation; can replace a live speaker in a setting where the presentation is run without a speaker present

navigate to use various methods to move among slides in a slide show presentation

Navigation bar located at the bottom of the Outlook window; contains buttons used to switch between Outlook views; also contains the Address bar in the Firefox window and in the Internet Explorer window when it is run in the Windows 8 user interface

Navigation pane a pane in File Explorer that lists folder and library locations; also a pane on the left side of the Access window; displays the names of all objects in the database

network the infrastructure for linking various computing devices to each other and to the Internet; uses a communications medium, such as a wireless signal or cable; can be used to share files, software, and resources, such as a printer

network adapter devices that give your computer the ability to connect to a wired or wireless network; a network interface card (NIC) is one kind of network adapter

No Markup a Track Changes setting in Word that displays the document as it would look with all changes accepted

Normal view the default PowerPoint view in which most of the work to build a slide show is done

note container the box around each block of text on a OneNote page

notebook a OneNote file that contains at least one section and one page

NotePad a text-editing app included with Windows 8

notes information entered in the Notes pane that is useful to a speaker but will not be visible to an audience during a presentation

notes master the view used to format and arrange the contents of printed speaker notes for a presentation

Notes Page view a PowerPoint view that displays the current slide with any added notes below it

notes pane a pane below the slide pane that provides a place to enter speaker notes

notification area located on the far right of the Taskbar; shows the status of certain system features

number format a setting you can apply to a cell or range to specify the appearance of a number, such as whether it includes a currency symbol, decimal places, or a thousands separator, or whether it appears in a date format; the default number format is General

Number in Excel, a number format that displays a value in a cell by including two decimal places by default; offers options for adding a thousands separator and changing how Excel displays negative values; in Access, a data type used to store numbers only

numbered list used for items with a logical order or sequence, such as a set of steps in a process

Office Clipboard a storage area for text and objects that have been cut or copied; the Office Clipboard can store up to 24 items; users can select text or objects to be pasted from the Office Clipboard

Office Theme the default theme applied to a blank document, workbook, or presentation

Office Web Apps web-based versions of the Microsoft Office applications Word, Excel, PowerPoint, and OneNote that can be accessed from a SkyDrive account

OneNote a Microsoft Office application used to create a digital notebook

OneNote Clipping Tool a tool used to capture the screen or a portion of the screen from within the Office 2013 applications

Online Pictures a Word feature and PowerPoint in which you can insert pictures from a variety of online sources including royalty-free clip art pictures from Office.com

Online Video a Word feature in which you can insert video from a variety of online websites, such as YouTube

operating system also known as OS, the most important piece of software used on a computer system; provides a user interface that allows a person to interact with the computer, manages the operations of the CPU and the computer's hardware devices, and supports the actions within application programs, such as opening and saving files

operator a mathematical symbol that specifies that a particular type of calculation be made in a formula

order of operations the sequence in which Excel processes calculations in a formula, based on operator type and other rules; follows the standard mathematical order of operations

Original a Track Changes setting in Word that displays the original content of the document before any markup was added

outline pane a pane in Outline view that displays the text contained on each slide in an outline format

Outline view a PowerPoint view used to create an outline or storyboard for a presentation

Outlook personal information management software

output devices devices that convert information from your computer into a usable form, such as visual (printout, monitor), audio (speakers), or digital (hard drive, CD/DVD drive, online cloud server) format

page an area in a notebook used to enter notes

page break a feature that allows you to manually indicate where one page stops and another begins

page orientation the setting that determines whether the longer side of a document runs along the top (landscape orientation) or bottom (portrait orientation) of a page

Paint a Windows 8 app that can be used to edit a screenshot or other graphic image

paste to insert an object from the Clipboard to a specified location

PDF a file format usually viewed using Adobe Reader or Adobe Acrobat; currently the standard for document sharing; may be opened and edited in Word 2013

Peeks an Outlook feature that allows you to view your Calendar, People, or Tasks without having to switch views

pen a presenter's tool used in Slide Show view to "write" on a slide

People an Outlook tool used to organize and save information about the people and businesses with whom your communicate

Percentage a number format that multiplies the cell value by 100 and adds the percent symbol (%)

Picture Border a feature you can use to add a line surrounding an object and modify the line's thickness and design

pie chart a circular chart resembling a pie that contains clearly defined slices; slices represent individual data values or percentages of the pie and illustrate how their relative sizes or data values in the series relate to the total

pinch a technique used to zoom out on a touch screen; the user touches the screen with two fingers spread apart and moves them toward each other

placeholder a holding place for contents defined by a layout that you use to enter text or objects into a slide presentation; empty placeholders are not visible during a slide show

plot area the area of the chart where the data series is displayed

populating the database the process of adding records to a database

portrait a page orientation where the width of the page is smaller than the height

Post to Social Networks an option in Word in which a document has been saved to your SkyDrive account where you can post the document to social networks, such as Facebook or Twitter

Power a setting that can be adjusted in Windows 8 to save the battery life of a laptop

PowerPoint the Microsoft Office slide presentation application

Present Online a PowerPoint feature that presents a presentation online in real time

Presenter View a PowerPoint view that allows you to see your notes while you are delivering your presentation

press and hold a technique used on a touch screen in which the user presses on the screen and holds it for a couple of seconds; equivalent to right-clicking with a mouse

Preview view an option on the View tab in File Explorer that allows you to see a thumbnail image of the file

primary key a designation assigned to a field in an Access table to make sure no two records in the table are the same; the primary key column cannot contain duplicate entries

Print Layout a feature in the Print backstage area in PowerPoint; allows you to choose whether to print slides, notes, a presentation outline, or handouts

Print Preview shows you what a printed document will look like before you print it

professional styles style sets by various organizations, such as the Modern Languages Association (MLA), for the correct or preferred way to reference or cite sources in a document and format a research paper

Publish as a Blog Post an option in Word used to post a document to a blogging site, such as WordPress or SharePoint

query a database object that, based on specified criteria, pulls or extracts data from one or more tables

query design grid the area of the window used to create a query in Design view

Query Wizard provides a series of dialog boxes that you can use to create a simple or select query

Quick Access Toolbar interface element in the top left corner of the window; contains the Save, Undo, and Redo buttons and can be customized by adding icons for actions that are used often

Quick Analysis a feature in Excel that allows you to analyze a range of data; select from tabs such as CHARTS to display the data in a graph format or FORMATTING to highlight values based on a criterion

Quick Tables a Word feature that enables you to apply common table styles to tables

range on a worksheet, a contiguous selection of cells identified by the cell addresses of the upper-left and lower-right cells, separated by a colon, such as the range B6:H11

Reading view a PowerPoint view that displays the slides in full-screen view and is often used to review a presentation

record a collection of related fields

Record Navigation bar a bar located at the bottom of a form that is used to navigate to different records and display a new blank form

record selection area an area to the left of a record in a table; can be clicked to select a record

Recycle Bin location where deleted files are held for a time; files in the Recycle Bin can be permanently deleted or restored to their original locations on the computer

Rehearse Timings a PowerPoint feature used to determine how long each slide should display before advancing to the next slide in an automatic slide show

Reject a button on the REVIEW tab of Word; allows you to reject some or all of the changes made by reviewers

relational database a type of database that uses related tables to organize data

relative reference in a formula, a cell reference that will automatically be adjusted when you fill or copy the formula; the cell reference in the destination cell formula will be adjusted by the displacement of the original cell to the destination cell; the default reference type

report an Access database object that presents database information in a professional-looking format

resize the ability to change the size of objects on a slide

restarting closes Windows, powers off the computer, then repowers the computer and reopens Windows; restart process begins by pressing Ctrl + Alt + Delete or by selecting Restart from the Power icon in the Settings panel on the Charms bar

Restore Down a button used to reduce the size of the window

Restrict Editing a tool in the Protect group of the REVIEW tab; allows you to restrict the types of edits reviewers can make to your document

ribbon an interface element that is displayed along the top of the application window and organized into a series of tabs designed to help you quickly find the commands that you need to complete a task

rotate a technique used on a touch screen in which the user rotates text or an image by touching the screen with two or more fingers and turning their hand

rotation handle a line and circle above the center middle handle on a selected object that you can drag to rotate an object

router a device that relays data among devices on a network

row heading the numbers down the left side of the sheet that are used to identify a particular row

ruler a feature that consists of a set of rulers (one vertical, the other horizontal) you can display in Word and use to set margins and tabs

run to display a slide show in Slide Show view

screen saver a moving picture or pattern that is automatically displayed on the monitor when the computer has been idle for a specified period of time

screenshot an image of some or all of the current display on your computer monitor

scroll a technique used to navigate a file that enables you to reach a specific location in the file

Search charm located on the Charms bar; can be clicked to open the Search pane where you can search for Apps, Settings, or Files

search engine an online service used to locate information on the Web; Google is an example of a search engine

Search pane a pane on the Start screen that allows you to search for apps, settings, and files

section consists of one or more pages in a digital notebook

select highlighting text to which your next action will apply, such as the action of applying Bold formatting or cutting the text to paste it elsewhere

selection area the area along the left side of a document used to select a line, a paragraph, or all text in the document with various clicking actions

Send Using E-mail an option in Word used to send a document as an attachment in an email message

separator a tab, comma, paragraph break, or single character such as a hyphen that can be used to indicate a new column when text is converted into a table

Settings charm located on the Charms bar; can be clicked to open the Settings pane, which provides access to basic PC settings such as power and volume as well as access to the PC settings window

Shadow an effect you can apply to make an object appear as if it has a shadow

Shake a Windows 8 feature that provides a quick way to minimize multiple windows

Shapes a Word feature that offers a gallery of shapes you can select and draw on your page

sheet (see *worksheet*)

sheet tab a tab at the bottom of a worksheet that displays the worksheet name; clicking on the tab selects the worksheet

Short date a brief date format that displays as in the following example: 1/8/2015

Short Text a data type that stores characters and numbers that do not require calculations, such as names and zip codes

Show/Hide ¶ a Word feature that displays formatting marks

Simple Markup a Track Changes feature in Word that shows you a cleaner version of the document and an indicator showing where changes have been made

SkyDrive a Microsoft service that allows you to upload files to an online storage area, which is referred to as a cloud

Sleep a Windows 8 feature that saves power without requiring you to close all of your files and shut down your computer

slide a technique used on a touch screen in which the user touches an object on the screen and drags it left, right, up, or down; equivalent to scrolling with a mouse

slide master a PowerPoint feature used to apply formatting and header/footer settings to every slide in a presentation; changes made to individual slides will override Slide Master settings

Slide Master view a PowerPoint view used to change the formatting of the slide master

slide pane a pane that includes a large view of an individual slide

slide show term for a PowerPoint presentation wherein slides are displayed to accompany a speaker or in a self-running show, possibly with recorded narration

Slide Show view a PowerPoint view used to run a presentation

Slide Sorter view a PowerPoint view that displays all the slides in the presentation on one screen as thumbnails; the view used most often for organizing slides

slide thumbnail pane a pane on the left of the Normal View in PowerPoint; allows you to scan and move through a presentation using slide thumbnails

slide transition animations that occur when you move from slide to slide in Slide Show view

SmartArt a Word feature that makes creating diagrams simple by first choosing from among many standard diagrams, such as work flow or organization charts, then drawing them on the page, and then modifying their text labels

Snap an App a Windows 8 feature you can use to dock an application window on the left or right side of your screen

Snipping Tool a Windows 8 app that you can use to capture the entire display or a portion of the display on your computer monitor

soft return pressing Shift + Enter to begin a new line without beginning a new paragraph

software a set of instructions that tells the computer what to do; types include operating system software and applications

sort a method of organizing data in alphabetical, numerical, or chronological order

Sound a PowerPoint feature that allows a sound file to be added to a slide transition

source refers to the original document or file from which information is copied

spacing the amount of white space between lines of text in a paragraph or between paragraphs

spelling checker a Microsoft Office feature that indicates possible spelling, grammar, or formatting errors and provides tools to correct them

spelling check dictionary the built-in set of words that the Microsoft Office spelling checker accesses to verify correct spelling in files; users can edit this dictionary

spyware a type of program that, without your knowledge, is installed on your computer to collect information about you and your online activities

Start charm located on the Charms bar; used to open the Start screen

Status bar located along the bottom of the Internet Explorer, Chrome, and Firefox windows, this bar displays status messages such as a web page's download progress

Sticky Notes a Windows 8 accessory program that lets you create electronic sticky notes that can appear on the desktop

storage devices used to save data that you want to use again; examples include cloud storage, DVD, and flash drives

stretch a technique used to zoom in on a touch screen; the user touches the screen with two fingers close together and moves them apart

style set predesigned group of fonts and paragraph properties used to quickly change the appearance of a document

styles formatting settings grouped together so that you can apply the whole group of settings with a single step

swipe a technique used on a touch screen in which the user uses quick, short movements to move from one part of the screen or another

tabs preset increments on the horizontal ruler that you can use to place text; the four kinds of tabs are left, right, center, and decimal; the first three align text to the left, right, or center of the tab position, respectively; a decimal tab aligns numbers based on the position of the decimal point within them

tab indicator the small box at the top of the vertical ruler; click to change the type of tab that you will insert when you click the ruler

tabbed browsing a browser feature that allows you to open more than one website in a single browser window

table an Access database object used to enter and organize data; in other Office programs, a feature that organizes sets of information into rows and columns

table style a Word feature that applies a set of predesigned formats to a table

tag a method of grouping and organizing notes by assigning a piece of information, such as *Important* or *To Do*, to a note

tap a technique used to navigate and select on a touch screen; equivalent to a mouse click

Taskbar contains buttons for apps that are currently opened on your computer; located along the bottom of the Windows 8 desktop

tattoo a Windows 8 screen background

template a predesigned document or presentation with formatting and graphical elements on which you can base a new document or presentation; a quick way to create a professional-looking document or presentation

text box a text container; in PowerPoint, the contents of a text box are not reflected in the presentation outline

text wrap a feature of Word that automatically begins a new line of text when the text reaches the right margin

theme a predesigned Windows 8 appearance setting that includes a desktop background, screen saver, window border color, and sound scheme; also in Excel, PowerPoint, and Word, predefined design element sets that include colors, fonts, and graphical elements

tiles rectangular graphics that can be clicked to open applications and files

toolbar located near the top or bottom of an application window; contains a variety of command buttons for an application

touch screen a screen that can be manipulated using your fingers or a stylus

Track Changes a Word feature that keeps a record of changes to a document by using colors and strikethroughs to indicate changed or added text, formatting, and objects

Troubleshooting a link in the Action Center window used to help solve computer problems

Uniform Resource Locator (URL) the address of a web page on the Internet

upload the process of transferring a file from your computer or other local device to a remote location such as the Internet

vertical axis the axis along the left side of a bar, column, or line chart; runs between the top and bottom of the chart

virus a program that can harm the programs and files stored on your computer

Weather bar an Outlook Calendar feature that displays the current weather forecast for a selected location

Web app an Access database that can be viewed, edited, and shared on the Web

web browser a software program that allows you to locate and view web pages

web page a single page or document in a website

website a collection of web pages

wide area network (WAN) a type of network that connects distant computers; the Internet is the largest of all WANs

Windows 8 the latest version of the Microsoft Windows operating system

Windows 8 Start screen provides a central "jumping off" point from which you can perform a variety of tasks, such as searching for and opening apps, watching videos, emailing friends, and checking local weather

Windows Accessories Windows 8 utility programs located in the Windows Accessories group; includes WordPad, Paint, Calculator, Sticky Notes, and Snipping Tool

Windows Firewall a Windows 8 utility program that performs firewall tasks and helps protect your computer network from outsiders

Windows Help and Support a feature that helps you explore and troubleshoot Windows 8 features

Windows Update allows you to download and install the latest updates to Windows 8 and other Microsoft products

wireless access point a device that relays data among devices on a network

Word the Microsoft Office word processing application

WordPad a Windows 8 app that provides simple word processor functionality

workbook an Excel file; contains one or more worksheets

works cited a page at the end of a document, listing all works quoted in the document

worksheet a collection of cells used to organize, store, and manipulate data; also known by the generic term *spreadsheet* or the shorter term *sheet*

Wrap Text a Word feature used to adjust how an object and text are arranged relative to one another; also in Excel, a format that tells long text entries to wrap to multiple lines in the cell

Zoom slider bar adjusts the magnification of the view in Microsoft Office programs

INDEX

Photo Credits: Page 65 motherboard, Courtesy of ASUSTeK Computer Inc.; tablet, Courtesy of Samsung; **Page 66** display (touch screen), Courtesy of Samsung; operating system, Courtesy of Intel Corporation; **Page 72** tablet, pressureUA/ iStockphoto; smartphone, Courtesy of Opera Software ASA; **Page 611** iPhone, Courtesy of Apple Inc.; **Page 631** chocolate dessert, © Lachlan Hardy; **Page 651** car-racing trophy, AlonzoDesign/iStockphoto.